The ENCYCLOPEDIA of HOCKEY

New and Revised Edition

by
Robert A. Styer

South Brunswick and New York: A. S. Barnes and Company
London: Thomas Yoseloff Ltd

A. S. Barnes and Co., Inc.
Cranbury, New Jersey 08512

Thomas Yoseloff Ltd
108 New Bond St.
London, W1Y OQX, England

ISBN: 0-498-01304-9
Printed in the United States of America

Contents

1	**Evolution of Hockey**	9
2	**The National Hockey League**	17
3	**History by Years**	28
4	**National Hockey League Records**	149
	Champions, 149; League Statistics, 149; Club Records, 151	
5	**Register of Players**	170
	Inactive Players, 171; Active Players, 228; League Leaders, 254; Player Records, 259	
6	**Register of Goaltenders**	266
	Register, 267; League Leaders, 289; Goaltenders Records, 291	
7	**Trophies**	299
	Club, 299; Player, 301	
8	**All-Star Teams**	308
9	**All-Star Games**	316
10	**Stanley Cup**	318
	Winners, 318; Club Records, 319	
11	**Register of Players (Stanley Cup)**	325
	Inactive Players, 326; Active Players, 352; Player Records, 364	
12	**Register of Goaltenders (Stanley Cup)**	370
	Register, 371; Career Records, 378	
13	**Officials**	381
14	**Hall of Fame**	384
15	**Playing Rule Changes**	387
16	**Amateur Champions**	390
	Olympics, 390; World, 391; Allan Cup, 392; Memorial Cup, 393	
17	**Father and Son(s)**	395
18	**Brothers**	396
19	**Pension Plan**	398
20	**Seating Diagrams**	399
21	**1972-1973 Season**	407

The
ENCYCLOPEDIA
of
HOCKEY

1
Evolution of Hockey

Hockey derives its name from field hockey, which has been played in England for several centuries. Ice hockey evolved from field hockey, bandy, hurley, and similar games that required the hitting of a ball with a stick between two uprights. It has been established that such games were played as early as 400 B.C.

There is evidence that Britons played a form of field hockey on ice called bandy. During the winter of 1813–14, this game was played at Bury Fen, in the English county of Huntingdonshire. Records reveal that a leg of mutton was offered to the winner of a match between Bury Fen and Willingham in 1827.

By the 1830s, bandy had acquired some rules that would later apply to hockey.

(1) No bandy stick shall be more than two inches wide in any part.
(2) No one is allowed to raise the bandy above his shoulder. Only the goalkeeper may hit the ball while it is in the air.
(3) No player is to be considered offside when within his own half of the playing ice.
(4) The game begins when the referee throws up the ball in the center of the ice.
(5) The team consists of eleven players.

There is little doubt that modern ice hockey was first played and developed in Canada, but where the first game was played has caused dispute among historians.

Ice skating is many centuries old. It is mentioned in Icelandic literature of 1100 A.D. In 1500, the Dutch were making iron skates. Early Canadian history indicates that Iroquois Indians chased deer across ice on skates made of bone.

In 1604, at St. Croix, some young men of De Mont's expedition to Acadia (Nova Scotia) went skating on the ponds. They may have been the first to skate in North America. *First Things in Acadia* also makes reference to hockey having been played in 1828, on the Chain Lakes at Dartmouth, Nova Scotia.

In his book *Warden of the North*, T. H. Raddell claims Nova Scotia as the birthplace of hockey.

Ice hockey, Canada's national game, began on the Dartmouth Lakes in the eighteenth century. Here, the garrison teams found the Indians playing a primitive form of hurley on the ice, adopted and adapted it, and later put the game on skates. When the soldiers were transferred

to military posts along the St. Lawrence and the Great Lakes, they took the game with them; and for some time afterwards continued to send to the Dartmouth Indians for the necessary sticke.

Kingston, Ontario, claims that the first hockey was played there. In an effort to determine where the first hockey was actually played the Canadian Amateur Hockey Association appointed a committee, which later reported:

The first hockey was played by the Royal Canadian Rifles, an Imperial unit, stationed in Halifax and Kingston in 1855; it is quite possible that English troops stationed in Kingston from 1783 to 1855 played hockey, as there is evidence in old papers, letters and legends that the men and officers located with the Imperial troops as early as the year 1783, were proficient skaters and participated in field hockey. It is more than likely that the pioneers played their field hockey in those early days on skates but it is not an established fact. The playing of hockey games as early as 1855 in Kingston is certain. Early manuscripts, letters, and even the sticks and a puck used in the early days of hockey have been located. With ice conditions more favourable in Kingston Harbour, which is situated at the terminus of the Great Lakes, than on the east coast, it is only logical that there was more hockey and skating in Cataraqui (the old Indian name for Kingston) than in Halifax.

Montreal contends that the first hockey was played there. Henry Roxborough in his book *The Stanley Cup Story* mentions a game between the Dorchester Club and the Uptown Club on the last Saturday in February of 1837, with eight men to a side; goal, point, cover-point, centre, rover, home, right side and left side.

McGill University (Montreal) also has a claim, for it was here that an attempt to draft some uniform rules was made. In 1879, W. L. Murray, W. F. Robertson and R. F. Smith selected from the rules of field hockey and rugby those that would be applicable to ice hockey. They suggested a flat, round puck instead of a ball, the type of uniforms to be worn, and the size of goals. They proposed nine men to a side and specified the duties of officials and length of a game. With the uniformity of the rules, hockey soon gained favor throughout eastern Canada. Its popularity became apparent in western Canada by 1896, when a club from Winnipeg not only challenged for the Stanley Cup but won it.

By the turn of the century, hockey clubs were being formed in the United States and several artificial ice rinks had been installed. Figure-skating had become quite popular in the 1860s and the first attempt at making artificial ice came about because of the smooth surface that figure-skating required. There was an artificial ice rink at Chelsea, England, in 1876. The first rink in North America was in the old Madison Square Garden in New York City, installed by Thomas L. Rankin and opened on February 12, 1879. Europe had several rinks in the 1880s, and in 1893 one was featured at the Chicago World's Fair. Later there was artificial ice at New York's Ice Palace on 181st Street and St. Nicholas Rink. The first hockey game on artificial ice may, in fact, have been played at the St. Nicholas Rink when some Canadian hockey clubs played there in 1896. There were no artificial rinks in Canada until 1911, when Frank and

Lester Patrick built their arenas in Vancouver and Victoria, British Columbia.

Around the turn of the century, the concept of professional athletics was introduced. Until this occured players generally played for the clubs in their home town; but the sponsors and owners of rinks were aware of the increased patronage that a winning club generated and offers began to be made.

At first, the better clubs had only a few members who were being paid, but as competition became more intense and the demand for a winning club increased, the clubs became more professionalized. The players moved around a lot, spending each season with the club that offered the best proposition.

Oddly, the first all-professional club was not in Canada but in the United States. This team was assembled in the little Michigan town of Houghton and was called the Portage Lake Hockey Club. After the 1896–97 season, the Berlin (Kitchener) club had been expelled by the Ontario Hockey Association for paying some of its players. Playing on this club had been a dentist, Dr. J. L. Gibson, who later migrated to Houghton where he set up a practice. In 1903–04, he and some associates imported some players from Canada, and formed one of the best clubs of that period.

Among these players were William "Riley" Hern, and "Hod" and Bruce Stuart. During that season they lost only two games, which were later avenged, and defeated the famed Montreal Wanderers twice. Two years later, in 1905–06, they had an even stronger club when Joseph Hall and Frederic "Cyclone" Taylor came from Canada to join them.

When Lord Stanley first presented the Stanley Cup in 1892, all clubs were amateur. The first winner was a club representing the Montreal Amateur Athletic Association. The prestige of winning this cup hastened the formation of professional clubs, and by 1907 Canada had many.

It was in 1907 that the Eastern Canadian Amateur Hockey Association removed the 'Amateur' from its title and became openly professional. This was a four-club league and consisted of the Montreal Shamrocks, Montreal Wanderers, Ottawa Senators and Quebec Bulldogs.

There was little chance that a truly amateur club would ever win the Stanley Cup again.

In 1908, William M. Northey encouraged Sir H. Montague Allan, a prominent Montreal industrialist and financier, to present a trophy for amateur competition. With the presentation of the Allan Cup, the Stanley Cup came into exclusive control of the professionals.

In 1909, the National Hockey Association was organized and included Cobalt, Haileybury, Montreal Canadiens, Montreal Wanderers and Renfrew Millionaires. The Eastern Canadian Hockey Association had by now changed its name to the Canadian Hockey Association and, although the Montreal Wanderers were now in the National Hockey Association, the former still had the Montreal Shamrocks, Ottawa Senators, and the Quebec Bulldogs, plus two other clubs from Montreal: the Montreal Nationals and All-Montreal.

Competition for players became so vigorous that both associations soon realized that neither would survive if they continued offering ever-higher

salaries to the players. To halt certain disaster they joined together, after two weeks of operating separately, under the National Hockey Association banner. The Ottawa Senators and Montreal Shamrocks joined with Cobalt, Haileybury, Montreal Canadiens, Montreal Wanderers and Renfrew Millionaires to become the top league in the country and win the Stanley Cup the next five years. Later the Quebec Bulldogs, Toronto Blueshirts and Toronto Tecumsehs (later the Ontarios and then Shamrocks) saw action in the league as Cobalt, Haileybury, Montreal Shamrocks and Renfrew Millionaires dropped out.

National Hockey Association

| | League Champions | Schedule | Leading Scorer | | |
			Player	Club	Goals
1916–17	Montreal Canadiens	20	Joseph Malone —	Quebec	
			Frank Nighbor (tie)	Ottawa	41
1915–16	Montreal Canadiens	24	Edouard Lalonde	Montreal	28
1914–15	Ottawa Senators	20	Thomas Smith	Quebec	39
1913–14	Toronto Blueshirts	20	Thomas Smith	Quebec	42
1912–13	Quebec Bulldogs	20	Joseph Malone	Quebec	43
1911–12	Quebec Bulldogs	18	Joseph Malone	Quebec	33
1910–11	Ottawa Senators	16	Martin Walsh	Ottawa	40
1909–10	Montreal Wanderers	12	Edouard Lalonde	Mont. Canadiens— Renfrew	34

Although the Patrick brothers were originally from Quebec, they lived at Nelson, British Columbia where their father, Joseph Patrick, was a lumber baron and Frank and Lester came East to play hockey each winter. They were not thirty years old when they approached their father about financing a league on the Pacific Coast. With his approval, the brothers started building arenas and recruiting players from the East.

Once again the National Hockey Association became involved in competition for players. This league was formed at Vancouver on December 7, 1911, and Frank and Lester Patrick named it the Pacific Coast Hockey Association. The first game was played at Victoria on January 5, 1912.

In the first season, three clubs entered (New Westminster, Vancouver and Victoria) and in later years Portland, Seattle and Spokane also played. Harry Hyland, "Newsy" Lalonde and "Cyclone" Taylor were among the players the Patricks induced to go West. Many had been enticed away from clubs in the National Hockey Association and relations between the two leagues had become strained.

In the summer of 1913, Frank Patrick came east and met with representatives of the National Hockey Association. It was agreed that once a player had signed to play for a certain club that club could retain him. This now prohibited players from changing clubs each season. It was also agreed that a series between each leagues' champion would be played for the Stanley Cup. This series would alternate yearly between East and West with the first one to take place in the East in 1914. The Pacific

Coast Hockey Association operated for 13 seasons, during which time its clubs won two Stanley Cups. A third series between the Montreal Canadiens and Seattle Metropolitans never reached a decision.

Leading Scorers of the Pacific Coast Hockey Association

	Player	Club	Goals	Assists	Points
1923–24	Arthur Duncan	Vancouver	19	9	28
1922–23	Frank Fredrickson	Victoria	39	15	54
1921–22	John James Adams	Vancouver	26	4	30
1920–21	Frank Fredrickson	Victoria	20	12	32
	Fred Harris	Vancouver	15	17	32
1919–20	Tommy Dunderdale	Victoria	26	7	33
1918–19	Frederic Wellington Taylor	Vancouver	23	13	36
1917–18	Frederic Wellington Taylor	Vancouver	32	11	43
1916–17	Bernard Patrick Morris	Seattle	37	17	54
1915–16	Frederic Wellington Taylor	Vancouver	22	14	36
1914–15	Frederic Wellington Taylor	Vancouver	23	22	45
1913–14	Frederic Wellington Taylor	Vancouver	24	15	39
1912–13	Tommy Dunderdale	Victoria	24	5	29
1911–12	Edouard Charles Lalonde	Vancouver	27	—*	27

* No assists were recorded in 1911–12.

Pacific Coast Hockey Association

League Champions

	Regular Schedule	Playoffs	*Won	*Lost	*Tied	*Points
1923–24	Seattle Metropolitans	Vancouver	14	16	0	28
1922–23	Vancouver Maroons	Vancouver	16	12	1	33
1921–22	Seattle Metropolitans	Vancouver	12	11	1	25
1920–21	Vancouver Millionaires	Vancouver	13	11	0	26
1919–20	Seattle Metropolitans	Seattle	12	10	0	24
1918–19	Vancouver Millionaires	Seattle	12	8	0	24
1917–18	Seattle Metropolitans	Vancouver	11	9	0	22
1916–17	Seattle Metropolitans	None	16	8	0	32
1915–16	Portland Rosebuds	None	13	5	0	26
1914–15	Vancouver Millionaires	None	13	4	0	26
1913–14	Victoria Capitals	None	10	6	0	20
1912–13	Victoria Capitals	None	10	5	0	20
1911–12	New Westminster Royals	None	9	6	0	18

* Regular Season

In 1921, the Western Canada Hockey League began operating with four cities from the Canadian prairie (Calgary, Edmonton, Regina and Saskatoon). Portland, Vancouver and Victoria later played in this league after the Pacific Coast Hockey Association folded. In 1925, while a member of this league, the Victoria Cougars won the Stanley Cup. This league operated for five seasons, and in 1926 was sold to the National Hockey League for $258,000.

Western Canada Hockey League

	League Champions		Leading Scorer	
	Regular Season	Playoffs	Player	Club
1925–26	Edmonton Eskimos	Victoria Cougars	William Cook	Saskatoon
1924–25	Calgary Tigers	Victoria Cougars	Duncan MacKay	Vancouver
1923–24	Calgary Tigers	Calgary Tigers	William Cook	Saskatoon
1922–23	Edmonton Eskimos	Edmonton Eskimos	Arthur Gagne	Edmonton
1921–22	Edmonton Eskimos	Regina Capitals	Gordon Keats	Edmonton

The National Hockey Association had completed its eighth season at the end of the 1916–17 season. There had been discord among the owners and general discontent prevailed. Before the next season, Frank Calder, the league secretary, arranged a meeting between the owners. The date was November 22, 1917, and before this meeting adjourned, the National Hockey Association had gone out of existence.

The Stanley Cup

At a banquet given to the Ottawa Club on March 18, 1892, in response to a toast by Lord Stanley, Lord Kilcoursie read a letter which states Lord Stanley's wish to present a cup for competition among Canada's hockey clubs.

I have for some time been thinking it would be a good thing if there were a challenge cup, which could be held from year to year by the leading hockey club in Canada. There does not appear to be outward or visible sign of the championship at present, and considering the interest that hockey matches now elicit, and the importance of having the games fairly played under generally recognized rules, I am willing to give a cup that shall be annually held by the winning club.

I am not quite certain that the present regulations governing the arrangement of matches gives entire satisfaction. It would be worth considering whether they could not be arranged so that each team would play once at home and once at the place where their opponents hail from.

Lord Stanley was Canada's Governor-General from 1888 until May, 1893, and his full title was: Right Honourable Sir Frederick Arthur Stanley, Baron Stanley of Preston, in the County of Lancaster, in the Peerage of Great Britain, Knight Grand Cross of the Most Honourable Order of the Bath.

The proposal to present this cup was greeted with wide approval and Lord Stanley instructed one of his aides in England, Captain Colville, to obtain one. Captain Colville selected a large gold-lined silver bowl resting on an ebony base costing ten guineas (approximately fifty dollars). Little did Lord Stanley visualize the vast arenas that would be built, nor the large sums of money spent by future generations of sportsmen, in a determined effort to win this cup.

Through the years the cup had become quite battered and the National Hockey League has had it replated. Today the cup rests on a high pedestal as a series of collars have been added on which the names of the clubs and players winning it are inscribed. The greatest honor that can come to any club or player is to have its or his name inscribed on this cup. It is not only the oldest trophy competed for on the North American continent but also the most famous.

The first trustees of the Stanley Cup were two Ottawa sportsmen, P. D. Ross and Sheriff Sweetland. Ross, who had been a forward on an early Ottawa club, referee, sports editor and publisher, was a trustee for fifty-six years. Lord Stanley suggested the following proposals to the first trustees:

(1) The winners shall give bond for the return of the cup in good order, when required by the trustees for the purpose of being handed over to any other team that may in turn win.

(2) Each winning team shall have at their own charge, engraved on a silver ring fitted on the cup for that purpose, the name of the team and the year won.

(3) The cup shall remain a challenge cup, and should not become the property of any team, even if won more than once.

(4) In case of any doubt as to the title of any club to claim the position of champions, the cup shall be held or awarded by the trustees as they may think right, their decision being absolute.

(5) Shall either trustee resign or otherwise drop out, the remaining trustee should nominate a substitute.

No winner was declared in 1893. The trustees had ordered the Ottawa Capitals to play Toronto's Osgoode Hall (college) at Toronto and the Ottawa club refused. On February 23, 1894, the trustees announced:

Arrangements have been completed whereby the Lord Stanley Hockey Cup will now pass into the hands of the Montreal Amateur Athletic Association. Some trouble arose last year about the acceptance, and the M.A.A.A. have had it in their possession ever since. The Montreal team will now officially take it over.

1894 Montreal Amateur Athletic Association

W. M. Barlow	A. A. Hodgson	A. T. Mussen	H. Routh
A. Cameron	G. R. James	E. M. O'Brien	A. C. Waud
H. G. Collins	A. B. Kingan		

The first Stanley Cup game ever played, took place on March 22, 1894, at the Victoria Rink in Montreal between the cup holding Montreal Amateur Athletic Association club and the Ottawa Capitals. The Montreal Amateur Athletic Association club defeated the Ottawa Capitals 3 goals to 1.

The following is a newspaper dispatch of this game from Montreal:

The hockey championship was decided tonight, and never before in the history of the game was there such a large crowd or so much enthusiasm. There were fully five thousand persons present at the match; and tin horns, strong lungs and a general rabble predominated. The match resulted in favour of Montreal by three goals to one. The referee forgot to see many things. The ice was fairly good.

In the first half, the play was of the rushing order, with Montreal getting slightly the best of it. The Ottawas, however, found an opening after about ten minutes play, and Russell scored. As soon as the puck was sent off again, Hodgson carried it to the Ottawa end and undertook to score; but the Ottawa defense were on the alert and saved the goal. A hard struggle ensued, and after ten minutes of rushing and hard hockey, Montreal scored. No other goal was taken in this half, and when the second half commenced, everyone settled down to see a great contest and they were not disappointed.

The Ottawas played with much more vim and made it lively for their opponents. The Montrealers were more fortunate, and through the offices of Hodgson and Barlow, two more goals were taken. The match concluded in a victory for the local team by three goals to one. After the match the winners were carried off the rink.

Through 1913, the holder of the cup was challenged each year by another club and in some years by several. In 1914, the Pacific Coast Hockey Association champions started meeting the National Hockey Association champions (later the National Hockey League) for the cup. In 1922, 1923 and 1924, the champions of the Western Canada Hockey League and the champions of the Pacific Coast Hockey Association competed with the National Hockey League champions for its possession.

The Pacific Coast Hockey Association folded after 1924 and for the next two years (1925 and 1926) the winner was decided in a series between the champions of the National Hockey League and the champions of the Western Canada Hockey League. After 1926, the Western Canada Hockey League was sold to the National Hockey League and the Stanley Cup came into its exclusive possession.

2
The National Hockey League

The National Hockey League came into existence during World War I and prevailed through wars, depressions and faltering franchises to become the ultimate in professional hockey.

For its first season (1917–18), George Kennedy of the Montreal Canadiens, Samuel E. Lichtenhein of the Montreal Wanderers and Michael J. Quinn of the Quebec Bulldogs were granted franchises. Thomas P. Gorman of the Ottawa Senators and Charles Laurens Querrie, accepting on behalf of a group from Toronto, were also awarded franchises. The Toronto Arenas were so called after the Mutual Street Arena in Toronto where their home games were played. They used this name for two seasons, then were known as the St. Patricks. Toronto was the only club that had artificial ice.

The league named Frank Calder as its first president and secretary-treasurer. Calder, a Scotsman, was a school teacher in England until 1900, when he came to Canada and became a sports writer in Montreal. He was an outstanding organizer and served the National Hockey League until his death at Montreal on February 4, 1943.

Although the Quebec Bulldogs held a franchise, they did not enter a club that first season (1917–18). The first games were played on December 19, 1917. On January 2, 1918, the Montreal Wanderers' Westmount arena burned and the team was forced to disband after playing only six games. In the first four seasons the league played a split schedule. In 1917–18, the Montreal Canadiens won the first half and the Toronto Arenas the second, with the Toronto club victorious in the playoffs.

Toronto then met the Vancouver Millionaires, the Pacific Coast Hockey Association champions, and defeated them for the Stanley Cup. Although the Stanley Cup didn't come into exclusive possession of the National Hockey League until 1926, their league champions were defeated only once when the Victoria Cougars of the Western Canada Hockey League, guided by Lester Patrick, won over the Montreal Canadiens in 1925.

The Quebec Bulldogs did not exercise their franchise in 1918–19, and the league operated with only three clubs and played an 18-game schedule. The Montreal Canadiens again won the first half and the Ottawa Senators the second half. The Canadiens won the playoffs and traveled to Seattle to meet the Seattle Metropolitans, champions of the Pacific Coast Hockey Association. The influenza epidemic was sweeping the country and several of the Montreal players contacted it. When two of them became critically

ill the Seattle Department of Health forbade any more playing. Five games had been played with each club winning two and one a tie.

The Quebec Bulldogs joined the league in the 1919–20 season and finished last in both halves. The Ottawa Senators won both halves and were automatically league champions. Seattle again won the Pacific Coast Hockey Association championship and came East to meet the Senators. This time the playoffs went to a conclusion with Ottawa winning the Stanley Cup.

For the 1920–21 season the Quebec Bulldogs were replaced by the Hamilton Tigers and the league was composed of those four clubs until the 1924–25 season.

During the first seven years of the National Hockey League, many of the great players of all time were in action. Harry Hyland and Arthur Ross played for the Montreal Wanderers. Toronto had John Adams, Harold Cameron, Samuel Crawford, Cecil Dye and Edward Noble. Dye led the league in total points twice and in goals scored three times. He was an outstanding athlete, having played professional baseball with Buffalo of the International Baseball League and football with Toronto Argonauts. The Ottawa Senators featured such future Hall of Fame members as Clinton Benedict, George Boucher, Harry Broadbent, John Darragh, Cyril Denneny, Edward Gerard and Frank Nighbor.

Skating for the Montreal Canadiens were goaltender Georges Vézina, Joseph Hall, Edouard Lalonde, Jean Laviolette, Joseph Malone and Didier Pitre. Vézina had been the Canadiens' goaltender from 1910 until he collapsed in the nets on November 28, 1925, in a game with Pittsburgh and died of tuberculosis four months later. Lalonde was another great athlete. In 1951, he was voted the outstanding lacrosse player of the first half century. In 365 professional games he scored 441 goals and was the leading scorer five times, for three different leagues.

Malone was the most prolific scorer ever to play in the National Hockey League. When "The Rocket" Richard scored 50 goals in 50 games in 1944–45, it was a great achievement, but Malone in 1917–18 had scored 44 goals in 20 games and in 1919–20, he scored 39 goals in 24 games.

At Quebec City, while a member of the Quebec Bulldogs, Malone scored seven goals on January 31, 1920, against the Toronto St. Patricks. Three of these were scored in the last two minutes of the third period. On three other occasions during the same season he scored five goals in one game and at one time his consecutive goal scoring streak reached 14 games. In 16 seasons in four different leagues he played 274 games and scored 354 goals. Joseph Malone's National Hockey League scoring record, averaging over two goals per game in 1917–18, has never even been approached by any other player.

In 1921, George Kennedy passed away and the Montreal Canadiens were purchased from his widow by Joseph Cattarinich, Joseph "Léo" Dandurand and Louis Letourneau. The Canadiens, organized in 1909, are the oldest professional hockey club. Their first game was played in January 1910 while a member of the National Hockey Association in Montreal's Jubilee Rink. The Canadian Arena Company, consisting of Sir Edward Beatty, Kenneth Dawes, Maj. McDougall, Herbert Molson, William M.

Northey, Sen. Donat Raymond and L. H. Timmins, built and financed the Montreal Forum in 1924. In 1935 the Canadian Arena Company bought the Canadiens' franchise, name, players, and equipment for $165,000.

Dandurand became the Canadiens' president and manager, and in 1922 traded Edouard Lalonde to Saskatoon of the Western Canada Hockey League for Aurèle Joliat. In 1923, he signed the player who would become their most famous, Howarth Morenz, to a Montreal Canadien contract. Joliat and Morenz joined with William Boucher to form the Montreal Canadiens' first great line in the National Hockey League.

Joliat became one of the greatest of all left wingers and Morenz's skills have never been surpassed. When their careers came to a close, each had scored 270 goals. When they started, the schedule was only 24 games a season and upon their departure had been increased to 48. Morenz was a fast skater with a hard, accurate shot who played the game in a reckless and exciting manner. His every action was performed with flair and flourish. It is he, with his spectacular efforts, who is generally recognized as bringing hockey to its place among the major sports. Later he was voted the hockey player of the first half century.

In the season of 1924–25, the Montreal Maroons and the Boston Bruins entered the National Hockey League. Montreal again had two clubs and Boston became the first United States entry. Charles F. Adams, owner of a chain of grocery stores, sportsman (he built Suffolk Downs racetrack in 1935), and devotee of hockey traveled to Montreal to watch the 1924 Stanley Cup playoffs. While there he investigated the possibility of a franchise for Boston and was awarded one. One of his first moves was to hire Arthur Ross as his general-manager and coach. Ross had played hockey for 29 years, 17 as a professional, and had been a National Hockey League referee. Boston played their first four seasons in the old Boston Arena on Huntington Avenue.

The Boston Bruins finished last their first season and fourth the next. In 1926, the Western Canada Hockey League was sold to the National Hockey League for $258,000. The National Hockey League distributed the players among the various clubs in the league. Among the players Boston received was a defenseman from Fort Qu'Appelle, Saskatchewan, by the name of Edward Shore. He was to become one of the greatest defensemen ever to lace up a skate. Shore was a terrific skater and his rink-long dashes thrilled the Boston fans. In 1928–29, goaltender Cecil Thompson and Ralph Wieland joined the Boston Bruins. The famous "Dynamite Line" was formed, with Weiland at center and Aubrey Clapper and Norman Gainor on the wings. Boston now had a contender.

Boston Garden was sold out for every game as more and more people flocked to see the great Shore. The largest crowd ever to see a game in Boston will never be known, for on November 20, 1928, the fans crashed the doors down to watch their Bruins play the Montreal Canadiens. When Arthur Ross retired in 1953, the Boston Bruins had won six N. H. L. championships and three Stanley Cups. Ross, who considered hockey to be the world's greatest sport, while officiating insisted the players abide by the rules, and while coaching instilled in them a desire to win. The goal nets and pucks now used are his innovations.

New York's Madison Square Garden was built in 1925 thanks to the efforts of George L. (Tex) Rickard, a famous boxing promoter; the Hamilton franchise was sold to New York interests. On December 15, 1925, the New York Americans and the Montreal Canadiens played the first major league hockey game in Madison Square Garden. The Americans lost 3–1, as Wilfred Green, New York American forward, scored the first goal in what later became the most famous of all sports arenas.

The Hamilton franchise's move to New York is the only instance in any professional sport in which a club had finished at the head of its league and then departed. In 1924–25, the Hamilton Tigers had completed the regular schedule on top of the league, but defaulted to the Montreal Canadiens in the playoffs when their players demanded more money. The Pittsburgh Pirates had also been given a franchise in 1925–26 bringing the United States entries to three.

The National Hockey League granted three more franchises for 1926–27, all to United States cities: Chicago, Detroit, and New York for the second time. These clubs received many of their players from the league when the Western Canada Hockey League players were allocated.

The Chicago Black Hawks played their first game on November 17, 1926, in the old Chicago Coliseum on South Wabash Street and defeated the Toronto St. Patricks 4–1. The Chicago Stadium was built by Patrick T. "Paddy" Harmon and some associates at a cost of $6 million and the Black Hawks played their first game there on December 16, 1929, defeating the Pittsburgh Pirates 3–1. Harmon had also bid for the Chicago franchise in the National Hockey League when he attended an expansion meeting in Montreal and stacked 50 $1,000 bills on the conference table. To the dismay of the club owners his offer had to be refused because they had already granted a franchise to Major McLaughlin for $12,000. (In 1967 the new clubs paid $2 million each for their franchises.)

The management of Madison Square Garden had noted the successful season of the Americans and the following season (1926–27) Col. John S. Hammond, vice-president of the Garden, was instrumental in getting the arena a franchise. The club was named Rangers in honor of (Tex) Rickard. Conn Smythe, who had coached Toronto University clubs to Canadian and world amateur titles, was signed to organize a club. Smythe, a Canadian World War I hero (Military Cross), began by signing what was to be the greatest Ranger line of all: Frank Boucher and the Cook brothers.

William Cook at right wing led the league in total points twice and in goals scored twice. Frank Boucher was an outstanding center who led the league in assists three times. Frederick Cook was not so talented as Boucher or his own brother, but he was more than able to contribute to their scientific attack. They were the first to use the drop-pass, which Frederick Cook claimed had come to him in a dream. He also was probably the first player to use the slap-shot. Clarence Abel and Ivan Johnson were also signed by Smythe, but before the season got under way Smythe was dismissed by the Garden management.

On October 25, 1926, Lester Patrick took over the Rangers as general-manager and coach. The Rangers' opening game was played in Madison Square Garden on November 16, 1926, and they defeated the Montreal

Maroons 1–0. In their second season the New York Rangers captured the National Hockey League championship and the Stanley Cup.

(Tex) Rickard, although he never had an interest in the club, was instrumental in bringing Chicago into the National Hockey League by persuading Major Frederic McLaughlin and a group of wealthy Chicagoans to apply for a franchise. The great Indian orator and chief of the Sauks was called Black Hawk and Major McLaughlin had served in the 333rd machine gun battalion of the 85th (Black Hawk) Division in World War I, so he called his club the Chicago Black Hawks.

In his first seven years as president of the club, the Major hired and fired nine coaches. It wasn't until 1934, with Thomas P. Gorman as general-manager and coach, that Chicago won its first Stanley Cup. Gorman went to the Montreal Maroons the following season and guided them to a Stanley Cup victory. Nobody in any sport had ever brought successive world titles to two different clubs before.

On September 25, 1926, a group of Detroit businessmen, which included such renowned names as Fisher, Ford, Kresge, and Scripps, was granted a franchise. Olympia Stadium was still under construction, so they played their first season in the Border Cities Arena across the Detroit River in Windsor, Ontario. After finishing last in their first season, the Detroit Cougars hired John Adams as general manager and coach.

Adams remained for 35 years, during which time Detroit won twelve National Hockey League championships and seven Stanley Cups. Even though the city's press representatives changed the team's name to Falcons at the start of the 1930–31 season, Detroit had little success in the early years. Detroit's first league championship came in 1933–34 after James D. Norris, a native of Montreal, and Arthur M. Wirtz bought the club. Norris had played hockey in Montreal and been a member of the Montreal Amateur Athletic Association, whose insignia was a winged wheel. He had admired this insignia, adopted it for his own club and called them the Detroit Red Wings.

During 1935–36 and 1936–37, Detroit featured their first great line of Lawrence Aurie, Martin Barry, and Herbert Lewis. With Sydney Howe leading another line and Ebenezer Goodfellow excelling on defense, Detroit won the league championship and the Stanley Cup both seasons. This was during the time when Detroit was known as "the city of champions." The city's baseball Tigers and football Lions had conquered all opponents and Joe Louis was on his way to boxing's heavyweight championship of the world.

Lawrence Aurie was the first player John Adams drafted when he came to Detroit, and James Norris admired the little right winger. Upon his retirement at the close of the 1938–39 season, Norris ordered that his number 6 uniform be retired. In the early 1940s, Detroit's "Liniment Line" of Sidney Abel, Donald Grosso, and Edward Wares appeared on the scene and they won the league championship and the Stanley Cup in 1942–43.

Conn Smythe had returned to Canada after his short sojourn with the New York Rangers and, with some friends, bought the Toronto St. Patrick franchise in 1927 from J. P. Bickell, Paul Ciceri, N. L. Nathanson and "Charlie" Querrie for $160,000. The first thing he did was select a name

not only synonymous with Toronto, but all of Canada: the Toronto Maple Leafs. Smythe had great faith in the future of hockey and at the height of the depression began building Maple Leaf Gardens. This building, known to Canadians everywhere, opened on November 12, 1931, and the Maple Leafs lost to the Chicago Black Hawks, 2–1.

The previous season (1930–31) Smythe had given the Ottawa Senators $35,000, along with Eric Pettinger and Arthur Smith, for the already great defenseman, but destined to be even greater, Michael ("The King") Clancy. In 1928–29 a rough and tough defenseman by the name of George Horner had joined the club. In 1929–30 three rookies made the club: Charles Conacher, Harvey Jackson, and Joseph Primeau. They became the fabled "Kid Line." Primeau, the center, became a master playmaker and Conacher, with his booming shot, led the league in goals scored five times. Jackson, in 1931–32, led the league in total points, the youngest player ever to do so. These players, all of them destined to be enshrined in the Hall of Fame, led the Maple Leafs to a Stanley Cup victory that first season in their gleaming new building. By December 1961 when Stafford Smythe took over the presidency from his father, the Toronto Maple Leafs had won seven Stanley Cups.

In 1928–29, the great goaltender of the Montreal Canadiens, George Hainsworth, in a 44 game season, allowed only 43 goals to be scored against him and registered 22 shutouts. In 1929–30, a rule change allowed players of the attacking side to enter the defending club's zone before the puck, although it had to be carried in by another player. If the defending club gained possession of the puck and carried or shot it out of their zone the attacking players had to leave that zone or be subject to a minor penalty.

This rule was intended to open up scoring opportunities. It certainly did; from a league total of 642 goals in 1928–29, 1301 were shot into the nets in 1929–30. The record stood until the 1967–68 season when there were 2476 goals scored. When a club gained possession of the puck, and it became apparent that the puck carrier could enter the defending zone, his teammates raced to positions around the goal. The goaltenders had little chance and the rule didn't last through the season.

By then, though, many players were on their way to large point totals. Ralph Weiland of the Boston Bruins finished the season with 73 points, a record which stood for 13 years. Douglas Bentley of the Chicago Black Hawks eventually tied it in 1942–43 after the schedule had been increased to 50 games. The following season Herbert Cain of Boston surpassed it with 82 points.

In 1930–31, the Pittsburgh Pirate franchise was transferred to Philadelphia, where they called themselves the Quakers and operated for one season. Benny Leonard, the great little lightweight boxer, lost heavily in both cities with this franchise. The Ottawa Senators, who had won four National Hockey League championships and four Stanley Cups in the first ten years of the National Hockey League, were also beginning to flounder. They withdrew in 1931–32 and returned in 1932–33 and 1933–34, but finished last both times. Then in 1934–35 the franchise was shifted to St.

Louis where they were called the Eagles. They finished last and the club disbanded.

The great depression had spread around the world and hockey was finding the going rough. But the National Hockey League had been born during World War I and this was just another challenge. During these hard times, throughout the length and breadth of the land, a voice could be heard every Saturday night. It was "Hockey Night in Canada," with Foster Hewitt reporting from Toronto. In cities, hamlets, and on farms everywhere radios were switched to this broadcast. It was sponsored by the Imperial Oil Company and was the most popular program in Canada. Canadians and their neighbors along the border, immobilized by ice and snow, eagerly awaited these weekly broadcasts throughout the winter.

Foster Hewitt, whose voice was familiar to Canadians everywhere, had begun broadcasting hockey games in 1923. (In recent years television has taken over and no games were broadcast from Toronto in 1965–66, but popular demand brought them back in 1966–67. November 12, 1966, was the first Saturday in 35 years that a regular season game wasn't scheduled in Toronto.)

With the coming of the New York Rangers, Chicago, and Detroit in 1926–27 the league was divided into two divisions: the American Division and the International Division. This system continued until the close of the 1937–38 season, when the Montreal Maroons folded.

During their 14 seasons in the National Hockey League, the Montreal Maroons won one N. H. L. championship and two Stanley Cups and displayed some outstanding players: the "Big S Line" of Nelson Stewart, Albert Siebert and Reginald Smith; goaltender Clinton Benedict; George Boucher, Harry Broadbent, Lionel Conacher, Mervyn Dutton, and Edward Noble.

Stewart and William Cook of the New York Rangers are the only rookies ever to have lead the league in scoring. Stewart scored goals at a terrific rate and when he retired after the 1939–40 season, he had scored 324, all in schedules of 48 games or less. He was the first player in the National Hockey League to score over 300 goals and not until "The Rocket" Richard scored his 324th goal in October 1952 was his record equalled. Siebert was the left winger on the Big S Line and he was one of the roughest left wings ever. He later became a defenseman and in the summer of 1939 was appointed coach of the Montreal Canadiens only to lose his life by drowning in August.

When Canada selected her athlete of the first half century, she chose Lionel Conacher. The Conacher family have contributed immensely to major league hockey. Charles and Roy were brothers of Lionel, and Murray Henderson and Charles, Jr. were nephews. Lionel's son, Brian, played for the Toronto Maple Leafs. Lionel, a defenseman, played for the Pittsburgh Pirates, New York Americans and Chicago Black Hawks in addition to the Maroons.

Lionel was the first defenseman to consistently drop to his knees to block shots. He also starred in football, lacrosse, soccer, and baseball, and was also voted Canada's *football* player of the first half century. It was

while a member of the Toronto Argonaut football club that he acquired the nickname Big Train. He played professional baseball with the Toronto Maple Leafs of the International Baseball League and soccer with the Toronto Scottish. For a while he wrestled professionally, and also boxed. Lionel Pretoria (Big Train) Conacher was certainly one of the world's great athletes.

The Americans played their last season in the National Hockey League in 1941–42. They had had an uphill struggle from the time the Rangers joined them in Madison Square Garden. The Rangers had won three league championships and three Stanley Cups while they hadn't won either.

Lester Patrick, one of the most beloved of all hockey men anywhere, was the Rangers general manager and coach. In their early years the Rangers had the smooth and efficient line of Frank Boucher and the Cook brothers, along with the colorful defenseman, Ivan "Ching" Johnson, to attract the New York fans.

Later they were to see another line with the Colville brothers and Alexander Shibicky. With this line Patrick revolutionized the style of penalty killing by attacking and attempting to play in the opponent's end.

The Patrick name is imbedded in New York hockey. Lester had been with the Rangers from the very first game they played. Later both his sons played for and coached the Rangers. They were both playing for the Rangers when they won their last Stanley Cup. Lynn was a left winger and played on the Broadway Line with Bryan Hextall and Phillipe Watson. Murray was a defenseman, and in addition to having coached the Rangers, was also their general manager for nine years.

In 1938, the league took over the New York Americans franchise and installed Mervyn Dutton, who had been their coach since 1936, to direct them in the league's behalf. During 1939–40 they acquired Edward Shore and in 1941–42 called themselves the Brooklyn Americans. It was all to no avail. Although the league had helped them financially, competing against the Rangers—who were owned by Madison Square Garden while they paid a high rental fee—forced them to fold. But many of the players who once wore the star-spangled uniform of the New York Americans will long be remembered for they are now enshrined in the Hall of Fame.

War was raging in Europe and Canada entered the conflict in 1939. The Canadian government decided to allow hockey to continue as long as it didn't interfere with the war effort. Two years later the United States became involved. The United States government also permitted hockey to carry on.

Into Boston Garden in 1937 had skated three players from the Kitchener-Waterloo district in Ontario. They were of German descent and were the second great line that Arthur Ross formed at Boston. This was the "Kraut Line." Robert Bauer, Woodrow Dumart, and Milton Schmidt dazzled the Boston fans and the rest of the league with their precision plays and clever stickhandling. This line enlisted as a unit in the Royal Canadian Air Force, as did Roy Conacher, a fine left winger, who had led the league in goals scored in 1938–39. Francis Brimsek, who with Cecil Thompson gave Boston 19 years of the finest goaltending any club could wish for, enlisted in the United States Coast Guard.

Lynn and Murray Patrick, who had become United States citizens, enlisted in the United States Army and Arthur Coulter joined the United States Coast Guard. When goaltender "Sugar Jim" Henry, the Colville brothers, Kilby MacDonald, Alfred Pike, and Alexander Shibicky returned to Canada to enlist, the New York Rangers fell apart. From a first place finish in 1941–42, they plummeted to the bottom and remained there for the next four years.

Douglas Bentley arrived in Chicago in 1939–40 and immediately set people to talking about his ability. His reply to these compliments was "If you think I'm good you should see my younger brother." The next season Chicago saw "Max" Bentley and he was everything that his brother had said he was—and more. "Max" Bentley was one of the most gifted stickhandlers ever to come out of western Canada. He carried the puck as though it were attached to his stick by an invisible string. He centered one of the finest lines the Chicago Black Hawks ever had, the Pony Line, with his brother and William Mosienko. "Max" Bentley won two scoring championships and performed his wizardry at Chicago for over five years.

The Toronto Maple Leafs had won the Stanley Cup in 1947. Conn Smythe had watched "Max" Bentley over the years and he knew that with Bentley he could win another Stanley Cup. He offered Chicago Norman Poile and James Stewart, both voted Second All-Star Team that season, August Bodnar, who was rookie of the year in 1943–44, and two defensemen, Ernest Dickens and Robert Goldham. The Maple Leafs didn't win one more Stanley Cup, they won two more and became the first National Hockey League club to win three consecutive Cups. During the next nine years the Chicago Black Hawks finished last seven times.

When Frank Calder passed away in 1943, the league remembered the fine job Mervyn Dutton had done for it with the Americans. Dutton, whose large construction firm in Western Canada demanded most of his time, agreed to accept the presidency on a temporary basis.

In 1946, Clarence S. Campbell, a native of Flemington, Saskatchewan, was elected president of the National Hockey League. Campbell had earned a Rhodes scholarship while attending the University of Alberta, had practiced law in Edmonton, had acted as counsel at the Nuremburg war crimes trials, and had officiated in the National Hockey League for three seasons during the late 1930s.

Upon James Norris's death in 1952, his two sons, James D. Norris, Jr. and Bruce A. and his daughter Marguerite inherited his vast fortune. Part of this fortune included the Olympia Stadium and Detroit Red Wings, the Chicago Stadium, a majority interest in Madison Square Garden, the St. Louis Arena, the Indianapolis Coliseum and the Omaha Arena. That same year James D. Norris, Jr. and Arthur M. Wirtz sold their interests in the Olympia Stadium and Detroit Red Wings to Bruce A. and Marguerite.

At Chicago, William J. Tobin and associates had bought controlling interest of the Black Hawks from the estate of Major McLaughlin who had died in 1944. Although Tobin had been with the Chicago Black Hawks in different capacities ever since the club was founded, it began to falter.

In 1952, when James D. Norris, Jr. and Arthur M. Wirtz took over the

club, attendance had fallen off so badly that in 1954–55 they played some home games in Omaha, St. Louis, and St. Paul. Under Tobin and his associates the club had only been in the play-offs once and five times finished last.

James D. Norris, Jr. turned to his old friend of many years in Detroit, John Adams. Adams recommended Thomas N. Ivan who had just won his sixth consecutive league championship as coach of the Detroit Red Wings. Norris signed Ivan as general manager of the Chicago Black Hawks on July 7, 1954. Ivan's first job was to build a farm system. Tobin and his associates had let it deteriorate to such an extent that Chicago controlled only about three dozen players while the other clubs in the league were controlling around 200. "Dick" Irvin, whom Thomas Ivan had hired as coach in May, 1955, was forced to resign just prior to the start of the 1956–57 season due to illness (he died in May 1957) and Ivan took on the added duty of coaching.

The Black Hawks remained in the cellar during the first three years of Thomas Ivan's management, but during this time he was rebuilding the farm system. In 1957–58, Chicago secured Glenn Hall, an outstanding goaltender, from the Detroit Red Wings. From the farm system came a muscular left winger, destined to be one of the great goal scorers, Bobby Hull. Pierre Pilote, a fine defenseman, had joined the Black Hawks in 1955–56 and Stan Mikita, a scrappy center, arrived through the farm system in 1959–60. The Chicago Black Hawks would now take their place among the league contenders.

During a practice in March, 1961 Mikita slightly broke the blade of his stick, which resulted in its being partially curved. He continued to use it and became aware that the puck was taking off in an odd and unusual manner. He began soaking, heating and bending the blades of his sticks. Hull became interested and began warping his blades, and in the 1961–62 season they began using them in league games. Soon other players began using these hooked blades, when they saw the results Hull and Mikita were achieving, and manufacturers began producing them to meet the demand this stick was creating among hockey players. It was this "banana blade" that drove a puck in such an unpredictable fashion and the increased use of the slap-shot that caused many of the goaltenders to turn to the face mask for protection.

The early 1950s were the Detroit Red Wings' most glorious years. From 1948–49 through 1954–55, they were the National Hockey League champions and won four Stanley Cups. John Adams had turned the coaching chores over to Thomas Ivan, a man who had never played major league hockey. He coached the Red Wings to six straight first place finishes before going to Chicago. James D. Skinner who, also, had never played major league hockey, replaced Ivan and coached the Red Wings to their seventh straight league title. Detroit didn't stand pat with these clubs. Each year new faces appeared. Gordie Howe, "Red" Kelly, "Ted" Lindsay and Martin Pavelich were the only players there throughout the seven years.

The Toronto Maple Leafs had finished last in 1957–58 and before the start of the next season acquired John Bower, a goaltender, from the

minors, Bert Olmstead from the Montreal Canadiens, and Allan Stanley from the Boston Bruins. On November 28, 1958, George (Punch) Imlach, Maple Leafs general-manager, dismissed William Reay and took over the coaching duties. In a dramatic fight for the fourth and last playoff spot Imlach brought the Maple Leafs on strong to overtake the slumping New York Rangers on the last day of the season.

Bert Olmstead, who on January 9, 1954, while himself a member of the Montreal Canadiens, tied "The Rocket's" record of eight points in one game, retired at the end of the 1961–62 season. Imlach continued to guide the Maple Leafs to Stanley Cup victories in 1963 and 1964, and became the second Toronto coach to win three Stanley Cups in succession.

William O'Ree, the first Negro to play in the National Hockey League, made his debut at the Montreal Forum on January 18, 1958, as a member of the Boston Bruins.

In the summer of 1966, the National Hockey League opened its first United States office at 575 Madison Avenue in New York City. Don V. Ruck, the director, was appointed supervisor over all public relations in both Canada and the United States. He was also to administer all television and radio enterprises. In February 1967 the Columbia Broadcasting System began telecasting games nationally.

In 1967–68, six more clubs entered the National Hockey League and the league was divided into two divisions, with the older clubs in the Eastern Division and the new clubs in the Western Division. The six new clubs were the Minnesota North Stars, Los Angeles Kings, Philadelphia Flyers, Pittsburgh Penguins, Oakland Seals, and St. Louis Blues. Each new club paid $2 million for their franchise and were permitted to draft 18 players and two goaltenders from the other clubs.

The Oakland club began its first season calling themselves the California Seals but in early November changed to the Oakland Seals. Frank D. Selke, son of a former Toronto Maple Leafs Executive and Managing-Director of Montreal Canadiens, was named President of the Seals.

The Western Division schedule ended with only 6 points separating the top 5 clubs. The Philadelphia Flyers emerged the winner under the most trying conditions. Wind damage to the roof of the Spectrum forced them to remain on the road from early in March until the end of the schedule.

In the Eastern Division the Toronto Maple Leafs repeated what they had done 23 years before by failing to make the Stanley Cup playoffs after winning the cup the previous season.

3
History by Years

1894 Montreal Amateur Athletic Association

W. M. Barlow   A. A. Hodgson   A. T. Mussen   H. Routh
A. Cameron   G. R. James   E. M. O'Brien   A. C. Waud
Herbert G. Collins A. B. Kingan

The first Stanley Cup game ever played took place on March 22, 1894, at the Victoria Rink in Montreal between the cup holding Montreal Amateur Athletic Association club and the Ottawa Capitals. The Montreal club defeated Ottawa, 3 goals to 1.

On March 9, 1895 the Montreal Amateur Athletic Association club defeated Queen's University (Kingston, Ont.), 5 goals to 1, at Montreal.

1895 Montreal Victorias

S. Davidson   D. H. Henderson   R. E. MacDougall
Charles Graham Drinkwater R. W. Jones   Norman S. Rankin
Michael Grant

By winning the Canadian Amateur Hockey Association Championship in 1894–95 the Montreal Victorias took possession of the Stanley Cup.

1896 Winnipeg Victorias

J. Armytage   Flett   Higginbotham
Donald H. "Dan" Bain   Howard   Merritt
Campbell

On February 14, 1896, the Winnipeg Victorias defeated the Montreal Victorias 2 goals to 0 at Montreal.

The Winnipeg Victorias traveled over 1350 miles by rail to play a sudden-death game and become the first western club to win the Stanley Cup. The following biographical sketches were written by an eastern Canadian sportswriter:

Armytage, Winnipeg Victorias' captain, plays forward. A good general and possessed of staying powers. He is at his best at the end of a hard thirty minutes.

Bain, center forward; a very solidly built man, with great pace;

stands like a rock on his skates, is quick on the puck, and an unpleasant man to tackle if body-checking is the game.

Howard and Campbell—side forwards. Cool, quick players, both well-drilled in the scientific work of buttressing the puck against the sides of the rink to pass an opponent, and capable of shooting true at any distance.

Higginbotham—cover-point. A veteran player of great resources and judgement, a smart check and a good lifter. He has at times a pleasant way of running through the field, with the puck at the end of his stick.

Flett—point. Steady and reliable, always in position and seldom misses his check. A quick stickhandler.

Merritt—goalkeeper. Clever between the posts and not easily tempted to leave his position.

The team as a whole thoroughly understands the art of forward combination play. Each man is a good stickhandler, with the knack of shooting the puck hard and instantly from right hand or left.

1897 Montreal Victorias

S. Davidson	D. T. Gillelan	G. G. Lewis
Charles Graham	Michael Grant	R. E. MacDougall
Drinkwater	D. H. Henderson	E. H. McLea

On December 30, 1896, the Montreal Victorias defeated the Winnipeg Victorias, 6 goals to 5, at Winnipeg.

1898 Montreal Victorias

Cam Davidson	Michael Grant	R. E. MacDougall
Charles Graham	G. G. Lewis	E. H. McLea
Drinkwater	H. B. MacDougall	F. Richardson

On December 27, 1897, the Montreal Victorias defeated the Ottawa Capitals, 15 goals to 2, at Montreal.

1899 Montreal Victorias

Russell Bowie	W. Ewing	E. H. McLea
Cam Davidson	Michael Grant	F. McRobie
Charles Graham	G. G. Lewis	F. Richardson
Drinkwater	R. E. MacDougall	

In a 2-game series, the Montreal Victorias outscored the Winnipeg Victorias, 5 goals to 3.

Feb. 15, 1899	Montreal	2	Winnipeg	1	at Montreal
Feb. 18, 1899	Montreal	3	Winnipeg	2	at Montreal

In the first game Montreal scored 2 goals in the last two minutes of play. In the second game, with 13 minutes left to play and Montreal leading 3–2, MacDougall viciously struck A. B. Gingras, Winnipeg right winger, across the knee, putting him out of the game. When referee Findlay gave MacDougall a minor penalty, instead of a game misconduct,

the Winnipeg players left the ice and refused to return. Later the Stanley Cup trustees upheld Findlay's decision.

1899 Montreal Shamrocks

J. P. Brannen	Fred Scanlan	Harry J. Trihey
Arthur F. Farrell	F. C. Tansey	F. Wall
J. H. McKenna		

By winning the Canadian Amateur Hockey Association Championship in 1898–99 the Montreal Shamrocks took possession of the Stanley Cup.

On March 14, 1899, the Montreal Shamrocks defeated Queen's University (Kingston, Ont.), 6 goals to 2, at Montreal.

1900 Montreal Shamrocks

J. P. Brannen	J. H. McKenna	Harry J. Trihey
Arthur F. Farrell	Fred Scanlan	F. Wall
C. Hoerner		

In a 2-out-of-3-game series, the Montreal Shamrocks defeated the Winnipeg Victorias, 2 games to 1.

Feb. 12, 1900	Montreal	3	Winnipeg	4
Feb. 14, 1900	Montreal	3	Winnipeg	2
Feb. 16, 1900	Montreal	5	Winnipeg	4

In the third game, Trihey scored the winning goal with a minute left to play.

In a 2-out-of-3-game series, the Montreal Shamrocks defeated the Halifax Crescents, 2 games to 0.

Mar. 5, 1900	Montreal	10	Halifax	2
Mar. 7, 1900	Montreal	11	Halifax	0

1901 Winnipeg Victorias

Donald H. Bain	M. L. Flett	Charles W. Johnstone
A. Brown	R. M. Flett	John Marshall
F. T. Cadham	A. B. Gingras	E. B. Wood

In a 2-out-of-3-game series, the Winnipeg Victorias defeated the Montreal Shamrocks, 2 games to 0.

Jan. 29, 1901	Winnipeg	4	Montreal	3
Jan. 31, 1901	Winnipeg	2*	Montreal	1

*Bain scored 4:00 in overtime.

In the first game checking was close and very hard. The following is a report by an observer:

Winnipeg's Bain made a run all alone. Wall of the Shamrocks made some extraordinary lifts. Then both of them got into a mix-up and were sent to the fence. The game was rough. Sticks on both sides were

cut to razor-like effectiveness and, in the slashing, ankles were temporarily rendered useless. Players on both teams tried to see how near the fence a man might be shouldered without being charged with manslaughter.

In the second game penalties were numerous as the clubs played bitterly.

In a 2-out-of-3-game series, the Winnipeg Victorias defeated the Toronto Wellingtons, 2 games to 0.

Jan. 21, 1902   Winnipeg   5   Toronto   3
Jan. 23, 1902   Winnipeg   5   Toronto   3

1902 Montreal Amateur Athletic Association

W. J. Bellingham   T. G. Hodge   John Marshall
Richard R. Boon   A. Hooper   W. C. Nicholson
R. R. Elliott   C. A. Liffiton   G. Smith
James Henry Gardner

In a 2-out-of-3-game series, the Montreal Amateur Athletic Association club defeated the Winnipeg Victorias, 2 games to 1.

Mar. 13, 1902   Montreal   0   Winnipeg   1
Mar. 15, 1902   Montreal   5   Winnipeg   0
Mar. 17, 1902   Montreal   2   Winnipeg   1

In a 2-out-of-3-game series, the Montreal Amateur Athletic Association club defeated the Winnipeg Victorias, 2 games to 1.

Jan. 29, 1903   Montreal   8   Winnipeg   1
Jan. 31, 1903   Montreal   2   Winnipeg   2

27 minutes of overtime was played in an attempt to break this tie.

Feb. 2, 1903   Montreal   2   Winnipeg   4
Feb. 4, 1903   Montreal   5   Winnipeg   1

1903 Ottawa Silver Seven

A. A. Fraser   John Bower Hutton   Alfred E. Smith
Dave J. Gilmour   Frank McGee   C. D. Spittall
Hamilton Livingstone   Art E. Moore   Harry Westwick
  Gilmour   E. Harvey Pulford   F. W. Wood
S. C. Gilmour   P. T. Sims

When a club won the championship of a league in which the Stanley Cup holder competed, it would then take possession of the cup. It was in this manner that the Ottawa Silver Seven gained the cup from the Montreal Amateur Athletic Association club.

In a 2-game series, the Ottawa Silver Seven outscored the Montreal Victorias, 9 goals to 1.

March 7, 1903   Ottawa   1   Montreal   1   at Montreal
March 10, 1903   Ottawa   8   Montreal   0   at Ottawa

In a 2-out-of-3-game series, the Ottawa Silver Seven defeated the Rat Portage (Kenora, Ont.) Thistles, 2 games to 0.

Mar. 12, 1903   Ottawa   6   Rat Portage   2
Mar. 14, 1903   Ottawa   4   Rat Portage   2

Six native sons played for this club: Hutton, goal; Moore, cover-point; McGee, center; H. Gilmour, rover; S. Gilmour, right wing; D. Gilmour, left wing. Later, four of them, along with Westwick, would be elected to Hockey's Hall of Fame. Frank McGee scored four goals in this series. Another honor would come 50 years later when this club would be voted "the outstanding hockey club of the first half century."

1904 Ottawa Silver Seven

A. A. Fraser	John Bower Hutton	E. Harvey Pulford
Dave J. Gilmour	Frank McGee	Alfred E. Smith
Hamilton Livingstone	J. McGee	Harry Westwick
Gilmour	Art E. Moore	F. W. Wood
S. C. Gilmour	P. T. Sims	

In a 2-out-of-3-game series, the Ottawa Silver Seven defeated the Winnipeg Rowing Club, 2 games to 1.

Dec. 30, 1903   Ottawa   9   Winnipeg   1
Jan. 1, 1904   Ottawa   2   Winnipeg   6
Jan. 4, 1904   Ottawa   2   Winnipeg   0

In the first game, Winnipeg was so eager to win that its players frequently over-skated the puck, collided with each other and constantly found themselves out of position. The game lasted almost three hours. In the first half, Westwick scored two goals in nine seconds.

In the second game, Ottawa suffered the first loss of only three games they would lose in defending the Stanley Cup. The third game was one of the bloodiest Stanley Cup games ever played. From the time referee Trihey dropped the first puck until there were only 15 minutes left there was no score, but the battered Winnipeg club eventually went down to defeat.

The Winnipeg *Free Press* carried the following casualty list:

Hospital cases of Rowing Club: P. Brown, lame; C. Richards, face swollen, leg hurt; C. Bennest, thumb broken, badly bruised; W. Breen, bruised and broken-up; J. Hall, cut on head; D. Kirby, cut on head; W. Bawlf, cut and bruised. Seven out of nine injured; two forced to retire from game, three forced to remain in bed after game; one out of hockey for season.

In a 2-out-of-3-game series, the Ottawa Silver Seven defeated the Toronto Marlboroughs, 2 games to 0.

Feb. 23, 1904   Ottawa   6   Toronto   3
Feb. 25, 1904   Ottawa   11   Toronto   2

In the first game, Toronto led, 3–1, at halftime but Ottawa came back

in the second half to score five goals. By the end of the game, the Toronto club had been severely crippled. "Tom" Phillips was barely able to skate at all, Winchester had a badly battered arm and MacLaren was in the hospital with a broken rib.

The following was reported by the *Toronto Globe:*

> Ottawa players slash, trip and practice the severest kind of cross-checking with a systematic hammering of hands and wrists. They hit a man on the head when the referee isn't looking, and they body a man into the boards after he has passed the puck. The rubber is not the objective, but the man must be stopped at all costs; if he is put out altogether, so much the better.

On March 2, 1904 the Ottawa Silver Seven tied with the Montreal Wanderers, 5 goals to 5, at Montreal.

Ottawa led 5–3 with 5 minutes left to play but Montreal tied the score and then wouldn't play any overtime unless referee Kearns was replaced. It was in this game that Montreal's huge goaltender, 300-pound "Billy" Nicholson, skated the length of the rink in an attempt to score. Game lasted 4 hours and 36 penalties were called. The series was abandoned when the Stanley Cup trustees ordered the next game to be played at Ottawa and Montreal refused to go.

In a 2-out-of-3-game series, the Ottawa Silver Seven defeated the Brandon (Man.) Wheat Kings, 2 games to 0.

Mar. 9, 1904   Ottawa   6   Brandon   3
Mar. 11, 1904   Ottawa   9   Brandon   3

Lester Patrick played for Brandon and it was in this series, while playing defense, that he rushed up the ice and scored a goal, to become the first defenceman ever to do so. Frank McGee scored 21 of Ottawa's 50 goals in these eight games.

1905 Ottawa Silver Seven

D. N. Finnie	Frank McGee	Alfred E. Smith
Hamilton Livingstone	Art E. Moore	Harry Westwick
Gilmour	E. Harvey Pulford	

In a 2-out-of-3-game series, the Ottawa Silver Seven defeated Dawson City (Yukon Territory), 2 games to 0.

Jan. 13, 1905   Ottawa   9   Dawson City   2
Jan. 16, 1905   Ottawa   23   Dawson City   2

The Dawson City club was formed by a group of young men who had gone to the Yukon to seek their fortune during the Klondike gold rush. Upon receiving their challenge, the Stanley Cup trustees notified them that they would have to meet the Ottawa Silver Seven in Ottawa.

On Dec. 19, 1904, they started walking; they stopped at Royal Canadian Northwest Mounted Police posts, they arrived at Whitehorse after nine days. There a storm delayed them for two days and they waited three

days in Skagway for a boat to take them to Seattle. From there they took a train and after three weeks and 4,000 miles arrived in Ottawa.

Frank McGee, Ottawa's brilliant center, scored only once in the first game, but in the second game he scored fourteen goals. Frequently skating from end to end he scored eight goals in succession and five in a little over three minutes. McGee had lost an eye in a game earlier in his career and later gave his life in the Battle of the Somme. His record has never been broken nor has any club ever traveled so far or been so soundly beaten.

In a 2-out-of-3-game series, the Ottawa Silver Seven defeated the Rat Portage (Kenora, Ont.) Thistles, 2 games to 1.

Mar. 7, 1905   Ottawa   3   Rat Portage   9
Mar. 9, 1905   Ottawa   4   Rat Portage   2
Mar. 11, 1905   Ottawa   5   Rat Portage   4

In the first game Ottawa lost the second of three games they would eventually lose in nine series in defence of the Stanley Cup. "Tom" Phillips scored four goals for Rat Portage in that first game. "Billy" Gilmour and Frank McGee hadn't played in the first game, but returned for the second and Ottawa won, 4–2.

The third game was brutal; when an exhausted Rat Portage player fell in front of his goal he was given a major penalty for obstructing the goal.

At half-time, Rat Portage led, 2–1, and with two minutes left in the game, the score was 4–4. With a minute and thirty seconds to go the great Frank McGee scored his third goal of the evening.

1905–06

In a 2-out-of-3-game series, the Ottawa Silver Seven defeated Queen's University (Kingston, Ont.) 2 games to 0.

Feb. 27, 1906   Ottawa   16   Queen's University   7
Feb. 28, 1906   Ottawa   12   Queen's University   7

In a 2-out-of-3-game series, the Ottawa Silver Seven defeated Smiths Falls (Ont.), 2 games to 0.

Mar. 6, 1906   Ottawa   6   Smiths Falls   5
Mar. 8, 1906   Ottawa   8   Smiths Falls   2

1906 Montreal Wanderers

Frank "Pud" Glass	T. R. "Rod" Kennedy	Ernest Russell
Ernest "Moose" Johnson	J. "Doc" Menard	W. S. "Billy" Strachan
	Lester Patrick	

In a 2-game series, the Montreal Wanderers outscored the Ottawa Silver Seven, 12 goals to 10.

Mar. 14, 1906   Montreal   9   Ottawa   1
Mar. 17, 1906   Montreal   3   Ottawa   9

Defensive play predominated with hard-hitting and close-checking until F. Glass scored with eight minutes gone. Near the 13-minute mark he

scored again and at halftime the Wanderers were leading, 4–0.

The rout continued as Glass scored again near the 11-minute mark of the second half and Russell followed with two more. Eventually Harry Smith scored for Ottawa, but Montreal came back to score twice within six minutes. It was a humiliating defeat for the club that had held the Stanley Cup since March of 1903. They had won nine consecutive series, had won 17 of 22 games and had outscored their opponents by 156 goals to 77.

Ottawa replaced "Billy" Hague with Percy LeSueur in goal and started the second game with a concerted attack. Lester Patrick scored the first goal after twelve minutes. The attack persisted and Frank McGee scored followed with two by Harry Smith. At the half-time, the score was 3–1 for Ottawa.

Ottawa had attacked strongly in the first half, but in the second half they began with a devastating onslaught. In a minute and 25 seconds, they had scored three goals. Harry Smith scored his fourth goal and the Wanderers lead slipped to 10–8. Near the 18-minute mark Harry Smith scored two goals to tie it up 10–10.

The Ottawa Silver Seven were now showing the class that had made them the world's champions for the past three years. With 10 minutes remaining, Smith scored his seventh goal, only to have referee Robert Meldrum rule it offside. Shortly thereafter, Smith drew a penalty and with Ottawa playing six men to seven and tiring, Lester Patrick scored for the Wanderers. A minute later he scored his third goal of the evening and the reign of the Silver Seven had come to a close.

In a 2-game series, the Montreal Wanderers outscored New Glasgow (N.S.), 17 goals to 5.

Dec. 27, 1906   Montreal   10   New Glasgow   3   at Montreal
Dec. 29, 1906   Montreal   7   New Glasgow   2   at Montreal

1907 Kenora Thistles

D. R. "Roxy" Beaudro   Charles Thomas   R. Phillips
E. Giroux   Hooper   "Tom" Phillips
Silas Seth Griffis   William George   Arthur Howey Ross
Joseph Henry Hall   McGimsie

In a 2-game series, the Kenora Thistles outscored the Montreal Wanderers, 12 goals to 8.

Jan. 17, 1907   Kenora   4   Montreal   2
Jan. 21, 1907   Kenora   8   Montreal   6

1907 Montreal Wanderers

Cecil W. Blatchford   E. Liffiton   H. C. Strachan
Frank Glass   John Marshall   W. S. Strachan
William Milton Hern   Lester Patrick   Bruce Stuart
Ernest Johnson   Ernest Russell   Hodgson Stuart
T. R. Kennedy   Walter Smaill

In a 2-game series, the Montreal Wanderers outscored the Kenora Thistles, 12 goals to 8.

Mar. 23, 1907 Montreal 7 Kenora 2
Mar. 25, 1907 Montreal 5 Kenora 6

Although Alfred E. Smith, Harry "Rat" Westwick and Fred Whitcroft, three future Hall of Fame members, joined Kenora for this series, the Thistles were unable to defeat the Wanderers.

1908 Montreal Wanderers

Cecil W. Blatchford	John Marshall	W. S. Strachan
Frank Glass	Arthur Howey Ross	Bruce Stuart
William Milton Hern	Ernest Russell	
Ernest Johnson	Walter Smaill	
E. Liffiton	H. C. Strachan	

In a 2-game series, the Montreal Wanderers outscored the Ottawa Victorias, 22 goals to 4.

Jan. 9, 1908 Montreal   9 Ottawa 3 at Montreal
Jan. 13, 1908 Montreal 13 Ottawa 1 at Montreal

In a 2-game series, the Montreal Wanderers outscored the Winnipeg Maple Leafs, 20 to 8.

Mar. 10, 1908 Montreal 11 Winnipeg 5
Mar. 12, 1908 Montreal   9 Winnipeg 3

On Mar. 14, 1908, the Montreal Wanderers defeated the Toronto Trolley Leaguers, 6 to 4, at Montreal.

1909 Ottawa Senators

Edgar Dey	Fred Lake	Frederic Wellington
Hamilton Livingstone	Percy LeSueur	Taylor
Gilmour	Bruce Stuart	Martin Walsh
Albert "Dubby" Kerr		

In a 2-game series the Montreal Wanderers outscored Edmonton, 13 goals to 10.

Dec. 28, 1908 Montreal 7 Edmonton 3 at Montreal
Dec. 30, 1908 Montreal 6 Edmonton 7 at Montreal

Every player on the Edmonton club was a 'ringer' except one. They included Harold McNamara, "Tom" Phillips, Didier Pitre and Lester Patrick, who captained the club.

On Mar. 3, 1909, the Ottawa Senators defeated the Montreal Wanderers, 8 to 3, at Ottawa.

As soon as referee Russell Bowie dropped the first puck, end to end rushes predominated and at 4:50 Ottawa scored. At 5:30, Bruce Stuart, Ottawa's rover, scored and at one time Ottawa had three men in the penalty box.

The half-time ended, tied 3–3. The second half started with Ottawa attacking and when the Wanderers had two men in the penalty box,

"Dubby" Kerr scored to put them in the lead, 4–3. When the game ended, Ottawa had scored four more goals.

1909–10

In a 2-game series, the Ottawa Senators outscored Galt (Ont.), 15 to 4.

Jan. 5, 1910   Ottawa   12   Galt   3
Jan. 7, 1910   Ottawa   3   Galt   1

In a 2-game series, the Ottawa Senators outscored Edmonton, 21 to 11.

Jan. 18, 1910   Ottawa   8   Edmonton   4
Jan. 20, 1910   Ottawa   13   Edmonton   7

1910 Montreal Wanderers

Cecil W. Blatchford	William Milton Hern	John Marshall
W. Chipchase	Harry M. Hyland	Ernest Russell
Frank Glass	Ernest Johnson	

On Mar. 5, 1910, the Montreal Wanderers defeated the Ottawa Senators, 3 goals to 1, at Ottawa.

On Mar. 12, 1910, the Montreal Wanderers defeated Berlin (Kitchener, Ont.), 7 goals to 3, at Montreal.

1911 Ottawa Senators

Alex Currie	Fred Lake	Bruce Stuart
John Proctor Darragh	Percy LeSueur	Martin Walsh
Horace Gaul	Bruce Ridpath	
Albert "Dubby" Kerr	Hamby Shore	

*On Mar. 13, 1911, the Ottawa Senators defeated Galt (Ont.), 7 goals to 4, at Ottawa.

*On Mar. 16, 1911, the Ottawa Senators defeated Port Arthur (Ont.), 13 to 4, at Ottawa.

In the third period, Walsh scored three goals in 40 seconds.

1912 Quebec Bulldogs

Joseph Henry Hall	"Jack" McDonald	George Prodgers
—— Leonard	Patrick Joseph Moran	Walter Rooney
Joseph Malone	Edward Oatman	
Jack Marks		

In a 2-out-of-3-game series, the Quebec Bulldogs defeated Moncton (N. B.), 2 to 0.

†Mar. 11, 1912   Quebec   9   Moncton   3
†Mar. 13, 1912   Quebec   8   Moncton   0

*These were the first Stanley Cup Games to be played in three 20-minute periods (all previous games were played in two 30-minute halves).
†These were the first Stanley Cup games to be played with 6 players a side (all previous games were played with 7 players a side).

1913 Quebec Bulldogs

Samuel Russell   Jeff Malone   Harry Mummery
  Crawford   Joseph Malone   Walter Rooney
Billy Creighton   Jack Marks   Thomas Smith
Joseph Henry Hall   Patrick Joseph Moran

In a 2-out-of-3-game series, the Quebec Bulldogs defeated the Sydney (N. S.) Millionaires, 2 to 0.

Mar. 8, 1913   Quebec   14   Sydney   3
Mar. 10, 1913   Quebec   6   Sydney   2

In the first game, Joseph Malone scored nine goals.

1914 Toronto Blueshirts

Harold Hugh Cameron   Frank C. Foyston   George McNamara
Con Corbeau   Harry Holmes   John Phillip Walker
Allan M. Davidson   F. Roy "Minnie"   Carol Wilson
                         McGiffen

In a 3-out-of-5-game series, the Toronto Blueshirts defeated the Victoria Capitals, 3 to 0.

Mar. 14, 1914   Toronto   5   Victoria   2
Mar. 17, 1914   Toronto   6*   Victoria   5
Mar. 19, 1914   Toronto   2   Victoria   1

(*McGiffen scored 15:00 in overtime)

1914—The 1st and 3rd games were played under National Hockey Association rules (6 players a side, no forward passing anywhere, substitute allowed for penalized player). The 2nd game was played under Pacific Coast Hockey Association rules (7 players a side, forward passing allowed in center zone, no substitute for penalized player).

This was the first series between the National Hockey Association champions and the Pacific Coast Hockey Association champions.

1915 Vancouver Millionaires

Lloyd Cook   Frank Nighbor   Frederic Wellington
Hugh Lehman   Frank A. Patrick   Taylor
Duncan MacKay   James Seaborn
Kenny Mallen   Russell Stanley

In a 3-out-of-5-game series, the Vancouver Millionaires defeated the Ottawa Senators, 3 to 0.

Mar. 22, 1915   Vancouver   6   Ottawa   2
Mar. 24, 1915   Vancouver   8   Ottawa   3
Mar. 26, 1915   Vancouver   12   Ottawa   3

1915—The 2nd game was played under National Hockey Association rules (6 players a side, no forward passing anywhere, substitute allowed for penalized player). The 1st and 3rd games were played under Pacific Coast Hockey Association rules (7 players a side, forward passing allowed in center zone, no substitute for penalized player).

Silas Seth Griffis, captain and outstanding defenceman of Vancouver, didn't play in this series due to a broken ankle which occurred in practice at the end of the regular season.

1916 Montreal Canadiens

Amos Arbour
Louis Berlinquette
Bert Corbeau
Jack Fournier
Edouard Charles
  Lalonde

Jean Baptiste
  Laviolette
Howard McNamara
Didier Pitre
George "Skinner"
  Poulin
George Prodgers

Skene Ronan
Georges Vezina

In a 3-out-of-5-game series, the Montreal Canadiens defeated the Portland Rosebuds, 3 to 2.

Mar. 20, 1916	Montreal	0	Portland	2
Mar. 22, 1916	Montreal	2	Portland	1
Mar. 25, 1916	Montreal	6	Portland	3
Mar. 28, 1916	Montreal	5	Portland	6
Mar. 30, 1916	Montreal	2	Portland	1

1916—The 1st, 3rd and 5th games were played under National Hockey Association rules (6 players a side, no forward passing anywhere, substitute allowed for penalized player). The 2nd and 4th games were played under Pacific Coast Hockey Association rules (7 players a side, forward passing allowed in center zone, no substitute for penalized player).

1917 Seattle Metropolitans

Everar L. Carpenter
Frank C. Foyston
Harry Holmes

Bernard Patrick
  Morris
Roy Rickey

James Riley
Robert Rowe
John Phillip Walker
Carol Wilson

In a 3-out-of-5-game series, the Seattle Metropolitans defeated the Montreal Canadiens, 3 to 1.

Mar. 17, 1917	Seattle	4	Montreal	8
Mar. 20, 1917	Seattle	6	Montreal	1
Mar. 23, 1917	Seattle	4	Montreal	1
Mar. 26, 1917	Seattle	9	Montreal	1

1917—The 2nd and 4th games were played under National Hockey Association rules (6 players a side, no forward passing anywhere, substitute allowed for penalized player). The 1st and 3rd games were played under Pacific Coast Hockey Association rules (7 players a side, forward passing allowed in centre zone, no substitute for penalized player).

This club, coached by Pete Muldoon, was the first United States club to win the Stanley Cup.

1917–18

The National Hockey League played a split schedule during its first 4 seasons. The winner of the first half met the winner of the second half to decide the league championship.

League Standings

First Half

	Games	Won	Lost	Tied	Points	Goals for	Goals against
Montreal	14	10	4	0	20	81	47
Toronto	14	8	6	0	16	71	75
Ottawa	14	5	9	0	10	67	79
Montreal Wanderers	6	1	5	0	2	17	35

The Montreal Wanderers withdrew from the league after playing 6 games when their Westmount Arena burned on January 2, 1918.

Second Half

	Games	Won	Lost	Tied	Points	Goals for	Goals against
Toronto	8	5	3	0	10	37	34
Ottawa	8	4	4	0	8	35	35
Montreal	8	3	5	0	6	34	37

In a 2 game series with the club scoring the most goals winning the league championship, Toronto outscored the Montreal Canadiens 10 to 7.

Mar. 11   Montreal   3   Toronto   7
Mar. 13   Montreal   4   Toronto   3

1918 Toronto Arenas

Harold Hugh Cameron
Corbett Denneny
Harry Holmes

Harry Meeking
Harry Mummery

Edward Reginald
  Noble
Kenneth Randall
Alf. Skinner

Stanley Cup

This was the first series between the National Hockey League champions and the Pacific Coast Hockey Association champions.

Mar. 20   Toronto   5   Vancouver   3
Mar. 23   Toronto   4   Vancouver   6
Mar. 26   Toronto   6   Vancouver   3
Mar. 28   Toronto   1   Vancouver   8
Mar. 30   Toronto   2   Vancouver   1

Winner: Toronto, 3–2.

1918—The 1st, 3rd & 5th games were played under National Hockey League rules (6 players a side, no forward passing anywhere, substitute allowed for penalized player). The 2nd & 4th games were played under Pacific Coast Hockey Association rules (7 players a side, forward passing allowed in centre zone, no substitute for penalized player).

"Jack" Adams and "Rusty" Crawford had signed with Toronto after the February 1st deadline and were not eligible to play in Stanley Cup games. Toronto's request that the rule be waived was denied by Vancouver.

Leaders

Goals: Joseph Malone (Montreal) 44; Assists: not recorded; Points: Joseph Malone 44——44; Penalty Minutes: not recorded.

Notes

National Hockey League organized at Montreal, November 22. First four teams were: Montreal Canadiens and Wanderers, Ottawa Senators, Toronto Arenas and the Quebec Bulldogs. Quebec failed to produce a team although it held a franchise.

The first official N.H.L. games were played December 19, 1917, and Toronto was the only city with an artificial ice arena.

Frank Calder was elected first president and also served as secretary-treasurer.

The N.H.L. played six-man hockey, eliminating the position of "Rover," who was a free-lancing forward, assigned to no specific position on attack or defense.

The first season demanded a schedule of 22 games for each team. Today the teams play a 76-game season.

Fire destroyed the arena used by the Montreal Wanderers and the team disbanded.

The league played a split schedule, 14 games in the first section, eight in the second with the two sectional winners meeting for a two-game championship playoff, decided by most-goals scored in the two games. The Toronto Arenas won the first title, outscoring the Montreal Canadiens, 10–7.

1918–19

League Standings

First Half

	Games	Won	Lost	Tied	Points	Goals for	Goals against
Montreal	10	7	3	0	14	57	50
Ottawa	10	5	5	0	10	39	40
Toronto	10	3	7	0	6	43	49

Second Half

	Games	Won	Lost	Tied	Points	Goals for	Goals against
Ottawa	8	7	1	0	14	32	14
Montreal	8	3	5	0	6	31	28
Toronto	8	2	6	0	4	22	43

In a 4-out-of-7-game series, Montreal defeated Ottawa, 4 games to 1.

Feb. 22	Montreal	8	Ottawa	4
Feb. 27	Montreal	5	Ottawa	3
March 1	Montreal	6	Ottawa	6
March 3	Montreal	3	Ottawa	6
March 6	Montreal	4	Ottawa	2

Stanley Cup: No Decision

Mar. 19, 1919	Montreal	0	Seattle	7	
Mar. 22, 1919	Montreal	4	Seattle	2	
Mar. 24, 1919	Montreal	2	Seattle	7	
Mar. 26, 1919	Montreal	0	Seattle	0	(Two 10-minute overtime
Mar. 29, 1919	Montreal	4*	Seattle	3	periods played)

*McDonald scored 15:57 in overtime.

1919—The 2nd, 4th and 5th games were played under National Hockey League rules (6 players a side, no forward passing anywhere, substitute allowed for penalized player). The 1st and 3rd games were played under Pacific Coast Hockey Association rules (7 players a side, forward passing allowed in center zone, no substitute for penalized player).

Playoff Action

Leaders

Goals: Edouard Lalonde (Montreal), Ogilvie Cleghorn (Montreal) 23 (tie)
Assists: Edouard Lalonde 9; Points: Edouard Lalonde 23-9-32; Penalty Minutes: Joseph Hall (Montreal) 85.

Notes

Schedule dropped to 18 games with only three teams in the league.

Assists were added as part of the scoring record.

Kicking the puck was allowed.

The Seattle Department of Health halted this series when so many of the Montreal Canadiens became ill with the Spanish influenza that was sweeping the country. Joseph Hall had stopped off at his home in Brandon, Man., and when he arrived at Seattle had to be hospitalized. "Bill" Coutu and "Jack" McDonald were also quite sick.

In the second game, "Newsy" Lalonde scored all the Canadien's goals. In the fifth game "Jack" McDonald, who had dressed but played only intermittently due to illness, came on the ice in an attempt to aid his sick and tired teammates, who were holding a 3–3 tie in overtime. He carried the puck into Seattle territory and after faking passes to Lalonde and Ogilvie Cleghorn, evaded the goaltender as he came out and scored.

On the day the sixth game was scheduled, five of the Canadiens were seriously ill, and Hall and McDonald were in critical condition. Joseph Hall never recovered. George Kennedy, Canadien manager, was also very ill and died from the effects two years later.

Had the Stanley Cup trustees been approached, they probably would have awarded the cup to Seattle, but Frank A. Patrick, the Pacific Coast Hockey Association president, refused to take advantage of a stricken foe.

1919–20

League Standings

First Half

	Games	Won	Lost	Tied	Points	Goals for	Goals against
Ottawa	12	9	3	0	18	59	23
Montreal	12	8	4	0	16	62	51
Toronto	12	5	7	0	10	52	62
Quebec	12	2	10	0	4	44	81

Second Half

	Games	Won	Lost	Tied	Points	Goals for	Goals against
Ottawa	12	10	2	0	20	62	41
Toronto	12	7	5	0	14	67	44
Montreal	12	5	7	0	10	67	62
Quebec	12	2	10	0	4	47	96

By winning both halves Ottawa was automatically league champion.

1920 Ottawa Senators

Clinton S. Benedict	Sprague Cleghorn	
George Boucher	John Proctor Darragh	Frank Nighbor
Harry L. Broadbent	Cyril Denneny	Edward George
Morley Bruce	Jack McKell	Gerard

Stanley Cup

March 22	Ottawa	3	Seattle	2
March 24	Ottawa	3	Seattle	0
March 27	Ottawa	1	Seattle	3
March 30	Ottawa	2	Seattle	5
April 1	Ottawa	6	Seattle	1

Winner: Ottawa, 3–2.

Last two games played on artificial ice at Toronto because of mild weather at Ottawa.

1920—The 1st, 3rd and 5th games were played under National Hockey League rules (6 players a side, no forward passing anywhere, substitute allowed for penalized player). The 2nd and 4th games were played under Pacific Coast Hockey Association rules (7 players a side, forward passing allowed in center zone, no substitute for penalized player).

Leaders

Goals: Joseph Malone (Quebec) 39; Assists: Corbett Denneny (Toronto) 12;
Points: Joseph Malone 39-6-45; Penalty Minutes: Carol Wilson (Toronto) 79.

Notes

The Quebec Bulldogs joined the league which now played a 24-game schedule with four teams.
The Toronto Arenas changed their name to St. Patricks.

1920–21

League Standings

First Half	Games	Won	Lost	Tied	Points	Goals for	Goals against
Ottawa	10	8	2	0	16	49	23
Toronto	10	5	5	0	10	39	47
Montreal	10	4	6	0	8	37	51
Hamilton	10	3	7	0	6	34	38

Second Half	Games	Won	Lost	Tied	Points	Goals for	Goals against
Toronto	14	10	4	0	20	66	53
Montreal	14	9	5	0	18	75	48
Ottawa	14	6	8	0	12	48	52
Hamilton	14	3	11	0	6	58	94

In a 2-game series, with the club scoring the most goals winning the league championship, Ottawa outscored Toronto, 7–0.

March 10   Ottawa   5   Toronto   0
March 14   Ottawa   2   Toronto   0

1921 Ottawa Senators

Clinton S. Benedict	Sprague Cleghorn	
George Boucher	John Proctor Darragh	Frank Nighbor
Harry L. Broadbent	Cyril Denneny	Edward George
Morley Bruce	Jack McKell	Gerard

Stanley Cup

March 21, 1921   Ottawa   1   Vancouver   3
March 24, 1921   Ottawa   4   Vancouver   3
March 28, 1921   Ottawa   3   Vancouver   2
March 31, 1921   Ottawa   2   Vancouver   3
April   4, 1921   Ottawa   2   Vancouver   1
   Winner: Ottawa, 3–2.

1921—The 1st game was played under National Hockey League rule (6 players a side) and Pacific Coast Hockey Association rules (forward passing allowed in center zone, no substitute for penalized player). The 2nd and 4th games were played under National Hockey League rules (6 players a side, no forward passing anywhere, substitute allowed for penalized player). The 3rd and 5th games were played under Pacific Coast Hockey Association rules (7 players a side, forward passing allowed in center zone, no substitute for penalized player).

Leaders

Goals: Cecil Dye (Toronto) 35; Assists: Louis Berlinquette (Montreal), Harold Cameron (Toronto), Joseph Matte (Hamilton) 9 (tie); Points: Edouard Lalonde (Montreal) 33-8-41; Penalty Minutes: Bert Corbeau (Montreal) 86.

Notes

Quebec's Bulldogs dropped out and were replaced by the Hamilton Tigers. Goaltenders were now allowed to pass forward in the defense zones.

1921–22

League Standings

The National Hockey League discarded the split schedule and for the next 3 seasons the first place club played the second place club in a 2 game series. The club scoring the most goals was declared the league champion.

Clubs	Games	Won	Lost	Tied	Points	Goals for	Goals against
Ottawa	24	14	8	2	30	106	84
Toronto	24	13	10	1	27	98	97
Montreal	24	12	11	1	25	88	94
Hamilton	24	7	17	0	14	88	105

Toronto outscored Ottawa, 5 goals to 4.
March 11, 1922   Ottawa   4   Toronto   5
March 13, 1922   Ottawa   0   Toronto   0

In a 2-game series, the Vancouver Millionaires defeated the Regina Capitals of the Western Canada Hockey League, 5 goals to 2. The first game was played under Pacific Coast Hockey Association rules (7 players to a side). The second was played under Western Canada Hockey League rules (6 players).

March 8, 1922   Vancouver   1   Regina   2
March 11, 1922   Vancouver   4   Regina   0

1922 Toronto St. Patricks

Lloyd Andrews
Harold Hugh Cameron
Corbett Denneny
Edward George
  Gerard
Cecil Dye
Edward Reginald
  Noble
Kenneth Randall
John Ross Roach
Roderick Smylie
Theodore Stackhouse
William Stuart

Stanley Cup: Toronto 3, Vancouver 2 (Games)

March 17   Toronto   3   Vancouver   4
March 21   Toronto   2   Vancouver   1   (Dye scored 4:45 in overtime)
March 23   Toronto   0   Vancouver   3
March 25   Toronto   6   Vancouver   0
March 28   Toronto   5   Vancouver   1

The 1st, 3rd and 5th games were played under N.H.L. rules (6 players to a side). The 2nd and 4th games were played under PCHA rules (7 players a side).

Leaders

Goals: Harry Broadbent (Ottawa) 32; Assists: Harry Broadbent, Leo Reise (Hamilton) 14 (tie); Points: Harry Broadbent 32-14-46; Penalty Minutes: Sprague Cleghorn (Montreal) 63.

Notes*

The Stanley Cup series between the Regina Capitals of the Western Canada Hockey League and the Vancouver Millionaires of the Pacific Coast Hockey Association was Western Canada's first attempt at the Cup.

In the Regina–Vancouver series, Arthur Duncan scored 3 goals in the 2nd game.

In the Toronto–Vancouver Cup playoff, John James Adams, playing for Vancouver and later to be Detroit's general-manager, scored six goals during the series and Cecil Dye scored nine, four of them in the fifth game.

With Harold Cameron and Kenneth Randall injured and unable to play, the Toronto St. Patricks were granted permission to use Edward Gerard, captain and outstanding defenseman of the Ottawa Senators, in the 4th game. In the 5th game, Cameron was able to return.

In this same series, Edward Oatman of the Victoria Aristocrats had been granted permission to play for the Vancouver Millionaires as a replacement for the injured Fred Harris.

1922–23

League Standings

Clubs	Games	Won	Lost	Tied	Points	Goals for	Goals against
Ottawa	24	14	9	1	29	77	54
Montreal	24	13	9	2	28	73	61
Toronto	24	13	10	1	27	82	88
Hamilton	24	6	18	0	12	81	110

Ottawa outscored Montreal, 3 goals to 2.

March 7	Montreal	0	Ottawa	2
March 9	Montreal	2	Ottawa	1

1923 Ottawa Senators

Clinton S. Benedict		
George Boucher	Cyril Denneny	Harry L. Broadbent
Francis Michael Clancy	Edward George Gerard	Lionel Hitchman
		Frank Nighbor

Stanley Cup: Ottawa 3, Vancouver 1 (Games)

March 16	Ottawa	1	Vancouver	0
March 19	Ottawa	1	Vancouver	4
March 23	Ottawa	3	Vancouver	2
March 26	Ottawa	5	Vancouver	1

* In 1922, 1923 and 1924 there were three major hockey leagues (Pacific Coast Hockey Association, National Hockey League and Western Canada Hockey League).
In 1922 the Pacific Coast Hockey Association and Western Canada Hockey League played first with the National Hockey League drawing the bye.
In 1923 the Pacific Coast Hockey Association and the National Hockey League played first with the Western Canada Hockey League drawing the bye.
In 1924 the Western Canada Hockey League again drew the bye.

March 29   Ottawa   2   *Edmonton Eskimos   1 (Denneny scored 2:08
March 31   Ottawa   1   Edmonton Eskimos   0   in overtime)
*Western Canada Hockey League champion.

Leaders

Goals: Cecil Dye (Toronto) 26; Assists: Edmond Bouchard (Hamilton)
12; Points: Cecil Dye 26–11–37; Penalty Minutes: William Boucher
(Montreal) 52.

Notes

John Darragh did not come west with the Ottawa Senators to compete
in the playoffs. Harry Helman, who hadn't played in the first two games,
received a badly cut cheek and injured nose when he fell on Nighbor's
skate during practice on March 21st. He was hospitalized and didn't play
in the next two games against Vancouver or in the series with Edmonton.

1923–24

League Standings

Clubs	Games	Won	Lost	Tied	Points	Goals for	Goals against
Ottawa	24	16	8	0	32	74	54
Montreal	24	13	11	0	26	59	48
Toronto	24	10	14	0	20	59	85
Hamilton	24	9	15	0	18	63	68

Montreal outscored Ottawa, 5 goals to 2.

March 8   Montreal   1   Ottawa   0
March 11   Montreal   4   Ottawa   2

1924 Montreal Canadiens

William Boucher	Ogilvie Cleghorn	Sylvio Mantha
William Bell	Sprague Cleghorn	Howarth W. Morenz
William Cameron	William Coutu	Georges Vézina
	Aurèle Joliat	

Stanley Cup: Montreal 2, Vancouver 0 (Games)

March 18   Montreal   3   Vancouver   2
March 20   Montreal   2   Vancouver   1

March 22   Montreal   6   Calgary Tigers   1   at Montreal
March 25   Montreal   3   Calgary Tigers   0   at Ottawa

The last game of this series was played on artificial ice in Ottawa's new arena when the natural ice at Montreal began to thaw. Montreal didn't have artificial ice until the following season **(1924–25)** when the Forum was built.

Leaders

Goals: Cyril Denneny (Ottawa) 22; Assists: Francis Clancy (Ottawa) 8; Points: Cyril Denneny 22–1–23; Penalty Minutes: Bert Corbeau (Toronto) 55.

Trophies

Hart: Frank Nighbor (Ottawa).

1924–25

League Standings

During the next 2 seasons, the second place club played the third place club in a 2-game series. The club scoring the most goals earned the right to meet the first place club in another 2-game series with the club scoring the most goals declared the league champions.

Clubs	Games	Won	Lost	Tied	Points	Goals for	Goals against
Hamilton	30	19	10	1	39	90	60
Toronto	30	19	11	0	38	90	84
Mont. Canadiens	30	17	11	2	36	93	56
Ottawa	30	17	12	1	35	83	66
Mont. Maroons	30	9	19	2	20	45	65
Boston	30	6	24	0	12	49	119

Playoffs: (Winner scored most goals, 2 games)

March 11	Mont. Canadiens	3	Toronto	2
March 13	Mont. Canadiens	2	Toronto	0
		5		2

The Montreal Canadiens were declared league champions when Hamilton defaulted.

1925 Victoria Cougars

"Jocko" Anderson
Frank C. Foyston
Gordon Fraser
Frank Fredrickson

Harold Halderson
Wilfred Hart
Harry Holmes

Clement Joseph
Loughlin
Harry Meeking
John Phillip Walker

Stanley Cup: Victoria 3, Montreal 1 (Games)

March 21	Victoria	5	Montreal	2
March 23	Victoria	3	Montreal	1
March 27	Victoria	2	Montreal	4
March 30	Victoria	6	Montreal	1

Leaders

Goals: Cecil Dye (Toronto) 38; Assists: Cyril Denneny (Ottawa) 15; Points: Cecil Dye 38-6-44; Penalty Minutes: William Boucher, Montreal) 92.

Trophies

Byng: Frank Nighbor (Ottawa); Hart: William Burch (Hamilton); Prince of Wales: Mont. Canadiens.

Notes

Boston Bruins, first U.S. based team, was added and a second Montreal team, the Maroons, made up a six-team league.

1925—26

League Standings

Clubs	Games	Won	Lost	Tied	Points	Goals for	Goals against
Ottawa	36	24	8	4	52	77	42
Mont. Maroons	36	20	11	5	45	91	73
Pittsburgh	36	19	16	1	39	82	70
Boston	36	17	15	4	38	92	85
N.Y. Americans	36	12	20	4	28	68	89
Toronto	36	12	21	3	27	92	114
Mont. Canadiens	36	11	24	1	23	79	108

Playoffs (Winner scored most goals, 2 games)

March 20	Mont. Maroons	3	Pittsburgh	1
March 23	Mont. Maroons	3	Pittsburgh	3
		6		4

League Championship (Winner scored most goals, 2 games)

March 25	Mont. Maroons	1	Ottawa	1
March 27	Mont. Maroons	1	Ottawa	0
		2		1

1926 Montreal Maroons

Clinton S. Benedict	Albert R. Holway	Merlyn J. Phillips
Harry L. Broadbent	Duncan B. Munro	Samuel Rothschild
Frank Carson	Edward Reginald	Albert Charles Siebert
Charles Dinsmore	Noble	Nelson Robert Stewart

Stanley Cup: Montreal 3, Victoria 1 (Games)

March 30	Montreal	3	Victoria	0
April	1	Montreal	3	Victoria	0
April	3	Montreal	2	Victoria	3
April	6	Montreal	2	Victoria	0

Leaders

Goals: Nelson Stewart (Mont. Maroons) 34; Assists: Frank Nighbor (Ottawa) 13; Points: Nelson Stewart 36-8-44; Penalty Minutes: Bert Corbeau (Toronto) 121.

Trophies

Byng: Frank Nighbor (Ottawa); Hart: Nelson Stewart (Mont. Maroons); Prince of Wales: Mont. Maroons.

Coaches

Cecil Hart replaced Dandurand at Montreal.

Notes

Schedule increased to 36 games.
Hamilton dropped out permanently and the franchise was sold to the New York Americans.
A third U.S. club, the Pittsburgh Pirates, was added.

1926–27

League Standings

The league was divided into two divisions in 1926–27; the American Division and the International Division. The Clubs played six games with the clubs in their own division and four games with each club in the other division. During the next two seasons, each division conducted playoffs for the division championship. The second place club played the third place club in a two-game series. The club scoring the most goals earned the right to meet the first place club in another two-game series with the club scoring the most goals declared the division champions. The division champions then met in a 2-out-of-3-game series in 1926–27 and a 3-out-of-5-game series in 1927–28 to decide the league championship. These series, also, decided the Stanley Cup winner for these two seasons.

American Division					Goals for	Goals against
	Games	Won	Lost	Tied	Points	
N. Y. Rangers	44	25	13	6	56	95	72
Boston	44	21	20	3	45	97	89
Chicago	44	19	22	3	41	115	116
Pittsburgh	44	15	26	3	33	79	108
Detroit	44	12	28	4	28	76	105

International Division					Goals for	Goals against
	Games	Won	Lost	Tied	Points	
Ottawa	44	30	10	4	64	86	69
Mont. Canadiens	44	28	14	2	58	99	67
Mont. Maroons	44	20	20	4	44	71	68
N. Y. Americans	44	17	25	2	36	82	91
Toronto	44	15	24	5	35	79	94

1927 Ottawa Senators

John James Adams
George Boucher
Francis Michael
  Clancy
Alexander Connell

Cyril Denneny
Frank Finnigan
Edwin Gorman
Milton Halliday

Hector Kilrea
Frank Nighbor
Alexander Smith
Reginald J. Smith

Playoffs: (Winners scored most goals, 2 games)

March 29   Boston   6   Chicago   1
March 31   Boston   4   Chicago   4
               ―――――   ――――
                  10   5

March 29   Mont. Canadiens   1   Mont. Maroons   1
March 31   Mont. Canadiens   1*   Mont. Maroons   0
                    ―――   ――
                     2   1

(*Morenz scored 12:05 overtime)

April 2   Ottawa   4   Mont. Canadiens   0
April 4   Ottawa   1   Mont. Canadiens   1
            ――――   ――――
              5   1

April 2   Boston   0   N.Y. Rangers   0
April 4   Boston   3   N.Y. Rangers   1
            ―――   ―――
             3   1

Championship and Stanley Cup

April 7   Ottawa   0   Boston   0 (20 minutes overtime failed to break tie)
April 9   Ottawa   3   Boston   1
April 11   Ottawa   1   Boston   1 (20 minutes overtime failed to break tie)
April 13   Ottawa   3   Boston   1

Leaders

Goals: William Cook (N.Y. Rangers) 33; Assists: James Irvin (Chicago) 18; Points: William Cook 33–4–37; Penalty Minutes: Nelson Stewart (Mont. Maroons) 133.

Trophies

Byng: William Burch (N.Y. Americans); Hart: Herbert Gardiner (Mont. Canadiens); Vezina: George Hainsworth (Mont. Canadiens); Prince of Wales: Ottawa.

Coaches

"Pete" Muldoon named first coach of Chicago Black Hawks; Arthur Duncan named first coach of Detroit Cougars; Lester Patrick named coach of N.Y. Rangers.

Notes

Three new U.S. teams, the Chicago Black Hawks, Detroit Cougars and New York Rangers, were added to make a 10-team league, split in two divisions.

1927–28

League Standings

The clubs played six games with the clubs in their own division and four games with each club in the other division.

American Division

	Games	Won	Lost	Tied	Points	Goals for	Goals against
Boston	44	20	13	11	51	77	70
N. Y. Rangers	44	19	16	9	47	94	79
Pittsburgh	44	19	17	8	46	67	76
Detroit	44	19	19	6	44	88	79
Chicago	44	7	34	3	17	68	134

International Division

	Games	Won	Lost	Tied	Points	Goals for	Goals against
Mont. Canadiens	44	26	11	7	59	116	48
Mont. Maroons	44	24	14	6	54	96	77
Ottawa	44	20	14	10	50	78	57
Toronto	44	18	18	8	44	89	88
N. Y. Americans	44	11	27	6	28	63	128

Playoffs: (Winners scored most goals, 2 games)

March 27	N.Y. Rangers	4	Pittsburgh	0	at New York
March 29	N.Y. Rangers	2	Pittsburgh	4	at New York
		6		4	

The 1st game of this series was Pittsburgh's home game, but due to the players sharing in the gate receipts in these play-offs the Pirates preferred to play in the much larger Madison Square Garden than in their small (4,000 seat) Duquesne Gardens in Pittsburgh.

March 27	Mont. Maroons	1	Ottawa	0
March 29	Mont. Maroons	2	Ottawa	1
		3		1

April 1	N.Y. Rangers	1	Boston	1
April 3	N.Y. Rangers	4	Boston	1
		5		2

March 31	Mont. Maroons	2	Mont. Canadiens	2
April 3	Mont. Maroons	1	Mont. Canadiens	0
		3		2

(Oatman scored 8:20 overtime)

**Championship and Stanley Cup: N.Y. Rangers 3,
Mont. Maroons 2 (Games)**

| April 5 | New York | 0 | Montreal | 2 |
| April 7 | New York | 2 | Montreal | 1 |

(F. Boucher scored 7:05 overtime)

April 10	New York	0	Montreal	2
April 12	New York	1	Montreal	0
April 14	New York	2	Montreal	1

1928 New York Rangers

Clarence Abel	Lorne Chabot	Ivan W. Johnson
Frank Xavier Boucher	Frederick Joseph Cook	Joseph Miller
Leo A. Bourgault	William Osser Cook	John Murray Murdoch
William G. Boyd	Alexander Gray	Lester Patrick
Francis C. W. Callighen		Paul I. Thompson

Leaders

Goals: Howarth Morenz (Mont. Canadiens) 33; Assists: Howarth Morenz 18; Points: Howarth Morenz 33–18–51; Penalty Minutes: Edward Shore (Boston) 166.

Trophies

Byng: Frank Boucher (N.Y. Rangers); Hart: Howarth Morenz (Mont. Canadiens); Vezina: George Hainsworth (Mont. Canadiens); Prince of Wales: Boston; Kendall: Mont. Canadiens.

Coaches

Barney Stanley and Hugh Lehman replaced Muldoon at Chicago; Jack Adams replaced Duncan at Detroit; Conn Smythe named Coach of Toronto Maple Leafs.

Notes

In the second Montreal-New York game, early in the 2nd period, Lorne Chabot was knocked out on a shot by (Nels) Stewart, which struck him over the eye; he was rushed to the hospital. In those days the clubs carried only one goaltender. Alexander Connell of the Ottawa Senators was in the stands and when Lester Patrick, New York Ranger general-manager, asked Edward Gerard, Montreal coach, if he could use him as a replacement, Gerard refused.

In the days when Lester Patrick played, if a goaltender was penalized, he had to go to the penalty box. A defenseman then dropped back and attempted to protect the goal. Patrick, having played defense, had occasionally done this. Patrick was now white-haired and 44 years old and no player that old had ever competed in a Stanley Cup game.

With Gerard's refusal, Lester Patrick had to do something quickly or forfeit the game, as the time allotted to replace an injured goaltender was about over. He began donning Chabot's sweaty, blood-soaked gear and led the Rangers back on the ice. The Rangers determinedly defended their gallant general-manager and at the end of the period there was no score.

Thirty seconds after the third period started (Bill) Cook scored and with 6 minutes left to play (Nels) Stewart tied it up. At 7:05 in overtime, Frank Boucher threaded his way through the Maroon defense, drew out Clinton Benedict, and scored.

Lester Patrick made 18 saves and as the tears rolled down his cheeks his joyous Rangers raised him to their shoulders and carried him to the dressing room.

Forward passing was now allowed in both the defense and center zones.
New type of goal nets, designed by Arthur Ross, became official.
Hockey sticks were limited to 53 inches.
Goaltenders' pads were cut down from 12 to 10 inches in width.

1928–29

League Standings

The clubs played six games with the clubs in their own division and

four games with each club in the other division.

From 1928–29 through 1937–38, the league championship was decided in a 3-out-of-5-game series between the leaders of each division.

American Division

	Games	Won	Lost	Tied	Points	Goals for	Goals against
Boston	44	26	13	5	57	89	52
N.Y. Rangers	44	21	13	10	52	72	65
Detroit	44	19	16	9	47	72	63
Pittsburgh	44	9	27	8	26	46	80
Chicago	44	7	29	8	22	33	85

International Division

	Games	Won	Lost	Tied	Points	Goals for	Goals against
Mont. Canadiens	44	22	7	15	59	71	43
N.Y. Americans	44	19	13	12	50	53	53
Toronto	44	21	18	5	47	85	69
Ottawa	44	14	17	13	41	54	67
Mont. Maroons	44	15	20	9	39	67	65

1929 Boston Bruins

William J. Carson	Lionel Hitchman	George Owen
Aubrey Victor Clapper	Lloyd Klein	Edward William Shore
Cyril Denneny	Myles J. Lane	Cecil Ralph Thompson
Norman Gainor	Duncan MacKay	Ralph Weiland
W. Percival Galbraith	Harold Oliver	

Stanley Cup: Boston 2, N.Y. Rangers 0 (Games)

March 28   Boston   2   N.Y. Rangers   0
March 29   Boston   2   N.Y. Rangers   1

From 1929 through 1938, the first place clubs in each division met to decide the league championship. The Second place clubs in each division met in a series as did the third place clubs. The winners in these series then played a series between themselves to decide who would meet the league champions for the Stanley Cup.

Championship: Boston 3, Mont. Canadiens 0 (Games)

March 19   Boston   1   Mont. Canadiens   0
March 21   Boston   1   Mont. Canadiens   0
March 23   Boston   2   Mont. Canadiens   1

Playoffs:

March 24   N.Y. Rangers   1   Toronto   0
March 26   N.Y. Rangers   2   Toronto   1
                                    (F. Boucher scored 2:03 overtime)

Playoffs: (Winners scored most goals in 2 games)

March 19	N.Y. Rangers	0	N.Y. Americans	0
March 21	N.Y. Rangers	1	N.Y. Americans	0
		1		0

(Keeling scored 29:50 overtime)

March 19	Toronto	3	Detroit	1
March 21	Toronto	4	Detroit	1
		7		2

Leaders

Goals: Irvin Bailey (Toronto) 22; Assists: Frank Boucher (N.Y. Rangers) 16; Points: Irvin Bailey 22–10–32; Penalty Minutes: Mervyn Dutton (Mont. Maroons) 139.

Trophies

Byng: Frank Boucher (N.Y. Rangers); Hart: Roy Worters (N.Y. Americans); Vezina: George Hainsworth (Mont. Canadiens); Prince of Wales: Boston; Kendall: Mont. Canadiens.

Coaches

Herbert Gardiner replaced Lehman at Chicago, who had in turn succeeded Stanley.

1929–30

League Standings

The clubs played 6 games with the clubs in their own division and 4 games with each club in the other division.

American Division	Games	Won	Lost	Tied	Points	Goals for	Goals against
Boston	44	38	5	1	77	179	98
Chicago	44	21	18	5	47	117	111
N.Y. Rangers	44	17	17	10	44	136	143
Detroit	44	14	24	6	34	117	133
Pittsburgh	44	5	36	3	13	102	185

International Division	Games	Won	Lost	Tied	Points	Goals for	Goals against
Mont. Maroons	44	23	16	5	51	141	114
Mont. Canadiens	44	21	14	9	51	142	114
Ottawa	44	21	15	8	50	138	118
Toronto	44	17	21	6	40	116	124
N.Y. Americans	44	14	25	5	33	113	161

1930 Montreal Canadiens

Martin Burke	J. Albert Leduc	Armand Mondou
Gerald Carson	Alfred Lépine	Howarth W. Morenz
George Hainsworth	Leon-Georges Mantha	Gus Rivers
Aurèle Joliat	Sylvio Mantha	Nicholas Wasnie
Wildore Larochelle	Albert McCaffrey	

Stanley Cup: Mont. Canadiens 2, Boston 0 (Games)

April 1   Canadiens   3   Boston   0
April 3   Canadiens   4   Boston   3

The first place clubs in each division met to decide the league championship. The second place clubs in each division met in a series as did the third place clubs. The winners of these series' then played a series between themselves to decide who would meet the league champions for the Stanley Cup.

Championship: Boston 3, Mont. Maroons 1 (Games)

March 20   Boston   2   Maroons   1   (Oliver scored 45:35 overtime)
March 22   Boston   4   Maroons   2
March 25   Boston   0   Maroons   1   (Wilcox scored 26:27 overtime)
March 27   Boston   5   Maroons   1

Playoffs:

March 28   Mont. Canadiens   2   N.Y. Rangers   1
                                              (Rivers scored 68:52 overtime)
March 30   Mont. Canadiens   2   N.Y. Rangers   0

Playoffs: (Winners scored most goals, 2 games)

March 23   Mont. Canadiens   1   Chicago   0
March 26   Mont. Canadiens   2   Chicago   2
                              ___   ___
                               3   2
                                        (Morenz scored 51:43 overtime)

March 20   N.Y. Rangers   1   Ottawa   1
March 23   N.Y. Rangers   5   Ottawa   2
                          ___   ___
                           6   3

Leaders

Goals: Ralph Weiland (Boston) 43; Assists: Frank Boucher (N.Y. Rangers) 36; Points: Ralph Weiland 43–30–73; Penalty Minutes: Joseph Lamb (Ottawa) 119.

Trophies

Byng: Frank Boucher (N.Y. Rangers); Hart: Nelson Stewart (Mont. Maroons); Vezina: Cecil Thompson (Boston); Prince of Wales: Boston; Kendall: Mont. Maroons.

Coaches

Thomas Shaughnessy and William Tobin at Chicago.

Notes

Forward passing permitted within all three zones.

1930–31

League Standings

The clubs played six games with the clubs in their own division and four games with each club in the other division.

American Division

	Games	Won	Lost	Tied	Points	Goals for	Goals against
Boston	44	28	10	6	62	143	90
Chicago	44	24	17	3	51	108	78
N.Y. Rangers	44	19	16	9	47	106	87
Detroit	44	16	21	7	39	102	105
Philadelphia	44	4	36	4	12	76	184

International Division

	Games	Won	Lost	Tied	Points	Goals for	Goals against
Mont. Canadiens	44	26	10	8	60	129	89
Toronto	44	22	13	9	53	118	99
Mont. Maroons	44	20	18	6	46	105	106
N.Y. Americans	44	18	16	10	46	76	74
Ottawa	44	10	30	4	24	91	142

1931 Montreal Canadiens

Martin Burke	J. Albert Leduc	Armand Mondou
Jean Gagnon	Alfred Lepine	Howarth W. Morenz
George Hainsworth	Arthur J. Lesieur	Jean Baptiste Pusie
Aurele Joliat	Leon-Georges Mantha	Gus Rivers
Wildore Larochelle	Sylvio Mantha	Nicholas Wasnie

Stanley Cup: Mont. Canadiens 3, Chicago 2 (Games)

April	3	Canadiens	2	Chicago	1
April	5	Canadiens	1	Chicago	2 (Gottselig scored 24:50 overtime)
April	9	Canadiens	2	Chicago	3 (Wentworth scored 53:50 overtime)
April	11	Canadiens	4	Chicago	2
April	14	Canadiens	2	Chicago	0

The first place clubs in each division met to decide the league championship. The second place clubs in each division met in a series as did

the third place clubs. The winners of these serieses would then play a series between themselves to decide who would meet the league champions for the Stanley Cup.

Championship: Mont. Canadiens 3, Boston 2 (Games)

March 24 Canadiens 4 Boston 5 (Weiland scored 18:56 overtime)
March 26 Canadiens 1 Boston 0
March 28 Canadiens 4 Boston 3 (L. Mantha scored 5:10 overtime)
March 30 Canadiens 1 Boston 3
April   1 Canadiens 3 Boston 2 (Larochelle scored 19:00 overtime)

Playoffs: (Winners scored most goals, 2 games)

March 29 Chicago 2 N.Y. Rangers 0
March 31 Chicago 1 N.Y. Rangers 0
                    ──   ──
                    3   0

March 24 Chicago 2 Toronto 2
March 26 Chicago 2 Toronto 1 (Adams scored 19:20 overtime)
                    ──   ──
                    4   3

March 24 N.Y. Rangers 5 Mont. Maroons 1
March 26 N.Y. Rangers 3 Mont. Maroons 0
                        ──   ──
                        8   1

Leaders

Goals: Charles Conacher (Toronto) 31; Assists: A. Joseph Primeau (Toronto) 32; Points: Howarth Morenz (Mont. Canadiens) 28–23–51; Penalty Minutes: Harvey Rockburn (Detroit) 118.

Trophies

Byng: Frank Boucher (N.Y. Rangers); Hart: Howarth Morenz (Mont. Canadiens); Vezina: Roy Worters (N.Y. Americans); Prince of Wales: Boston; Kendall: Mont. Canadiens.

Coaches

Arthur Duncan replaced Smythe at Toronto.

Notes

Pittsburgh dropped out with franchise going to new team, the Philadelphia Quakers. This team won four of 44 games and lasted one season. Detroit changed name from Cougars to Falcons.

1931–32

League Standings

The clubs played eight games with the clubs in their own division and six games with each club in the other division.

American Division	Games	Won	Lost	Tied	Points	Goals for	Goals against
N.Y. Rangers	48	23	17	8	54	134	112
Chicago	48	18	19	11	47	86	101
Detroit	48	18	20	10	46	95	108
Boston	48	15	21	12	42	122	117

International Division	Games	Won	Lost	Tied	Points	Goals for	Goals against
Mont. Canadiens	48	25	16	7	57	128	111
Toronto	48	23	18	7	53	155	127
Mont. Maroons	48	19	22	7	45	142	139
N.Y. Americans	48	16	24	8	40	95	142

1932 Toronto Maple Leafs

Irvin W. Bailey
Andrew Blair
Lorne Chabot
Francis Michael Clancy
Charles William
    Conacher

E. Harold Cotton
Harold Darragh
Clarence Henry Day
Frank Finnigan
Robert J. Gracie
George Reginald
    Horner

Harvey Jackson
Alexander Levinsky
Earl Miller
A. Joseph Primeau
Fred Robertson

Stanley Cup: Toronto 3, N.Y. Rangers 0 (Games)

April 5	Toronto	6	Rangers	4
April 7	Toronto	6	Rangers	2
April 9	Toronto	6	Rangers	4

The first place clubs in each division met to decide the league championship. The second place clubs in each division met in a series as did the third place clubs. The winners of these series' then played a series between themselves to decide who would meet the league champions for the Stanley Cup.

Championship: N.Y. Rangers 3, Mont. Canadiens 1 (Games)

March 24	Rangers	3	Canadiens	4	
March 26	Rangers	4	Canadiens	3	(F. Cook scored 59:32 overtime)
March 27	Rangers	1	Canadiens	0	
March 29	Rangers	5	Canadiens	2	

Playoffs: (Winners scored most goals, 2 games)

March 31	Toronto	1	Mont. Maroons	1
April	2	Toronto	3	Mont. Maroons	2
			4		3

(Gracie scored 17:59 overtime)

March 27	Toronto	0	Chicago	1
March 29	Toronto	6	Chicago	1
		6		2

March 27	Mont. Maroons	1	Detroit	1
March 29	Mont. Maroons	2	Detroit	0
		3		1

Leaders

Goals: Charles Conacher (Toronto) 34; Assists: A. Joseph Primeau (Toronto) 37; Points: Harvey Jackson (Toronto) 28–25–53; Penalty Minutes: Mervyn Dutton (N.Y. Americans) 107.

Trophies

Byng: A. Joseph Primeau (Toronto); Calder: Howarth Morenz (Mont. Canadiens); Vezina: Charles Gardiner (Chicago); Prince of Wales: N.Y. Rangers; Kendall: Mont. Canadiens.

Notes

The Ottawa Senators dropped out for one year.
Schedule increased from 44 to 48 games.

1932–33

League Standings

The clubs played 6 games with each club in both divisions.

American Division

	Games	Won	Lost	Tied	Points	Goals for	Goals against
Boston	48	25	15	8	58	124	88
Detroit	48	25	15	8	58	111	93
N.Y. Rangers	48	23	17	8	54	135	107
Chicago	48	16	20	12	44	88	101

International Division

	Games	Won	Lost	Tied	Points	Goals for	Goals against
Toronto	48	24	18	6	54	119	111
Mont. Maroons	48	22	20	6	50	135	119
Mont. Canadiens	48	18	25	5	41	92	115
N.Y. Americans	48	15	22	11	41	91	118
Ottawa	48	11	27	10	32	88	131

1933 New York Rangers

Andrew Aitkenhead
Oscar Asmundson
Frank Xavier Boucher
Douglas R. Brennan
Frederick Joseph Cook
William Osser Cook
Cecil Gordon Dillon
Ehrhardt Henry Heller
Ivan W. Johnson
Melville Sydney Keeling
John Murray Murdoch
Gordon R. Pettinger
Earl Walter Seibert
Albert Charles Siebert
Arthur E. Somers

Stanley Cup: N.Y. Rangers 3, Toronto 1 (Games)

April	4	Rangers	5	Toronto	1	
April	8	Rangers	3	Toronto	1	
April	11	Rangers	2	Toronto	3	
April	13	Rangers	1	Toronto	0	(W. Cook scored 7:33 overtime)

The first place clubs in each division met to decide the league championship. The second place clubs in each division met in a series as did the third place clubs. The winners of these series then played a series between themselves to decide who would meet the league champions for the Stanley Cup.

Championship: Toronto 3, Boston 2 (Games)

March	25	Toronto	1	Boston	2	(Barry scored 14:14 overtime)
March	28	Toronto	1	Boston	0	(Jackson scored 15:03 overtime)
March	30	Toronto	1	Boston	2	(Shore scored 4:23 overtime)
April	1	Toronto	5	Boston	3	
April	3	Toronto	1	Boston	0	(Doraty scored 104:46 overtime)

Playoffs: (Winners scored most goals, 2 games)

March 30	N.Y. Rangers	2	Detroit	0
April 2	N.Y. Rangers	4	Detroit	3
		6		3

March 26	N.Y. Rangers	5	Mont. Canadiens	2
March 28	N.Y. Rangers	3	Mont. Canadiens	3
		8		5

March 25	Detroit	2	Mont. Maroons	0
March 28	Detroit	3	Mont. Maroons	2
		5		2

Playoff Action

The final game of the Championship series was the second longest game ever played. Through regulation time and five 20-minute overtime periods there had been no score. Referee Ogilvie Cleghorn had disallowed three goals; one by Toronto and another by Alexander Smith of the Bruins near the 14-minute mark in the third period, due to an offside. The third by Francis ("The King") Clancy of Toronto in overtime was, also, called back for being offside.

The winner of this game was scheduled to play the New York Rangers in a sold out Madison Square Garden the following evening in the final series for the Stanley Cup. Toronto had drawn six consecutive penalties, but had still been able to stave off defeat. Edward Shore of Boston, except when in the penalty box, had been on the ice most of the time.

A suggestion that a coin be tossed to decide the victor was rejected by Frank Calder, league President. He also denied a proposal that both goaltenders leave their nets. Lorne Chabot of the Maple Leafs and "Tiny" Thompson of the Bruins had stopped over 200 shots. At 4:46 of the sixth overtime, Andrew Blair of Toronto intercepted a pass by Shore to Joseph Lamb and passed ahead to little Kenneth Doraty. Doraty, who only weighed 127 pounds, skated in and shot the puck across the net in front of Thompson and it caught the corner just inside the goal post. It was 1:50 in the morning.

Leaders

Goals: William Cook (N.Y. Rangers) 28; Assists: Frank Boucher (N.Y. Rangers) 28; Points: William Cook 28-22-50; Penalty Minutes: George Horner (Toronto) 144.

Trophies

Byng: Frank Boucher (N.Y. Rangers); Calder: Carl Voss (N.Y. Rangers—Detroit); Hart: Edward Shore (Boston); Vezina: Cecil Thompson (Boston); Prince of Wales: Boston; Kendall: Mont. Maroons.

Coaches

Edouard Lalonde replaced Hart at Mont. Canadiens.

Notes

Ottawa returned to action, creating an unbalanced league with five teams in the International Division, four in the American.

Detroit changed name from Falcons to Red Wings.

1933–34

League Standings

The clubs played 6 games with each club in both divisions.

American Division

	Games	Won	Lost	Tied	Points	Goals for	Goals against
Detroit	48	24	14	10	58	113	98
Chicago	48	20	17	11	51	88	83
N.Y. Rangers	48	21	19	8	50	120	113
Boston	48	18	25	5	41	111	130

International Division

	Games	Won	Lost	Tied	Points	Goals for	Goals against
Toronto	48	26	13	9	61	174	119
Mont. Canadiens	48	22	20	6	50	99	101
Mont. Maroons	48	19	18	11	49	117	112
N.Y. Americans	48	15	23	10	40	104	132
Ottawa	48	13	29	6	32	115	143

1934 Chicago Black Hawks

Clarence Abel
Lionel Pretoria Conacher
Thomas John Cook
Arthur Edmund Coulter
Rosario Couture

Charles Robert Gardiner
Leroy D. Goldsworthy
John P. Gottselig
Roger Jenkins
William Kendall
Harold March

Donald McFadyen
Elwin Nelson Romnes
Jake O. Sheppard
Paul I. Thompson
Louis Napoleon Trudel

Stanley Cup: Chicago 3, Detroit 1 (Games)

April	3	Chicago	2	Detroit	1	(Thompson scored 21:05 overtime)
April	5	Chicago	4	Detroit	1	
April	8	Chicago	2	Detroit	5	
April	10	Chicago	1	Detroit	0	(March scored 30:05 overtime)

The first place clubs in each division met to decide the league championship. The second place clubs in each division met in a series as did the third place clubs. The winners of these series then played a series between themselves to decide who would meet the league champions for the Stanley Cup.

Championship: Detroit 3, Toronto 2 (Games)

March 22	Detroit	2	Toronto	1	(Lewis scored 1:33 overtime)
March 24	Detroit	6	Toronto	3	
March 26	Detroit	1	Toronto	3	
March 28	Detroit	1	Toronto	5	
March 30	Detroit	1	Toronto	0	

Playoffs: (Winners scored most goals, 2 games)

March 28	Chicago	3	Mont. Maroons	0
April 1	Chicago	3	Mont. Maroons	2
		6		2

March 22	Chicago	3	Mont. Canadiens	2	(March scored 11:05
March 25	Chicago	1	Mont. Canadiens	1	overtime)
		4		3	

March 20	Mont. Maroons	0	N.Y. Rangers	0
March 25	Mont. Maroons	2	N.Y. Rangers	1
		2		1

Leaders

Goals: Charles Conacher (Toronto) 32; Assists: A. Joseph Primeau (Toronto) 32; Points: Charles Conacher 32-20-52; Penalty Minutes: George Horner (Toronto) 146.

Trophies

Byng: Frank Boucher (N.Y. Rangers); Calder: Russell Blinco (Mont. Maroons); Hart: Aurèle Joliat (Mont. Canadiens); Vezina: Charles Gardiner (Chicago); Prince of Wales: Detroit; Kendall: Mont. Maroons.

1934–35

League Standings

The clubs played 6 games with each club in both divisions.

American Division					Goals	Goals
	Games	Won	Lost	Tied	Points	for	against
Boston	48	26	16	6	58	129	112
Chicago	48	26	17	5	57	118	88
N.Y. Rangers	48	22	20	6	50	137	139
Detroit	48	19	22	7	45	127	114

International Division

	Games	Won	Lost	Tied	Points	Goals for	Goals against
Toronto	48	30	14	4	64	157	111
Mont. Maroons	48	24	19	5	53	123	92
Mont. Canadiens	48	19	23	6	44	110	145
N.Y. Americans	48	12	27	9	33	100	142
St. Louis	48	11	31	6	28	86	144

1935 Montreal Maroons

Russell Percival Blinco	Robert J. Gracie	Allan Shields
Herbert J. Cain	August Marker	Reginald J. Smith
Lionel Pretoria Con-	Samuel McManus	David T. Trottier
acher	William Miller	James William Ward
Alexander Connell	Lawrence Northcott	Marvin P. Wentworth
Stewart Evans	Earl Robinson	

Stanley Cup: Mont. Maroons 3, Toronto 0 (Games)

April 4	Mont. Maroons	3	Toronto	2	(Trottier scored 5:28 over-
April 6	Mont. Maroons	3	Toronto	1	time)
April 9	Mont. Maroons	4	Toronto	1	

The first place clubs in each division met to decide the league champion-ship. The second place clubs in each division met in a series as did the third place clubs. The winners of these series then played a series between themselves to decide who would meet the league champions for the Stanley Cup.

Championship: Toronto 3, Boston 1 (Games)

March 23	Toronto	0	Boston	1	(Clapper scored 33:26 overtime)
March 26	Toronto	2	Boston	0	
March 28	Toronto	3	Boston	0	
March 30	Toronto	2*	Boston	1	(*Kelly scored 1:36 overtime)

Playoffs: (Winners scored most goals, 2 games)

March 28	Mont. Maroons	2	N.Y. Rangers	1
March 30	Mont. Maroons	3	N.Y. Rangers	3
		—		—
		5		4

March 23	Mont. Maroons	0	Chicago	0	
March 26	Mont. Maroons	1	Chicago	0	(Northcott scored 4:02
		—		—	overtime)
		1		0	

March 24	N.Y. Rangers	2	Mont. Canadiens	1
March 26	N.Y. Rangers	4	Mont. Canadiens	4
		—		—
		6		5

Playoff Action

During the second period, Bill Cook was penalized and on his way to the penalty box when he became involved in a fight with Nelson Crutchfield and a free-for-all erupted. Cook was carried from the ice unconscious with blood flowing from a head wound. In the third period he returned to take a pass from Frank Boucher and score the winning goal.

After the overtime of the Montreal-Chicago game on March 26 started, "Lolo" Couture drew a major penalty from referee Gerald Goodman when he struck David Trottier in the face. In ten seconds the game was over as the five Maroons attacked including the defensemen Evans and Wentworth. Gracie had won the draw from John Gottselig and after faking a pass to Ward slid the puck over to Northcott. Northcott calmly drew Lorne Chabot to the ice and then fired the puck high into the net.

Leaders

Goals: Charles Conacher (Toronto) 36; Assists: Arthur Chapman (N.Y. Americans) 34; Points: Charles Conacher 36-21-57; Penalty Minutes: George Horner (Toronto) 125.

Trophies

Byng: Frank Boucher (N.Y. Rangers); Calder: David Schriner (N.Y. Americans); Hart: Edward Shore (Boston); Vezina: Lorne Chabot (Chicago); Prince of Wales: Boston; Kendall: Mont. Canadiens.

Coaches

Frank Patrick replaced Ross at Boston; Leo Dandurand replaced Lalonde at Mont. Canadiens.

Notes

Ottawa dropped out again with franchise going to the St. Louis Eagles, a team which also expired after one season.

1935–36

League Standings

The clubs played 8 games with the clubs in their own division and 6 games with each club in the other division.

American Division	Games	Won	Lost	Tied	Points	Goals for	Goals against
Detroit	48	24	16	8	56	124	103
Boston	48	22	20	6	50	92	83
Chicago	48	21	19	8	50	93	92
N.Y. Rangers	48	19	17	12	50	91	96

| *International Division* | | | | | | Goals | Goals |
	Games	Won	Lost	Tied	Points	for	against
Mont. Maroons	48	22	16	10	54	114	106
Toronto	48	23	19	6	52	126	106
N.Y. Americans	48	16	25	7	39	109	122
Mont. Canadiens	48	11	26	11	33	82	123

1936 Detroit Red Wings

Lawrence Aurie	Sydney Harris Howe	Wilfred K. McDonald
Martin J. Barry	Peter Kelly	Gordon R. Pettinger
Ralph Bowman	Hector Kilrea	Norman E. Smith
Modere Fernand Bruneteau	Walter Kilrea	John Arthur Sorrell
Ebenezer R. Good-fellow	Herbert Lewis	Douglas C. Young

Stanley Cup: Detroit 3, Toronto 1 (Games)

April	5	Detroit	3	Toronto	1	
April	7	Detroit	9	Toronto	4	
April	9	Detroit	3	Toronto	4	(Boll scored 0.31 overtime)
April	11	Detroit	3	Toronto	2	

The first place clubs in each division met to decide the league championship. The second place clubs in each division met in a series as did the third place clubs. The winners of these series then played a series between themselves to decide who would meet the league champions for the Stanley Cup.

Championship: Detroit 3, Mont. Maroons 0 (Games)

March	24	Detroit	1	Mont. Maroons	0	(M. Bruneteau scored
March	26	Detroit	3	Mont. Maroons	0	116:30 overtime)
March	29	Detroit	2	Mont. Maroons	1	

Playoffs

March	28	Toronto	3	N.Y. Americans	1
March	31	Toronto	0	N.Y. Americans	1
April	2	Toronto	3	N.Y. Americans	1

March	24	Toronto	0	Boston	3
March	26	Toronto	8	Boston	3

			8	6	(Winner based on total goals)

March	24	N.Y. Americans	3	Chicago	0
March	26	N.Y. Americans	4	Chicago	5

		7	5	(Winner based on total goals)

Playoff Action

The first championship game was the longest ever played. Through regulation time the checking had been hard and close. Near the end of the fifth 20-minute overtime, Detroit came very close to scoring when Herbert Lewis had Lorne Chabot beaten, after taking a pass from Martin Barry, only to see his shot hit the goal post.

It rebounded to "Hooley" Smith of Montreal who skated back quickly and passed to Lawrence Northcott. Norman Smith got a pad on his shot. Douglas Young recovered the puck and skated back for the Red Wings. His shot struck Lionel Conacher's skate and almost deflected into the net. As the period ended, Young was attempting to get his stick on the loose puck as Chabot came out and dove on it.

In the sixth overtime Hector Kilrea recovered a rebound after Norman Smith had just repelled a four-man Maroon attack. He quickly skated back with Modere Bruneteau and, as Bruneteau rounded the Montreal defense, fed him the puck. It was 16:30 of the sixth overtime and 2:25 in the morning as he shot the puck into the net.

During the game Norman Smith had made 90 saves.

During this series "Bucko" McDonald was outstanding on defense as he checked "Hooley" Smith. Smith, Montreal's leading scorer in the regular season, was held scoreless. In the Detroit nets Norman Smith was also outstanding as he turned in two successive shutouts.

Leaders

Goals: Charles Conacher (Toronto), William Thoms (Toronto) 23 (tie); Assists: Arthur Chapman (N.Y. Americans) 28; Points: David Schriner (N.Y. Americans) 19-26-45; Penalty Minutes: George Horner (Toronto) 167.

Trophies

Byng: Elwin Romnes (Chicago); Calder: Michael Karakes (Chicago); Hart: Edward Shore (Boston); Vezina: Cecil Thompson (Boston); Prince of Wales: Detroit; Kendall: Mont. Maroons.

Coaches

Sylvio Mantha replaced Dandurand at Mont. Canadiens.

Notes

League of eight teams played 48-game schedule.

1936–37

League Standings

The clubs played eight games with the clubs in their own division and six games with each club in the other division.

American Division

	Games	Won	Lost	Tied	Points	Goals for	Goals against
Detroit	48	25	14	9	59	128	102
Boston	48	23	18	7	53	120	110
N.Y. Rangers	48	19	20	9	47	117	106
Chicago	48	14	27	7	35	99	131

International Division

	Games	Won	Lost	Tied	Points	Goals for	Goals against
Mont. Canadiens	48	24	18	6	54	115	111
Mont. Maroons	48	22	17	9	53	126	110
Toronto	48	22	21	5	49	119	115
N.Y. Americans	48	15	29	4	34	122	161

1937 Detroit Red Wings

Martin J. Barry
Ralph Bowman
Modere Fernand
  Bruneteau
James R. Franks
John Gallagher
Ebenezer R. Good-
  fellow

Sydney Harris Howe
Peter Kelly
Hector Kilrea
Walter Kilrea
Herbert Lewis
Howard Mackie
Wilfred K. McDonald
Gordon R. Pettinger

Earl Cooper Robertson
John Sherf
Norman E. Smith
John Arthur Sorrell

Stanley Cup: Detroit 3, N.Y. Rangers 2 (Games)

April	6	Detroit	1	N.Y. Rangers	5
April	8	Detroit	4	N.Y. Rangers	2
April	11	Detroit	0	N.Y. Rangers	1
April	13	Detroit	1	N.Y. Rangers	0
April	15	Detroit	3	N.Y. Rangers	0

The first place clubs in each division met to decide the league champion-ship. The second place clubs in each division met in a series as did the third place clubs. The winners of these series then played a series between themselves to decide who would meet the league champions for the Stanley Cup.

Championship: Detroit 3, Mont. Canadiens 2 (Games)

March	23	Detroit	4	Mont. Canadiens	0	
March	25	Detroit	5	Mont. Canadiens	1	
March	27	Detroit	1	Mont. Canadiens	3	
March	30	Detroit	1	Mont. Canadiens	3	
April	1	Detroit	2	Mont. Canadiens	1	(H. Kilrea scored 51:49 overtime)

Playoffs:

April 1	N.Y. Rangers	1	Mont. Maroons	0
April 3	N.Y. Rangers	4	Mont. Maroons	0

March 23	Mont. Maroons	4	Boston	1
March 25	Mont. Maroons	0	Boston	4
March 28	Mont. Maroons	4	Boston	1

| March 23 | N.Y. Rangers | 3 | Toronto | 0 | |
| March 25 | N.Y. Rangers | 2 | Toronto | 1 | (Pratt scored 13:05 over-time) |

Leaders

Goals: Lawrence Aurie (Detroit), Nelson Stewart (Boston—N.Y. Americans) 23 (tie); Assists: Charles Apps (Toronto) 29; Points: David Schriner (N.Y. Americans) 21-25-46; Penalty Minutes: George Horner (Toronto) 124.

Trophies

Byng: Martin Barry (Detroit); Calder: Charles Apps (Toronto); Hart: Albert Siebert (Mont. Canadiens); Vezina: Norman Smith (Detroit); Prince of Wales: Detroit; Kendall: Mont. Maroons.

Coaches

Arthur Ross replaced Frank Patrick at Boston; Cecil Hart replaced Mantha at Mont. Canadiens.

1937–38

League Standings

The clubs played eight games with the clubs in their own division and six games with each club in the other division.

American Division	Games	Won	Lost	Tied	Points	Goals for	Goals against
Boston	48	30	11	1	67	142	89
N.Y. Rangers	48	27	15	6	60	149	96
Chicago	48	14	25	9	37	97	139
Detroit	48	12	25	11	35	99	133
International Division	Games	Won	Lost	Tied	Points	Goals for	Goals against
Toronto	48	24	15	9	57	151	127
N.Y. Americans	48	19	18	11	49	110	111
Mont. Canadiens	48	18	17	13	49	123	128
Mont. Maroons	48	12	30	6	30	101	149

1938 Chicago Black Hawks

Albert P. Connolly	Michael Karakas	Earl Walter Seibert
Carl Dahlstrom	Alexander Levinsky	John W. Shill
Paul Goodman	William K. MacKenzie	Paul I. Thompson
John P. Gottselig	Harold March	Louis Napoleon Trudel
Harold R. Jackson	Alfred Ernest Moore	Carl Voss
Roger Jenkins	Peter Palangio	Arthur Walter Ronald
Virgil Johnson	Elwin Nelson Romnes	Wiebe

Stanley Cup: Chicago 3, Toronto 1 (Games)

April	5	Chicago	3	Toronto	1
April	7	Chicago	1	Toronto	5
April	10	Chicago	2	Toronto	1
April	12	Chicago	4	Toronto	1

The first place clubs in each division met to decide the league championship. The second place clubs in each division met in a series as did the third place clubs. The winners of these series then played a series between themselves to decide who would meet the league champions for the Stanley Cup.

Championship: Toronto 3, Boston 0 (Games)

March 24   Toronto   1   Boston   0   (Parsons scored 21:31 overtime)
March 26   Toronto   2   Boston   1
March 29   Toronto   3   Boston   2   (Drillon scored 10.04 overtime)

Playoffs:

March 29   Chicago   1   N.Y. Americans   3
March 31   Chicago   1   N.Y. Americans   0   (Dahlstrom scored 13:01
April   3   Chicago   3   N.Y. Americans   2   overtime)

March 22   Chicago   4   Montreal   6
March 24   Chicago   4   Montreal   0
March 26   Chicago   3   Montreal   2   (P. Thompson scored 11:49
                                              overtime)

March 22   N.Y. Americans   2*   N.Y. Rangers   1
March 24   N.Y. Americans   3   N.Y. Rangers   4
March 27   N.Y. Americans   3   N.Y. Rangers   2   (Carr scored
                                                        60:40 overtime)

(*Sorrell scored 21:25 overtime)

Playoff Action

In the first game of the Stanley Cup, Alfred Moore replaced Michael Karakas in the Chicago nets. Karakas had suffered a broken toe in the final game of the series with the New York Americans. In less than two minutes Toronto scored, but Moore shut them out from then on to become the hero of the game.

Leaders

Goals: Gordon Drillon (Toronto) 26; Assists: Charles Apps (Toronto) 29; Points: Gordon Drillon 26-26-52; Penalty Minutes: George Horner (Toronto) 92.

Trophies

Byng: Gordon Drillon (Toronto); Calder: Carl Dahlstrom (Chicago); Hart: Edward Shore (Boston); Prince of Wales: Boston; Kendall: Mont. Canadiens; MacBeth: N.Y. Rangers.

1938–39

League Standings

In 1938–39, the National Hockey League discarded the two division system and through 1966–67 the first place club was declared the league champion.

Clubs	Games	Won	Lost	Tied	Points	Goals for	Goals against
Boston	48	36	10	2	74	156	76
N.Y. Rangers	48	26	16	6	58	149	105
Toronto	48	19	20	9	47	114	107
N.Y. Americans	48	17	21	10	44	119	157
Detroit	48	18	24	6	42	107	128
Montreal	48	15	24	9	39	115	146
Chicago	48	12	28	8	32	91	132

1939 Boston Bruins

Robert T. Bauer
Francis Charles Brimsek
Aubrey Victor Clapper
Roy G. Conacher
William Mailes Cowley
John Shea Crawford

Woodrow W. C. Dumart
Raymond Getliffe
Robert George Hamill
John Melvin Hill
William Hollett
Gordon R. Pettinger

John Frederick Portland
Charles H. Sands
Milton Conrad Schmidt
Edward William Shore
Ralph Weiland

Stanley Cup: Boston 4, Toronto 1 (Games)

April	6	Boston	2	Toronto	1
April	9	Boston	2	Toronto	3	(Romnes scored 10:38 overtime)
April	11	Boston	3	Toronto	1
April	13	Boston	2	Toronto	0
April	16	Boston	3	Toronto	1

The first and second place clubs played a 4-out-of-7-game series. The third and fourth place clubs and the fifth and sixth place clubs played a 2-out-of-3-game series. The winners of these 2-out-of-3-game series then met in another 2-out-of-3-game series. The winner of this series then met the winner of the series between the first and second place clubs in a 4-out-of-7-game series for the Stanley Cup.

Playoffs:

March	21	Boston	2	N.Y. Rangers	1	(Hill scored 59:25 overtime)
March	23	Boston	3	N.Y. Rangers	2	(Hill scored 8:24 overtime)
March	26	Boston	4	N.Y. Rangers	1	
March	28	Boston	1	N.Y. Rangers	2	
March	30	Boston	1	N.Y. Rangers	2	(C. Smith scored 17:19 over-
April	1	Boston	1	N.Y. Rangers	3	time)
April	2	Boston	2	N.Y. Rangers	1	(Hill scored 48:00 overtime)

March	28	Toronto	4	Detroit	1	
March	30	Toronto	1	Detroit	3	
April	1	Toronto	5	Detroit	4	(Drillon scored 5:42 overtime)

March	21	Toronto	4	N.Y. Americans	0
March	23	Toronto	2	N.Y. Americans	0

March	21	Detroit	0	Montreal	2	
March	23	Detroit	7	Montreal	3	
March	26	Detroit	1	Montreal	0	(Barry scored 7:47 overtime)

Playoff Action

It was in this series John Hill, Boston, gained the nickname "Sudden Death." He scored, in overtime, in the first, second, and seventh games.

Leaders

Goals: Roy Conacher (Boston) 26; Assists: William Cowley (Boston) 34; Points: Hector Blake (Montreal) 24-23-47; Penalty Minutes: George Horner (Toronto) 85.

Trophies

Byng: Clinton Smith (N.Y. Rangers); Calder: Francis Brimsek (Boston); Hart: Hector Blake (Montreal); Vezina: Francis Brimsek; Prince of Wales: Boston; MacBeth: N.Y. Rangers.

Coaches

Jules Dugal replaced Hart at Montreal Canadiens.

Notes

League reduced to one division of seven teams.

Penalty shot rule revised to allow shooter to take shot from as close to the goal as he wished, instead of from 28 feet out, as previously.

Lineman added to team of officials.

Montreal Maroons dropped out.

1939–40

League Standings

Clubs	Games	Won	Lost	Tied	Points	Goals for	Goals against
Boston	48	31	12	5	67	170	98
N.Y. Rangers	48	27	11	10	64	136	77
Toronto	48	25	17	6	56	134	110
Chicago	48	23	19	6	52	112	120
Detroit	48	16	26	6	38	90	126
N.Y. Americans	48	15	29	4	34	106	140
Montreal	48	10	33	5	25	90	167

1940 New York Rangers

Matthew L. Colville
MacNeil Colville
Arthur Edmund
  Coulter
Erhardt Henry Heller
Bryan Aldwin Hextall
Wilbert Carl Hiller

David Alexander Kerr
James Allan Kilby
  MacDonald
Joseph Lynn Patrick
Frederick Murray
  Patrick
Alfred G. Pike

Walter Pratt
Alexander Dimitri
  Shibicky
Clinton J. Smith
Phillipe Henri Watson

Stanley Cup: N.Y. Rangers 4, Toronto 2 (Games)

April 2	N.Y. Rangers	2	Toronto	1	(Pike scored 15:30 overtime)
April 3	N.Y. Rangers	6	Toronto	2	
April 6	N.Y. Rangers	1	Toronto	2	
April 9	N.Y. Rangers	0	Toronto	3	
April 11	N.Y. Rangers	2	Toronto	1	(M. Patrick scored 11:43 overtime)
April 13	N.Y. Rangers	3	Toronto	2	(Hextall scored 2:07 overtime)

The first and second place clubs played a 4-out-of-7-game series. The third and fourth place clubs and the fifth and sixth place clubs played a 2-out-of-3-game series. The winners of these 2-out-of-3-game serieses

then met in another 2-out-of-3-game series. The winner of this series then met the winner of the series between the 1st and 2nd place clubs in a 4-out-of-7-game series for the Stanley Cup.

Playoffs:

March 19	N.Y. Rangers	4	Boston	0
March 21	N.Y. Rangers	2	Boston	4
March 24	N.Y. Rangers	3	Boston	4
March 26	N.Y. Rangers	1	Boston	0
March 28	N.Y. Rangers	1	Boston	0
March 30	N.Y. Rangers	4	Boston	1
March 26	Toronto	2	Detroit	1
March 28	Toronto	3	Detroit	1
March 19	Toronto	3	Chicago	2 (Apps scored 6:53 overtime)
March 21	Toronto	2	Chicago	1
March 19	Detroit	2	N.Y. Americans	1 (S. Howe scored 0:25 overtime)
March 22	Detroit	4	N.Y. Americans	5
March 24	Detroit	3	N.Y. Americans	1

Playoff Action

In the first game of the Stanley Cup series, Alfred Pike swept the puck into his own goal trying to clear it. The goal was given to "Red" Heron of Toronto. In the fifth game, "Muzz" Patrick scored his third goal of the playoffs in the overtime. He had only scored two during the regular season.

Leaders

Goals: Bryan Hextall (N.Y. Rangers) 24; Assists: Milton Schmidt (Boston) 30; Points: Milton Schmidt 22–30–52; Penalty Minutes: George Horner (Toronto) 87.

Trophies

Byng: Robert Bauer (Boston); Calder: James MacDonald (N.Y. Rangers); Hart: Ebenezer Goodfellow (Detroit); Vezina: David Kerr (N.Y. Rangers); Prince of Wales: Boston; MacBeth: N.Y. Rangers.

Coaches

Ralph Weiland replaced Ross at Boston; Alfred Lepine replaced Dugal at Mont. Canadiens; Frank Boucher replaced Lester Patrick at N.Y. Rangers.

1940–41

League Standings

Clubs	Games	Won	Lost	Tied	Points	Goals for	Goals against
Boston	48	27	8	13	67	168	102
Toronto	48	28	14	6	62	145	99
Detroit	48	21	16	11	53	112	102
N.Y. Rangers	48	21	19	8	50	143	125
Chicago	48	16	25	7	39	112	139
Montreal	48	16	26	6	38	121	147
N.Y. Americans	48	8	29	11	27	99	186

1941 Boston Bruins

Robert T. Bauer
Francis Charles Brimsek
Herbert J. Cain
Aubrey Victor Clapper
Roy G. Conacher
William Mailes Cowley
John Shea Crawford

Woodrow W. C. Dumart
John Melvin Hill
William Hollett
Arthur Jackson
Patrick Joseph McReavy

Terrence George Reardon
Milton Conrad Schmidt
Desmond Patrick Smith
Edward Randall Wiseman

Stanley Cup: Boston 4, Detroit 0 (Games)

April	6	Boston	3	Detroit 2
April	8	Boston	2	Detroit 1
April	10	Boston	4	Detroit 2
April	12	Boston	3	Detroit 1

The first and second place clubs played a 4-out-of-7-game series. The third and fourth place clubs and the fifth and sixth place clubs played a 2-out-of-3-game series. The winners of these 2-out-of-3-game serieses then met in another 2-out-of-3-game series. The winner of this series then met the winner of the series between the first and second place clubs in a 4-out-of-7-game series for the Stanley Cup.

Playoffs:

March 20	Boston	3	Toronto	0
March 22	Boston	3	Toronto	5
March 25	Boston	2	Toronto	7
March 27	Boston	2	Toronto	1
March 29	Boston	1	Toronto	2 (Langelle scored 17:31 overtime)
April 1	Boston	2	Toronto	1
April 3	Boston	2	Toronto	1

March 27	Detroit	3	Chicago	1
March 30	Detroit	2	Chicago	1 (Giesebrecht scored 9:15 overtime)

March 20	Detroit	2	N.Y. Rangers	1 (Giesebrecht scored 12:01
				overtime)
March 23	Detroit	1	N.Y. Rangers	3
March 25	Detroit	3	N.Y. Rangers	2
March 20	Chicago	2	Montreal	1
March 22	Chicago	3	Montreal	4 (Sands scored 34:04 overtime)
March 25	Chicago	3	Montreal	2

Leaders

Goals: Bryan Hextall (N.Y. Rangers) 26; Assists: William Cowley (Boston) 45; Points: William Cowley 17–45–62; Penalty Minutes: James Orlando (Detroit) 99.

Trophies

Byng: Robert Bauer (Boston); Calder: John Quilty (Montreal); Hart: William Cowley (Boston); Vezina: Walter Broda (Toronto); Prince of Wales: Boston; MacBeth: N.Y. Rangers.

Coaches

Dick Irvin replaced Lepine at Montreal; Clarence Day replaced Irvin at Toronto.

Notes

New rule demanded flooding of ice surface between each period.

1941–42

League Standings

Clubs	Games	Won	Lost	Tied	Points	Goals for	Goals against
New York	48	29	17	2	60	177	143
Toronto	48	27	18	3	57	158	136
Boston	48	25	17	6	56	160	118
Chicago	48	22	23	3	47	145	155
Detroit	48	19	25	4	42	140	147
Montreal	48	18	27	3	39	134	173
Brooklyn	48	16	29	3	35	133	175

1942 Toronto Maple Leafs

Charles Joseph
Sylvanus Apps
Walter Edward Broda
Lorne Carr
Robert Davidson
Ernest L. Dickens
Gordon Drillon

Robert J. Goldham
Henry Goldup
Rudolph Kampman
Peter Langelle
John McCreedy
Wilfred K. McDonald
Donald Maurice Metz

Nicholas J. Metz
David Schriner
Walter P. Stanowski
James Gaye Stewart
William Taylor

Stanley Cup: Toronto 4, Detroit 3 (Games)

April   4   Toronto   2   Detroit   3
April   7   Toronto   2   Detroit   4
April   9   Toronto   2   Detroit   5
April 12   Toronto   4   Detroit   3
April 14   Toronto   9   Detroit   3
April 16   Toronto   3   Detroit   0
April 18   Toronto   3   Detroit   1

The first and second place clubs played a 4-out-of-7-game series. The third and fourth place clubs and the fifth and sixth place clubs played a 2-out-of-3-game series. The winners of these 2-out-of-3-game serieses then met in another 2-out-of-3-game series. The winner of this series then met the winner of the series between the first and second place clubs in a 4-out-of-7-game series for the Stanley Cup.

Playoffs:

March 21   Toronto   3   New York   1
March 22   Toronto   4   New York   2
March 24   Toronto   0   New York   3
March 28   Toronto   2   New York   1
March 29   Toronto   1   New York   3
March 31   Toronto   3   New York   2

March 29   Detroit   6   Boston   4
March 31   Detroit   3   Boston   1

March 22   Detroit   2   Montreal   1
March 24   Detroit   0   Montreal   5
March 26   Detroit   6   Montreal   2

March 22   Boston   2   Chicago   1   (Smith scored 6:51 overtime)
March 24   Boston   0   Chicago   4
March 26   Boston   3   Chicago   2

Playoff Action

Sparked by Donald Grosso, the Red Wings took the first three games of the Stanley Cup. In the third game Edward Bush of Detroit set a scoring record for defensemen in a Stanley Cup game by scoring one goal and assisting on the other four.

In the fourth game, Detroit scored two goals early in the second period but Lorne Carr and Davidson tied it up for Toronto before the period ended. Liscombe scored for Detroit near the 10-minute mark of the third period to give the Red Wings a 3-2 lead. Before the final whistle blew "Syl" Apps had scored the tieing goal and set up the winner for Toronto's first victory in the series. This quick victory by Toronto caused some of the Detroit players and fans to become slightly unhinged. Grosso

and Edward Wares were later fined for berating the referee, and general-manager John Adams received a suspension for punching him.

In the fifth game the newly formed line of "Syl" Apps and the Metz brothers scored six goals; with Donald Metz scoring three of them.

In the sixth game "Turk" Broda slammed the door on Detroit with a 3–0 shut-out.

In the seventh game, the Red Wings scored early in the second period. However, (Sweeney) Schriner scored when he jabbed a loose puck that went through a group of players at 7:47 in the third period. Later he scored another and when Peter Langelle saw John McCreedy's backhander, which had been deflected upward, land in front of the Detroit net he swirled in and drilled it home.

With this victory the Toronto Maple Leafs had done what no other club before or since have been able to do; come back to win four games after being down three. This feat was voted the sports comeback of the first half-century by Canadian sports writers.

Leaders

Goals: Lynn Patrick (New York) 32; Assists: Phillipe Watson (New York) 37; Points: Bryan Hextall (New York) 24–32–56; Penalty Minutes: Martin Egan (Brooklyn) 124.

Trophies

Byng: Charles Apps (Toronto); Calder: Grant Warwick (New York); Hart: Thomas Anderson (Brooklyn); Vezina: Francis Mrimsek (Boston); Prince of Wales: New York; MacBeth: New York.

Coaches

Arthur Ross replaced Weiland at Boston.

Notes

New York Americans franchise was renamed the Brooklyn Americans, an attempt to create a Brooklyn-New York rivalry. However, the team continued to play at Madison Square Garden, and lasted only one more season.

1942–43

League Standings

Clubs	Games	Won	Lost	Tied	Points	Goals for	Goals against
Detroit	50	25	14	11	61	169	124
Boston	50	24	17	9	57	195	176
Toronto	50	22	19	9	53	198	159
Montreal	50	19	19	12	50	181	191
Chicago	50	17	18	15	49	179	180
New York	50	11	31	8	30	161	253

1943 Detroit Red Wings

Sidney Gerald Abel	Donald Joseph Grosso	James V. Orlando
Adam Brown	Sydney Harris Howe	John C. Simon
Modere F. Bruneteau	Harold R. Jackson	John Sherratt Stewart
Joseph G. Carveth	Harry Carl Liscombe	Edward Wares
Lester Douglas	Alexander E. Motter	Harry P. Watson
Joseph Fisher	John T. Mowers	

From 1943 through 1967 the first and third place clubs and the second and fourth place clubs each played a 4-out-of-7-game series. The winners of these series then met in another 4-out-of-7-game series for the Stanley Cup.

Stanley Cup: Detroit 4, Boston 0 (Games)

April 1	Detroit	6	Boston	2
April 4	Detroit	4	Boston	3
April 7	Detroit	4	Boston	0
April 8	Detroit	2	Boston	0

Playoffs:

March 21	Detroit	4	Toronto	2	
March 23	Detroit	2	Toronto	3	(McLean scored 70:18 overtime)
March 25	Detroit	4	Toronto	2	
March 27	Detroit	3	Toronto	6	
March 28	Detroit	4	Toronto	2	
March 30	Detroit	3	Toronto	2	(Brown scored 9:21 overtime)

March 21	Boston	5	Montreal	4	(Gallinger scored 12:30 overtime)
March 23	Boston	5	Montreal	3	
March 25	Boston	3	Montreal	2	(Jackson scored 3:20 overtime)
March 27	Boston	0	Montreal	4	
March 30	Boston	5	Montreal	4	(DeMarco scored 3:41 overtime)

Leaders

Goals: Douglas Bentley (Chicago) 33; Assists: William Cowley (Boston) 45; Points: Douglas Bentley 33–40–73; Penalty Minutes: James Orlando (Detroit) 99.

Trophies

Byng: Maxwell Bentley (Chicago); Calder: James Stewart (Toronto); Hart: William Cowley (Boston); Vezina: John Mowers (Detroit); Prince of Wales: Detroit.

Notes

From 1943 through 1967, the 1st and 3rd place clubs and the 2nd and 4th place clubs each played a 4-out-of-7-game series. The winner of these series' then met in another 4-out-of-7-game series for the Stanley Cup.

With Brooklyn out, a six team league played a 50 game schedule.

Overtime games during regular schedule were discontinued; previously, one overtime period would be played before a tie was declared.

Frank Calder, first NHL president, died in February and was replaced by Mervyn "Red" Dutton.

1943–44

League Standings

Clubs	Games	Won	Lost	Tied	Points	Goals for	Goals against
Montreal	50	38	5	7	83	234	109
Detroit	50	26	18	6	58	214	177
Toronto	50	23	23	4	50	214	174
Chicago	50	22	23	5	49	178	187
Boston	50	19	26	5	43	223	268
New York	50	6	39	5	17	162	310

1944 Montreal Canadiens

Hector Blake
Emile Joseph
  Bouchard
Erwin Groves
  Chamberlain
William Ronald
  Durnan

Robert L. Fillion
Raymond Getliffe
Glen David Harmon
Gerald Heffernan
Elmer James Lach
Leo P. Lamoureux
Fernand Majeau

Michael C. McMahon
Herbert W. O'Connor
Joseph Henri Maurice
  Richard
Phillipe Henri Watson

Stanley Cup: Montreal 4, Chicago 0 (Games)

April	4	Montreal	5	Chicago	1	
April	6	Montreal	3	Chicago	1	
April	9	Montreal	3	Chicago	2	
April	13	Montreal	5	Chicago	4	(Blake scored 9:12 overtime)

Playoffs:

March	21	Montreal	1	Toronto	3
March	23	Montreal	5	Toronto	1
March	25	Montreal	2	Toronto	1
March	28	Montreal	4	Toronto	1
March	30	Montreal	11	Toronto	0

March	21	Chicago	2	Detroit	1
March	23	Chicago	1	Detroit	4
March	26	Chicago	2	Detroit	0
March	28	Chicago	7	Detroit	1
March	30	Chicago	5	Detroit	2

Playoff Action

In the second game of the Montreal-Toronto series, Joseph Richard scored all five goals beating Paul Bibeault, Toronto goaltender, three times when he broke in alone. Hector Blake, on his left wing, assisted on all five and Elmer Lach, his center, assisted on four. In the fifth game, J. Richard scored two goals as Montreal routed the Maple Leafs 11–0. During this game the Canadiens scored five goals in less than four minutes in the third period.

Leaders

Goals: Douglas Bentley (Chicago) 38; Assists: Clinton Smith (Chicago) 49; Points: Herbert Cain (Boston) 36–46–82; Penalty Minutes: Michael McMahon (Montreal) 98.

Trophies

Byng: Clinton Smith (Chicago); Calder: August Bodnar (Toronto); Hart: Walter Pratt (Toronto); Vezina: William Durnan (Montreal); Prince of Wales: Montreal.

Notes

Red line added in middle of center zone to speed action.

1944–45

League Standings

Clubs	Games	Won	Lost	Tied	Points	Goals for	Goals against
Montreal	50	38	8	4	80	228	121
Detroit	50	31	14	5	67	218	161
Toronto	50	24	22	4	52	183	161
Boston	50	16	30	4	36	179	219
Chicago	50	13	30	7	33	141	194
New York	50	11	29	10	32	154	247

1945 Toronto Maple Leafs

August Bodnar	Theodore S. Kennedy	Elwyn Morris
Lorne Carr	Frank McCool	Walter Pratt
Robert Davidson	John McCreedy	David Schriner
Reginald Hamilton	Jack McLean	Walter P. Stanowski
John Melvin Hill	Donald Maurice Metz	
Arthur Jackson	Nicholas J. Metz	

Stanley Cup: Toronto 4, Detroit 3 (Games)

April 6 Toronto 1 Detroit 0
April 8 Toronto 2 Detroit 0

April 12	Toronto	1	Detroit	0	
April 14	Toronto	3	Detroit	5	
April 19	Toronto	0	Detroit	2	
April 21	Toronto	0	Detroit	1	(E. Bruneteau scored 14:16 overtime)
April 22	Toronto	2	Detroit	1	

Playoffs:

March 20	Toronto	1	Montreal	0	
March 22	Toronto	3	Montreal	2	
March 24	Toronto	1	Montreal	4	
March 27	Toronto	4	Montreal	3	(Bodnar scored 12:36 overtime)
March 29	Toronto	3	Montreal	10	
March 31	Toronto	3	Montreal	2	

March 20	Detroit	3	Boston	4	
March 22	Detroit	2	Boston	4	
March 25	Detroit	3	Boston	2	
March 27	Detroit	3	Boston	2	
March 29	Detroit	3	Boston	2	(M. Bruneteau scored 17:12 overtime)
April 1	Detroit	3	Boston	5	
April 3	Detroit	5	Boston	3	

Playoff Action

In the fourth game of the Stanley Cup series, Theodore Kennedy scored Toronto's three goals. In the seventh game, midway through the third period with the score tied 1–1, Frank McCool, Toronto goaltender who had been discharged from the armed forces due to a stomach disorder, became so nervous that he was permitted to leave the ice for ten minutes.

After McCool's return, Walter Pratt scored the winning goal. McCool had been superb in shutting out Detroit for three consecutive games. When William Hollett scored at 8:35 of the first period in the fourth game, it was the first goal he had allowed since March 31st when (Butch) Bouchard of the Montreal Canadiens scored at 15:26 of the third period: a span of 193 minutes and 9 seconds.

Leaders

Goals: Maurice Richard (Montreal) 50; Assists: Elmer Lach (Montreal) 54; Points: Elmer Lach 26–54–80; Penalty Minutes: Martin Egan (Boston) 86.

Trophies

Byng: William Mosienko (Chicago); Calder: Frank McCool (Toronto); Hart: Elmer Lach (Montreal); Vezina: William Durnan (Montreal); Prince of Wales: Montreal.

Coaches

John Gottselig replaced Thompson at Chicago.

Hall of Fame

Players: Donald Bain, Hobart Baker, Russell Bowie, Aubrey Clapper, Charles Gardiner, Eddie Gerard, Aurel Joliat, Frank McGee, Howarth Morenz, Frank Nighbor, Lester Patrick, Tommy Phillips, Harvey Pulford, Arthur Ross, Edward Shore, Hod Stuart, Frederic Taylor, Georges Vézina.

Builders: Sir Montague Allan, Frank Calder, William Hewitt, Francis Nelson, William Northey, John Robertson, Claude Robinson, Lord Stanley of Preston, Capt. James Sutherland.

1945–46

League Standings

Clubs	Games	Won	Lost	Tied	Points	Goals for	Goals against
Montreal	50	28	17	5	61	172	134
Boston	50	24	18	8	56	167	156
Chicago	50	23	20	7	53	200	178
Detroit	50	20	20	10	50	146	159
Toronto	50	19	24	7	45	174	185
New York	50	13	28	9	35	144	191

1946 Montreal Canadiens

Hector Blake
Emile Joseph Bouchard
Erwin Groves Chamberlain
William Ronald Durnan
Frank H. Eddolls
Robert L. Fillion
Glen David Harmon
Wilbert Carl Hiller
Elmer James Lach
Leo P. Lamoureux
Kenneth Mosdell
Herbert W. O'Connor
James Meldrum Peters
Gerard R. Plamondon
Kenneth Joseph Reardon
William T. Reay
Joseph Henri Maurice Richard

Stanley Cup: Montreal 4, Boston 1 (Games)

March	30	Montreal	4	Boston	3 (M. Richard scored 9:08 overtime)
April	2	Montreal	3	Boston	2 (Peters scored 16:55 overtime)
April	4	Montreal	4	Boston	2
April	7	Montreal	2	Boston	3 (Reardon scored 15:13 overtime)
April	9	Montreal	6	Boston	3

Playoffs:

March	19	Montreal	6	Chicago	2
March	21	Montreal	5	Chicago	1
March	24	Montreal	8	Chicago	2
March	26	Montreal	7	Chicago	2

March 19   Boston   3   Detroit   1
March 21   Boston   0   Detroit   3
March 24   Boston   5   Detroit   2
March 26   Boston   4   Detroit   1
March 28   Boston   4   Detroit   3   (Gallinger scored 9:51 overtime)

Leaders

Goals: James Stewart (Toronto) 37; Assists: Elmer Lach (Montreal) 34; Points: Max Bentley (Chicago) 31–30–61; Penalty Minutes: John Stewart (Detroit) 73.

Trophies

Byng: Hector Blake (Montreal); Calder: Edgar Laprade (New York); Hart: Maxwell Bentley (Chicago); Vezina: William Durnan (Montreal); Prince of Wales: Montreal.

Coaches

Aubrey "Dit" Clapper replaced Arthur Ross at Boston.

Notes

New ruling created officiating crew of one referee and two linesmen.

1946–47

League Standings

Clubs	Games	Won	Lost	Tied	Points	Goals for	Goals against
Montreal	60	34	16	10	17	189	138
Toronto	60	31	19	10	72	209	172
Boston	60	26	23	11	63	190	175
Detroit	60	22	27	11	55	190	193
New York	60	22	32	6	50	167	186
Chicago	60	19	37	4	42	193	274

1947 Toronto Maple Leafs

Charles Joseph Sylvanus Apps
William Barilko
August Bodnar
Garth Vernon Boesch
Walter Edward Broda
William Ezinicki
Theodore S. Kennedy
Joseph Francis Klukay
Victor I. Lynn
Howard William Meeker
Donald Maurice Metz
Nicholas J. Metz
James Angus Gerald Mortson
Norman Robert Poile
Walter P. Stanowski
James Gaye Stewart
James R. Thomson
Harry P. Watson

Stanley Cup: Toronto 4, Montreal 2 (Games)

April 8	Toronto	0	Montreal	6
April 10	Toronto	4	Montreal	0
April 12	Toronto	4	Montreal	2
April 15	Toronto	2	Montreal	1	(Apps scored 16:36 overtime)
April 17	Toronto	1	Montreal	3
April 19	Toronto	2	Montreal	1

Playoffs:

March 26	Toronto	3	Detroit	2	(Meeker scored 3:05 overtime)
March 29	Toronto	1	Detroit	9
April 1	Toronto	4	Detroit	1
April 3	Toronto	4	Detroit	1
April 5	Toronto	6	Detroit	1

March 25	Montreal	3	Boston	1
March 27	Montreal	2	Boston	1	(Mosdell scored 5:38 overtime)
March 29	Montreal	2	Boston	4
April 1	Montreal	5	Boston	1
April 3	Montreal	4	Boston	3	(Quilty scored 36:40 overtime)

Playoff Action

In the fourth Stanley Cup game, late in the third period, with the score tied 1–1, "The Rocket" Richard missed an open net after picking up a rebound. Hector Blake, also, had an open net to shoot at after he picked up Richard's rebound only to have a Toronto player dive in front of his shot. Later (Syl) Apps scored for Toronto in overtime.

It was during this series that Richard exploded against Victor Lynn and later William Ezinicki. He struck Ezinicki with his stick and drew a match misconduct penalty and later was fined and suspended for one game.

Leaders

Goals: Maurice Richard (Montreal) 45; Assists: William Taylor (Detroit) 46; Points: Max Bentley (Detroit) 29–43–72; Penalty Minutes: James Mortson (Toronto) 133.

Trophies

Byng: Robert Bauer (Boston); Calder: Howard Meeker (Toronto); Hart: Maurice Richard (Montreal); Vezina: William Durnan (Montreal); Prince of Wales: Montreal.

Notes

Mervyn Dutton retired as NHL president and was succeeded by Clarence S. Campbell.

Schedule increased to 60 games.

1947–48

League Standings

Clubs	Games	Won	Lost	Tied	Points	Goals for	Goals against
Toronto	60	32	15	13	77	182	143
Detroit	60	30	18	12	72	187	148
Boston	60	23	24	13	59	167	168
New York	60	21	26	13	55	176	201
Montreal	60	20	29	11	51	147	169
Chicago	60	20	34	6	46	196	225

1948 Toronto Maple Leafs

Charles Joseph Sylvanus Apps
William Barilko
Maxwell Herbert Lloyd Bentley
Garth Vernon Boesch
Walter Edward Broda
Lester John Thomas Costello

William Ezinicki
Theodore S. Kennedy
Joseph Francis Klukay
Victor I. Lynn
Howard William Meeker
Donald Maurice Metz
Nicholas J. Metz

James Angus Gerald Mortson
Philip L. Samis
Sidney J. Smith
Walter P. Stanowski
James R. Thomson
Harry P. Watson

Stanley Cup: Toronto 4, Detroit 0 (Games)

April	7	Toronto	5	Detroit	3
April	10	Toronto	4	Detroit	2
April	11	Toronto	2	Detroit	0
April	14	Toronto	7	Detroit	2

Playoffs:

March	24	Toronto	5	Boston	4	(Metz scored 17:03 overtime)
March	27	Toronto	5	Boston	3	
March	30	Toronto	5	Boston	1	
April	1	Toronto	2	Boston	3	
April	3	Toronto	3	Boston	2	

March	24	Detroit	2	New York	1
March	26	Detroit	5	New York	2
March	28	Detroit	2	New York	3
March	30	Detroit	1	New York	3
April	1	Detroit	3	New York	1
April	4	Detroit	4	New York	2

Leaders

Goals: Robert Lindsay (Detroit) 33; Assists: Douglas Bentley (Chicago) 37; Points: Elmer Lach (Montreal) 30-31-61; Penalty Minutes: William Barilko (Toronto) 147.

Trophies

Byng: Herbert O'Connor (New York); Calder: James McFadden (Detroit); Hart: Herbert O'Connor; Ross: Elmer Lach (Montreal); Vezina: Walter Broda (Toronto); Prince of Wales: Toronto.

Coaches

Charles Conacher replaced Gottselig at Chicago; Thomas Ivan replaced Adams at Detroit.

1948–49

League Standings

Clubs	Games	Won	Lost	Tied	Points	Goals for	Goals against
Detroit	60	34	19	7	75	195	145
Boston	60	29	23	8	66	178	163
Montreal	60	28	23	9	65	152	126
Toronto	60	22	25	13	57	147	161
Chicago	60	21	31	8	50	173	211
New York	60	18	31	11	47	133	172

1949 Toronto Maple Leafs

William Barilko
Maxwell Herbert
  Lloyd Bentley
Garth Vernon Boesch
Walter Edward Broda
Robert J. Dawes
William Ezinicki
Calvin Pearly Gardner

William Juzda
Theodore S. Kennedy
Joseph Francis Klukay
Victor I. Lynn
Fleming David Mackell
Donald Maurice Metz

James Angus Gerald
  Mortson
Sidney J. Smith
Harry Taylor
James R. Thomson
Raymond C. Timgren
Harry P. Watson

Stanley Cup: Toronto 4, Detroit 0 (Games)

April	8	Toronto	3	Detroit	2
April	10	Toronto	3	Detroit	1
April	13	Toronto	3	Detroit	1
April	16	Toronto	3	Detroit	1

Playoffs:

March	22	Toronto	3	Boston	0	(Klukay scored 17:31 overtime)
March	24	Toronto	3	Boston	2	
March	26	Toronto	4	Boston	5	(Dumart scored 16:14 overtime)
March	29	Toronto	3	Boston	1	
March	30	Toronto	3	Boston	2	

March 22 Detroit 2 Montreal 1 (McNab scored 44:52 overtime)
March 24 Detroit 3 Montreal 4 (Plamondon scored 2:59 over
March 26 Detroit 2 Montreal 3   time)
March 29 Detroit 3 Montreal 1
March 31 Detroit 3 Montreal 1
April   2 Detroit 1 Montreal 3
April   5 Detroit 3 Montreal 1

Playoff Action

In the second game of the Stanley Cup finals, Sidney Smith scored Toronto's three goals.

With this victory the Maple Leafs became the only club ever to win the Stanley Cup after finishing in fourth place during the regular schedule.

Clarence ("Happy") Day was the first coach to coach a National Hockey League club to three consecutive Stanley Cup titles.

Leaders

Goals: Sidney Abel (Detroit) 28; Assists: Douglas Bentley (Chicago) 43; Points: Roy Conacher (Chicago) 26-42-68; Penalty Minutes: William Ezinicki (Toronto) 145.

Trophies

Byng: Hubert Quackenbush (Detroit) ; Calder: Pentti Lund (New York) ; Hart: Sidney Abel (Detroit) ; Ross: Roy Conacher (Chicago) ; Vezina: William Durnan (Montreal) ; Prince of Wales: Detroit.

Coaches

Lynn Patrick replaced Boucher at New York.

Notes

National Hockey League Pension Society formed.

1949–50

League Standings

Clubs	Games	Won	Lost	Tied	Points	Goals for	Goals against
Detroit	70	37	19	14	88	229	164
Montreal	70	29	22	19	77	172	150
Toronto	70	31	27	12	74	176	173
New York	70	28	31	11	67	170	189
Boston	70	22	32	16	60	198	228
Chicago	70	22	38	10	54	203	244

1950 Detroit Red Wings

Sidney Gerald Abel
Peter Joseph Babando
Stephen Black
Joseph G. Carveth
Gerald J. W. A.
  Couture
Albert P. Dewsbury
Lidio J. Fogolin
George Gee

Gordon Haidy
Gordon Howe
Leonard Patrick Kelly
Robert Blake Theodore
  Lindsay
Harry Lumley
George Clare Martin
James A. McFadden
Doug McKay

Maxwell D. McNab
Martin N. Pavelich
James Meldrum Peters
Joseph Rene Prono-
  vost
Leo C. Reise, Jr.
John Sherratt Stewart
John Edward Wilson
Lawrence Wilson

Stanley Cup: Detroit 4, New York 3 (Games)

April 11	Detroit	4	New York	1	
April 13	Detroit	1	New York	3	
April 15	Detroit	4	New York	0	
April 18	Detroit	3	New York	4	(Raleigh scored 8:34 overtime)
April 20	Detroit	1	New York	2	(Raleigh scored 1:38 overtime)
April 22	Detroit	5	New York	4	
April 23	Detroit	4	New York	3	(Babando scored 28:31 over-time)

Playoffs:

March 28	Detroit	0	Toronto	5	
March 30	Detroit	3	Toronto	1	
April 1	Detroit	0	Toronto	2	
April 4	Detroit	2	Toronto	1	(Reise scored 20:38 overtime)
April 6	Detroit	0	Toronto	2	
April 8	Detroit	4	Toronto	0	
April 9	Detroit	1	Toronto	0	(Reise scored 8:39 overtime)
March 29	New York	3	Montreal	1	
April 1	New York	3	Montreal	2	
April 2	New York	4	Montreal	1	
April 4	New York	2	Montreal	3	(Lach scored 15:19 overtime)
April 6	New York	3	Montreal	0	

Playoff Action

In the first game of the Detroit-Toronto series, with Toronto leading 4–0 in the third period, Gordon Howe was seriously hurt as a result of having crashed headlong into the boards. His skull was fractured, along with his right cheekbone and nose, and his right eyeball was scratched. A brain specialist prepared to operate immediately. He was on the critical list for several days. Thomas Ivan, Detroit coach, charged Theodore Kennedy with butt-ending Howe. Toronto claimed Howe had missed checking Kennedy and had instead crashed into the boards.

In the second game the Detroit players were out to avenge Howe. Near the end of the second period Lindsay tripped Kennedy and another Red Wing struck him over the head. After Howe's injury, Clarence S. Campbell, league president, came to Detroit to conduct an inquiry. Referee George Gravel said it was an "extremely unfortunate accident." After films of the game were reviewed the league exonerated Kennedy.

In the seventh game, in overtime, Leo Reise shot from the blue-line and William Barilko accidentally deflected the puck past "Turk" Broda into the Toronto goal. Reise had scored only four goals during the regular season and this was his second overtime goal in the playoffs.

A circus had taken over Madison Square Garden and the Rangers were without home ice for the Stanley Cup finals. Choosing Toronto for their temporary home, they played the second and third games there. Despite their handicap, the New York Rangers very nearly became the second club to finish fourth in the regular schedule and then come on to win the Stanley Cup.

In the first game, although Detroit was without the services of Gordon Howe and Lindsay, out with an injured back, they defeated New York 4–1 on goals by Carveth, Couture, Gee and McFadden. "Buddy" O'Connor scored New York's lone goal.

In the second game Lindsay returned but New York tied the series with a 3–1 win.

In the third game Lumley turned in an outstanding performance as he shut out the Rangers, 4–0. In the fourth game, in overtime, "Bones" Raleigh, while laying on the ice, guided a pass from Edward Slowinski into the Detroit net to win for New York.

In the fifth game, Raleigh came to the rescue with his second overtime goal to send New York into the lead, 3 games to 2.

In the sixth game, the Rangers at one time commanded a two-goal lead on goals by Fisher and Allan Stanley early in the first period. Detroit fought back to win 5–4 on two goal efforts by Abel and Lindsay. Abel backhanded the winning goal past Claude Rayner at 10:34 in the third period.

In the seventh and final game, New York again took a two-goal lead in the first period. Near the five minute mark of the second period, in 21 seconds, Detroit had tied it. Once again New York went ahead as O'Connor took a pass from (Nick) Mickoski at 11:42. At 15:57, McFadden tied the score on a play with Peters and the clubs went through the third period without a score.

During this third period the tension became so intense that John Adams, Detroit general-manager, left the arena and walked the streets outside until the game was over.

In the first overtime Detroit forced the play and Lumley made five stops while Rayner had eleven. In the second overtime, Rayner made a brilliant save as he came 15 feet out of his goal to stop George Gee who had taken a pass from Babando and broken in the clear. Martin Pavelich had had a chance to end it all when his shot went over the top of the open net.

The last face-off took place in the Ranger zone. Gee won the draw from O'Connor and flipped the puck to Babando. Babando let go with a back-

hander and Rayner, whose view was blocked by his own defensemen, never saw it until it was in the net.

Leaders

Goals: Maurice Richard (Montreal) 43; Assists: Robert Lindsay (Detroit) 55; Points: Robert Lindsay 23-55-78; Penalty Minutes: William Ezinicki (Toronto) 144.

Trophies

Byng: Edgar Laprade (New York); Calder: John Gelineau (Boston); Hart: Claude Rayner (New York); Ross: Robert Lindsay (Detroit); Vezina: William Durnan (Montreal); Prince of Wales: Detroit.

Coaches

George "Buck" Boucher replaced Clapper at Boston.

Hall of Fame

Players: Allan Davidson, Charles Drinkwater, Michael Grant, Silas Griffis, Edouard Lalonde, Joseph Malone, George Richardson, Col. Harry Trihey.

Notes

70-game schedule introduced.
Ice surface painted white. Clubs allowed to dress 17 players exclusive of goalkeepers for a game.

1950–51

League Standings

Clubs	Games	Won	Lost	Tied	Points	Goals for	Goals against
Detroit	70	44	13	13	101	236	139
Toronto	70	41	16	13	95	212	138
Montreal	70	25	30	15	65	173	184
Boston	70	22	30	18	62	178	197
New York	70	20	29	21	61	169	201
Chicago	70	13	47	10	36	171	280

1951 Toronto Maple Leafs

William Barilko
Maxwell Herbert
   Lloyd Bentley
Walter Edward Broda
Ferdinand Charles
   Flaman
Calvin Pearly Gardner
William Juzda

Theodore S. Kennedy
Joseph Francis Klukay
Daniel Lewicki
Fleming David
   Mackell
Howard William
   Meeker

James Angus Gerald
   Mortson
Elwin Ira Rollins
Aloysius Martin Sloan
Sidney J. Smith
James R. Thomson
Raymond C. Timgren
Harry P. Watson

Stanley Cup: Toronto 4, Montreal 1 (Games)

April 11	Toronto	3	Montreal	2	(Smith scored 5:51 overtime)
April 14	Toronto	2	Montreal	3	(M. Richard scored 2:55 overtime)
April 17	Toronto	2	Montreal	1	(Kennedy scored 4:47 overtime)
April 19	Toronto	3	Montreal	2	(Watson scored 5:15 overtime)
April 21	Toronto	3	Montreal	2	(Barilko scored 2:53 overtime)

Playoffs:

March 28	Toronto	0	Boston	2	
March 31	Toronto	1	Boston	1	(Tie—after one overtime—curfew
April 1	Toronto	3	Boston	0	law)
April 3	Toronto	3	Boston	1	
April 7	Toronto	4	Boston	1	
April 8	Toronto	6	Boston	0	

March 27	Montreal	3	Detroit	2	(M. Richard scored 61:09 overtime)
March 29	Montreal	1	Detroit	0	(M. Richard scored 42:20 overtime)
March 31	Montreal	0	Detroit	2	
April 3	Montreal	1	Detroit	4	
April 5	Montreal	5	Detroit	2	
April 7	Montreal	3	Detroit	2	

Playoff Action

This was an exciting Stanley Cup series; all the games went into overtime.

In the second game, in overtime, "The Rocket" Richard took a pass from Douglas Harvey and carried it over the blue line. As he rounded the Toronto defense, he lost the puck and "Turk" Broda came out after it. Richard beat him to it and scored.

In the fifth game, Toronto pressed the attack in the first period. Rollins only had four saves to 14 for Gerard McNeil in the Montreal nets. At 8:56 of the second period "The Rocket" took the puck at center ice and scored.

With one goal in the lead Montreal went on the defensive as Toronto rifled 19 shots at McNeil.

Joseph Primeau, Maple Leaf coach, pulled Rollins with a minute and 33 seconds left. With 61 seconds left, Rollins returned to his goal as the face-off was outside the Montreal zone. Kennedy won the draw and shot the puck into the Canadien's area where a scramble forced another face-off. Rollins again left his goal with 39 seconds left.

Max Bentley fired through a group of players and the puck bounced to Sidney Smith. Smith swiped at it and it hit the goal post. It lit at Tod Sloan's feet and he smacked it in with 32 seconds left.

In overtime, Calvin Gardner carried the puck into the Montreal end and Meeker shot it out to William Barilko who zoomed it into the net.

Leaders

Goals: Gordon Howe (Detroit) 43; Assists: Gordon Howe, Theodore Kennedy (Toronto) 43 (tie); Points: Gordon Howe 43-43-86; Penalty Minutes: James Mortson (Toronto) 142.

Trophies

Byng: Leonard Kelly (Detroit); Calder: Terrance Sawchuk (Detroit); Hart: Milton Schmidt (Boston); Ross: Gordon Howe (Detroit); Vezina: Elwin Rollins (Toronto); Prince of Wales: Detroit.

Coaches

Lynn Patrick replaced Boucher at Boston; Ebenezer Goodfellow replaced Conacher at Chicago; Neil Colville replaced Patrick at New York; Joseph Primeau replaced Day at Toronto.

Notes

William Barilko, Toronto star, flew north with a companion on a fishing trip in August. They vanished and were found, in the wreckage of the plane, 11 years later, near Cochrane, Ont.

1951–52

League Standings

Clubs	Games	Won	Lost	Tied	Points	Goals for	Goals against
Detroit	70	44	14	12	100	215	133
Montreal	70	34	26	10	78	195	164
Toronto	70	29	25	16	74	168	157
Boston	70	25	29	16	66	162	176
New York	70	23	34	13	59	192	219
Chicago	70	17	44	9	43	158	241

1952 Detroit Red Wings

Sidney Gerald Abel
Alexander Peter Delvecchio
Robert J. Goldham
Gordon Howe
Leonard Patrick Kelly
Anthony J. Leswick

Robert Blake Theodore Lindsay
Martin N. Pavelich
Joseph Rene Marcel Pronovost
Metro Prystai
Leo C. Reise, Jr.

Terrance Gordon Sawchuk
Glen Frederick Skov
Victor John Stasiuk
John Edward Wilson
Benedict Francis Woit
Lazarus Zeidel

Stanley Cup: Detroit 4, Montreal 0 (Games)

April 10	Detroit	3	Montreal	1
April 12	Detroit	2	Montreal	1
April 13	Detroit	3	Montreal	0
April 15	Detroit	3	Montreal	0

Playoffs:

March	25	Detroit	3	Toronto	0
March	27	Detroit	1	Toronto	0
March	29	Detroit	6	Toronto	2
April	1	Detroit	3	Toronto	1

March	25	Montreal	5	Boston	1	
March	27	Montreal	4	Boston	0	
March	30	Montreal	1	Boston	4	
April	1	Montreal	2	Boston	3	
April	3	Montreal	0	Boston	1	
April	6	Montreal	3	Boston	2	(Masnick scored 27:49 overtime)
April	8	Montreal	3	Boston	1	

Playoff Action

In the second game of the Toronto-Detroit series, although "Turk" Broda had been sensational, Toronto lost 1–0. John Wilson, playing on a line with Delvecchio and Prystai, scored the only goal in the second period. Delvecchio had shot from far out and Broda had come out of his net to make the save. The puck slithered through his pads and dropped behind him as Wilson came racing in from the side to pick it up and slip it into the goal.

In the seventh Montreal-Boston game, during the second period, "The Rocket" Richard was knocked out in a collision with Leo LaBine and Bill Quackenbush. He was taken to the Clinic in Montreal's Forum and didn't appear on the Canadien's bench until later in the third period.

With the score tied 1–1 and around four minutes left to play, "Dick" Irvin, Canadien coach, let Richard go out on the ice. (Butch) Bouchard laid a pass on his stick and "The Rocket" moved into high gear. He sped over the blue line and cut sharply around Quackenbush and bore in on "Sugar Jim" Henry, the Boston goaltender. Henry, who had suffered a broken nose and two black eyes earlier in the game, had no more than started his sprawl when Richard had it in the net.

The Associated Press called this goal "one of the most sensational ever scored in Stanley Cup play!" The final score was 3–1 as William Reay scored an open-net goal at 19:46.

Leaders

Goals: Gordon Howe (Detroit) 47; Assists: Elmer Lach (Montreal) 50; Points: Gordon Howe 47-39-86; Penalty Minutes: Walter Kyle (Boston) 127.

Trophies

Byng: Sidney Smith (Toronto); Calder: Bernard Geoffrion (Montreal); Hart: Gordon Howe (Detroit); Ross: Gordon Howe; Vezina: Terrance Sawchuck (Detroit); Prince of Wales: Detroit.

Coaches

William Cook replaced Colville at New York.

Hall of Fame

Players: Richard Boon, William Cook, Frank Goheen, Ernest Johnson, Duncan MacKay.

Notes

Goal crease enlarged from three-by-seven feet to four-by-eight; face-off circle enlarged from a 10-foot to a 15-foot radius.

1952–53

League Standings

Clubs	Games	Won	Lost	Tied	Points	Goals for	Goals against
Detroit	70	36	16	18	90	222	133
Montreal	70	28	23	19	75	155	148
Boston	70	28	29	13	69	152	172
Chicago	70	27	18	15	69	169	175
Toronto	70	27	30	13	67	156	167
New York	70	17	37	16	50	152	211

1953 Montreal Canadiens

Douglas Anderson
Emile Joseph Bou-
  chard
Floyd James Curry
Lorne Austin Davis
Richard Frank Gamble
Bernard Andre
  Geoffrion
Douglas Norman
  Harvey

Thomas Christian
  Johnson
Elmer James Lach
Calum MacKay
James Albert Mac-
  Pherson
Paul Andrew Masnick
Edward Joseph Mazur
John R. McCormack
Paul C. Meger

Gerard George McNeil
Richard Winston
  Moore
Kenneth Mosdell
Murray Bert Olmstead
Jacques Plante
William T. Reay
Joseph Henri Maurice
  Richard
Dollard Herve St.
  Laurent

Stanley Cup: Montreal 4, Boston 1 (Games)

April	9	Montreal	4	Boston	2	
April	11	Montreal	1	Boston	4	
April	12	Montreal	3	Boston	0	
April	14	Montreal	7	Boston	3	
April	16	Montreal	1	Boston	0	(Lach scored 1:22 overtime)

Playoffs:

March	24	Montreal	3	Chicago	1	
March	26	Montreal	4	Chicago	3	
March	29	Montreal	1	Chicago	2	(Dewsbury scored 5:18 over-
March	31	Montreal	1	Chicago	3	time)
April	2	Montreal	2	Chicago	4	
April	4	Montreal	3	Chicago	0	
April	7	Montreal	4	Chicago	1	

March	24	Boston	0	Detroit	7	
March	26	Boston	5	Detroit	3	
March	29	Boston	2	Detroit	1	(McIntyre scored 12:29 overtime)
March	31	Boston	6	Detroit	2	
April	2	Boston	4	Detroit	6	
April	5	Boston	4	Detroit	2	

Playoff Action

In the fourth game of the Stanley Cup series, "The Rocket" Richard scored three goals on Gordon Henry in the Boston nets. In the fifth game, there was no score as the third period ended. Defensive play and hard body-checking predominated throughout the three periods with the Canadiens having 28 shots on goal to the Bruins 21.

"Dick" Irvin sent the Punch Line out to start the overtime. Woodrow Dumart had taken a shot on the Montreal goal and Edward Mazur of Montreal then picked up the puck, skated back and shot just before he reached the Boston blue-line. "Bill" Quackenbush, in an effort to block the shot, only deflected it and it rebounded off "Sugar Jim" Henry's pads. Racing in "The Rocket" picked it up and as Henry lunged he passed to Lach, who rifled a backhander into the net. Note: Boston used Gordon Henry and "Sugar Jim" Henry in goal during this series. Plante played the first two games of this series for the Canadiens and Gerard McNeil was in goal for the last three.

Leaders

Goals: Gordon Howe (Detroit) 49; Assists: Gordon Howe 46; Points: Gordon Howe 49-46-95; Penalty Minutes: Maurice Richard (Montreal) 112.

Trophies

Byng: Leonard Kelly (Detroit); Calder: Lorne Worsley (New York); Hart: Gordon Howe (Detroit); Ross: Gordon Howe; Vezina: Terrance Sawchuk (Detroit); Prince of Wales: Detroit.

Coaches

Sidney Abel replaced Goodfellow at Chicago.

1953–54

League Standings

Clubs	Games	Won	Lost	Tied	Points	Goals for	Goals against
Detroit	70	37	19	14	88	191	132
Montreal	70	35	24	11	81	195	141
Toronto	70	32	24	14	78	152	131
Boston	70	32	28	10	74	177	181
New York	70	29	31	10	68	161	182
Chicago	70	12	51	7	31	133	242

1954 Detroit Red Wings

Courtney Keith Allen
Alexander Peter Del-
   vecchio
William Patrick
   Dineen
Joseph Gilles Dube
Robert J. Goldham
Gordon Howe

Leonard Patrick Kelly
Anthony J. Leswick
Robert Blake Theodore
   Lindsay
Martin N. Pavelich
James Meldrum Peters
Joseph Rene Marcel
   Pronovost

Metro Prystai
Earl Reibel
Terrance Sawchuk
Glen Frederick Skov
John Edward Wilson
Benedict Francis Woit

Stanley Cup: Detroit 4, Montreal 3 (Games)

April	4	Detroit	3	Montreal	1	
April	6	Detroit	1	Montreal	3	
April	8	Detroit	5	Montreal	2	
April	10	Detroit	2	Montreal	0	
April	11	Detroit	0	Montreal	1	(Mosdell scored 5:45 overtime)
April	13	Detroit	1	Montreal	4	
April	16	Detroit	2	Montreal	1	(Leswick scored 4:29 overtime)

Playoffs:

March	23	Detroit	5	Toronto	0	
March	25	Detroit	1	Toronto	3	
March	27	Detroit	3	Toronto	1	
March	30	Detroit	2	Toronto	1	
April	1	Detroit	4	Toronto	3	(Lindsay scored 21:01 overtime)
March	23	Montreal	2	Boston	0	
March	25	Montreal	8	Boston	1	
March	28	Montreal	4	Boston	3	
March	30	Montreal	2	Boston	0	

Playoff Action

In the second game of the Boston-Montreal series, Jean Beliveau, playing on a line with Bernard Geoffrion and Richard Moore, began the game facing off against Milton Schmidt of Boston. Beliveau won the draw and

drove the puck into a Boston corner. Geoffrion raced the Bruin defenders for it and passed it back out to Moore. Moore beat "Sugar Jim" Henry, Boston goaltender, and the game was now 10 seconds old. Moore's record for scoring the fastest goal from the start of a Stanley Cup game didn't even get in the record books.

A week later, on April 1, Gordon Howe of Detroit scored nine seconds from the opening face-off against Toronto. However, Moore scored two goals and had four assists in this game and his line-mates each had two goals and three assists. It was a rough game as referee Jack Mehlenbacher called 23 penalties; 3 misconducts, 8 majors and 12 minors.

In the second game of the finals, Montreal scored three goals in 56 seconds of the first period; "The Rocket" Richard scored two and Richard Moore the other.

In the seventh game, in overtime, Leswick sent a shot in from the blue line. It deflected off Douglas Harvey's glove and bounced over Gerard McNeil's shoulder into the net. McNeil had been injured a month before the regular season ended. Jacques Plante played the four games against Boston and the first four against Detroit. With the Canadiens down three games to one, McNeil returned. He shut out the Red Wings in the fifth game and Montreal won the sixth as he gave up only one goal.

Leaders

Goals: Maurice Richard (Montreal) 37; Assists: Gordon Howe (Detroit) 48; Points: Gordon Howe 33-48-81; Penalty Minutes: James Mortson (Chicago) 132.

Trophies

Byng: Leonard Kelly (Detroit); Calder: Camille Henry (New York); Hart: Elwin Rollins (Chicago); Norris: Leonard Kelly; Ross: Gordon Howe (Detroit); Vezina: Harry Lumley (Toronto); Prince of Wales: Detroit.

Coaches

General Manager Frank Boucher temporarily replaced Cook at New York; in January, "Muzz" Patrick succeeded Boucher. "King" Clancy replaced Primeau at Toronto.

1954–55

League Standings

Clubs	Games	Won	Lost	Tied	Points	Goals for	Goals against
Detroit	70	42	17	11	95	204	134
Montreal	70	41	18	11	93	228	157
Toronto	70	24	24	22	70	147	135
Boston	70	23	26	21	67	169	188
New York	70	17	35	18	52	150	210
Chicago	70	13	40	17	43	161	235

1955 Detroit Red Wings

Marcel Bonin	Gordon Howe	Earl Reibel
Alexander Peter Del-	Leonard Patrick Kelly	Terrance Sawchuk
vecchio	Anthony J. Leswick	Glen Frederick Skov
William Patrick	Robert Blake Theodore	Victor John Stasiuk
Dineen	Lindsay	John Edward Wilson
Robert J. Goldham	Martin N. Pavelich	Benedict Francis Woit
James Alexander Hay	Joseph Rene Marcel	
Larry Morley Hillman	Pronovost	

Stanley Cup: Detroit 4, Montreal 3 (Games)

April	3	Detroit	4	Montreal	2
April	5	Detroit	7	Montreal	1
April	7	Detroit	2	Montreal	4
April	9	Detroit	3	Montreal	5
April	10	Detroit	5	Montreal	1
April	12	Detroit	3	Montreal	6
April	14	Detroit	3	Montreal	1

Playoffs:

March	22	Detroit	7	Toronto	4
March	24	Detroit	2	Toronto	1
March	26	Detroit	2	Toronto	1
March	29	Detroit	3	Toronto	0

March	22	Montreal	2	Boston	0	
March	24	Montreal	3	Boston	1	
March	27	Montreal	2	Boston	4	
March	29	Montreal	4	Boston	3	(Marshall scored 3:05 overtime)
March	31	Montreal	5	Boston	1	

Playoff Action

In the first game of the Stanley Cup playoff, Richard Moore became involved in a brawl with the Detroit players, fans and his own team-mates that lasted for ten minutes. When it was over a police escort was needed to accompany him off the ice.

In the second game, Lindsay scored four goals; one against Charles Hodge and three against Jacques Plante, who were alternating in the Canadien net.

In the third game, Bernard Geoffrion scored three goals for Montreal.

In the fifth game, Gordon Howe scored three goals on Plante.

In the seventh game, Howe scored the first goal followed with two more by Alexander Delvecchio. Howe had five goals and seven assists in this series. "The Rocket" Richard did not play in the playoffs for the Canadiens as he had been suspended for striking an official near the end of the regular schedule.

Leaders

Goals: Bernard Geoffrion (Montreal), Maurice Richard (Montreal) 38 (tie); Assists: Murray Olmstead (Montreal) 48; Points: Bernard Geoffrion 38-37-75; Penalty Minutes: Ferdinand Flaman (Boston) 150.

Trophies

Byng: Sidney Smith (Toronto); Calder: Edward Litzenberger (Montreal—Chicago); Hart: Theodore Kennedy (Toronto); Norris: Douglas Harvey (Montreal); Ross: Bernard Geoffrion (Montreal); Vezina: Terrance Sawchuk (Detroit); Prince of Wales: Detroit.

Coaches

Milton Schmidt replaced Patrick at Boston; Frank Eddolls replaced Abel at Chicago; James Skinner replaced Ivan at Detroit.

Notes

Intra-league draft modified to provide effective means of assuring availability of players.

1955–56

League Standings

Clubs	Games	Won	Lost	Tied	Points	Goals for	Goals against
Montreal	70	45	15	10	100	222	131
Detroit	70	30	24	16	76	183	148
New York	70	32	28	10	74	204	203
Toronto	70	24	33	13	61	153	181
Boston	70	23	34	13	59	147	185
Chicago	70	19	39	12	50	155	216

1956 Montreal Canadiens

Jean Marc Beliveau
Emile Joseph Bouchard
Floyd James Curry
Bernard Andre Geoffrion
Douglas Norman Harvey
Thomas Christian

Johnson
John Louis LeClair
Donald Robert Marshall
Richard Winston Moore
Kenneth Mosdell
Murray Bert Olmstead
Jacques Plante

Claude Provost
Henri Richard
Joseph Henri Maurice Richard
Dollard Herve St. Laurent
Jean-Guy Talbot
Robert George Turner

Stanley Cup: Montreal 4, Detroit 1 (Games)

March 31	Montreal	6	Detroit	4
April 3	Montreal	5	Detroit	1
April 5	Montreal	1	Detroit	3
April 8	Montreal	3	Detroit	0
April 10	Montreal	3	Detroit	1

Playoffs:

March 20	Montreal	7	New York	1
March 22	Montreal	2	New York	4
March 24	Montreal	3	New York	1
March 25	Montreal	5	New York	3
March 27	Montreal	7	New York	0

March 20	Detroit	3	Toronto	2	
March 22	Detroit	3	Toronto	1	
March 24	Detroit	5	Toronto	4	(Lindsay scored 4:22 overtime)
March 27	Detroit	0	Toronto	2	
March 29	Detroit	3	Toronto	1	

Playoff Action

In the first game of the finals, with his club down 4–2 after two periods, Hector Blake, Canadiens coach, gave his players a tongue lashing. They came out in the third period and scored four goals, with the third line of Floyd Curry, John Leclair, and Claude Provost each scoring once.

Jean Beliveau scored seven goals in this series and Olmstead had eight assists.

This was Henri Richard's first appearance in Stanley Cup play and he scored four goals and had four assists during the playoffs.

Leaders

Goals: Jean Beliveau (Montreal) 47; Assists: Murray Olmstead (Montreal) 56; Points: Jean Beliveau 47–41–88; Penalty Minutes: Louis Fortinato (New York) 202.

Trophies

Byng: Earl Reibel (Detroit); Calder: Glenn Hall (Detroit); Hart: Jean Beliveau (Montreal); Norris: Douglas Harvey (Montreal); Ross: Jean Beliveau; Vezina: Jacques Plante (Montreal); Prince of Wales: Montreal.

Coaches

James Dickenson "Dick" Irvin replaced Eddolls at Chicago; Hector Blake replaced Irvin at Montreal; Philip Watson replaced Patrick at New York.

1956–57

League Standings

Clubs	Games	Won	Lost	Tied	Points	Goals for	Goals against
Detroit	70	38	20	12	88	198	157
Montreal	70	35	23	12	82	210	155
Boston	70	34	24	12	80	195	174
New York	70	26	30	14	66	184	227
Toronto	70	21	34	15	57	174	192
Chicago	70	16	39	15	47	169	225

1957 Montreal Canadiens

Jean Arthur Béliveau
Connell Broden
Floyd James Curry
Bernard Andre Geoffrion
Phillipe Goyette
Douglas Norman Harvey
Thomas Christian

Johnson
Donald Robert Marshall
Richard Winston Moore
Murray Bert Olmstead
Jacques Plante
Joseph Armand Andre Pronovost

Claude Provost
Henri Richard
Joseph Henri Maurice Richard
Dollard Herve St. Laurent
Jean-Guy Talbot
Robert George Turner

Stanley Cup: Montreal 4, Boston 1 (Games)

April	6	Montreal	5	Boston	1
April	9	Montreal	1	Boston	0
April	11	Montreal	4	Boston	2
April	14	Montreal	0	Boston	2
April	16	Montreal	5	Boston	1

Playoffs:

March	26	Montreal	4	New York	1	
March	28	Montreal	3	New York	4	(Hebenton scored 13:38 overtime)
March	30	Montreal	8	New York	3	
April	2	Montreal	3	New York	1	
April	4	Montreal	4	New York	3	(M. Richard scored 1:11 overtime)

March	26	Boston	3	Detroit	1
March	28	Boston	2	Detroit	7
March	31	Boston	4	Detroit	3
April	2	Boston	2	Detroit	0
April	4	Boston	4	Detroit	3

Playoff Action

In the fifth game of the series with Detroit, Boston was trailing 2–1 until Leo LaBine scored, assisted by Donald McKenney, in the third

period. Later Douglas Mohns scored on a pass from McKenney to put the Bruins ahead 3–2. They went on to a 4–3 victory and into the final series against Montreal.

In the first game of the finals, "The Rocket" Richard scored four goals.

Donald Simmons was outstanding in goal for Boston against both Detroit and the Canadiens.

Leaders

Goals: Gordon Howe (Detroit) 44; Assists: Robert Lindsay (Detroit) 55; Points: Gordon Howe 44–45–89; Penalty Minutes: James Mortson (Chicago) 147.

Trophies

Byng: Andrew Hebenton (New York); Calder: Lawrence Regan (Boston); Hart: Gordon Howe (Detroit); Norris: Douglas Harvey (Montreal); Ross: Gordon Howe; Vezina: Jacques Plante (Montreal); Prince of Wales: Detroit.

Coaches

Thomas Ivan replaced Irvin at Chicago; Howard Meeker replaced Clancy at Toronto.

Notes

Player serving minor penalty allowed to return to ice after goal is scored by opposing team.

1957–58

League Standings

Clubs	Games	Won	Lost	Tied	Points	Goals for	Goals against
Montreal	70	43	17	10	96	250	158
New York	70	32	25	13	77	195	188
Detroit	70	29	29	12	70	176	207
Boston	70	27	28	15	69	199	194
Chicago	70	24	39	7	55	163	202
Toronto	70	21	38	11	53	192	226

1958 Montreal Canadiens

Jean Arthur Béliveau
Marcel Bonin
Connell Broden
Floyd James Curry
Bernard Andre
 Geoffrion
Phillipe Goyette
Douglas Norman
 Harvey
Thomas Christian

Johnson
Albert Langlois
Donald Robert
 Marshall
Alvin Brian McDonald
Richard Winston
 Moore
Murray Bert Olmstead
Jacques Plante
Joseph Armand Andre

Pronovost
Claude Provost
Henri Richard
Joseph Henri Maurice
 Richard
Dollard Herve
 St. Laurent
Jean-Guy Talbot
Robert George Turner

Stanley Cup: Montreal 4, Boston 2 (Games)

April	8	Montreal	2	Boston	1	
April	10	Montreal	2	Boston	5	
April	13	Montreal	3	Boston	0	
April	15	Montreal	1	Boston	3	
April	17	Montreal	3	Boston	2	(Maurice Richard scored 5:45
April	20	Montreal	5	Boston	3	overtime)

Playoffs:

March	25	Montreal	8	Detroit	1	
March	27	Montreal	5	Detroit	1	
March	30	Montreal	2	Detroit	1	(J. A. Pronovost scored 11:52
April	1	Montreal	4	Detroit	3	overtime)

March	25	Boston	3	New York	5	
March	27	Boston	4	New York	3	(Toppazzini scored 4:46
March	29	Boston	5	New York	0	overtime)
April	1	Boston	2	New York	5	
April	3	Boston	6	New York	1	
April	5	Boston	8	New York	2	

Playoff Action

In the first game of the Detroit-Montreal series, Goyette scored three goals. In the fourth game, "The Rocket" Richard scored three goals. One of the first two was scored after he had been wrestled to the ice by Warren Godfrey, Detroit defenseman, whom he had cut around. As the puck slid toward Terrance Sawchuk, Red Wing goaltender, Richard rose to one knee and, lunging with his stick extended full length, poked it by him. His third goal was the Canadiens' fourth and winning one. He scored seven goals in this series.

In the second game of the Boston-New York series, Donald McKenney tied the score at 2–2 when he scored on a long shot after stealing the puck from defenseman "Jack" Evans.

McKenney again tied the score for Boston at 3–3 when his shot got by Lorne Worsley, Ranger goaltender, half way through the third period. Toppazzini's score in overtime won the game for Boston.

In the sixth game, McKenney tied the assist record for a Stanley Cup game with five. Toppazzini had three goals and Mackell had two. During the series, Toppazzini scored eight goals and Mackell had four goals and ten assists.

In the fifth game of the finals, Henri Richard assisted on his brother's overtime goal. "The Rocket" had four goals in this series for a total of eleven in the playoffs.

Leaders

Goals: Richard Moore (Montreal) 36; Assists: Henri Richard (Montreal) 32; Points: Richard Moore 36–48–84; Penalty Minutes: Louis Fortinato (New York) 152.

Trophies

Byng: Camille Henry (New York); Calder: Francis Mahovlich (Toronto); Hart: Gordon Howe (Detroit); Norris: Douglas Harvey (Montreal); Ross: Richard Moore (Montreal); Vezina: Jacques Plante (Montreal); Prince of Wales: Montreal.

Coaches

Rudolph Pilous replaced Ivan at Chicago; Sidney Abel replaced Skinner at Detroit; William Reay replaced Meeker at Toronto.

Hall of Fame

Players: Frank Boucher, Francis Clancy, Sprague Cleghorn, Alex Connell, Mervyn Dutton, Frank Foyston, Frank Fredrickson, Herbert Gardiner, George Hay, James Irvin, Ivan Johnson, Gordon Keats, Hugh Lehman, George McNamara, Patrick Moran.
Builders: George Dudley, James Norris, Sr., Frank Patrick, Allan Pickard, Sen. Donat Raymond, Conn Smythe, Lloyd Turner.

Notes

First ten years of Pension Plan completed and Plan revised with greatly increased benefits.
Players' Playoff awards substantially increased.
Owner-Player Council established.

1958–59

League Standings

Clubs	Games	Won	Lost	Tied	Points	Goals for	Goals against
Montreal	70	39	18	13	91	258	158
Boston	70	32	29	9	73	205	215
Chicago	70	28	29	13	69	197	208
Toronto	70	27	32	11	65	189	201
New York	70	26	32	12	64	201	217
Detroit	70	25	37	8	58	167	218

1959 Montreal Canadiens

Ralph Backstrom
Jean Arthur Béliveau
Marcel Bonin
Bernard Andre Geoffrion
Phillipe Goyette
Douglas Norman Harvey
William Lawrence Hicke

Thomas Christian Johnson
Albert Langlois
Donald Robert Marshall
Alvin Brian McDonald
Richard Winston Moore
Kenneth Mosdell
Jacques Plante

Joseph Armand Andre Pronovost
Claude Provost
Henri Richard
Joseph Henri Maurice Richard
Jean-Guy Talbot
Robert George Turner

Stanley Cup: Montreal 4, Toronto 1 (Games)

April 9   Montreal 5   Toronto 3
April 11   Montreal 3   Toronto 1
April 14   Montreal 2   Toronto 3   (Duff scored 10:06 overtime)
April 16   Montreal 3   Toronto 2
April 18   Montreal 5   Toronto 3

Playoffs:

March 24   Montreal 4   Chicago 2
March 26   Montreal 5   Chicago 1
March 28   Montreal 2   Chicago 4
March 31   Montreal 1   Chicago 3
April 2   Montreal 4   Chicago 2
April 4   Montreal 5   Chicago 4

March 24   Toronto 1   Boston 5
March 26   Toronto 2   Boston 4
March 28   Toronto 3   Boston 2   (Ehman scored 5:02 overtime)
March 31   Toronto 3   Boston 2   (Mahovlich scored 11:21 overtime)
April 2   Toronto 4   Boston 1
April 4   Toronto 4   Boston 5
April 7   Toronto 3   Boston 2

Playoff Action

With Jean Beliveau and "The Rocket" Richard injured during the playoffs and missing most of the games, Marcel Bonin sparked the Canadiens with a 10 goal effort. Toronto had gained the fourth and last playoff spot by one point over the New York Rangers.

In the third game of the Chicago-Montreal series, Jean Beliveau received a fractured vertebrae when Glen Skov slammed him into the boards and he missed the rest of the playoffs. In the sixth game, with Pronovost in the penalty box, Claude Provost tied the score at 3–3 while helping to kill the penalty. Provost, also, scored the winning goal with only two minutes left when Phillipe Goyette passed the puck out to him from behind the Chicago net.

In the first Toronto-Boston game, early in the second period, Leo Boivin of Boston hit Olmstead with a terrific body-check. He continued playing the second period but didn't appear in the third.

In the fourth game, near the nine-minute mark in overtime, Jean-Guy Gendron drew a major penalty for cross-checking Gerald Ehman. On the power play, Olmstead dug the puck out of a corner and passed to Mahovlich who scored.

In the sixth game, Boston scored two goals early in the first period only to have Toronto tie it up midway in the second period. On a pass from Bronco Horvath, John Bucyk scored his first goal of the series only to have Mahovlich tie it for Toronto 3–3. Again Bucyk took a pass from Horvath and scored for Boston and again Mahovlich tied it up.

Eventually, with only a few minutes left, Horvath scored the winning goal.

In the seventh game, during the second minute of the second period, Harry Lumley, Boston's goaltender, took a drive from Richard Duff's stick flush in the mouth. He lost two teeth and stopped another shot by George Armstrong before the whistle halted play. He skated off, took seven stitches and returned to thwart Robert Baun with a great save and stop two in a row by Gerald Ehman when Ehman regained his own rebound.

Toronto outplayed Boston in the second period but the Bruins scored two goals; one a brilliant solo effort by Boivin. In the third period, John Bower made a couple of great saves to hold Boston scoreless while Toronto scored three goals.

Ehman scored the winner assisted by Mahovlich.

Leaders

Goals: Jean Beliveau (Montreal) 45; Assists: Richard Moore (Montreal) 55; Points: Richard Moore 41–55–96; Penalty Minutes: Ted Lindsay (Chicago) 184.

Trophies

Byng: Alexander Delvecchio (Detroit); Calder: Ralph Backstrom (Montreal); Hart: Andrew Bathgate (New York); Norris: Thomas Johnson (Montreal); Ross: Richard Moore (Montreal); Vezina: Jacques Plante (Montreal); Prince of Wales: Montreal.

Coaches

George Imlach replaced Reay at Toronto.

Hall of Fame

Players: John Adams, Cyril Denneny, Cecil Thompson.

1959–60

League Standings

Clubs	Games	Won	Lost	Tied	Points	Goals for	Goals against
Montreal	70	40	18	12	92	255	178
Toronto	70	35	26	9	79	199	195
Chicago	70	28	29	13	69	191	180
Detroit	70	26	29	15	67	186	197
Boston	70	28	34	8	64	220	241
New York	70	17	38	15	49	187	247

1960 Montreal Canadiens

Ralph Backstrom
Jean Arthur Béliveau
Marcel Bonin
Bernard Andre
  Geoffrion
Phillipe Goyette
Douglas Norman
  Harvey
William Lawrence

Hicke
Thomas Christian
  Johnson
Albert Langlois
Donald Robert
  Marshall
Richard Winston
  Moore
Jacques Plante

Joseph Armand Andre
  Pronovost
Claude Provost
Henri Richard
Joseph Henri Maurice
  Richard
Jean-Guy Talbot
Robert George Turner

Stanley Cup: Montreal 4, Toronto 0 (Games)

April	7	Montreal	4	Toronto	2
April	9	Montreal	2	Toronto	1
April	12	Montreal	5	Toronto	2
April	14	Montreal	4	Toronto	0

Playoffs:

March 24   Montreal   4   Chicago   3
March 26   Montreal   4   Chicago   3   (Harvey scored 8:38 overtime)
March 29   Montreal   4   Chicago   0
March 31   Montreal   2   Chicago   0

March 23   Toronto   1   Detroit   2
March 26   Toronto   4   Detroit   2
March 27   Toronto   5   Detroit   4   (Mahovlich scored 43:00 overtime)
March 29   Toronto   1   Detroit   2   (Melnyk scored 1:54 overtime)
April   2   Toronto   5   Detroit   4
April   3   Toronto   4   Detroit   2

Playoff Action

In the second Chicago-Montreal game, with Montreal leading 3–2, and just a little over a minute left to play in the third period, Harvey attempted to pass out from his own zone. William Hay of Chicago intercepted the puck and scored at 18:58 to send the game into overtime.

Harvey redeemed himself when he broke in on the Chicago goal with Moore and Henri Richard. He took Richard's pass and drilled a low drive past Glenn Hall.

In the third game, with no score in the second period, Hector Blake, Montreal Coach, began using Backstrom, Hicke and Marshall on a forward line. They accounted for three of the Canadiens' four goals. Hicke and Marshall each scored and Backstrom and Marshall assisted on one by Talbot. Geoffrion scored the other.

In the second Toronto-Detroit game, Gordon Howe had John Bower, Toronto goaltender, beaten in the second period only to hit the goal

post. Robert Pulford scored Toronto's fourth goal in the last minute, after Terrance Sawchuk had been removed from the Detroit goal, when he shot from his own side of center ice.

In the third game, Toronto scored three quick goals in the second period but the Red Wings fought back to tie the score. The Maple Leafs scored their fourth goal only to have Detroit score again and send the game into overtime. In the second overtime, Bower made a spectacular stop on Gordon Howe. In the third overtime, "Red" Kelly's shot hit Peter Goegan of Detroit. He shot again and Mahovlich tipped it in.

In the sixth game Richard Duff gave Toronto a two-goal lead with about three minutes left in the third period when he scored their fourth goal.

In the first Montreal-Toronto game, Plante was brilliant in the Canadien nets, especially in stopping "Red" Kelly and Robert Pulford.

In the second game, Richard Moore scored Montreal's first goal when he deflected Henri Richard's shot from a difficult angle. John Bower made a sensational save on Henri Richard in the third period.

In the third game, "The Rocket" Richard scored the last goal of his fabulous career. Moore carried the puck out of the Montreal zone and passed ahead to Henri Richard. Henri and his brother sped over the Toronto blue line and at 11:07 in the third period "The Rocket" took Henri's pass and beat John Bower. It was his only goal of the playoffs and he immediately went into the net for the puck.

In the fourth game, Beliveau scored the first, and what turned out to be the winning goal, at 8:16 of the first period.

Plante was outstanding in this series as were Harvey and Johnson on defense. Marshall and Provost excelled as penalty killers. By taking the playoffs in eight straight games, the Canadiens duplicated the performance of the Detroit Red Wings in 1952.

Leaders

Goals: Bronco Horvath (Boston), Robert Hull (Chicago) 39 (tie); Assists: Donald McKenney (Boston) 49; Points: Robert Hull 39–42–81; Penalty Minutes: Carl Brewer (Toronto) 150.

Trophies

Byng: Donald McKenney (Boston); Calder: William Hay (Chicago); Hart: Gordon Howe (Detroit); Norris: Douglas Harvey (Montreal); Ross: Robert Hull (Chicago); Vezina: Jacques Plante (Montreal); Prince of Wales: Montreal.

Coaches

Alfred Pike replaced Watson at New York.

Hall of Fame

Players: George Boucher, Sylvio Mantha, John Walker.
Builders: Charles Adams, Gen. John Kilpatrick, Frank Selke.

1960–61

League Standings

Clubs	Games	Won	Lost	Tied	Points	Goals for	Goals against
Montreal	70	41	19	10	92	254	188
Toronto	70	39	19	12	90	234	176
Chicago	70	29	24	17	75	198	180
Detroit	70	25	29	16	66	195	215
New York	70	22	38	10	54	204	248
Boston	70	15	42	13	43	176	254

1961 Chicago Black Hawks

Alger Arbour
Earl Frederick Balfour
Murray Lewis Balfour
William John Evans
Reginald Stephen
  Fleming
Glenn Henry Hall
William Charles Hay
Wayne Wilson Hicks

Wayne James Hillman
Robert Marvin Hull
Edward C. J.
  Litzenberger
Ronald Patrick Maki
Alvin Brian McDonald
Stanley Mikita
Robert Ronald Murphy
Eric Paul Nesterenko

Pierre Paul Pilote
Dollard Herve
  St. Laurent
Aloysius Martin Sloan
Elmer Vasko
Kenneth Malcolm
  Wharram

Stanley Cup: Chicago 4, Detroit 2 (Games)

April	6	Chicago	3	Detroit	2
April	8	Chicago	1	Detroit	3
April	10	Chicago	3	Detroit	1
April	12	Chicago	1	Detroit	2
April	14	Chicago	6	Detroit	3
April	16	Chicago	5	Detroit	1

Playoffs:

March 21 Chicago 2 Montreal 6
March 23 Chicago 4 Montreal 3
March 26 Chicago 2 Montreal 1 (Balfour scored 52:12 overtime)
March 28 Chicago 2 Montreal 5
April 1 Chicago 3 Montreal 0
April 4 Chicago 3 Montreal 0

March 22 Detroit 2 Toronto 3 (Armstrong scored 24:51 overtime)
March 25 Detroit 4 Toronto 2
March 26 Detroit 2 Toronto 0
March 28 Detroit 4 Toronto 1
April 1 Detroit 3 Toronto 2

Playoff Action

In the first Chicago-Montreal game, William Hicke was rushed to a hospital with a concussion when his head hit the ice after a hard body-check by St. Laurent.

In the second game, Litzenberger scored the winning goal with about three minutes left in the game.

In the third game, Murray Balfour scored for Chicago in the second period. With Hall stopping everything shot at him, Hector Blake, Canadiens' coach, began altering his lines. The score was still 1–0 with about 45-seconds left in the third period when Blake pulled Jacques Plante. With a faceoff in the Chicago end, Phillipe Goyette won the draw. He passed to Henri Richard and at 19:24 Richard tied the score.

In the second overtime, a Montreal player scored but referee Dalton McArthur ruled "no goal" because his stick was above his shoulder. Early in the third overtime, the Canadiens were stopped by Hall on several good chances. At 11:44, Richard Moore drew a tripping penalty and 28 seconds later, from a pile-up in front of the Montreal net, Murray Balfour scored the winner. Immediately Blake rushed across the ice and swung a solid right at referee McArthur. Clarence S. Campbell, league president, after reviewing the events fined Blake $2,000—the highest fine ever assessed.

In the fifth game, Glenn Hall was outstanding as McDonald, Mikita, and Vasko scored for Chicago.

In the sixth game, Hall turned in another brilliant performance and the Chicago scorers were Hay, Hull, and Nesterenko. Hall had been superb throughout the series, making over 200 stops. The Canadiens had finished the regular season 17 points ahead of Chicago and had been in every final series since 1951.

In the fourth Detroit-Toronto game, Detroit's first goal came when David Keon accidentally deflected the puck past John Bower. Their second goal came when Carl Brewer passed right onto Victor Stasiuk's stick, who in turn passed it to Gordon Howe. Their third goal was scored when Bower came out of his net to check Marcel Pronovost who was skating in on him. He upended Pronovost but missed the puck, which slid slowly over the goal line. Their fourth goal was scored into an empty net after Bower had been removed.

Terrance Sawchuk, Detroit goaltender, was outstanding in this series. Toronto was leading the league as the schedule drew to a close but after "Red" Kelly was injured they slipped two points back of Montreal. Kelly played in only two games of this series.

Terrance Sawchuk was injured in the Detroit-Chicago series and Henry Bassen replaced him for three and two-thirds games. Marcel Pronovost, whose ankle was broken by teammate Norman Ullman's shot in practice, played four games on it while it was frozen with pain-killer.

In the sixth game, with a Chicago player in the penalty box and Detroit using their power-play, Reginald Fleming gained control of the puck

in the Detroit end and bulled his way in on Bassen to score and tie the game at 1–1. Near the middle of the second period, Glenn Hall made fine saves on Leo LaBine and Howard Young.

Chicago scored with about a minute left in the second period and added three more in the third.

Leaders

Goals: Bernard Geoffrion (Montreal) 50; Assists: Jean Beliveau (Montreal) 58; Points: Bernard Geoffrion 50–45–95; Penalty Minutes: Pierre Pilote (Chicago) 165.

Trophies

Byng: Leonard Kelly (Toronto); Calder: David Keon (Toronto); Hart: Bernard Geoffrion (Montreal); Norris: Douglas Harvey (Montreal); Ross: Bernard Geoffrion; Vezina: John Bower (Toronto); Prince of Wales: Montreal.

Hall of Fame

Players: Charles Apps, Charles Conacher, Clarence Day, George Hainsworth, Joseph Hall, Percy LeSueur, Frank Rankin, Joseph Richard, Milton Schmidt, Oliver Seibert, Bruce Stuart.
Builders: George Brown, Paul Loicq, Fred Waghorne.
Referees: Chaucer Elliott, Frederick Ion, J. Cooper Smeaton.

Notes

Arrangements completed with Canadian National Exhibition and City of Toronto for construction of Hockey Hall of Fame at CNE.

1961–62

League Standings

Clubs	Games	Won	Lost	Tied	Points	Goals for	Goals against
Montreal	70	42	14	14	98	259	166
Toronto	70	37	22	11	85	232	180
Chicago	70	31	26	13	75	217	186
New York	70	26	32	12	64	195	207
Detroit	70	23	33	14	60	184	219
Boston	70	15	47	8	38	177	306

1962 Toronto Maple Leafs

Alger Arbour
George Edward
  Armstrong
Robert Neil Baun
John William Bower
Carl Thomas Brewer
Terrance Richard Duff
William Harris
Myles Gilbert Horton

Leonard Patrick Kelly
David Michael Keon
Edward C. J.
  Litzenberger
John Stewart
  MacMillan
Francis William
  Mahovlich
Robert Frank Nevin

Murray Bert Olmstead
Robert Pulford
Edward Steven Phillip
  Shack
Donald Simmons
Allan Herbert Stanley
Ronald George
  Stewart

Stanley Cup: Toronto 4, Chicago 2 (Games)

April 10	Toronto	4	Chicago	1
April 12	Toronto	3	Chicago	2
April 15	Toronto	0	Chicago	3
April 17	Toronto	1	Chicago	4
April 19	Toronto	8	Chicago	4
April 22	Toronto	2	Chicago	1

Playoffs:

March 27	Chicago	1	Montreal	2	
March 29	Chicago	3	Montreal	4	
April 1	Chicago	4	Montreal	1	
April 3	Chicago	5	Montreal	3	
April 5	Chicago	4	Montreal	3	
April 8	Chicago	2	Montreal	0	
March 27	Toronto	4	New York	2	
March 29	Toronto	2	New York	1	
April 1	Toronto	4	New York	5	
April 3	Toronto	2	New York	4	
April 5	Toronto	3	New York	2	(Kelly scored 24:23 overtime)
April 7	Toronto	7	New York	1	

Playoff Action

In the third Chicago-Montreal game, Stanley Mikita teased Louis Fontinato into charging penalties twice during the first period. Each time Chicago's power-play scored to send them off to a 2–0 lead.

Henri Richard of the Canadiens missed this series due to an injured arm. Ralph Backstrom missed one game, from a shoulder separation, for the Canadiens.

Mikita had 10 assists in this series.

In the first Toronto-New York game, with the Maple Leafs leading 2–1 in the second period and killing a penalty, "Tim" Horton scored what turned out to be the winning goal on passes from Nevin and Pulford. With

Lorne Worsley removed from the Ranger net, Horton also set up George Armstrong for Toronto's final goal.

In the third game, John Wilson scored for the Rangers at 19:50 in the second period to give New York a 2–1 lead.

In the fourth game, Rodrigue Gilbert stole a Toronto pass and scored on John Bower 41 seconds after the opening faceoff. He scored again 15 minutes later.

In the fifth game, during the second overtime, Toronto controlled the play and New York didn't even get a shot on goal. Toronto's fourth shot on goal in the second overtime was a vicious blast by Frank Mahovlich. With an acrobatic effort, Lorne Worsley stopped the shot and the puck lay under his shoulder as he fell on his back. When referee Edward Powers, Jr. didn't whistle the play dead, Worsley, in trying to find where the puck was, rose up. At that instant "Red" Kelly, who had assisted on Toronto's two other goals, lifted it over him into the net.

During the game Worsley made 56 saves to 39 for Bower.

In the third Chicago-Toronto game, Chicago resorted to some heavy body-checking and won 3–0.

In the fourth game, John Bower injured his thigh doing the splits while stopping a drive by Robert Hull in the eighth minute of the first period. Three minutes later Hull deflected Stanley Mikita's shot by him. Four minutes later, at 14:40, with Chicago leading 1–0, he left the game. Donald Simmons replaced him for the rest of the game and series.

In the fifth game, Pulford scored at the 17-second mark in the first period. He scored again and then Murray Balfour with one and Alvin McDonald with two put Chicago in front 3–2. In the second period, Mahovlich in the Chicago end sent the puck back to Horton. Horton drove a shot at the Chicago goal that glanced off Mahovlich's knee and William Harris deflected it in. Slightly over a minute later another drive by Horton was stopped by Glenn Hall but Keon and Mahovlich kept banging at the loose puck with Keon putting it in.

The fifth and winning goal was scored by Mahovlich when he beat Hall to the puck after Hall had stopped a shot by "Red" Kelly that fell in the crease. Pulford scored three goals in this game.

In the sixth game, Robert Hull scored for Chicago midway in the third period. Nevin tied the score assisted by Mahovlich. Near the 14-minute mark, Eric Nesterenko drew a holding penalty and Toronto sent out their power-play.

About 45 seconds later, Keon won a faceoff and shot the puck back to Horton near the blue line. He passed to Armstrong who immediately sent it back to him. Horton then saw Duff uncovered about 20 feet out from the goal and passed to him. The pass was behind Duff but he swung around and drove the puck in the net.

Leaders

Goals: Robert Hull (Chicago) 50; Assists: Andrew Bathgate (New York) 56; Points: Andrew Bathgate 28-56-84, Robert Hull 50-34-84 (tie); Penalty Minutes: Louis Fontinato (Montreal) 167.

Trophies

Byng: David Keon (Toronto); Calder: Robert Rousseau (Montreal); Hart: Jacques Plante (Montreal); Norris: Douglas Harvey (New York); Ross: Robert Hull (Chicago); Vezina: Jacques Plante; Prince of Wales: Montreal.

Coaches

Philip Watson replaced Schmidt at Boston; Douglas Harvey replaced Pike at New York.

Hall of Fame

Players: Harry Broadbent, Harold Cameron, Samuel Crawford, John Darragh, James Gardiner, Hamilton Gilmour, Wilfred Green, William Hern, Charles Hooper, John Hutton, Harry Hyland, Jean Laviolette, Fred Maxwell, William McGimsie, Edward Noble, Didier Pitre, J. D. Ruttan, David Schriner, Harold Simpson, Alfred Smith, Russell Stanley, Nelson Stewart, Martin Walsh, Harry Watson, Harry Westwick, Fred Whitcroft, Gordon Wilson.
Builders: Thomas Ahearn, Walter Brown, Fred Hume, James Norris, John O'Brien, Frank Smith.
Referees: Michael Rodden.

Notes

Hockey Hall of Fame officially opened on August 26, by Prime Minister John F. Diefenbaker and U.S. Ambassador Livingston T. Merchant.
Clubs allowed to dress 16 players exclusive of goalkeeper for a game.

1962–63

League Standings

Clubs	Games	Won	Lost	Tied	Points	Goals for	Goals against
Toronto	70	35	23	12	82	221	180
Chicago	70	32	21	17	81	194	178
Montreal	70	28	19	23	79	225	183
Detroit	70	32	25	13	77	200	194
New York	70	22	36	12	56	211	233
Boston	70	14	39	17	45	198	281

1963 Toronto Maple Leafs

George Edward Armstrong
Robert Neil Baun
John William Bower
Carl Thomas Brewer
Kent Gemmell Douglas
Terrance Richard Duff
William Harris
Myles Gilbert Horton
Leonard Patrick Kelly
David Michael Keon
Edward C. J. Litzenberger
John Stewart MacMillan
Francis William Mahovlich
Robert Frank Nevin
Robert Pulford
Edward Steven Phillip Shack
Allan Herbert Stanley
Ronald George Stewart

Stanley Cup: Toronto 4, Detroit 1 (Games)

April	9	Toronto	4	Detroit	2
April	11	Toronto	4	Detroit	2
April	14	Toronto	2	Detroit	3
April	16	Toronto	4	Detroit	2
April	18	Toronto	3	Detroit	1

Playoffs:

March	26	Toronto	3	Montreal	1
March	28	Toronto	3	Montreal	2
March	30	Toronto	2	Montreal	0
April	2	Toronto	1	Montreal	3
April	4	Toronto	5	Montreal	0

March	26	Detroit	4	Chicago	5
March	28	Detroit	2	Chicago	5
March	31	Detroit	4	Chicago	2
April	2	Detroit	4	Chicago	1
April	4	Detroit	4	Chicago	2
April	7	Detroit	7	Chicago	4

Playoff Action

In the second Chicago-Detroit game, Bruce MacGregor of Detroit, in swinging around, caught Robert Hull flush on the nose with his stick. The blow broke the orbalrim bones under his eyes and he missed the third game. He returned for the last three games, although he could barely see out of one eye, and scored five goals.

In the sixth game, he scored three goals and assisted on the other. He had scored three goals in the first two games for a total of eight in the series.

Chicago had led the league for most of the regular schedule.

In the first Detroit-Toronto game, Duff scored twice within 19 seconds in the first period; at 0:49 and 1:08.

In the second game, Mahovlich was hurt and Litzenberger starred as his replacement.

In the fifth game, Keon scored Toronto's first goal while they were playing a man short. Shack scored the Maple Leafs' second goal—which turned out to be the winner—and at the end of the second period Toronto led 2–1. In the third period, when Sidney Abel, Detroit general-manager and coach, changed lines, Gordon Howe ignored him on several occasions and remained on the ice. Late in the period Howe and Norman Ullman worked the puck into Toronto's end. Howe in attempting to jam the puck by Bower became entangled with him and they fell to the ice. Ullman, fighting with the Toronto players for the loose puck, managed to get a shot off at the open net only to have it hit Howe's leg. Keon scored the other Maple Leaf goal.

The Toronto players had so admired Howe's durable performance that they invited him to their dressing room to drink from the Stanley Cup.

Brewer, who had played a major role in the Toronto victory, broke his arm late in the last game.

Only five points at the close of the regular schedule separated the four clubs that entered the playoffs.

Leaders

Goals: Gordon Howe (Detroit) 38; Assists: Henri Richard (Montreal) 50; Points: Gordon Howe 38-48-86; Penalty Minutes: Howard Young (Detroit) 273.

Trophies

Byng: David Keon (Toronto); Calder: Kent Douglas (Toronto); Hart: Gordon Howe (Detroit); Norris: Pierre Pilote (Chicago); Ross: Gordon Howe; Vezina: Glenn Hall (Chicago); Prince of Wales: Toronto.

Coaches

Milton Schmidt replaced Watson at Boston; Murray Patrick temporarily replaced Harvey at New York, until George Sullivan was signed in December.

Hall of Fame

Players: Ebenezer Goodfellow, A. Joseph Primeau, Earl Seibert. Builders: Joseph Dandurand, Thomas Gorman, Maj. Frederic McLaughlin. Referees: Robert Hewitson.

1963–64

League Standings

Clubs	Games	Won	Lost	Tied	Points	Goals for	Goals against
Montreal	70	36	21	13	85	209	167
Chicago	70	36	22	12	84	218	169
Toronto	70	33	25	12	78	192	172
Detroit	70	30	29	11	71	191	204
New York	70	22	38	10	54	186	242
Boston	70	18	40	12	48	170	212

1964 Toronto Maple Leafs

Alger Arbour
George Edward Armstrong
Andrew James Bathgate
Robert Neil Baun
John William Bower
Carl Thomas Brewer
Gerald Joseph Ehman

William Harris
Larry Morley Hillman
Myles Gilbert Horton
Leonard Patrick Kelly
David Michael Keon
Edward C. J. Litzenberger
Francis William Mahovlich

Donald Hamilton McKenney
James Joseph Pappin
Robert Pulford
Edward Steven Phillip Shack
Allan Herbert Stanley
Ronald George Stewart

Stanley Cup: Toronto 4, Detroit 3 (Games)

April 11	Toronto	3	Detroit	2	
April 14	Toronto	3	Detroit	4	(Jeffrey scored 7:52 overtime)
April 16	Toronto	3	Detroit	4	
April 18	Toronto	4	Detroit	2	
April 21	Toronto	1	Detroit	2	
April 23	Toronto	4	Detroit	3	(Baun scored 1:43 overtime)
April 25	Toronto	4	Detroit	0	

Playoffs:

March 26	Detroit	1	Chicago	4	
March 29	Detroit	5	Chicago	4	
March 31	Detroit	3	Chicago	0	
April 2	Detroit	2	Chicago	3	(Balfour scored 8:21 overtime)
April 5	Detroit	2	Chicago	3	
April 7	Detroit	7	Chicago	2	
April 9	Detroit	4	Chicago	2	

March 26	Toronto	0	Montreal	2
March 28	Toronto	2	Montreal	1
March 31	Toronto	2	Montreal	3
April 2	Toronto	5	Montreal	3
April 4	Toronto	2	Montreal	4
April 7	Toronto	3	Montreal	0
April 9	Toronto	3	Montreal	1

Playoff Action

In the first Montreal-Toronto game, Charles Hodge shut out Toronto as Ralph Backstrom and Bernard Geoffrion scored for Montreal.

In the second game, Frank Mahovlich scored a goal and assisted on the other in a 2–1 win for the Maple Leafs.

In the third game, with Toronto leading 2–1 late in the third period, Henri Richard and Jean-Claude Tremblay scored two quick goals for Montreal.

In the fourth game, Frank Mahovlich scored two and assisted on three of Toronto's five goals.

In the seventh game, Keon scored all three goals for Toronto. He scored at 8:22 of the first period and three minutes later scored again. Ralph Backstrom scored Montreal's goal near the eight-minute mark of the third period. After Hodge was removed from the goal, Keon scored in the empty net at 19:49. Jean Beliveau, with an injured knee, played in only five games.

In the second Chicago-Detroit game, Norman Ullman of Detroit scored three goals. In the sixth game he again scored three goals—two against Glenn Hall and one against Denis DeJordy, who replaced Hall at the start of the third period.

In the first Toronto-Detroit game, Robert Pulford broke from his own blue line and scored Toronto's winning goal at 19:58 of the third period.

In the second game, in overtime, Howe carried the puck behind the Toronto goal and passed crisply to Jeffrey, who scored the winning goal for the Red Wings.

In the fourth game, midway in the third period with the score 2–2, Kelly passed to Mahovlich in the Toronto end. Mahovlich passed to Bathgate along the boards who carried it over the Detroit blue line where he faked a pass to Kelly and scored from about 45 feet out.

In the sixth game, Howe had scored a goal and assisted on another, and Hubert Martin had scored Detroit's third goal, when Bathgate tied the score for Toronto in the third period.

From a faceoff with six minutes left, Howe drove a booming shot that hit Baun on the ankle. He was carried from the ice and given a pain killer and was able to return in the overtime.

Detroit started the overtime with a rush and Edward Joyal's shot hit the goalpost. Toronto carried the puck back in the Detroit end and Pulford passed to Baun. He took a shot from the blue line that went through a group of players, hit William Gadsby's stick, and was deflected by Terrance Sawchuk for the winning goal. X-rays later revealed a hair-line fracture in Baun's ankle.

Although the Maple Leafs were injury plagued, they won the seventh game 4–0. Baun was skating on a right ankle that would later show a fracture, Armstrong had a painful shoulder injury, Brewer was suffering with a rib separation that had already caused him to miss two games, and Kelly had strained ligaments in his left knee. McKenney had been knocked out of the series altogether with torn ligaments in his knee.

Bathgate scored for Toronto after picking up a loose puck, and at the end of two periods Toronto led 1–0. Keon scored early in the third period and soon after Mahovlich recovered his own rebound that had missed the net. He passed back to Armstrong who scored. A few minutes later Mahovlich carried the puck down the side and faked a shot at Sawchuk. Instead he passed to Kelly who scored Toronto's fourth goal.

Leaders

Goals: Robert Hull (Chicago) 43; Assists: Andrew Bathgate (New York-Toronto) 58; Points: Stanley Mikita (Chicago) 39-50-89; Penalty Minutes: Victor Hadfield (New York) 151.

Trophies

Byng: Kenneth Wharram (Chicago); Calder: Jacques Laperriére (Montreal); Hart: Jean Béliveau (Montreal); Norris: Pierre Pilote (Chicago); Ross: Stanley Mikita (Chicago); Vezina: Charles Hodge (Montreal); Prince of Wales: Montreal.

Coaches

William Reay replaced Pilous at Chicago.

Hall of Fame

Players: Douglas Bentley, William Durnan, Albert Siebert, John Stewart.
Builders: Angus Campbell, Francis Dilio.
Referees: William Chadwick.

1964–65

League Standings

Clubs	Games	Won	Lost	Tied	Points	Goals for	Goals against
Detroit	70	40	23	7	87	224	175
Montreal	70	36	23	11	83	211	185
Ch'cago	70	34	28	8	76	224	176
Toronto	70	30	26	14	74	204	173
New York	70	20	38	12	52	179	246
Boston	70	21	43	6	48	166	253

1965 Montreal Canadiens

Ralph Backstrom
David Alexander Balon
Jean Arthur Béliveau
Gordon Berenson
Yvan Cournoyer
Terrance Richard Duff
John Bowie Ferguson
Jean Phillipe Gauthier
Terrance Victor

Harper
Edward Alexander
Harris
Charles Edward
Hodge
Jacques Laperriére
Claude David Larose
Jean Noël Picard
Claude Provost

Henri Richard
James Wilfred Roberts
Joseph Jean-Paul
Robert Rousseau
Jean-Guy Talbot
Jean-Claude Tremblay
Lorne Worsley

Stanley Cup: Montreal 4, Chicago 3 (Games)

April 17	Montreal	3	Chicago	2
April 20	Montreal	2	Chicago	0
April 22	Montreal	1	Chicago	3
April 25	Montreal	1	Chicago	5
April 27	Montreal	6	Chicago	0
April 29	Montreal	1	Chicago	2
May 1	Montreal	4	Chicago	0

Playoffs:

April 1	Chicago	3	Detroit	4
April 4	Chicago	3	Detroit	6
April 6	Chicago	5	Detroit	2
April 8	Chicago	2	Detroit	1
April 11	Chicago	2	Detroit	4
April 13	Chicago	4	Detroit	0
April 15	Chicago	4	Detroit	2

April 1 Montreal 3 Toronto 2
April 3 Montreal 3 Toronto 1
April 6 Montreal 2 Toronto 3 (Keon scored 4:17 overtime)
April 8 Montreal 2 Toronto 4
April 10 Montreal 3 Toronto 1
April 13 Montreal 4 Toronto 3 (Provost scored 16:33 overtime)

Playoff Action

In the first Montreal-Toronto game, Rousseau broke a 1–1 tie in the third period when he drove a 55-foot slap shot past John Bower.

In the second game, he stopped Kelly, Keon, and Pulford with outstanding defensive efforts. He deflected Keon's shot by diving full length in front of the net.

In the third game, Keon beat Worsley unassisted in the overtime. Frank Mahovlich, Toronto's leading scorer during the regular season, failed to score in this series.

Gilles Tremblay was out of the entire playoffs for Montreal with a broken leg and Laperrière broke his in the last game of this series.

In the first Montreal-Chicago game, Cournoyer scored the winning goal in the third period assisted by Beliveau. Provost was used to check Hull, and in the first game Hull only had one shot on goal.

In the second game, Hull had four shots on goal.

In the fourth game, Hull scored two goals in the third period but Provost had just put in a shift on the power play and was not on the ice. Hull's first goal was a blast from the red line that got by Hodge. His second came when he took the puck in his own end and skated up and around Jean-Claude Tremblay to score.

In the seventh game, all the goals were scored in the first period with Beliveau scoring 14 seconds after the game got under way. Beliveau had gone to the bench after taking a hard body-check. Duff scored on Hall with a shot around the knees.

Worsley had hurt his thigh in the third game and Hodge had played the fourth, fifth and sixth games. Hector Blake, Canadiens coach, used Worsley in this game because he had not allowed Hull to score on him during the regular schedule and so far in this series. Henri Richard scored Montreal's third goal, and near the 17-minute mark Cournoyer took a pass from Rousseau during a power play and scored on a breakaway.

Stanley Mikita of Chicago failed to score in this series. Beliveau scored four game winning goals in the playoffs, three of them came in this series.

Worsley shut out Chicago in the second and seventh game, and the Canadiens power-play worked for 21 goals in their 13 games.

In the fifth game of the Chicago-Detroit series, Norman Ullman scored two goals in five seconds, scoring on Glenn Hall at 17:35 and 17:40 in the second period. He scored three goals during the game.

In the seventh game, late in the second period with Detroit leading 2–1, Stanley Mikita passed to Douglas Mohns who went around a de-

fenseman and scored on Roger Crozier to tie the score. Half way through the third period, Mohns passed to Mikita who scored the winning goal.

Robert Hull of Chicago had eight goals and five assists in this series.

Leaders

Goals: Norman Ullman (Detroit) 42; Assists: Stanley Mikita (Chicago) 59; Points: Stanley Mikita 28–59–87; Penalty Minutes: Carl Brewer (Toronto) 177.

Trophies

Byng: Robert Hull (Chicago); Calder: Roger Crozier (Detroit); Hart: Robert Hull; Norris: Pierre Pilote (Chicago); Ross: Stanley Mikita (Chicago); Smythe: Jean Beliveau (Montreal); Vezina: John Bower (Toronto), Terrance Sawchuk (Toronto); Prince of Wales: Detroit.

Hall of Fame

Players: Martin Barry, Clinton Benedict, Arthur Farrell, George Horner, Sydney Howe, John Marshall, William Mosienko, Blair Russell, Ernest Russell, Fred Scanlan.

Builders: Foster Hewitt, Thomas Lockhart.

Notes

Rules modified to provide no bodily contact on faceoffs.

1965–66

League Standings

Clubs	Games	Won	Lost	Tied	Points	Goals for	Goals against
Montreal	70	41	21	8	90	239	173
Chicago	70	37	25	8	82	240	187
Toronto	70	34	25	11	79	208	187
Detroit	70	31	27	12	74	221	194
Boston	70	21	43	6	48	174	275
New York	70	18	41	11	47	195	261

1966 Montreal Canadiens

Ralph Backstrom
David Alexander Balon
Jean Arthur Béliveau
Yvan Cournoyer
Terrance Richard Duff
John Bowie Ferguson
Terrance Victor
  Harper

Edward Alexander
  Harris
Claude David Larose
Garry Noel Price
Claude Provost
Henri Richard
James Wilfred Roberts
Léon Rochefort

Joseph Jean-Paul
  Robert Rousseau
Jean-Guy Talbot
Gilles Tremblay
Jean-Claude Tremblay
Lorne Worsley

Stanley Cup: Montreal 4, Detroit 2 (Games)

April 24	Montreal	2	Detroit	3
April 26	Montreal	2	Detroit	5
April 28	Montreal	4	Detroit	2
May 1	Montreal	2	Detroit	1
May 3	Montreal	5	Detroit	1
May 5	Montreal	3	Detroit	2 (Richard scored 2:20 overtime)

Playoffs:

April 7	Montreal	4	Toronto	3
April 9	Montreal	2	Toronto	0
April 12	Montreal	5	Toronto	2
April 14	Montreal	4	Toronto	1
April 7	Detroit	1	Chicago	2
April 10	Detroit	7	Chicago	0
April 12	Detroit	1	Chicago	2
April 14	Detroit	5	Chicago	1
April 17	Detroit	5	Chicago	3
April 19	Detroit	3	Chicago	2

Playoff Action

In the second Detroit-Montreal game, Bryan Watson coaxed John Ferguson into an elbowing penalty and the Red Wings tied the score at 1–1.

In the third game, with less than a minute left in the first period, Beliveau stole the puck from Alexander Delvecchio. He skated in alone, and as Roger Crozier came out of his goal, Beliveau scored to put the Canadiens out in front 2–1.

In the fourth game, Crozier had his knee sprained and his ankle twisted when his leg was jammed against the goal post at 5:48 in the first period; he was replaced by Henry Bassen. Norman Ullman scored for Detroit half way through the second period. With nine seconds left in the second period, Jean-Claude Tremblay shot from the blue-line and Beliveau tipped it in to tie the score. Backstrom took a pass from Roberts to score the winning goal at 13:37.

In the fifth game, the Canadiens scored four of their five goals in the first two periods. Larose had been replaced on the line with Balon and Richard by Leon Rochefort after the second game and in this game, Rochefort assisted on a goal by Balon.

In the sixth game after Beliveau scored early in the first period, the game turned into a brilliant duel between Crozier in the Detroit nets and Worsley of Montreal.

Gilles Tremblay, the left winger, had to guard Howe and held him to one goal during the series and it came while he was off the ice.

In the first Montreal-Toronto game, Allan Stanley of Toronto reinjured his knee during his first shift on the ice and was out the rest of the

series. With three weeks of the regular schedule remaining, he had torn a cartilage in his knee in a collision with Forbes Kennedy of Boston and hadn't played since.

In the first Chicago-Detroit game, Robert Hull scored a goal but for the rest of the series Sidney Abel, Detroit coach, had Bryan Watson checking him and he scored only one more goal and that while Watson was off the ice.

The line of Alexander Delvecchio, Gordon Howe and Dean Prentice was a major factor in Detroit's win. Paul Henderson scored two game winning goals for Detroit.

Leaders

Goals: Robert Hull (Chicago) 54; Assists: Jean Beliveau (Montreal), Stanley Mikita (Chicago), Robert Rousseau (Montreal) 48 (tie); Points: Robert Hull 54–43–97; Penalty Minutes: Reginald Fleming (Boston-New York) 166.

Trophies

Byng: Alexander Delvecchio (Detroit); Calder: Briton Selby (Toronto); Hart: Robert Hull (Chicago); Norris: Jacques Laperriere (Montreal); Ross: Robert Hull; Smythe: Roger Crozier (Detroit); Patrick: John Adams (Detroit); Vezina: Charles Hodge (Montreal), Lorne Worsley (Montreal); Prince of Wales: Montreal.

Coaches

Emile Francis replaced Sullivan at New York.

Hall of Fame

Players: Maxwell Bentley, Hector Blake, Emile Bouchard, Francis Brimsek, Theodore Kennedy, Elmer Lach, Robert Lindsay, Walter Pratt, Kenneth Reardon.
Builders: Clarence Sutherland Campbell.

1966–67

League Standings

Clubs	Games	Won	Lost	Tied	Points	Goals for	Goals against
Chicago	70	41	17	12	94	264	170
Montreal	70	32	25	13	77	202	188
Toronto	70	32	27	11	75	204	211
New York	70	30	28	12	72	188	189
Detroit	70	27	39	4	58	212	241
Boston	70	17	43	10	44	182	253

1967 Toronto Maple Leafs

George Edward
   Armstrong
Robert Neil Baun
John William Bower
Brian Kennedy
   Conacher
Ronald John Edward
   Ellis
Autry Raymond
   Erickson
Larry Morley Hillman

Myles Gilbert Horton
Lawrence Joseph
   Jeffrey
Leonard Patrick Kelly
David Michael Keon
Francis William
   Mahovlich
Milan Marcetta
James Joseph Pappin
Joseph Réne Marcel
   Pronovost

Robert Pulford
Terrance Gordon
   Sawchuk
Edward Steven Phillip
   Shack
Allan Herbert Stanley
Peter David
   Stemkowski
Michael Robert Walton

Stanley Cup: Toronto 4, Montreal 2 (Games)

April 20	Toronto	2	Montreal	6	
April 22	Toronto	3	Montreal	0	
April 25	Toronto	3	Montreal	2	(Pulford scored 28:26 overtime)
April 27	Toronto	2	Montreal	6	
April 29	Toronto	4	Montreal	1	
May 2	Toronto	3	Montreal	1	

Playoffs:

April 6	Toronto	2	Chicago	5
April 8	Toronto	3	Chicago	1
April 11	Toronto	3	Chicago	1
April 13	Toronto	3	Chicago	4
April 15	Toronto	4	Chicago	2
April 18	Toronto	3	Chicago	1

April 6	Montreal	6	New York	4	
April 8	Montreal	3	New York	1	
April 11	Montreal	3	New York	2	
April 13	Montreal	2	New York	1	(Ferguson scored 6:28 overtime)

Playoff Action

John Bower's little finger was smashed stopping a shot by Mahovlich in practice and Sawchuk tended goal for Toronto in the first four games in the Chicago series. In the fourth game, Hall, Chicago, goaltender, was struck in the mouth on a drive by Pappin late in the third period; 25 stitches were required. Denis DeJordy finished the game in his place.

In the fifth game, Bower started but didn't appear sharp; so with the score tied 2–2 at the end of the first period, Toronto coach, George "Punch" Imlach, replaced him with Sawchuk. The first shot on Sawchuk was a blistering blast from 15 feet out by Robert Hull that struck him

on the shoulder and dropped him to the ice. He arose to stop 36 more shots and shut out Chicago's great scorers for the rest of the game. The Black Hawks had outshot Toronto, 49–31, in this game. In the sixth game Brian Conacher, son of the immortal "Big Train," replaced the injured George Armstrong and scored two goals.

Toronto's best line in this series was Pappin, Pulford, and Stemkowski with Pappin scoring three goals and four assists. Toronto's penalty killing, lead by Keon was outstanding in this department. His persistent forechecking throughout the series was also a contributing factor in the Maple Leaf victory.

When New York faced Montreal in their first game, New York led 4–1 with 11 minutes left to play only to have the Canadiens score 3 goals within 1 minute and 51 seconds and the winner less than two minutes later.

In the fourth game, although outshooting the Canadiens, 34–29, the Rangers were eliminated. Rogatien Vachon, rookie Montreal goaltender, was in goal in all four games.

Montreal then faced Toronto and in the first game Imlach replaced Sawchuk with Bower early in the third period as the Canadiens outskated the Maple Leafs.

In the second game, Bower was outstanding as he shut out the Canadiens 3–0. In the third game, Bower again excelled as both clubs, tied 2–2, went into overtime and attacked with little regard for defense. Bower stopped 60 shots in this game, three of them on Yvan Cournoyer on breakaways.

Finally at 8:26 of the second overtime, Pulford drove Pappin's pass by Vachon. It was the second longest overtime game ever played in Maple Leaf Gardens.

In the fourth game, Bower pulled a muscle in the warm-up and Sawchuk replaced him and appeared unsteady as the Canadiens tied the series.

In the 5th game, Lorne Worsley relieved Vachon for the 3rd period and Sawchuk came up with a brilliant performance as Montreal outshot Toronto, 38–29.

In the sixth game, Sawchuk again stood out as he blocked seventeen shots in the 1st period. Worsley was in goal for Montreal as the Canadiens outshot the Maple Leafs again 41–36. The Canadiens had outshot the Maple Leafs in five games of this six game series and had 206 shots to Toronto's 175. Pappin was the leading playoff scorer with seven goals and eight assists.

Beliveau, Henri Richard, and Vachon were outstanding for the Canadiens with Beliveau being the leading Canadien playoff scorer with six goals and five assists.

Leaders

Goals: Robert Hull (Chicago) 52; Assists: Stanley Mikita (Chicago) 62; Points: Stanley Mikita 35–62–97; Penalty Minutes: John Ferguson (Montreal) 177.

Trophies

Byng: Stanley Mikita (Chicago); Calder: Robert Orr (Boston); Hart: Stanley Mikita; Norris: Henry Howell (New York); Ross: Stanley Mikita; Smythe: David Keon (Toronto); Patrick: Gordon Howe (Detroit); Vezina: Denis DeJordy (Chicago), Glenn Hall (Chicago); Prince of Wales: Chicago.

Coaches

Harry Sinden replaced Schmidt at Boston.

Hall of Fame

Players: Walter Broda, Neil Colville, Harry Oliver.
Referees: Roy Storey.

Notes

Substitution allowed on coincidental major penalties.

1967–68

League President—Clarence Sutherland Campbell
Referee-in-Chief—Ian "Scotty" Morrison
Eastern Supervisor of Officials—Frank Udvari
Western Supervisor of Officials—William "Dutch" van Deelen

League Standings

The clubs played 10 games with the clubs in their own division and 4 games with each club in the other division.

East Division

Clubs	Games	Won	Lost	Tied	Points	Goals for	Goals against	Shut-outs	PiM
Mont. Canadiens	74	42	22	10	94	236	167	10	700
N.Y. Rangers	74	39	23	12	90	226	183	9	673
Boston Bruins	74	37	27	10	84	259	216	4	1043
Chi. Black Hawks	74	32	26	16	80	212	222	6	606
Tor. Maple Leafs	74	33	31	10	76	209	176	9	634
Det. Red Wings	74	27	35	12	66	245	257	1	759
						1387		39	4415

February 11, 1968—N.Y. Rangers played their final game in Madison Square Garden (Detroit 3 N.Y. Rangers 3).
February 18, 1968—N.Y. Rangers played their first game in Madison Square Garden Center (N.Y. Rangers 3 Philadelphia 1).

	General-Mgr.	Asst. General-Mgr.	Coach
Boston	Milton Schmidt	none	Harry Sinden
Chicago	Thomas N. Ivan	none	William T. Reay
Detroit	Sidney G. Abel	Aldege Bastien	Abel

Montreal   Samuel Pollock   none   Hector Blake
N.Y. Rangers   Emile P. Francis   John Gordon   Francis
Toronto   George F. Imlach   Francis M. Clancy Imlach

Note: Bastien coached Detroit in most of their games.
February 3, 1968—Clancy coached Toronto as they tied Pittsburgh 3-3 at Pittsburgh.

West Division

Clubs	Games	Won	Lost	Tied	Points	Goals for	Goals against	Shut-outs	PiM
Phila. Flyers	74	31	32	11	73	173	179	8	987
L.A. Kings	74	31	33	10	72	200	224	4	810
St.L. Blues	74	27	31	16	70	177	191	6	792
Minn. N. Stars	74	27	32	15	69	191	226	6	738
Pitt. Penguins	74	27	34	13	67	195	216	7	554
Calif. Seals*	74	15	42	17	47	153	219	5	787
						1089		36	4668

*Changed name to Oakland Seals on November 6, 1967.
Los Angeles played their first 17 home games in the Long Beach Arena at Long Beach, Calif. (6 games) and in the Los Angeles Sports Arena at Los Angeles (11 games). They played their first game in The Forum at Inglewood, Calif. on December 30, 1967 (Los Angeles 0 Philadelphia 2).
Philadelphia played their final 7 home games away due to wind damage to the roof of The Spectrum: March 3rd at New York (Oakland 1 Philadelphia 1), March 7th at Toronto (Boston 2 Philadelphia 1) and March 10th, 14th, 17th, 28th and 30th at Quebec City.

	General-Mgr.	Asst. General-Mgr.	Coach
California	M. Bert Olmstead	Gordon Fashoway	Olmstead
Los Angeles	Lawrence Regan	none	Leonard P. Kelly
Minnesota	Wren A. Blair	John Mariucci	Blair
Philadelphia	Norman R. Poile	none	C. Keith Allen
Pittsburgh	John T. Riley	none	George Sullivan
St. Louis	J. Lynn Patrick	W. Scott Bowman	J. Lynn Patrick

November 22, 1967—Bowman replaced Patrick as coach (St. Louis had won 4—lost 10—tied 2).
December 23, 1967—Fashoway coached Oakland as they lost to Montreal 4-2 at Montreal and in final 21 games of season (won 5—lost 10—tied 6).
January 24, 1968—Mariucci coached Minnesota as they lost to St. Louis 5-2 at St. Louis (Blair on scouting trip).

Player Transactions

October 19, 1967—Detroit traded Robert McCord to Minnesota for Jean-Guy Talbot
November 28, 1967—N.Y. Rangers traded Gordon Berenson to St. Louis for Ronald Attwell and Ronald Stewart
December 26, 1967—Minnesota traded George Harris to Toronto for Jean-Paul Parisé
January 9, 1968—Detroit traded John Brenneman, Edward Hampson and Albert Marshall to Oakland for Kent Douglas

January 12, 1968—Detroit waived Jean-Guy Talbot to St. Louis
February 27, 1968—Philadelphia traded Wayne Hicks to Pittsburgh
                   for Arthur Stratton
   March   4, 1968—Detroit traded Paul Henderson, Floyd Smith and
                   Norman Ullman to Toronto for Francis Mahovlich,
                   Peter Stemkowski and Garry Unger

1968 Stanley Cup

Montreal Canadiens

Ralph Gerald Backstrom
Jean Arthur Béliveau
Yvan Serge Cournoyer
Terrance Richard Duff
John Bowie Ferguson
Daniel Frederick Grant
Terrance Victor Harper
Edward Alexander Harris
Joseph Jacques Hugues Laperriére
Claude David Larose
Jacques Gerard Lemaire

Joseph Antoine Claude Provost
Michael Edward Redmond
Joseph Henri Richard
Joseph Jean-Paul Robert Rousseau
Serge A. Savard
Jean-Claude Tremblay
Joseph Jean-Gilles Tremblay
Rogatien Rosaire Vachon
Carol Marcel Vadnais
Lorne John Worsley

The first and third and second and fourth place clubs in each division met in a 4 out of 7 game series. The winners of these series then met in another 4 out of 7 game series. These division winners then met in a 4 out of 7 game series.

Montreal (first in East Division) vs. Boston (third in East Division)

April 4, 1968 at Montreal	Montreal 2	Boston 1
April 6, 1968 at Montreal	Montreal 5	Boston 3
April 9, 1968 at Boston	Montreal 5	Boston 2
April 11, 1968 at Boston	Montreal 3	Boston 2

N.Y. Rangers (second in East Division) vs. Chicago (fourth in East Division)

April 4, 1968 at New York	N.Y. Rangers 3	Chicago 1
April 9, 1968 at New York	N.Y. Rangers 2	Chicago 1
April 11, 1968 at Chicago	N.Y. Rangers 4	Chicago 7
April 13, 1968 at Chicago	N.Y. Rangers 1	Chicago 3
April 14, 1968 at New York	N.Y. Rangers 1	Chicago 2
April 16, 1968 at Chicago	N.Y. Rangers 1	Chicago 4

Montreal (eliminated Boston) vs. Chicago (eliminated N.Y. Rangers)

April 18, 1968 at Montreal	Montreal 9	Chicago 2
April 20, 1968 at Montreal	Montreal 4	Chicago 1
April 23, 1968 at Chicago	Montreal 4	Chicago 2
April 25, 1968 at Chicago	Montreal 1	Chicago 2
April 28, 1968 at Montreal	Montreal 4*	Chicago 3

*Jacques Lemaire scored at 2:14 in overtime

Philadelphia (first in West Division) vs. St. Louis (third in West Division)

April 4, 1968 at Philadelphia	Philadelphia 0	St. Louis 1
April 6, 1968 at Philadelphia	Philadelphia 4	St. Louis 3
April 10, 1968 at St. Louis	Philadelphia 2	St. Louis 3*

*Lawrence Keenan scored at 24:10 in overtime

April 11, 1968 at St. Louis	Philadelphia 2	St. Louis 5
April 13, 1968 at Philadelphia	Philadelphia 6	St. Louis 1
April 16, 1968 at St. Louis	Philadelphia 2*	St. Louis 1

*J. Donald Blackburn scored at 31:18 in overtime

April 18, 1968 at Philadelphia	Philadelphia 1	St. Louis 3

Los Angeles (second in West Division) vs. Minnesota (fourth in West Division)

April 4, 1968 at Inglewood, Calif.	Los Angeles 2	Minnesota 1
April 6, 1968 at Inglewood, Calif.	Los Angeles 2	Minnesota 0
April 9, 1968 at Bloomington, Minn.	Los Angeles 5	Minnesota 7
April 11, 1968 at Bloomington, Minn.	Los Angeles 2	Minnesota 3
April 13, 1968 at Inglewood, Calif.	Los Angeles 3	Minnesota 2
April 16, 1968 at Bloomington, Minn.	Los Angeles 3	Minnesota 4*

*Milan Marcetta scored at 9:11 in overtime

April 18, 1968 at Inglewood, Calif.	Los Angeles 4	Minnesota 9

St. Louis (eliminated Philadelphia) vs. Minnesota (eliminated Los Angeles)

April 21, 1968 at St. Louis	St. Louis 5	Minnesota 3
April 22, 1968 at Bloomington, Minn.	St. Louis 2	Minnesota 3*

*C. Parker MacDonald scored at 3:41 in overtime

April 25, 1968 at St. Louis	St. Louis 1	Minnesota 5
April 27, 1968 at St. Louis†	St. Louis 4*	Minnesota 3

*Gary Sabourin scored at 1:32 in overtime

April 29, 1968 at St. Louis	St. Louis 3*	Minnesota 2

*William McCreary scored at 17:27 in overtime

May 1, 1968 at Bloomington, Minn.	St. Louis 1	Minnesota 5
May 3, 1968 at St. Louis	St. Louis 2*	Minnesota 1

*Ronald Schock scored at 22:50 in overtime

†Minnesota's home game (Ice Follies in their Metropolitan Sports Center)

Montreal (East Division winner) vs. St. Louis (West Division winner)

May 5, 1968 at St. Louis	Montreal 3* St. Louis 2

*Jacques Lemaire scored at 1:41 in overtime

May 7, 1968 at St. Louis	Montreal 1 St. Louis 0
May 9, 1968 at Montreal	Montreal 4* St. Louis 3

*J. J. Robert Rousseau scored at 1:13 in overtime

May 11, 1968 at Montreal	Montreal 3 St. Louis 2

1968–69

League Standings

The clubs played 8 games with the clubs in their own division and 6 games with each club in the other division.

East Division

Clubs	Games	Won	Lost	Tied	Points	Goals for	Goals against	Shut-outs	PiM
Mont. Canadiens	76	46	19	11	103	271	202	9	780
Boston Bruins	76	42	18	16	100	303	221	5	1297
N.Y. Rangers	76	41	26	9	91	231	196	7	806
Tor. Maple Lfs.	76	36	26	15	85	234	217	5	961
Det. Red Wings	76	33	31	12	78	239	221	4	885
Chi. Blk. Hawks	76	34	33	9	77	280	246	5	842
						1558		35	5571

	General-Mgr.	Asst. General-Mgr.	Coach
Boston	Milton Schmidt	Thomas C. Johnson	Harry Sinden
Chicago	Thomas N. Ivan	none	William T. Reay
Detroit	Sidney G. Abel	none	William A. Gadsby
Montreal	Samuel Pollock	none	Claude Ruel
N.Y. Rangers	Emile P. Francis	John Gordon	Bernard Geoffrion
Toronto	George F. Imlach	Francis M. Clancy	Imlach

Gordon left N.Y. Rangers in late November to become General-Manager of Cleveland Barons in minor American Hockey League.

January 17, 1969—Geoffrion collapsed in dressing-room at Oakland—had influenza and complications from ulcer operation in May, 1968 (N.Y. Rangers had won 22—lost 18—tied 3). Francis coached club rest of season.

Abel coached Detroit twice in March on orders from Bruce A. Norris, club President, in effort to make play-offs (lost 1—tied 1).

West Division

Clubs	Games	Won	Lost	Tied	Points	Goals for	Goals against	Shut-outs	PiM
St. Louis Blues	76	37	25	14	88	204	157	13	838
Oakland Seals	76	29	36	11	69	219	251	4	811
Phila. Flyers	76	20	35	21	61	174	225	2	964
L.A. Kings	76	24	42	10	58	185	260	4	698
Pitt. Penguins	76	20	45	11	51	189	252	2	677
Minn. N. Stars	76	18	43	15	51	189	270	1	862
						1160		26	4850

Oakland played 5 home games in San Francisco's Cow Palace due to schedule problem.

	General-Mgr.	Asst. General-Mgr.	Coach
Los Angeles	Lawrence Regan	none	Leonard P. Kelly
Minnesota	Wren A. Blair	John Mariucci	Blair
Oakland	Frank D. Selke	none	Frederick Glover

Philadelphia	Norman R. Poile	none	C. Keith Allen
Pittsburgh	John T. Riley	none	George Sullivan
St. Louis	W. Scott Bowman	none	Bowman

John Muckler coached Minnesota from November 6th through January 19th (won 6—lost 23—tied 6).

Player Transactions

November 12, 1968—Los Angeles acquired Ronald Anderson from Detroit

November 15, 1968—Montreal acquired Lawrence Hillman from Minnesota

November 29, 1968—Oakland traded William Harris to Pittsburgh for Robert Dillabough

January 6, 1969—St. Louis waived Myron Stankiewicz to Philadelphia ($30,000)

January 24, 1969—Minnesota traded Duane Rupp to Pittsburgh for Leo Boivin

January 30, 1969—Oakland traded George Swarbrick and Bryan Watson to Pittsburgh for Earl Ingarfield, Richard Mattiussi and Eugene Ubriaco

February 14, 1969—Chicago traded William Orban and A. Thomas Reid to Minnesota for André Boudrais and Michael McMahon

February 14, 1969—Detroit traded Daniel Lawson to Minnesota for Wayne Connelly

March 3, 1969—Philadelphia traded Forbes Kennedy and R. Briton Selby to Toronto for Michael Byers, Gerald Meehan and William Sutherland

August 15, 1968—Hartland deM. Molson and Thomas H. P. Molson (brothers) sold controlling interest in Canadian Arena Company (included Montreal Canadiens) to another branch of the Molson family—J. David, Peter and William Molson (also brothers).

1969 Stanley Cup

Montreal Canadiens

Ralph Gerard Backstrom
Jean Arthur Béliveau
Christian Gerard Bordeleau
Yvan Serge Cournoyer
Terrance Richard Duff
John Bowie Ferguson
Lucien S. J. Grenier
Terrance Victor Harper
Edward Alexander Harris
Lawrence Morley Hillman

Joseph Jacques Hugues Laperriére
Jacques Gerard Lemaire
Joseph Antoine Claude Provost
Michael Edward Redmond
Joseph Henri Richard
Joseph Jean-Paul Robert Rousseau
Serge A. Savard
Jean-Claude Tremblay
Rogatien Rosaire Vachon
Lorne John Worsley

The first and third and second and fourth place clubs in each division met in a 4 out of 7 game series. The winners of these series then met in another 4 out of 7 game series. These division winners then met in a 4 out of 7 game series.

Montreal (first in East Division) vs. N.Y. Rangers (third in East Division)

April 2, 1969 at Montreal	Montreal	3	N.Y. Rangers	1
April 3, 1969 at Montreal	Montreal	5	N.Y. Rangers	2
April 5, 1969 at New York	Montreal	4	N.Y. Rangers	1
April 6, 1969 at New York	Montreal	4	N.Y. Rangers	3

Boston (second in East Division) vs. Toronto (fourth in East Division)

April 2, 1969 at Boston	Boston	10	Toronto	0
April 3, 1969 at Boston	Boston	7	Toronto	0
April 5, 1969 at Toronto	Boston	4	Toronto	3
April 6, 1969 at Toronto	Boston	3	Toronto	2

Montreal (eliminated N.Y. Rangers) vs. Boston (eliminated Toronto)

| April 10, 1969 at Montreal | Montreal | 3* | Boston | 2 |

*Ralph Backstrom scored at 0:42 in overtime

| April 13, 1969 at Montreal | Montreal | 4* | Boston | 3 |

*Michael Redmond scored at 4:55 in overtime

April 17, 1969 at Boston	Montreal	0	Boston	5
April 20, 1969 at Boston	Montreal	2	Boston	3
April 22, 1969 at Montreal	Montreal	4	Boston	2
April 24, 1969 at Boston	Montreal	2*	Boston	1

*Jean Béliveau scored at 31:28 in overtime

St. Louis (first in West Division) vs. Philadelphia (third in West Division)

April 2, 1969 at St. Louis	St. Louis	5	Philadelphia	2
April 3, 1969 at St. Louis	St. Louis	5	Philadelphia	0
April 5, 1969 at Philadelphia	St. Louis	3	Philadelphia	0
April 6, 1969 at Philadelphia	St. Louis	4	Philadelphia	1

Oakland (second in West Division) vs. Los Angeles (fourth in West Division)

| April 2, 1969 at Oakland | Oakland | 4 | Los Angeles | 5* |

*Edward Irvine scored at 0:19 in overtime

April 3, 1969 at Oakland	Oakland	4	Los Angeles	2
April 5, 1969 at Inglewood, Calif.	Oakland	5	Los Angeles	2
April 6, 1969 at Inglewood, Calif.	Oakland	2	Los Angeles	4
April 9, 1969 at Oakland	Oakland	4	Los Angeles	1
April 10, 1969 at Inglewood, Calif.	Oakland	3	Los Angeles	4
April 13, 1969 at Oakland	Oakland	3	Los Angeles	5

St. Louis (eliminated Philadelphia) vs. Los Angeles (eliminated Oakland)

April 15, 1969 at St. Louis	St. Louis 4	Los Angeles 0
April 17, 1969 at St. Louis	St. Louis 3	Los Angeles 2
April 19, 1969 at Inglewood, Calif.	St. Louis 5	Los Angeles 2
April 20, 1969 at Inglewood, Calif.	St. Louis 4	Los Angeles 1

Montreal (East Division winner) vs. St. Louis (West Division winner)

April 27, 1969 at Montreal	Montreal 3	St. Louis 1
April 29, 1969 at Montreal	Montreal 3	St. Louis 1
May 1, 1969 at St. Louis	Montreal 4	St. Louis 0
May 4, 1969 at St. Louis	Montreal 2	St. Louis 1

1969–70

League Standings

The clubs played 8 games with the clubs in their own division and 6 games with each club in the other division.

East Division

Clubs	Games	Won	Lost	Tied	Points	Goals for	Goals against	Shut-outs	PiM
Chi. Blk. Hawks	76	45	22	9	99	250	170	15	901
Boston Bruins	76	40	17	19	99	277	216	7	1196
Det. Red Wings	76	40	21	15	95	246	199	2	907
N.Y. Rangers	76	38	22	16	92	246	189	7	853
Mont. Canadiens	76	38	22	16	92	244	201	4	892
Tor. Maple Lfs.	76	29	34	13	71	222	242	6	898
						1485		41	5647

	General-Mgr.	Asst. General-Mgr.	Coach
Boston	Milton Schmidt	Thomas C. Johnson	Harry Sinden
Chicago	Thomas N. Ivan	none	William T. Reay
Detroit	Sidney G. Abel	none	William Gadsby
Montreal	Samuel Pollock	Floyd J. Curry	Claude Ruel
N.Y. Rangers	Emile P. Francis	Bernard Geoffrion	Francis
Toronto	James Gregory	none	D. John McLellan

October 16, 1969—Gadsby replaced by Abel about an hour before start of Detroit's third game of season (Detroit had won both games).

October 25, 1969—Francis Clancy, Toronto Vice-President, coached Toronto as they defeated St. Louis 4-2 at Toronto (McLellan had influenza).

West Division

Clubs	Games	Won	Lost	Tied	Points	Goals for	Goals against	Shut-outs	PiM
St.L. Blues	76	37	27	12	86	224	179	10	876
Pitt. Penguins	76	26	38	12	64	182	238	5	1038
Minn. N. Stars	76	19	35	22	60	224	257	4	1008
Oakland Seals	76	22	40	14	58	169	243	2	845
Phila. Flyers	76	17	35	24	58	197	225	4	1123
L.A. Kings	76	14	52	10	38	168	290	3	969
						1164		28	5859

	General-Mgr.	Asst. General-Mgr.	Coach
Los Angeles	Lawrence Regan	none	Harold R. Laycoe
Minnesota	Wren A. Blair	John Mariucci	Blair
Oakland	Frank D. Selke	none	Frederick Glover
Philadelphia	Norman R. Poile	C. Keith Allen	Victor Stasiuk
Pittsburgh	John T. Riley	Jack Button	Leonard P. Kelly
St. Louis	W. Scott Bowman	Clifford Fletcher	Bowman

December 14, 1969—Laycoe replaced by John Wilson (Los Angeles had won 5—lost 18—tied 1) and Douglas Harvey named Assistant Coach.

December 18, 1969—Poile replaced by Allen.

December 29, 1969—Blair succeeded as coach by Charles Burns, who retired as a player (Minnesota had won 9—lost 13—tied 10). On March 1, 1970 Burns became a player-coach when he began playing again.

Alger Arbour, St. Louis Captain, coached 3 games while Bowman was on scouting trip to Canada—

March 21, 1970—St. Louis 0 Toronto 2 at St. Louis
March 22, 1970—St. Louis 0 Chicago 1 at Chicago
March 24, 1970—St. Louis 4 Los Angeles 0 at Los Angeles

Player Transactions

October 28, 1969—Pittsburgh acquired Michael McMahon from Detroit

December 9, 1969—Boston traded James Harrison to Toronto for K. Wayne Carleton

December 15, 1969—Chicago traded Howard Ménard to Oakland for Eugene Ubriaco

January 23, 1970—Los Angeles acquired T. Richard Duff from Montreal

February 20, 1970—Chicago traded Denis DeJordy and J. Gilles Marotte to Los Angeles for Bryan Campbell, Gerard Desjardins and William White

February 20, 1970—Detroit traded Garry Monahan and Matthew Ravlich to Los Angeles for Gary Croteau and Dale Rolfe

February 27, 1970—Los Angeles traded Edward Irvine to N.Y. Rangers for Réal Lemieux and Juha Widing

February 27, 1970—Minnesota acquired Lorne Worsley from Montreal

March 2, 1970—N.Y. Rangers acquired Myles Horton from Toronto

New Rules: Curvature of stick blade limited to 1 inch.
              Player leaving bench to enter altercation—automatic $100.
              fine (had previously been $50.).
Robert Hull voted "Player of the Decade" (1960–70) in poll of sports-writers and broadcasters by Associated Press.

1970 Stanley Cup

Boston Bruins

Donald William Awrey	Donald Michel Marcotte
John Paul Bucyk	John Albert McKenzie
Kenneth Wayne Carleton	Robert Gordon Orr
Wayne John Cashman	Derek Michael Sanderson
Gerald Michael Cheevers	Daniel Patrick Schock
Gary Walter Doak	Dallas Earl Smith
Philip Anthony Esposito	Richard Allan Smith
Kenneth Raymond Hodge	Francis William Speer
Edward Joseph Johnston	Frederic William Stanfield
William Anton Lesuk	Vernon Edwin Westfall
James Peter Lorentz	

The first and third and second and fourth place clubs in each division met in a 4 out of 7 game series. The winners of these series then met in another 4 out of 7 game series. These division winners then met in a 4 out of 7 game series.

Chicago (first in East Division) vs. Detroit (third in East Division)

April 8, 1870 at Chicago	Chicago 4	Detroit 2
April 9, 1970 at Chicago	Chicago 4	Detroit 2
April 11, 1970 at Detroit	Chicago 4	Detroit 2
April 12, 1970 at Detroit	Chicago 4	Detroit 2

Boston (second in East Division) vs. N.Y. Rangers (fourth in East Division)

April 8, 1970 at Boston	Boston 8	N.Y. Rangers 2
April 9, 1970 at Boston	Boston 5	N.Y. Rangers 3
April 11, 1970 at New York	Boston 3	N.Y. Rangers 4
April 12, 1970 at New York	Boston 2	N.Y. Rangers 4
April 14, 1970 at Boston	Boston 3	N.Y. Rangers 2
April 16, 1970 at New York	Boston 4	N.Y. Rangers 1

Chicago (eliminated Detroit) vs. Boston (eliminated N.Y. Rangers)

April 19, 1970 at Chicago	Chicago 3	Boston 6
April 21, 1970 at Chicago	Chicago 1	Boston 4
April 23, 1970 at Boston	Chicago 2	Boston 5
April 26, 1970 at Boston	Chicago 4	Boston 5

St. Louis (first in West Division) vs. Minnesota (third in West Division)

April 8, 1970 at St. Louis	St. Louis 6	Minnesota 2
April 9, 1970 at St. Louis	St. Louis 2	Minnesota 1
April 11. 1970 at Bloomington, Minn.	St. Louis 2	Minnesota 4
April 12, 1970 at Bloomington, Minn.	St. Louis 0	Minnesota 4
April 14, 1970 at St. Louis	St. Louis 6	Minnesota 3
April 16, 1970 at Bloomington, Minn.	St. Louis 4	Minnesota 2

Pittsburgh (second in West Division) vs. Oakland (fourth in West Division)

April 8, 1970 at Pittsburgh	Pittsburgh 2	Oakland 1
April 9, 1970 at Pittsburgh	Pittsburgh 3	Oakland 1
April 11, 1970 at Oakland	Pittsburgh 5	Oakland 2
April 12, 1970 at Oakland	Pittsburgh 3*	Oakland 2

*Michel Briere scored at 8:28 in overtime

St. Louis (eliminated Minnesota) vs. Pittsburgh (eliminated Oakland)

April 19, 1970 at St. Louis	St. Louis 3	Pittsburgh 1
April 21, 1970 at St. Louis	St. Louis 4	Pittsburgh 1
April 23, 1970 at Pittsburgh	St. Louis 2	Pittsburgh 3
April 26, 1970 at Pittsburgh	St. Louis 1	Pittsburgh 2
April 28, 1970 at St. Louis	St. Louis 5	Pittsburgh 0
April 30, 1970 at Pittsburgh	St. Louis 4	Pittsburgh 3

Boston (East Division winner) vs. St. Louis (West Division winner)

May 3, 1970 at St. Louis	Boston 6	St. Louis 1
May 5, 1970 at St. Louis	Boston 6	St. Louis 2
May 7, 1970 at Boston	Boston 4	St. Louis 1 ·
May 10, 1970 at Boston	Boston 4*	St. Louis 3

*Robert Orr scored at 0:40 in overtime

1970–71

League Standings

The clubs played 6 games with each club in both divisions.

East Division

Clubs	Games	Won	Lost	Tied	Points	Goals for	Goals against	Shut-outs	PiM
Boston Bruins	78	57	14	7	121	399	207	7	1156
N.Y. Rangers	78	49	18	11	109	259	177	12	952
Mont. Canadiens	78	42	23	13	97	291	216	3	1271
Tor. Maple Lfs.	78	37	33	8	82	248	211	8	1133
Buffalo Sabres	78	24	39	15	63	217	291	2	1188
Van. Canucks	78	24	46	8	56	229	296	0	1371
Det. Red Wings	78	22	45	11	55	209	308	1	988
						1852		33	8059

	General-Mgr.	Asst. General-Mgr.	Coach
Boston	Milton Schmidt	none	Thomas C. Johnson
Buffalo	George F. Imlach	Frederick T. Hunt	Imlach
Detroit	Sidney G. Abel	Aldege Bastien	Nevin D. Harkness
Montreal	Samuel Pollock	Floyd J. Curry	Claude Ruel
N.Y. Rangers	Emile P. Francis	none	Francis
Toronto	James Gregory	none	D. John McLellan
Vancouver	Norman R. Poile	none	Harold R. Laycoe

December 3, 1970—Ruel replaced by Allister MacNeil (Montreal had won 8—lost 11—
tied 4)—and Curry replaced by Ronald Caron.
January 6, 1971—Abel resigned. January 8, 1971—Harkness named General-Manager
(Detroit had won 12—lost 22—tied 4). January 10, 1971—N. Douglas
Barkley officially named coach (he had coached Detroit as they de-
feated Buffalo 3-2 at Detroit on January 9th).

West Division

Clubs	Games	Won	Lost	Tied	Points	Goals for	Goals against	Shut-outs	PiM
Chi. Blk. Hawks	78	49	20	9	107	277	184	6	1280
St.L. Mlues	78	34	25	19	78	223	208	6	1092
Phila. Flyers	78	28	33	17	73	207	225	4	1060
Minn. N. Stars	78	28	34	16	72	191	223	5	898
L.A. Kings	78	25	40	13	63	239	303	1	775
Pitt. Penguins	78	21	37	20	62	221	240	4	1079
Oakland Seals*	78	20	53	5	45	199	320	2	937
						1557		28	7121

*Prior to start of season name was changed from Bay Area Seals back to Oakland
Seals and on October 15, 1970 to California Golden Seals.

	General-Mgr.	Asst. General-Mgr.	Coach
Chicago	Thomas N. Ivan	none	William T. Reay
Los Angeles	Lawrence Regan	none	Regan
Minnesota	Wren A. Blair	John Mariucci	John Gordon
Oakland	Frank D. Selke	none	Frederick Glover
Philadelphia	C. Keith Allen	none	Victor Stasiuk
Pittsburgh	Leonard P. Kelly	Jack Button	Kelly
St. Louis	W. Scott Bowman	Clifford Fletcher	Alger J. Arbour

November 12, 1970—Selke resigned. November 13, 1970—William A. Torrey named General-Manager and resigned on November 25th. November 26, 1970—
Glover named General-Manager (and coach).
February 6, 1971—Arbour replaced by Bowman (St. Louis had won 21—lost 15—tied
14). Arbour returned to playing.

Player Transactions

October 19, 1970—Philadelphia sold William Sutherland to St. Louis
October 30, 1970—Detroit traded Peter Stemkowski to N.Y. Rangers
for Larry Brown
November 2, 1970—Detroit acquired Donald Luce from N.Y. Rangers

November   3, 1970—California waived Paul Andrea to Buffalo ($30,-
                  000.)
November   3, 1970—Detroit waived Robert Baun to Buffalo
November   4, 1970—Buffalo traded Robert Baun to St. Louis for Law-
                  rence Keenan and Jean-Guy Talbot
November 13, 1970—St. Louis traded Robert Baun to Toronto for R.
                  Briton Selby (Baun didn't play for St. Louis)
November 23, 1970—Minnesota waived Daniel Seguin to Vancouver
November 24, 1970—Buffalo acquired T. Richard Duff and Edward
                  Shack from Los Angeles
December   3, 1970—Vancouver sold John Arbour to St. Louis
December 28, 1970—Buffalo waived Clifford Schmautz to Philadelphia
 January 13, 1971—Detroit traded Francis Mahovlich to Montreal for
                  Guy Charron, William Collins and Michael Red-
                  mond
 January 22, 1971—Philadelphia acquired Daniel Schock from Boston
 January 26, 1971—Los Angeles traded W. Gordon Labossiere to Mont-
                  real for Ralph Backstrom
 January 26, 1971—Minnesota acquired W. Gordon Labossiere from
                  Montreal
 January 26, 1971—N.Y. Rangers traded Sylvanus Apps to Pittsburgh
                  for Glen Sather
 January 28, 1971—St. Louis acquired A. Francis Huck from Montreal
 February   1, 1971—Philadelphia traded Bernard Parent to Toronto for
                  Bruce Gamble and Michael Walton
 February   1, 1971—Boston acquired Michael Walton from Phila-
                  delphia
 February   1, 1971—Detroit traded Larry Brown and Bruce MacGregor
                  to N.Y. Rangers for S. Arnold Brown and Michael
                  Robitaille
 February   5, 1971—California sold Henry Howell to Los Angeles
 February   6, 1971—Detroit traded Wayne Connelly and Garry Unger
                  to St. Louis for Gordon Berenson and Timothy
                  Ecclestone
 February 22, 1971—Chicago traded Douglas Mohns to Minnesota for
                  Daniel O'Shea
 February 23, 1971—California traded Edward Hampson to Minnesota
                  for Thomas Williams
    March   2, 1971—Detroit traded Dale Rolfe to N.Y. Rangers for
                  James Krulicki
    March   8, 1971—California traded J. Wayne Muloin to Minnesota
                  for Richard Redmond

New Rules: Curvature of stick blade limited to ½ inch.
            Clubs allowed to dress 19 (17 players and 2 goaltenders)
            to November 1st.
            Fines: misconduct (from $25. to $50.), game misconduct
            (from $50. to $100.) and match misconduct (from

$100. to $200.). Previous fines had been in effect since 1947.

December   1, 1970—National Hockey League took control of Pittsburgh club from Donald H. Parsons and his associates.

January 19, 1971—National Hockey League Writers' Association (organized four seasons ago) changed name to Professional Hockey Writers' Association.

April 21, 1971—Peter H. Block, A. H. Burchfield III, Elmore L. Keener and Thayer R. Potter bought Pittsburgh club.

1971 Stanley Cup

Montreal Canadiens

Jean Arthur Béliveau
Pierre Bouchard
Yvan Serge Cournoyer
Kenneth Wayne Dryden
John Bowie Ferguson
Terrance Victor Harper
Réjean Houle
Joseph Jacques Hugues Lapierriére
Guy Gerard Lapointe
Claude David Larose
Charles Thomas Lefley

Jacques Gerard Lemaire
Francis William Mahovlich
Peter Joseph Mahovlich
Robert John Murdoch
Joseph Henri Richard
Phillip Roberto
Léon Joseph Fernand Rochefort
Robert Richard Sheehan
Marc Tardif
Jean-Claude Tremblay

The first and third and second and fourth place clubs in each division met in a 4 out of 7 game series. The winner of the first and third place clubs in the East Division then met the winner of the second and fourth place clubs in the West Division and the winner of the first and third place clubs in the West Division then met the winner of the second and fourth place clubs in the East Division in a 4 out of 7 game series. These winners then met in a 4 out of 7 game series.

Boston (first in East Division) vs. Montreal (third in East Division)

April 7, 1971 at Boston	Boston	3	Montreal	1
April 8, 1971 at Boston	Boston	5	Montreal	7
April 10, 1971 at Montreal	Boston	1	Montreal	3
April 11, 1971 at Montreal	Boston	5	Montreal	2
April 13, 1971 at Boston	Boston	7	Montreal	3
April 15, 1971 at Montreal	Boston	3	Montreal	8
April 18, 1971 at Boston	Boston	2	Montreal	4

N.Y. Rangers (second in East Division) vs. Toronto (fourth in East Division)

April 7, 1971 at New York	N.Y. Rangers	5	Toronto	4
April 8, 1971 at New York	N.Y. Rangers	1	Toronto	4
April 10, 1971 at Toronto	N.Y. Rangers	1	Toronto	3
April 11, 1971 at Toronto	N.Y. Rangers	4	Toronto	2
April 13, 1971 at New York	N.Y. Rangers	3	Toronto	1
April 15, 1971 at Toronto	N.Y. Rangers	2*	Toronto	1

*Robert Nevin scored at 9:07 in overtime

Chicago (first in West Division) vs. Philadelphia (third in West Division)

April 7, 1971 at Chicago	Chicago 5	Philadelphia 2
April 8, 1971 at Chicago	Chicago 6	Philadelphia 2
April 10, 1971 at Philadelphia	Chicago 3	Philadelphia 2
April 11, 1971 at Philadelphia	Chicago 6	Philadelphia 2

St. Louis (second in West Division) vs. Minnesota (fourth in West Division)

April 7, 1971 at St. Louis	St. Louis 2	Minnesota 3
April 8, 1971 at St. Louis	St. Louis 4	Minnesota 2
April 10, 1971 at Bloomington, Minn.	St. Louis 3	Minnesota 0
April 11, 1971 at Bloomington, Minn.	St. Louis 1	Minnesota 2
April 13, 1971 at St. Louis	St. Louis 3	Minnesota 4
April 15, 1971 at Bloomington, Minn.	St. Louis 2	Minnesota 5

Montreal (eliminated Boston) vs. Minnesota (eliminated St. Louis)

April 20, 1971 at Montreal	Montreal 7	Minnesota 2
April 22, 1971 at Montreal	Montreal 3	Minnesota 6
April 24, 1971 at Bloomington, Minn.	Montreal 6	Minnesota 3
April 25, 1971 at Bloomington, Minn.	Montreal 2	Minnesota 5
April 27, 1971 at Montreal	Montreal 6	Minnesota 1
April 29, 1971 at Bloomington, Minn.	Montreal 3	Minnesota 2

Chicago (eliminated Philadelphia) vs. N.Y. Rangers (eliminated Toronto)

April 18, 1971 at Chicago	Chicago 1	N.Y. Rangers 2*
	*Peter Stemkowski scored at 1:37 in overtime	
April 20, 1971 at Chicago	Chicago 3	N.Y. Rangers 0
April 22, 1971 at New York	Chicago 1	N.Y. Rangers 4
April 25, 1971 at New York	Chicago 7	N.Y. Rangers 1
April 27, 1971 at Chicago	Chicago 3*	N.Y. Rangers 2
	*Robert Hull scored at 6:35 in overtime	
April 29, 1971 at New York	Chicago 2	N.Y. Rangers 3*
	*Peter Stemkowski scored at 41:29 in overtime	
May 2, 1971 at Chicago	Chicago 4	N.Y. Rangers 2

Montreal (eliminated Minnesota) vs. Chicago (eliminated N.Y. Rangers)

May 4, 1971 at Chicago	Montreal 1	Chicago 2*
	*James Pappin scored at 21:11 in overtime	
May 6, 1971 at Chicago	Montreal 3	Chicago 5
May 9, 1971 at Montreal	Montreal 4	Chicago 2
May 11, 1971 at Montreal	Montreal 5	Chicago 2
May 13, 1971 at Chicago	Montreal 0	Chicago 2
May 16, 1971 at Montreal	Montreal 4	Chicago 3
May 18, 1971 at Chicago	Montreal 3	Chicago 2

1971–72

League President—Clarence Sutherland Campbell
Referee-in-Chief—Ian "Scotty" Morrison
Supervisors of Officials—William "Dutch" van Deelen, Dan McLeod &
Frank Udvari

League Standings

The clubs played 6 games with each club in both divisions.

East Division

Clubs	Games	Won	Lost	Tied	Points	Goals for	Goals against	Shut-outs	PiM
Boston Bruins	78	54	13	11	119	330	204	4	1112
N.Y. Rangers	78	48	17	13	109	317	192	4	1010
Mont. Canadiens	78	46	16	16	108	307	205	8	783
Tor. Maple Lfs.	78	33	31	14	80	209	208	5	887
Det. Red Wings	78	33	35	10	76	261	262	4	850
Buffalo Sabres	78	16	43	19	51	204	289	2	831
Van. Canucks	78	20	50	8	48	203	297	1	1094
						1830		28	6567

	General-Mgr.	Asst. General-Mgr.	Coach
Boston	Milton Schmidt	none	Thomas C. Johnson
Buffalo	George F. Imlach	Frederick T. Hunt	Imlach
Detroit	Nevin Harkness	Aldege Bastien	N. Douglas Barkley
Montreal	Samuel Pollock	Ronald Caron	W. Scott Bowman
N.Y. Rangers	Emile P. Francis	none	Francis
Toronto	James Gregory	none	D. John McLellan
Vancouver	Norman R. Poile	none	Harold R. Laycoe

November 1, 1971—Barkley replaced by John Wilson (Detroit had won 3—lost 8).
January 7, 1972—Imlach had heart attack (Buffalo had won 8—lost 23—tied 10).
January 9, 1972—Floyd Smith coached Buffalo as they lost 2-1 to Toronto at Buffalo.
January 10, 1972—Joseph R. Crozier named coach and Hunt became General-Manager (Crozier had coached Buffalo on November 27, 1971 as they lost 5-2 to Vancouver at Vancouver).
February 23, 1972—McLellan hospitalized with ulcer (Toronto had won 24—lost 27—tied 11). Francis Clancy, Toronto Vice-President, coached club rest of season except for March 24, 1972 when McLellan coached club as they lost 5-3 to Vancouver at Vancouver.

West Division

Clubs	Games	Won	Lost	Tied	Points	Goals for	Goals against	Shut-outs	PiM
Chi. Blk. Hawks	78	46	17	15	107	256	166	14	884
Minn. N. Stars	78	37	29	12	86	212	191	5	853
St. Louis Blues	78	28	39	11	67	208	247	2	1150
Pitt. Penguins	78	26	38	14	66	220	258	1	978
Phila. Flyers	78	26	38	14	66	200	236	7	1233
Cal. Gold. Seals	78	21	39	18	60	216	288	4	1009
L.A. Kings	78	20	49	9	49	206	305	2	719
						1518		35	6786

	General-Mgr.	Asst. General-Mgr.	Coach
California	Garry F. Young	none	Frederick Glover
Chicago	Thomas N. Ivan	none	William T. Reay
Los Angeles	Lawrence Regan	none	Regan
Minnesota	Wren A. Blair	John Mariucci	John Gordon
Philadelphia	C. Keith Allen	none	Frederick Shero
Pittsburgh	Leonard P. Kelly	Jack Button	Kelly
St. Louis	J. Lynn Patrick	Alger J. Arbour	Sidney G. Abel

October 14, 1971—Glover replaced by Victor Stasiuk (California had lost 1—tied 2).
October 29, 1971—Regan replaced by Glover as coach (Los Angeles had won 2—lost 7—tied 1).
October 31, 1971—Patrick replaced by Abel (Patrick remained a Vice-President) and William McCreary named coach (St. Louis had won 3—lost 6—tied 1).
December 24, 1971—McCreary replaced Arbour and Arbour named coach (St. Louis had won 9—lost 20—tied 5).
January 29, 1972—Kelly resigned as General-Manager (remained coach) and John T. Riley replaced him.

Player Transactions

October 21, 1971—California traded Ronald Stackhouse to Detroit for Thomas Webster

November 4, 1971—Los Angeles traded Denis DeJordy and Dale Hoganson to Montreal for Rogatien Vachon

November 8, 1971—St. Louis sold William Sutherland to Detroit

November 15, 1971—N.Y. Rangers traded John Egers to St. Louis for Eugene Carr, Wayne Connelly and James Lorentz

November 16, 1971—N.Y. Rangers traded David Balon and Wayne Connelly to Vancouver for Gary Doak

November 16, 1971—Buffalo traded Lawrence Keenan to Philadelphia for R. Larry Mickey

November 17, 1971—California acquired Ivan Boldirev from Boston

November 22, 1971—Vancouver waived Michael Corrigan to Los Angeles

November 22, 1971—Vancouver waived Daniel Johnson to Detroit

December 8, 1971—St. Louis waived Michel Parizeau to Philadelphia

December 13, 1971—Montreal traded Phillip Roberto to St. Louis for James Roberts

December 17, 1971—Buffalo traded Douglas Barrie to Los Angeles for Michael Byers and Lawrence Hillman

January 11, 1972—Los Angeles traded J. Allison McDonough to Pittsburgh for Robert Woytowich

January 14, 1972—Buffalo acquired James Lorentz from N.Y. Rangers

January 28, 1972—Los Angeles traded William Flett, Edward Joyal, Ross Lonsberry and Jean Potvin to Philadelphia for Serge Bernier, N. James Johnson and William Lesuk

February 7, 1972—Chicago traded Daniel O'Shea to St. Louis for Christian Bordeleau

February 20, 1972—N.Y. Rangers traded Pierre Jarry to Toronto for R. James Dorey

February 23, 1972—Boston traded Reginald Leach, Richard Smith and Robert Stewart to California for Carol Vadnais

March   3, 1972—Buffalo waived Kevin O'Shea to St. Louis

March   5, 1972—Buffalo traded Edward Shack to Pittsburgh for Rene Robert and cash

March   6, 1972—St. Louis acquired Christopher Evans from Buffalo

March   6, 1972—Vancouver sold Ronald Stewart to N.Y. Rangers

March   6, 1972—Buffalo sold J. G. Phillipe Goyette to N.Y. Rangers

New Rules: Third player to enter altercation—automatic game misconduct.

First player leaving bench to enter altercation—automatic game misconduct.

Players clearing bench to enter altercation—automatic double-minor penalty to club.

December 30, 1971—J. David, Peter and William Molson sold controlling interest in Canadian Arena Company (included Montreal Canadiens) to John Bassett, Edward and Peter Bronfman and E. Jacques Courtois.

1972 Stanley Cup

Boston Bruins

Donald William Awrey	Donald Michel Marcotte
Garnet Edward Bailey	John Albert McKenzie
John Paul Bucyk	Robert Gordon Orr
Wayne John Cashman	Garry Lorne Peters
Gerald Michael Cheevers	Derek Michael Sanderson
Philip Anthony Esposito	Dallas Earl Smith
Edward Joseph Green	Frederic William Stanfield
Christopher Joseph Hayes	Carol Marcel Vadnais
Kenneth Raymond Hodge	Michael Robert Walton
Edward Joseph Johnston	Vernon Edwin Westfall

The first and fourth and second and third place clubs in each division met in a 4 out of 7 game series. The winner of the first and fourth place clubs in the East Division then met the winner of the second and third place clubs in the West Division and the winner of the first and fourth place clubs in the West Division then met the winner of the second and third place clubs in the East Division in a 4 out of 7 game series. These winners then met in a 4 out of 7 game series.

Boston (First in East Division) vs. Toronto (fourth in East Division)

April 5, 1972 at Boston	Boston	5	Toronto	0
April 6, 1972 at Boston	Boston	3	Toronto	4*

*James Harrison scored at 2:58 in overtime

April 8, 1972 at Toronto	Boston	2	Toronto	0
April 9, 1972 at Toronto	Boston	5	Toronto	4
April 11, 1972 at Boston	Boston	3	Toronto	2

N.Y. Rangers (second in East Division) vs. Montreal (third in East Division)

April	5, 1972 at New York	N.Y. Rangers	3	Montreal	2
April	6, 1972 at New York	N.Y. Rangers	5	Montreal	2
April	8, 1972 at Montreal	N.Y. Rangers	1	Montreal	2
April	9, 1972 at Montreal	N.Y. Rangers	6	Montreal	4
April	11, 1972 at New York	N.Y. Rangers	1	Montreal	2
April	13, 1972 at Montreal	N.Y. Rangers	3	Montreal	2

Chicago (first in West Division) vs. Pittsburgh (fourth in West Division)

April	5, 1972 at Chicago	Chicago	3	Pittsburgh	1
April	6, 1972 at Chicago	Chicago	3	Pittsburgh	2
April	8, 1972 at Pittsburgh	Chicago	2	Pittsburgh	0
April	9, 1972 at Pittsburgh	Chicago	6*	Pittsburgh	5

*H. Jacques Martin scored at 0:12 in overtime

Minnesota (second in West Division) vs. St. Louis (third in West Division)

| April | 5, 1972 at Bloomington, Minn. | Minnesota | 3 | St. Louis | 0 |
| April | 6, 1972 at Bloomington, Minn. | Minnesota | 6* | St. Louis | 5 |

*William Goldsworthy scored at 1:36 in overtime

April	8, 1972 at St. Louis	Minnesota	1	St. Louis	2
April	9, 1972 at St. Louis	Minnesota	3	St. Louis	3
April	11, 1972 at Bloomington, Minn.	Minnesota	4	St. Louis	3
April	13, 1972 at St. Louis	Minnesota	2	St. Louis	4
April	16, 1972 at Bloomington, Minn.	Minnesota	1	St. Louis	2*

*Kevin O'Shea scored at 10:07 in overtime

Boston (eliminated Toronto) vs. St. Louis (eliminated Minnesota)

April 20, 1972 at Boston	Boston	10	St. Louis	2
April 18, 1972 at Boston	Boston	6	St. Louis	1
April 23, 1972 at St. Louis	Boston	7	St. Louis	2
April 25, 1972 at St. Louis	Boston	5	St. Louis	3

Chicago (eliminated Pittsburgh) vs. N.Y. Rangers (eliminated Montreal)

April 16, 1972 at Chicago	Chicago	2	N.Y. Rangers	3
April 18, 1972 at Chicago	Chicago	3	N.Y. Rangers	5
April 20, 1972 at New York	Chicago	2	N.Y. Rangers	3
April 23, 1972 at New York	Chicago	2	N.Y. Rangers	6

Boston (eliminated St. Louis) vs. N.Y. Rangers (eliminated Chicago)

April 30, 1972 at Boston	Boston	6	N.Y. Rangers	5
May	2, 1972 at Boston	Boston	2	N.Y. Rangers	1
May	4, 1972 at New York	Boston	2	N.Y. Rangers	5
May	7, 1972 at New York	Boston	3	N.Y. Rangers	2
May	9, 1972 at Boston	Boston	2	N.Y. Rangers	3
May	11, 1972 at New York	Boston	3	N.Y. Rangers	0

4
National Hockey League Records

National Hockey League Champions

1917–18	Toronto Arenas	1945–46	Montreal Canadiens
1918–19	Montreal Canadiens	1946–47	Montreal Canadiens
1919–20	Ottawa Senators	1947–48	Toronto Maple Leafs
1920–21	Ottawa Senators	1948–49	Detroit Red Wings
1921–22	Toronto St. Patricks	1949–50	Detroit Red Wings
1922–23	Ottawa Senators	1950–51	Detroit Red Wings
1923–24	Montreal Canadiens	1951–52	Detroit Red Wings
1924–25	Montreal Canadiens	1952–53	Detroit Red Wings
1925–26	Montreal Maroons	1953–54	Detroit Red Wings
1926–27	Ottawa Senators	1954–55	Detroit Red Wings
1927–28	New York Rangers	1955–56	Montreal Canadiens
1928–29	Boston Bruins	1956–57	Detroit Red Wings
1929–30	Boston Bruins	1957–58	Montreal Canadiens
1930–31	Montreal Canadiens	1958–59	Montreal Canadiens
1931–32	New York Rangers	1959–60	Montreal Canadiens
1932–33	Toronto Maple Leafs	1960–61	Montreal Canadiens
1933–34	Detroit Red Wings	1961–62	Montreal Canadiens
1934–35	Toronto Maple Leafs	1962–63	Toronto Maple Leafs
1935–36	Detroit Red Wings	1963–64	Montreal Canadiens
1936–37	Detroit Red Wings	1964–65	Detroit Red Wings
1937–38	Toronto Maple Leafs	1965–66	Montreal Canadiens
1938–39	Boston Bruins	1966–67	Chi. Black Hawks
1939–40	Boston Bruins	1967–68	Montreal Canadiens
1940–41	Boston Bruins	1968–69	Montreal Canadiens
1941–42	New York Rangers	1969–70	Chi. Black Hawks
1942–43	Detroit Red Wings	1970–71	Boston Bruins
1943–44	Montreal Canadiens	1971–72	Boston Bruins
1944–45	Montreal Canadiens		

League Statistics

Season	Clubs	Schedule	Games Played	Goals	Assists	Points	Pen in Min.
1971–72	14	78	546	3,348	5,404	8,752	13,353
1970–71	14	78	546	3,409	5,570	8,979	15,180
1969–70	12	76	456	2,649	4,276	6,925	11,506
1968–69	12	76	456	2,718	4,477	7,195	10,421

Season	Clubs	Schedule	Games Played	Goals	Assists	Points	Pen in Min.
1968–69	12	76	456	2,718	4,477	7,195	10,394
1967–68	12	74	444	2,476	4,020	6,496	9,083
1966–67	6	70	210	1,252	2,054	3,306	4,519
1965–66	6	70	210	1,277	2,114	3,391	4,997
1964–65	6	70	210	1,208	1,960	3,168	5,979
1963–64	6	70	210	1,166	1,915	3,081	5,370
1962–63	6	70	210	1,249	2,024	3,273	4,730
1961–62	6	70	210	1,264	2,090	3,354	4,538
1960–61	6	70	210	1,261	2,080	3,341	4,783
1959–60	6	70	210	1,238	2,061	3,299	4,905
1958–59	6	70	210	1,217	1,987	3,204	4,838
1957–58	6	70	210	1,175	1,943	3,118	5,100
1956–57	6	70	210	1,130	1,821	2,951	5,012
1955–56	6	70	210	1,064	1,692	2,756	5,488
1954–55	6	70	210	1,059	1,651	2,710	4,993
1953–54	6	70	210	1,009	1,556	2,565	5,099
1952–53	6	70	210	1,006	1,513	2,519	4,046
1951–52	6	70	210	1,090	1,630	2,720	3,956
1950–51	6	70	210	1,139	1,637	2,776	4,269
1949–50	6	70	210	1,148	1,664	2,812	3,984
1948–49	6	60	180	978	1,332	2,310	3,651
1947–48	6	60	180	1,054	1,444	2,498	3,642
1946–47	6	60	180	1,138	1,479	2,617	3,121
1945–46	6	50	150	1,003	1,138	2,141	1,779
1944–45	6	50	150	1,103	1,321	2,424	1,898
1943–44	6	50	150	1,225	1,748	2,973	1,934
1942–43	6	50	150	1,083	1,648	2,731	2,197
1941–42	7	48	168	1,047	1,623	2,670	2,824
1940–41	7	48	168	900	1,348	2,248	2,290
1939–40	7	48	168	838	1,228	2,066	2,510
1938–39	7	48	168	851	1,316	2,167	2,196
1937–38	8	48	192	972	1,364	2,336	2,766
1936–37	8	48	192	946	1,198	2,144	2,679
1935–36	8	48	192	831	1,163	1,994	3,363
1934–35	9	48	216	1,087	1,420	2,507	3,222
1933–34	9	48	216	1,041	1,178	2,219	3,447
1932–33	9	48	216	983	1,189	2,172	4,379
1931–32	8	48	192	957	1,001	1,958	4,026
1930–31	10	44	220	1,054	973	2,027	4,975
1929–30	10	44	220	1,301	1,083	2,384	5,122
1928–29	10	44	220	642	382	1,024	4,515
1927–28	10	44	220	836	416	1,252	4,860
1926–27	10	44	220	879	414	1,293	4,608
1925–26	7	36	126	581	215	796	2,582
1924–25	6	30	90	450	161	611	1,811
1923–24	4	24	48	255	82	337	559
1922–23	4	24	48	313	158	471	744
1921–22	4	24	48	380	188	568	463
1920–21	4	24	48	406	128	534	874
1919–20	4	24	48	460	138	598	791
1918–19	3	18	27	224	82	306	711
1917–18	4	22	36*	342	**	342	**
			11,075	61,712			

* The Montreal Wanderers withdrew from the league after playing 6 games when their Westmount Arena burned on January 2, 1918.
** Assists and Penalties were not recorded in 1917-18.

Club Records

Most Wins

1970–71	Boston	57
1971–72	Boston	54
1970–71	Chicago	49
1970–71	N.Y. Rangers	49
1971–72	N.Y. Rangers	48
1968–69	Montreal	46
1971–72	Chicago	46
1971–72	Montreal	46
1955–56	Montreal	45
1969–70	Chicago	45
1950–51	Detroit	44
1951–52	Detroit	44
1957–58	Montreal	43
1954–55	Detroit	42
1961–62	Montreal	42
1967–68	Montreal	42
1968–69	Boston	42
1970–71	Montreal	42
1950–51	Toronto	41
1954–55	Montreal	41
1960–61	Montreal	41
1965–66	Montreal	41
1966–67	Chicago	41
1968–69	N.Y. Rangers	41

Most Losses

1970–71	California	53
1969–70	Los Angeles	52
1953–54	Chicago	51
1971–72	Vancouver	50
1971–72	Los Angeles	49
1950–51	Chicago	47
1961–62	Boston	47
1970–71	Vancouver	46
1968–69	Pittsburgh	45
1970–71	Detroit	45
1951–52	Chicago	44
1964–65	Boston	43
1965–66	Boston	43
1966–67	Boston	43
1968–69	Minnesota	43
1971–72	Buffalo	43
1960–61	Boston	42
1967–68	Oakland	42
1968–69	Los Angeles	42
1965–66	N.Y. Rangers	41
1954–55	Chicago	40
1963–64	Boston	40
1969–70	Oakland	40
1970–71	Los Angeles	40

Most Ties

1969–70	Philadelphia	24
1962–63	Montreal	23
1954–55	Toronto	22
1969–70	Minnesota	22
1950–51	N.Y. Rangers	21
1954–55	Boston	21
1968–69	Philadelphia	21
1970–71	Pittsburgh	20
1949–50	Montreal	19
1952–53	Montreal	19
1969–70	Boston	19
1970–71	St. Louis	19
1971–72	Buffalo	19
1950–51	Boston	18
1952–53	Detroit	18
1954–55	N.Y. Rangers	18
1971–72	California	18
1954–55	Chicago	17
1960–61	Chicago	17
1962–63	Boston	17
1962–63	Chicago	17
1967–68	Oakland	17
1970–71	Philadelphia	17

Most Points

		won lost tied	
1970–71	Boston	(57—14— 7)	121
1971–72	Boston	(54—13—11)	119
1970–71	N.Y. Rangers	(49—18—11)	109
1971–72	N.Y. Rangers	(48—17—13)	109
1971–72	Montreal	(46—16—16)	108
1970–71	Chicago	(49—20— 9)	107
1970–72	Chicago	(46—17—15)	107
1968–69	Montreal	(46—19—11)	103
1950–51	Detroit	(44—13—13)	101
1951–52	Detroit	(44—14—12)	100
1955–56	Montreal	(45—15—10)	100
1968–69	Boston	(42—18—16)	100
1969–70	Boston	(40—17—19)	99
1969–70	Chicago	(45—22— 9)	99
1961–62	Montreal	(42—14—14)	98
1970–71	Montreal	(42—23—13)	97
1957–58	Montreal	(43—17—10)	96
1950–51	Toronto	(41—16—13)	95
1954–55	Detroit	(42—17—11)	95
1969–70	Detroit	(40—21—15)	95
1966–67	Chicago	(41—17—12)	94
1967–68	Montreal	(42—22—10)	94
1954–55	Montreal	(41—18—11)	93

Most Goals

1970–71	Boston	399
1971–72	Boston	330
1971–72	N.Y. Rangers	317
1971–72	Montreal	307
1968–69	Boston	303
1970–71	Montreal	291
1968–69	Chicago	280
1969–70	Boston	277
1970–71	Chicago	277
1968–69	Montreal	271
1966–67	Chicago	264
1971–72	Detroit	261
1961–62	Montreal	259
1967–68	Boston	259
1970–71	N.Y. Rangers	259
1958–59	Montreal	258
1971–72	Chicago	256
1959–60	Montreal	255

Most Assists

1970–71	Boston	697
1971–72	Boston	560
1971–72	N.Y. Rangers	531
1968–69	Boston	497
1970–71	Chicago	482
1968–69	Chicago	474
1971–72	Montreal	467
1969–70	Boston	460
1970–71	Montreal	455
1958–59	Montreal	439
1966–67	Chicago	437
1968–69	Montreal	432
1957–58	Montreal	430
1959–60	Montreal	430
1967–68	Boston	429
1971–72	Detroit	428
1970–71	N.Y. Rangers	426
1969–70	Chicago	423
1961–62	Montreal	422
1971–72	Chicago	419
1960–61	Montreal	410
1969–70	N.Y. Rangers	409

Most Points (Scoring)

		goals assists	
1970–71	Boston	(399—697)	1096
1971–72	Boston	(330—560)	890
1971–72	N.Y. Rangers	(317—531)	848
1968–69	Boston	(303—497)	800
1971–72	Montreal	(307—467)	774
1970–71	Chicago	(277—482)	759
1968–69	Chicago	(280—474)	754
1970–71	Montreal	(291—455)	746
1969–70	Boston	(277—460)	737
1968–69	Montreal	(271—432)	703
1966–67	Chicago	(264—437)	701
1958–59	Montreal	(258—439)	697
1971–72	Detroit	(261—428)	689
1967–68	Boston	(259—429)	688
1959–60	Montreal	(255—430)	685
1970–71	N.Y. Rangers	(259—426)	685
1961–62	Montreal	(259—422)	681
1957–58	Montreal	(250—430)	680
1971–72	Chicago	(256—419)	675
1969–70	Chicago	(250—423)	673
1960–61	Montreal	(254—410)	664

Most Goals-Against

1970–71	California	320
1943–44	N.Y. Rangers	310
1970–71	Detroit	308
1961–62	Boston	306
1971–72	Los Angeles	305
1970–71	Los Angeles	303
1971–72	Vancouver	297
1970–71	Vancouver	296
1970–71	Buffalo	291
1969–70	Los Angeles	290
1971–72	Buffalo	289
1971–72	California	288
1962–63	Boston	281
1950–51	Chicago	280
1965–66	Boston	275
1946–47	Chicago	274
1968–69	Minnesota	270

Most Penalties in Minutes

1970–71	Vancouver	1371
1968–69	Boston	1297
1970–71	Chicago	1280
1970–71	Montreal	1271
1971–72	Philadelphia	1233
1969–70	Boston	1196
1970–71	Buffalo	1188
1970–71	Boston	1156
1971–72	St. Louis	1150
1970–71	Toronto	1133
1969–70	Philadelphia	1123
1964–65	Detroit	1121
1963–64	Chicago	1116
1971–72	Boston	1112
1971–72	Vancouver	1094
1970–71	St. Louis	1092
1970–71	Pittsburgh	1079
1964–65	Toronto	1068

Most Shut-Outs

1928–29	Mont. Canadiens	22
1928–29	N.Y. Americans	16
1925–26	Ottawa	15
1927–28	Boston	15
1927–28	Ottawa	15
1969–70	Chicago	15
1926–27	Mont. Canadiens	14
1971–72	Chicago	14
1926–27	Mont. Maroons	13
1926–27	Ottawa	13
1927–28	Mont. Canadiens	13
1928–29	N.Y. Rangers	13
1953–54	Detroit	13
1953–54	Toronto	13
1968–69	St. Louis	13

Game Records

Most Goals (both clubs)

Jan. 10, 1920	Montreal Canadiens (14) & Toronto St. Patricks (7)	21
Dec. 19, 1917	Montreal Wanderers (10) & Toronto Arenas (9)	19
Mar. 3, 1920	Montreal Canadiens (16) & Quebec Bulldogs (3)	19
Mar. 4, 1944	Boston Bruins (10) & New York Rangers (9)	19
Mar. 16, 1944	Boston Bruins (9) & Detroit Red Wings (10)	19
Jan. 11, 1938	Montreal Canadiens (7) & Montreal Maroons (11)	18
Mar. 17, 1946	Detroit Red Wings (7) & Toronto Maple Leafs (11)	18

Most Goals (1 club)

Mar. 3, 1920 at Quebec City	Montreal Canadiens	16
Jan. 23, 1944 at Detroit	Detroit Red Wings	15
Jan. 10, 1920 at Montreal	Montreal Canadiens	14
Jan. 21, 1945 at Boston	Boston Bruins	14
Mar. 16, 1957 at Toronto	Toronto Maple Leafs	14
Nov. 21, 1943 at Montreal	Montreal Canadiens	13
Jan. 2, 1944 at New York	Boston Bruins	13
Jan. 2, 1971 at Toronto	Toronto Maple Leafs	13

Most Assists (both clubs)

Feb. 18, 1936	Montreal Maroons (16) & New York Americans (20)	36
Nov. 5, 1942	Detroit Red Wings (21) & New York Rangers (7)	28
Mar. 28, 1971	California Golden Seals (8) & Vancouver Canucks (20)	28
Jan. 11, 1938	Montreal Canadiens (10) & Montreal Maroons (17)	27
Mar. 4, 1944	Boston Bruins (15) & New York Rangers (12)	27
Oct. 16, 1968	Chicago Black Hawks (20) & Minnesota North Stars (7)	27

Most Assists (1 club)

Mar. 16, 1957 at Toronto	Toronto Maple Leafs	23
Nov. 21, 1971 at New York	New York Rangers	23
Jan. 23, 1944 at Detroit	Detroit Red Wings	22
Jan. 2, 1971 at Toronto	Toronto Maple Leafs	22
Nov. 5, 1942 at Detroit	Detroit Red Wings	21
Mar. 15, 1967 at Montreal	Montreal Canadiens	21

Most Points (both clubs)

Feb. 18, 1936	Montreal Maroons (24) & New York Americans (28)	52
Mar. 4, 1944	Boston Bruins (25) & New York Rangers (21)	46
Jan. 11, 1938	Montreal Canadiens (17) & Montreal Maroons (28)	45
Nov. 5, 1942	Detroit Red Wings (33) & New York Rangers (12)	45
Mar. 28, 1971	California Golden Seals (13) & Vancouver Canucks (31)	44
Mar. 17, 1946	Detroit Red Wings (16) & Toronto Maple Leafs (26)	42
Mar. 16, 1947	Chicago Black Hawks (17) & Detroit Red Wings (25)	42

Most Points (1 club)

Jan. 23, 1944 at Detroit	Detroit Red Wings (15 goals—22 assists)	37
Mar. 16, 1957 at Toronto	Toronto Maple Leafs (14 goals—23 assists)	37
Jan. 2, 1971 at Toronto	Toronto Maple Leafs (13 goals—22 assists)	35
Nov. 21, 1971 at New York	New York Rangers (12 goals—23 assists)	35
Nov. 5, 1942 at Detroit	Detroit Red Wings (12 goals—21 assists)	33
Mar. 15, 1967 at Montreal	Montreal Canadiens (11 goals—21 assists)	32

Most Penalties (both clubs)

Mar. 11, 1961	Chi. Black Hawks (20) & Tor. Maple Leafs (20)	40
Jan. 10, 1970	L.A. Kings (21) & Minn. North Stars (18)	39
Dec. 9, 1970	Mont. Canadiens (21) & Tor. Maple Leafs (16)	37
Dec. 9, 1953	Mont. Canadiens (18) & Tor. Maple Leafs (18)	36
Feb. 26, 1971	Chi. Black Hawks (21) & Calif. Golden Seals (15)	36
Nov. 12, 1931	Mont. Canadiens (12) & New York Rangers (21)	33
Dec. 3, 1967	Boston Bruins (17) & Mont. Canadiens (16)	33
Jan. 1, 1961	Boston Bruins (14) & Mont. Canadiens (18)	32
Mar. 24, 1962	Chi. Black Hawks (15) & Mont. Canadiens (16)	31
Jan. 30, 1958	Det. Red Wings (16) & Mont. Canadiens (14)	30
Dec. 7, 1963	Chi. Black Hawks (16) & Tor. Maple Leafs (14)	30
Mar. 13, 1965	Det. Red Wings (16) & Mont. Canadiens (14)	30
Jan. 9, 1971	St. Louis Blues (14) & Vancouver Canucks (16)	30

Most Penalties (1 club)

Nov. 12, 1931 at Montreal	New York Rangers	21
Jan. 10, 1970 at Bloomington, Minn.	Los Angeles Kings	21
Dec. 9, 1970 at Toronto	Montreal Canadiens	21
Feb. 26, 1971 at Oakland	Chicago Black Hawks	21
Mar. 11, 1961 at Toronto	Chicago Black Hawks	20
Mar. 11, 1961 at Toronto	Toronto Maple Leafs	20
Dec. 9, 1953 at Toronto	Montreal Canadiens	18
Dec. 9, 1953 at Toronto	Toronto Maple Leafs	18
Jan. 1, 1961 at Boston	Montreal Canadiens	18
Jan. 10, 1970 at Bloomington, Minn.	Minnesota North Stars	18

Most Penalties in Minutes (both clubs)

Dec. 9, 1953   Montreal Canadiens (106) & Toronto Maple Leafs (98)   204

Most Penalties in Minutes (1 club)

Dec. 9, 1953 at Toronto   Mont. Canadiens (8 misc.—2 maj.— 8 min.)   106
Dec. 9, 1970 at Toronto   Mont. Canadiens (6 misc.—5 maj.—10 min.)   105
Dec. 9, 1953 at Toronto   Tor. Maple Leafs (7 misc.—2 maj.— 9 min.)   98

Most Goals-Against

Mar. 3, 1920 at Quebec City	Quebec Bulldogs	16
Jan. 23, 1944 at Detroit	New York Rangers	15
Jan. 10, 1920 at Montreal	Toronto St. Patricks	14
Jan. 21, 1945 at Boston	New York Rangers	14
Mar. 16, 1957 at Toronto	New York Rangers	14
Nov. 21, 1943 at Montreal	Boston Bruins	13
Jan. 2, 1944 at New York	New York Rangers	13
Jan. 2, 1971 at Toronto	Detroit Red Wings	13

Most Shots on Net

Mar. 4, 1941 at Boston	Boston Bruins	83
Dec. 26, 1925 at New York	New York Americans	73
Dec. 10. 1970 at Boston	Boston Bruins	72
Dec. 26, 1925 at New York	Pittsburgh Pirates	68
Feb. 7, 1971 at Boston	Boston Bruins	67
Apr 5, 1970 at New York	New York Rangers	65
Nov. 10, 1969 at Boston	Boston Bruins	63
Dec. 14, 1930 at New York	Detroit Falcons	62

Period Records

Most Goals (both clubs)

Mar. 16, 1939	N.Y. Americans (3) & N.Y. Rangers (7)	3rd period	10
Jan. 11, 1938	Mont. Canadiens (2) & Mont. Maroons (7)	1st period	9
Jan. 21, 1943	N.Y. Rangers (4) & Tor. Maple Leafs (5)	3rd period	9
Mar. 16, 1943	Boston Bruins (6) & N.Y. Rangers (3)	3rd period	9
Mar. 17, 1946	Det. Red Wings (4) & Tor. Maple Leafs (5)	3rd period	9
Dec. 20, 1959	Chi. Blk. Hawks (7) & Tor. Maple Leafs (2)	2nd period	9
Mar. 16, 1969	Boston Bruins (8) & Tor. Maple Leafs (1)	2nd period	9
Mar. 30, 1969	Chi. Blk. Hawks (6) & Det. Red Wings (3)	2nd period	9
Oct. 18, 1969	Mont. Canadiens (6) & N.Y. Rangers (3)	3rd period	9

Most Goals (1 club)

Jan. 23, 1944 at Detroit	Detroit Red Wings	3rd period	8
Mar. 16, 1969 at Boston	Boston Bruins	2nd period	8
Nov. 21, 1971 at New York	New York Rangers	3rd period	8
Jan. 10, 1920 at Montreal	Montreal Canadiens	1st period	7
Feb. 9, 1930 at Detroit	Detroit Cougars	3rd period	7
Jan. 11, 1938 at Montreal	Montreal Maroons	1st period	7
Mar. 16, 1939 at New York	New York Rangers	3rd period	7
Jan. 28, 1943 at Chicago	Chicago Black Hawks	3rd period	7

Dec. 20, 1959 at Chicago	Chicago Black Hawks	2nd period 7
Feb. 13, 1960 at Toronto	Toronto Maple Leafs	3rd period 7
Apr. 5, 1970 at Chicago	Chicago Black Hawks	3rd period 7
Nov. 7, 1970 at Montreal	Montreal Canadiens	2nd period 7
Jan. 2, 1971 at Toronto	Toronto Maple Leafs	3rd period 7

Most Assists (both clubs)

Mar. 30, 1969	Chi. Blk. Hawks (12) & Det. Red Wings (5)	2nd period 17
Mar. 16, 1939	N.Y. Americans (6) & N.Y. Rangers (10)	3rd period 16
Jan. 21, 1943	N.Y. Rangers (7) & Tor. Maple Leafs (9)	3rd period 16
Mar. 16, 1969	Boston Bruins (14) & Tor. Maple Leafs (2)	2nd period 16

Most Assists (1 club)

Nov. 21, 1971 at New York	New York Rangers	3rd period 15
Jan. 23, 1944 at Detroit	Detroit Red Wings	3rd period 14
Mar. 16, 1969 at Boston	Boston Bruins	2nd period 14
Jan. 28, 1943 at Chicago	Chicago Black Hawks	3rd period 12
Mar. 30, 1969 at Chicago	Chicago Black Hawks	2nd period 12
Nov. 7, 1970 at Montreal	Montreal Canadiens	2nd period 12

Most Points (both clubs)

Mar. 16, 1939	N.Y. Americans (9) & N.Y. Rangers (17)	3rd period 26
Mar. 30, 1969	Chi. Blk. Hawks (18) & Det. Red Wings (8)	2nd period 26
Jan. 21, 1943	N.Y. Rangers (11) & Tor. Maple Lfs. (14)	3rd period 25
Mar 16, 1969	Boston Bruins (22) & Tor. Maple Lfs. (3)	2nd period 25

Most Points (1 club)

Nov. 21, 1971 at New York	N.Y. Rangers	3rd per. (8 goals—15 assists) 23
Jan. 23, 1944 at Detroit	Det. Red. Wings	3rd per. (8 goals—14 assists) 22
Mar. 16, 1969 at Boston	Boston Bruins	2nd per. (8 goals—14 assists) 22
Jan. 28, 1943 at Chicago	Chi. Blk. Hawks	3rd per. (7 goals—12 assists) 19
Nov. 7, 1970 at Montreal	Mont. Canadiens	2nd per. (7 goals—12 assists) 19

Most Penalties (both clubs)

Dec. 9, 1953	Mont. Canadiens (13) & Tor. Maple Leafs (13)	3rd period 26
Dec. 9, 1970	Mont. Canadiens (14) & Tor. Maple Leafs (11)	1st period 25
Jan. 30, 1958	Det. Red Wings (11) & Mont. Canadiens (10)	3rd period 21
Mar. 11, 1961	Chi. Blk. Hawks (11) & Tor. Maple Leafs (10)	3rd period 21
Dec. 7, 1963	Chi. Blk. Hawks (12) & Tor. Maple Leafs (9)	3rd period 21
Dec. 29, 1963	Mont. Canadiens (9) & N.Y. Rangers (11)	3rd period 20
Oct. 18, 1970	Buffalo Sabres (12) & Pitt. Penguins (8)	1st period 20

Most Penalties (1 club)

Dec. 9, 1970 at Toronto	Montreal Canadiens	1st period 14
Dec. 9, 1953 at Toronto	Montreal Canadiens	3rd period 13
Dec. 9, 1953 at Toronto	Toronto Maple Leafs	3rd period 13
Dec. 7, 1963 at Toronto	Chicago Black Hawks	3rd period 12
Oct. 18, 1970 at Buffalo	Buffalo Sabres	1st period 12

Most Penalties in Minutes (both clubs)

Dec. 9, 1953	Mont. Canadiens (96) & Tor. Maple Lfs. (88)	3rd period	184
Mar. 11, 1961	Chi. Blk. Hawks (74) & Tor. Maple Lfs. (61)	3rd period	135
Dec. 7, 1963	Chi. Blk. Hawks (76) & Tor. Maple Lfs. (59)	3rd period	135
Dec. 9, 1970	Mont. Canadiens (72) & Tor. Maple Lfs. (58)	1st period	130
Jan. 24, 1971	Det. Red Wings (64) & Van. Canucks (64)	3rd period	128

Most Penalties in Minutes (1 club)

Dec. 9, 1953 at Tor.	Mont. Canadiens	3rd period	(8 misc.—2 maj.—3 min.)	96
Dec. 9, 1953 at Tor.	Tor. Maple Lfs.	3rd period	(7 misc.—2 maj.—4 min.)	88
Dec. 7, 1963 at Tor.	Chi. Blk. Hawks	3rd period	(5 misc.—4 maj.—3 min.)	76
Mar. 11, 1961 at Tor.	Chi. Blk. Hawks	3rd period	(5 misc.—4 maj.—2 min.)	74
Dec. 9, 1970 at Tor.	Mont. Canadiens	1st period	(4 misc.—4 maj.—6 min.)	72
Jan. 24, 1971 at Det.	Det. Red Wings.	3rd period	(5 misc.—2 maj.—2 min.)	64
Jan. 24, 1971 at Det.	Van. Canucks	3rd period	(5 misc.—2 maj.—2 min.)	64
Mar. 11, 1961 at Tor.	Tor. Maple Lfs.	3rd period	(4 misc.—3 maj.—3 min.)	61
Dec. 7, 1963 at Tor.	Tor. Maple Lfs.	3rd period	(4 misc.—3 maj.—2 min.)	59
Dec. 9, 1970 at Tor.	Tor. Maple Lfs.	1st period	(3 misc.—4 maj.—4 min.)	58

Most Goals-Against

Jan. 23, 1944 at Detroit	New York Rangers	3rd period	8
Mar. 16, 1969 at Boston	Toronto Maple Leafs	2nd period	8
Nov. 21, 1971 at New York	California Golden Seals	3rd period	8
Jan. 10, 1920 at Montreal	Toronto St. Patricks	1st period	7
Feb. 9, 1930 at Detroit	Pittsburgh Pirates	3rd period	7
Jan. 11, 1938 at Montreal	Montreal Canadiens	1st period	7
Mar. 16, 1939 at New York	New York Americans	3rd period	7
Jan. 28, 1943 at Chicago	New York Rangers	3rd period	7
Dec. 20, 1959 at Chicago	Toronto Maple Leafs	2nd period	7
Feb. 13, 1960 at Toronto	Detroit Red Wings	3rd period	7
Apr. 5, 1970 at Chicago	Montreal Canadiens	3rd period	7
Nov. 7, 1970 at Montreal	Buffalo Sabres	2nd period	7
Jan. 2, 1971 at Toronto	Detroit Red Wings	3rd period	7

Most Shots on Net

Mar. 4, 1941 at Boston	Boston Bruins	1st period	37
Dec. 14, 1930 at New York	Detroit Falcons	2nd period	31
Dec. 10, 1970 at Boston	Boston Bruins	3rd period	30

Consecutive Game Records

Won

started Dec. 3, 1929—ended Jan. 12, 1930	Boston Bruins	14
started Feb. 23, 1971—ended Mar. 21, 1971	Boston Bruins	13
started Jan. 6, 1968—ended Feb. 4, 1968	Montreal Canadiens	12
started Feb. 24, 1927—ended Mar. 26, 1927	Montreal Canadiens	11
started Feb. 4, 1930—ended Mar. 13, 1930	Boston Bruins	11
started Dec. 19, 1939—ended Jan. 14, 1940	New York Rangers	10
started Feb. 17, 1944—ended Mar. 12, 1944	Montreal Canadiens	10
started Dec. 5, 1970—ended Dec. 26, 1970	Boston Bruins	10

Won or Tied

started Dec. 22, 1940—ended Feb. 25, 1941 Bos. Bruins (won 15—tied 8) 23
started Mar. 4, 1943—ended Dec. 5, 1943 Mont. Can. (won 13—tied 7) 20
started Nov. 23, 1939—ended Jan. 14, 1940 N.Y. Rang. (won 14—tied 5) 19
started Nov. 30, 1927—ended Jan. 21, 1928 Mont. Can. (won 15—tied 3) 18
started Jan. 6, 1945—ended Mar. 3, 1945 Mont. Can. (won 16—tied 2) 18
started Dec. 28, 1968—ended Feb. 6, 1969 Bos. Bruins (won 13—tied 5) 18

Lost

started Nov. 29, 1930—ended Jan. 10, 1931   Philadelphia Quakers   15
started Feb. 13, 1926—ended Mar. 16, 1926   Montreal Canadiens   12
started Jan. 4, 1951—ended Feb. 1, 1951   Chicago Black Hawks   12
started Dec. 3, 1924—ended Jan. 10, 1925   Boston Bruins   11
started Oct. 30, 1943—ended Nov. 28, 1943   New York Rangers   11
started Jan. 24, 1925—ended Feb. 28, 1925   Montreal Maroons   10
started Mar. 5, 1927—ended Nov. 26, 1927   New York Americans   10
started Nov. 22, 1941—ended Dec. 18, 1941   Brooklyn Americans   10
started Jan. 3, 1962—ended Jan. 31, 1962   New York Rangers   10
started Jan. 15, 1967—ended Feb. 11, 1967   Toronto Maple Leafs   10

Lost or Tied

started Jan. 23, 1944—ended Nov. 11, 1944 N.Y. Rangs. (lost 21—tied 4) 25
started Dec. 17, 1950—ended Feb. 1, 1951 Chi. B. Hks. (lost 18—tied 3) 21
started Jan. 28, 1962—ended Mar. 15, 1962 Bos. Bruins (lost 16—tied 4) 20
started Jan. 15, 1970—ended Mar. 1, 1970 Minn. N. St. (lost 15—tied 5) 20
started Dec. 31, 1942—ended Feb. 21, 1943 N.Y. Rangs. (lost 14—tied 5) 19
started Jan. 29, 1970—ended Mar. 7, 1970 L.A. Kings (lost 13—tied 4) 17

Shut-Out

started Feb. 7, 1929—ended Mar. 2, 1929   Chicago Black Hawks   8
started Feb. 7, 1928—ended Feb. 23, 1928   New York Rangers   4
started Feb. 14, 1928—ended Feb. 28, 1928   Montreal Canadiens   4
started Dec. 6, 1928—ended Dec. 20, 1928   Pittsburgh Pirates   4
started Dec. 27, 1967—ended Jan. 4, 1968   Oakland Seals   4

Not Shut-Out

started Mar. 14, 1970—ended   Chicago Black Hawks   168*
started Nov. 8, 1968—ended Mar. 4, 1970   New York Rangers   126
started Nov. 2, 1940—ended Dec. 31, 1942   New York Rangers   117
started Feb. 21, 1945—ended Nov. 30, 1946   Chicago Black Hawks   74
started Mar. 17, 1931—ended Jan. 17, 1933   New York Rangers   71
started Feb. 12, 1942—ended Nov. 14, 1943   Detroit Red Wings   68

*hasn't ended—will continue in 1972–73 season

Club Standings (Season by Season)

The position of these clubs is based on their record in the regular schedule.

For the first 4 seasons, 1917–20, when they played a split schedule, their positions are arrived at by combining both halves.

For the 12 seasons that the league was divided into 2 divisions (1926–27 through 1937–38), the positions of the clubs are as they would have been had the league not been divided. The same applies since 1967–68 when the league was again divided into 2 divisions.

Montreal

Season	Games	Won	Lost	Tied	Points	Goals for	Goals against	Position
1971–72	78	46	16	16	108	307	205	3rd
1970–71	78	42	23	13	97	291	216	4th
1969–70	76	38	22	16	92	244	201	5th
1968–69	76	46	19	11	103	271	202	1st
1967–68	74	42	22	10	94	236	167	1st
1966–67	70	32	25	13	77	202	188	2nd
1965–66	70	41	21	8	90	239	173	1st
1964–65	70	36	23	11	83	211	185	2nd
1963–64	70	36	21	13	85	209	167	1st
1962–63	70	28	19	23	79	225	183	3rd
1961–62	70	42	14	14	98	259	166	1st
1960–61	70	41	19	10	92	254	188	1st
1959–60	70	40	18	12	92	255	178	1st
1958–59	70	39	18	13	91	258	158	1st
1957–58	70	43	17	10	96	250	158	1st
1956–57	70	35	23	12	82	210	155	2nd
1955–56	70	45	15	10	100	222	131	1st
1954–55	70	41	18	11	93	228	157	2nd
1953–54	70	35	24	11	81	195	141	2nd
1952–53	70	28	23	19	75	155	148	2nd
1951–52	70	34	26	10	78	195	164	2nd
1950–51	70	25	30	15	65	173	184	3rd
1949–50	70	29	22	19	77	172	150	2nd
1948–49	60	28	23	9	65	152	126	3rd
1947–48	60	20	29	11	51	147	169	5th
1946–47	60	34	16	10	78	189	138	1st
1945–46	50	28	17	5	61	172	134	1st
1944–45	50	38	8	4	80	228	121	1st
1943–44	50	38	5	7	83	234	109	1st
1942–43	50	19	19	12	50	181	191	4th
1941–42	48	18	27	3	39	134	173	6th
1940–41	48	16	26	6	38	121	147	6th
1939–40	48	10	33	5	25	90	167	7th L
1938–39	48	15	24	9	39	115	146	6th
1937–38	48	18	17	13	49	123	128	5th
1936–37	48	24	18	6	54	115	111	2nd

Season	Games	Won	Lost	Tied	Points	Goals for	Goals against	Position
1935–36	48	11	26	11	33	82	123	8th L
1934–35	48	19	23	6	44	110	145	7th
1933–34	48	22	20	6	50	99	101	4th
1932–33	48	18	25	5	41	92	115	7th
1931–32	48	25	16	7	57	128	111	1st
1930–31	44	26	10	8	60	129	89	2nd
1929–30	44	21	14	9	51	142	114	3rd
1928–29	44	22	7	15	59	71	43	1st
1927–28	44	26	11	7	59	116	48	1st
1926–27	44	28	14	2	58	99	67	2nd
1925–26	36	11	24	1	23	79	108	7th L
1924–25	30	17	11	2	36	93	56	3rd
1923–24	24	13	11	0	26	59	48	2nd
1922–23	24	13	9	2	28	73	61	2nd
1921–22	24	12	11	1	25	88	94	3rd
1920–21	24	13	11	0	26	112	99	3rd
1919–20	24	13	11	0	26	129	113	2nd
1918–19	18	10	8	0	20	88	78	2nd
1917–18	22	13	9	0	26	115	84	1st
	2,996	1,503	1,011	482	3,488	9,166	7,522	

Boston

Season	Games	Won	Lost	Tied	Points	Goals for	Goals against	Position
1971–72	78	54	13	11	119	330	204	1st
1970–71	78	57	14	7	121	399	207	1st
1969–70	76	40	17	19	99	277	216	2nd
1968–69	76	42	18	16	100	303	221	2nd
1967–68	74	37	27	10	84	259	216	3rd
1966–67	70	17	43	10	44	182	253	6th L
1965–66	70	21	43	6	48	174	275	5th
1964–65	70	21	43	6	48	166	253	6th L
1963–64	70	18	40	12	48	170	212	6th L
1962–63	70	14	39	17	45	198	281	6th L
1961–62	70	15	47	8	38	177	306	6th L
1960–61	70	15	42	13	43	176	254	6th L
1959–60	70	28	34	8	64	220	241	5th
1958–59	70	32	29	9	73	205	215	2nd
1957–58	70	27	28	15	69	199	194	4th
1956–57	70	34	24	12	80	195	174	3rd
1955–56	70	23	34	13	59	147	185	5th
1954–55	70	23	26	21	67	169	188	4th
1953–54	70	32	28	10	74	177	181	4th
1952–53	70	28	29	13	69	152	172	3rd
1951–52	70	25	29	16	66	162	176	4th
1950–51	70	22	30	18	62	178	197	4th
1949–50	70	22	32	16	60	198	228	5th
1948–49	60	29	23	8	66	178	163	2nd
1947–48	60	23	24	13	59	167	168	3rd

Season	Games	Won	Lost	Tied	Points	Goals for	Goals against	Position
1946–47	60	26	23	11	63	190	175	3rd
1945–46	50	24	18	8	56	167	156	2nd
1944–45	50	16	30	4	36	179	219	4th
1943–44	50	19	26	5	43	223	268	5th
1942–43	50	24	17	9	57	195	176	2nd
1941–42	48	25	17	6	56	160	118	3rd
1940–41	48	27	8	13	67	168	102	1st
1939–40	48	31	12	5	67	170	98	1st
1938–39	48	36	10	2	74	156	76	1st
1937–38	48	30	11	7	67	142	89	1st
1936–37	48	23	18	7	53	120	110	3rd
1935–36	48	22	20	6	50	92	83	4th
1934–35	48	26	16	6	58	129	112	2nd
1933–34	48	18	25	5	41	111	130	7th
1932–33	48	25	15	8	58	124	88	1st
1931–32	48	15	21	12	42	122	117	7th
1930–31	44	28	10	6	62	143	90	1st
1929–30	44	38	5	1	77	179	98	1st
1928–29	44	26	13	5	57	89	52	2nd
1927–28	44	20	13	11	51	77	70	3rd
1926–27	44	21	20	3	45	97	89	4th
1925–26	36	17	15	4	38	92	85	4th
1924–25	30	6	24	0	12	49	119	6th L
	2,836	1,242	1,143	451	2,935	8,332	8,100	

Buffalo Sabres

Season	Games	Won	Lost	Tied	Points	Goals for	Goals against	Position
1971–72	78	16	43	19	51	203	289	12th
1970–71	78	24	39	15	63	217	291	10th
	156	40	82	34	114	420	580	

Chicago

Season	Games	Won	Lost	Tied	Points	Goals for	Goals against	Position
1971–72	78	46	17	15	107	256	166	4th
1970–71	78	49	20	9	107	277	184	3rd
1969–70	76	45	22	9	99	250	170	1st
1968–69	76	34	33	9	77	280	246	7th
1967–68	74	32	26	16	80	212	222	4th
1966–67	70	41	17	12	94	264	170	1st
1965–66	70	37	25	8	82	240	187	2nd
1964–65	70	34	28	8	76	224	176	3rd
1963–64	70	36	22	12	84	218	169	2nd
1962–63	70	32	21	17	81	194	178	2nd
1961–62	70	31	26	13	75	217	186	3rd
1960–61	70	29	24	17	75	198	180	3rd
1959–60	70	28	29	13	69	191	180	3rd

Season	Games	Won	Lost	Tied	Points	Goals for	Goals against	Position
1958–59	70	28	29	13	69	197	208	3rd
1957–58	70	24	39	7	55	163	202	5th
1956–57	70	16	39	15	47	169	225	6th L
1955–56	70	19	39	12	50	155	216	6th L
1954–55	70	13	40	17	43	161	235	6th L
1953–54	70	12	51	7	31	133	242	6th L
1952–53	70	27	28	15	69	169	175	4th
1951–52	70	17	44	9	43	158	241	6th L
1950–51	70	13	47	10	36	171	280	6th L
1949–50	70	22	38	10	54	203	244	6th L
1948–49	60	21	31	8	50	173	211	5th
1947–48	60	20	34	6	46	195	225	6th L
1946–47	60	19	37	4	42	193	274	6th L
1945–46	50	23	20	7	53	200	178	3rd
1944–45	50	13	30	7	33	141	194	5th
1943–44	50	22	23	5	49	178	187	4th
1942–43	50	17	18	15	49	179	180	5th
1941–42	48	22	23	3	47	145	155	4th
1940–41	48	16	25	7	39	112	139	5th
1939–40	48	23	19	6	52	112	120	4th
1938–39	48	12	28	8	32	91	132	7th L
1937–38	48	14	25	9	37	97	139	6th
1936–37	48	14	27	7	35	99	131	7th
1935–36	48	21	19	8	50	93	92	5th
1934–35	48	26	17	5	57	118	88	3rd
1933–34	48	20	17	11	51	88	83	3rd
1932–33	48	16	20	12	44	88	101	6th
1931–32	48	18	19	11	47	86	101	4th
1930–31	44	24	17	3	51	108	78	4th
1929–30	44	21	18	5	47	117	111	5th
1928–29	44	7	29	8	22	33	85	10th L
1927–28	44	7	34	3	17	68	134	10th L
1926–27	44	19	22	3	41	115	116	6th
	2,770	1,080	1,256	434	2,594	7,529	7,936	

Detroit

Season	Games	Won	Lost	Tied	Points	Goals for	Goals against	Position
1971–72	78	33	35	10	76	261	262	7th
1970–71	78	22	45	11	55	209	308	13th
1969–70	76	40	21	15	95	246	199	3rd
1968–69	76	33	31	12	78	239	221	6th
1967–68	74	27	35	12	66	245	257	11th
1966–67	70	27	39	4	58	212	241	5th
1965–66	70	31	27	12	74	221	194	4th
1964–65	70	40	23	7	87	224	175	1st
1963–64	70	30	29	11	71	191	204	4th
1962–63	70	32	25	13	77	200	194	4th

Season	Games	Won	Lost	Tied	Points	Goals for	Goals against	Position
1961–62	70	23	33	14	60	184	219	5th
1960–61	70	25	29	16	66	195	215	4th
1959–60	70	26	29	15	67	186	197	4th
1958–59	70	25	37	8	58	167	218	6th L
1957–58	70	29	29	12	70	176	207	3rd
1956–57	70	38	20	12	88	198	157	1st
1955–56	70	30	24	16	76	183	148	2nd
1954–55	70	42	17	11	95	204	134	1st
1953–54	70	37	19	14	88	191	132	1st
1952–53	70	36	16	18	90	222	133	1st
1951–52	70	44	14	12	100	215	133	1st
1950–51	70	44	13	13	101	236	139	1st
1949–50	70	37	19	14	88	229	164	1st
1948–49	60	34	19	7	75	195	145	1st
1947–48	60	30	18	12	72	187	148	2nd
1946–47	60	22	27	11	55	190	193	4th
1945–46	50	20	20	10	50	146	159	4th
1944–45	50	31	14	5	67	218	161	2nd
1943–44	50	26	18	6	58	214	177	2nd
1942–43	50	25	14	11	61	169	124	1st
1941–42	48	19	25	4	42	140	147	5th
1940–41	48	21	16	11	53	112	102	3rd
1939–40	48	16	26	6	38	90	126	5th
1938–39	48	18	24	6	42	107	128	5th
1937–38	48	12	25	11	35	99	133	7th
1936–37	48	25	14	9	59	128	102	1st
1935–36	48	24	16	8	56	124	103	1st
1934–35	48	19	22	7	45	127	114	6th
1933–34	48	24	14	10	58	113	98	2nd
1932–33	48	25	15	8	58	111	93	2nd
1931–32	48	18	20	10	46	95	108	5th
1930–31	44	16	21	7	39	102	105	8th
1929–30	44	14	24	6	34	117	133	8th
1928–29	44	19	16	9	47	72	63	6th
1927–28	44	19	19	6	44	88	79	7th
1926–27	44	12	28	4	28	76	105	10th L
	2,770	1,240	1,064	466	2,946	7,854	7,297	

Los Angeles

Season	Games	Won	Lost	Tied	Points	Goals for	Goals against	Position
1971–72	78	20	49	9	49	206	305	13th
1970–71	78	25	40	13	63	239	303	9th
1969–70	76	14	52	10	38	168	290	12th L
1968–69	76	24	42	10	58	185	260	10th
1967–68	74	31	33	10	72	200	224	7th
	382	114	216	52	280	998	1,382	

Minnesota

Season	Games	Won	Lost	Tied	Points	Goals for	Goals against	Position
1971–72	78	37	29	12	86	212	191	5th
1970–71	78	28	34	16	72	191	223	8th
1969–70	76	19	35	22	60	224	257	9th
1968–69	76	18	43	15	51	189	270	12th L
1967–68	74	27	32	15	69	191	226	9th
	382	129	173	80	338	1,007	1,167	

New York Rangers

Season	Games	Won	Lost	Tied	Points	Goals for	Goals against	Position
1971–72	78	48	17	13	109	317	192	2nd
1970–71	78	49	18	11	109	259	177	2nd
1969–70	76	38	22	16	92	246	189	4th
1968–69	76	41	26	9	91	231	196	3rd
1967–68	74	39	23	12	90	226	183	2nd
1966–67	70	30	28	12	72	188	189	4th
1965–66	70	18	41	11	47	195	261	6th L
1964–65	70	20	38	12	52	179	246	5th
1963–64	70	22	38	10	54	186	242	5th
1962–63	70	22	36	12	56	211	233	5th
1961–62	70	26	32	12	64	195	207	4th
1960–61	70	22	38	10	54	204	248	5th
1959–60	70	17	38	15	49	187	247	6th L
1958–59	70	26	32	12	64	201	217	5th
1957–58	70	32	25	13	77	195	188	2nd
1956–57	70	26	30	14	66	184	227	4th
1955–56	70	32	28	10	74	204	203	3rd
1954–55	70	17	35	18	52	150	210	5th
1953–54	70	29	31	10	68	161	182	5th
1952–53	70	17	37	16	50	152	211	6th L
1951–52	70	23	34	13	59	192	219	5th
1950–51	70	20	29	21	61	169	201	5th
1949–50	70	28	31	11	67	170	189	4th
1948–49	60	18	31	11	47	133	172	6th L
1947–48	60	21	26	13	55	176	201	4th
1946–47	60	22	32	6	50	167	186	5th
1945–46	50	13	28	9	35	144	191	6th L
1944–45	50	11	29	10	32	154	247	6th L
1943–44	50	6	39	5	17	162	310	6th L
1942–43	50	11	31	8	30	161	253	6th L
1941–42	48	29	17	2	60	177	143	1st
1940–41	48	21	19	8	50	143	125	4th
1939–40	48	27	11	10	64	136	77	2nd
1938–39	48	26	16	6	58	149	105	2nd
1937–38	48	27	15	6	60	149	96	2nd
1936–37	48	19	20	9	47	117	106	6th
1935–36	48	19	17	12	50	91	96	6th
1934–35	48	22	20	6	50	137	139	5th
1933–34	48	21	19	8	50	120	113	5th

Season	Games	Won	Lost	Tied	Points	Goals for	Goals against	Position
1932–33	48	23	17	8	54	135	107	4th
1931–32	48	23	17	8	54	134	112	2nd
1930–31	44	19	16	9	47	106	87	5th
1929–30	44	17	17	10	44	136	143	6th
1928–29	44	21	13	10	52	72	65	3rd
1927–28	44	19	16	9	47	94	79	5th
1926–27	44	25	13	6	56	95	72	3rd
	2,770	1,102	1,186	482	2,686	7,690	8,082	

Oakland

Season	Games	Won	Lost	Tied	Points	Goals for	Goals against	Position
1971–72	78	21	39	18	60	216	288	11th
1970–71	78	20	53	5	45	199	320	14th L
1969–70	76	22	40	14	58	169	243	10th
1968–69	76	29	36	11	69	219	251	8th
1967–68	74	15	42	17	47	153	219	12th L
	382	107	210	65	279	956	1,321	

Philadelphia Flyers

Season	Games	Won	Lost	Tied	Points	Goals for	Goals against	Position
1971–72	78	26	38	14	66	200	236	10th
1970–71	78	28	33	17	73	207	225	7th
1969–70	76	17	35	24	58	197	225	11th
1968–69	76	20	35	21	61	174	225	9th
1967–68	74	31	32	11	73	173	179	6th
	382	122	173	87	331	951	1,090	

Pittsburgh Penguins

Season	Games	Won	Lost	Tied	Points	Goals for	Goals against	Position
1971–72	78	26	38	14	66	220	258	9th
1970–71	78	21	37	20	62	221	240	11th
1969–70	76	26	38	12	64	182	238	8th
1968–69	76	20	45	11	51	189	252	11th
1967–68	74	27	34	13	67	195	216	10th
	382	120	192	70	310	1,007	1,204	

St. Louis Blues

Season	Games	Won	Lost	Tied	Points	Goals for	Goals against	Position
1971–72	78	28	39	11	67	208	247	8th
1970–71	78	34	25	19	87	223	208	5th
1969–70	76	37	27	12	86	224	179	6th
1968–69	76	37	25	14	88	204	157	4th
1967–68	74	27	31	16	70	177	191	8th
	382	163	147	72	398	1,036	982	

Toronto

Season	Games	Won	Lost	Tied	Points	Goals for	Goals against	Position
1971–72	78	33	31	14	80	209	208	6th
1970–71	78	37	33	8	82	248	211	6th
1969–70	76	29	34	13	71	222	242	7th
1968–69	76	35	26	15	85	234	217	5th
1967–68	74	33	31	10	76	209	176	5th
1966–67	70	32	27	11	75	204	211	3rd
1965–66	70	34	25	11	79	208	187	3rd
1964–65	70	30	26	14	74	204	173	4th
1963–64	70	33	25	12	78	192	172	3rd
1962–63	70	35	23	12	82	221	180	1st
1961–62	70	37	22	11	85	232	180	2nd
1960–61	70	39	19	12	90	234	176	2nd
1959–60	70	35	26	9	79	199	195	2nd
1958–59	70	27	32	11	65	189	201	4th
1957–58	70	21	38	11	53	192	226	6th L
1956–57	70	21	34	15	57	174	192	5th
1955–56	70	24	33	13	61	153	181	4th
1954–55	70	24	24	22	70	147	135	3rd
1953–54	70	32	24	14	78	152	131	3rd
1952–53	70	27	30	13	67	156	167	5th
1951–52	70	29	25	16	74	168	157	3rd
1950–51	70	41	16	13	95	212	138	2nd
1949–50	70	31	27	12	74	176	173	3rd
1948–49	60	22	25	13	57	147	161	4th
1947–48	60	32	15	13	77	182	143	1st
1946–47	60	31	19	10	72	209	172	2nd
1945–46	50	19	24	7	45	174	185	5th
1944–45	50	24	22	4	52	183	161	3rd
1943–44	50	23	23	4	50	214	174	3rd
1942–43	50	22	19	9	53	198	159	3rd
1941–42	48	27	18	3	57	158	136	2nd
1940–41	48	28	14	6	62	145	99	2nd
1939–40	48	25	17	6	56	134	110	3rd
1938–39	48	19	20	9	47	114	107	3rd
1937–38	48	24	15	9	57	151	127	3rd
1936–37	48	22	21	5	49	119	115	5th
1935–36	48	23	19	6	52	126	106	3rd
1934–35	48	30	14	4	64	157	111	1st
1933–34	48	26	13	9	61	174	119	1st
1932–33	48	24	18	6	54	119	111	3rd
1931–32	48	23	18	7	53	155	127	3rd
1930–31	44	22	13	9	53	118	99	3rd
1929–30	44	17	21	6	40	116	124	7th
1928–29	44	21	18	5	47	85	69	5th
1927–28	44	18	18	8	44	89	88	8th
1926–27	44	15	24	5	35	79	94	8th
1925–26	36	12	21	3	27	92	114	6th
1924–25	30	19	11	0	38	90	84	2nd
1923–24	24	10	14	0	20	59	85	3rd
1922–23	24	13	10	1	27	82	88	3rd

Season	Games	Won	Lost	Tied	Points	Goals for	Goals against	Position
1921–22	24	13	10	1	27	98	97	2nd
1920–21	24	15	9	0	30	105	100	1st
1919–20	24	12	12	0	24	119	106	3rd
1918–19	18	5	13	0	10	65	92	3rd L
1917–18	22	13	9	0	26	108	109	2nd
	2,996	1,368	1,168	460	3,196	8,699	8,001	

Vancouver Canucks

Season	Games	Won	Lost	Tied	Points	Goals for	Goals against	Position
1971–72	78	20	50	8	48	203	297	14th L
1970–71	78	24	46	8	56	229	296	12th
	156	44	96	16	104	432	593	

Mont. Maroons

Season	Games	Won	Lost	Tied	Points	Goals for	Goals against	Position
1937–38	48	12	30	6	30	101	149	8th L
1936–37	48	22	17	9	53	126	110	4th
1935–36	48	22	16	10	54	114	106	2nd
1934–35	48	24	19	5	53	123	92	4th
1933–34	48	19	18	11	49	117	122	6th
1932–33	48	22	20	6	50	135	119	5th
1931–32	48	19	22	7	45	142	139	6th
1930–31	44	20	18	6	46	105	106	6th
1929–30	44	23	16	5	51	141	114	2nd
1928–29	44	15	20	9	39	67	65	8th
1927–28	44	24	14	6	54	96	77	2nd
1926–27	44	20	20	4	44	71	68	5th
1925–26	36	20	11	5	45	91	73	2nd
1924–25	30	9	19	2	20	45	65	5th
	622	271	260	91	633	1,474	1,405	

Mont. Wanderers

Season	Games	Won	Lost	Tied	Points	Goals for	Goals against	Position
1917–18	6	1	5	0	2	17	35	4th L

Quebec

Season	Games	Won	Lost	Tied	Points	Goals for	Goals against	Position
1919–20	24	4	20	0	8	91	177	4th L

Hamilton

Season	Games	Won	Lost	Tied	Points	Goals for	Goals against	Position
1924–25	30	19	10	1	39	90	60	1st
1923–24	24	9	15	0	18	63	68	4th L
1922–23	24	6	18	0	12	81	110	4th L
1921–22	24	7	17	0	14	88	105	4th L
1920–21	24	6	18	0	12	92	132	4th L
	126	47	78	1	95	414	475	

N.Y. Americans

Season	Games	Won	Lost	Tied	Points	Goals for	Goals against	Position
1941–42	48	16	29	3	35	133	175	7th L
1940–41	48	8	29	11	27	99	186	7th L
1939–40	48	15	29	4	34	106	140	6th
1938–39	48	17	21	10	44	119	157	4th
1937–38	48	19	18	11	49	110	111	4th
1936–37	48	15	29	4	34	122	161	8th L
1935–36	48	16	25	7	39	109	122	7th
1934–35	48	12	27	9	33	100	142	8th L
1933–34	48	15	23	10	40	104	132	8th L
1932–33	48	15	22	11	41	91	118	8th L
1931–32	48	16	24	8	40	95	142	8th L
1930–31	44	18	16	10	46	76	74	7th
1929–30	44	14	25	5	33	113	161	9th
1928–29	44	19	13	12	50	53	53	4th
1927–28	44	11	27	6	28	63	128	9th
1926–27	44	17	25	2	36	82	91	7th
1925–26	36	12	20	4	28	68	89	5th
	784	255	402	127	637	1,643	2,182	

Ottawa

Season	Games	Won	Lost	Tied	Points	Goals for	Goals against	Position
1933–34	48	13	29	6	32	115	143	9th L
1932–33	48	11	27	10	32	88	131	9th L
1931–32	No competition							
1930–31	44	10	30	4	24	91	142	9th
1929–30	44	21	15	8	50	138	118	4th
1928–29	44	14	17	13	41	54	67	7th
1927–28	44	20	14	10	50	78	57	4th
1926–27	44	30	10	4	64	86	69	1st
1925–26	36	24	8	4	52	77	42	1st
1924–25	30	17	12	1	35	83	66	4th
1923–24	24	16	8	0	32	74	54	1st
1922–23	24	14	9	1	29	77	54	1st
1921–22	24	14	8	2	30	106	84	1st
1920–21	24	14	10	0	28	97	75	2nd
1919–20	24	19	5	0	38	121	64	1st
1918–19	18	12	6	0	24	71	54	1st
1917–18	22	9	13	0	18	102	114	3rd
	542	258	221	63	579	1,458	1,334	

Philadelphia Quakers

Season	Games	Won	Lost	Tied	Points	Goals for	Goals against	Position
1930–31	44	4	36	4	12	76	184	10th L

Pittsburgh Pirates

Season	Games	Won	Lost	Tied	Points	Goals for	Goals against	Position
1929–30	44	5	36	3	13	102	185	10th L
1928–29	44	9	36	3	13	46	80	9th
1927–28	44	19	17	8	46	67	76	6th
1926–27	44	15	26	3	33	79	108	9th
1925–26	36	19	16	1	39	82	70	3rd
	212	67	122	23	157	376	519	

St. Louis Eagles

Season	Games	Won	Lost	Tied	Points	Goals for	Goals against	Position
1934–35	48	11	31	6	28	86	144	9th L

Composite Club Totals

Clubs	Seasons	Games	Won	Lost	Tied	Points	Goals for	Goals against
Montreal Canadiens	55	2,996	1,503	1,011	482	3,488	9,166	7,522
Toronto	55	2,996	1,368	1,168	460	3,196	8,699	8,001
Boston Bruins	48	2,836	1,242	1,143	451	2,935	8,332	8,100
Chicago Black Hawks	46	2,770	1,080	1,256	434	2,594	7,529	7,936
Detroit	46	2,770	1,240	1,064	466	2,946	7,854	7,297
New York Rangers	46	2,770	1,102	1,186	482	2,686	7,690	8,082
New York Americans	17	784	255	402	127	637	1,643	2,182
Ottawa Senators	16	542	258	221	63	579	1,458	1,334
Montreal Maroons	14	622	271	260	91	633	1,474	1,405
Los Angeles Kings	5	382	114	216	52	280	998	1,382
Minnesota North Stars	5	382	129	173	80	338	1,007	1,167
Oakland	5	382	107	210	65	279	956	1,321
Philadelphia Flyers	5	382	122	173	87	331	951	1,090
Pittsburgh Penguins	5	382	120	192	70	310	1,007	1,204
St. Louis Blues	5	382	163	147	72	398	1,036	982
Pittsburgh Pirates	5	212	67	122	23	157	376	519
Hamilton Tigers	5	126	47	78	1	95	414	475
Buffalo Sabres	2	156	40	82	34	114	420	580
Vancouver Canucks	2	156	44	96	16	104	432	593
St. Louis Eagles	1	48	11	31	6	28	86	144
Philadelphia Quakers	1	44	4	36	4	12	76	184
Quebec Bulldogs	1	24	4	20	0	8	91	177
Montreal Wanderers	1	6	1	5	0	2	17	35
		11,075*	9,292	9,292	1,783*		61,712	61,712

* These figures are arrived at by totalling the number of games played by each club and dividing by two. Obviously two clubs participated in each game played and in each tie game.

5
Register of Players

Inactive Players (excluding goaltenders)   **171**
Active Players (excluding goaltenders)   **228**

Inactive Players (Excluding Goaltenders)

This section includes players whose careers ended prior to the 1968–69 season. For players active after 1968–69 see page 228.

Abbreviations

The following appear after names of players:

LW—Left Wing
RW—Right Wing
C—Center
D—Defense
SL—Shoots left
SR—Shoots right

The following appear as headings:

Sea.—Season
Ga.—Games
Go.—Goals
A.—Assists
P.—Points
PM.—Penalties in Minutes

A blank column indicates that information is unavailable.

Sea. Club	Ga.	Go.	A.	P.	PM.

ABBOTT, REGINALD, C-SL

Sea. Club	Ga.	Go.	A.	P.	PM.
1952-53 Montreal	3	0	0	0	0

ABEL, CLARENCE J., D-SL
Born: Sault Ste. Marie, Mich. May 28, 1900

Sea. Club	Ga.	Go.	A.	P.	PM.
1926-27 N. Y. Rangers		8	4	12	78
1927-28 "		0	1	1	28
1928-29 "		3	1	4	41
1929-30 Chicago		3	3	6	42
1930-31 "		0	1	1	45
1931-32 "		4	3	7	34
1932-33 "		0	4	4	63
1933-34 "		2	1	3	28
8 Years		20	18	38	359

ABEL, GERALD SCOTT, LW
Born: Detroit, Mich. Dec. 25, 1944

Sea. Club	Ga.	Go.	A.	P.	PM.
1966-67 Detroit	1	0	0	0	0

ABEL, SIDNEY GERALD, LW & C-SL
Born: Melville, Sask. Feb. 22, 1918

Sea. Club	Ga.	Go.	A.	P.	PM.
1938-39 Detroit	15	1	1	2	0
1939-40 "	24	1	5	6	4
1940-41 "	47	11	22	33	29
1941-42 "	48	18	31	49	45
1942-43 "	49	18	24	42	33
1943-45 Military Ser.					
1945-46 Detroit	7	0	2	2	0
1946-47 "	60	19	29	48	29
1947-48 "	60	14	30	44	69
1948-49 "	60	*28	26	54	49
1949-50 "	69	34	35	69	46
1950-51 "	69	23	38	61	30
1951-52 "	62	17	36	53	32
1952-53 Chicago	39	5	4	9	6
1953-54 "	3	0	0		4
14 Years	612	189	283	472	376

*League Leader
1941-42 2nd All-Star Team
1948-49 1st All-Star Team, Hart Trophy
1949-50 " " " "
1950-51 2nd " " "
1969 Hall of Fame

ACHTYMICHUK, EUGENE EDWARD, C-SL
Born: Lamont, Alb. Sept. 7, 1932

Sea. Club	Ga.	Go.	A.	P.	PM.
1951-52 Montreal	1	0	0	0	0
1956-57 "	3	0	0	0	0
1957-58 "	16	3	5	8	2
1958-59 Detroit	12	0	0	0	0
4 Years	32	3	5	8	2

ADAM, DOUGLAS P. LW

Sea. Club	Ga.	Go.	A.	P.	PM.
1949-50 New York	4	0	1	1	0

ADAMS, JOHN E. LW-SL
Born: Calgary, Alb. May 5, 1920

Sea. Club	Ga.	Go.	A.	P.	PM.
1940-41 Montreal		6	12	18	11

ADAMS, JOHN JAMES C-SR
Born: Fort William, Ont. June 14, 1895

Sea. Club	Ga.	Go.	A.	P.	PM.
1917-18 Toronto		0		0	
1918-19 "		3	3	6	17
1922-23 "		19	9	28	42
1923-24 "		13	3	16	49
1924-25 "		21	8	29	66
1925-26 "		21	5	26	52
1926-27 Ottawa		5	1	6	66
7 Years		82	29	111	292

1959 Hall of Fame

ADAMS, STEWART LW

Sea. Club	Ga.	Go.	A.	P.	PM.
1929-30 Chicago		4	6	10	16
1930-31 "		5	13	18	18
1931-32 "		0	5	5	26
1932-33 Toronto		0	2	2	0
4 Years		9	26	35	60

AILSBY, LLOYD D
Born: Vesper, Sask.

Sea. Club	Ga.	Go.	A.	P.	PM.
1951-52 New York Rangers	3	0	0	0	2

ALBRIGHT, CLINTON H. RW-SL

Sea. Club	Ga.	Go.	A.	P.	PM.
1948-49 N. Y. Rangers	59	14	5	19	19

ALDCORN, GARY WILLIAM LW-SL
Born: Shaunavon, Sask. Mar. 7, 1935

Sea. Club	Ga.	Go.	A.	P.	PM.
1956-57 Toronto	22	5	1	6	4
1957-58 "	59	10	14	24	12
1958-59 "	5	0	3	3	2
1959-60 Detroit	70	22	29	51	32
1960-61 Detroit-Boston	70	4	9	13	28
5 Years	226	41	56	97	78

ALEXANDRE, ARTHUR, C

Sea. Club	Ga.	Go.	A.	P.	PM.
1931-32 Montreal Canadiens		0	2	2	8

ALLEN, COURTNEY KEITH D
Born: Saskatoon, Sask. Aug. 21, 1923

Sea. Club	Ga.	Go.	A.	P.	PM.
1953-54 Detroit	10	0	4	4	2
1954-55 "	18	0	0	0	6
2 Years	28	0	4	4	8

ALLEN, GEORGE LW-SL
Born: Bayfield, N. Bruns. July 27, 1914

Sea. Club	Ga.	Go.	A.	P.	PM.
1938-39 N. Y. Rangers		6	6	12	10
1939-40 Chicago		10	12	22	26
1940-41 "		14	17	31	22
1941-42 "	43	7	13	20	31
1942-43 "	47	10	14	24	26
1943-44 "	45	17	24	41	36
1945-46 "	44	11	15	26	16
1946-47 Montreal	49	7	14	21	12
8 Years		82	115	197	179

ALLEN, VIVAN M. RW
Born: Bayfield, N. Bruns.

Sea. Club	Ga.	Go.	A.	P.	PM.
1940-41 N. Y. Americans		0	1	1	0

ALLUM, WILLIAM D
Born: Winnipeg, Man.

Sea. Club	Ga.	Go.	A.	P.	PM.
1940-41 N. Y. Rangers	1	0	1	1	0

ANDERSON, DALE NORMAN D-SL
Born: Regina, Sask. Mar. 5, 1932

Sea. Club	Ga.	Go.	A.	P.	PM.
1956-57 Detroit	13	0	0	0	6

ANDERSON, JAMES WILLIAM LW-SL
Born: Pembroke, Ont., Dec. 1, 1930

Sea. Club	Ga.	Go.	A.	P.	PM.
1967-68 Los Angeles	7	1	2	3	2

ANDERSON, THOMAS LINTON, LW&D-SL
Born: Edinburgh, Scotland, July 9, 1911

Sea. Club	Ga.	Go.	A.	P.	PM.
1934-35 Detroit		5	2	7	16
1935-36 N. Y. Americans		3	2	5	20
1936-37 " " "		10	15	25	24
1937-38 " " "		4	21	25	22
1938-39 " " "		13	27	40	14
1939-40 " " "		12	19	31	22
1940-41 " " "		3	12	15	8
1941-42 Brooklyn		12	29	41	64
8 Years		62	127	189	190

1941-42 1st All-Star Team, Hart Trophy

ANDREWS, LLOYD

Sea. Club	Ga.	Go.	A.	P.	PM.
1921-22 Toronto	11	0	0	0	0
1922-23 "	23	5	4	9	10
1923-24 "	12	2	1	3	0
1924-25 "	7	1	0	1	0
4 Years	53	8	5	13	10

ANSLOW, HUBERT W. LW

Sea. Club	Ga.	Go.	A.	P.	PM.
1947-48 New York	2	0	0	0	0

APPS, CHARLES JOSEPH SYLVANUS C-SL
Born: Paris, Ontario, Jan. 18, 1915

Sea. Club	Ga.	Go.	A.	P.	PM.
1936-37 Toronto		16	*29	45	10
1937-38 "		21	*29	50	9
1938-39 "		15	25	40	4
1939-40 "		13	17	30	5
1940-41 "		20	24	44	6
1941-42 "		18	23	41	0
1942-43 "	29	23	17	40	2
1943-45 Military Ser.					
1945-46 Toronto	40	24	16	40	2
1946-47 "	54	25	24	49	6
1947-48 "	55	26	27	53	12
10 Years		201	231	432	56

*League Leader
1936-37 Frank Calder Trophy
1937-38 2nd All-Star Team
1938-39 1st All-Star Team
1940-41 2nd " " "

(continued)

Sea. Club	Ga.	Go.	A.	P.	PM.
1941-42 1st " " ":Lady Byng Trophy					
1942-43 2nd " " "					
1961 Hall of Fame					
ARBOUR, AMOS LW					
Born: Victoria Harbour, Ont.					
1918-19 Montreal	1	0	0	0	0
1919-20 "	20	22	4	26	10
1920-21 "	22	14	3	17	40
1921-22 Hamilton	23	8	3	11	6
1922-23 "	23	6	1	7	6
1923-24 Toronto	20	1	2	3	4
6 Years	109	51	13	64	66
ARBOUR, ERNEST LW					
1926-27 Pittsburgh		7	8	15	10
1927-28 Pitts.-Chicago		5	5	10	32
1928-29 Chicago		3	4	7	32
1929-30 "		10	8	18	26
1930-31 "		3	3	6	12
5 Years		28	28	56	112
ARBOUR, JOHN A. D					
1926-27 Detroit		4	1	5	46
1928-29 Toronto		1	0	1	10
2 Years		5	1	6	56
ARMSTRONG, MURRAY A. C-SL					
Born: Manor, Sask. Jan. 1, 1916					
1938-39 Toronto		0	1	1	0
1939-40 N. Y. Americans		16	20	36	12
1940-41 " " "		10	14	24	6
1941-42 Brooklyn	45	6	22	28	15
1943-44 Detroit	28	12	22	34	4
1944-45 "	50	15	24	39	21
1945-46 "	40	8	18	26	4
7 Years		67	121	188	62
ARMSTRONG, NORMAN LW&D SL					
Born: Owen Sound, Ont., Oct. 17, 1938					
1962-63 Toronto	7	1	1	2	2
ARMSTRONG, ROBERT RICHARD D-SR					
Born: Toronto, Ont. Apr. 7, 1931					
1950-51 Boston	2	0	0	0	2
1952-53 "	55	0	8	8	45
1953-54 "	64	2	10	12	81
1954-55 "	57	1	3	4	38
1955-56 "	68	0	12	12	122
1956-57 "	57	1	15	16	79
1957-58 "	47	1	4	5	66
1958-59 "	60	1	9	10	50
1959-60 "	69	5	14	19	96
1960-61 "	54	0	10	10	72
1961-62 "	9	2	1	3	20
11 Years	542	13	86	99	671
ARUNDEL, JOHN O. RW SL					
Born: Winnipeg, Man.					
1949-50 Toronto	3	0	0	0	9
ASHWORTH, FRANK LW					
1946-47 Chicago	18	5	4	9	2
ASMUNDSON, OSCAR C					
Born: Red Deer, Alb.					
1932-33 N. Y. Rangers		5	10	15	20
1933-34 "		2	6	8	8
1934-35 St. Louis		4	7	11	2
3 Years		11	23	34	30
ATANAS, WALTER RW-SR					
1944-45 N. Y. Rangers	49	13	8	21	40
ATTWELL, RONALD ALLAN RW-SR					
Born: Humber Summit, Ont. Feb. 9, 1935					
1967-68 St. Louis-New York	22	1	7	8	8
AUBUCHON, OSCAR LW-SL					
Born: St. Hyacinthe, Que.					
1942-43 Boston	3	3	0	3	0
1943-44 Boston–New York	47	17	12	29	4
2 Years	50	20	12	32	4

Sea. Club	Ga.	Go.	A.	P.	PM.
AURIE, LAWRENCE RW-SR					
Born: Sudbury, Ont. 1905					
1927-28 Detroit	13	3	16	43	
1928-29 "	1	1	2	26	
1929-30 "	14	5	19	28	
1930-31 "	12	6	18	23	
1931-32 "	13	8	21	18	
1932-33 "	12	11	23	25	
1933-34 "	16	19	35	36	
1934-35 "	17	29	46	24	
1935-36 "	16	18	34	17	
1936-37 "	*23	20	43	20	
1937-38 "	10	9	19	19	
1938-39 "	1	0	1	0	
12 Years	148	129	277	279	
*League Leader					
1936-37 1st All-Star Team					
AYRES, THOMAS VERNON D					
Born: Toronto, Ont.					
1930-31 N. Y. Americans		2	1	3	54
1931-32 " " "		2	4	6	82
1932-33 " " "		0	0	0	97
1933-34 Mont. Maroons		0	0	0	19
1934-35 St. Louis		2	2	4	60
1935-36 N. Y. Rangers		0	4	4	38
6 Years		6	11	17	350
BABANDO, PETER JOSEPH LW-SL					
Born: Braeburn, Penna. May 10, 1925					
1947-48 Boston	60	23	11	34	52
1948-49 "	58	19	14	33	34
1949-50 Detroit	56	6	6	12	25
1950-51 Chicago	70	18	19	37	36
1951-52 "	49	11	14	25	29
1952-53 "-N. York	58	9	9	18	18
6 Years	351	86	73	159	194
BACKOR, PETER D					
1944-45 Toronto	36	4	5	9	6
BAILEY, IRVIN W. RW-SR					
Born: Bracebridge, Ont. July 3, 1903					
1926-27 Toronto		15	13	28	82
1927-28 "		9	3	12	72
1928-29 "		*22	10	*32	78
1929-30 "		22	21	43	69
1930-31 "		23	19	42	46
1931-32 "		8	5	13	62
1932-33 "		10	8	18	52
1933-34 "		2	3	5	11
8 Years		111	82	193	472
*League Leader					
BAILEY, ROBERT ALLEN RW-SR					
Born: Kenora, Ont. May 29, 1931					
1953-54 Toronto	48	2	7	9	70
1954-55 "	32	4	2	6	52
1955-56 "	6	0	0	0	6
1957-58 Chicago-Detroit	63	9	12	21	79
4 Years	149	15	21	36	207
BALDWIN, DOUGLAS D-SR					
1945-46 Toronto	15	0	1	1	6
1946-47 Detroit	4	0	0	0	0
1947-48 Chicago	5	0	0	0	2
3 Years	24	0	1	1	8
BALFOUR, EARL FREDERICK LW-SL					
Born: Toronto, Ont. Jan. 4, 1933					
1951-52 Toronto	3	0	0	0	2
1953-54 "	17	0	1	1	6
1955-56 "	59	14	5	19	40
1957-58 "	1	0	0	0	0
1958-59 Chicago	70	10	8	18	10
1959-60 "	70	3	5	8	16
1960-61 "	68	3	3	6	4
7 Years	288	30	22	52	78

Sea. Club	Ga.	Go.	A.	P.	PM.
BALFOUR, MURRAY LEWIS RW-SR					
Born: Regina, Sask. Aug. 24, 1936					
1956-57 Montreal	2	0	0	0	2
1957-58 "	3	1	1	2	4
1959-60 Chicago	61	18	12	30	55
1960-61 "	70	21	27	48	123
1961-62 "	49	15	15	30	72
1962-63 "	65	10	23	33	75
1963-64 "	41	2	10	12	36
1964-65 Boston	15	0	2	2	26
8 Years	306	67	90	157	393
BALIUK, STANLEY C-SL					
Born: Port Arthur, Ont. Oct. 5, 1935					
1959-60 Boston	7	0	0	0	2
BARBE, ANDRE J. RW					
1950-51 Toronto	1	0	0	0	2
BARILKO, WILLIAM D-SR					
Born: Timmins, Ont.					
1946-47 Toronto	18	3	7	10	33
1947-48 "	57	5	9	14	*147
1948-49 "	60	5	4	9	95
1949-50 "	59	7	10	17	85
1950-51 "	58	6	6	12	96
5 Years	252	26	36	62	456
*League Leader					
BARKLEY, NORMAN DOUGLAS D-SR					
Born: Lethbridge, Alb. Jan. 6, 1937					
1957-58 Chicago	3	0	0	0	0
1959-60 "	3	0	0	0	2
1962-63 Detroit	70	3	24	27	78
1963-64 "	67	11	21	32	115
1964-65 "	67	5	20	25	122
1965-66 "	43	5	15	20	65
6 Years	253	24	80	104	382
BARRY, EDWARD F					
Born: U. S. A.					
1946-47 Boston	19	1	3	4	2
BARRY, MARTIN J. C-SL					
Born: St. Gabriel, Que. Dec. 8, 1905					
1927-28 N. Y. Americans	1	0	1	1	2
1929-30 Boston	18	15	33	33	34
1930-31 "	20	11	31	26	
1931-32 "	21	17	38	22	
1932-33 "	24	13	37	40	
1933-34 "	27	12	39	12	
1934-35 "	20	20	40	33	
1935-36 Detroit	21	19	40	16	
1936-37 "	17	27	44	6	
1937-38 "	9	20	29	34	
1938-39 "	13	28	41	4	
1939-40 Montreal	4	10	14	2	
12 Years	195	192	387	231	
1936-37 1st All-Star Team, Lady Byng Trophy					
1965 Hall of Fame					
BARRY, WILLIAM R. C					
1951-52 Boston	18	1	2	3	6
BARTLETT, JAMES BAKER LW-SL					
Born: Verdun, Que. May 27, 1932					
1954-55 Montreal	2	0	0	0	4
1955-56 New York	12	0	1	1	8
1958-59 " "	70	11	9	20	118
1959-60 " "	44	8	4	12	48
1960-61 Boston	63	15	9	24	95
5 Years	191	34	23	57	273
BARTON, CLIFFORD J. RW					
Born: Port Arthur, Ont.					
1929-30 Pittsburgh		4	2	6	4
1930-31 Phila.		6	7	13	18
1939-40 N. Y. Rangers		0	0	0	0
3 Years		10	9	19	22
BATHGATE, FRANK D. C					
1952-53 New York	2	0	0	0	2
BAUER, ROBERT T. RW-SR					
Born: Waterloo, Ont. Feb. 16, 1915					
1936-37 Boston		1	0	1	0
1937-38 "		20	14	34	9
1938-39 "		13	18	31	4
1939-40 "		17	26	43	2
1940-41 "		17	22	39	2
1941-42 "		13	22	35	11
1942-45 Military Service					
1945-46 Boston	39	11	10	21	4
1946-47 "	58	30	24	54	4
1951-52 "	1	1	1	2	0
9 Years		123	137	260	36
1938-39 2nd All-Star Team					
1939-40 " " " " ; Lady Byng Trophy					
1940-41 " " " " ; " " "					
1946-47 " " " " ; " " "					
BEATTIE, JOHN C & LW-SL					
Born: Ibstock, England Oct. 2, 1907					
1930-31 Boston		10	11	21	25
1932-33 "		8	12	20	12
1933-34 "		9	13	22	26
1934-35 "		9	18	27	27
1935-36 "		14	18	32	27
1936-37 "		8	7	15	10
1937-38 Detroit-N. Y. Americans		4	6	10	5
1938-39 N. Y. Americans		0	0	0	5
8 Years		62	85	147	137
BECKETT, ROBERT OWEN C&LW-SL					
Born: Unionville, Ont. April 8, 1936					
1956-57 Boston	18	0	3	3	2
1957-58 "	9	0	0	0	2
1961-62 "	34	7	2	9	14
1963-64 "	7	0	1	1	0
4 Years	68	7	6	13	18
BEDARD, JAMES L. D					
1949-50 Chicago	· 6	0	0	0	2
1950-51 "	17	1	1	2	6
2 Years	23	1	1	2	8
BEHLING, CLARENCE RICHARD D-SR					
1940-41 Detroit		0	0	0	0
1942-43 "	2	1	0	1	2
2 Years		1	0	1	2
BEISLER, FRANK D					
Born: New Haven, Conn.					
1936-37 N. Y. Americans		0	0	0	0
BELISLE, DANIEL GEORGE LW—SL					
Born: South Porcupine, Ont. May 9, 1937					
1960-61 New York	4	2	0	2	0
BELL, HARRY D					
1946-47 New York	1	0	1	1	0
BELL, JOSEPH A. LW-SL					
1942-43 New York	15	2	5	7	6
1946-47 New York	47	6	4	10	12
2 Years	62	8	9	17	18
BELL, WILLIAM E.					
1917-18 Mont. Wanderers-Mont. Canad.	8	1	0	1	0
1918-19 Montreal Canadiens	1	0	0	0	0
1920-21 " "	4	0	0	0	0
1921-22 " " -Ottawa	23	2	1	3	4
1922-23 " "	15	0	0	0	0
1923-24 " "	10	0	0	0	0
6 Years	61	3	1	4	4

Sea. Club	Ga.	Go.	A.	P.	PM.
BELLEFEUILLE, PETER RW					
1925-26 Toronto		14	2	16	22
1926-27 Toronto-Detroit		6	0	6	26
1928-29 Detroit		1	0	1	0
1929-30		4	2	6	10
4 Years		25	4	29	58
BELLEMER, ANDREW D					
Born: Penetang, Ont.					
1932-33 Mont. Maroons		0	0	0	0
BEND, JOHN LINTHWAITE C					
1942-43 New York	8	3	1	4	2
BENNETT, FRANK D					
1943-44 Detroit	7	0	1	1	2
BENNETT, MAX RW					
Born: Cobalt, Ont.					
1935-36 Mont. Canadiens		0	0	0	0
BENOIT, JOSEPH RW					
Born: St. Albert, Alb.					
1940-41 Montreal		16	16	32	32
1941-42 "	46	20	16	36	27
1942-43 "	49	30	27	57	23
1945-46 "	39	9	10	19	8
1946-47 "	6	0	0	0	4
5 Years		75	69	144	94
BENSON, ROBERT D					
1924-25 Boston	8	0	1	1	4
BENSON, WILLIAM L. C					
Born: Winnipeg, Man.					
1940-41 N. Y. Americans		3	4	7	4
1941-42 Brooklyn	45	8	21	29	31
2 Years		11	25	36	35
BENTLEY, DOUGLAS WAGNER LW&C-SL					
Born: Delisle, Sask. Sept. 3, 1916					
1939-40 Chicago		12	7	19	12
1940-41 "		8	20	28	12
1941-42 "	38	12	14	26	11
1942-43 "	50	*33	40	*73	18
1943-44 "	50	*38	39	77	22
1945-46 "	36	19	21	40	16
1946-47 "	52	21	34	55	18
1947-48 "	60	20	*37	57	16
1948-49 "	58	23	*43	66	38
1949-50 "	64	20	33	53	28
1950-51 "	44	9	23	32	20
1951-52 "	8	2	3	5	4
1953-54 New York	20	2	10	12	2
13 Years		219	324	543	217
*League Leader					
1942-43 1st All-Star Team					
1943-44 " " " "					
1946-47 " " " "					
1948-49 2nd All-Star Team					
1964 Hall of Fame					
BENTLEY, MAXWELL HERBERT LLOYD C-SL					
Born: Delisle, Sask. Mar. 1, 1920					
1940-41 Chicago	36	7	10	17	6
1941-42 "	39	13	17	30	2
1942-43 "	47	26	44	70	2
1945-46 "	47	31	30	*61	6
1946-47 "	60	29	43	*72	12
1947-48 Chicago-Toronto	59	26	28	54	14
1948-49 Toronto	60	19	22	41	18
1949-50 "	69	23	18	41	14
1950-51 "	67	21	41	62	34
1951-52 "	69	24	17	41	40
1952-53 "	36	12	11	23	16
1953-54 New York	57	14	18	32	15
12 Years	646	245	299	544	179
*League Leader					
1942-43 Lady Byng Trophy					
1945-46 1st All-Star Team; Hart Trophy					
1946-47 2nd All-Star Team					
1966 Hall of Fame					

Sea. Club	Ga.	Go.	A.	P.	PM.
BENTLEY, REGINALD RW-SL					
Born: Delisle, Sask.					
1942-43 Chicago	11	1	2	3	2
BERGDINON – –					
1925-26 Boston	2	0	0	0	0
BERLINQUETTE, LOUIS LW					
1917-18 Montreal Canadiens	20	2	0	2	
1918-19 "	18	5	3	8	9
1919-20 "	24	7	7	14	36
1920-21 "	24	12	*9	21	24
1921-22 "	24	12	5	17	8
1922-23 "	24	2	3	5	4
1924-25 Mont. Maroons	29	4	2	6	22
1925-26 Pittsburgh	30	0	0	0	8
8 Years	193	44	29	73	111
* League Leader					
BESLER, PHILIP R. RW-SR					
Born: Melville, Sask. 1911					
1938-39 Chicago-Detroit		1	4	5	18
BESSONE, PETER D-SL					
Born: Springfield, Mass.					
1937-38 Detroit		0	1	1	6
BETTIO, SILVIO ANGELO LW-SL					
Born: Copper Cliff, Ont. Dec. 1, 1928					
1949-50 Boston	44	9	12	21	32
BIONDA, JACK ARTHUR D-SL					
Born: Huntsville, Ont. Sept. 18, 1933					
1955-56 Toronto	13	0	1	1	18
1956-57 Boston	35	2	3	5	43
1957-58 "	42	1	4	5	50
1958-59 "	3	0	1	1	2
4 Years	93	3	9	12	113
BLACK, STEPHEN LW					
1949-50 Detroit	69	7	14	21	53
1950-51 Detroit-Chicago	44	4	6	10	24
2 Years	113	11	20	31	77
BLADE, HENRY G. C					
1946-47 Chicago	18	1	3	4	2
1947-48 "	6	1	0	1	0
2 Years	24	2	3	5	2
BLAINE, GARY JAMES LW-SR					
Born: St. Boniface, Man. Apr. 19, 1933					
1954-55 Montreal	1	0	0	0	0
BLAIR, ANDREW DRYDEN C-SL					
Born: Winnipeg, Man. 1908					
1928-29 Toronto		12	15	27	41
1929-30 "		11	10	21	27
1930-31 "		11	8	19	32
1931-32 "		9	14	23	35
1932-33 "		6	9	15	38
1933-34 "		14	9	23	35
1934-35 "		6	14	20	22
1935-36 "		5	4	9	60
1936-37 Chicago		0	3	3	33
9 Year•		74	86	160	323
BLAIR, CHARLES RW-SR					
Born: Scotland, July 23, 1928					
1948-49 Toronto	1	0	0	0	0
BLAIR, GEORGE C-SR					
Born: South Porcupine, Ont. Sept. 15, 1929					
1950-51 Toronto	2	0	0	0	0
BLAKE, FRANCIS J. D					
Born: Kingston, Ont.					
1934-35 St. Louis		1	1	2	2
1935-36 Toronto		0	0	0	2
2 Years		1	1	2	4
BLAKE, HECTOR LW-SL					
Born: Victoria Mines, Ont. Aug. 21, 1912					
1934-35 Mont. Maroons	3	0	0	0	0

(continued)

Sea.	Club	Ga.	Go.	A.	P.	PM.
1935-36	Mont. Canadiens		1	2	3	28
1936-37	" "		10	12	22	12
1937-38	" "		17	16	33	33
1938-39	" "		24	23	*47	10
1939-40	" "		17	19	36	48
1940-41	" "		12	20	32	49
1941-42	" "	48	17	28	45	29
1942-43	" "	48	23	36	59	26
1943-44	" "	41	26	33	59	10
1944-45	" "	49	29	38	67	25
1945-46	" "	50	29	21	50	2
1946-47	" "	60	21	29	50	6
1947-48	" "	32	9	15	24	4
14 Years			235	292	527	282

*League Leader

1937-38 2nd All-Star Team
1938-39 1st All-Star Team; Hart Trophy
1939-40 " " "
1944-45 1st All-Star Team
1945-46 2nd " " "; Lady Byng Trophy
1966 Hall of Fame

BLINCO, RUSSELL PERCIVAL C-SL
Born: Grand Mere, Que. Mar. 12, 1908

Sea.	Club	Ga.	Go.	A.	P.	PM.
1933-34	Mont. Maroons		14	9	23	2
1934-35	" "		13	14	27	4
1935-36	" "		13	10	23	10
1936-37	" "		6	12	18	2
1937-38	" "		10	9	19	4
1938-39	Chicago		3	12	15	2
6 Years			59	66	125	24

1933-34 Rookie of the Year

BODNAR, AUGUST C&RW-SR
Born: Fort William, Ont.

Sea.	Club	Ga.	Go.	A.	P.	PM.
1943-44	Toronto	50	22	40	62	18
1944-45	"	49	8	36	44	18
1945-46	"	49	14	23	37	14
1946-47	"	39	4	6	10	10
1947-48	Chicago	46	13	22	35	23
1948-49	"	59	19	26	45	14
1949-50	"	70	11	28	39	6
1950-51	"	44	8	12	20	8
1951-52	"	69	14	26	40	26
1952-53	"	66	16	13	29	26
1953-54	Chicago-Boston	59	9	18	27	30
1954-55	Boston	67	4	4	8	14
12 Years		667	142	254	396	207

1943-44 Calder Trophy

BOEHM, RONALD JOHN LW-SL
Born: Allan, Sask., Aug. 14, 1943

Sea.	Club	Ga.	Go.	A.	P.	PM.
1967-68	Oakland	16	2	1	3	10

BOESCH, GARTH VERNON D-SR
Born: Milestone, Sask. Oct. 8, 1920

Sea.	Club	Ga.	Go.	A.	P.	PM.
1946-47	Toronto	35	4	5	9	47
1947-48	"	45	2	7	9	52
1948-49	"	59	1	10	11	43
1949-50	"	58	?	6	8	63
4 Years		197	9	28	37	205

BOILEAU, MARC CLAUDE LW&C-SL
Born: Pointe Claire, Que. Sept. 3, 1932

Sea.	Club	Ga.	Go.	A.	P.	PM.
1961-62	Detroit	54	5	6	11	8

BOILEAU (Drinkwater), RENE

Sea.	Club	Ga.	Go.	A.	P.	PM.
1925-26	N. Y. Americans	7	0	0	0	0

BOLL, FRANK THORMAN LW-SL
Born: Fillmore, Sask. Mar. 6, 1911

Sea.	Club	Ga.	Go.	A.	P.	PM.
1933-34	Toronto		12	8	20	21
1934-35	"		14	4	18	4
1935-36	"		15	13	28	14
1936-37	"		6	3	9	12
1937-38	"		14	11	25	18
1939-40	N. Y. Americans		5	10	15	18
1940-41	" " "		12	14	26	16
1941-42	Brooklyn		11	15	26	23
1942-43	Boston	43	25	27	52	20
1943-44	"	39	19	25	44	2
10 Years			133	130	263	148

BOLTON, HUGH E. D-SR

Sea.	Club	Ga.	Go.	A.	P.	PM.
1949-50	Toronto	2	0	0	0	2
1950-51	"	13	1	3	4	4

(continued)

Sea.	Club	Ga.	Go.	A.	P.	PM.
1951-52	"	60	3	13	16	73
1952-53	"	9	0	0	0	10
1953-54	"	9	0	0	0	10
1954-55	"	69	2	19	21	55
1955-56	"	67	4	16	20	65
1956-57	"	6	0	0	0	2
8 Years		235	10	51	61	221

BONIN, MARCEL LW&RW-SL
Born: Montreal, Que. Sept. 7, 1931

Sea.	Club	Ga.	Go.	A.	P.	PM.
1952-53	Detroit	37	4	9	13	14
1953-54	"	1	0	0	0	0
1954-55	"	69	16	20	36	53
1955-56	Boston	67	9	9	18	49
1957-58	Montreal	66	15	24	39	37
1958-59	"	57	13	30	43	38
1959-60	"	59	17	34	51	59
1960-61	"	65	16	35	51	45
1961-62	"	33	7	14	21	41
9 Years		454	97	175	272	336

BOONE, CARL GEORGE RW-SR
Born: Kirkland Lake, Ont. Sept. 11, 1932

Sea.	Club	Ga.	Go.	A.	P.	PM.
1957-58	Boston	34	5	3	8	28

BOOTHMAN, GEORGE E. D-SR
Born: Calgary, Alb.

Sea.	Club	Ga.	Go.	A.	P.	PM.
1942-43	Toronto	9	1	1	2	4
1943-44	"	49	16	18	34	14
2 Years		58	17	19	36	18

BOSTROM, HELGE D

Sea.	Club	Ga.	Go.	A.	P.	PM.
1929-30	Chicago		0	1	1	8
1930-31	"		2	2	4	32
1931-32	"		0	0	0	4
1932-33	"		1	0	1	14
4 Years			3	3	6	58

BOUCHARD, EDMOND LW

Sea.	Club	Ga.	Go.	A.	P.	PM.
1921-22	Montreal		1	4	5	4
1922-23	Hamilton		5	*12	17	32
1923-24	Montreal-Hamilton		5	0	5	2
1924-25	Hamilton		2	2	4	14
1925-26	N. Y. Americans		3	1	4	10
1926-27	" " "		2	1	3	12
1927-28	" " "		1	0	1	37
1928-29	N. Y. Americans—Pittsburgh		0	0	0	4
8 Years			19	20	39	115

*League Leader

BOUCHARD, EMILE JOSEPH D-SR
Born: Montreal, Que. Sept. 11, 1920

Sea.	Club	Ga.	Go.	A.	P.	PM.
1941-42	Montreal	44	0	6	6	38
1942-43	"	45	2	16	18	47
1943-44	"	39	5	14	19	52
1944-45	"	50	11	23	34	34
1945-46	"	45	7	10	17	52
1946-47	"	60	5	7	12	60
1947-48	"	60	4	6	10	78
1948-49	"	27	3	3	6	42
1949-50	"	69	1	7	8	88
1950-51	"	52	3	10	13	80
1951-52	"	60	3	9	*12	45
1952-53	"	58	2	8	10	55
1953-54	"	70	1	10	11	89
1954-55	"	70	2	16	18	81
1955-56	"	36	0	0	0	22
15 Years		785	49	145	194	863

1943-44 2nd All-Star Team
1944-45 1st " " "
1945-46 1st " " "
1946-47 1st " " "
1966 Hall of Fame

BOUCHARD, RICHARD RW-SR
Born: Lettelier, Man. Dec. 2, 1934

Sea.	Club	Ga.	Go.	A.	P.	PM.
1954-55	New York	1	0	0	0	0

BOUCHER, FRANK XAVIER C-SL
Born: Ottawa, Ont. Oct. 7, 1901

Sea.	Club	Ga.	Go.	A.	P.	PM.
1921-22	Ottawa	24	9	1	10	4
1926-27	N. Y. Rangers	44	13	15	28	17
1927-28	" " "	44	23	12	35	12
1928-29	" " "	44	10	*16	26	8
1929-30	" " "	42	26	*36	62	16
1930-31	" " "	44	12	27	39	20

(continued)

Sea. Club	Ga.	Go.	A.	P.	PM.
1931-32 " " "	48	12	23	35	18
1932-33 " " "	46	7	*28	35	4
1933-34 " " "	48	14	30	44	4
1934-35 " " "	48	13	32	45	2
1935-36 " " "	48	11	18	29	2
1936-37 " " "	44	7	13	20	5
1937-38 " " "	18	0	1	1	2
1943-44 " " "	15	4	10	14	2
14 Years	557	161	262	423	116

*League Leader
1927-28 Lady Byng Trophy
1928-29 " " "
1929-30 " " "
1930-31 2nd All-Star Team; Lady Byng Trophy
1932-33 1st " " "; " " "
1933-34 " " " " ; " " "
1934-35 " " " " ; " " "
1958 Hall of Fame

BOUCHER, GEORGE D-SL
Born: Ottawa, Ont., 1895

Sea. Club	Ga.	Go.	A.	P.	PM.
1917-18 Ottawa		9		9	
1918-19 "		5	2	7	21
1919-20 "		10	4	14	34
1920-21 "		12	5	17	43
1921-22 "		12	8	20	10
1922-23 "		15	9	24	44
1923-24 "		14	5	19	28
1924-25 "		15	4	19	80
1925-26 "		8	4	12	64
1926-27 "		8	3	11	115
1927-28 "		7	5	12	78
1928-29 Ottawa-Mont. Maroons		4	2	6	70
1929-30 Mont. Maroons		2	6	8	50
1930-31 " "		0	0	0	25
1931-32 Chicago		1	5	6	50
15 Years		122	62	184	712

1960 Hall of Fame

BOUCHER, ROBERT F

Sea. Club	Ga.	Go.	A.	P.	PM.
1923-24 Montreal	12	0	0	0	0

BOUCHER, WILLIAM RW-SR

Sea. Club	Ga.	Go.	A.	P.	PM.
1921-22 Montreal Canadiens		17	5	22	18
1922-23 " "		23	4	27	*52
1923-24 " "		16	6	22	33
1924-25 " " "		18	13	31	*92
1925-26 " " "		8	5	13	112
1926-27 Mont. Canadiens-Boston		6	0	6	26
1927-28 N. Y. Americans		5	2	7	62
7 Years		93	35	128	395

*League Leader

BOURCIER, CONRAD

Sea. Club	Ga.	Go.	A.	P.	PM.
1935-36 Montreal Canadiens		0	0	0	0

BOURCIER, JEAN-LOUIS

Sea. Club	Ga.	Go.	A.	P.	PM.
1935-36 Mont. Canadiens		0	1	1	0

BOURGAULT, LEO A. D&RW

Sea. Club	Ga.	Go.	A.	P.	PM.
1926-27 Toronto-N. Y. Rangers		2	1	3	72
1927-28 N. Y. Rangers		7	0	7	72
1928-29 " " "		2	3	5	59
1929-30 " " "		7	6	13	54
1930-31 N. Y. Rangers-Ottawa		0	5	5	40
1932-33 Ottawa-Mont. Canadiens		2	2	4	27
1933-34 Mont. Canadiens		4	3	7	10
7 Years		24	20	44	334

BOWCHER, CLARENCE D

Sea. Club	Ga.	Go.	A.	P.	PM.
1926-27 N. Y. Americans		0	1	1	4
1927-28 " " "		2	1	3	106
2 Years		2	2	4	110

BOWMAN, RALPH D-SL
Born: Winnipeg, Man. Jan. 12, 1911

Sea. Club	Ga.	Go.	A.	P.	PM.
1933-34 Ottawa		0	2	2	64
1934-35 St. Louis-Detroit		3	5	8	72
1935-36 Detroit		3	2	5	44
1936-37 "		0	1	1	24
1937-38 "		0	2	2	26
1938-39 "		2	3	5	26
1939-40 "		0	2	2	4
7 Years		8	17	25	260

BOWNASS, JOHN D-SL
Born: Winnipeg, Man. July 27, 1930

Sea. Club	Ga.	Go.	A.	P.	PM.
1957-58 Montreal	4	0	1	1	0
1958-59 New York	35	1	2	3	20
1959-60 " "	37	2	5	7	34
1961-62 " "	4	0	0	0	4
4 Years	80	3	8	11	58

BOYD, IRVIN RW
Born: Phila., Penna.

Sea. Club	Ga.	Go.	A.	P.	PM.
1931-32 Boston		2	1	3	10
1934-35 Detroit		2	3	5	14
1942-43 Boston	20	6	5	11	6
1943-44 "	5	0	1	1	0
4 Years		10	10	20	30

BOYD, WILLIAM G. RW

Sea. Club	Ga.	Go.	A.	P.	PM.
1926-27 N. Y. Rangers		4	1	5	40
1927-28 " " "		4	0	4	13
1928-29 " " "		0	0	0	5
1929-30 " " Americans		7	6	13	16
4 Years		15	7	22	74

BRACKENBOROUGH, JOHN C

Sea. Club	Ga.	Go.	A.	P.	PM.
1925-26 Boston	7	0	0	0	0

BRADLEY, BARTON W. F

Sea. Club	Ga.	Go.	A.	P.	PM.
1949-50 Boston	1	0	0	0	0

BRANIGAN, ANDREW JOHN D-SL
Born: Winnipeg, Man. April 11, 1922

Sea. Club	Ga.	Go.	A.	P.	PM.
1940-41 N. Y. Americans		1	0	1	5
1941-42 Brooklyn	21	0	2	2	26
2 Years		1	2	3	31

BRAYSHAW, RUSSELL A. LW
Born: Rosthern, Sask.

Sea. Club	Ga.	Go.	A.	P.	PM.
1944-45 Chicago	43	5	9	14	24

BRENNAN, DOUGLAS R. D

Sea. Club	Ga.	Go.	A.	P.	PM.
1931-32 N. Y. Rangers		4	3	7	40
1932-33 " " "		5	4	9	94
1933-34 " " "		0	0	0	18
3 Years		9	7	16	152

BRENNAN, THOMAS F

Sea. Club	Ga.	Go.	A.	P.	PM.
1943-44 Boston	11	2	1	3	2
1944-45 "	1	0	1	1	0
2 Years	12	2	2	4	2

BRETTO, JOSEPH D
Born: Hibbing, Minn.

Sea. Club	Ga.	Go.	A.	P.	PM.
1944-45 Chicago	3	0	0	0	4

BRIDEN, ARCHIE W

Sea. Club	Ga.	Go.	A.	P.	PM.
1926-27 Boston-Detroit		5	2	7	36
1929-30 Pittsburgh		4	3	7	20
2 Years		9	5	14	56

BRINK, MILTON
Born: U. S. A.

Sea. Club	Ga.	Go.	A.	P.	PM.
1936-37 Chicago	0	0	0	0	0

BRISSON, GERALD RW-SL
Born: St. Boniface, Man. Sept. 3, 1937

Sea. Club	Ga.	Go.	A.	P.	PM.
1962-63 Montreal	4	0	2	2	4

BROADBENT, HARRY L. RW-SR
Born: Ottawa, Ont., 1892

Sea. Club	Ga.	Go.	A.	P.	PM.
1918-19 Ottawa		4	2	6	12
1919-20 "		19	4	23	39
1920-21 "		4	1	5	6
1921-22 "		*32	*14	*46	24
1922-23 "		14	0	14	32
1923-24 "		9	4	13	44
1924-25 Mont. Maroons		15	4	19	75
1925-26 " "		12	5	17	112
1926-27 " "		9	5	14	88
1927-28 Ottawa		3	2	5	62

Sea. Club	Ga.	Go.	A.	P.	PM.
1928-29 N. Y. Americans		1	4	5	59
11 Years		122	45	167	553
*League Leader					
1962 Hall of Fame					
BRODEN, CONNELL C					
1935-56 Montreal	3	0	0	0	2
1957-58 "	3	2	1	3	0
2 Years	6	2	1	3	2
BROPHY, BERNARD W					
Born: Collingwood, Ont.					
1925-26 Mont. Maroons	10	0	0	0	0
1928-29 Detroit		2	4	6	23
1929-30 "		2	0	2	2
3 Years		4	4	8	25
BROWN, ADAM LW					
Born: Scotland, February 4, 1920					
1941-42 Detroit	28	6	9	15	15
1943-44 "	50	24	18	42	56
1945-46 "	48	20	11	31	27
1946-47 Detroit-Chicago	64	19	30	49	87
1947-48 Chicago	32	7	10	17	41
1948-49 "	58	8	12	20	69
1949-50 "	25	2	2	4	16
1950-51 "	53	10	12	22	61
1951-52 Boston	33	8	9	17	6
9 Years	391	104	113	217	378
BROWN, FRED					
1927-28 Mont. Maroons		1	0	1	0
BROWN, GEORGE C&LW-SL					
Born: Winnipeg, Man. 1914					
1936-37 Mont. Canadiens		4	6	10	10
1937-38 " "		1	7	8	14
1938-39 " "		1	9	10	10
3 Years " "		6	22	28	34
BROWN, GERALD W. J. C					
1941-42 Detroit	13	4	4	8	0
1945-46 "	10	0	1	1	2
2 Years	23	4	5	9	2
BROWN, HAROLD F. LW					
Born: Brandon, Man.					
1945-46 New York	13	2	1	3	2
BROWN, PATRICK CONWAY C-SL					
Born: Vankleek Hill, Ont. Jan. 11, 1917					
1938-39 Detroit		1	0	1	0
1939-40 "		8	3	11	2
1940-41 "		1	2	3	0
1941-42 "	9	0	3	3	4
1942-43 "	23	5	16	21	6
5 Years		15	24	39	12
BROWN, STANLEY D					
1926-27 N. Y. Rangers		6	2	8	14
1927-28 Detroit		2	0	2	4
2 Years		8	2	10	18
BROWNE, CECIL LW-SL					
1927-28 Chicago		2	0	2	4
BRUCE, ARTHUR GORDON RW					
Born: Ottawa, Ont.					
1940-41 Boston		0	1	1	2
1941-42 "	15	4	8	12	11
1945-46 "	5	0	0	0	0
3 Years		4	9	13	13
BRUCE, MORLEY F					
1917-18 Ottawa		0		0	
1919-20 "		1	0	1	2
1920-21 "		3	1	4	23
1921-22 "		4	0	4	2
4 Years		8	1	9	27

Sea. Club	Ga.	Go.	A.	P.	PM.
BRUNETEAU, EDWARD E. H. RW					
1940-41 Detroit	12	1	1	2	2
1943-44 "	2	0	1	1	0
1944-45 "	42	12	13	25	6
1945-46 "	46	17	12	29	11
1946-47 "	60	9	14	23	14
1947-48 "	18	1	1	2	2
1948-49 "	1	0	0	0	0
7 Years	181	40	42	82	35
BRUNETEAU, MODERE FERNAND RW-SR					
Born: St. Boniface, Man. Nov. 28, 1914					
1935-36 Detroit		2	0	2	2
1936-37 "		9	7	16	18
1937-38 "		3	6	9	16
1938-39 "		3	7	10	0
1939-40 "		10	14	24	10
1940-41 "		11	17	28	12
1941-42 "	48	14	19	33	8
1942-43 "	50	23	22	45	2
1943-44 "	39	35	18	53	4
1944-45 "	43	23	24	47	6
1945-46 "	28	6	4	10	2
11 Years		139	138	277	80
BRYDGE, WILLIAM HENRY D-SR					
Born: Renfrew, Ont.					
1926-27 Toronto		6	3	9	76
1928-29 Detroit		2	2	4	59
1929-30 N. Y. Americans		2	6	8	64
1930-31 " " "		2	5	7	70
1931-32 " " "		2	8	10	77
1932-33 " " "		4	15	19	60
1933-34 " " "		6	7	13	44
1934-35 " " "		2	6	8	29
1935-36 " " "		0	0	0	27
9 Years		26	52	78	506
BRYDSON, GLENN RW-SR					
Born: Swansea, Ont. Nov. 7, 1910					
1930-31 Mont. Maroons		0	0	0	4
1931-32 " "		10	13	23	44
1932-33 " "		11	17	28	26
1933-34 " "		4	5	9	19
1934-35 St. Louis		11	18	29	45
1935-36 N. Y. Rangers-Chicago		10	16	26	39
1936-37 Chicago		7	7	14	20
1937-38 "		1	3	4	6
8 Years		54	79	133	203
BRYDSON, GORDON					
1929-30 Toronto		2	0	2	8
BUCHANAN, ALLASTER W. LW-SL					
1948-49 Toronto	3	0	1	1	2
1949-50 "	1	0	0	0	0
2 Years	4	0	1	1	2
BUCHANAN, MICHAEL D					
1951-52 Chicago	1	0	0	0	0
BUCHANAN, RALPH L. C&W					
1948-49 New York	2	0	0	0	0
BUKOVICH, ANTHONY J. LW					
Born: U. S. A.					
1943-44 Detroit	3	0	1	1	0
1944-45 "	14	7	2	9	6
2 Years	17	7	3	10	6
BULLER, HYMAN D					
1943-44 Detroit	7	0	3	3	4
1944-45 "	2	0	0	0	2
1951-52 New York	68	12	23	35	96
1952-53 " "	70	7	18	25	73
1953-54 " "	41	3	14	17	40
5 Years	188	22	58	80	215
1951-52 2nd All-Star Team					
BURCH, WILLIAM C-SL					
Born: Yonkers, N. Y.					
1922-23 Hamilton		6	2	8	2

(continued)

Sea. Club	Ga.	Go.	A.	P.	PM.
1923-24 "	16	2	18		4
1924-25 "	20	4	24		10
1925-26 N. Y. Americans	22	3	25		33
1926-27 " " "	19	8	27		40
1927-28 " " "	10	2	12		36
1928-29 " " "	11	5	16		45
1929-30 " " "	7	3	10		22
1930-31 " " "	14	8	22		35
1931-32 " " "	7	15	22		20
1932-33 Boston	5	1	6		6
11 Years	137	53	190		253
1924-25 Hart Trophy					
1926-27 Lady Byng Trophy					

BURCHELL, FREDERICK C&LW-SL
Born: Montreal, Que. Jan. 9, 1931

	Ga.	Go.	A.	P.	PM.
1950-51 Montreal	2	0	0	0	0
1953-54 "	2	0	0	0	2
2 Years	4	0	0	0	2

BUREGA, WILLIAM R. D-SL
Born: Winnipeg, Man. Mar. 13, 1932

	Ga.	Go.	A.	P.	PM.
1955-56 Toronto	4	0	1	1	4

BURKE, EDWARD W

	Ga.	Go.	A.	P.	PM.
1931-32 Boston		3	0	3	12
1932-33 N. Y. Americans		2	0	2	4
1933-34 " " "		20	10	30	24
1934-35 " " "		4	10	14	15
4 Years		29	20	49	55

BURKE, MARTIN D-SL

	Ga.	Go.	A.	P.	PM.
1927-28 Mont. Canadiens-Pitts.		2	1	3	61
1928-29 Mont. Canadiens		4	2	6	68
1929-30 " "		2	11	13	71
1930-31 " "		2	5	7	91
1931-32 " "		3	6	9	50
1932-33 Mont. Canadiens-Ottawa		2	5	7	36
1933-34 Mont. Canadiens		1	4	5	28
1934-35 Chicago		2	4	29	29
1935-36 "		0	3	3	49
1936-37 "		1	3	4	28
1937-38 Chicago-Mont. Canadiens		0	5	5	39
11 Years		19	47	66	550

BURMISTER, ROY F

	Ga.	Go.	A.	P.	PM.
1929-30 N. Y. Americans		1	1	2	2
1930-31 " " "		0	0	0	0
1931-32 " " "		3	2	5	2
3 Years		4	3	7	4

BURNETT, JAMES KELVIN C-SL
Born: Lachine, Que. June 16, 1926

	Ga.	Go.	A.	P.	PM.
1952-53 New York	3	1	0	1	0

BURNS, NORMAN C. C

	Ga.	Go.	A.	P.	PM.
1941-42 New York	11	0	4	4	2

BURNS, ROBERT W

	Ga.	Go.	A.	P.	PM.
1928-29 Chicago		0	0	0	6
1929-30 "		1	0	1	2
2 Years		1	0	1	8

BURTON, CUMMING SCOTT RW-SR
Born: Sudbury, Ont. May 12, 1936

	Ga.	Go.	A.	P.	PM.
1955-56 Detroit	3	0	0	0	0
1957-58 "	26	0	1	1	12
1958-59 "	14	0	1	1	9
3 Years	43	0	2	2	21

BUSH, EDWARD WEBSTER D-SR
Born: Collingwood, Ont. July 11, 1918

	Ga.	Go.	A.	P.	PM.
1938-39 Detroit		0	0	0	0
1941-42 "	18	4	6	10	50
2 Years		4	6	10	50

BUSWELL, WALTER D-SL
Born: Montreal, Que. 1908

	Ga.	Go.	A.	P.	PM.
1932-33 Detroit		2	4	6	16
1933-34 "		1	2	3	8
1934-35 "		1	3	4	32
1935-36 Mont. Canadiens		0	2	2	34
1936-37 " "		0	4	4	30
1937-38 " "		2	15	17	24
1938-39 " "		3	7	10	10
1939-40 " "		1	3	4	10
8 Years		10	40	50	164

BUTLER, JOHN R. RW

	Ga.	Go.	A.	P.	PM.
1947-48 Chicago	7	2	0	2	0

BUTTREY, GORDON RW

	Ga.	Go.	A.	P.	PM.
1943-44 Chicago	10	0	0	0	0

BYERS, GORDON C. F

	Ga.	Go.	A.	P.	PM.
1949-50 Boston	1	0	1	1	0

CAFFERY, JOHN C-SR
Born: Kingston, Ont. June 30, 1934

	Ga.	Go.	A.	P.	PM.
1954-55 Toronto	3	0	0	0	0
1956-57 Boston	47	2	2	4	20
1957-58 "	7	1	0	1	2
3 Years	57	3	2	5	22

CAHILL, CHARLES

	Ga.	Go.	A.	P.	PM.
1925-26 Boston	31	0	1	1	4

CAIN, HERBERT J. LW-SL
Born: Newmarket, Ont., 1912

	Ga.	Go.	A.	P.	PM.
1933-34 Mont. Maroons		4	5	9	14
1934-35 " "		20	7	27	13
1935-36 " "		5	13	18	16
1936-37 " "		13	17	30	18
1937-38 " "		11	19	30	10
1938-39 Montreal Canadiens		13	14	27	26
1939-40 Boston		21	10	31	30
1940-41 "		8	10	18	6
1941-42 "		8	10	18	2
1942-43 "	45	18	18	36	19
1943-44 "	48	36	46	*82	4
1944-45 "	50	32	13	45	16
1945-46 "	48	17	12	29	4
13 Years		206	194	400	178
*League Leader					
1943-44 2nd All-Star Team					

CAIN, JAMES F. D

	Ga.	Go.	A.	P.	PM.
1924-25 Mont. Maroons	28	4	0	4	27
1925-26 Toronto	33	0	0	0	8
2 Years	61	4	0	4	35

CALLADINE, NORMAN C
Born: Peterborough, Ont.

	Ga.	Go.	A.	P.	PM.
1942-43 Boston	3	0	1	1	0
1943-44 "	49	16	27	43	8
1944-45 "	11	3	1	4	0
3 Years	63	19	29	48	8

CALLIGHEN, FRANCIS C. W. D

	Ga.	Go.	A.	P.	PM.
1927-28 N. Y. Rangers	36	0	0	0	32

CAMERON, ANGUS C
Born: Prince Albert, Sask.

	Ga.	Go.	A.	P.	PM.
1942-43 New York	35	8	11	19	0

CAMERON, HAROLD HUGH D
Born: Pembroke, Ont. Feb. 6, 1890

	Ga.	Go.	A.	P.	PM.
1917-18 Toronto	20	17		17	
1918-19 Toronto-Ottawa	14	11	3	14	35
1919-20 Toronto-Montreal	23	16	1	17	11
1920-21 Toronto	24	18	*9	27	35
1921-22 "	24	19	8	27	18
1922-23 "	22	9	6	15	21
6 Years	127	90	27	117	120
* League Leader					
1962 Hall of Fame					

CAMERON, WILLIAM

	Ga.	Go.	A.	P.	PM.
1923-24 Mont. Canadiens	18	0	0	0	2
1925-26 N. Y. Americans	21	0	0	0	0
2 Years	39	0	0	0	2

CAMPBELL, DAVID

	Ga.	Go.	A.	P.	PM.
1920-21 Montreal	3	0	0	0	0

CAMPBELL, DONALD F-SL

	Ga.	Go.	A.	P.	PM.
1943-44 Chicago	17	1	3	4	8

CAMPBELL, EARL

	Ga.	Go.	A.	P.	PM.
1923-24 Ottawa Senators	18	4	1	5	6
1924-25 " "	30	0	0	0	0
1925-26 N. Y. Americans	29	1	0	1	6
3 Years	77	5	1	6	12

CAMPEAU, JEAN C. C

	Ga.	Go.	A.	P.	PM.
1943-44 Montreal	2	0	0	0	0

(continued)

Sea. Club	Ga.	Go.	A.	P.	PM.
1947-48 "	14	2	2	4	4
1948-49 "	26	3	7	10	12
3 Years	42	5	9	14	16
CARBOL, LEO D-SR					
1942-43 Chicago	6	0	1	1	4
CARDIN, CLAUDE LW-SL					
Born: Sorel, Que., Feb. 17, 1941					
1967-68 St. Louis	1	0	0	0	0
CAREY, GEORGE RW					
1919-20 Quebec Bulldogs	20	11	5	16	4
1920-21 Hamilton Tigers	20	7	1	8	8
1921-22 " "	23	3	2	5	2
1922-23 " "	5	1	0	1	0
1923-24 Toronto St. Patricks	4	0	0	0	0
5 Years	72	22	8	30	14
CARPENTER, EVERAR L. D-SR					
1919-20 Quebec	24	8	3	11	19
1920-21 Hamilton	20	2	1	3	17
2 Years	44	10	4	14	36
CARR, ---- F					
1919-20 Quebec		0	0	0	0
CARR, ALFRED GEORGE LW					
Born: Winnipeg, Man.					
1943-44 Toronto Maple Leafs	5	0	1	1	4
CARR, LORNE RW-SR					
Born: Stoughton, Sask. July 2, 1910					
1933-34 N. Y. Rangers		0	0	0	0
1934-35 " " Americans		17	14	31	14
1935-36 " "		8	10	18	4
1936-37 " " "		18	16	34	22
1937-38 " " "		16	7	23	12
1938-39 " " "		19	18	37	16
1939-40 " " "		8	17	25	17
1940-41 " " "		13	19	32	10
1941-42 Toronto		16	17	33	4
1942-43 "	50	27	33	60	15
1943-44 "	50	36	38	74	9
1944-45 "	47	21	25	46	7
1945-46 "	42	5	8	13	2
13 Years		204	222	426	132
1942-43 1st All-Star Team					
1943-44 " " " "					
CARRIGAN, EUGENE C					
Born: Edmonton, Alb.					
1930-31 N. Y. Rangers		2	0	2	13
1934-35 St. Louis		0	1	1	0
2 Years		2	1	3	13
CARROLL, GEORGE D					
1924-25 Mont. Maroons-Boston	15	0	0	0	9
CARRUTHERS, GORDON DWIGHT D–SR					
Born: Lashburn, Sask. Nov. 7, 1944					
1965-66 Detroit	1	0	0	0	0
1967-68 Philadelphia	1	0	0	0	0
2 Years	2	0	0	0	0
CARSE, ROBERT ALLISON LW-SL					
Born: Edmonton, Alb., July 19, 1919					
1939-40 Chicago		3	5	8	11
1940-41 "		9	9	18	9
1941-42 "		7	16	23	10
1942-43 "	47	10	22	32	6
1947-48 Montreal	22	3	3	6	16
5 Years		32	55	87	52
CARSE, WILLIAM ALEXANDER C&LW-SL					
Born: Edmonton, Alb., May 29, 1914					
1938-39 N. Y. Rangers		0	1	1	0
1939-40 Chicago		10	13	23	10
1940-41 "		5	15	20	12
1941-42 "	43	13	14	27	16
4 Years		28	43	71	38
CARSON, FRANCIS W. RW					
Born: Bracebridge, Ont. 1902					
1925-26 Mont. Maroons		2	1	3	6
1926-27 " "		2	3	5	12
1927-28 " "		0	1	1	10
1930-31 N. Y. Americans		6	7	13	36

(continued)

Sea. Club	Ga.	Go.	A.	P.	PM.
1931-32 Detroit		10	14	24	31
1932-33 "		12	13	25	35
1933-34 "		10	9	19	36
7 Years		42	48	90	166
CARSON, GERALD GEORGE D					
Born: Parry Sound, Ont. October 10, 1903					
1928-29 Mont. Canadiens-N.Y. Rangers		0	0		9
1929-30 Mont. Canadiens		1	0	1	8
1932-33 Mont. Canadiens		5	2	7	53
1933-34 " "		5	1	6	51
1934-35 " "		0	5	5	56
1936-37 " Maroons		1	3	4	28
6 Years		12	11	23	205
CARSON, WILLIAM J. C					
1926-27 Toronto		16	6	22	41
1927-28 "		20	6	26	36
1928-29 Toronto-Boston		11	8	19	55
1929-30 Boston		7	4	11	24
4 Years		54	24	78	156
CARTER, WILLIAM GORDON C-SL					
Born: Cornwall, Ont. Dec. 2, 1937					
1957-58 Montreal	1	0	0	0	0
1960-61 Boston	8	0	0	0	2
1961-62 Montreal	7	0	0	0	4
3 Years	16	0	0	0	6
CARVETH, JOSEPH G. RW-SR					
Born: Regina, Sask.					
1940-41 Detroit	19	2	1	3	2
1941-42 "	29	6	11	17	2
1942-43 "	43	18	18	36	6
1943-44 "	46	21	35	56	6
1944-45 "	50	26	28	54	6
1945-46 "	48	17	18	35	10
1946-47 Boston	51	21	15	36	18
1947-48 Boston-Montreal	57	9	19	28	8
1948-49 Montreal	60	15	22	37	8
1949-50 Montreal-Detroit	71	14	18	32	15
1950-51 Detroit	30	1	4	5	0
11 Years	504	150	189	339	81
CERESINO, RAYMOND LW-SR					
1948-49 Toronto	12	1	1	2	2
CHAD, JOHN RW-SR					
Born: Provost, Alb., Sept. 16, 1919					
1939-40 Chicago		8	3	11	11
1940-41 "		7	18	25	16
1941-45 Military Service					
1945-46 Chicago	13	0	1	1	2
3 Years		15	22	37	29
CHALMERS, WILLIAM C&LW-SL					
Born: Stratford, Ont. Jan. 24, 1934					
1953-54 New York	1	0	0	0	0
CHAMBERLAIN, ERWIN GROVES C&LW-SL					
Born: Shawville, Que. Feb. 14, 1915					
1937-38 Toronto		4	12	16	51
1938-39 "		10	16	26	32
1939-40 "		5	17	22	63
1940-41 Montreal	36	10	15	25	75
1941-42 Montreal-Brooklyn	36	12	12	24	46
1942-43 Boston	45	9	24	33	67
1943-44 Montreal	47	15	32	47	85
1944-45 "	32	2	12	14	38
1945-46 "	40	12	14	26	42
1946-47 "	49	10	10	20	97
1947-48 "	30	6	3	9	62
1948-49 "	54	5	8	13	111
12 Years		100	175	275	769
CHAMPAGNE, ANDRE JOSEPH ORIUS LW-SL					
Born: Eastview, Ont. Sept. 19, 1943					
1962-63 Toronto	2	0	0	0	0
CHAPMAN, ARTHUR V. C-SL					
Born: Winnipeg, Man. May 26, 1907					
1930-31 Boston		7	7	14	22
1931-32 "		11	14	25	18
1932-33 "		3	6	9	19
1933-34 Boston-N. Y. Americans		5	12	17	15
1934-35 N. Y. Americans		9	*34	43	4
1935-36 " " "		10	*28	38	14

(continued)

Sea. Club	Ga.	Go.	A.	P.	PM.
1936-37 " "	8	23	31		36
1937-38 " "	2	27	29		8
1938-39 " "	3	19	22		2
1939-40 " "	4	6	10		2
10 Years	62	176	238		140

*League Leader
1936-37 2nd All-Star Team

CHARLEBOIS, ROBERT RICHARD LW-SL
Born: Cornwall Ont. May 27, 1944

1967-68 Minnesota	7	1	0	1	0

CHECK, LUDE LW
Born: Brandon, Man.

1943-44 Detroit	1	0	0	0	0
1944-45 Chicago	26	6	2	8	4
2 Years	27	6	2	8	4

CHEVREFILS, REAL LW-SL
Born: Timmins, Ont. May 2, 1932

1951-52 Boston	33	8	17	25	8
1952-53 "	69	19	14	35	44
1953-54 "	14	4	1	5	2
1954-55 "	64	18	22	40	30
1955-56 Detroit-Boston	63	14	12	26	34
1956-57 Boston	70	31	17	48	38
1957-58 "	44	9	9	18	21
1958-59 "	30	1	5	6	8
8 Years	387	104	97	201	185

1956-57 2nd All-Star Team

CHISHOLM, ALEXANDER RW-SR
Born: Galt, Ont. Apr. 1, 1915

1939-40 Toronto		6	8	14	22
1940-41 "		4	0	4	8
2 Years		10	8	18	30

CHISHOLM, ARTHUR C

1960-61 Boston	3	0	0	0	0

CHOUINARD, JEAN

1927-28 Ottawa	2	0	0	-	0

CHRYSTAL, ROBERT H. D

1953-54 New York	64	5	5	10	44
1954-55 " "	68	6	9	15	68
2 Years	132	11	14	25	112

CHURCH, JOHN D-SR
Born: Kamsack, Sask. May 24, 1915

1938-39 Toronto		0	2	2	2
1939-40 "		1	4	5	62
1940-41 "		0	1	1	22
1941-42 Toronto-Brooklyn	42	1	6	7	40
1945-46 Boston	43	2	6	8	28
5 Years		4	19	23	154

CIESLA, HENRY EDWARD C-SL
Born: St. Catharines, Ont. Oct. 15, 1934

1955-56 Chicago	70	8	23	31	22
1956-57 "	70	10	8	18	28
1957-58 New York	60	2	6	8	16
1958-59 " "	69	6	14	20	21
4 Years	269	26	51	77	87

CLANCY, FRANCIS MICHAEL D-SL
Born: Ottawa, Ont. Feb. 25, 1903

1921-22 Ottawa		4	5	9	19
1922-23 "		3	1	4	20
1923-24 "		9	*8	17	18
1924-25 "		14	5	19	61
1925-26 "		8	4	12	80
1926-27 "		9	10	19	78
1927-28 "		8	7	15	73
1928-29 "		13	2	15	89
1929-30 "		17	23	40	83
1930-31 Toronto		7	14	21	63
1931-32 "		10	9	19	61
1932-33 "		13	12	25	79
1933-34 "		11	17	28	62
1934-35 "		5	16	21	53
1935-36 "		5	10	15	61
1936-37 "		1	0	1	4
16 Years		137	143	280	904

*League Leader
1930-31 1st All-Star Team
1931-32 2nd " " "

(continued)

Sea. Club	Ga.	Go.	A.	P.	PM.
1932-33 2nd " " "					
1933-34 1st " " "					
1958 Hall of Fame					

CLAPPER, AUBREY VICTOR RW&D-SR
Born: Newmarket, Ont. Feb. 9, 1907

1927-28 Boston		4	1	5	20
1928-29 "		9	2	11	48
1929-30 "		41	20	61	48
1930-31 "		22	8	30	50
1931-32 "		17	22	39	21
1932-33 "		14	14	28	42
1933-34 "		10	12	22	6
1934-35 "		21	16	37	21
1935-36 "		12	13	25	14
1936-37 "		17	8	25	25
1937-38 "		6	9	15	24
1938-39 "		13	13	26	22
1939-40 "		10	18	28	25
1940-41 "		8	18	26	24
1941-42 "		3	12	15	31
1942-43 "	38	5	18	23	12
1943-44 "	50	6	25	31	13
1944-45 "	46	8	14	22	16
1945-46 "	30	2	3	5	0
1946-47 "	6	0	0	0	0
20 Years		228	246	474	462

1930-31 2nd All-Star Team
1934-35 " " "
1938-39 1st All-Star Team
1939-40 " " " "
1940-41 " " " "
1943-44 2nd All-Star Team
1945 Hall of Fame

CLEGHORN, J. OGILVIE C-SR

1918-19 Montreal Canadiens	*23	6	29	33	
1919-20 " "	19	3	22	30	
1920-21 " "	5	4	9	8	
1921-22 " "	21	3	24	26	
1922-23 " "	19	7	26	14	
1923-24 " "	3	3	6	14	
1924-25 " "	3	2	5	14	
1925-26 Pittsburgh	2	1	3	4	
1926-27 " "	0	0	0	0	
1927-28 "	0	0	0	4	
10 Years	95	29	124	147	

*League Leader

CLEGHORN, SPRAGUE D-SL
Born: Montreal, Que., 1890

1918-19 Ottawa		6	6	12	27
1919-20 "		16	5	21	62
1920-21 "		5	5	10	35
1921-22 Montreal		17	7	24	*63
1922-23 "		9	4	13	34
1923-24 "		8	3	11	39
1924-25 "		8	1	9	82
1925-26 Boston		6	5	11	49
1926-27 "		7	1	8	84
1927-28 "		2	2	4	14
10 Years		84	39	123	489

*League Leader
1958 Hall of Fame

CLINE, BRUCE RW-SR
Born: Massawippi, Que. Nov. 14, 1931

1956-57 New York	30	2	3	5	10

CLUNE, WALTER JAMES D-SR
Born: Toronto, Ont. Feb. 20, 1930

1955-56 Montreal	5	0	0	0	6

COFLIN, HUGH ALEXANDER D-SL
Born: Blaine Lake, Sask. Dec. 15, 1928

1950-51 Chicago	31	0	3	3	33

COLLINGS, NORMAN

1934-35 Mont. Canadiens		0	1	1	0

COLVILLE, MATTHEW L. RW-SR
Born: Edmonton, Alb., Jan. 8, 1916

1935-36 N. Y. Rangers		1	4	5	6
1936-37 " " "		7	12	19	10

(continued)

Sea. Club	Ga.	Go.	A.	P.	PM.
1937-38 " " "		14	14	28	18
1938-39 " " "		7	21	28	24
1939-40 " " "		7	14	21	12
1940-41 " " "		14	17	31	18
1941-42 " " "	46	14	16	30	26
1942-45 Military Service					
1945-46 New York	39	7	6	13	8
1946-47 " "	14	0	0	0	8
9 Years		71	104	175	130

COLVILLE, NEIL MacNEIL C&D-SR
Born: Edmonton, Alb. Aug. 4 1914

1935-36 N. Y. Rangers		0	0	0	0
1936-37 " " "		10	18	28	33
1937-38 " " "		17	19	36	11
1938-39 " " "		18	19	37	12
1939-40 " " "		19	19	38	22
1940-41 " " "		14	28	42	28
1941-42 " " "	48	8	25	33	37
1942-44 Military Service					
1944-45 New York	4	0	1	1	2
1945-46 " "	49	5	4	9	25
1946-47 " "	60	4	16	20	16
1947-48 " "	55	4	12	16	25
1948-49 " "	14	0	5	5	2
12 Years		99	166	265	213

1938-39 2nd All-Star Team
1939-40 " " " "
1947-48 " " " "
1967 Hall of Fame

COLWILL, LESLIE JOHN RW-SR
Born: Divide, Sask. Jan. 1, 1935

1958-59 New York	69	7	6	13	16

COMIER, ROGER W

1925-26 Mont. Canadiens		0	0	0	0

CONACHER, CHARLES WILLIAM RW-SR
Born: Toronto, Ont. Dec. 10, 1909

1929-30 Toronto		20	9	29	48
1930-31 "		*31	12	43	78
1931-32 "		*34	14	48	66
1932-33 "		14	19	33	64
1933-34 "		*32	20	*52	38
1934-35 "		*36	21	*57	24
1935-36 "		*23	15	38	74
1936-37 "		3	5	8	13
1937-38 "		7	9	16	6
1938-39 Detroit		8	15	23	39
1939-40 N. Y. Americans		10	18	28	41
1940-41 " " "		7	16	23	32
12 Years		225	173	398	523

*League Leader
1931-32 2nd All-Star Team
1932-33 " " " "
1933-34 1st All-Star Team
1934-35 " " " "
1935-36 " " " "
1961 Hall of Fame

CONACHER, CHARLES WILLIAM Jr. LW-SL
Born: Toronto, Ont. July 29, 1932

1951-52 Chicago	2	0	1	1	0
1952-53 "	41	5	6	11	7
1953-54 "	70	19	9	28	23
1954-55 Chicago-N. Y.	70	12	11	23	12
1955-56 New York	41	11	11	22	10
1957-58 Toronto	5	0	1	1	5
6 Years	229	47	39	86	57

CONACHER, JAMES C-SL

1945-46 Detroit	20	1	5	6	6
1946-47 "	33	16	13	29	2
1947-48 "	60	17	23	40	2
1948-49 Detroit-Chicago	59	26	23	49	43
1949-50 Chicago	66	13	20	33	14
1950-51 "	52	10	27	37	16
1951-52 Chicago-New York	21	1	2	3	2
1952-53 New York	17	1	4	5	2
8 Years	328	85	117	202	87

Sea. Club	Ga.	Go.	A.	P.	PM.
CONACHER, LIONEL PRETORIA D-SL					
Born: Toronto, Ont. May 24, 1901					
1925-26 Pittsburgh		9	4	13	64
1926-27 Pitts.-N.Y. Americans		8	9	17	93
1927-28 N. Y. Americans		11	6	17	82
1928-29 " " "		5	2	7	132
1929-30 " " "		4	6	10	73
1930-31 Mont. Maroons		4	3	7	57
1931-32 " "		7	9	16	60
1932-33 " "		7	21	28	61
1933-34 Chicago		10	13	23	87
1934-35 Mont. Maroons		2	6	8	44
1935-36 " "		7	7	14	65
1936-37 " "		6	19	25	64
12 Years		80	105	185	882

1932-33 2nd All-Star Team
1933-34 1st " " "
1936-37 2nd All-Star Team

CONACHER, ROY G. LW—SL
Born: Toronto, Ont. Oct. 5, 1916

1938-39 Boston		*26	11	37	12
1939-40 "		18	12	30	9
1940-41 "		24	14	38	7
1941-42 "		24	13	37	12
1942-45 Military Service					
1945-46 Boston	4	2	1	3	0
1946-47 Detroit	60	30	24	54	6
1947-48 Chicago	52	22	27	49	4
1948-49 "	60	26	42	*68	8
1949-50 "	70	25	31	56	16
1950-51 "	70	26	24	50	16
1951-52 "	12	3	1	4	0
11 Years		226	200	426	90

*League Leader
1948-49 1st All-Star Team, Ross Trophy

CONN, MAITLAND D
Born: Saskatoon, Sask.

1933-34 N. Y. Americans		4	17	21	12
1934-35 " " "		5	11	16	10
2 Years		9	28	37	22

CONNOLLY, ALBERT P. C-SL
Born: Montreal, Que. 1909

1934-35 N. Y. Rangers		10	11	21	23
1935-36 " " "		2	2	4	10
1937-38 Chicago		1	2	3	4
3 Years		13	15	28	37

CONNOR, HARRY LW

1927-28 Boston		9	1	10	36
1928-29 N. Y. Americans		6	2	8	83
1929-30 Ottawa-Boston		1	2	3	26
1930-31 Ottawa		0	0	0	4
4 Years		16	5	21	149

CONNORS, ROBERT LW

1926-27 N. Y. Americans		1	0	1	0
1928-29 Detroit		13	3	16	68
1929-30 "		3	7	10	42
3 Years		17	10	27	110

CONVEY, EDWARD C-SL
Born: Toronto, Ont.

1930-31 N. Y. Americans		0	0	0	2
1931-32 " " "		1	0	1	21
2 Years		1	0	1	23

COOK, ALEX C
Born: Kingston, Ont.

1931-32 Boston		4	4	8	14
1933-34 Ottawa		1	0	1	8
1934-35 St. Louis		0	0	0	0
3 Years		5	4	9	22

COOK, FREDERICK JOSEPH LW-SL
Born: Kingston, Ont. Sept. 18, 1903

1926-27 N. Y. Rangers		14	9	23	42
1927-28 " " "		14	14	28	43
1928-29 " " "		13	5	18	70
1929-30 " " "		24	18	42	55
1930-31 " " "		18	17	35	72
1931-32 " " "		14	20	34	43
1932-33 " " "		22	15	37	35
1933-34 " " "		18	15	33	36
1934-35 " " "		13	21	34	26

(continued)

Sea. Club	Ga.	Go.	A.	P.	PM.
1935-36 " " "		4	5	9	12
1936-37 Boston		4	5	9	8
11 Years		158	144	302	442
1930-31 2nd All-Star Team					

COOK, LLOYD D-SL

Sea. Club	Ga.	Go.	A.	P.	PM.
1924-25 Boston	4	1	0	1	0

•

COOK, THOMAS JOHN C-SL
Born: Fort William, Ont. Oct. 5, 1900

Sea. Club	Ga.	Go.	A.	P.	PM.
1929-30 Chicago		14	16	30	16
1930-31 "		15	14	29	34
1931-32 "		12	13	25	36
1932-33 "		12	14	26	30
1933-34 "		5	9	14	15
1934-35 "		13	18	31	33
1935-36 "		4	8	12	20
1936-37 "		0	2	2	0
1937-38 Mont. Maroons		2	4	6	0
9 Years		77	98	175	184

COOK, WILLIAM OSSER RW-SR
Born: Brantford, Ont. Oct. 9, 1896

Sea. Club	Ga.	Go.	A.	P.	PM.
1926-27 N. Y. Rangers		*33	4	*37	58
1927-28 " " "		18	6	24	42
1928-29 " " "		15	8	23	41
1929-30 " " "		29	30	59	56
1930-31 " " "		30	12	42	39
1931-32 " " "		33	14	47	33
1932-33 " " "		*28	22	*50	51
1933-34 " " "		13	13	26	21
1934-35 " " "		21	15	36	23
1935-36 " " "		7	10	17	16
1936-37 " " "		1	4	5	6
11 Years		228	138	366	386

*League Leader
1930-31 1st All-Star Team
1931-32 " " " "
1932-33 " " " "
1933-34 2nd " " "
1952 Hall of Fame

COOPER, CARSON RW-SR
Born: Cornwall, Ont.

Sea. Club	Ga.	Go.	A.	P.	PM.
1924-25 Boston		5	3	8	4
1925-26 "		28	3	31	10
1926-27 Boston-Mont. Canadiens		9	3	12	16
1927-28 Detroit		15	2	17	32
1928-29 "		18	9	27	14
1929-30 "		18	18	36	14
1930-31 "		14	14	28	10
1931-32 "		3	5	8	11
8 Years		110	57	167	111

COOPER, HAROLD RW

Sea. Club	Ga.	Go.	A.	P.	PM.
1944-45 New York	8	0	0	0	2

COOPER, JOSEPH D-SR
Born: Winnipeg, Man. Dec. 14, 1914

Sea. Club	Ga.	Go.	A.	P.	PM.
1935-36 N. Y. Rangers		0	0	0	0
1936-37 " " "		0	3	3	42
1937-38 " " "		3	2	5	56
1938-39 Chicago		3	3	6	10
1939-40 "		4	7	11	59
1940-41 "		5	5	10	66
1941-42 "	47	6	14	20	58
1943-44 "	13	1	0	1	17
1944-45 "	50	4	17	21	50
1945-46 "	50	2	7	9	46
1946-47 New York	59	2	8	10	38
11 Years		30	66	96	442

COPP, ROBERT A. D-SL

Sea. Club	Ga.	Go.	A.	P.	PM.
1942-43 Toronto	28	3	9	12	24
1950-51 "	2	0	0	0	2
2 Years	30	3	9	12	26

CORBEAU, BERT D

Sea. Club	Ga.	Go.	A.	P.	PM.
1917-18 Montreal		8		8	
1918-19 "		2	1	3	51
1919-20 "		11	5	16	59
1920-21 "		12	1	13	*86
1921-22 "		4	7	11	26
1922-23 Hamilton		10	3	13	36
1923-24 Toronto		8	6	14	*55
1924-25 "		4	3	7	67
1925-26 "		5	5	10	*121

(continued)

Sea. Club	Ga.	Go.	A.	P.	PM.
1926-27 "		1	2	3	88
10 Years		65	33	98	589

*League Leader

CORCORAN, NORMAN C&RW-SR
Born: Toronto, Ont. Aug. 15, 1931

Sea. Club	Ga.	Go.	A.	P.	PM.
1949-50 Boston	1	0	0	0	0
1952-53 "	1	0	0	0	0
1954-55 "	2	0	0	0	2
1955-56 Detroit-Chicago	25	1	3	4	19
4 Years	29	1	3	4	21

CORRIGAN, CHARLES H. P. RW
Born: Moosomin, Sask.

Sea. Club	Ga.	Go.	A.	P.	PM.
1940-41 N. Y. Americans		2	2	4	2

CORRIVEAU, FRED ANDRE RW

Sea. Club	Ga.	Go.	A.	P.	PM.
1953-54 Montreal	3	0	1	1	0

COSTELLO, J. MURRAY C&W-SR

Sea. Club	Ga.	Go.	A.	P.	PM.
1953-54 Chicago	40	3	2	5	6
1954-55 Boston	54	4	11	15	25
1955-56 Boston-Detroit	65	6	6	12	23
1956-57 Detroit	3	0	0	0	0
4 Years	162	13	19	32	54

COSTELLO, LESTER JOHN THOMAS LW-SL

Sea. Club	Ga.	Go.	A.	P.	PM.
1948-49 Toronto	15	2	3	5	11

COTCH, CHARLES

Sea. Club	Ga.	Go.	A.	P.	PM.
1924-25 Hamilton Tigers	11	1	0	1	0

COTTON, E. HAROLD LW—SL
Born: Toronto, Ont. Nov. 5, 1902

Sea. Club	Ga.	Go.	A.	P.	PM.
1925-26 Pittsburgh		7	1	8	22
1926-27 "		5	0	5	17
1927-28 "		9	3	12	40
1928-29 Pitts.-Toronto		4	4	8	46
1929-30 Toronto		21	17	38	47
1930-31 "		12	17	29	45
1931-32 "		5	13	18	41
1932-33 "		10	11	21	29
1933-34 "		8	14	22	46
1934-35 "		11	14	25	36
1935-36 N. Y. Americans		7	9	16	27
1936-37 " " "		2	0	2	23
12 Years		101	103	204	419

COUGHLIN, JACK

Sea. Club	Ga.	Go.	A.	P.	PM.
1917-18 Toronto Arenas	6	2		2	
1919-20 Quebec-Mont. Canadiens	11	0	0	0	0
1924-25 Hamilton Tigers	2	0	0	0	0
3 Years	19	2	0	2	0

COULSON, D'ARCY D

Sea. Club	Ga.	Go.	A.	P.	PM.
1930-31 Philadelphia		0	0	0	103

COULTER, ARTHUR EDMUND D-SR
Born: Winnipeg, Man. May 31, 1909

Sea. Club	Ga.	Go.	A.	P.	PM.
1931-32 Chicago		0	1	1	23
1932-33 "		3	2	5	53
1933-34 "		5	2	7	39
1934-35 "		4	8	12	68
1935-36 Chicago-N. Y. Rangers		1	7	8	44
1936-37 N. Y. Rangers		1	5	6	27
1937-38 " " "		5	10	15	80
1938-39 " " "		4	8	12	58
1939-40 " " "		1	9	10	68
1940-41 " " "		5	14	19	42
1941-42 " " "		1	16	17	31
11 Years		30	82	112	533

1934-35 2nd All-Star Team
1937-38 " " " "
1938-39 " " " "
1939-40 " " " "

COUTU, WILLIAM D-SL
Born: Sault Ste. Marie, Ont.

Sea. Club	Ga.	Go.	A.	P.	PM.
1917-18 Montreal Canadiens		2		2	
1918-19 " "		1	1	2	18
1919-20 " "		4	0	4	30
1920-21 Hamilton		8	4	12	74

(continued)

Sea.	Club	Ga.	Go.	A.	P.	PM.
1921-22	Montreal Canadiens		4	3	7	4
1922-23	" "		5	2	7	37
1923-24	" "		3	1	4	8
1924-25	Mont. Canadiens		3	2	5	49
1925-26	" "		2	4	6	95
1926-27	Boston		1	1	2	35
10 Years			33	18	51	350

COUTURE, GERALD J. W. A. RW-SR
Born: Saskatoon, Sask.

Sea.	Club	Ga.	Go.	A.	P.	PM.
1945-46	Detroit	43	3	7	10	18
1946-47	"	30	5	10	15	0
1947-48	"	19	3	6	9	2
1948-49	"	51	19	10	29	6
1949-50	"	69	24	7	31	21
1950-51	"	53	7	6	13	2
1951-52	Montreal	10	0	1	1	4
1952-53	Chicago	70	19	18	37	22
1953-54	"	40	6	5	11	14
9 Years		385	86	70	156	89

COUTURE, ROSARIO RW

Sea.	Club	Ga.	Go.	A.	P.	PM.
1928-29	Chicago		1	3	4	22
1929-30	"		8	8	16	63
1930-31	"		8	11	19	30
1931-32	"		9	9	18	8
1932-33	"		10	7	17	26
1933-34	"		5	8	13	21
1934-35	"		7	9	16	14
1935-36	Mont. Canadiens		0	1	1	0
8 Years			48	56	104	184

COWLEY, WILLIAM MAILES C-SL
Born: Bristol, Que. June 12, 1912

Sea.	Club	Ga.	Go.	A.	P.	PM.
1934-35	St. Louis	43	5	7	12	10
1935-36	Boston	48	11	10	21	17
1936-37	"	46	13	22	35	4
1937-38	"	48	17	22	39	8
1938-39	"	34	8	*34	42	2
1939-40	"	48	13	27	40	24
1940-41	"	46	17	*45	*62	16
1941-42	"	28	4	23	27	6
1942-43	"	48	27	*45	72	10
1943-44	"	36	30	41	71	12
1944-45	"	49	25	40	65	12
1945-46	"	26	12	12	24	6
1946-47	"	51	13	25	38	16
13 Years		551	195	353	548	143

*League Leader
1937-38 1st All-Star Team
1940-41 " " " & Hart Trophy
1942-43 " " " " & Hart Trophy
1943-44 " " " "
1944-45 2nd " " "
1968 Hall of Fame

COX, DANIEL S. LW

Sea.	Club	Ga.	Go.	A.	P.	PM.
1926-27	Toronto		0	1	1	4
1927-28	"		9	6	15	27
1928-29	"		12	7	19	14
1929-30	Toronto-Ottawa		4	6	10	20
1930-31	Ottawa		9	12	21	12
1931-32	Detroit		4	6	10	23
1932-33	Ottawa		4	7	11	8
1933-34	Ottawa-N. Y. Rangers		5	4	9	2
8 Years			47	49	96	110

CRAWFORD, JOHN SHEA D-SR
Born: Dublin, Ont. Oct. 26, 1916

Sea.	Club	Ga.	Go.	A.	P.	PM.
1938-39	Boston		4	8	12	12
1939-40	"		1	4	5	26
1940-41	"	45	2	8	10	27
1941-42	"	43	2	9	11	37
1942-43	"	49	5	18	23	24
1943-44	"	34	4	16	20	8
1944-45	"	40	5	19	24	10
1945-46	"	48	7	9	16	10
1946-47	"	58	1	17	18	16
1947-48	"	45	3	11	14	10
1948-49	"	55	2	13	15	14
1949-50	"	46	2	8	10	8
12 Years			38	140	178	202

1942-43 2nd All-Star Team
1945-46 1st " " "

CRAWFORD, SAMUEL RUSSELL RW-SL
Born: Cardinal, Ont. Nov. 7, 1885

(continued)

Sea.	Club	Ga.	Go.	A.	P.	PM.
1917-18	Ottawa-Toronto	20	3		3	
1918-19	Toronto	18	7	3	10	51
2 Years		38	10	3	13	51

1962 Hall of Fame

CREIGHTON, DAVID THEODORE C-SL
Born: Port Arthur, Ont. June 24, 1930

Sea.	Club	Ga.	Go.	A.	P.	PM.
1948-49	Boston	12	1	3	4	0
1949-50	"	64	18	13	31	13
1950-51	"	56	5	4	9	4
1951-52	"	49	20	17	37	18
1952-53	"	45	8	8	16	14
1953-54	"	69	20	20	40	27
1954-55	Toronto-Chicago	62	9	8	17	14
1955-56	New York	70	20	31	51	43
1956-57	" "	70	18	21	39	42
1957-58	" "	70	17	35	52	40
1958-59	Toronto	34	3	9	12	4
1959-60	"	14	1	5	6	4
12 Years		615	140	174	314	223

CREIGHTON, JAMES A F

Sea.	Club	Ga.	Go.	A.	P.	PM.
1930-31	Detroit	9	1	0	1	2

CRESSMAN, GLEN RW-SR
Born: Peterborough, Ont. Aug 29, 1934

Sea.	Club	Ga.	Go.	A.	P.	PM.
1956-57	Montreal	4	0	0	0	2

CROGHAN, MAURICE

Sea.	Club	Ga.	Go.	A.	P.	PM.
1937-38	Mont. Maroons		0	0	0	4

CROSSETT, STANLEY D

Sea.	Club	Ga.	Go.	A.	P.	PM.
1930-31	Philadelphia		0	0	0	10

CROZIER, JOSEPH RICHARD D-SR
Born: Winnipeg, Man. Feb. 19, 1929

Sea.	Club	Ga.	Go.	A.	P.	PM.
1959-60	Toronto	5	0	3	3	2

CRUTCHFIELD, NELSON C

Sea.	Club	Ga.	Go.	A.	P.	PM.
1934-35	Mont. Canadiens		5	5	10	20

CULLEN, BRIAN JOSEPH C-SL
Born: Ottawa, Ont. Nov. 11, 1933

Sea.	Club	Ga.	Go.	A.	P.	PM.
1954-55	Toronto	27	3	5	8	6
1955-56	"	21	2	6	8	8
1956-57	"	46	8	12	20	27
1957-58	"	67	20	23	43	29
1958-59	"	59	4	14	18	10
1959-60	New York	64	8	21	29	6
1960-61	" "	42	11	19	30	6
7 Years		326	56	100	156	92

CULLEN, CHARLES FRANCIS RW-SR
Born: Ottawa, Ont. June 16, 1935

Sea.	Club	Ga.	Go.	A.	P.	PM.
1955-56	Toronto	3	0	0	0	4
1956-57	"	51	6	10	16	30
1957-58	"	70	16	25	41	37
1958-59	"	40	6	8	14	17
1959-60	Detroit	55	4	9	13	23
5 Years		219	32	52	84	111

CUNNINGHAM, LESLIE ROY C-SL
Born: Calgary, Alb., Oct. 4, 1913

Sea.	Club	Ga.	Go.	A.	P.	PM.
1936-37	N. Y. Americans		1	8	9	19
1939-40	Chicago		6	11	17	2
2 Years			7	19	26	21

CUNNINGHAM, ROBERT GORDON C-SL
Born: Welland, Ont. Feb. 26, 1941

Sea.	Club	Ga.	Go.	A.	P.	PM.
1960-61	New York	3	0	1	1	0
1961-62	" "	1	0	0	0	0
2 Years		4	0	1	1	0

CUPOLO, WILLIAM D. RW

Sea.	Club	Ga.	Go.	A.	P.	PM.
1944-45	Boston	47	11	13	24	10

CURRIE, HUGH ROY D-SR
Born: Saskatoon, Sask. Oct. 22, 1925

Sea.	Club	Ga.	Go.	A.	P.	PM.
1950-51	Montreal	1	0	0	0	0

CURRY, FLOYD JAMES RW-SR
Born: Chapleau, Ont. Aug. 11, 1925

Sea.	Club	Ga.	Go.	A.	P.	PM.
1947-48	Montreal	31	1	5	6	0
1949-50	"	49	8	8	16	8
1950-51	"	69	13	14	27	23
1951-52	"	64	20	18	38	10

(continued)

Sea. Club	Ga.	Go.	A.	P.	PM.
1952-53 "	68	16	6	22	10
1953-54 "	70	13	8	21	22
1954-55 "	68	11	10	21	36
1955-56 "	70	14	18	32	10
1956-57 "	70	7	9	16	20
1957-58 "	42	2	3	5	8
10 Years	601	105	99	204	147

CUSHENAN, IAN ROBERTSON D-SL
Born: Hamilton, Ont. Nov. 29, 1933

Sea. Club	Ga.	Go.	A.	P.	PM.
1956-57 Chicago	11	0	0	0	13
1957-58 "	61	2	8	10	67
1958-59 Montreal	35	1	2	3	28
1959-60 New York	17	0	1	1	22
1963-64 Detroit	5	0	0	0	4
5 Years	129	3	11	14	134

CUSSON, JEAN LW-SL
Born: Verdun, Que., Oct. 5, 1942

Sea. Club	Ga.	Go.	A.	P.	PM.
1967-68 Oakland	2	0	0	0	0

DAHLSTROM, CARL C-SL
Born: Minneapolis, Minn. July 3, 1913

Sea. Club	Ga.	Go.	A.	P.	PM.
1937-38 Chicago		10	9	19	11
1938-39 "		6	14	20	2
1939-40 "		11	19	30	15
1940-41 "		11	14	25	10
1941-42 "		13	14	27	6
1942-43 "	38	11	13	24	10
1943-44 "	50	20	22	42	8
1944-45 "	40	6	13	19	0
8 Years		88	118	206	62

1937-38 Calder Trophy

DALEY, FRANK PATRICK C&LW
Born: Port Arthur, Ont.

Sea. Club	Ga.	Go.	A.	P.	PM.
1928-29 Detroit Cougars		0	0	0	0

DAME, AURELIA N. LW
Born: Edmonton, Alb.

Sea. Club	Ga.	Go.	A.	P.	PM.
1941-42 Montreal		2	5	7	4

D'AMORE, HENRY F

Sea. Club	Ga.	Go.	A.	P.	PM.
1943-44 New York	4	1	0	1	2

DARRAGH, HAROLD RW-SR

Sea. Club	Ga.	Go.	A.	P.	PM.
1925-26 Pittsburgh		10	7	17	6
1926-27 "		12	3	15	4
1927-28 "		13	2	15	10
1928-29 "		9	3	12	6
1929-30 "		15	17	32	6
1930-31 Phila.-Boston		3	5	8	6
1931-32 Toronto		5	10	15	6
1932-33 "		1	2	3	0
8 Years		68	49	117	44

DARRAGH, JOHN PROCTOR RW&LW-SL
Born: Ottawa, Ont. Dec. 4, 1890

Sea. Club	Ga.	Go.	A.	P.	PM.
1917-18 Ottawa	18	14	-	14	-
1918-19 "	14	12	1	13	27
1919-20 "	22	22	5	27	22
1920-21 "	24	11	8	19	20
1922-23 "	24	7	7	14	13
1923-24 "	18	2	0	2	2
6 Years	120	68	21	89	84

1962 Hall of Fame

DAVIDSON, GORDON JOHN D-SL
Born: Stratton, Ont.

Sea. Club	Ga.	Go.	A.	P.	PM.
1942-43 New York	35	2	3	5	4
1943-44 " "	16	1	3	4	4
2 Years	51	3	6	9	8

DAVIDSON, ROBERT E. LW-SL
Born: Toronto, Ont. Feb. 10, 1912

Sea. Club	Ga.	Go.	A.	P.	PM.
1934-35 Toronto		0	0	0	6
1935-36 "		4	4	8	32
1936-37 "		8	7	15	43
1937-38 Toronto		3	17	20	52
1938-39 "		4	10	14	29
1939-40 "		8	18	26	56
1940-41 "		3	6	9	39
1941-42 "		6	20	26	39
1942-43 "	50	13	23	36	20
1943-44 "	47	19	28	47	21
1944-45 "	50	17	18	35	49
1945-46 "	41	9	9	18	12
12 Years		94	160	254	398

DAVIE, ROBERT H.

Sea. Club	Ga.	Go.	A.	P.	PM.
1933-34 Boston		0	0	0	6
1934-35 "		0	1	1	17
1935-36 "		0	0	0	2
3 Years		0	1	1	25

DAVIS, LORNE AUSTIN RW&D-SR
Born: Regina, Sask. July 20, 1930

Sea. Club	Ga.	Go.	A.	P.	PM.
1951-52 Montreal	3	1	1	2	2
1953-54 "	37	6	4	10	2
1954-55 Chicago-Detroit	30	0	5	5	6
1955-56 Boston	15	0	1	1	0
1959-60 "	10	1	1	2	10
5 Years	95	8	12	20	20

DAVIS, ROBERT

Sea. Club	Ga.	Go.	A.	P.	PM.
1932-33 Detroit		0	0	0	4

DAVISON, MURRAY D-SR
Born: Brantford, Ont. June 10, 1938

Sea. Club	Ga.	Go.	A.	P.	PM.
1965-66 Boston	1	0	0	0	0

DAWES, ROBERT J. C
Born: Saskatoon, Sask. 1924

Sea. Club	Ga.	Go.	A.	P.	PM.
1946-47 Toronto	1	0	0	0	0
1948-49 "	5	1	0	1	0
1,949-50 "	11	1	2	3	2
1950-51 Montreal	15	0	5	5	4
4 Years	32	2	7	9	6

DAY, CLARENCE HENRY LW&D-SL
Born: Owen Sound, Ont. June 14, 1901

Sea. Club	Ga.	Go.	A.	P.	PM.
1924-25 Toronto		10	12	22	27
1925-26 "		14	2	16	26
1926-27 "		11	5	16	50
1927-28 "		9	8	17	48
1928-29 "		6	6	12	85
1929-30 "		7	14	21	77
1930-31 "		1	13	14	56
1931-32 "		7	8	15	33
1932-33 "		6	14	20	46
1933-34 "		9	10	19	35
1934-35 "		2	4	6	38
1935-36 "		1	13	14	41
1936-37 "		3	4	7	20
1937-38 N. Y. Americans		0	3	3	14
14 Years		86	116	202	596

1961 Hall of Fame

DEACON, DONALD C-SL
Born: Regina, Sask. June 2, 1913

Sea. Club	Ga.	Go.	A.	P.	PM.
1936-37 Detroit		0	0	0	2
1938-39 "		1	3	4	2
1939-40 "		5	1	6	2
3 Years		6	4	10	6

DELMONTE, ARMAND R. RW

Sea. Club	Ga.	Go.	A.	P.	PM.
1945-46 Boston	1	0	0	0	0

DeLORY, VALENTINE A. F

Sea. Club	Ga.	Go.	A.	P.	PM.
1948-49 New York	1	0	0	0	0

DeMARCO ALBERT RW&C-SR
Born: North Bay, Ont. May 10, 1916

Sea. Club	Ga.	Go.	A.	P.	PM.
1938-39 Chicago		1	0	1	0
1939-40 "		0	5	5	17
1942-43 Toronto-Boston	7	4	2	6	0
1943-44 Boston-New York	39	14	19	33	2
1944-45 New York	50	24	30	54	10
1945-46 " "	50	20	27	47	20
1946-47 " "	44	9	10	19	4
7 Years		72	93	165	53

DEMERS, ANTONIO RW-SR
Born: Chambly Basin, Que. July 22, 1917

Sea. Club	Ga.	Go.	A.	P.	PM.
1939-40 Montreal		2	3	5	2
1940-41 "		13	10	23	17
1941-42 "		3	4	7	4
1942-43 "	9	2	5	7	0
1943-44 New York	1	0	0	0	0
5 Years		20	22	42	23

DENIS, JEAN-PAUL RW-SR
Born: Montreal, Que. Feb. 28, 1924

Sea. Club	Ga.	Go.	A.	P.	PM.
1946-47 New York	6	0	1	1	0
1949-50 " "	4	0	1	1	2
2 Years	10	0	2	2	2

Sea. Club	Ga.	Go.	A.	P.	PM.
DENIS, LOUIS GILBERT RW-SR					
Born: Vonda, Sask. June 7, 1928					
1949-50 Montreal	2	0	1	1	0
1950-51 "	1	0	0	0	0
2 Years	3	0	1	1	0
DENNENY, CORBETT C					
1917-18 Toronto	20		20		
1918-19 "	7	3	10	15	
1919-20 "	23	*12	35	18	
1920-21 "	17	6	23	27	
1921-22 "	19	7	26	28	
1922-23 "	1	0	1	0	
1923-24 Hamilton	0	0	0	6	
1926-27 Toronto	7	1	8	24	
1927-28 Chicago	5	0	5	16	
9 Years	99	29	128	134	
*League Leader					
DENNENY, CYRIL LW-SL					
Born: Farran's Point, Ont. 1891					
1917-18 Ottawa	36		36		
1918-19 "	18	4	22	43	
1919-20 "	16	2	18	21	
1920-21 "	34	5	39	0	
1921-22 "	27	12	39	18	
1922-23 "	21	10	31	20	
1923-24 "	*22	1	*23	10	
1924-25 "	27	*15	42	16	
1925-26 "	24	12	36	18	
1926-27 "	17	6	23	16	
1927-28 "	3	0	3	12	
1928-29 Boston	1	2	3	2	
12 Years	246	69	315	176	
*League Leader					
1959 Hall of Fame					
DENOIRD, GERALD					
1922-23 Toronto	15	0	0	0	0
DESAULNIERS, GERARD C-SL					
Born: Shawinigan Falls, Que. Dec. 31, 1928					
1950-51 Montreal	3	0	1	1	2
1952-53 "	2	0	1	1	2
1953-54 "	3	0	0	0	0
3 Years	8	0	2	2	4
DESILETS, JOFFRE WILFRED RW-SR					
Born: Capreol, Ont. Apr. 16, 1915					
1935-36 Mont. Canadiens	7	6	13	0	
1936-37 " "	7	12	19	17	
1937-38 " "	6	7	13	6	
1938-39 Chicago	11	13	24	28	
1939-40 "	6	7	13	6	
5 Years	37	45	82	57	
DESJARDINS, VICTOR A. C SL					
Born: Sault Ste. Marie, Mich.					
1930-31 Chicago	3	12	15	11	
1931-32 N. Y. Rangers	3	3	6	16	
2 Years	6	15	21	27	
DESLAURIERS, JACQUES D-SL					
Born: Montreal, Que. Sept. 3, 1928					
1955-56 Montreal	2	0	0	0	0
DEWAR, THOMAS D					
Born: Frobisher, Sask.					
1943-44 New York	9	0	2	2	4
DEWSBURY, ALBERT P. D-SL					
1946-47 Detroit	23	2	1	3	12
1949-50 "	11	2	2	4	2
1950-51 Chicago	67	5	14	19	79
1951-52 "	69	7	17	24	99
1952-53 "	69	5	16	21	97
1953-54 "	69	6	15	21	44
1954-55 "	12	0	1	1	10
1955-56 "	37	3	12	15	22
8 Years	357	30	78	108	365
DHEERE, MARCEL A. LW					
1942-43 Montreal	11	1	2	3	2
DIACHUK, EDWARD LW-SL					
Born: Vegreville, Alb., Aug. 16, 1936					
1960-61 Detroit	12	0	0	0	19

Sea. Club	Ga.	Go.	A.	P.	PM.
DICK, HARRY D					
1946-47 Chicago	12	0	1	1	12
DICKENS, ERNEST L. D-SL					
Born: Winnipeg, Man.					
1941-42 Toronto	10	2	2	4	6
1945-46 "	15	1	3	4	6
1947-48 Chicago	54	5	15	20	30
1948-49 "	59	2	3	5	14
1949-50 "	70	0	13	13	22
1950-51 "	70	2	8	10	20
6 Years	278	12	44	56	98
DICKENSON, JOHN H. RW					
1951-52 New York	37	14	13	27	8
1952-53 " "	11	4	4	8	2
2 Years	48	18	17	35	10
DILL, ROBERT E. D					
Born: U. S. A.					
1943-44 New York	28	6	10	16	66
1944-45 " "	48	9	5	14	69
2 Years	76	15	15	30	135
DILLON, CECIL GORDON RW-SL					
Born: Toledo, Ohio Apr. 26, 1908					
1930-31 N. Y. Rangers	7	3	10	8	
1931-32 " " "	23	15	38	22	
1932-33 " " "	21	10	31	12	
1933-34 " " "	13	26	39	10	
1934-35 " " "	25	9	34	4	
1935-36 " " "	18	14	32	12	
1936-37 " " "	20	11	31	13	
1937-38 " " "	21	18	39	6	
1938-39 " " "	12	15	27	6	
1939-40 Detroit	7	10	17	12	
10 Years	167	131	298	105	
1935-36 2nd All-Star Team					
1936-37 " " " "					
1937-38 1st " " "					
DINEEN, WILLIAM PATRICK RW-SR					
Born: Arvida, Que. Sept. 18, 1932					
1953-54 Detroit	70	17	8	25	34
1954-55 "	69	10	9	19	36
1955-56 "	70	12	7	19	30
1956-57 "	51	6	7	13	12
1957-58 Detroit-Chicago	63	6	13	19	10
5 Years	323	51	44	95	122
DINSMORE, CHARLES F					
1924-25 Mont. Maroons	2	1	3	26	
1925-26 " "	3	1	4	18	
1926-27 " "	1	0	1	6	
1929-30 " "	0	0	0	0	
4 Years	6	2	8	50	
DONNELLY, BABE D					
1926-27 Mont. Maroons	0	1	1	14	
DORAN, JOHN M. D-SR					
Born: Toronto Ont. May 24, 1910					
1933-34 N. Y. Americans	1	4	5	40	
1935-36 " " "	4	2	6	44	
1936-37 " " "	0	1	1	10	
1937-38 Detroit	0	0	0	10	
1939-40 Montreal	0	3	3	6	
5 Years	5	10	15	110	
DORAN, LLOYD G. C					
1946-47 Detroit	24	3	2	5	10
DORATY, KENNETH RW					
1926-27 Chicago	0	0	0	0	
1932-33 Toronto	5	11	16	16	
1933-34 "	9	10	19	6	
1934-35 "	1	4	5	0	
1937-38 Detroit	0	1	1	2	
5 Years	15	26	41	24	
DOROHOY, EDWARD C-SL					
Born: Medicine Hat. Alb., Mar. 13, 1929					
1948-49 Montreal	16	0	0	0	6
DOUGLAS, LESTER C					
Born: Perth, Ont.					

(continued)

Sea. Club	Ga.	Go.	A.	P.	PM.
1940-41 Detroit	18	1	2	3	2
1942-43 "	21	5	8	13	4
1945-46 "	1	0	0	0	0
1946-47 "	12	0	2	2	2
4 Years	52	6	12	18	8

DOWNIE, DAVID M. RW
Born: Burks Falls, Ont.

1932-33 Toronto		0	1	1	2

DRAPER, BRUCE C-SL
Born: Toronto, Ont. Oct. 2, 1940

1962-63 Toronto	1	0	0	0	0

DRILLON (Drillen), GORDON RW-SR
Born: Moncton, N. Bruns. Oct. 23, 1914

1936-37 Toronto		16	17	33	2
1937-38 "		*26	26	*52	4
1938-39 "		18	16	34	15
1939-40 "		21	19	40	13
1940-41 "		23	21	44	2
1941-42 "		23	18	41	6
1942-43 Montreal	49	28	22	50	14
7 Years		155	139	294	56

*League Leader
1937-38 1st All-Star Team, Lady Byng Trophy
1938-39 " " " "
1941-42 2nd " " "

DRINKWATER, RAINY BOILEAU — See BOILEAU, RENE

DROUILLARD, CLARENCE C
Born: Windsor, Ont.

1937-38 Detroit		0	1	1	0

DROUIN, PAUL EMILE C&LW-SL
Born: Verdun, Que. 1916

1935-36 Mont. Canadiens		1	8	9	19
1937-38 " "		7	13	20	8
1938-39 " "		7	11	18	2
1939-40 " "		4	11	15	51
1940-41 " "		4	7	11	0
5 Years		23	50	73	80

DRUMMOND, JAMES HENRY D-SL
Born: Toronto, Ont.

1944-45 New York	2	0	0	0	0

DRURY, HERBERT J. LW

1925-26 Pittsburgh		6	2	8	40
1926-27 "		5	1	6	48
1927-28 "		6	4	10	44
1928-29 "		5	4	9	49
1929-30 "		2	0	2	12
1930-31 Philadelphia		0	2	2	10
6 Years		24	13	37	203

DUBE, JOSEPH GILLES LW

1949-50 Montreal	12	1	2	3	2

DUGGAN, JACK

1925-26 Ottawa	27	0	0	0	2

DUGUID, LORNE WALLACE LW
Born: Bolton, Ont. April 4, 1910

1931-32 Mont. Maroons		0	0	0	6
1932-33 " "		4	7	11	38
1933-34 " "		0	1	1	0
1934-35 Detroit		3	3	6	9
1935-36 Boston		1	4	5	2
1936-37 "		1	0	1	2
6 Years		9	15	24	57

DUMART, WOODROW W. C. LW-SL
Born: Kitchener, Ont. Dec. 23, 1916

1936-37 Boston		4	4	8	2
1937-38 "		13	14	27	6
1938-39 "		14	15	29	2
1939-40 "		22	21	43	16
1940-41 "	40	18	15	33	2
1941-42 "	35	14	15	29	8
1942-45 Military Service					
1945-46 Boston	50	22	12	34	2
1946-47 "	60	24	28	52	12
1947-48 "	59	21	16	37	14
1948-49 "	59	11	12	23	6

(continued)

Sea. Club	Ga.	Go.	A.	P.	PM.
1949-50 "	69	14	25	39	14
1950-51 "	70	20	21	41	7
1951-52 "	39	5	8	13	0
1952-53 "	62	5	9	14	2
1953-54 "	69	4	3	7	6
15 Years		211	218	429	99

1939-40 2nd All-Star Team
1940-41 " " " "
1946-47 " " " "

DUNCAN, ARTHUR D-SR

1926-27 Detroit		3	2	5	26
1927-28 Toronto		7	5	12	97
1928-29 "		4	4	8	53
1929-30 "		.4	5	9	49
4 Years		18	16	34	225

DUNLAP, FRANK D

1943-44 Toronto	5	0	1	1	2

DUSSAULT, JOSEPH NORMAND LW
Born: Springfield, Mass.

1947-48 Montreal	28	5	10	15	4
1948-49 "	47	9	8	17	6
1949-50 "	67	13	24	37	22
1950-51 "	64	4	20	24	15
4 Years	206	31	62	93	47

DUTKOWSKI, LAUDES JOSEPH F&D
Born: Ragina, Sask. August 31, 1902

1926-27 Chicago		3	2	5	22
1929-30 "		7	10	17	42
1930-31 Chicago-N. Y. Americans		2	4	6	40
1932-33 N. Y. Americans		4	7	11	43
1933-34 N. Y. Americans-Chicago-					
N. Y. Rangers		0	7	7	31
5 Years		16	30	46	178

DUTTON, MERVYN A. D-SR
Born: Russell, Man. July 23, 1898

1926-27 Mont. Maroons		4	4	8	108
1927-28 " "		7	6	13	94
1928-29 " "		1	3	4	*139
1929-30 " "		3	13	16	98
1930-31 N. Y. Americans		1	11	12	71
1931-32 " " "		3	5	8	*107
1932-33 " " "		0	2	2	74
1933-34 " " "		2	8	10	65
1934-35 " " "		3	7	10	46
1935-36 " " "		5	8	13	69
10 Years		29	67	96	871

*League Leader
1958 Hall of Fame

DYCK, HENRY R. C
Born: Swift Current, Sask.

1943-44 New York	1	0	0	0	0

DYE, CECIL RW-SR
Born: Hamilton, Ont. May 13, 1898

1919-20 Toronto		12	3	15	10
1920-21 Hamilton-Toronto		*35	2	37	32
1921-22 Toronto		30	7	37	18
1922-23 "		*26	11	*37	19
1923-24 "		17	2	19	23
1924-25 "		*38	6	*44	41
1925-26 "		18	5	23	26
1926-27 Chicago		25	5	30	14
1927-28 "		0	0	0	0
1928-29 N. Y. Americans		1	0	1	17
1930-31 Toronto		0	0	0	0
11 Years		202	41	243	200

*League Leader
Hall of Fame

DYTE, JOHN D
Born: Kingston, Ont.

1943-44 Chicago	27	1	0	1	31

EDDOLLS, FRANK H. D-SL
Born: Lachine, Que. July 5, 1921

1944-45 Montreal	43	5	8	13	20
1945-46 "	8	0	1	1	6
1946-47 "	6	0	0	0	0
1947-48 New York	58	6	13	19	16
1948-49 " "	34	4	2	6	10

(continued)

Sea.	Club	Ga.	Go.	A.	P.	PM.
1949-50	" "	58	2	6	8	20
1950-51	" "	68	3	8	11	24
1951-52	" "	42	3	5	8	18
8 Years		317	23	43	66	114

EDMUNDSON, GARRY FRANK LW&C-SL
Born: Sexsmith, Alb. May 6, 1932

Sea.	Club	Ga.	Go.	A.	P.	PM.
1951-52	Montreal	1	0	0	0	2
1959-60	Toronto	39	4	6	10	47
1960-61	"	3	0	0	0	0
3 Years		43	4	6	10	49

EGAN, MARTIN JOSEPH D-SR
Born: Blackie, Alb. Apr. 26, 1918

Sea.	Club	Ga.	Go.	A.	P.	PM.
1939-40	N. Y. Americans		4	3	7	6
1940-41	" " "		4	9	13	51
1941-42	Brooklyn	48	8	20	28	*124
1942-43	Military Service					
1943-44	Detroit-Boston	48	15	28	43	95
1944-45	Boston	48	7	15	22	*86
1945-46	"	41	8	10	18	32
1946-47	"	60	7	18	25	89
1947-48	"	60	8	11	19	81
1948-49	"	60	6	18	24	92
1949-50	New York	70	5	11	16	50
1950-51	" "	70	5	10	15	70
11 Years			77	153	230	776

*League Leader
1941-42 2nd All-Star Team

ELIK, BORIS LW-SL
Born: Geraldton, Ont. Oct. 17, 1929

Sea.	Club	Ga.	Go.	A.	P.	PM.
1962-63	Detroit	3	0	0	0	0

ELLIOTT, FRED RW

Sea.	Club	Ga.	Go.	A.	P.	PM.
1928-29	Ottawa		2	0	2	6

EMMS, LEIGHTON LW&D
Born: Barrie, Ont. Jan. 12, 1905

Sea.	Club	Ga.	Go.	A.	P.	PM.
1926-27	Mont. Maroons		0	0		0
1927-28	" "		0	1	1	8
1930-31	N. Y. Americans		5	4	9	56
1931-32	N. Y. Americans-Detroit		7	9	16	38
1932-33	Detroit		9	13	22	63
1933-34	"		7	7	14	51
1934-35	Boston-N. Y. Americans		3	3	6	27
1935-36	N. Y. Americans		1	5	6	12
1936-37	" " "		4	8	12	48
1937-38	" " "		1	3	4	6
10 Years			37	53	90	309

ENIO – See SCLISIZZI

EVANS, STEWART D-SL
Born: Ottawa, Ont. June 19, 1908

Sea.	Club	Ga.	Go.	A.	P.	PM.
1930-31	Detroit		1	4	5	14
1932-33	"		2	6	8	74
1933-34	Detroit-Mont. Maroons		4	2	6	55
1934-35	Mont. Maroons		5	7	12	54
1935-36	" "		3	5	8	57
1936-37	" "		6	7	13	54
1937-38	" "		5	11	16	59
1938-39	Montreal Canadiens		2	7	9	58
8 Years			28	49	77	425

EVANS, WILLIAM JOHN D-SL
Born: Garnant, S. Wales Apr. 21, 1928

Sea.	Club	Ga.	Go.	A.	P.	PM.
1948-49	New York	3	0	0	0	4
1949-50	" "	2	0	0	0	2
1950-51	" "	49	1	0	1	95
1951-52	" "	52	1	6	7	83
1953-54	" "	44	4	4	8	73
1954-55	" "	47	0	5	5	91
1955-56	" "	70	2	9	11	104
1956-57	" "	70	3	6	9	110
1957-58	" "	70	4	8	12	108
1958-59	Chicago	70	1	8	9	75
1959-60	"	68	0	4	4	60
1960-61	"	69	0	8	8	58
1961-62	"	70	3	14	17	80
1962-63	"	68	0	8	8	46
14 Years		752	19	80	99	989

EZINICKI, WILLIAM RW-SR
Born: Winnipeg, Man. March 11, 1924

Sea.	Club	Ga.	Go.	A.	P.	PM.
1944-45	Toronto	8	1	4	5	17
1945-46	"	24	4	8	12	29
1946-47	"	60	17	20	37	93
1947-48	"	60	11	20	31	97
1948-49	"	52	13	15	28	*145
1949-50	"	67	10	12	22	*144
1950-51	Boston	53	16	19	35	119
1951-52	"	28	5	5	10	47
1954-55	New York	16	2	2	4	22
9 Years		368	79	105	184	713

* League Leader

FAHEY, JOHN TREVOR LW-SL
Born: New Waterford, Nova Scotia Jan. 4, 1944

Sea.	Club	Ga.	Go.	A.	P.	PM.
1964-65	New York	1	0	0	0	0

FARRANT, WALTER LESLIE F

Sea.	Club	Ga.	Go.	A.	P.	PM.
1943-44	Chicago	1	0	0	0	0

FASHOWAY, GORDON LW-SL
Born: Portage la Prairie, Man. June 16, 1926

Sea.	Club	Ga.	Go.	A.	P.	PM.
1950-51	Chicago	13	3	2	5	14

FAULKNER, SELM ALEXANDER C-SL
Born: Bishop's Falls, Newfoundland May 21, 1936

Sea.	Club	Ga.	Go.	A.	P.	PM.
1961-62	Toronto	1	0	0	0	0
1962-63	Detroit	70	10	10	20	6
1963-64	"	30	5	7	12	9
3 Years		101	15	17	32	15

FERGUSON, LORNE ROBERT LW&RW-SL
Born: Palmerston, Ont. May 26, 1930

Sea.	Club	Ga.	Go.	A.	P.	PM.
1949-50	Boston	3	1	1	2	0
1950-51	"	70	16	17	33	31
1951-52	"	27	3	4	7	14
1954-55	"	69	20	14	34	24
1955-56	Boston-Detroit	63	15	12	27	30
1956-57	Detroit	70	13	10	23	26
1957-58	Detroit-Chicago	53	7	12	19	24
1958-59	Chicago	67	7	10	17	44
8 Years		422	82	80	162	193

FIELD, WILFRED S. D-SR
Born: Winnipeg, Man. Apr. 29, 1916

Sea.	Club	Ga.	Go.	A.	P.	PM.
1938-39	N. Y. Americans		1	3	4	37
1939-40	" " "		1	3	4	28
1940-41	" " "		5	6	11	31
1941-42	Brooklyn	41	6	9	15	23
1944-45	Montreal-Chicago	48	4	4	8	32
5 Years			17	25	42	151

FIELDER, GUYLE ABNER C-SL
Born: Potlach, Idaho Nov. 21, 1930

Sea.	Club	Ga.	Go.	A.	P.	PM.
1950-51	Chicago	3	0	0	0	0
1957-58	Detroit	6	0	0	0	2
2 Years		9	0	0	0	2

FILLION, MARCEL F

Sea.	Club	Ga.	Go.	A.	P.	PM.
1944-45	Boston	1	0	0	0	0

FILLION, ROBERT L. LW

Sea.	Club	Ga.	Go.	A.	P.	PM.
1943-44	Montreal	41	7	23	30	14
1944-45	"	31	6	8	14	12
1945-46	"	50	10	6	16	12
1946-47	"	57	6	3	9	16
1947-48	"	32	9	9	18	8
1948-49	"	59	3	9	12	14
1949-50	"	57	1	3	4	8
7 Years		327	42	61	103	84

FILMORE, THOMAS RW
Born: Thamesford, Ont.

Sea.	Club	Ga.	Go.	A.	P.	PM.
1930-31	Detroit		7	2	9	10
1931-32	Detroit-N. Y. Americans		9	6	15	14
1932-33	N. Y. Americans		1	4	5	9
3 Years			17	12	29	33

FINKBEINER, LLOYD

Sea.	Club	Ga.	Go.	A.	P.	PM.
1940-41	N. Y. Americans		0	0	0	0

FINNEY, JOSEPH SIDNEY C-SL
Born: Banbridge, Ireland May 1, 1929

Sea.	Club	Ga.	Go.	A.	P.	PM.
1951-52	Chicago	35	6	5	11	0
1952-53	"	18	4	2	6	4
1953-54	"	6	0	0	0	0
3 Years		59	10	7	17	4

Sea. Club	Ga.	Go.	A.	P.	PM.
FINNIGAN, EDWARD					
1934-35 St. Louis	1	1	2		2
FINNIGAN, FRANK RW-SR					
Born: Shawville, Que. July 9, 1903					
1923-24 Ottawa		0	0	0	0
1924-25 "		0	0	0	20
1925-26 "		2	0	2	24
1926-27 "		15	1	16	52
1927-28 "		20	5	25	34
1928-29 "		15	4	19	71
1929-30 "		21	15	36	46
1930-31 "		9	8	17	40
1931-32 Toronto		8	13	21	45
1932-33 Ottawa		4	14	18	37
1933-34 "		10	10	20	10
1934-35 St. Louis-Toronto		7	5	12	12
1935-36 Toronto		2	6	8	10
1936-37 "		2	7	9	4
14 Years		115	88	203	405
FISHER, ALVIN					
1924-25 Toronto	9	1	0	1	4
FISHER, DUNCAN ROBERT RW-SR					
Born: Regina, Sask. Aug. 30, 1927					
1948-49 New York	60	9	16	25	40
1949-50 " "	70	12	21	33	42
1950-51 New York-Boston	65	9	20	29	20
1951-52 Boston	65	15	12	27	2
1952-53 "	7	0	1	1	0
1958-59 Detroit	8	0	0	0	0
6 Years	275	45	70	115	104
FISHER, JOSEPH RW-SR					
Born: Medicine Hat. Alb., July 4, 1916					
1939-40 Detroit		2	4	6	2
1940-41 "		5	8	13	11
1941-42 "		0	0	0	0
1942-43 "	1	1	0	1	0
4 Years		8	12	20	13
FITZPATRICK, ALEXANDER STEWART C-SL					
Born: Paisley, Scotland Dec. 22, 1944					
1964-65 New York	4	0	0	0	2
1967-68 Minnesota	18	3	6	9	6
2 Years	22	3	6	9	8
FLAMAN, FERDINAND CHARLES D-SR					
Born: Dysart, Sask. Jan. 25, 1927					
1944-45 Boston	1	0	0	0	0
1945-46 "	1	0	0	0	0
1946-47 "	23	1	4	5	41
1947-48 "	56	4	6	10	69
1948-49 "	60	4	12	16	62
1949-50 "	69	2	5	7	122
1950-51 Boston-Toronto	53	3	7	10	101
1951-52 Toronto	61	0	7	7	110
1952-53 "	66	2	6	8	110
1953-54 "	62	0	8	8	84
1954-55 Boston	70	4	14	18	*150
1955-56 "	62	4	17	21	70
1956-57 "	68	6	25	31	108
1957-58 "	66	0	15	15	71
1958-59 "	70	0	21	21	101
1959-60 "	60	2	18	20	112
1960-61 "	62	2	9	11	59
17 Years	910	34	174	208	1370
*League Leader					
1954-55 2nd All-Star Team					
1956-57 " " " "					
1957-58 " " " "					
FLESCH, --					
1920-21 Hamilton	1	0	0	0	0
FOGOLIN, LIDIO J. D-SL					
1948-49 Detroit	43	1	2	3	59
1949-50 "	63	4	8	12	63
1950-51 Detroit—Chicago	54	3	11	14	79
1951-52 Chicago	69	0	9	9	96
1952-53 "	70	2	8	10	79
1953-54 "	68	0	1	1	95
1954-55 "	9	0	1	1	16
1955-56 "	51	0	8	8	88
8 Years	427	10	48	58	575
FOLK, WILLIAM JOSEPH D-SL					
Born: Regina, Sask. July 11, 1927					
1951-52 Detroit	4	0	0	0	2
1952-53 "	8	0	0	0	2
2 Years	12	0	0	0	4
FONTINATO, LOUIS D-SL					
Born: Guelph, Ont. Jan. 20, 1932					
1954-55 New York	27	2	2	4	60
1955-56 " "	70	3	15	18	*202
1956-57 " "	70	3	12	15	139
1957-58 " "	70	3	8	11	*152
1958-59 " "	64	7	6	13	149
1959-60 " "	64	2	11	13	137
1960-61 " "	53	2	3	5	100
1961-62 Montreal	54	2	13	15	*167
1962-63 "	63	2	8	10	141
9 Years	535	26	78	104	1247
*League Leader					
FORSEY, JACK RW&LW					
1942-43 Toronto	19	7	9	16	10
FORSLUND, GUS					
1932-33 Ottawa		4	9	13	2
FORTIER, CHARLES					
1923-24 Montreal	1	0	0	0	0
FOSTER, HARRY C. D					
Born: Guelph, Ont.					
1929-30 N. Y. Rangers		0	0	0	10
1931-32 Boston		1	2	3	12
1933-34 Detroit		0	0	0	2
1934-35 "		2	0	2	8
4 Years		3	2	5	32
FOSTER, HERBERT S. LW					
Born: Brockville, Ont.					
1940-41 New York Rangers	4	1	0	1	5
1947-48 " " "	1	0	0	0	0
2 Years	5	1	0	1	5
FOWLER, JAMES D-SR					
Born: Toronto, Ont. Apr. 6, 1915					
1936-37 Toronto		7	11	18	22
1937-38 "		10	12	22	8
1938-39 "		1	6	7	9
3 Years		18	29	47	39
FOWLER, THOMAS LW					
1946-47 Chicago	24	0	1	1	18
FOYSTON, FRANK C&LW-SL					
Born: Minesing, Ont. Feb. 1891					
1926-27 Detroit		10	5	15	16
1927-28 "		7	2	9	16
2 Years		17	7	24	32
1958 Hall of Fame					
FRAMPTON, ROBERT P. J. LW					
1949-50 Montreal	2	0	0	0	0
FRASER, ----					
1923-24 Hamilton	1	0	0	0	0
FRASER, ARCHIBALD M. C					
Born: Souris, Man.					
1943-44 New York	3	0	1	1	0
FRASER, GORDON D-SL					
1926-27 Chicago		14	6	20	89
1927-28 Chicago-Detroit		4	2	6	60
1928-29 Detroit		0	0	0	12
1929-30 Mont. Canadiens-Pitts.		6	4	10	41
1930-31 Philadelphia		0	0	0	22
5 Years		24	12	36	224
FRASER, HARVEY C					
Born: Souris, Man.					
1944-45 Chicago	21	5	4	9	0
FREDRICKSON, FRANK C-SL					
Born: Winnipeg, Man.					
1926-27 Detroit-Boston		18	13	31	46
1927-28 Boston		10	4	14	83
1928-29 Boston-Pittsburgh		6	8	14	52
1929-30 Pittsburgh		4	7	11	20

(continued)

Sea. Club	Ga.	Go.	A.	P.	PM.
1930-31 Detroit		1	2	3	6
5 Years		39	34	73	207
1958 Hall of Fame					
FREW, IRVINE D					
Born: Scotland					
1933-34 Mont. Maroons		2	1	3	41
1934-35 St. Louis		0	2	2	89
1935-36 Mont. Canadiens		0	2	2	16
3 Years		2	5	7	146
FROST, HARRY RW					
Born: New Liskeard, Ont.					
1938-39 Boston	-	0	0	0	0
FRYDAY, ROBERT G. LW					
1949-50 Montreal	2	1	0	1	0
1951-52 "	3	0	0	0	0
2 Years	5	1	0	1	0
GADSBY, WILLIAM ALEXANDER D-SL					
Born: Calgary, Alb. Aug. 8, 1927					
1946-47 Chicago	48	8	10	18	31
1947-48 "	60	6	10	16	66
1948-49 "	50	3	10	13	85
1949-50 "	70	10	24	34	138
1950-51 "	25	3	7	10	32
1951-52 "	59	7	15	22	87
1952-53 "	68	2	20	22	84
1953-54 "	70	12	29	41	108
1954-55 Chicago-New York	70	11	13	24	61
1955-56 New York	70	9	42	51	84
1956-57 " "	70	4	37	41	72
1957-58 " "	65	14	32	46	48
1958-59 " "	70	5	46	51	56
1959-60 " "	65	9	22	31	60
1960-61 " "	65	9	26	35	49
1961-62 Detroit	70	7	30	37	88
1962-63 "	70	4	24	28	116
1963-64 "	64	2	16	18	80
1964-65 "	61	0	12	12	122
1965-66 "	58	5	12	17	72
20 Years	1248	130	437	567	1539
1952-53 2nd All-Star Team					
1953-54 " " " "					
1955-56 1st All-Star Team					
1956-57 2nd " " "					
1957-58 1st " " "					
1958-59 " " " "					
1964-65 2nd " " "					
Hall of Fame					
GAGNE, ARTHUR RW					
1926-27 Mont. Canadiens	-	14	3	17	42
1927-28 " "	-	20	10	30	75
1928-29 " "	-	7	3	10	52
1929-30 Boston-Ottawa	-	6	5	11	38
1930-31 Ottawa	-	19	11	30	50
1931-32 Detroit	-	1	1	2	0
6 Years		67	33	100	257
GAGNE, PIERRE REYNAUD LW-SL					
Born: North Bay, Ont., June 5, 1940					
1959-60 Boston	2	0	0	0	0
GAGNON, JEAN RW-SR					
Born: Chicoutimi, Que. June 8, 1905					
1930-31 Mont. Canadiens	-	18	7	25	43
1931-32 " "	-	19	18	37	40
1932-33 " "	-	12	23	35	64
1933-34 " "	-	9	15	24	25
1934-35 Boston-Mont. Canadiens	-	2	6	8	11
1935-36 Mont. Canadiens	-	7	9	16	42
1936-37 " "	-	20	16	36	38
1937-38 " "	-	13	17	30	9
1938-39 " "	-	12	22	34	23
1939-40 Mont. Canad.-N. Y. Americans	-	8	8	16	0
10 Years		120	141	261	295
GAINOR, NORMAN LW					
1927-28 Boston	-	8	4	12	35
1928-29 "	-	14	5	19	30
1929-30 "	-	18	31	49	39
1930-31 "	-	8	3	11	14
1931-32 N. Y. Rangers	-	3	9	12	9
1934-35 Mont. Maroons	-	0	4	4	2
6 Years		51	56	107	129

Sea. Club	Ga.	Go.	A.	P.	PM.
GALBRAITH, W. PERCIVAL LW					
1926-27 Boston	-	9	8	17	26
1927-28 "	-	6	5	11	26
1928-29 "	-	2	1	3	44
1929-30 "	-	7	9	16	38
1930-31 "	-	2	3	5	28
1931-32 "	-	2	1	3	28
1932-33 "	-	1	2	3	28
1933-34 "	-	2	0	2	6
8 Years		31	29	60	224
GALLAGHER, JOHN D-SL					
Born: Kenora, Ont. 1909					
1930-31 Mont. Maroons	-	4	2	6	35
1931-32 " "	-	1	0	1	18
1932-33 Mont. Maroons-Detroit	-	4	6	10	48
1936-37 N. Y. Americans-Detroit	-	1	0	1	12
1937-38 N. Y. Americans	-	3	6	9	18
1938-39 " "	-	1	5	6	22
6 Years		14	19	33	153
GALLINGER, DONALD C. C					
1942-43 Boston	48	14	20	34	16
1943-44 "	23	13	5	18	6
1945-46 "	50	17	23	40	18
1946-47 "	47	11	19	30	12
1947-48 "	54	10	21	31	37
5 Years	222	65	88	153	89
GAMBLE, RICHARD FRANK LW-SL					
Born: Moncton, N. Bruns. Nov. 16, 1928					
1950-51 Montreal	1	0	0	0	0
1951-52 "	64	23	17	40	8
1952-53 "	69	11	13	24	26
1953-54 "	32	4	8	12	18
1954-55 Chicago	14	2	0	2	6
1955-56 Montreal	12	0	3	3	8
1965-66 Toronto	2	1	0	1	0
1966-67 "	1	0	0	0	0
8 Years	195	41	41	82	66
GARDINER, HERBERT MARTIN D-SL					
Born: Winnipeg, Man. May 1891					
1927-28 " "	-	4	3	7	22
1928-29 Chic.-Montreal Canadiens	-	0	0	0	0
3 Years		10	9	19	48
1926-27 Hart Trophy					
1958 Hall of Fame					
GARDNER, CALVIN PEARLY C-SL					
Born: Transcona, Man. Oct. 30, 1924					
1945-46 New York	16	8	2	10	2
1946-47 " "	52	13	16	29	30
1947-48 " "	58	7	18	25	71
1948-49 Toronto	53	13	22	35	35
1949-50 "	31	7	19	26	12
1950-51 "	66	23	28	51	42
1951-52 "	70	15	26	41	40
1952-53 Chicago	70	11	24	35	60
1953-54 Boston	70	14	20	34	62
1954-55 "	70	16	22	38	40
1955-56 "	70	15	21	36	57
1956-57 "	70	12	20	32	66
12 Years	696	154	238	392	517
GARIEPY, RAYMOND D					
Born: Toronto, Ont.					
1953-54 Boston	35	1	6	7	39
1955-56 Toronto	1	0	0	0	4
2 Years	36	1	6	7	43
GARRETT, DUDLEY D-SL					
1942-43 New York	23	1	1	2	18
GAUDREAULT, ARMAND G. LW					
1944-45 Boston	44	15	9	24	27
GAUDREAULT, LEO C					
Born: Chicoutimi, Que.					
1927-28 Mont. Canadiens	-	6	2	8	24
1928-29 " "	-	0	0	0	4
1932-33 " "	-	2	2	4	2
3 Years		8	4	12	30
GAUTHIER, ARTHUR					
1926-27 Mont. Canadiens	13	0	0	0	0

Sea. Club	Ga.	Go.	A.	P.	PM.
GAUTHIER, RENE FERNAND RW					
1943-44 New York	33	14	10	24	0
1944-45 Montreal	50	18	13	31	23
1945-46 Detroit	30	9	8	17	6
1946-47 "	40	1	12	13	2
1947-48 "	35	1	5	6	2
1948-49 "	41	3	2	5	2
6 Years	229	46	50	96	35
GEE, GEORGE C&LW-SL					
1945-46 Chicago	35	14	15	29	12
1946-47 "	60	20	20	40	26
1947-48 "	60	14	25	39	18
1948-49 Chicago−Detroit	51	7	14	21	31
1949-50 Detroit	69	17	21	38	42
1950-51 "	70	17	20	37	19
1951-52 Chicago	70	18	31	49	39
1952-53 "	67	18	21	39	99
1953-54 "	69	10	16	26	59
9 Years	551	135	183	318	345
GEOFFRION, BERNARD ANDRE RW-SR					
Born: Montreal, Que. Feb. 16, 1931					
1950-51 Montreal	18	8	6	14	9
1951-52 "	67	30	24	54	66
1952-53 "	65	22	17	39	37
1953-54 "	54	29	25	54	87
1954-55 "	70	*38	37	*75	57
1955-56 "	59	29	33	62	66
1956-57 "	41	19	21	40	18
1957-58 "	42	27	23	50	51
1958-59 "	59	22	44	66	30
1959-60 "	59	30	41	71	36
1960-61 "	64	*50	45	*95	29
1961-62 "	62	23	36	59	36
1962-63 "	51	23	18	41	73
1963-64 "	55	21	18	39	41
1966-67 New York	58	17	25	42	42
1967-68 " "	59	5	16	21	11
16 Years	883	393	429	822	689
*League Leader					
1951-52 Calder Trophy					
1954-55 2nd All-Star Team; Ross Trophy					
1959-60 2nd All-Star Team					
1960-61 Hart Trophy					
1960-61 1st All-Star Team; Ross Trophy					
Hall of Fame					
GERAN, GEORGE P.					
Born: U. S. A.					
1917-18 Mont. Wanderers	4	0		0	
1925-26 Boston	33	5	1	6	6
2 Years	37	5	1	6	6
GERARD, EDWARD GEORGE D					
Born: Ottawa, Ont. Feb. 22, 1890					
1917-18 Ottawa		13		13	
1918-19 "		4	6	10	17
1919-20 "		9	3	12	19
1920-21 "		11	4	15	18
1921-22 "		7	9	16	16
1922-23 "		6	8	14	24
6 Years		50	30	80	94
1945 Hall of Fame					
GETLIFFE, RAYMOND LW&C-SL					
Born: Galt, Ont. Apr. 3, 1914					
1935-36 Boston		0	0	0	2
1936-37 "		16	15	31	28
1937-38 "		11	13	24	16
1938-39 "		10	12	22	11
1939-40 Montreal		11	12	23	29
1940-41 "		15	10	25	25
1941-42 "		11	15	26	45
1942-43 "	50	18	28	46	26
1943-44 "	44	28	25	53	44
1944-45 "	41	16	7	23	54
10 Years		136	137	273	260
GIESEBRECHT, ROY GEORGE C-SL					
Born: Petawawa, Ont. Sept. 16, 1918					
1938-39 Detroit		10	10	20	2
1939-40 "		4	7	11	2
1940-41 "		7	18	25	7
1941-42 "	34	6	16	22	2
4 Years		27	51	78	13

Sea. Club	Ga.	Go.	A.	P.	PM
GILBERT, JEANNOT ELMOURT C-SL					
Born: Grande Baie, Que. Dec. 29, 1940					
1962-63 Boston	5	0	0	0	4
1964-65 "	4	0	1	1	0
2 Years	9	0	1	1	4
GILLIE, FARRAND					
1928-29 Detroit		0	0		0
GIRARD, KENNETH RW-SR					
Born: Toronto, Ont. Dec. 8, 1936					
1956-57 Toronto	3	0	1	1	2
1957-58 "	3	0	0	0	0
1959-60 "	1	0	0	0	0
3 Years	7	0	1	1	2
GIROUX, ARTHUR RW-SR					
Born: Binscarth, Man.					
1932-33 Mont. Canadiens		5	2	7	14
1934-35 Boston		1	0	1	0
1935-36 Detroit		0	2	2	0
3 Years		6	4	10	14
GLADU, JOSEPH JEAN-PAUL LW					
1944-45 Boston	40	6	14	20	2
GLOVER, FREDERICK AUSTIN C&RW-SR					
Born: Toronto, Ont. Jan. 5, 1928					
1949-50 Detroit	7	0	0	0	0
1951-52 "	54	9	9	18	25
1952-53 Chicago	31	4	2	6	37
3 Years	92	13	11	24	62
GODFREY, WARREN EDWARD D-SL					
Born: Toronto, Ont. Mar. 23, 1931					
1952-53 Boston	60	1	13	14	40
1953-54 "	70	5	9	14	71
1954-55 "	62	1	17	18	58
1955-56 Detroit	67	2	6	8	86
1956-57 "	69	1	8	9	103
1957-58 "	67	2	16	18	56
1958-59 "	69	6	4	10	44
1959-60 "	69	5	9	14	60
1960-61 "	63	3	16	19	62
1961-62 "	69	4	13	17	84
1962-63 Boston	66	2	9	11	56
1963-64 Detroit	4	0	0	0	2
1964-65 "	11	0	0	0	8
1965-66 "	26	0	4	4	22
1966-67 "	2	0	0	0	0
1967-68 "	12	0	1	1	0
16 Years	786	32	125	157	752
GODIN, H. GABRIEL "Sam" W					
Born: Rockland, Ont. September 20, 1909					
1927-28 Ottawa		0	0	0	0
1928-29 "		2	1	3	21
1933-34 Mont. Canadiens		2	2	4	15
3 Years		4	3	7	36
GOEGAN, PETER JOHN D-SL					
Born: Fort William, Ont. Mar. 6, 1934					
1957-58 Detroit	14	0	2	2	28
1958-59 "	67	1	11	12	109
1959-60 "	21	3	0	3	6
1960-61 "	67	5	29	34	78
1961-62 Detroit-New York	46	5	7	12	30
1962-63 Detroit	62	1	8	9	48
1963-64 "	12	0	0		8
1964-65 "	4	1	0	1	2
1965-66 "	13	0	2	2	14
1966-67 "	31	2	6	8	12
1967-68 Minnesota	46	1	2	3	30
11 Years	383	19	67	86	365
GOLDHAM, ROBERT J. D-SR					
Born: Georgetown, Ont. May 12, 1922					
1941-42 Toronto	19	4	7	11	25
1945-46 "	49	7	14	21	44
1946-47 "	11	1	1	2	10
1947-48 Chicago	38	2	9	11	38
1948-49 "	60	1	10	11	43
1949-50 "	67	2	10	12	57
1950-51 Detroit	61	5	18	23	31
1951-52 "	69	0	14	14	24
1952-53 "	70	1	13	14	32
1953-54 "	69	1	15	16	50
1954-55 "	69	1	16	17	14
1955-56 "	68	3	16	19	31
12 Years	650	28	143	171	400
1954-55 2nd All-Star Team					

Sea. Club	Ga.	Go.	A.	P.	PM.
GOLDSWORTHY, LEROY D. RW-SR					
Born: Two Harbors, Minn. Oct. 18, 1908					
1929-30 N. Y. Rangers		4	1	5	16
1930-31 Detroit		1	0	1	2
1932-33 "		3	6	9	6
1933-34 Chicago		3	3	6	0
1934-35 Mont. Canadiens		20	9	29	15
1935-36 " "		15	11	26	8
1936-37 Boston		8	6	14	8
1937-38 "		9	10	19	14
1938-39 N. Y. Americans		3	11	14	10
9 Years		66	57	123	79
GOLDUP, HENRY LW-SL					
Born: Kingston, Ont. Oct. 29, 1918					
1939-40 Toronto		6	4	10	2
1940-41 "		10	5	15	9
1941-42 "	44	12	18	30	13
1942-43 Toronto-New York	44	12	27	39	37
1943-44 Military Service					
1944-45 New York	48	17	25	42	25
1945-46 " "	19	6	1	7	11
6 Years		63	80	143	97
GOODEN, WILLIAM F. C. LW					
1942-43 New York	11	0	3	3	0
1943-44 " "	41	9	8	17	15
2 Years	52	9	11	20	15
GOODFELLOW, EBENEZER R. C&D-SL					
Born: Ottawa, Ont. Apr. 9, 1907					
1929-30 Detroit		17	17	34	54
1930-31 "		25	23	48	32
1931-32 "		14	16	30	56
1932-33 "		12	8	20	47
1933-34 "		13	13	26	45
1934-35 "		12	24	36	44
1935-36 "		5	18	23	69
1936-37 "		9	16	25	43
1937-38 "		0	7	7	13
1938-39 "		8	8	16	36
1939-40 "		11	17	28	31
1940-41 "		5	17	22	35
1941-42 "		2	2	4	2
1942-43 "	11	1	4	5	4
14 Years		134	190	324	511
1935-36 2nd All-Star Team					
1936-37 1st All-Star Team					
1939-40 " " " " & Hart Trophy					
1963 Hall of Fame					
GORDON, FRED F					
1926-27 Detroit		5	5	10	28
1927-28 Boston		3	2	5	44
2 Years		8	7	15	72
GORDON, JOHN C-SR					
Born: Winnipeg, Man. Mar. 3, 1928					
1948-49 New York	31	3	9	12	0
1949-50 " "	1	0	0	0	0
1950-51 " "	4	0	1	1	0
3 Years	36	3	10	13	0
GORMAN, EDWIN F. D-SL					
1924-25 Ottawa	30	11	3	14	49
1925-26 "	23	2	1	3	12
1926-27 "	39	1	0	1	17
1927-28 Toronto	18	0	1	1	30
4 Years	110	14	5	19	108
GOTTSELIG, JOHN P. LW-SL					
Born: Odessa, Russia June 24, 1906					
1928-29 Chicago		5	3	8	26
1929-30 "		21	4	25	28
1930-31 "		20	12	32	14
1931-32 "		14	15	29	28
1932-33 Chicago		11	11	22	6
1933-34 "		16	14	30	4
1934-35 "		19	18	37	16
1935-36 "		14	15	29	4
1936-37 "		9	21	30	10
1937-38 "		13	19	32	22
1938-39 "		16	23	39	15
1939-40 "		8	15	23	7
1940-41 "		1	4	5	5
1942-43 "	10	2	6	8	12
1943-44 "	45	8	15	23	6
1944-45 "	1	0	0	0	0
16 Years		177	195	372	203
1938-39 2nd All-Star Team					

Sea. Club	Ga.	Go.	A.	P.	PM.
GOUPILLE, CLIFFORD D-SL					
Born: Three Rivers, Que. Sept. 2, 1915					
1937-38 Mont. Canadiens		4	5	9	44
1938-39 " "		0	2	2	24
1939-40 " "		2	10	12	48
1940-41 " "		3	6	9	81
1941-42 " "		1	5	6	51
1942-43 " "	6	2	0	2	8
6 Years		12	28	40	256
GOYER, GERALD FRANCIS C-SL					
Born: Belleville, Ont. Oct. 20, 1936					
1967-68 Chicago	40	1	2	3	4
GRABOSKI, ANTHONY D-SL					
1940-41 Montreal		4	3	7	12
1941-42 "		2	5	7	8
1942-43 "	9	0	2	2	4
3 Years		6	10	16	24
GRACIE, ROBERT J. C&LW-SL					
Born: North Bay, Ont. Nov. 8, 1910					
1930-31 Toronto		4	2	6	4
1931-32 "		13	8	21	29
1932-33 "		9	13	22	27
1933-34 Boston-N. Y. Americans		6	12	18	20
1934-35 N. Y. Amer.-Mont. Maroons		12	9	21	15
1935-36 Mont. Maroons		11	14	25	31
1936-37 " "		11	25	36	18
1937-38 " "		12	19	31	32
1938-39 Montreal—Canadiens		4	7	11	31
9 Years		82	109	191	207
GRAHAM, EDWARD DIXON D					
Born: Owen Sound, Ont. January 30, 1906					
1927-28 Chicago		1	0	1	8
1929-30 "		1	2	3	23
1930-31 "		0	7	7	38
1931-32 "		0	3	3	40
1932-33 "		3	8	11	57
1933-34 Mont. Maroons-Detroit		3	1	4	39
1934-35 Detroit-St. Louis		0	2	2	28
1935-36 Boston		4	1	5	37
1936-37 N. Y. Americans		2	1	3	20
9 Years		14	25	39	290
GRAHAM, LETH LW					
1920-21 Ottawa Senators	13	0	0	0	0
1921-22 " "	2	2	0	2	0
1922-23 Hamilton Tigers	4	1	0	1	0
1923-24 Ottawa Senators	3	0	0	0	0
1924-25 " "	3	0	0	0	0
1925-26 " "	1	0	0	0	0
6 Years	26	3	0	3	0
GRAVELLE, JOSEPH G. LEO RW					
1946-47 Montreal	53	16	14	30	12
1947-48 "	15	0	0	0	0
1948-49 "	36	4	6	10	6
1949-50 "	70	19	10	29	18
1950-51 Montreal-Detroit	49	5	4	9	6
5 Years	223	44	34	78	42
GRAY, ALEXANDER C					
1927-28 N. Y. Rangers		7	0	7	28
1928-29 Toronto		0	0	0	2
2 Years		7	0	7	30
GREEN, REDVERS LW					
1923-24 Hamilton		11	0	11	20
1924-25 "		19	4	23	63
1925-26 N. Y. Americans		13	4	17	42
1926-27 " " "		10	4	14	53
1927-28 " " "		6	1	7	67
1928-29 Boston		0	0	0	16
6 Years		59	13	72	261
GREEN, WILFRED THOMAS RW-SR					
Born: Sudbury, Ont. July 17, 1896					
1923-24 Hamilton		7	2	9	19
1924-25 "		18	1	19	75
1925-26 N. Y. Americans		6	4	10	40
1926-27 " " "		2	1	3	17
4 Years		33	8	41	151
1962 Hall of Fame					
GRIGOR, GEORGE C-SR					
Born: Edinburgh, Scotland					
1943-44 Chicago	2	1	0	1	0

Sea. Club	Ga.	Go.	A.	P.	PM.
GRONSDAHL, LLOYD G. RW					
1941-42 Boston	10	1	2	3	0
GROSS, LLOYD LW					
Born: Kitchener, Ont.					
1926-27 Toronto		1	1	2	0
1933-34 N. Y. Amer.-Boston-Detroit	9	4	13		18
1934-35 Detroit	1	0	1		2
3 Years	11	5	16		20
GROSSO, DONALD JOSEPH LW&C-SL					
Born: Sault Ste. Marie, Ont. Apr. 12, 1915					
1938-39 Detroit		1	1	2	0
1939-40 "		2	3	5	11
1940-41 "		8	7	15	14
1941-42 "	48	23	30	53	13
1942-43 "	50	15	17	32	10
1943-44 "	42	16	31	47	13
1944-45 Detroit-Chicago	41	15	16	31	10
1945-46 Chicago	47	7	10	17	17
1946-47 Boston	33	0	2	2	2
9 Years		87	117	204	90
GROSVENOR, LEONARD C					
1927-28 Ottawa		1	2	3	18
1928-29 "		3	2	5	16
1929-30 "		0	3	3	19
1930-31 "		5	4	9	25
4 Years		9	11	20	78
GUIDOLIN, ALDO RENO RW&D-SR					
Born: Forks of Credit, Ont. June 6, 1932					
1952-53 New York	30	4	4	8	24
1953-54 " "	68	2	6	8	51
1954-55 " "	70	2	5	7	34
1955-56 " "	14	1	0	1	8
4 Years	182	9	15	24	117
GUIDOLIN, ARMAND LW&C-SL					
Born: Timmins, Ont. December 9, 1925					
1942-43 Boston	42	7	15	22	53
1943-44 "	47	17	25	42	58
1944-45 Canadian Armed Forces					
1945-46 "	50	15	17	32	62
1946-47 "	56	10	13	23	73
1947-48 Detroit	58	12	10	22	78
1948-49 Detroit-Chicago	60	4	17	21	116
1949-50 Chicago	70	17	34	51	42
1950-51 "	69	12	22	34	56
1951-52 "	67	13	18	31	78
9 Years	519	107	171	278	616
HADDON, LLOYD WARD D-SL					
Born: Sarnia, Ont., Aug. 10, 1938					
1959-60 Detroit	8	0	0	0	2
HAGGARTY, JAMES LW					
Born: Port Arthur, Ont.					
1941-42 Montreal		1	1	2	0
HALDERSON, HAROLD D					
1926-27 Detroit-Toronto		3	2	5	65
HALEY, LEONARD FRANK RW-SR					
Born: Edmonton, Alb., Sept. 15, 1931					
1959-60 Detroit	27	1	2	3	12
1960-61 "	3	1	0	1	2
2 Years	30	2	2	4	14
HALL, GARY WAYNE LW-SL					
Born: Melita, Man. May 22, 1939					
1960-61 New York	4	0	0	0	0
HALL, JOSEPH HENRY D-SR					
Born: Staffordshire, England, 1882					
1917-18 Montreal Canadiens	20	8		8	
1918-19 " "	17	7	1	8	*85
2 Years	37	15	1	16	85
*League Leader					
1961 Hall of Fame					
HALL, ROBERT G. "Red" C					
1925-26 N. Y. Americans	8	0	0	0	0

Sea. Club	Ga.	Go.	A.	P.	PM.
HALLIDAY, MILTON					
1926-27 Ottawa		1	0	1	2
1927-28 "		0	0	0	2
1928-29 Ottawa Senators		0	0	0	0
3 Years		1	0	1	4
HAMEL, HERBERT F					
1930-31 Toronto		0	0	0	4
HAMILL, ROBERT GEORGE LW-SL					
Born: Toronto, Ont. Jan. 11, 1917					
1937-38 Boston		0	1	1	2
1938-39 "		0	1	1	0
1939-40 "		10	8	18	16
1940-41 "		0	1	1	0
1941-42 Boston-Chicago	43	24	12	36	23
1942-43 Chicago	50	28	16	44	44
1945-46 "	38	20	17	37	23
1946-47 "	60	21	19	40	12
1947-48 "	60	11	13	24	18
1948-49 "	57	8	4	12	16
1949-50 "	59	6	2	8	6
1950-51 "	2	0	0	0	0
12 Years		128	94	222	160
HAMILTON, CHARLES C&D SL					
Born: Kirkland Lake, Ont. Jan. 18, 1939					
1961-62 Montreal	1	0	0	0	0
HAMILTON, JOHN M. LW&C-SL					
1942-43 Toronto	13	1	6	7	4
1943-44 "	49	20	17	37	4
1945-46 "	40	7	9	16	12
3 Years	102	28	32	60	20
HAMILTON, REGINALD D-SL					
Born: Toronto, Ont. Apr. 29, 1914					
1936-37 Toronto		3	7	10	32
1937-38 "		1	4	5	43
1938-39 "		0	7	7	54
1939-40 "		2	2	4	23
1940-41 "		3	12	15	59
1941-42 "	22	0	4	4	27
1942-43 "	48	4	17	21	68
1943-44 "	39	4	12	16	32
1944-45 "	50	3	12	15	41
1945-46 Chicago	48	1	7	8	31
1946-47 "	10	0	3	3	2
11 Years		21	87	108	412
HANNA, JOHN D-SR					
Born: Sydney, Nova Scotia Apr. 5, 1935					
1958-59 New York	70	1	10	11	83
1959-60 " "	61	4	8	12	87
1960-61 " "	46	1	8	9	34
1963-64 Montreal	6	0	0	0	2
1967-68 Philadelphia	15	0	0	0	0
5 Years	198	6	26	32	206
HANNIGAN, JOHN GORDON LW-SL					
1952-53 Toronto	65	17	18	35	51
1953-54 "	35	4	4	8	18
1954-55 "	13	0	2	2	8
1955-56 "	48	8	7	15	40
4 Years	161	29	31	60	117
HANNIGAN, RAYMOND J. RW-SR					
1948-49 Toronto	3	0	0	0	2
HANSON, EMIL D					
Born: Rapid City, S. Dakota					
1932-33 Detroit		0	0	0	6
HANSON, OSCAR SL					
Born: U. S. A.					
1937-38 Chicago		0	0	0	0
HARMON, GLEN DAVID D-SL					
Born: Holland, Man. Jan. 2, 1921					
1942-43 Montreal	27	5	9	14	25
1943-44 "	43	5	16	21	36
1944-45 "	42	5	8	13	41

(continued)

Sea. Club	Ga.	Go.	A.	P.	PM.
1945-46 ''	49	7	10	17	28
1946-47 ''	57	5	9	14	53
1947-48 ''	56	10	4	14	52
1948-49 ''	59	8	12	20	44
1949-50 ''	62	3	16	19	28
1950-51 ''	57	2	12	14	27
9 Years	452	50	96	146	334
1944-45 2nd All-Star Team					
1948-49 '' '' '' ''					

HARMS, JOHN RW

1943-44 Chicago	1	0	0	0	0
1944-45 ''	43	5	5	10	21
2 Years	44	5	5	10	21

HARNOTT, WALTER W

1933-34 Boston		0	0	0	2

HARRINGTON, LELAND LW-SL
Born: U. S. A.

1925-26 Boston		7	2	9	6
1927-28 ''		1	0	1	7
1932-33 Mont. Canadiens		1	1	2	2
3 Years		9	3	12	15

HARRIS, FRED LW-SL
Born: Kenora, Ont.

1924-25 Boston	6	3	1	4	8

HARRIS, GEORGE FRANCIS RW-SL
Born: Sarnia, Ont. Feb. 25, 1942

1967-68 Minn-Toronto	26	1	4	5	4

HARRIS, HENRY LW-SL

1930-31 Boston		2	4	6	20

HARRISON, EDWARD F. RW

1947-48 Boston	52	6	7	13	8
1948-49 ''	59	5	5	10	20
1949-50 ''	70	14	12	26	23
1950-51 Boston-New York	13	2	0	2	2
4 Years	194	27	24	51	53

HART, WILFRED LW

1926-27 Mont. Canadiens		3	3	6	8
1927-28 '' ''		3	2	5	4
1932-33 '' ''		0	3	3	0
3 Years		6	8	14	12

HASSARD, ROBERT H. RW&C-SR

1949-50 Toronto	1	0	0	0	0
1950-51 ''	12	0	1	1	0
1952-53 ''	70	8	23	31	14
1953-54 ''	26	1	4	5	4
1954-55 Chicago	17	0	0	0	4
5 Years	126	9	28	37	22

HAWORTH, GORDON JOSEPH C-SL
Born: Drummondville, Que. Feb. 20, 1932

1952-53 New York	2	0	1	1	0

HAY, GEORGE LW-SL
Born: Listowel, Ont. Jan. 1898

1926-27 Chicago		14	8	22	12
1927-28 Detroit		22	13	35	20
1928-29 ''		11	8	19	14
1929-30 ''		18	15	33	8
1930-31 ''		8	10	18	24
1932-33 ''		1	6	7	6
6 Years		74	60	134	84
1958 Hall of Fame					

HAY, JAMES ALEXANDER D-SR
Born: Saskatoon, Sask. May 15, 1931

1952-53 Detroit	42	1	4	5	2
1953-54 ''	12	0	0	0	0
1954-55 ''	21	0	1	1	20
3 Years	75	1	5	6	22

HAY, WILLIAM CHARLES C-SL
Born: Saskatoon, Sask. Dec. 8, 1935

1959-60 Chicago	70	18	37	55	31
1960-61 ''	69	11	48	59	45

(continued)

Sea. Club	Ga.	Go.	A.	P.	PM.
1961-62 ''	60	11	52	63	34
1962-63 ''	64	12	33	45	36
1963-64 ''	70	23	33	56	30
1964-65 ''	69	11	26	37	36
1965-66 ''	68	20	31	51	20
1966-67 ''	36	7	13	20	12
8 Years	506	113	273	388	244
1959-60 Calder Trophy					

HAYNES, PAUL C-SL
Born: Montreal, Que. Mar. 1, 1910

1930-31 Mont. Maroons		1	0	1	0
1931-32 '' ''		1	0	1	0
1932-33 '' ''		16	25	41	18
1933-34 '' ''		5	4	9	18
1934-35 Mont. Maroons-Boston		5	5	10	8
1935-36 Mont. Canadiens		5	19	24	24
1936-37 '' ''		8	18	26	24
1937-38 '' ''		13	22	35	25
1938-39 '' ''		5	33	38	27
1939-40 '' ''		2	8	10	8
1940-41 '' ''		0	0	0	12
11 Years		61	134	195	164

HEAD, GALEN RUSSELL RW-SR
Born: Grande Prairie, Alb. Apr. 16, 1947

1967-68 Detroit	1	0	0	0	0

HEADLEY, FERN

1924-25 Boston-Mont. Canadiens	27	1	1	2	6

HEALEY, RICHARD THOMAS D-SL
Born: Vancouver, Br. Col. Mar. 12, 1938

1960-61 Detroit	1	0	0	0	2

HEBENTON, ANDREW ALEX RW-SL
Born: Winnipeg, Man. Oct. 3, 1929

1955-56 New York	70	24	14	38	8
1956-57 '' ''	70	21	23	44	10
1957-58 '' ''	70	21	24	45	17
1958-59 '' ''	70	33	29	62	8
1959-60 '' ''	70	19	27	46	4
1960-61 '' ''	70	26	28	54	10
1961-62 '' ''	70	18	24	42	10
1962-63 '' ''	70	15	22	37	8
1963-64 Boston	70	12	11	23	8
9 Years	630	189	202	391	83
1956-57 Lady Byng Trophy					

HEFFERNAN, FRANK

1919-20 Toronto	17	0	0	0	0

HEFFERNAN, GERALD RW-SR

1941-42 Montreal		5	15	20	15
1943-44 ''	43	28	20	48	12
2 Years		33	35	68	27

HEINRICH, LIONEL G. RW&D

1955-56 Boston	35	1	1	2	33

HELLER, EHRHARDT HENRY D-SR
Born: Kitchener, Ont. June 2, 1910

1931-32 N. Y. Rangers	21	2	2	4	9
1932-33 '' '' ''	40	5	7	12	31
1933-34 '' '' ''	48	2	5	7	29
1934-35 '' '' ''	47	3	11	14	31
1935-36 '' '' ''	43	2	11	13	40
1936-37 '' '' ''	48	5	12	17	42
1937-38 '' '' ''	48	2	14	16	68
1938-39 '' '' ''	48	0	23	23	42
1939-40 '' '' ''	47	5	14	19	26
1940-41 '' '' ''	48	2	16	18	42
1941-42 '' '' ''	35	6	5	11	22
1942-43 '' '' ''	45	4	14	18	14
1943-44 '' '' ''	50	8	27	35	29
1944-45 '' '' ''	45	7	12	19	26
1945-46 '' '' ''	34	2	3	5	14
15 Years	647	55	176	231	465
1940-41 2nd All-Star Team					

HELMAN, HARRY

1922-23 Ottawa Senators	24	0	0	0	5
1923-24 '' ''	17	1	0	1	2
1924-25 '' ''	1	0	0	0	0
3 Years	42	1	0	1	7

Sea. Club	Ga.	Go.	A.	P.	PM
HEMMERLING, E. C. LW-SL					
Born: Landis, Sask. Aug. 11, 1914					
1935-36 N. Y. Americans		0	0	0	0
1936-37 " "		3	3	6	4
2 Years		3	3	6	4
HENDERSON, JOHN MURRAY D-SL					
1944-45 Boston	5	0	1	1	4
1945-46 "	48	4	11	15	30
1946-47 "	57	5	12	17	63
1947-48 "	49	6	8	14	50
1948-49 "	60	2	9	11	28
1949-50 "	64	3	8	11	42
1950-51 "	66	4	7	11	37
1951-52 "	56	0	6	6	51
8 Years	405	24	62	86	305
HENDRICKSON, JOHN GUNNARD D-SR					
Born: Kingston, Ont. Dec. 5, 1936					
1957-58 Detroit	1	0	0	0	0
1958-59 "	3	0	0	0	2
1961-62 "	1	0	0	0	2
3 Years	5	0	0	0	4
HERBERTS, JAMES C					
1924-25 Boston		17	5	22	50
1925-26 "		26	5	31	47
1926-27 "		15	7	22	51
1927-28 Boston-Toronto		15	4	19	64
1928-29 Detroit		9	5	14	34
1929-30 "		1	3	4	4
6 Years		83	29	112	250
HERCHENRATTER, AUGGIE RW					
Born: Kitchener, Ont.					
1940-41 Detroit		1	2	3	2
HERGERTS, FRED					
1934-35 N. Y. Americans		2	4	6	2
HERGESHEIMER, PHILIP RW-SR					
Born: Winnipeg, Man. July 9, 1915					
1939-40 Chicago		9	11	20	6
1940-41 "		8	16	24	9
1941-42 Chicago-Boston	26	3	11	14	14
1942-43 Chicago	9	1	3	4	0
4 Years		21	41	62	29
HERGESHEIMER, WALTER E. RW-SR					
Born: Winnipeg, Man. Jan. 8, 1927					
1951-52 New York	68	26	12	38	6
1952-53 " "	70	30	29	59	10
1953-54 " "	66	27	16	43	42
1954-55 " "	14	4	2	6	4
1955-56 " "	70	22	18	40	26
1956-57 Chicago	41	2	8	10	12
1958-59 New York	22	3	0	3	6
7 Years	351	114	85	199	106
HERON, ROBERT G. LW-SL					
Born: Toronto, Ont. Dec. 31, 1917					
1939-40 Toronto		11	12	23	12
1940-41 "		9	5	14	12
1941-42 Montreal-Brooklyn	23	1	2	3	14
3 Years		21	19	40	38
HEXIMER, ORVILLE R. W					
1929-30 N. Y. Rangers		1	0	1	4
1932-33 Boston		7	5	12	12
1934-35 N. Y. Americans		5	2	7	0
3 Years		13	7	20	16
HEXTALL, BRYAN ALDWIN RW-SL					
Born: Grenfell, Sask. July 31, 1913					
1936-37 New York Rangers	1	0	1	1	0
1937-38 " " "	48	17	4	21	6
1938-39 " " "	48	20	15	35	18
1939-40 " " "	48	*24	15	39	52
1940-41 " " "	48	*26	18	44	16
1941-42 " " "	48	24	32	*56	30
1942-43 " " "	50	27	32	59	28
1943-44 " " "	50	21	33	54	41
1945-46 " " "	3	0	1	1	0
1946-47 " " "	60	20	10	30	18
1947-48 " " "	43	8	14	22	18
(continued)					

Sea. Club	Ga.	Go.	A.	P.	PM
11 Years	447	187	175	362	227
*League Leader					
1939-40 1st All-Star Team					
1940-41 " " " "					
1941-42 " " " "					
1942-43 2nd " " "					
1969 Hall of Fame					
HEYLIGER, VICTOR F-SL					
Born: U. S. A.					
1943-44 Chicago	26	2	3	5	2
HICKS, HAROLD D					
1928-29 Mont. Maroons		2	0	2	27
1929-30 Detroit		3	2	5	35
1930-31 "		0	0	0	10
3 Years		5	2	7	72
HICKS, WAYNE WILSON RW-SR					
Born: Aberdeen, Wash. Apr. 9, 1937					
1960-61 Chicago	1	0	0	0	0
1962-63 Boston	65	7	9	16	14
1963-64 Montreal	2	0	0	0	0
1967-68 Phila.-Pittsburgh	47	6	14	20	8
4 Years	115	13	23	36	22
HILDEBRAND, ISAAC BRUCE RW-SR					
Born: New Westminster, Br. Col.					
1953-54 New York-Chicago	38	7	11	18	16
1954-55 Chicago	3	0	0	0	0
2 Years	41	7	11	18	16
HILL, JOHN MELVIN RW-SR					
Born: Glenboro, Man. Feb. 15, 1914					
1937-38 Boston		2	0	2	2
1938-39 "		10	10	20	16
1939-40 "		9	11	20	19
1940-41 "		5	4	9	4
1941-42 Brooklyn	47	14	23	37	10
1942-43 Toronto	49	17	27	44	47
1943-44 "	17	9	10	19	16
1944-45 "	45	18	17	35	14
1945-46 "	35	5	7	12	10
9 Years		89	109	198	138
HILLER, WILBERT CARL LW-SL					
Born: Kitchener, Ont. May 11, 1915					
1937-38 N. Y. Rangers	1	0	1	1	2
1938-39 " " "		10	19	29	22
1939-40 " " "		13	18	31	57
1940-41 " " "		8	10	18	20
1941-42 Detroit-Boston	50	7	10	17	19
1942-43 Boston-Montreal	42	8	6	14	4
1943-44 New York	50	18	22	40	15
1944-45 Montreal	48	20	16	36	20
1945-46 "	45	7	11	18	4
9 Years		91	113	204	163
HILLMAN, FLOYD ARTHUR D-SL					
Born: Ruthven, Ont. Nov. 19, 1933					
1956-57 Boston	6	0	0	0	10
HIMES, NORMAN C-SR					
Born: Galt, Ont. April 13, 1903					
1926-27 N. Y. Americans		9	2	11	14
1927-28 " " "		14	5	19	22
1928-29 " " "		10	0	10	25
1929-30 " " "		28	22	50	15
1930-31 " " "		15	9	24	18
1931-32 " " "		7	21	28	9
1932-33 " " "		9	25	34	12
1933-34 " " "		9	16	25	10
1934-35 " " "		5	13	18	2
9 Years		106	113	219	127
HINSE, JOSEPH CHARLES ANDRE LW SL					
Born: Trois Rivieres, Que. April 19, 1945					
1967-68 Toronto	4	0	0	0	0
HIRSCHFELD, JOHN A. LW					
1949-50 Montreal	13	1	2	3	2
1950-51 "	20	0	2	2	0
2 Years	33	1	4	5	2

HITCHMAN, F. LIONEL D-SL
Born: Toronto, Ont. 1903

Sea. Club	Ga.	Go.	A.	P.	PM.
1922-23 Ottawa		0	1	1	12
1923-24 "		2	6	8	24
1924-25 Ottawa-Boston		3	0	3	24
1925-26 Boston		7	4	11	70
1926-27 "		3	6	9	70
1927-28 "		5	3	8	87
1928-29 "		1	0	1	64
1929-30 "		2	7	9	58
1930-31 "		0	2	2	40
1931-32 "		3	3	6	36
1932-33 "		0	1	1	34
1933-34 "		1	0	1	4
12 Years		27	33	60	523

HODGSON, THEODORE JAMES RW-SR
Born: Hobbema, Alb. June 30, 1945

Sea. Club	Ga.	Go.	A.	P.	PM.
1966-67 Boston	4	0	0	0	0

HOEKSTRA, CECIL THOMAS LW-SL
Born: Winnipeg, Man. Apr. 2, 1935

Sea. Club	Ga.	Go.	A.	P.	PM.
1959-60 Montreal Canadiens	4	0	0	0	0

HOEKSTRA, EDWARD ADRIAN C-SL
Born: Winnipeg, Man. Nov. 4, 1937

Sea. Club	Ga.	Go.	A.	P.	PM.
1967-68 Philadelphia	70	15	21	36	6

HOFFINGER, VICTOR D

Sea. Club	Ga.	Go.	A.	P.	PM.
1927-28 Chicago		0	1	1	18
1928-29 "		0	0	0	12
2 Years		0	1	1	30

HOLLETT, WILLIAM D-SL
Born: N. Sydney, Nova Scotia, Apr. 13, 1912

Sea. Club	Ga.	Go.	A.	P.	PM.
1933-34 Toronto-Ottawa		7	4	11	25
1934-35 Toronto		10	16	26	38
1935-36 Toronto-Boston		2	6	8	10
1936-37 Boston		3	7	10	22
1937-38 "		4	10	14	54
1938-39 "		10	17	27	35
1939-40 "		10	18	28	18
1940-41 "		9	15	24	23
1941-42 "	46	19	14	33	21
1942-43 "	50	19	25	44	19
1943-44 Boston-Detroit	52	15	19	34	38
1944-45 Detroit	50	20	21	41	39
1945-46 "	38	4	9	13	16
13 Years		132	181	313	358

1942-43 2nd All-Star Team
1944-45 1st All-Star Team

HOLLINGWORTH, GORDON D-SL
Born: Verdun, Que. July 24, 1933

Sea. Club	Ga.	Go.	A.	P.	PM.
1954-55 Chicago	70	3	9	12	135
1955-56 Detroit	41	0	2	2	28
1956-57 "	25	0	1	1	16
1957-58 "	27	1	2	3	22
4 Years	163	4	14	18	201

HOLMES, CHARLES FRANK RW-SR
Born: Edmonton, Alb. Sept. 21, 1934

Sea. Club	Ga.	Go.	A.	P.	PM.
1958-59 Detroit	15	0	3	3	6
1961-62 "	8	1	0	1	4
2 Years	23	1	3	4	10

HOLMES, LOUIS CHARLES CARTER C
Born: Edmonton, Alb.

Sea. Club	Ga.	Go.	A.	P.	PM.
1931-32 Chicago		1	4	5	6
1932-33 "		0	0	0	2
2 Years		1	4	5	8

HOLMES, WILLIAM
Born: Portage la Prairie, Man.

Sea. Club	Ga.	Go.	A.	P.	PM.
1925-26 Montreal Canadiens	9	1	0	1	2
1929-30 N. Y. Americans	42	5	4	9	33
2 Years	51	6	4	10	35

HOLOTA, JOHN O. C
Born: Hamilton, Ont.

Sea. Club	Ga.	Go.	A.	P.	PM.
1942-43 Detroit	12	2	0	2	0
1945-46 "	3	0	0	0	0
2 Years	15	2	0	2	0

HOLWAY, ALBERT R. D

Sea. Club	Ga.	Go.	A.	P.	PM.
1923-24 Toronto		1	0	1	0
1924-25 Toronto-Mont. Maroons		2	2	4	20
1925-26 Mont. Maroons		0	0	0	6

(continued)

Sea. Club	Ga.	Go.	A.	P.	PM.
1926-27 " "		0	0	0	2
1928-29 Pittsburgh		4	0	4	20
5 Years		7	2	9	48

HORECK, PETER RW-SL

Sea. Club	Ga.	Go.	A.	P.	PM.
1944-45 Chicago	50	20	16	36	44
1945-46 "	50	20	21	41	34
1946-47 Chicago-Detroit	56	16	19	35	71
1947-48 Detroit	50	12	17	29	44
1948-49 "	60	14	16	30	46
1949-50 Boston	34	5	5	10	22
1950-51 "	66	10	13	23	57
1951-52 Chicago	60	9	11	20	22
8 Years	426	106	118	224	340

HORNE, GEORGE

Sea. Club	Ga.	Go.	A.	P.	PM.
1925-26 Mont. Maroons		0	0	0	2
1928-29 Toronto		9	3	12	32
2 Years		9	3	12	34

HORNER, GEORGE REGINALD D-SR
Born: Lynden, Ont. May 28, 1909

Sea. Club	Ga.	Go.	A.	P.	PM.
1928-29 Toronto		0	0	0	30
1929-30 "		2	7	9	96
1930-31 "		1	11	12	71
1931-32 "		7	9	16	97
1932-33 "	48	3	8	11	*144
1933-34 "	42	11	10	21	*146
1934-35 "	46	4	8	12	*125
1935-36 "	43	2	9	11	*167
1936-37 "	48	3	9	12	*124
1937-38 "	47	4	20	24	*92
1938-39 "	48	4	10	14	*85
1939-40 "	30	1	9	10	*87
12 Years		42	110	152	1264

*League Leader
1965 Hall of Fame

HORVATH, BRONCO JOSEPH C-SL
Born: Port Colborne, Ont. Mar. 12, 1930

Sea. Club	Ga.	Go.	A.	P.	PM.
1955-56 New York	66	12	17	29	40
1956-57 New York-Montreal	8	1	2	3	4
1957-58 Boston	67	30	36	66	71
1958-59 "	45	19	20	39	58
1959-60 "	68	*39	41	80	60
1960-61 "	47	15	15	30	15
1961-62 Chicago	68	17	29	46	21
1962-63 New York-Toronto	51	7	19	26	46
1967-68 Minnesota	14	1	6	7	4
9 Years	434	141	185	326	319

*League Leader
1959-60 2nd All-Star Team

HOWARD, JACK F.

Sea. Club	Ga.	Go.	A.	P.	PM.
1936-37 Toronto	2	0	0	0	0

HOWE, SYDNEY HARRIS LW&C-SL
Born: Ottawa, Ont. Sept. 28, 1911

Sea. Club	Ga.	Go.	A.	P.	PM.
1929-30 Ottawa		1	1	2	0
1930-31 Philadelphia		9	11	20	20
1932-33 Ottawa		12	12	24	17
1933-34 "		13	7	20	18
1934-35 St. Louis-Detroit		22	25	47	34
1935-36 Detroit		16	14	30	26
1936-37 "		17	10	27	10
1937-38 "		8	19	27	14
1938-39 "		16	20	36	11
1939-40 "		14	23	37	17
1940-41 "		20	24	44	8
1941-42 "	48	16	19	35	6
1942-43 "	50	20	35	55	10
1943-44 "	46	32	28	60	6
1944-45 "	46	17	36	53	6
1945-46 "	26	4	7	11	9
16 Years		237	291	528	212

1944-45 2nd All-Star Team
1965 Hall of Fame

HOWE, VICTOR S. RW

Sea. Club	Ga.	Go.	A.	P.	PM.
1950-51 New York	3	1	0	1	0
1953-54 " "	1	0	0	0	0
1954-55 " "	29	2	4	6	10
3 Years	33	3	4	7	10

HOWELL, RONALD RW-SR
Born: Hamilton, Ont. Dec. 4, 1935

Sea. Club	Ga.	Go.	A.	P.	PM.
1954-55 New York	3	0	0	0	0

(continued)

Sea. Club	Ga.	Go.	A.	P.	PM.
1955-56 " "	1	0	0	0	0
2 Years	4	0	0	0	0
HRYMNAK, STEPHEN D					
1951-52 Chicago	18	2	1	3	4
HUARD, ROLAND F					
1930-31 Toronto	1	1	0	1	0
HUCUL, FREDERICK ALBERT D-SL					
Born: Tubrose, Sask. Dec. 3, 1931					
1950-51 Chicago	3	1	0	1	2
1951-52 "	34	3	7	10	37
1952-53 "	57	5	7	12	25
1953-54 "	27	0	3	3	19
1967-68 St. Louis	43	2	13	15	30
5 Years	164	11	30	41	113
HUDSON, RONALD RW					
1937-38 Detroit		5	2	7	2
HUGGINS, ALLAN C					
1930-31 Mont. Maroons		1	1	2	2
HUGHES, ALBERT C					
1930-31 N. Y. Americans		5	7	12	14
1931-32 " " "		1	1	2	8
2 Years		6	8	14	22
HUGHES, J.					
1929-30 Detroit		0	1	1	48
HUNT, FREDERICK TENNYSON RW-SR					
Born: Brantford, Ont. Jan. 17, 1918					
1940-41 N. Y. Americans		2	5	7	0
1944-45 New York Rangers	44	13	9	22	6
2 Years		15	14	29	6
HURST, RONALD RW-SR					
Born: Toronto, Ont. May 18, 1931					
1955-56 Toronto	50	7	5	12	62
1956-57 "	14	2	2	4	8
2 Years	64	9	7	16	70
HUTCHINSON, RONALD WAYNE LW-SL					
Born: Flin Flon, Man. Oct. 24, 1936					
1960-61 New York	9	0	0	0	0
HUTTON, WILLIAM DAVID RW					
Born: Calgary, Alb.					
1929-30 Boston-Ottawa		2	1	3	2
1930-31 Boston-Philadelphia		1	1	2	4
2 Years		3	2	5	6
HYLAND, HARRY M. RW					
Born: Montreal, Que. Jan. 2, 1889					
1917-18 Mont. Wanderers-Ottawa	16	14	-	14	-
1962 Hall of Fame					
IMLACH, BRENT C					
Born: Quebec City, Que. Nov. 16, 1946					
1965-66 Toronto	2	0	0	0	0
1966-67 "	1	0	0	0	0
2 Years	3	0	0	0	0
INGOLDSBY, JACK LW-SR					
1942-43 Toronto	6	0	1	1	0
1943-44 "	21	5	0	5	15
2 Years	27	5	1	6	15
INGRAM, FRANK RW					
1924-25 Boston		0	0	0	0
1929-30 Chicago		6	10	16	28
1930-31 "		17	4	21	37
1931-32 "		1	2	3	4
4 Years		24	16	40	69
INGRAM, RONALD WALTER D-SR					
Born: Toronto, Ont. July 5, 1933					
1956-57 Chicago	45	1	6	7	21
1963-64 Detroit-New York	66	4	9	13	58
1964-65 New York	3	0	0	0	2
3 Years	114	5	15	20	81

Sea. Club	Ga.	Go.	A.	P.	PM.
IRVIN, JAMES DICKENSON C-SL					
Born: Limestone Ridge, Ont. July 19, 1892					
1926-27 Chicago		18	*18	36	34
1927-28 "		5	4	9	12
1928-29 "		6	1	7	30
3 Years		29	23	52	76
*League Leader					
1958 Hall of Fame					
IRWIN, IVAN DUANE D-SL					
Born: Chicago, Ill. Mar. 13, 1927					
1952-53 Montreal	4	0	1	1	0
1953-54 New York	56	2	12	14	109
1954-55 " "	60	0	13	13	85
1955-56 " "	34	0	1	1	20
1957-58 " "	1	0	0	0	0
5 Years	155	2	27	29	214
JACKSON, ARTHUR C-SL					
Born: Toronto, Ont. Dec. 15, 1915					
1934-35 Toronto		1	3	4	4
1935-36 "		5	15	20	14
1936-37 "		2	0	2	2
1937-38 Boston		9	3	12	24
1938-39 N. Y. Americans		12	13	25	15
1939-40 Boston		7	18	25	6
1940-41 "		17	15	32	10
l1941-42 "		6	18	24	25
1942-43 "	50	22	31	53	20
1943-44 "	49	28	41	69	8
1944-45 Boston-Toronto	50	14	21	35	16
11 Years		123	178	301	144
JACKSON, HAROLD R. D					
Born: Cedar Springs, Ont.					
1936-37 Chicago		1	3	4	6
1937-38 "		0	0	0	0
1940-41 Detroit		0	0	0	0
1942-43 Detroit	4	0	4	4	6
1943-44 "	50	7	12	19	76
1944-45 "	50	5	6	11	45
1945-46 "	36	3	4	7	36
1946-47 "	37	1	5	6	39
8 Years		17	34	51	208
JACKSON, HARVEY LW-SL					
Born: Toronto, Ont. Jan. 17, 1911					
1929-30 Toronto		12	6	18	29
1930-31 "		18	13	31	81
1931-32 "		28	25	*53	63
1932-33 "		27	17	44	43
1933-34 "		20	18	38	38
1934-35 "		22	22	44	27
1935-36 "		11	11	22	19
1936-37 "		21	19	40	12
1937-38 "		17	17	34	18
1938-39 "		10	17	27	12
1939-40 N. Y. Americans		12	8	20	10
1940-41 " " "		8	18	26	4
1941-42 Boston		5	7	12	18
1942-43 "	44	19	15	34	38
1943-44 "	42	11	21	32	25
15 Years		241	234	475	437
*League Leader					
1931-32 1st All-Star Team					
1932-33 2nd " " " "					
1933-34 1st " " " "					
1934-35 " " " " "					
1936-37 " " " " "					
Hall of Fame					
JACKSON, JOHN A. D					
1946-47 Chicago	48	2	5	7	38
JACKSON, LLOYD LW&C-SL					
Born: Ottawa, Ont. 1913					
1936-37 N. Y. Americans		1	1	2	0
JACKSON, STANTON LW					
1921-22 Toronto		0	0	0	0
1923-24 "		1	1	2	6
1924-25 Toronto-Boston		5	0	5	36
1925-26 Boston		3	3	6	30
1926-27 Ottawa		0	0	0	2
5 Years		9	4	13	74

Sea. Club	Ga.	Go.	A.	P.	PM.
JACKSON, WALTER LW					
1932-33 N. Y. Americans		10	2	12	6
1933-34 " " "		6	9	15	12
2 Years		16	11	27	18
JACOBS, – –					
1918-19 Toronto	1	0	0	0	0
JAMES, GERALD EDWIN RW-SR					
Born: Regina, Sask. Oct. 22, 1934					
1954-55 Toronto	1	0	0	0	0
1955-56 "	46	3	3	6	50
1956-57 "	53	4	12	16	90
1957-58 "	15	3	2	5	61
1959-60 "	34	4	9	13	56
5 Years	149	14	26	40	257
JAMIESON, JAMES F					
1943-44 New York	1	0	1	1	0
JANKOWSKI, LOUIS CASIMER RW-SR					
Born: Regina, Sask. June 27, 1931					
1950-51 Detroit	1	0	1	1	0
1952-53 "	22	1	2	3	0
1953-54 Chicago	68	15	13	28	7
1954-55 "	36	3	2	5	8
4 Years	127	19	18	37	15
JARVIS, JAMES A. LW					
1929-30 Pittsburgh		11	8	19	32
1930-31 Philadelphia		5	7	12	30
1936-37 Toronto		1	0	1	0
3 Years		17	15	32	62
JENKINS, ROGER RW&D-SR					
Born: Appleton, Wis. Nov. 18, 1911					
1930-31 Toronto-Chicago		0	1	1	16
1932-33 Chicago		3	10	13	42
1933-34 "		2	2	4	37
1934-35 Mont. Canadiens		4	6	10	63
1935-36 Boston		2	6	8	51
1936-37 Mont. Canadiens-N. Y. Americans		1	4	5	14
1937-38 Chicago		1	8	9	26
1938-39 Chicago-N. Y. Americans		2	2	4	6
8 Years		15	39	54	255
JENNINGS, JOSEPH W. RW					
1940-41 Detroit		1	5	6	2
1941-42 "	16	2	1	3	6
1942-43 "	8	3	3	6	2
1943-44 "	33	6	11	17	10
1944-45 Boston	39	20	13	33	25
5 Years		32	33	65	45
JEREMIAH, EDWARD J.					
Born: U. S. A.					
1931-32 N. Y. Americans		0	1	1	0
JERWA, FRANK C					
Born: Poland					
1931-32 Boston		4	5	9	14
1932-33 "		3	4	7	23
1933-34 "		0	0	0	2
1934-35 St. Louis		4	7	11	14
4 Years		11	16	27	53
JERWA, JOSEPH D-SL					
Born: Bankhead, Alb. Jan. 20, 1908					
1930-31 N. Y. Rangers		4	7	11	72
1931-32 Boston		0	0	0	8
1935-36 N. Y. Americans		9	12	21	65
1936-37 Boston-N. Y. Americans		9	13	22	57
1937-38 N. Y. Americans		3	14	17	53
1938-39 " "		4	12	16	52
6 Years		29	58	87	307
JOANETTE, ROSARIO F					
1944-45 Montreal	2	0	1	1	4
JOHNS, DONALD ERNEST D-SR					
Born: Brantford, Ont. Dec. 13, 1937					
1960-61 New York	63	1	7	8	34
1962-63 " "	6	0	4	4	6
1963-64 " "	57	1	9	10	26
1964-65 " "	22	0	1	1	4
1965-66 Montreal	1	0	0	0	0
1967-68 Minnesota	4	0	0	0	6
6 Years	153	2	21	23	76

Sea. Club	Ga.	Go.	A.	P.	PM.
JOHNSON, ALLAN EDMUND RW-SR					
Born: Winnipeg, Man. Mar. 30, 1935					
1956-57 Montreal	2	0	1	1	2
1960-61 Detroit	70	16	21	37	14
1961-62 "	31	5	6	11	14
1962-63 "	2	0	0	0	0
4 Years	105	21	28	49	30
JOHNSON, EARL O. SL					
Born: Fort Francis, Ont. June 28, 1931					
1953-54 Detroit	1	0	0	0	0
JOHNSON, IVAN W. D-SL					
Born: Winnipeg, Man. Dec. 17, 1897					
1926-27 N. Y. Rangers		3	2	5	66
1927-28 " " "		10	6	16	146
1928-29 " " "		0	0	0	14
1929-30 " " "		3	3	6	82
1930-31 " " "		2	6	8	77
1931-32 " " "		3	10	13	106
1932-33 " " "		8	9	17	127
1933-34 " " "		2	6	8	86
1934-35 " " "		2	3	5	34
1935-36 " " "		5	3	8	58
1936-37 " " "		0	0	0	2
1937-38 " " Americans		0	0	0	10
12 Years		38	48	86	808
1930-31 2nd All-Star Team					
1931-32 1st " " "					
1932-33 " " " "					
1933-34 2nd " " "					
1958 Hall of Fame					
JOHNSON, NORMAN BRUCE C-SL					
Born: Moose Jaw, Sask. Nov. 27, 1932					
1957-58 Boston	15	2	3	5	8
1958-59 Boston-Chicago	46	3	17	20	33
2 Years	61	5	20	25	41
JOHNSON, THOMAS CHRISTIAN D-SL					
Born: Baldur, Man. Feb. 18, 1928					
1947-48 Montreal	1	0	0	0	0
1950-51 "	70	2	8	10	128
1951-52 "	67	0	7	7	76
1952-53 "	70	3	8	11	63
1953-54 "	70	7	11	18	85
1954-55 "	70	6	19	25	74
1955-56 "	64	3	10	13	75
1956-57 "	70	4	11	15	59
1957-58 "	66	3	18	21	75
1958-59 "	70	10	29	39	76
1959-60 "	64	4	25	29	59
1960-61 "	70	1	15	16	54
1961-62 "	62	1	17	18	45
1962-63 "	43	3	5	8	28
1963-64 Boston	70	4	21	25	33
1964-65 "	51	0	9	9	30
16 Years	978	51	213	264	960
1955-56 2nd All-Star Team					
1958-59 1st All-Star Team & Norris Trophy					
Hall of Fame					
JOHNSON, VIRGIL D					
Born: Minneapolis, Minn.					
1937-38 Chicago		0	2	2	2
1943-44 "	49	1	8	9	23
1944-45 "	2	0	1	1	2
3 Years		1	11	12	27
JOHNSON, WILLIAM C-SR					
1949-50 Toronto	1	0	0	0	0
JOHNSTON, GEORGE J. RW					
Born: St. Charles, Man.					
1941-42 Chicago	2	2	0	2	0
1942-43 "	30	10	7	17	0
1945-46 "	16	5	4	9	2
1946-47 "	10	3	1	4	0
4 Years	58	20	12	32	2
JOHNSTONE, ROBERT ROSS D					
1943-44 Toronto	18	2	0	2	6
1944-45 "	24	3	4	7	8
2 Years	42	5	4	9	14

Sea. Club	Ga.	Go.	A.	P.	PM.
JOLIAT, AURELE LW-SL					
Born: Ottawa Ont. Aug. 29, 1901					
1922-23 Mont. Canadiens		13	9	22	31
1923-24 " "		15	5	20	19
1924-25 " "		29	11	40	85
1925-26 " "		17	9	26	52
1926-27 " "		14	4	18	79
1927-28 " "		28	11	39	105
1928-29 " "		12	5	17	59
1929-30 " "		19	12	31	40
1930-31 " "		13	22	35	73
1931-32 " "		15	24	39	46
1932-33 " "		18	21	39	53
1933-34 " "		22	15	37	27
1934-35 " "		17	12	29	18
1935-36 " "		15	8	23	16
1936-37 " "		17	15	32	30
1937-38 " "		6	7	13	24
16 Years		270	190	460	757
1930-31 1st All-Star Team					
1931-32 2nd " " "					
1933-34 " " " & Hart Trophy					
1934-35 " " " "					
1945 Hall of Fame					
JOLIAT, RENE					
1924-25 Mont. Canadiens	1	0	0	0	0
JONES, ALVIN B. D-SR					
Born: Owen Sound, Ont. Aug. 17, 1918					
1938-39 Detroit	11	0	1	1	6
1941-42 "	21	2	1	3	8
1942-43 Toronto	16	0	0	0	22
3 Years	48	2	2	4	36
JUCKES, WINSTON B. LW					
1947-48 New York	2	0	0	0	0
1949-50 " "	14	2	1	3	6
2 Years	16	2	1	3	6
JUZDA, WILLIAM D-SR					
Born: Winnipeg, Man.					
1940-41 N. Y. Rangers	5	0	0	0	2
1941-42 " " "	45	4	8	12	29
1945-46 " " "	32	1	3	4	17
1946-47 " " "	45	3	5	8	60
1947-48 " " "	60	3	9	12	70
1948-49 Toronto	38	1	2	3	23
1949-50 "	62	1	14	15	68
1950-51 "	65	0	9	9	64
1951-52 "	46	1	4	5	65
9 Years	398	14	54	68	398
KABEL, ROBERT GERALD C&RW-SR					
Born: Dauphin, Man. Nov. 11, 1934					
1959-60 New York	44	5	11	16	32
1960-61 " "	4	0	2	2	2
2 Years	48	5	13	18	34
KACHUR, EDWARD CHARLES RW-SR					
Born: Fort William, Ont. Apr. 22, 1934					
1956-57 Chicago	34	5	7	12	21
1957-58 "	62	5	7	12	14
2 Years	96	10	14	24	35
KAISER, VERNON C. LW					
Born: Preston, Ont.					
1950-51 Montreal	50	7	5	12	33
KALBFLEISH, WALTER D					
Born: New Hambury, Ont.					
1933-34 Ottawa		0	4	4	20
1934-35 St. Louis		0	0	0	6
1935-36 N. Y. Americans		0	0	0	2
1936-37 " " "		0	0	0	4
4 Years		0	4	4	32
KALETA, ALEXANDER LW-SL					
Born: Canmore, Alb.					
1941-42 Chicago	48	7	21	28	24
1945-46 "	49	19	27	46	17
1946-47 "	57	24	20	44	37
1947-48 "	52	10	16	26	40
1948-49 New York	56	12	19	31	18
1949-50 " "	67	17	14	31	40
1950-51 " "	58	3	4	7	26
7 Years	387	92	121	213	202

Sea. Club	Ga.	Go.	A.	P.	PM.
KAMINSKY, MAX C					
Born: Niagara Falls, Ont. Apr. 19, 1913					
1933-34 Ottawa		9	17	26	14
1934-35 Boston		12	15	27	4
1935-36 "		1	2	3	20
3 Years		22	34	56	38
KAMPMAN, RUDOLPH D-SR					
Born: Kitchener, Ont. Mar. 12, 1914					
1937-38 Toronto		1	2	3	56
1938-39 "		2	8	10	52
1939-40 "		6	9	15	59
1940-41 "		1	4	5	53
1941-42 "	38	4	7	11	67
5 Years		14	30	44	287
KANE, FRANCIS J. D					
1943-44 Detroit	2	0	0	0	0
KEATING, JOHN R. C					
Born: Newcastle, New Bruns.					
1931-32 N. Y. Americans		5	3	8	6
1932-33 " " "		0	2	2	11
2 Years		5	5	10	17
KEATING, JOHN THOMAS LW&C-SL					
Born: Kitchener, Ont. Oct. 9, 1918					
1938-39 Detroit		1	0	1	2
1939-40 "		2	0	2	2
2 Years		3	0	3	4
KEATS, GORDON BLANCHARD C-SR					
Born: Montreal, Que. Mar. 1, 1895					
1926-27 Boston-Detroit		16	8	24	52
1927-28 Detroit-Chicago		14	10	24	60
1928-29 Chicago		0	1	1	0
3 Years		30	19	49	112
1958 Hall of Fame					
KEELING, MELVILLE SYDNEY C&LW-SL					
Born: Owen Sound, Ont. Aug. 8, 1905					
1926-27 Toronto		11	2	13	29
1927-28 "		10	6	16	52
1928-29 N. Y. Rangers		6	3	9	35
1929-30 " " "		19	7	26	34
1930-31 " " "		13	9	22	35
1931-32 " " "		17	3	20	38
1932-33 " " "		8	6	14	22
1933-34 " " "		15	5	20	20
1934-35 " " "		15	4	19	14
1935-36 " " "		13	5	18	22
1936-37 " " "		22	4	26	18
1937-38 " "		8	9	17	12
12 Years		157	63	220	331
KELLER, RALPH D-SR					
Born: Wilkie, Sask. Feb. 6, 1936					
1962-63 New York	3	1	0	1	6
KELLY, LEONARD PATRICK D-SL					
Born: Simcoe, Ont. July 9, 1927					
1947-48 Detroit	60	6	14	20	13
1948-49 "	59	5	11	16	10
1949-50 "	70	15	25	40	9
1950-51 "	70	17	37	54	24
1951-52 "	67	16	31	47	16
1952-53 "	70	19	27	46	8
1953-54 "	62	16	33	49	18
1954-55 "	70	15	30	45	28
1955-56 "	70	16	34	50	39
1956-57 "	70	10	25	35	16
1957-58 "	61	13	18	31	26
1958-59 "	67	8	13	21	34
1959-60 Detroit-Toronto	68	12	17	29	16
1960-61 Toronto	64	20	50	70	12
1961-62 "	58	22	27	49	
1962-63 "	66	20	40	60	8
1963-64 "	70	11	34	45	16
1964-65 "	70	18	28	46	8
1965-66 "	63	8	24	32	12
1966-67 "	61	14	24	38	
20 Years	1316	281	542	823	32
1949-50 2nd All-Star Team					

(continued)

Sea. Club	Ga.	Go.	A.	P.	PM.
1950-51 1st All-Star Team & Lady Byng Trophy					
1951-52 " " " "					
1952-53 " " " " & Lady Byng Trophy					
1953-54 " " " " & Lady Byng & Norris Trophies					
1954-55 " " " "					
1955-56 2nd " " "					
1956-57 1st " " "					
1960-61 Lady Byng Trophy					
1969 Hall of Fame					

KELLY, PETER RW-SR
Born: Winnipeg, Man. May 22, 1912

Sea. Club	Ga.	Go.	A.	P.	PM.
1934-35 St. Louis		3	10	13	14
1935-36 Detroit	6	8	14		30
1936-37 "	5	4	9		12
1937-38 "	0	1	1		2
1938-39 "	4	9	13		4
1940-41 N. Y. Americans	3	5	8		2
1941-42 Brooklyn	0	1	1		4
7 Years	21	38	59		68

KELLY, REGIS J. RW-SR
Born: North Bay, Ont. Jan. 17, 1914

Sea. Club	Ga.	Go.	A.	P.	PM.
1934-35 Toronto		11	8	19	14
1935-36 "		11	8	19	24
1936-37 Toronto-Chicago		15	4	19	8
1937-38 Toronto		9	10	19	25
1938-39 "		11	11	22	12
1939-40 "		11	9	20	15
1940-41 Chicago		5	3	8	7
1941-42 Brooklyn		1	0	1	0
8 Years		74	53	127	105

KEMP, STANLEY D

Sea. Club	Ga.	Go.	A.	P.	PM.
1948-49 Toronto	1	0	0	0	2

KENDALL, WILLIAM RW

Sea. Club	Ga.	Go.	A.	P.	PM.
1933-34 Chicago		3	0	3	0
1934-35 "		6	4	10	16
1935-36 "		2	1	3	0
1936-37 Toronto-Chicago		5	4	9	10
1937-38 Chicago		0	1	1	2
5 Years		16	10	26	28

KENNEDY, THEODORE S. C-SR
Born: Humberstone, Ont. Dec. 12, 1925

Sea. Club	Ga.	Go.	A.	P.	PM.
1942-43 Toronto	2	0	1	1	0
1943-44 "	49	26	23	49	2
1944-45 "	49	29	25	54	14
1945-46 "	21	3	2	5	4
1946-47 "	60	28	32	60	27
1947-48 "	60	25	21	46	32
1948-49 "	59	18	21	39	25
1949-50 "	53	20	24	44	34
1950-51 "	63	18	*43	61	32
1951-52 "	70	19	33	52	33
1952-53 "	43	14	23	37	42
1953-54 "	67	15	23	38	78
1954-55 "	70	10	42	52	74
1956-57 "	30	6	16	22	35
14 Years	696	231	329	560	432

*League Leader
1949-50 2nd All-Star Team
1950-51 " " " "
1953-54 " " " "
1954-55 Hart Trophy
1966 Hall of Fame

KENNY, WILLIAM ERNEST D
Born: Vermilion, Alb.

Sea. Club	Ga.	Go.	A.	P.	PM.
1930-31 N. Y. Rangers	0	0	0		0
1934-35 Chicago	0	0	0		18
2 Years	0	0	0		18

KILREA, BRIAN BLAIR SR
Born: Ottawa, Ont. Oct. 21, 1934

Sea. Club	Ga.	Go.	A.	P.	PM.
1957-58 Detroit	1	0	0	0	0
1967-68 Los Angeles	25	3	5	8	12
2 Years	26	3	5	8	12

KILREA, HECTOR LW-SL
Born: Blackburn, Ont. June 11, 1907

Sea. Club	Ga.	Go.	A.	P.	PM.
1925-26 Ottawa		5	0	5	12
1926-27 "		11	7	18	48
1927-28 "		19	4	23	66
1928-29 "		5	7	12	36

(continued)

Sea. Club	Ga.	Go.	A.	P.	PM.
1929-30 "		36	22	58	72
1930-31 "		14	8	22	44
1931-32 Detroit		13	3	16	28
1932-33 Ottawa		14	8	22	26
1933-34 Toronto		10	13	23	15
1934-35 "		11	13	24	16
1935-36 Detroit		6	17	23	37
1936-37 "		6	9	15	20
1937-38 "		9	9	18	10
1938-39 "		8	9	17	8
1939-40 "		0	0	0	0
15 Years		167	129	296	438

KILREA, KENNETH ARMSTRONG LW&C-SL
Born: Ottawa, Ont. Jan. 16, 1919

Sea. Club	Ga.	Go.	A.	P.	PM.
1938-39 Detroit		0	0	0	0
1939-40 "		10	8	18	4
1940-41 "		2	0	2	0
1941-42 "	21	3	12	15	4
1943-44 "	14	1	3	4	0
5 Years		16	23	39	8

KILREA, WALTER C-SR
Born: Ottawa, Ont. Feb. 18, 1909

Sea. Club	Ga.	Go.	A.	P.	PM.
1929-30 Ottawa		4	2	6	4
1930-31 Philadelphia		8	12	20	22
1931-32 N. Y. Americans		3	8	11	18
1932-33 Ottawa-Mont. Maroons		5	12	17	16
1933-34 Mont. Maroons		3	1	4	7
1935-36 Detroit		4	10	14	10
1936-37 "		8	13	21	6
1937-38 "		0	0	0	4
8 Years		35	58	93	87

KING, FRANK E. C

Sea. Club	Ga.	Go.	A.	P.	PM.
1950-51 Montreal	10	1	0	1	2

KINSELLA, THOMAS R.

Sea. Club	Ga.	Go.	A.	P.	PM.
1930-31 Ottawa		0	0		0

KIRK, ROBERT H. RW-SR
Born: Belfast, Ireland Aug. 8, 1910

Sea. Club	Ga.	Go.	A.	P.	PM.
1937-38 N. Y. Rangers	39	4	8	12	14

KIRKPATRICK, ROBERT D. C-SL
Born: Regina, Sask.

Sea. Club	Ga.	Go.	A.	P.	PM.
1942-43 New York	49	12	12	24	6

KITCHEN, C. HOBART D

Sea. Club	Ga.	Go.	A.	P.	PM.
1925-26 Mont. Maroons		5	2	7	16
1926-27 Detroit		0	2	2	42
2 Years		5	4	9	58

KLEIN, LLOYD RW-SL
Born: Saskatoon, Sask. Jan. 13, 1910

Sea. Club	Ga.	Go.	A.	P.	PM.
1928-29 Boston		1	0	1	5
1931-32 "		1	0	1	0
1932-33 N. Y. Americans		2	2	4	4
1933-34 " " "		13	9	22	34
1934-35 " " "		7	3	10	9
1935-36 " " "		4	8	12	14
1936-37 " " "		2	1	3	2
1937-38 " " "		0	1	1	0
8 Years		30	24	54	68

KLINGBEIL, ERNEST
Born: U. S. A.

Sea. Club	Ga.	Go.	A.	P.	PM.
1936-37 Chicago		1	2	3	2

KLUKAY, JOSEPH FRANCIS LW-SL
Born: Sault Ste. Marie, Ont. Nov. 6, 1922

Sea. Club	Ga.	Go.	A.	P.	PM.
1946-47 Toronto	55	9	20	29	12
1947-48 "	59	15	15	30	28
1948-49 "	45	11	10	21	11
1949-50 "	70	15	16	31	19
1950-51 "	70	14	16	30	16
1951-52 "	43	4	8	12	6
1952-53 Boston	70	13	16	29	20
1953-54 "	70	20	17	37	27
1954-55 Boston-Toronto	66	8	8	16	48
1955-56 Toronto	18	0	1	1	2
10 Years	566	109	127	236	189

KNIBBS, WILLIAM ARTHUR C-SL
Born: Toronto, Ont. Jan. 24, 1942

Sea. Club	Ga.	Go.	A.	P.	PM.
1964-65 Boston	53	7	10	17	4

Sea. Club	Ga.	Go.	A.	P.	PM.
KNOTT, WILLIAM E. C					
Born: Oshawa, Ont.					
1941-42 Brooklyn	14	3	1	4	9
KNOX, PAUL RW					
Born: Toronto, Ont. November 23, 1933					
1954-55 Toronto	1	0	0	0	0
KONIK, GEORGE SAMUEL LW-SL					
Born: Flin Flon, Man. May 4, 1938					
1967-68 Pittsburgh	52	7	8	15	26
KOPAK, RUSSELL C					
1943-44 Boston	24	7	9	16	0
KOTANEN, EINO R. E. D					
1948-49 New York	1	0	0	0	0
1950-51 " "	1	0	0	0	0
2 Years	2	0	0	0	0
KOZAK, LESTER LW					
Born: Dauphin, Man. Oct. 28, 1940					
1961-62 Toronto	12	1	0	1	2
KRAFTCHECK, STEPHEN S. D-SR					
Born: Tinturn, Ont. Mar. 3, 1929					
1950-51 Boston	22	0	0	0	8
1951-52 New York	58	8	9	17	30
1952-53 " "	69	2	9	11	45
1958-59 Toronto	8	1	0	1	0
4 Years	157	11	18	29	83
KROL, JOSEPH LW-SL					
Born: Winnipeg, Man. Aug. 13, 1915					
1936-37 N. Y. Rangers		0	0	0	0
1938-39 " " "		1	1	2	0
1941-42 Brooklyn		9	3	12	8
3 Years		10	4	14	8
KRYZANOWSKI, EDWARD L. D					
1948-49 Boston	36	1	3	4	10
1949-50 "	57	6	10	16	12
1950-51 "	69	3	6	9	10
1951-52 "	70	5	3	8	33
1952-53 Chicago	5	0	0	0	0
5 Years	237	15	22	37	65
KUHN, GORDON RW					
Born: Windsor, Nova Scotia					
1932-33 N. Y. Americans		1	1	2	4
KUKULOWICZ, ADOLPH F. C					
1952-53 New York	3	1	0	1	0
1953-54 " "	1	0	0	0	0
2 Years	4	1	0	1	0
KULLMAN, ARNOLD EDWIN C-SL					
Born: Winnipeg, Man. Oct. 9, 1927					
1947-48 Boston	1	0	0	0	0
1949-50 Boston	12	0	1	1	11
2 Years	13	0	1	1	11
KULLMAN, EDWARD G. RW					
1947-48 New York	51	15	17	32	32
1948-49 " "	18	4	5	9	14
1950-51 " "	70	14	18	32	88
1951-52 " "	64	11	10	21	59
1952-53 " "	70	8	10	18	61
1953-54 " "	70	4	10	14	44
6 Years	343	56	70	126	298
KUNTZ, ALAN R. LW					
Born: Toronto, Ont.					
1941-42 New York	31	10	11	21	10
1945-46 " "	14	0	1	1	2
2 Years	45	10	12	22	12
KWONG, LAWRENCE					
1947-48 New York	1	0	0	0	0
KYLE, WALTER L. D					
Born: Dysart, Sask.					
1949-50 New York	70	3	5	8	143
1950-51 " "	64	2	3	5	92
1951-52 Boston	69	1	12	13	*127
3 Years	203	6	20	26	362
*League Leader					

Sea. Club	Ga.	Go.	A.	P.	PM.
KYLE, WILLIAM LW					
1949-50 New York	2	0	0	0	0
1950-51 " "	1	0	3	3	0
2 Years	3	0	3	3	0
LABADIE, JOSEPH GILLES MICHEL RW-SR					
Born: St. Francis d'Assisis, Que. Aug. 17, 1932					
1952-53 New York	3	0	0	0	0
LaBINE, LEO GERALD RW-SR					
Born: Haileybury, Ont. July 22, 1931					
1951-52 Boston	15	2	4	6	9
1952-53 "	51	8	15	23	69
1953-54 "	68	16	19	35	57
1954-55 "	67	24	18	42	75
1955-56 "	68	16	18	34	104
1956-57 "	67	18	29	47	128
1957-58 "	62	7	14	21	60
1958-59 "	70	9	23	32	74
1959-60 "	63	16	28	44	58
1960-61 Boston-Detroit	64	9	21	30	66
1961-62 Detroit	48	3	4	7	30
11 Years	643	128	193	321	730
LABOVICH, MAX C					
1943-44 New York	5	0	0	0	4
LABRIE, GUY D					
1943-44 Boston	15	2	7	9	2
1944-45 New York	27	2	2	4	14
2 Years	42	4	9	13	16
LACH, ELMER JAMES C-SL					
Born: Nokomis, Sask. Jan. 22, 1918					
1940-41 Montreal	43	7	14	21	16
1941-42 "	1	0	1	1	0
1942-43 "	45	18	40	58	14
1943-44 "	48	24	48	72	23
1944-45 "	50	26	*54	*80	37
1945-46 "	50	13	*34	47	34
1946-47 "	31	14	16	30	22
1947-48 "	60	30	31	*61	72
1948-49 "	36	11	18	29	59
1949-50 "	64	15	33	48	33
1950-51 "	65	21	24	45	48
1951-52 "	70	15	*50	65	36
1952-53 "	53	16	25	41	56
1953-54 "	48	5	20	25	28
14 Years	664	215	408	623	478
*League Leader					
1943-44 2nd All-Star Team					
1944-45 1st " " " & Hart Trophy					
1945-46 2nd " " "					
1947-48 1st " " " & Ross Trophy					
1951-52 " " " "					
1966 Hall of Fame					
LaFLEUR, RENE					
1924-25 Montreal Canadiens	1	0	0	0	0
LaFORCE, ERNEST D					
1942-43 Montreal	1	0	0	0	0
LaFRANCE, ADELARD F					
1933-34 Mont. Canadiens		0	0	0	2
LaFRANCE, LEO C&LW					
1926-27 Mont. Canadiens	4	0	0	0	0
1927-28 Mont. Canadiens-Chicago	27	2	0	2	6
2 Years	31	2	0	2	6
LAFRENIERE, ROGER JOSEPH D-SL					
Born: Montreal, Que. July 24, 1942					
1962-63 Detroit	3	0	0	0	4
LALANDE, HECTOR C-SL					
Born: North Bay, Ont. Nov. 24, 1934					
1953-54 Chicago	2	0	0	0	2
1955-56 "	65	8	18	26	70
1956-57 "	50	11	17	28	38
1957-58 Chicago-Detroit	34	2	4	6	12
4 Years	151	21	39	60	122

Sea. Club	Ga.	Go.	A.	P.	PM.
LALONDE, EDOUARD CHARLES C-SR					
Born: Cornwall, Ont. October 31, 1887					
1917-18 Montreal Canadiens	14	23		23	
1918-19 " "	17	*23	*9	*32	40
1919-20 "	23	36	6	42	33
1920-21 " "	24	33	8	*41	36
1921-22 " "	20	9	4	13	11
1926-27 N. Y. Americans	1	0	0	0	2
6 Years	99	124	27	151	122
*League Leader					
1950 Hall of Fame					
LAMB, JOSEPH GORDON C&RW-SR					
Born: Sussex, New Bruns. June 18, 1906					
1927-28 Mont. Maroons		8	5	13	39
1928-29 Mont. Maroons-Ottawa		4	1	5	52
1929-30 Ottawa		29	20	49	*119
1930-31 "		11	14	25	91
1931-32 N. Y. Americans		14	11	25	71
1932-33 Boston		11	8	19	68
1933-34 "		10	15	25	47
1934-35 St. L.-Mont. Canadiens		14	14	28	23
1935-36 Mont. Maroons		0	3	3	12
1936-37 N. Y. Americans		3	9	12	53
1937-38 N. Y. Americans-Detroit		4	1	5	26
11 Years		108	101	209	601
*League Leader					
LAMIRANDE, JEAN-PAUL LW					
1946-47 New York	14	1	1	2	14
1947-48 " "	18	0	1	1	6
1949-50 " "	16	4	3	7	6
1954-55 Montreal	1	0	0	0	0
4 Years	49	5	5	10	26
LAMOUREUX, LEO P. D-SL					
Born: Espanola, Ont.					
1941-42 Mont. Canadiens	1	0	0	0	0
1942-43 Montreal "	46	2	16	18	53
1943-44 " "	44	8	23	31	32
1944-45 " "	49	2	22	24	58
1945-46 " "	45	5	7	12	18
1946-47 " "	50	2	11	13	14
6 Years	235	19	79	98	175
LANCIEN, JOHN G. D					
1946-47 New York	1	0	0	0	0
1949-50 " "	43	1	4	5	27
1950-51 " "	19	0	1	1	8
3 Years	63	1	5	6	35
LANE, MYLES J. D-SL					
Born: Melrose, Mass. October 2, 1905					
1928-29 N. Y. Rangers-Boston		2	0	2	24
1929 Boston Bruins		0	0	0	0
1933-34 Boston		2	1	3	17
3 Years		4	1	5	41
LANGELLE, PETER C-SL					
Born: Winnipeg, Man. Nov. 4, 1917					
1938-39 Toronto		1	0	1	0
1939-40 "		7	14	21	2
1940-41 "		4	15	19	0
1941-42 "		10	22	32	9
4 Years		22	51	73	11
LANGLOIS, ALBERT D-SL					
Born: Magog, Que. Nov. 6, 1934					
1957-58 Montreal	1	0	0	0	0
1958-59 "	48	0	3	3	26
1959-60 "	67	1	14	15	48
1960-61 "	61	1	12	13	56
1961-62 New York	69	7	18	25	90
1962-63 " "	60	2	14	16	62
1963-64 New York-Detroit	61	5	8	13	45
1964-65 Detroit	65	1	12	13	107
1965-66 Boston	65	4	10	14	54
9 Years	497	21	91	112	488
LANGLOIS, CHARLES D-SR					
1924-25 Hamilton		6	1	7	59
1925-26 N. Y. Americans		9	1	10	76
1926-27 N. Y. Amer.-Pittsburgh		7	1	8	44
1927-28 Pitts.-Mont. Canadiens		0	0	0	22
4 Years		22	3	25	201

Sea. Club	Ga.	Go.	A.	P.	PM.
LANYON, EDWARD GEORGE D-SL					
Born: Winnipeg, Man. June 11, 1939					
1967-68 Pittsburgh	5	0	0	0	4
LAPRADE, EDGAR L. C-SL					
Born: Port Arthur, Ont.					
1945-46 New York	49	15	19	34	0
1946-47 " "	58	15	25	40	9
1947-48 " "	59	13	34	47	7
1948-49 " "	56	18	12	30	12
1949-50 " "	60	22	22	44	2
1950-51 " "	42	10	13	23	0
1951-52 " "	70	9	29	38	8
1952-53 " "	11	2	1	3	2
1953-54 " "	35	1	6	7	2
1954-55 " "	60	3	11	14	0
10 Years	500	108	172	280	42
1945-46 Calder Trophy					
1949-50 Lady Byng Trophy					
LaPRAIRIE, BUN					
Born: U. S. A.					
1936-37 Chicago		0	0	0	0
LAROCHELLE, WILDORE RW-SR					
Born: Sorel, Que. Sept. 3, 1906					
1925-26 Mont. Canadiens		2	1	3	10
1926-27 " "		0	1	1	6
1927-28 " "		3	1	4	30
1928-29 " "		0	0	0	0
1929-30 " "		14	11	25	28
1930-31 " "		8	5	13	35
1931-32 " "		18	8	26	16
1932-33 " "		11	4	15	27
1933-34 " "		16	11	27	27
1934-35 " "		9	19	28	12
1935-36 Mont. Canadiens-Chicago		2	3	5	14
1936-37 Chicago		9	10	19	6
12 Years		92	74	166	211
LAROSE, CHARLES					
1925-26 Boston	6	0	0	0	0
LARSON, NORMAN L. RW					
Born: Moose Jaw, Sask.					
1940-41 N. Y. Americans		9	9	18	6
1941-42 Brooklyn	40	16	9	25	6
1946-47 New York	1	0	0	0	0
3 Years		25	18	43	12
LATREILLE, PHILIP RW					
Born: Montreal, Que.					
1960-61 New York	4	0	0	0	2
LAUDER, MARTIN					
1927-28 Boston	3	0	0	0	2
LAVIOLETTE, JEAN BAPTISTE LW-SL					
Born: Belleville, Ont. July 27, 1879					
1917-18 Montreal Canadiens	18	2		2	
1962 Hall of Fame					
LAYCOE, HAROLD RICHARDSON D-SL					
Born: Sutherland Sask. June 23, 1922					
1945-46 New York	17	0	2	2	6
1946-47 " "	58	1	12	13	25
1947-48 Montreal	14	1	2	3	4
1948-49 "	51	3	5	8	31
1949-50 "	30	0	2	2	21
1950-51 Montreal-Boston	44	1	3	4	29
1951-52 Boston	70	5	7	12	61
1952-53 "	54	2	10	12	36
1953-54 "	58	3	16	19	29
1954-55 "	70	4	13	17	34
1955-56 "	65	5	5	10	16
11 Years	531	25	77	102	292
LEACH, LAWRENCE RAYMOND C&LW-SL					
Born: Lloydminster, Sask. June 18, 1936					
1958-59 Boston	29	4	12	16	26
1959-60 "	69	7	12	19	47
1961-62 "	28	2	5	7	18
3 Years	126	13	29	42	91

LEBRUN, ALBERT IVAN D-SR
Born: Timmins, Ont. Dec. 1, 1940

Sea. Club	Ga.	Go.	A.	P.	PM.
1960-61 New York	4	0	2	2	4
1965-66 " "	2	0	0	0	0
2 Years	6	0	2	2	4

LECLAIR, JOHN LOUIS C-SL
Born: Quebec City, Que. May 30, 1929

Sea. Club	Ga.	Go.	A.	P.	PM.
1954-55 Montreal	59	11	22	33	12
1955-56 "	54	6	8	14	30
1956-57 "	47	3	10	13	14
3 Years	160	20	40	60	56

LEDUC, J. ALBERT D-SR
Born: Valleyfield, Que. 1902

Sea. Club	Ga.	Go.	A.	P.	PM.
1925-26 Mont. Canadiens		10	3	13	62
1926-27 " "		5	2	7	62
1927-28 " "		8	5	13	73
1928-29 " "		9	2	11	79
1929-30 " "		7	8	15	90
1930-31 " "		8	6	14	82
1931-32 " "		5	3	8	60
1932-33 " "		5	3	8	62
1933-34 Ottawa-N. Y. Rangers		1	3	4	40
1934-35 Mont. Canadiens		0	0	0	4
10 Years		58	35	93	614

LEE, ROBERT C

Sea. Club	Ga.	Go.	A.	P.	PM.
1942-43 Montreal	1	0	0	0	0

LEGER, ROGER D-SR

Sea. Club	Ga.	Go.	A.	P.	PM.
1943-44 New York	7	1	2	3	2
1946-47 Montreal	49	4	18	22	12
1947-48 "	48	4	14	18	26
1948-49 "	28	6	7	13	10
1949-50 "	55	3	12	15	21
5 Years	187	18	53	71	71

LEIER, EDWARD C

Sea. Club	Ga.	Go.	A.	P.	PM.
1949-50 Chicago	5	0	1	1	0
1950-51 "	11	2	0	2	2
2 Years	16	2	1	3	2

LEMIEUX, ROBERT LYNNE D-SL
Born: Montreal, Que. Dec. 16, 1944

Sea. Club	Ga.	Go.	A.	P.	PM.
1967-68 Oakland	19	0	1	1	12

LEPINE, ALFRED C-SL
Born: Ste. Anne de Bellevue, Que. July 30, 1901

Sea. Club	Ga.	Go.	A.	P.	PM.
1925-26 Mont. Canadiens		9	1	10	18
1926-27 " "		16	1	17	20
1927-28 " "		4	1	5	6
1928-29 " "		6	1	7	48
1929-30 " "		24	9	33	47
1930-31 " "		17	7	24	63
1931-32 " "		19	11	30	42
1932-33 " "		8	8	16	45
1933-34 " "		10	8	18	44
1934-35 " "		12	19	31	16
1935-36 " "		6	10	16	4
1936-37 " "		7	8	15	15
1937-38 " "		5	14	19	24
13 Years		143	98	241	392

LEPINE, HECTOR

Sea. Club	Ga.	Go.	A.	P.	PM.
1925-26 Mont. Canadiens	33	5	2	7	2

LESIEUR, ARTHUR J. D-SR
Born: Fall River, Mass. September 13, 1907

Sea. Club	Ga.	Go.	A.	P.	PM.
1928-29 Mont. Canadiens-Chicago		0	0	0	0
1930-31 Mont. Canadiens		2	0	2	14
1931-32 " "		1	2	3	12
1935-36 " "		1	0	1	24
4 Years		4	2	6	50

LESWICK, ANTHONY J. LW-SR
Born: Humboldt, Sask.

Sea. Club	Ga.	Go.	A.	P.	PM.
1945-46 New York	50	15	9	24	26
1946-47 " "	59	27	14	41	51
1947-48 " "	60	24	16	40	76
1948-49 " "	60	13	14	27	70
1949-50 " "	69	19	25	44	85
1950-51 " "	70	15	11	26	112
1951-52 Detroit	70	9	10	19	93

(continued)

Sea. Club	Ga.	Go.	A.	P.	PM.
1952-53 "	70	15	12	27	87
1953-54 "	70	6	18	24	90
1954-55 "	70	10	17	27	137
1955-56 Chicago	70	11	11	22	71
1957-58 Detroit	22	1	2	3	2
12 Years	740	165	159	324	900

1949-50 2nd All-Star Team

LESWICK, JACK

Sea. Club	Ga.	Go.	A.	P.	PM.
1933-34 Chicago		1	7	8	16

LESWICK, PETER P. C&RW-SR
Born: Saskatoon, Sask.

Sea. Club	Ga.	Go.	A.	P.	PM.
1936-37 N. Y. Americans		1	0	1	0
1944-45 Boston	2	0	0	0	0
2 Years		1	0	1	0

LEVANDOSKI, JOSEPH T. RW

Sea. Club	Ga.	Go.	A.	P.	PM.
1946-47 New York	8	1	1	2	0

LEVINSKY, ALEXANDER D-SR
Born: Syracuse, N. Y. Feb. 2, 1910

Sea. Club	Ga.	Go.	A.	P.	PM.
1930-31 Toronto		0	1	1	2
1931-32 "		5	5	10	29
1932-33 "		1	4	5	61
1933-34 "		5	11	16	38
1934-35 N. Y. Rangers-Chicago		3	8	11	22
1935-36 Chicago		1	7	8	69
1936-37 "		0	8	8	32
1937-38 "		3	2	5	18
1938-39 "		1	3	4	36
9 Years		19	49	68	307

LEWICKI, DANIEL LW-SL
Born: Fort William, Ont. Mar. 12, 1931

Sea. Club	Ga.	Go.	A.	P.	PM.
1950-51 Toronto	61	16	18	34	26
1951-52 "	51	4	9	13	26
1952-53 "	4	1	3	4	2
1953-54 "	7	0	1	1	12
1954-55 New York	70	29	24	53	8
1955-56 " "	70	18	27	45	26
1956-57 " "	70	18	20	38	47
1957-58 " "	70	11	19	30	26
1958-59 Chicago	58	8	14	22	4
9 Years	461	105	135	240	177

1954-55 2nd All-Star Team

LEWIS, DOUGLAS LW
Born: Winnipeg, Man.

Sea. Club	Ga.	Go.	A.	P.	PM.
1946-47 Montreal	3	0	0	0	0

LEWIS, HERBERT LW-SL
Born: Calgary, Alb. Apr. 17, 1906

Sea. Club	Ga.	Go.	A.	P.	PM.
1928-29 Detroit		9	5	14	33
1929-30 "		20	11	31	36
1930-31 "		15	6	21	38
1931-32 "		5	14	19	21
1932-33 "		20	14	34	20
1933-34 "		16	15	31	15
1934-35 "		16	27	43	26
1935-36 "		14	23	37	25
1936-37 "		14	18	32	14
1937-38 "		13	18	31	12
1938-39 "		6	10	16	8
11 Years		148	161	309	248

LICARI, ANTHONY RW

Sea. Club	Ga.	Go.	A.	P.	PM.
1946-47 Detroit	9	0	1	1	0

LINDSAY, ROBERT BLAKE THEODORE LW-SL
Born: Renfrew, Ont. July 29, 1925

Sea. Club	Ga.	Go.	A.	P.	PM.
1944-45 Detroit	45	17	6	23	43
1945-46 "	47	7	10	17	14
1946-47 "	59	27	15	42	57
1947-48 "	60	*33	19	52	95
1948-49 "	50	26	28	54	97
1949-50 "	69	23	*55	*78	141
1950-51 "	67	24	35	59	110
1951-52 "	70	30	39	69	123
1952-53 "	70	32	39	71	111
1953-54 "	70	26	36	62	110
1954-55 "	49	19	19	38	85
1955-56 "	67	27	23	50	161
1956-57 "	70	30	*55	85	103
1957-58 Chicago	68	15	24	39	110
1958-59 "	70	22	36	58	*184
1959-60 "	68	7	19	26	91

(continued)

Sea. Club	Ga.	Go.	A.	P.	PM.
1964-65 Detroit	69	14	14	28	173
17 Years	1068	379	472	851	1808

*League Leader
1947-48 1st All-Star Team
1948-49 2nd " " "
1949-50 1st " " " & Ross Trophy
1950-51 1st All-Star Team
1951-52 " " " "
1952-53 " " " "
1953-54 " " " "
1955-56 " " " "
1956-57 " " " "
1966 Hall of Fame

LISCOMBE, HARRY CARL LW-SL
Born: Perth, Ont. May 17, 1915

Sea. Club	Ga.	Go.	A.	P.	PM.
1937-38 Detroit		14	10	24	30
1938-39 "		8	18	26	13
1939-40 "		2	7	9	4
1940-41 "		10	10	20	0
1941-42 "	47	13	17	30	14
1942-43 "	50	19	23	42	19
1943-44 "	50	36	37	73	17
1944-45 "	42	23	9	32	18
1945-46 "	44	12	9	21	2
9 Years	-	137	140	277	117

LITZENBERGER, EDWARD C. J. RW&C-SR
Born: Neudorf, Sask. July 15, 1932

Sea. Club	Ga.	Go.	A.	P.	PM.
1952-53 Montreal	2	1	0	1	2
1953-54 "	3	0	0	0	0
1954-55 Montreal-Chicago	73	23	28	51	40
1955-56 Chicago	70	10	29	39	36
1956-57 "	70	32	32	64	48
1957-58 "	70	32	30	62	63
1958-59 "	70	33	44	77	37
1959-60 "	52	12	18	30	15
1960-61 "	62	10	22	32	14
1961-62 Detroit-Toronto	69	18	22	40	14
1962-63 Toronto	58	5	13	18	10
1963-64 "	19	2	0	2	0
12 Years	618	178	238	416	279

1954-55 Calder Trophy
1956-57 2nd All-Star Team

LOCAS, JACQUES RW-SR
Born: Montreal, Que. Feb. 12, 1926

Sea. Club	Ga.	Go.	A.	P.	PM.
1947-48 Montreal	56	7	8	15	66
1948-49 "	3	0	0	0	0
2 Years	59	7	8	15	66

LOCKING, NORMAN LW
Born: Owen Sound, Ont.

Sea. Club	Ga.	Go.	A.	P.	PM.
1934-35 Chicago		2	5	7	19
1935-36 "		0	1	1	7
2 Years		2	6	8	26

LORRAIN, RODRIGUE RW-SR
Born: Buckingham, Que. July 1915

Sea. Club	Ga.	Go.	A.	P.	PM.
1935-36 Mont. Canadiens		0	0	0	2
1936-37 " "		3	6	9	8
1937-38 " "		13	19	32	14
1938-39 " "		10	9	19	0
1939-40 " "		1	5	6	6
1941-42 " "		1	0	1	0
6 Years		28	39	67	30

LOUGHLIN, CLEMENT JOSEPH D-SR
Born: Winnipeg, Man. Nov. 15, 1893

Sea. Club	Ga.	Go.	A.	P.	PM.
1926-27 Detroit		7	3	10	40
1927-28 "		1	2	3	21
1928-29 Chicago		0	1	1	16
3 Years		8	6	14	77

LOUGHLIN, WILFRED D

Sea. Club	Ga.	Go.	A.	P.	PM.
1923-24 Toronto	14	0	0	0	2

LOWE, NORMAN E. C-SR

Sea. Club	Ga.	Go.	A.	P.	PM.
1948-49 New York	1	0	0	0	0
1949-50 " "	3	1	1	2	0
2 Years	4	1	1	2	0

LOWE, ROSS R. D

Sea. Club	Ga.	Go.	A.	P.	PM.
1949-50 Boston	3	0	0	0	0
1950-51 "	43	5	3	8	40
1951-52 Montreal	31	1	5	6	42
3 Years	77	6	8	14	82

LOWREY, EDDIE

Sea. Club	Ga.	Go.	A.	P.	PM.
1917-18 Ottawa		2	-	2	-
1918-19 "		0	0	0	3
2 Years		2	0	2	3

LOWREY, FREDERICK JOHN FROCK "Frank"

Sea. Club	Ga.	Go.	A.	P.	PM.
1924-25 Mont. Maroons		0	0	0	6
1925-26 Pittsburgh		1	0	1	4
2 Years		1	0	1	10

LOWREY GERALD C
Born: Ottawa, Ont. 1906

Sea. Club	Ga.	Go.	A.	P.	PM.
1927-28 Toronto		6	5	11	29
1928-29 Toronto-Pittsburgh		5	12	17	30
1929-30 Pittsburgh		16	14	30	50
1930-31 Philadelphia		13	14	27	27
1931-32 Chicago		8	3	11	32
5 Years		48	48	96	168

LUCAS, DAVID CHARLES D-SL
Born: Downeyville, Ont. Mar. 22, 1932

Sea. Club	Ga.	Go.	A.	P.	PM.
1962-63 Detroit	1	0	0	0	0

LUND, PENTTI A. RW-SR
Born: Finland

Sea. Club	Ga.	Go.	A.	P.	PM.
1948-49 New York	59	14	16	30	16
1949-50 " "	64	18	9	27	16
1950-51 " "	59	4	16	20	6
1951-52 Boston	23	0	5	5	0
1952-53 "	54	8	9	17	2
5 Years	259	44	55	99	40

1948-49 Calder Trophy

LUNDY, PATRICK A. C

Sea. Club	Ga.	Go.	A.	P.	PM.
1945-46 Detroit	4	3	2	5	2
1946-47 "	59	17	17	34	10
1947-48 "	11	4	1	5	6
1948-49 "	15	4	3	7	4
1950-51 Chicago	61	9	9	18	9
5 Years	150	37	32	69	31

LYNN, VICTOR I. LW-SL
Born: Saskatoon, Sask.

Sea. Club	Ga.	Go.	A.	P.	PM.
1943-44 Detroit	3	0	0	0	4
1945-46 Montreal	2	0	0	0	0
1946-47 Toronto	31	6	14	20	44
1947-48 "	60	12	22	34	53
1948-49 "	52	7	9	16	36
1949-50 "	70	7	13	20	39
1950-51 Boston	56	14	6	20	69
1951-52 "	12	2	2	4	4
1952-53 Chicago	29	0	10	10	23
1953-54 "	11	1	0	1	2
10 Years	326	49	76	125	274

LYON, RONALD LW

Sea. Club	Ga.	Go.	A.	P.	PM.
1930-31 Boston-Philadelphia		2	4	6	29

MacDONALD, JAMES ALLAN KILBY LW&C-SL
Born: Ottawa, Ont. Sept. 6, 1914

Sea. Club	Ga.	Go.	A.	P.	PM.
1939-40 N. Y. Rangers		15	13	28	19
1940-41 " " "		5	6	11	12
1941-43 Military Service					
1943-44 New York	24	7	9	16	4
1944-45 " "	36	9	6	15	12
4 Years		36	34	70	47

1939-40 Calder Trophy

MACEY, HUBERT LW-SL
Born: Big River, Sask.

Sea. Club	Ga.	Go.	A.	P.	PM.
1941-42 N. Y. Rangers	9	3	5	8	0
1942-43 " "	9	3	3	6	0
1946-47 Montreal	12	0	1	1	0
3 Years	30	6	9	15	0

Sea. Club	Ga.	Go.	A.	P.	PM.
MacKAY, CALUM LW					
1946-47 Detroit	5	0	0	0	0
1948-49 "	1	0	0	0	0
1949-50 Montreal	52	8	10	18	44
1950-51 "	70	18	10	28	69
1951-52 "	12	0	1	1	8
1953-54 "	47	10	13	23	54
1954-55 "	50	14	21	35	39
7 Years	237	50	55	105	214
MacKAY, DAVID D					
Born: Edmonton, Alb.					
1940-41 Chicago		3	0	3	26
MacKAY, DUNCAN C-SL					
Born: Chesley Ont. May 21, 1894					
1926-27 Chicago ·		14	8	22	23
1927-28 "		17	4	21	23
1928-29 Pittsburgh-Boston		9	2	11	20
1929-30 Boston		4	5	9	13
4 Years		44	19	63	79
1952 Hall of Fame					
MacKAY, MURDO J. RW&C					
Born: Fort William, Ont.					
1945-46 Montreal	5	0	1	1	0
1947-48 "	14	0	2	2	0
2 Years	19	0	3	3	0
MACKELL, FLEMING DAVID C-SL					
Born: Montreal, Que. Apr. 30, 1929					
1947-48 Toronto	3	0	0	0	2
1948-49 "	11	1	1	2	6
1949-50 "	36	7	13	20	24
1950-51 "	70	12	13	25	40
1951-52 Toronto-Boston	62	3	16	19	40
1952-53 Boston	65	27	17	44	63
1953-54 "	67	15	32	47	60
1954-55 "	60	11	24	35	76
1955-56 "	52	7	9	16	59
1956-57 "	65	22	17	39	73
1957-58 "	70	20	40	60	72
1958-59 "	57	17	23	40	28
1959-60 "	47	7	15	22	19
13 Years	665	149	220	369	562
1952-53 1st All-Star Team					
MacKENZIE, WILLIAM K. D-SR					
Born: Winnipeg, Man. Dec. 12, 1912					
1932-33 Chicago		4	4	8	13
1933-34 Mont. Maroons		4	3	7	20
1934-35 Mont. Maroons-N. Y. Rangers		1	0	1	10
1936-37 Mont. Maroons-Mont. Canadiens		4	4	8	28
1937-38 Mont. Canadiens-Chicago		1	2	3	24
1938-39 Chicago		1	0	1	36
1939-40 "		0	1	1	14
7 Years		15	14	29	145
MACKEY, REGINALD D					
1926-27 N. Y. Rangers	34	0	0	0	16
MACKIE, HOWARD D					
Born: Kitchener, Ont.					
1936-37 Detroit		1	0	1	4
MacKINTOSH, IAN R. RW					
1952-53 New York	4	0	0	0	4
MacMILLAN, JOHN STEWART RW-SL					
Born: Lethbridge, Alb. Oct. 25, 1935					
1960-61 Toronto	31	3	5	8	8
1961-62 "	31	1	0	1	8
1962-63 "	6	1	1	2	6
1963-64 Toronto-Detroit	33	0	3	3	10
1964-65 Detroit	3	0	1	1	0
5 Years	104	5	10	15	32
MacNEIL, ALLISTER WENCES D-SL					
Born: Sydney, Nova Scotia Sept. 27, 1935					
1955-56 Toronto	1	0	0	0	2
1956-57 "	53	4	8	12	84
1957-58 "	13	0	0	0	9
1959-60 "	4	0	0	0	2

(continued)

Sea. Club	Ga.	Go.	A.	P.	PM.
1961-62 Montreal	61	1	7	8	74
1962-63 Chicago	70	2	19	21	100
1963-64 "	70	5	19	24	91
1964-65 "	69	3	7	10	119
1965-66 "	51	0	1	1	34
1966-67 New York	58	0	4	4	44
1967-68 Pittsburgh	74	2	10	12	58
11 Years	524	17	75	92	617
MacPHERSON, JAMES ALBERT D-SL					
Born: Edmonton, Alb. Mar. 21, 1927					
1948-49 Montreal	3	0	0	0	2
1950-51 "	62	0	16	16	40
1951-52 "	54	2	1	3	24
1952-53 "	59	2	3	5	67
1953-54 "	41	0	5	5	41
1954-55 "	30	1	8	9	55
1956-57 "	10	0	0	0	4
7 Years	259	5	33	38	233
MAHAFFY, JOHN C-SR					
1942-43 Montreal	9	2	5	7	4
1943-44 New York	28	9	20	29	0
2 Years	37	11	25	36	4
MAILLEY, - - - - D					
1942-43 Montreal	1	0	0	0	0
MAJEAU, FERNAND LW					
1943-44 Montreal	44	20	18	38	39
1944-45 "	12	2	6	8	4
2 Years	56	22	24	46	43
MALONE, CLIFFORD F					
1951-52 Montreal	3	0	0	0	0
MALONE, JOSEPH LW&C-SL					
Born: Quebec City, Que., Feb. 28, 1890					
1917-18 Montreal Canadiens	20	*44		*44	
1918-19 " "	8	7	1	8	3
1919-20 Quebec	24	*39	6	*45	12
1920-21 Hamilton	20	30	4	34	2
1921-22 "	24	25	7	32	4
1922-23 Montreal Canadiens	20	1	0	1	2
1923-24 " "	9	0	0	0	0
7 Years	125	146	18	164	23
*League Leader					
1950 Hall of Fame					
MALONEY, PHILIP FRANCIS C-SL					
Born: Ottawa, Ont. Oct. 6, 1927					
1949-50 Boston	70	15	31	46	6
1950-51 Boston-Toronto	14	3	0	3	2
1952-53 Toronto	29	2	6	8	2
1958-59 Chicago	24	2	2	4	6
1959-60 Chicago	21	6	4	10	0
5 Years	158	28	43	71	16
MANASTERSKY, TIMOTHY D					
Born: Montreal, Que.					
1950-51 Montreal	6	0	0	0	11
MANCUSO, FELIX RW-SR					
Born: Niagara Falls, Ont. Apr. 11, 1914					
1937-38 Mont. Canadiens		1	1	2	4
1939-40 "		0	0	0	6
1942-43 New York	21	6	8	14	13
3 Years		7	9	16	23
MANN, JOHN E. K. C					
Born: Winnipeg, Man.					
1943-44 New York	3	0	0	0	0
1944-45 " "	6	3	4	7	0
2 Years	9	3	4	7	0
MANN, NORMAN RW-SR					
Born: Bradford, Eng. 1913					
1938-39 Toronto		0	0	0	2
1940-41 "		0	3	3	2
2 Years		0	3	3	4
MANNERS, RENNISON F					
1929-30 Pittsburgh		3	2	5	14
1930-31 Philadelphia		0	0	0	0
2 Years		3	2	5	14

Sea. Club	Ga.	Go.	A.	P.	PM.
MANSON, RAYMOND C. LW					
1947-48 Boston	1	0	0	0	0
1948-49 New York	1	0	1	1	0
2 Years	2	0	1	1	0
MANTHA, LEON-GEORGES LW-SL					
Born: Lachine, Que. Nov. 29, 1908					
1928-29 Mont. Canadiens		0	0	0	8
1929-30 " "		5	2	7	16
1930-31 " "		11	6	17	25
1931-32 " "		1	7	8	8
1932-33 " "		3	6	9	10
1933-34 " "		6	9	15	12
1934-35 " "		12	10	22	14
1935-36 " "		1	12	13	14
1936-37 " "		13	14	27	17
1937-38 " "		23	19	42	12
1938-39 "		5	5	10	6
1939-40 "		9	11	20	6
1940-41 "		0	1	1	0
13 Years		89	102	191	148
MANTHA, SYLVIO D-SR					
Born: Montreal, Que. April 14, 1903					
1923-24 Montreal Canadiens		1	0	1	9
1924-25 " "		2	0	2	16
1925-26 Mont. Canadiens		2	1	3	66
1926-27 " "		10	5	15	77
1927-28 " "		4	11	15	61
1928-29 " "		9	4	13	56
1929-30 " "		13	11	24	108
1930-31 " "		4	7	11	75
1931-32 " "		5	5	10	62
1932-33 " "		4	7	11	50
1933-34 " "		4	6	10	24
1934-35 " "		3	11	14	36
1935-36 " "		2	4	6	25
1936-37 Boston		0	0	0	2
14 Years		63	72	135	667
1930-31 2nd All-Star Team					
1931-32 " " " "					
1960 Hall of Fame					
MARACLE, HENRY ELMER					
1930-31 N. Y. Rangers	11	1	3	4	4
MARCH, HAROLD RW-SR					
Born: Silton, Sask. Oct. 18, 1908					
1928-29 Chicago		3	3	6	6
1929-30 "		8	7	15	48
1930-31 "		11	6	17	36
1931-32 "		12	10	22	59
1932-33 "		9	11	20	38
1933-34 "		4	13	17	26
1934-35 "		13	17	30	48
1935-36 "		16	19	35	42
1936-37 "		11	6	17	31
1937-38 "		11	17	28	16
1938-39 "		10	11	21	29
1939-40 "		9	14	23	49
1940-41 "		8	9	17	16
1941-42 "		6	26	32	22
1942-43 "	50	7	29	36	46
1943-44 "	48	10	27	37	16
1944-45 "	38	5	5	10	12
17 Years		153	230	383	540
MARCON, LOUIS ANGELO D-SR					
Born: Fort William, Ont. May 28, 1935					
1958-59 Detroit	21	0	1	1	12
1959-60 "	38	0	3	3	30
1962-63 "	1	0	0	0	0
3 Years	60	0	4	4	42
MARIO, FRANK G. C					
Born: Esterhazy, Sask.					
1941-42 Boston	9	1	1	2	0
1944-45 "	44	8	18	26	24
2 Years	53	9	19	28	24

Sea. Club	Ga.	Go.	A.	P.	PM.
MARIUCCI, JOHN D-SL					
Born: U. S. A.					
1940-41 Chicago	23	0	5	5	33
1941-42 "	47	5	8	13	64
1945-46 "	50	3	8	11	58
1946-47 "	52	2	9	11	110
1947-48 "	51	1	4	5	63
5 Years	223	11	34	45	328
MARKER, AUGUST RW-SR					
Born: Wetaskiwin, Alb. Aug. 1, 1907					
1932-33 Detroit		1	1	2	8
1933-34 "		1	0	1	2
1934-35 Mont. Maroons		11	4	15	18
1935-36 " "		7	12	19	10
1936-37 " "		10	12	22	22
1937-38 " "		9	15	24	35
1938-39 Toronto		9	6	15	11
1939-40 "		10	9	19	15
1940-41 "		4	5	9	10
1941-42 Brooklyn		2	5	7	2
10 Years		64	69	133	133
MARKLE, JOHN RW					
Born: Thessalon, Ont.					
1935-36 Toronto		0	1	1	0
MARKS, JACK					
1917-18 Montreal Wanderers-Toronto		0			
1919-20 Quebec		0	0		4
2 Years		0	0		4
MARQUESS, CLARENCE E. RW					
1946-47 Boston	27	5	4	9	6
MARSHALL, WILLMOTT CHARLES C-SL					
Born: Kirkland Lake, Ont. Dec. 1, 1931					
1952-53 Toronto	2	0	0	0	0
1954-55 "	16	1	4	5	0
1955-56 "	6	0	0	0	0
1958-59 "	9	0	1	1	2
4 Years	33	1	5	6	2
MARTIN, FRANCIS WILLIAM D-SL					
Born: Cayuga, Ont. May 1, 1933					
1952-53 Boston	14	0	2	2	6
1953-54 "	68	3	17	20	38
1954-55 Chicago	66	4	8	12	35
1955-56 "	61	3	11	14	21
1956-57 "	70	1	8	9	12
1957-58 "	3	0	0	0	10
6 Years	282	11	46	57	122
MARTIN, GEORGE CLARE D-SR					
Born: Waterloo, Ont.					
1941-42 Boston	13	0	1	1	4
1946-47 "	6	3	0	3	0
1947-48 "	59	5	13	18	34
1949-50 Detroit	64	2	5	7	14
1950-51 "	50	1	6	7	12
1951-52 Chicago-New York	45	1	3	4	14
6 Years	237	12	28	40	78
MARTIN, JACK RAYMOND C-SL					
Born: St. Catharines, Ont. Nov. 29, 1940					
1960-61 Toronto	1	0	0	0	0
MARTIN, RONALD RW					
Born: Calgary, Alb.					
1932-33 N. Y. Americans		5	7	12	6
1933-34 " " "		8	9	17	30
2 Years		13	16	29	36
MARTIN, THOMAS RAYMOND RW-SR					
Born: Toronto, Ont., Oct. 16, 1947					
1967-68 Toronto	3	1	0	1	0
MASNICK, PAUL ANDREW C-SR					
Born: Regina, Sask. Apr. 14, 1931					
1950-51 Montreal	43	4	1	5	14
1951-52 "	15	1	2	3	2
1952-53 "	53	5	7	12	44
1953-54 "	50	5	21	26	57
1954-55 Montreal-Chicago	30	1	1	2	8
1957-58 Toronto	41	2	9	11	14
6 Years	232	18	41	59	139

Sea. Club	Ga.	Go.	A.	P.	PM.
MASON, CHARLES C. RW&LW-SR					
Born: Seaforth, Ont.February 1, 1911					
1934-35 N. Y. Rangers		5	9	14	14
1935-36 " " "		1	5	6	30
1937-38 N. Y. Americans		0	0	0	0
1938-39 Detroit-Chicago		1	3	4	0
4 Years		7	17	24	44
MASSECAR, GEORGE LW					
1929-30 N. Y. Americans		7	3	10	18
1930-31 " " "		4	7	11	16
1931-32 " " "		1	1	2	12
3 Years		12	11	23	46
MASTERTON, WILLIAM C-SR					
Born: Winnipeg, Man. Aug. 16 1938					
1967-68 Minnesota	38	4	8	12	4
MATHERS, FRANK SYDNEY D-SL					
Born: Winnipeg, Man. Mar. 29, 1924					
1948-49 Toronto	15	1	2	3	2
1949-50 "	6	0	1	1	2
1951-52 "	2	0	0	0	0
3 Years	23	1	3	4	4
MATTE, JOSEPH RW&D					
Born: Bourget, Ont.					
1919-20 Toronto	16	8	2	10	12
1920-21 Hamilton	19	7	*9	16	27
1921-22 "	20	3	3	6	4
1925-26 Boston Bruins	9	0	0	0	0
4 Years	64	18	14	32	43
*League Leader					
MATTE, JOSEPH D					
1942-43 Chicago	12	0	2	2	8
MATTE, ROLAND					
1929-30 Detroit		0	1	1	0
MATZ, JEAN F					
1924-25 Montreal Canadiens	30	3	2	5	0
MAXNER, WAYNE DOUGLAS LW-SL					
Born: Halifax, Nova Scotia, Sept. 27, 1942					
1964-65 Boston	54	7	6	13	42
1965-66 "	8	1	3	4	6
2 Years	62	8	9	17	48
MAXWELL, WALLY C-SL					
1952-53 Toronto	2	0	0	0	0
MAYER, SHEPPARD E. RW-SR					
1942-43 Toronto	2	1	2	3	4
MAZUR, EDWARD JOSEPH LW-SL					
Born: Winnipeg, Man. July 25, 1929					
1953-54 Montreal	67	7	14	21	95
1954-55 "	25	1	5	6	21
1956-57 Chicago	15	0	1	1	4
3 Years	107	8	20	28	120
McADAM, SAMUEL LW					
Born: Winnipeg, Man.					
1930-31 N. Y. Rangers	5	0	0	0	0
McANDREW, HAZEN D					
1941-42 Brooklyn	7	0	1	1	6
McATEE, JEROME LW					
1942-43 Detroit		0	0	0	0
1943-44 "	1	0	2	2	0
1944-45 "	44	15	11	26	6
3 Years		15	13	28	6
McATEE, NORMAN J. C-SL					
1946-47 Boston	13	0	1	1	0
McBRIDE, ––					
1928-29 Mont. Maroons		0	0	0	0
McBURNEY, JAMES C -SL					
1952-53 Chicago	1	0	1	1	0

Sea. Club	Ga.	Go.	A.	P.	PM.
McCABE, STANLEY W					
1929-30 Detroit		7	3	10	23
1930-31 "		2	1	3	22
1933-34 Mont. Maroons		0	0	0	4
3 Years		9	4	13	49
McCAFFREY, ALBERT J. D					
1924-25 Toronto		9	6	15	12
1925-26 "		14	7	21	42
1926-27 "		5	5	10	43
1927-28 Toronto-Pittsburgh		7	4	11	23
1928-29 Pittsburgh		1	0	1	34
1929-30 Pittsburgh-Mont. Canadiens		4	7	11	38
1930-31 Mont. Canadiens		2	1	3	10
7 Years		42	30	72	202
McCAIG, DOUGLAS D-SR					
1941-42 Detroit	9	0	1	1	6
1945-46 "	6	0	1	1	12
1946-47 "	47	2	4	6	62
1947-48 "	29	3	3	6	37
1948-49 Detroit-Chicago	56	1	3	4	60
1949-50 Chicago	63	0	4	4	49
1950-51 "	53	2	5	7	29
7 Years	263	8	21	29	255
McCALMON, EDWARD RW					
1927-28 Chicago		2	0	2	8
1930-31 Philadelphia		3	0	3	6
2 Years		5	0	5	14
McCARTHY, THOMAS RW-SL					
1919-20 Quebec	12	11	2	13	0
1920-21 Hamilton	22	8	1	9	10
2 Years	34	19	3	22	10
McCARTHY, THOMAS PATRICK FRANCIS LW-SL					
Born: Toronto, Ont. Sept. 15, 1934					
1956-57 Detroit	3	0	0	0	0
1957-58 "	18	2	1	3	4
1958-59 "	15	2	3	5	4
1960-61 Boston	24	4	5	9	0
4 Years	60	8	9	17	8
McCARTNEY, R.					
1932-33 Mont. Canadiens		0	0	0	0
McCASKILL, EDWARD JOEL C-SL					
Born: Kapuskasing, Ont., Oct. 29, 1936					
1967-68 Minnesota	4	0	2	2	0
McCORMACK, JOHN R. C-SL					
1947-48 Toronto	3	0	1	1	0
1948-49 "	1	0	0	0	0
1949-50 "	34	6	5	11	0
1950-51 "	46	6	7	13	2
1951-52 Montreal	54	2	10	12	4
1952-53 "	59	1	9	10	9
1953-54 "	51	5	10	15	12
1954-55 Chicago	63	5	7	12	8
8 Years	311	25	49	74	35
McCREEDY, JOHN LW-SR					
Born: Winnipeg, Man					
1941-42 Toronto		15	8	23	14
1944-45 "	17	2	4	6	11
2 Years		17	12	29	25
McCURRY, FRANCIS J. ("Duke") LW					
1925-26 Pittsburgh		13	4	17	32
1926-27 "		3	3	6	23
1927-28 "		5	3	8	60
1928-29 "		0	1	1	4
4 Years		21	11	32	119
McDONAGH, WILLIAM J. LW					
1949-50 New York	4	0	0	0	0
McDONALD, BYRON R. LW-SL					
Born: Moose Jaw, Sask. Nov. 21, 1916					
1939-40 Detroit		1	6	7	2
1944-45 Detroit-Chicago	29	7	14	21	0
2 Years		8	20	28	2

Sea. Club	Ga.	Go.	A.	P.	PM.
McDONALD, "JACK" C					
1917-18 Mont. Wanderers-Mont. Canad.	12	12	XX	12	
1918-19 " Canadiens	18	8	4	12	9
1919-20 Quebec Bulldogs	24	7	6	13	4
1920-21 Montreal Canadiens	17	0	1	1	0
1921-22 " "	2	0	0	0	0
5 Years	73	27	11	38	13
McDONALD, JOHN A. RW-SR					
Born: Swan River, Man.					
1943-44 New York	43	10	9	19	6
McDONALD, ROBERT F					
1943-44 New York	1	0	0	0	0
McDONALD, WILFRED K. D-SL					
Born: Fergus, Ont. Oct. 31, 1914					
1934-35 Detroit		1	2	3	8
1935-36 "		4	6	10	32
1936-37 "		3	5	8	20
1937-38 "		3	7	10	14
1938-39 Detroit-Toronto		3	3	6	22
1939-40 Toronto		2	5	7	13
1940-41 "		6	11	17	12
1941-42 "	48	2	19	21	24
1942-43 "	40	2	11	13	39
1943-44 Toronto-New York	50	7	10	17	22
1944-45 New York	40	2	9	11	0
11 Years		35	88	123	206
1941-42 2nd All-Star Team					
McDONNELL, MOYLAN J.					
1920-21 Hamilton	20	1	1	2	0
McFADDEN, JAMES A. C-SL					
Born: Belfast, Ire.					
1947-48 Detroit	60	24	24	48	12
1948-49 "	55	12	20	32	10
1949-50 "	68	14	16	30	8
1950-51 "	70	14	18	32	10
1951-52 Chicago	70	10	24	34	14
1952-53 "	70	23	21	44	29
1953-54 "	19	3	3	6	6
7 Years	412	100	126	226	89
1947-48 Calder Trophy					
McFADYEN, DONALD					
1932-33 Chicago		5	9	14	20
1933-34 "		1	3	4	20
1934-35 "		2	5	7	4
1935-36 "		4	16	20	33
4 Years		12	33	45	77
McGIBBON, IRVING RW					
1942-43 Montreal	1	0	0	0	2
McGILL, JACK J. W-SL					
1934-35 Mont. Canadiens		9	1	10	34
1935-36 " "		13	7	20	28
1936-37 " "		5	2	7	9
3 Years		27	10	37	71
McGILL, JOHN G. C-SL					
Born: Edmonton, Alb.					
1941-42 Boston	13	8	11	19	2
1944-45 "	14	4	2	6	0
1945-46 "	46	6	14	20	21
1946-47 "	24	5	9	14	19
4 Years	97	23	36	59	42
McGREGOR, DONALD ALEXANDER RW-SR					
Born: Toronto, Ont. Mar. 30, 1939					
1963-64 New York	2	0	0	0	2
McGUIRE, MICKEY					
1926-27 Pittsburgh		3	0	3	6
1927-28 "		0	0	0	0
2 Years		3	0	3	6
McINENLY, BERTRAM "Bert" D					
Born: Ottawa, Ont. May 6, 1906					
1930-31 Detroit		3	5	8	48
1931-32 Detroit-N. Y. Americans		12	7	19	60
1932-33 Ottawa		2	2	4	8
1933-34 Boston		0	0	0	4
1934-35 "		2	1	3	24
5 Years		19	15	34	144

Sea. Club	Ga.	Go.	A.	P.	PM.
McINTYRE, JOHN ARCHIBALD LW-SL					
Born: Brussels, Ont. Sept. 8, 1930					
1949-50 Boston	1	0	1	1	0
1951-52 "	52	12	19	31	18
1952-53 "	70	7	15	22	31
1953-54 Chicago	23	8	3	11	4
1954-55 "	65	16	13	29	40
1955-56 "	46	10	5	15	14
1956-57 "	70	18	14	32	32
1957-58 Chicago-Detroit	68	15	11	26	14
1958-59 Detroit	55	15	14	29	14
1959-60 "	49	8	7	15	6
10 Years	499	109	102	211	173
McKELL, JACK F					
1919-20 Ottawa	21	2	0	2	20
1920-21 "	21	2	1	3	22
2 Years	42	4	1	5	42
McKENNEY, DONALD HAMILTON C&LW-SL					
Born: Smiths Falls, Ont. Apr. 30, 1934					
1954-55 Boston	69	22	20	42	34
1955-56 "	65	10	24	34	20
1956-57 "	69	21	39	60	31
1957-58 Boston	70	28	30	58	22
1958-59 "	70	32	30	62	20
1959-60 "	70	20	*49	69	28
1960-61 "	68	26	23	49	22
1961-62 "	70	22	33	55	10
1962-63 Boston-New York	62	22	35	57	6
1963-64 New York-Toronto	70	18	23	41	8
1964-65 Toronto	52	6	13	19	6
1965-66 Detroit	24	1	6	7	0
1967-68 St. Louis	39	9	20	29	4
13 Years	798	237	345	582	211
*League Leader					
1959-60 Lady Byng Trophy					
McKINNON, ALEXANDER RW					
1924-25 Hamilton		8	2	10	45
1925-26 N. Y. Americans		5	3	8	34
1926-27 " " "		2	1	3	29
1927-28 " " "		3	3	6	71
1928-29 Chicago		0	1	2	56
5 Years		19	10	29	235
McKINNON, JOHN D					
Born: Guysborough, N.S. July 15, 1902					
1925-26 Mont. Canadiens		0	0	0	0
1926-27 Pittsburgh		13	0	13	21
1927-28 "		3	1	4	46
1928-29 "		1	0	1	44
1929-30 "		10	7	17	42
1930-31 Philadelphia		1	1	2	46
6 Years		28	9	37	199
McKINNON, ROBERT					
1928-29 Chicago		1	1	2	56
McLEAN, - - - -					
1919-20 Quebec	7	0	0	0	2
1920-21 Hamilton Tigers	2	0	0	0	0
2 Years	9	0	0	0	2
McLEAN, JACK RW					
Born: Winnipeg, Man.					
1942-43 Toronto	27	9	8	17	33
1943-44 "	32	3	15	18	30
1944-45 "	8	2	1	3	13
3 Years	67	14	24	38	76
McLELLAN, DANIEL JOHN SL					
Born: South Porcupine, Ont. Aug. 6, 1928					
1951-52 Toronto	1	0	0	0	0
McLENAHAN, ROLAND J. D					
1945-46 Detroit	9	2	1	3	10
McLEOD, ROBERT JOHN RW-SR					
Born: Regina, Sask. Apr. 30, 1930					
1949-50 New York	38	6	9	15	2
1950-51 " "	41	5	10	15	4

(continued)

Sea. Club	Ga.	Go.	A.	P.	PM.
1951-52 " "	13	2	3	5	2
1952-53 " "	3	0	0	0	2
1954-55 " "	11	1	1	2	2
5 Years	106	14	23	37	10
McMAHON, MICHAEL C. D-SL					
1943-44 Montreal	42	7	17	24	*98
1945-46 Montreal-Boston	15	0	1	1	4
2 Years	57	7	18	25	102
*League Leader					
McMANUS, SAMUEL LW					
Born: Belfast, Ire.					
1934-35 Mont. Maroons		0	1	1	8
McNAB, MAXWELL D. C-SL					
Born: Saskatoon, Sask.					
1947-48 Detroit	12	2	2	4	2
1948-49 "	51	10	13	23	14
1949-50 "	65	4	4	8	8
3 Years	128	16	19	35	24
McNAMARA, HOWARD D					
1919-20 Montreal	11	1	0	1	2
McNAUGHTON, GEORGE					
1919-20 Quebec	1	0	0	0	0
McNEILL, STUART C-SL					
Born: Port Arthur, Ont. Sept. 25, 1938					
1957-58 Detroit	2	0	0	0	0
1958-59 "	3	1	1	2	2
1959-60 "	5	0	0	0	0
3 Years	10	1	1	2	2
McNEILL, WILLIAM RONALD RW&C-SR					
Born: Edmonton, Alb. Jan. 26, 1936					
1956-57 Detroit	64	5	10	15	34
1957-58 "	35	5	10	15	29
1958-59 "	54	2	5	7	32
1959-60 "	47	5	13	18	33
1962-63 "	42	3	7	10	12
1963-64 "	15	1	1	2	2
6 Years	257	21	46	67	142
McREAVY, PATRICK JOSEPH C-SR					
Born: Blind River, Ont. Jan. 16, 1918					
1939-40 Boston		0	0	0	2
1940-41 "		0	1	1	2
1941-42 Boston-Detroit	40	5	9	14	0
3 Years		5	10	15	4
McVEIGH, CHARLES RW-SL					
Born: Kenora, Ont. March 29, 1898					
1926-27 Chicago		12	4	16	23
1927-28 "		6	7	13	10
1928-29 N. Y. Americans		6	2	8	16
1929-30 " " "		14	14	28	32
1930-31 " " "		5	11	16	23
1931-32 " " "		12	15	27	16
1932-33 " " "		7	12	19	10
1933-34 " " "		15	12	27	4
1934-35 " " "		7	11	18	4
9 Years		84	88	172	138
McVICAR, JOHN D-SR					
1930-31 Mont. Maroons		2	4	6	35
1931-32 " "		0	0	0	28
2 Years		2	4	6	63
MEEKER, HOWARD WILLIAM RW-SR					
1946-47 Toronto	55	27	18	45	76
1947-48 "	58	14	20	34	62
1948-49 "	30	7	7	14	56
1949-50 "	70	18	22	40	35
1950-51 "	49	6	14	20	24
1951-52 "	54	9	14	23	50
1952-53 "	25	1	7	8	26
1953-54 "	5	1	0	1	0
8 Years	346	83	102	185	329
1946-47 Calder Trophy					
MEEKING, HARRY LW					
Born: Kitchener, Ont.					
1917-18 Toronto	20	10		10	
1918-19 "	14	7	3	10	32
1926-27 Detroit-Boston	29	1	0	1	10
3 Years	63	18	3	21	42

Sea. Club	Ga.	Go.	A.	P.	PM.
MEGER, PAUL C. LW-SL					
1950-51 Montreal	17	2	4	6	6
1951-52 "	69	24	18	42	44
1952-53 "	69	9	17	26	38
1953-54 "	44	4	9	13	24
1954-55 "	13	0	4	4	6
5 Years	212	39	52	91	118
MEISSNER, RICHARD DONALD RW-SR					
Born: Kindersley, Sask. Jan. 6, 1940					
1959-60 Boston	60	5	6	11	22
1960-61 "	9	0	1	1	2
1961-62 "	66	3	3	6	13
1963-64 New York	35	3	5	8	0
1964-65 " "	1	0	0	0	0
5 Years	171	11	15	26	37
MELNYK, MICHAEL GERALD C-SR					
Born: Edmonton, Alb. Sept. 16, 1934					
1959-60 Detroit	63	10	10	20	12
1960-61 "	70	9	16	25	2
1961-62 Chicago	63	5	16	21	6
1967-68 St. Louis	73	15	35	50	14
4 Years	269	39	77	116	34
MENARD, HILLARY LW-SL					
Born: Timmins, Ont. Jan. 15, 1934					
1953-54 Chicago	1	0	0	0	0
MERONEK, WILLIAM C-SL					
Born: Stony Mountain, Man. Apr. 5, 1917					
1939-40 Montreal		2	2	4	0
1942-43 "	12	3	6	9	0
2 Years		5	8	13	0
MERRILL, HORACE D					
1917-18 Ottawa	4	0		0	
1919-20 "	7	0	0	0	0
2 Years	11	0	-	0	-
METZ, DONALD MAURICE RW-SR					
Born: Wilcox, Sask. Jan. 10, 1916					
1939-40 Toronto		1	1	2	4
1940-41 "		4	10	14	6
1941-42 "	25	2	3	5	8
1945-46 "	7	1	0	1	0
1946-47 "	40	4	9	13	10
1947-48 "	26	4	6	10	2
1948-49 "	33	4	6	10	12
7 Years		20	35	55	42
METZ, NICHOLAS J. LW&C-SL					
Born: Wilcox, Sask. Feb. 16, 1914					
1934-35 Toronto		2	2	4	4
1935-36 "		14	6	20	14
1936-37 "		9	11	20	19
1937-38 "		15	7	22	12
1938-39 "		11	10	21	15
1939-40 "		6	5	11	2
1940-41 "		14	21	35	10
1941-42 "	30	11	9	20	20
1944-45 "	50	22	13	35	26
1945-46 "	41	11	11	22	4
1946-47 "	60	12	16	28	15
1947-48 "	60	4	8	12	8
12 Years	131	119	250	149	
MICHALUK, ARTHUR D					
1947-48 Chicago	5	0	0	0	0
MICHALUK, JOHN F					
1950-51 Chicago	1	0	0	0	0
MICKOSKI, NICHOLAS C&LW-SL					
Born: Winnipeg, Man. Dec. 7, 1927					
1948-49 New York	54	13	9	22	20
1949-50 " "	45	10	10	20	10
1950-51 " "	64	20	15	35	12
1951-52 " "	43	7	13	20	20
1952-53 " "	70	19	16	35	39
1953-54 " "	68	19	16	35	22
1954-55 New York-Chicago	70	10	32	42	48
1955-56 Chicago	70	19	20	39	52
1956-57 "	70	16	20	36	24
1957-58 Chicago-Detroit	65	13	18	31	50
1958-59 Detroit	66	11	15	26	20

(continued)

Sea. Club	Ga.	Go.	A.	P.	PM.
1959-60 Boston	18	1	0	1	2
12 Years	703	158	184	342	319

MIGAY, RUDOLPH JOSEPH C-SL
Born: Fort William, Ont. Nov. 18, 1928

Sea. Club	Ga.	Go.	A.	P.	PM.
1949-50 Toronto	18	1	5	6	8
1951-52 "	19	2	1	3	12
1952-53 "	40	5	4	9	22
1953-54 "	70	8	15	23	60
1954-55 "	67	8	16	24	66
1955-56 "	70	12	16	28	52
1956-57 "	66	15	20	35	51
1957-58 "	48	7	14	21	18
1958-59 "	19	1	1	2	4
1959-60 "	1	0	0	0	0
10 Years	418	59	92	151	293

MIKOL, JOHN STANLEY RW-SR
Born: Kitchener, Ont. June 11, 1938

Sea. Club	Ga.	Go.	A.	P.	PM.
1962-63 Toronto	4	0	1	1	2
1964-65 New York	30	1	3	4	6
2 Years	34	1	4	5	8

MILKS, HIBBERT C
Born: Eardley, Ont. April 1, 1902

Sea. Club	Ga.	Go.	A.	P.	PM.
1925-26 Pittsburgh		14	5	19	17
1926-27 "		16	6	22	18
1927-28 "		18	3	21	34
1928-29 "		9	3	12	22
1929-30 "		13	11	24	36
1930-31 Philadelphia		17	6	23	42
1931-32 N. Y. Rangers		0	4	4	12
1932-33 Ottawa		0	3	3	0
8 Years		87	41	128	181

MILLAR, HUGH A. RW
Born: Bear Lake, Alb.

Sea. Club	Ga.	Go.	A.	P.	PM.
1946-47 Detroit	4	0	0	0	0

MILLER, EARL LW

Sea. Club	Ga.	Go.	A.	P.	PM.
1927-28 Chicago		1	1	2	32
1928-29 "		1	1	2	24
1929-30 "		11	5	16	50
1930-31 "		3	4	7	8
1931-32 Chicago-Toronto		3	3	6	10
5 Years		19	14	33	124

MILLER, JACK L. LW

Sea. Club	Ga.	Go.	A.	P.	PM.
1949-50 Chicago	6	0	0	0	0
1950-51 "	11	0	0	0	4
2 Years	17	0	0	0	4

MILLER, WILLIAM

Sea. Club	Ga.	Go.	A.	P.	PM.
1934-35 Mont. Maroons		3	0	3	2
1935-36 " Canadiens		1	2	3	2
1936-37 " "		3	1	4	12
3 Years		7	3	10	16

MITCHELL, HERBERT D

Sea. Club	Ga.	Go.	A.	P.	PM.
1924-25 Boston	27	3	0	3	42
1925-26 "	26	3	0	3	14
2 Years	53	6	0	6	56

MITCHELL, WILLIAM D

Sea. Club	Ga.	Go.	A.	P.	PM.
1941-42 Chicago	1	0	0	0	4
1942-43 "	42	1	1	2	47
1944-45 "	40	3	4	7	16
3 Years	83	4	5	9	67

MITCHELL, WILLIAM D

Sea. Club	Ga.	Go.	A.	P.	PM.
1963-64 Detroit	1	0	0	0	0

MOE, WILLIAM C. D-SL
Born: Boston, Mass. October 2, 1916

Sea. Club	Ga.	Go.	A.	P.	PM.
1944-45 New York	35	2	4	6	14
1945-46 " "	48	4	4	8	14
1946-47 " "	59	4	10	14	44
1947-48 " "	59	1	15	16	31
1948-49 " "	60	0	9	9	60
5 Years	261	11	42	53	163

MOFFATT, RONALD LW-SL
Born: West Hope, N. D.

Sea. Club	Ga.	Go.	A.	P.	PM.
1932-33 Detroit		1	1	2	6
1933-34 "		0	0	0	2
2 Years		1	1	2	8

MOHNS, LLOYD W. F

Sea. Club	Ga.	Go.	A.	P.	PM.
1943-44 New York	1	0	0	0	0

MOLYNEAUX, LAWRENCE S. D-SR
Born: Sutton West, Ont. July 9, 1912

Sea. Club	Ga.	Go.	A.	P.	PM.
1937-38 N. Y. Rangers		0	0	0	2
1938-39 " " "		0	1	1	18
2 Years		0	1	1	20

MONDOU, ARMAND LW&C-SL
Born: Yamaska, Que. June 27, 1905

Sea. Club	Ga.	Go.	A.	P.	PM.
1928-29 Mont. Canadiens		3	4	7	6
1929-30 " "		3	5	8	24
1930-31 " "		5	4	9	10
1931-32 " "		6	12	18	22
1932-33 " "		1	3	4	15
1933-34 " "		5	3	8	4
1934-35 " "		9	15	24	6
1935-36 " "		7	11	18	10
1936-37 " "		1	1	2	0
1937-38 " "		2	4	6	0
1938-39 " "		3	7	10	2
1939-40 " "		2	2	4	0
12 Years		47	71	118	99

MOORE, RICHARD WINSTON LW-SL
Born: Montreal, Que. Jan. 6, 1931

Sea. Club	Ga.	Go.	A.	P.	PM.
1951-52 Montreal	33	18	15	33	44
1952-53 "	18	2	6	8	19
1953-54 "	13	1	4	5	12
1954-55 "	67	16	20	36	32
1955-56 "	70	11	39	50	55
1956-57 "	70	29	29	58	56
1957-58 "	70	*36	48	*84	65
1958-59 "	70	41	*55	*96	61
1959-60 "	62	22	42	64	54
1960-61 "	57	35	34	69	62
1961-62 "	57	19	22	41	54
1962-63 "	67	24	26	50	61
1964-65 Toronto	38	2	4	6	68
1967-68 St. Louis	27	5	3	8	9
14 Years	719	261	347	608	652

*League Leader
1957-58 1st All-Star Team & Ross Trophy
1958-59 " " " & Ross Trophy
1960-61 2nd All-Star Team

MORAN, AMBROSE JASON D

Sea. Club	Ga.	Go.	A.	P.	PM.
1926-27 Mont. Canadiens		0	0	0	10
1927-28 Chicago		1	1	2	14
2 Years		1	1	2	24

MORENZ, HOWARTH W. C-SL
Born: Mitchell, Ont. Sept. 21, 1902

Sea. Club	Ga.	Go.	A.	P.	PM.
1923-24 Montreal Canadiens	-	13	3	16	20
1924-25 " "	-	27	7	34	31
1925-26 " "	-	23	3	26	39
1926-27 " "	-	25	7	32	49
1927-28 " "	-	*33	*18	*51	66
1928-29 " "	-	17	10	27	47
1929-30 " "	-	40	10	50	72
1930-31 " "	-	28	23	*51	49
1931-32 " "	-	24	25	49	46
1932-33 " "	-	14	21	35	32
1933-34 " "	-	8	13	21	21
1934-35 Chicago	-	8	26	34	21
1935-36 Chicago-N. Y. Rangers	-	6	15	21	26
1936-37 Mont. Canadiens	-	4	16	20	12
14 Years	-	270	197	467	531

*League Leader
1927-28 Hart Trophy
1930-31 1st All-Star Team & Hart Trophy
1931-32 " " " & Hart Trophy
1932-33 2nd All-Star Team
1945 Hall of Fame

MORIN, PETER LW-SL

Sea. Club	Ga.	Go.	A.	P.	PM.
1941-42 Montreal		10	12	22	7

MORRIS, BERNARD PATRICK RW-SR

Sea. Club	Ga.	Go.	A.	P.	PM.
1924-25 Boston	6	2	0	2	0

MORRIS, ELWYN D

Sea. Club	Ga.	Go.	A.	P.	PM.
1943-44 Toronto	50	12	21	33	22
1944-45 "	29	0	2	2	18
1945-46 "	38	1	5	6	10
1948-49 New York	18	0	1	1	8
4 Years	135	13	29	42	58

Sea. Club	Ga.	Go.	A.	P.	PM.
MORRISON, DONALD M. C					
Born: Saskatoon, Sask.					
1947-48 Detroit	40	10	15	25	6
1948-49 "	13	0	1	1	0
1950-51 Chicago	59	8	12	20	6
3 Years	112	18	28	46	12
MORRISON, JOHN F-SR					
1925-26 N. Y. Americans	18	0	0	0	0
MORRISON, RODERICK F. RW					
Born: Saskatoon, Sask.					
1947-48 Detroit	34	8	7	15	4
MORTSON, JAMES ANGUS GERALD D-SL					
Born: New Liskeard, Ont. Jan. 24, 1925					
1946-47 Toronto	60	5	13	18	*133
1947-48 "	58	7	11	18	118
1948-49 "	60	2	13	15	85
1949-50 "	67	3	14	17	125
1950-51 "	60	3	10	13	*142
1951-52 "	65	1	10	11	106
1952-53 Chicago	68	5	18	23	88
1953-54 "	68	5	13	18	*132
1954-55 "	65	2	11	13	133
1955-56 "	52	5	10	15	87
1956-57 "	70	5	18	23	*147
1957-58 "	67	3	10	13	62
1958-59 Detroit	36	0	1	1	22
13 Years	796	46	152	198	1380
*League Leader					
1949-50 1st All-Star Team					
MOSDELL, KENNETH C-SL					
Born: Montreal, Que. July 13, 1922					
1941-42 Brooklyn	41	7	9	16	16
1942-44 in Military Service					
1944-45 Montreal	31	12	6	18	16
1945-46 "	13	2	1	3	8
1946-47 "	54	5	10	15	50
1947-48 "	23	1	0	1	19
1948-49 "	60	17	9	26	50
1949-50 "	67	15	12	27	42
1950-51 "	66	13	18	31	24
1951-52 "	44	5	11	16	19
1952-53 "	63	5	14	19	27
1953-54 "	67	22	24	46	64
1954-55 "	70	22	32	54	82
1955-56 "	67	13	17	30	48
1956-57 Chicago	25	2	4	6	10
1957-58 Montreal	2	0	1	1	0
15 Years	693	141	168	309	475
1953-54 1st All-Star Team					
1954-55 2nd " " "					
MOSIENKO, WILLIAM RW-SR					
Born: Winnipeg, Man. Nov. 2, 1921					
1941-42 Chicago	12	6	8	14	4
1942-43 "	2	2	0	2	0
1943-44 "	50	32	38	70	10
1944-45 "	50	28	26	54	0
1945-46 "	40	18	30	48	12
1946-47 "	59	25	27	52	2
1947-48 "	40	16	9	25	0
1948-49 "	60	17	25	42	6
1949-50 "	69	18	28	46	10
1950-51 "	65	21	15	36	18
1951-52 "	70	31	22	53	10
1952-53 "	65	17	20	37	8
1953-54 "	65	15	19	34	17
1954-55 "	64	12	15	27	24
14 Years	711	258	282	540	121
1944-45 2nd All-Star Team & Lady Byng Trophy					
1945-46 " " " "					
1965 Hall of Fame					

Sea. Club	Ga.	Go.	A.	P.	PM.
MOTTER, ALEXANDER E. C&D-SL					
Born: Melville, Sask. June 20, 1913					
1935-36 Boston		1	4	5	4
1937-38 Boston-Detroit		5	17	22	6
1938-39 Detroit		5	11	16	17
1939-40 "		7	12	19	28
1940-41 "		13	12	25	18
1941-42 "	30	2	4	6	20
1942-43 "	50	6	4	10	42
7 Years		39	64	103	135
MUMMERY, HARRY D-SL					
1917-18 Toronto	18	3		3	
1918-19 "	13	2	0	2	27
1919-20 Quebec	24	9	6	15	42
1920-21 Montreal	24	15	5	20	68
1921-22 Hamilton	20	4	2	6	20
1922-23 "	7	0	0	0	4
6 Years	106	33	13	46	161
MUNRO, DUNCAN B. D-SL					
Born: Toronto, Ont.					
1924-25 Mont. Maroons		5	1	6	14
1925-26 " "		4	6	10	55
1926-27 " "		6	5	11	42
1927-28 " "		5	2	7	35
1928-29 " "		0	0	0	0
1929-30 " "		7	2	9	10
1930-31 " "		0	1	1	0
1931-32 " Canadiens		1	1	2	14
8 Years		28	18	46	170
MUNRO, GERALD					
1924-25 Mont. Maroons	29	1	0	1	22
1925-26 Toronto St. Patricks	4	0	0	0	0
2 Years	33	1	0	1	22
MURDOCH, JOHN MURRAY C&LW-SL					
Born: Lucknow, Ont. May 19, 1904					
1926-27 N. Y. Rangers	44	6	4	10	12
1927-28 " " "	44	7	3	10	14
1928-29 " " "	44	8	6	14	18
1929-30 " " "	44	13	13	26	22
1930-31 " " "	44	7	7	14	8
1931-32 " " "	48	5	16	21	32
1932-33 " " "	48	5	11	16	23
1933-34 " " "	48	17	10	27	29
1934-35 " " "	48	14	15	29	14
1935-36 " " "	48	2	9	11	9
1936-37 " " "	48	0	14	14	16
11 Years	508	84	108	192	197
MURRAY, ALLAN D-SL					
Born: Stratford, Ont. Nov. 10, 1908					
1933-34 N. Y. Americans		1	1	2	20
1934-35 " " "		2	1	3	36
1935-36 " " "		1	0	1	33
1936-37 " " "		0	2	2	22
1937-38 " " "		0	1	1	34
1938-39 " " "		0	0	0	8
1939-40 " " "		1	4	5	10
7 Years		5	9	14	163
MURRAY, JAMES ARNOLD D-SL					
Born: Virden, Man. Nov. 25, 1943					
1967-68 Los Angeles	30	0	2	2	14
MURRAY, LEO C-SL					
1932-33 Mont. Canadiens		0	0	0	2
MYLES, VICTOR R. D					
Born: Fairlight, Sask.					
1942-43 New York	45	6	9	15	57
NATTRASS, RALPH W. D-SL					
1946-47 Chicago	35	4	5	9	34
1947-48 "	60	5	12	17	79
1948-49 "	60	4	10	14	99
1949-50 "	68	5	11	16	96
4 Years	223	18	38	56	308

Sea. Club	Ga.	Go.	A.	P.	PM.
NEVILLE, - - - -					
1917-18 Toronto		1		1	
NEVILLE, MICHAEL C					
1924-25 Toronto		1	0	1	4
1925-26 "		3	3	6	8
1930-31 N. Y. Americans		1	0	1	2
3 Years		5	3	8	14
NEWMAN, JOHN C					
1930-31 Detroit		1	1	2	0
NICHOLSON, ALLAN DOUGLAS LW-SL					
Born: Estevan, Sask. Apr. 26, 1936					
1955-56 Boston	14	0	0	0	4
1956-57 "	5	0	1	1	0
2 Years	19	0	1	1	4
NICHOLSON, EDWARD G. D					
1947-48 Detroit	1	0	0	0	0
NICHOLSON, JOHN IVAN "Hickey" LW					
Born: Prince Edward Island					
1937-38 Chicago		1	0	1	0
NIGHBOR, FRANK J. C-SL					
Born: Pembroke, Ont. January 26, 1893					
1917-18 Ottawa	11		11		
1918-19 "	18	4	22	27	
1919-20 "	26	7	33	18	
1920-21 "	18	3	21	10	
1921-22 "	8	8	16	2	
1922-23 "	11	5	16	16	
1923-24 "	10	3	13	14	
1924-25 "	5	2	7	18	
1925-26 "	12	*13	25	40	
1926-27 "	6	6	12	26	
1927-28 "	8	5	13	46	
1928-29 "	1	4	5	22	
1929-30 Ottawa-Toronto	2	0	2	2	
13 Years	136	60	196	241	
*League Leader					
1923-24 Hart Trophy					
1924-25 Lady Byng Trophy					
1925-26 " " "					
1945 Hall of Fame					
NOBLE, EDWARD REGINALD LW&D-SL					
Born: Collingwood, Ont., June 23, 1895					
1917-18 Toronto	28		28		
1918-19 "	11	3	14	35	
1919-20 "	24	7	31	51	
1920-21 "	20	6	26	54	
1921-22 "	17	8	25	10	
1922-23 "	12	10	22	41	
1923-24 "	12	3	15	23	
1924-25 Toronto-Mont. Maroons	8	6	14	62	
1925-26 Mont. Maroons	9	9	18	96	
1926-27 " "	3	3	6	112	
1927-28 Detroit	6	8	14	63	
1928-29 "	6	4	10	52	
1929-30 "	6	4	10	72	
1930-31 "	2	5	7	42	
1931-32 "	3	3	6	72	
1932-33 Detroit-Mont. Maroons	0	0	0	22	
16 Years	167	79	246	807	
1962 Hall of Fame					
NOLAN, PATRICK					
1921-22 Toronto	2	0	0	0	0
NORTHCOTT, LAWRENCE LW-SL					
Born: Calgary, Alb. Sept. 7, 1908					
1928-29 Mont. Maroons	0	0	0	0	
1929-30 Mont. Maroons	10	1	11	6	
1930-31 " "	7	3	10	15	
1931-32 " "	19	6	25	33	
1932-33 " "	22	21	43	30	
1933-34 " "	20	13	33	27	
1934-35 " "	9	14	23	44	
1935-36 " "	15	21	36	41	
1936-37 " "	15	14	29	18	
1937-38 " "	11	12	23	50	
1938-39 Chicago	5	7	12	9	
11 Years	133	112	245	273	
1932-33 1st All-Star Team					

Sea. Club	Ga.	Go.	A.	P.	PM.
NYKOLUK, MICHAEL C-SR					
Born: Toronto, Ont. Dec. 11, 1934					
1956-57 Toronto	32	3	1	4	20
OATMAN, WARREN RUSSELL C					
1926-27 Detroit-Mont. Maroons		11	4	15	42
1927-28 Mont. Maroons		7	4	11	36
1928-29 Mont. Maroons-N. Y. Rangers		2	1	3	22
3 Years		20	9	29	100
O'BRIEN, ELLARD JOHN LW-SL					
Born: St. Catharines, Ont. May 27, 1930					
1955-56 Boston	2	0	0	0	0
O'CONNOR, HERBERT W. C-SL					
Born: Montreal, Que.					
1941-42 Montreal	36	9	16	25	4
1942-43 "	50	15	43	58	2
1943-44 "	44	12	42	54	6
1944-45 "	50	21	23	44	2
1945-46 "	45	11	11	22	2
1946-47 "	46	10	20	30	6
1947-48 New York	60	24	36	60	8
1948-49 " "	46	11	24	35	0
1949-50 " "	66	11	22	33	4
1950-51 " "	66	16	20	36	0
10 Years	509	140	257	397	34
1947-48 2nd All-Star Team ; Hart & Lady Byng Trophies.					
O'FLAHERTY, JOHN B. RW-SR					
1940-41 N. Y. Americans	5	4	0	4	0
1941-42 Brooklyn	11	1	1	2	0
2 Years	16	5	1	6	0
O'GRADY, GEORGE					
1917-18 Montreal Wanderers	4	0		0	
OLIVER, HAROLD RW-SR					
Born: Selkirk, Man. Oct. 26, 1900					
1926-27 Boston		18	6	24	17
1927-28 "		13	5	18	20
1928-29 "		17	6	23	24
1929-30 "		16	5	21	12
1930-31 "		16	14	30	18
1931-32 "		13	7	20	22
1932-33 "		11	7	18	10
1933-34 "		5	9	14	6
1934-35 N. Y. Americans		7	9	16	4
1935-36 " "		9	16	25	12
1936-37 " " "		2	1	3	2
11 Years		127	85	212	147
1967 Hall of Fame					
OLMSTEAD, MURRAY BERT LW-SL					
Born: Sceptre, Sask. Sept. 4, 1926					
1948-49 Chicago	9	0	2	2	4
1949-50 "	70	20	29	49	40
1950-51 Chicago-Montreal	54	18	23	41	50
1951-52 Montreal	69	7	28	35	49
1952-53 "	69	17	28	45	83
1953-54 "	70	15	37	52	85
1954-55 "	70	10	*48	58	103
1955-56 "	70	14	*56	70	94
1956-57 "	64	15	33	48	74
1957-58 "	57	9	28	37	71
1958-59 Toronto	70	10	31	41	74
1959-60 "	53	15	21	36	63
1960-61 "	67	18	34	52	84
1961-62 "	56	13	23	36	10
14 Years	848	181	421	602	884
*League Leader					
1952-53 2nd All-Star Team					
1955-56 " " " "					
OLSON, DENNIS C-SR					
Born: Kenora, Ont. Nov. 9, 1934					
1957-58 Detroit	4	0	0	0	0
O'NEIL, JAMES BEATON RW&C-SR					
Born: Semans, Sask. 1912					
1933-34 Boston		2	2	4	15
1934-35 "		2	11	13	35
1935-36 "		2	11	13	49
1936-37 "		0	2	2	6
1940-41 Montreal		0	3	3	0
1941-42 "	4	0	1	1	4
6 Years		6	30	36	109

Sea. Club	Ga.	Go.	A.	P.	PM.
O'NEILL, THOMAS B. RW					
1943-44 Toronto	33	8	7	15	29
1944-45 "	33	2	5	7	24
2 Years	66	10	12	22	53
O'REE, WILLIAM ELDON LW-SL					
Born: Fredericton, N. Bruns. Oct. 15, 1935					
1957-58 Boston	2	0	0	0	0
1960-61 "	43	4	10	14	26
2 Years	45	4	10	14	26
ORLANDO, JAMES V. D-SR					
Born: Montreal, Que. Feb. 27, 1916					
1936-37 Detroit		0	1	1	8
1937-38 "		0	0	0	4
1939-40 "		1	3	4	54
1940-41 "	48	1	10	11	*99
1941-42 "	48	1	7	8	111
1942-43 "	40	3	4	7	*99
6 Years		6	25	31	375
*League Leader					
OUELLETTE, ADELAND LW					
Born: Ottawa, Ont.					
1935-36 Chicago		3	2	5	11
OUELLETTE, GERALD ADRIAN RW-SR					
Born: Grand Falls, N. Bruns. Nov. 1, 1938					
1960-61 Boston	34	5	4	9	0
OWEN, GEORGE D-SL					
Born: Hamilton, Ont. December 1901					
1928-29 Boston		5	4	9	48
1929-30 "		9	4	13	31
1930-31 "		12	13	25	33
1931-32 "		12	10	22	29
1932-33 "		6	2	8	10
5 Years		44	33	77	151
PALANGIO, PETER LW					
Born: North Bay, Ont. September 10, 1908					
1926-27 Montreal Canadiens		0	0	0	0
1927-28 Detroit		3	0	3	8
1928-29 Montreal Canadiens		0	0	0	0
1936-37 Chicago		8	9	17	16
1937-38 "		2	1	3	4
5 Years		13	10	23	28
PALAZZARI, ALDO F					
1943-44 Boston-New York	35	8	3	11	4
PANAGABKO, EDWIN ARNOLD LW&C-SL					
Born: Norquay, Sask. May 17, 1934					
1955-56 Boston	28	0	3	3	38
1956-57 "	1	0	0	0	0
2 Years	29	0	3	3	38
PAPIKE, JOSEPH RW					
Born: Eveleth, Minn.					
1940-41 Chicago		2	2	4	2
1941-42 "		1	0	1	0
1944-45 "	2	0	1	1	2
3 Years		3	3	6	4
PARGETER, GEORGE W. LW					
1946-47 Montreal	4	0	0	0	0
PARKES, ERNEST LW-SR					
1924-25 Mont. Maroons	17	0	0	0	2
PARSONS, GEORGE LW-SL					
Born: Toronto, Ont. June 28, 1914					
1937-38 Toronto		5	6	11	6
1938-39 "		7	7	14	14
2 Years		12	13	25	20
PATRICK, FREDERICK MURRAY D-SR					
Born: Victoria B. C. June 28, 1915					
1937-38 N. Y. Rangers	1	0	2	2	0
1938-39 " " "	48	1	10	11	72
1939-40 " " "	46	2	4	6	44
1940-41 " " "	47	2	8	10	21
1941-45 in Military Service					
1945-46 New York	24	0	2	2	4
5 Years	166	5	26	31	141

Sea. Club	Ga.	Go.	A.	P.	PM.
PATRICK, JOSEPH LW-SL					
Born: Victoria, B. C. Feb. 3, 1912					
1934-35 N. Y. Rangers	48	9	13	22	17
1935-36 " " "	48	11	14	25	29
1936-37 " " "	45	8	16	24	23
1937-38 " " "	48	15	19	34	24
1938-39 " " "	35	8	21	29	25
1939-40 " " "	48	12	16	28	34
1940-41 " " "	48	20	24	44	12
1941-42 " " "	47	*32	22	54	18
1942-43 " " "	50	22	39	61	28
1943-45 in Military Service					
1945-46 New York	38	8	6	14	30
10 Years	455	145	190	335	240
*League Leader					
1941-42 1st All-Star Team					
1942-43 2nd " " "					
PATRICK, LESTER D					
Born: Drummondville, Que. Dec. 30, 1883					
1926-27 N. Y. Rangers		0	0	0	2
1945 Hall of Fame					
PATTERSON, GEORGE RW					
Born: Fort William, Ont.					
1926-27 Toronto		4	2	6	17
1927-28 Toronto-Mont. Canadiens		1	1	2	14
1928-29 Mont. Canadiens		4	5	9	34
1929-30 N. Y. Americans		13	4	17	24
1930-31 " " "		8	6	14	67
1931-32 " " "		6	0	6	26
1932-33 " " "		12	7	19	26
1933-34 N. Y. Americans-Boston		3	1	4	8
1934-35 Detroit-St. Louis		0	1	1	2
9 Years		51	27	78	218
PAUL, ARTHUR STEWART C-SR					
Born: Rocky Mountain House, Alb. Sept. 11, 1943					
1964-65 Detroit	3	0	0	0	0
PAULHUS, ROLAND					
1925-26 Mont. Canadiens	33	0	0	0	0
PAVELICH, MARTIN N. LW-SL					
1947-48 Detroit	41	4	8	12	10
1948-49 "	60	10	16	26	40
1949-50 "	65	8	15	23	58
1950-51 "	67	9	20	29	41
1951-52 "	68	17	19	36	54
1952-53 "	64	13	20	33	49
1953-54 "	65	9	20	29	57
1954-55 "	70	15	15	30	59
1955-56 "	70	5	13	18	38
1956-57 "	64	3	13	16	48
10 Years	634	93	159	252	454
PAYER, - - - -					
1917-18 Montreal Canadiens	1	0		0	
PEARSON, GEORGE ALEXANDER MELVIN LW-SL					
Born: Flin Flon, Man. Apr. 29, 1938					
1959-60 New York	23	1	5	6	13
1961-62 " "	3	0	0	0	2
1962-63 " "	5	1	0	1	6
1964-65 " "	5	0	0	0	4
1967-68 Pittsburgh	2	0	1	1	0
5 Years	38	2	6	8	25
PEIRSON, JOHN F. RW					
1946-47 Boston	5	0	0	0	0
1947-48 "	15	4	2	6	0
1948-49 "	59	22	21	43	45
1949-50 "	57	27	25	52	49
1950-51 "	70	19	19	38	43
1951-52 "	68	20	30	50	30
1952-53 "	49	14	15	29	32
1953-54 "	68	21	19	40	55
1955-56 "	33	11	14	25	41
1956-57 "	68	13	26	39	41
1957-58 "	53	2	2	4	10
11 Years	545	153	173	326	315
PELLETIER, JOSEPH GEORGES ROGER D-SR					
Born: Montreal, Que. June 22, 1945					
1967-68 Philadelphia	1	0	0	0	0

Sea. Club	Ga.	Go.	A.	P.	PM.
PENNINGTON, CLIFFORD C-SR					
Born: Winnipeg, Man. Apr. 18, 1940					
1960-61 Montreal	4	1	0	1	0
1961-62 Boston	70	9	32	41	2
1962-63 "	27	7	10	17	4
3 Years	101	17	42	59	6
PERREAULT, FERNAND LW					
1947-48 New York	2	0	0	0	0
1949-50 " "	1	0	0	0	0
2 Years	3	0	0	0	0
PETERS, FRANK J. D					
1930-31 N. Y. Rangers	43	0	0	0	59
PETERS, JAMES MELDRUM RW-SR					
1945-46 Montreal	47	11	19	30	10
1946-47 "	60	11	13	24	27
1947-48 Montreal-Boston	59	13	18	31	44
1948-49 Boston	60	16	15	31	8
1949-50 Detroit	70	14	16	30	20
1950-51 "	68	17	21	38	14
1951-52 Chicago	70	15	21	36	16
1952-53 "	69	22	19	41	16
1953-54 Chicago-Detroit	71	6	8	14	31
9 Years	574	125	150	275	186
PETTINGER, ERIC F					
1928-29 Boston-Toronto		3	3	6	41
1929-30 Toronto		4	9	13	40
1930-31 Ottawa		0	0	0	2
3 Years		7	12	19	83
PETTINGER, GORDON R. LW&C-SL					
Born: Regina, Sask. Nov. 17, 1911					
1932-33 N. Y. Rangers		1	2	3	18
1933-34 Detroit		3	14	17	14
1934-35 "		2	3	5	2
1935-36 "		8	7	15	6
1936-37 "		7	15	22	13
1937-38 Detroit-Boston		8	13	21	14
1938-39 Boston		11	14	25	8
1939-40 "		2	6	8	2
8 Years		42	74	116	77
PHILLIPS, CHARLES D					
1942-43 Montreal	17	0	0	0	6
PHILLIPS, MERLYN J. RW					
1925-26 Mont. Maroons		3	1	4	6
1926-27 " "		15	1	16	45
1927-28 " "		7	5	12	33
1928-29 " "		6	5	11	41
1929-30 " "		13	10	23	48
1930-31 " "		6	1	7	38
1931-32 " "		1	1	2	11
1932-33 N. Y. Americans		1	7	8	10
8 Years		52	31	83	232
PHILLIPS, W. J.					
1929-30 Mont. Maroons		1	1	2	6
PICARD, ADRIEN ROGER RW					
Born: Montreal, Que. Jan 13, 1935					
1967-68 St. Louis	15	2	2	4	21
PICKETTS, FRED HAROLD RW					
Born: Asquith, Sask.					
1933-34 N. Y. Americans		3	1	4	32
PIDHIRNY, HARRY C-SL					
Born: Toronto, Ont. Mar. 5, 1928					
1957-58 Boston	2	0	0	0	0
PIKE, ALFRED G. C&D-SL					
Born: Winnipeg, Man. Sept. 15, 1917					
1939-40 N. Y. Rangers		8	9	17	38
1940-41 " " "		6	13	19	23
1941-42 " " "	34	8	19	27	16
1942-43 " " "	41	6	16	22	48
1943-45 in Military Service					
1945-46 New York Rangers	33	7	9	16	18
1946-47 " " "	31	7	11	18	2
6 Years	-	42	77	119	145

Sea. Club	Ga.	Go.	A.	P.	PM.
PITRE, DIDIER RW-SR					
Born: Valleyfield, Que. 1884					
1917-18 Montreal Canadiens	19	17		17	
1918-19 " "	17	14	4	18	9
1919-20 " "	22	15	7	22	6
1920-21 " "	23	15	1	16	23
1921-22 " "	23	2	3	5	12
1922-23 " "	23	1	2	3	0
6 Years	127	64	17	81	50
1962 Hall of Fame					
PLAMONDON, GERARD R. LW					
1945-46 Montreal	6	0	2	2	2
1947-48 "	3	1	1	2	0
1948-49 "	27	5	5	10	8
1949-50 "	37	1	5	6	0
1950-51 "	1	0	0	0	0
5 Years	74	7	13	20	10
PLAXTON, HUGH					
1932-33 Mont. Maroons		1	2	3	4
PODOLSKY, NELSON LW					
1948-49 Detroit	1	0	0	0	0
POETA, ANTHONY J. RW					
1951-52 Chicago	1	0	0	0	0
POILE, DONALD B. C-SL					
Born: Fort William, Ont. June 1, 1932					
1954-55 Detroit	4	0	0	0	0
1957-58 "	62	7	9	16	12
2 Years	66	7	9	16	12
POILE, NORMAN ROBERT RW-SR					
Born: Ft. William, Ont. Feb. 10, 1924					
1942-43 Toronto	48	16	19	35	24
1943-44 "	11	6	8	14	9
1944-45 In Military Service					
1945-46 Toronto	9	1	8	9	0
1946-47 "	59	19	17	36	19
1947-48 Toronto-Chicago	58	25	29	54	17
1948-49 Chicago-Detroit	60	21	21	42	8
1949-50 New York-Boston	66	19	20	39	14
7 Years	311	107	122	229	91
1947-48 2nd All-Star Team					
POIRIER, GORDON ARTHUR C-SL					
Born: Maple Creek, Sask. Oct. 27, 1914					
1939-40 Montreal		0	1	1	0
POLICH, JOHN RW-SR					
Born: Hibbing, Minn. July 8, 1916					
1939-40 N. Y. Rangers		0	0	0	0
1940-41 " " "		0	1	1	0
2 Years		0	1	1	0
POLIZIANI, DANIEL RW-SR					
Born: Sydney, Nova Scotia, Jan. 8, 1935					
1958-59 Boston	1	0	0	0	0
POPEIN, LAWRENCE THOMAS C&LW-SL					
Born: Yorkton, Sask. Aug. 11, 1930					
1954-55 New York	70	11	17	28	27
1955-56 " "	64	14	25	39	37
1956-57 " "	67	11	19	30	20
1957-58 " "	70	12	22	34	22
1958-59 " "	61	13	21	34	28
1959-60 " "	66	14	22	36	16
1960-61 " "	4	0	1	1	0
1967-68 Oakland	47	5	14	19	12
8 Years	449	80	141	221	162
PORTLAND, JOHN FREDERICK D-SL					
Born: Collingwood, Ont. July 30, 1912					
1933-34 Mont. Canadiens		0	2	2	10
1934-35 Mont. Canadiens-Boston		1	1	2	4
1936-37 Boston		2	4	6	58
1937-38 "		0	5	5	26
1938-39 "		4	5	9	46
1939-40 Boston-Chicago		1	9	10	36
1940-41 Chicago-Montreal		2	7	9	38
1941-42 Montreal		2	9	11	53
1942-43 "	49	3	14	17	52
9 Years		15	56	71	323

Sea. Club	Ga.	Go.	A.	P.	PM.
POWELL, RAYMOND H. C-SL					
Born: Timmins, Ont.					
1950-51 Chicago	31	7	15	22	2
POWIS, GEOFFREY CHARLES C-SL					
Born: Winnipeg, Man. June 14, 1945					
1967-68 Chicago	2	0	0	0	0
PRATT, JACK C					
Born: Edinburgh, Scot.					
1930-31 Boston		2	0	2	36
1931-32 "		0	0	0	6
2 Years		2	0	2	42
PRATT, WALTER D-SL					
Born: Stony Mountain, Man. Jan. 7, 1916					
1935-36 N. Y. Rangers	17	1	1	2	16
1936-37 " " "	47	8	7	15	23
1937-38 " " "	47	5	14	19	56
1938-39 " " "	48	2	19	21	20
1939-40 " " "	48	4	13	17	61
1940-41 " " "	48	3	17	20	52
1941-42 " " "	47	4	24	28	65
1942-43 New York-Toronto	44	12	27	39	50
1943-44 Toronto	50	17	40	57	30
1944-45 "	50	18	23	41	39
1945-46 "	41	5	20	25	36
1946-47 Boston	31	4	4	8	25
12 Years	518	83	209	292	473
1943-44 1st All-Star Team; & Hart Trophy					
1944-45 2nd All-Star Team					
1966 Hall of Fame					
PRENTICE, ERIC D.					
1943-44 Toronto	5	0	0	0	4
PRICE, - - - -					
1919-20 Ottawa	1	0	0	0	0
PRICE, JOHN REES D-SL					
Born: Goderich, Ont. May 8, 1932					
1951-52 Chicago	1	0	0	0	0
1952-53 "	10	0	0	0	2
1953-54 "	46	4	6	10	22
3 Years	57	4	6	10	24
PRIMEAU, A. JOSEPH C-SL					
Born: Lindsay, Ont. Jan. 29, 1906					
1927-28 Toronto	1	0	0	0	0
1928-29 "		0	1	1	2
1929-30 "		5	21	26	22
1930-31 "		9	*32	41	18
1931-32 "		13	*37	50	25
1932-33 "		11	21	32	4
1933-34 "		14	*32	46	8
1934-35 "		10	20	30	16
1935-36 "		4	13	17	10
9 Years		66	177	243	105
*League Leader					
1931-32 Lady Byng Trophy					
1933-34 2nd All-Star Team					
1963 Hall of Fame					
PRINGLE, ELLIS D					
1930-31 N. Y. Americans		0	0	0	0
PRODGERS, GEORGE "Goldy" F					
1919-20 Toronto	16	8	6	14	2
1920-21 Hamilton	23	18	8	26	8
1921-22 "	24	15	4	19	4
1922-23 "	23	13	3	16	13
1923-24 "	23	9	1	10	6
1924-25 "	1	0	0	0	0
1925-26 Montreal Canadiens		0	0	0	0
7 Years	110	63	22	85	33
PRONOVOST, JOSEPH ARMAND ANDRE LW-SL					
Born: Shawinigan Falls, Que. July 9, 1936					
1956-57 Montreal	64	10	11	21	58
1957-58 "	66	16	12	28	55
1958-59 "	70	9	14	23	48
1959-60 "	69	12	19	31	61
1960-61 " – Boston	68	12	16	28	34
1961-62 Boston	70	15	8	23	74
1962-63 " – Detroit	68	13	7	20	24
1963-64 Detroit	70	7	16	23	54
1964-65 "	3	0	1	1	0
1967-68 Minnesota	8	0	0	0	0
10 Years	556	94	104	198	408

Sea. Club	Ga.	Go.	A.	P.	PM
PRYSTAI, METRO RW-SL					
Born: Yorkton, Sask., Nov. 7, 1927					
1947-48 Chicago	54	7	11	18	25
1948-49 "	59	12	7	19	19
1949-50 "	65	29	22	51	31
1950-51 Detroit	62	20	17	37	27
1951-52 "	69	21	22	43	16
1952-53 "	70	16	34	50	12
1953-54 "	70	12	15	27	26
1954-55 Detroit-Chicago	69	13	16	29	37
1955-56 Chicago-Detroit	71	13	19	32	18
1956-57 Detroit	70	7	15	22	16
1957-58 "	15	1	1	2	4
11 Years	674	151	179	330	231
PUDAS, ALBERT					
1926-27 Toronto St. Patricks	3	0	0	0	0
PURPUR, CLIFFORD RW					
Born: U. S. A.					
1934-35 St. Louis		1	2	3	8
1941-42 Chicago		0	0	0	0
1942-43 "	50	13	16	29	14
1943-44 "	40	9	10	19	13
1944-45 "	21	2	7	9	11
5 Years		25	35	60	46
PUSIE, JEAN BAPTISTE D-SL					
Born: Montreal, Que. October 15, 1910					
1930-31 Montreal Canadiens		0	0	0	0
1933-34 N. Y. Rangers		0	2	2	17
1934-35 Boston		1	0	1	0
1935-36 Mont. Canadiens		0	2	2	11
4 Years		1	4	5	28
QUACKENBUSH, HUBERT G. D-SL					
Born: Toronto, Ont.					
1942-43 Detroit	10	1	1	2	4
1943-44 "	43	4	14	18	6
1944-45 "	50	7	14	21	10
1945-46 "	48	11	10	21	6
1946-47 "	44	5	17	22	6
1947-48 "	58	6	16	22	17
1948-49 "	60	6	17	23	0
1949-50 Boston	70	8	17	25	4
1950-51 "	70	5	24	29	12
1951-52 "	69	2	17	19	6
1952-53 "	69	2	16	18	6
1953-54 "	45	0	17	17	6
1954-55 "	68	2	20	22	8
1955-56 "	70	3	22	25	4
14 Years	774	62	222	284	95
1946-47 2nd All-Star Team					
1947-48 1st " " "					
1948-49 " " " " & Lady Byng Trophy					
1950-51 " " " "					
1952-53 2nd " " "					
QUACKENBUSH, MAXWELL J. D					
1950-51 Boston	47	4	6	10	26
1951-52 Chicago	14	0	1	1	4
2 Years	61	4	7	11	30
QUENNEVILLE, LEO					
1929-30 N. Y. Rangers	25	0	3	3	10
QUILTY, JOHN F. C					
Born: Ottawa, Ont.					
1940-41 Montreal		18	16	34	31
1941-42 "		12	12	24	44
1946-47 "	3	1	1	2	0
1947-48 Montreal-Boston	26	5	5	10	6
4 Years		36	34	70	81
1940-41 Calder Trophy					
RADLEY, HARRY J.					
1930-31 N. Y. Americans		0	0	0	0
1936-37 Mont. Maroons		0	1	1	13
2 Years		0	1	1	13
RAGLAN, CLARENCE E. D					
1950-51 Detroit	33	3	1	4	14
1951-52 Chicago	35	0	5	5	28
1952-53 "	32	1	3	4	10
3 Years	100	4	9	13	52

Sea. Club	Ga.	Go.	A.	P.	PM.
RALEIGH, JAMES DONALD C-SL					
1943-44 New York	15	2	2	4	2
1947-48 " "	52	15	18	33	2
1948-49 " "	41	10	16	26	8
1949-50 " "	70	12	25	37	11
1950-51 " "	64	15	24	39	18
1951-52 " "	70	19	42	61	14
1952-53 " "	55	4	18	22	2
1953-54 " "	70	15	30	45	16
1954-55 " "	69	8	32	40	19
1955-56 " "	29	1	12	13	4
10 Years	535	101	219	320	96
RAMSAY, LES LW					
Born: Montreal, Que.					
1944-45 Chicago	11	2	2	4	2
RAMSEY, W. BEATTIE D					
1927-28 Toronto		0	2	2	10
RANDALL, KENNETH D					
1917-18 Toronto	20	12		12	
1918-19 "	14	7	6	13	27
1919-20 "	21	10	7	17	43
1920-21 "	21	6	1	7	58
1921-22 "	24	10	6	16	20
1922-23 "	24	3	5	8	51
1923-24 Hamilton	24	7	1	8	18
1924-25 "	30	8	0	8	49
1925-26 N. Y. Americans	34	4	2	6	94
1926-27 " " "	5	0	0	0	0
10 Years	217	67	28	95	360
RANIERI, GEORGE DOMINIC LW-SL					
Born: Toronto, Ont. Jan. 14, 1936					
1956-57 Boston	2	0	0	0	0
RAYMOND, ARMAND D-SL					
Born: Montreal, Que. Jan. 12, 1913					
1937-38 Mont. Canadiens		0	2	2	4
1939-40 " "		0	1	1	10
2 Years		0	3	3	14
RAYMOND, PAUL MARCEL					
1933-34 Mont. Canadiens		1	0	1	2
1934-35 " "		1	1	2	0
2 Years		2	1	3	2
READ, MELVIN D. C					
1946-47 New York	6	0	0	0	8
REARDON, KENNETH JOSEPH D-SL					
Born: Winnipeg, Man. Apr. 1, 1921					
1940-41 Montreal	34	2	8	10	41
1941-42 "	41	3	12	15	93
1945-46 "	43	5	4	9	45
1946-47 "	52	5	17	22	84
1947-48 "	58	7	15	22	129
1948-49 "	46	3	13	16	103
1949-50 "	67	1	27	28	109
7 Years	341	26	96	122	604
1945-46 2nd All-Star Team					
1946-47 1st All-Star Team					
1947-48 2nd " " "					
1948-49 " " " "					
1949-50 1st " " "					
1966 Hall of Fame					
REARDON, TERRENCE GEORGE C-SR					
Born: Winnipeg, Man. Apr. 6, 1919					
1939-40 Boston		0	0	0	0
1940-41 "		6	5	11	19
1941-42 Montreal	33	17	17	34	24
1942-43 "	13	6	6	12	2
1943-45 in Military Service					
1945-46 Boston	49	12	11	23	21
1946-47 "	60	6	14	20	17
6 Years		47	53	100	83
REAY, WILLIAM T. C-SL					
Born: Winnipeg, Man. Aug. 21, 1918					
1943-44 Detroit	2	2	0	2	0
1944-45 "	2	0	0	0	0
1945-46 Montreal	44	17	12	29	10
1946-47 "	59	22	20	42	17
1947-48 "	60	6	14	20	24
1948-49 "	60	22	23	45	33
1949-50 "	68	19	26	45	48
1950-51 "	60	6	18	24	24
1951-52 "	68	7	34	41	20
1952-53 "	56	4	15	19	26
10 Years	479	105	162	267	202
REDAHL, GORDON CHARLES LW-SL					
Born: Kinistino, Sask. Aug. 28, 1935					
1958-59 Boston	18	0	1	1	2
REDDING, GEORGE					
1924-25 Boston	27	3	2	5	10
1925-26 "	8	0	0	0	0
2 Years	35	3	2	5	10
REGAN, LAWRENCE EMMETT C&RW-SR					
Born: North Bay, Ont. Aug. 9, 1930					
1956-57 Boston	69	14	19	33	29
1957-58 "	59	11	28	39	22
1958-59 Boston-Toronto	68	9	27	36	12
1959-60 Toronto	47	4	16	20	6
1960-61 "	37	3	5	8	2
5 Years	280	41	95	136	71
1956-57 Calder Trophy					
REGAN, WILLIAM D. D					
1929-30 N. Y. Rangers		0	0	0	4
1930-31 " " "		2	1	3	49
1932-33 " " Americans		1	1	2	14
3 Years		3	2	5	67
REIBEL, EARL C-SR					
Born: Kitchener, Ont. July 21, 1930					
1953-54 Detroit	69	15	33	48	18
1954-55 "	70	25	41	66	15
1955-56 "	68	17	39	56	10
1956-57 "	70	13	23	36	6
1957-58 Detroit-Chicago	69	8	17	25	10
1958-59 Boston	63	6	8	14	16
6 Years	409	84	161	245	75
1955-56 Lady Byng Trophy					
REID, DAVID C					
1952-53 Toronto	2	0	0	0	0
1954-55 "	1	0	0	0	0
1955-56 "	4	0	0	0	0
3 Years	7	0	0	0	0
REID, GORDON J. D					
Born: Mount Albert, Ont.					
1936-37 N. Y. Americans		0	0	0	2
REID, REGINALD S.					
1924-25 Toronto	28	2	0	2	2
1925-26 "	12	0	0	0	2
2 Years	40	2	0	2	4
REIGLE, EDMOND D&F-SL					
Born: Winnipeg, Man.					
1950-51 Boston	17	0	2	2	25
REINIKKA, OLIVER M. F-SR					
1926-27 N. Y. Rangers	16	0	0	0	0
REISE, LEO C. SR. D-SR					
Born: Pembroke, Ont. June 1, 1892					
1920-21 Hamilton		2	0	2	8
1921-22 "		9	*14	23	8
1922-23 "		6	6	12	35
1923-24 "		0	0	0	0
1926-27 N. Y. Americans		7	6	13	24
1927-28 " " "		8	1	9	60
1928-29 " " "		4	1	5	32
1929-30 N. Y. Americans-N. Y. Rangers		3	3	6	20
8 Years		39	31	70	187
*League Leader					
REISE, LEO C. Jr. D-SL					
1945-46 Chicago	6	0	0	0	6
1946-47 Chicago-Detroit	48	4	6	10	32

(continued)

Sea. Club	Ga.	Go.	A.	P.	PM.
1947-48 Detroit	58	5	4	9	30
1948-49 "	59	3	7	10	60
1949-50 "	70	4	17	21	46
1950-51 "	68	5	16	21	67
1951-52 "	54	0	11	11	34
1952-53 New York	61	4	15	19	53
1953-54 " "	70	3	5	8	71
9 Years	494	28	81	109	399
1949-50 2nd All-Star Team					
1950-51 " " "					

RICHARD, JOSEPH HENRI MAURICE RW-SL
Born: Montreal, Que. Aug. 4, 1921

1942-43 Montreal	16	5	6	11	4
1943-44 "	46	32	22	54	45
1944-45 "	50	*50	23	73	46
1945-46 "	50	27	21	48	50
1946-47 "	60	*45	26	71	69
1947-48 "	53	28	25	53	89
1948-49 "	59	20	18	38	110
1949-50 "	70	*43	22	65	114
1950-51 "	65	42	24	66	97
1951-52 "	48	27	17	44	44
1952-53 "	70	28	33	61	*112
1953-54 "	70	*37	30	67	112
1954-55 "	67	*38	36	74	125
1955-56 "	70	38	33	71	89
1956-57 "	63	33	29	62	74
1957-58 "	28	15	19	34	28
1958-59 "	42	17	21	38	27
1959-60 "	51	19	16	35	50
18 Years	978	544	421	965	1285

*League Leader
1943-44 2nd All-Star Team
1944-45 1st " " "
1945-46 " " " "
1946-47 " " " " & Hart Trophy
1947-48 " " " "
1948-49 " " " "
1949-50 " " " "
1950-51 2nd " " "
1951-52 " " " "
1952-53 " " " "
1953-54 " " " "
1954-55 1st " " "
1955-56 " " " "
1956-57 2nd " " "
1961 Hall of Fame

RICHARDSON, DAVID GEORGE LW-SL
Born: St. Boniface, Man. Dec. 11, 1940

1963-64 New York	34	3	1	4	21
1964-65 " "	7	0	1	1	4
1965-66 Chicago	3	0	0	0	2
1967-68 Detroit	1	0	0	0	0
4 Years	45	3	2	5	27

RILEY, JACK

1933-34 Mont. Canadiens		6	11	17	4
1934-35 " "		4	11	15	4
2 Years		10	22	32	8

RILEY, JAMES NORMAN LW-SL
Born: Bayfield, N. B. May 25, 1897

1926-27 Chicago-Detroit		0	2	2	14

RIOPELLE, HOWARD J. LW-SL

1947-48 Montreal	55	5	2	7	12
1948-49 "	48	10	6	16	34
1949-50 "	66	12	8	20	27
3 Years	169	27	16	43	73

RIPLEY, VICTOR M. C
Born: Elgin, Ont.

1928-29 Chicago		11	2	13	31
1929-30 "		8	8	16	33
1930-31 "		8	4	12	9
1931-32 "		12	6	18	47
1932-33 Chicago-Boston		4	9	13	27
1933-34 Boston-N. Y. Rangers		7	13	20	16
1934-35 N. Y. Rangers-St. Louis		1	7	8	10
7 Years		51	49	100	173

RITCHIE, DAVID

1917-18 Montreal Wanderers-Ottawa	17	9		9	

(continued)

Sea. Club	Ga.	Go.	A.	P.	PM.
1918-19 Toronto Arenas	4	0	0	0	9
1919-20 Quebec Bulldogs	21	6	3	9	18
1920-21 Montreal Canadiens	5	0	0	0	0
1924-25 " "	5	0	0	0	0
1925-26 " "	2	0	0	0	0
6 Years	54	15	3	18	27

RITSON, ALEXANDER C. C-SL

1944-45 New York	1	0	0	0	0

RITTINGER, ALAN W. RW

1943-44 Boston	19	3	7	10	0

RIVARD, JOSEPH ROBERT C-SL
Born: Sherbrooke, Que. Aug. 1, 1939

1967-68 Pittsburgh	27	5	12	17	4

RIVERS (DESRIVIERES), GUSTAVE RW

1929-30 Mont. Canadiens		1	0	1	2
1930-31 " "		2	5	7	6
1931-32 " "		1	0	1	4
3 Years		4	5	9	12

ROACH, "MICKEY" C

1919-20 Toronto		10	2	12	4
1920-21 Hamilton Tigers		9	7	16	0
1921-22 Hamilton		14	3	17	7
1922-23 "		17	8	25	8
1923-24 "		5	3	8	0
1924-25 "		6	4	10	4
1925-26 N. Y. Americans		3	0	3	4
1926-27 " " "		11	0	11	14
8 Years		75	27	102	41

ROBERT, CLAUDE LW&C

1950-51 Montreal	23	1	0	1	9

ROBERT, SAMMY

1917-18 Ottawa		0			

ROBERTSON, FRED D
Born: Carlisle, Eng.

1931-32 Toronto		0	0	0	23
1933-34 Detroit		1	0	1	12
2 Years		1	0	1	35

ROBERTSON, GEORGE T. C

1947-48 Montreal	1	0	0	0	0
1948-49 "	30	2	5	7	6
2 Years	31	2	5	7	6

ROBINSON, EARL RW-SR
Born: Montreal, Que. Mar. 11, 1907

1928-29 Mont. Maroons		2	1	3	2
1929-30 " "		1	2	3	10
1931-32 " "		0	3	3	2
1932-33 " "		15	9	24	6
1933-34 " "		12	16	28	14
1934-35 " "		17	18	35	23
1935-36 " "		6	14	20	27
1936-37 " "		16	18	34	19
1937-38 " "		4	7	11	13
1938-39 Chicago		9	6	15	18
1939-40 Montreal Canadiens		1	4	5	4
11 Years		83	98	181	138

ROCCO — See REINIKKA

ROCHE, DESMOND "DEESE" RW

1930-31 Mont. Maroons		0	1	1	6
1932-33 Ottawa		3	6	9	6
1933-34 "		14	10	24	22
1934-35 St. Louis-Mont. Canadiens-Detroit		3	1	4	10
4 Years		20	18	38	44

ROCHE, EARL LW
Born: Swansea, Ont.

1930-31 Mont. Maroons		2	0	2	18
1932-33 Ottawa		4	5	9	6
1933-34 "		13	16	29	22
1934-35 St. Louis-Detroit		6	6	12	2
4 Years		25	27	52	48

ROCHE, ERNEST CHARLES D-SL
Born: Montreal, Que. Feb. 4, 1930

1950-51 Montreal	4	0	0	0	2

Sea. Club	Ga.	Go.	A.	P.	PM.
ROCHEFORT, DAVID JOSEPH C-SL					
Born: Red Deer, Alb. July 22, 1946					
1966-67 Detroit	1	0	0	0	0
ROCKBURN, HARVEY D					
1929-30 Detroit		4	0	4	97
1930-31 "		0	1	1	*118
1932-33 Ottawa		0	1	1	39
3 Years		4	2	6	254
*League Leader					
RODDEN, EDMUND A. RW					
Born: Mar., 1902					
1926-27 Chicago		3	3	6	0
1927-28 Chicago-Toronto		3	8	11	42
1928-29 Boston		0	0	0	10
1930-31 N. Y. Rangers		0	3	3	8
4 Years		6	14	20	60
ROMNES, ELWIN NELSON LW&C-SL					
Born: White Bear, Minn. Jan. 1, 1908					
1930-31 Chicago		5	7	12	8
1931-32 "		1	0	1	6
1932-33 "		10	12	22	2
1933-34 "		7	21	28	6
1934-35 "		10	14	24	8
1935-36 "		13	25	38	6
1936-37 "		4	14	18	2
1937-38 "		10	22	32	4
1938-39 Chicago-Toronto		7	20	27	0
1939-40 N. Y. Americans		0	1	1	0
10 Years		67	136	203	42
1935-36 Lady Byng Trophy					
RONAN, SKENE					
1918-19 Ottawa	11	0	0	0	0
RONTY, PAUL C-SL					
1947-48 Boston	24	3	11	14	0
1948-49 "	60	20	29	49	11
1949-50 "	70	23	36	59	8
1950-51 "	70	10	22	32	20
1951-52 New York	65	12	31	43	16
1952-53 " "	70	16	38	54	20
1953-54 " "	70	13	33	46	18
1954-55 New York-Montreal	59	4	11	15	10
8 Years	488	101	211	312	103
ROSS, ARTHUR HOWEY D					
Born: Naughton, Ont. Jan. 13, 1886					
1917-18 Montreal Wanderers	3	1		1	
1945 Hall of Fame					
ROSS, JAMES D-SR					
1951-52 New York	51	2	9	11	25
1952-53 " "	11	0	2	2	4
2 Years	62	2	11	13	29
ROSSIGNOL, ROLAND RW					
1943-44 Detroit	1	0	1	1	0
1944-45 Montreal	5	2	2	4	2
1945-46 Detroit	8	1	2	3	4
3 Years	14	3	5	8	6
ROTHSCHILD, SAMUEL SL					
1924-25 Mont. Maroons		5	4	9	4
1925-26 " "		2	1	3	8
1926-27 " "		1	1	2	8
1927-28 Pittsburgh-N. Y. Americans		0	0	0	10
4 Years		8	6	14	30
ROULSTON, WILLIAM ORVILLE D-SL					
Born: Toronto, Ont. 1912					
1936-37 Detroit		0	5	5	10
1937-38 "		0	1	1	0
2 Years		0	6	6	10
ROUSSEAU, GUY LUCIEN LW-SL					
Born: Montreal, Que. Dec. 21, 1934					
1954-55 Montreal	2	0	1	1	0
1956-57 "	2	0	0	0	2
2 Years	4	0	1	1	2
ROUSSEAU, ROLAND D					
1952-53 Montreal	2	0	0	0	0
ROWE, ROBERT D-SL					
1924-25 Boston	4	1	0	1	0

Sea. Club	Ga.	Go.	A.	P.	PM.
ROWE, RONALD N. LW					
1947-48 New York	5	1	0	1	0
ROZZINI, GINO C					
1944-45 Boston	31	5	10	15	20
RUELLE, BERNARD E. RW					
1943-44 Detroit	2	1	0	1	0
RUNGE, PAUL LW-SL					
Born: Edmonton, Alb. 1908					
1930-31 Boston	1	0	0	0	0
1931-32 "		0	1	1	8
1934-35 Mont. Canadiens		0	0	0	2
1935-36 Mont. Canadiens-Boston		8	4	12	18
1936-37 " "-Mont. Maroons		5	10	15	8
1937-38 Mont. Maroons		5	7	12	21
6 Years		18	22	40	57
RUSSELL, CHURCHILL D. LW-SL					
1945-46 New York	17	0	5	5	2
1946-47 " "	54	20	8	28	8
1947-48 " "	19	0	3	3	2
3 Years	90	20	16	36	12
SABOURIN, ROBERT RW-SL					
Born: Sudbury, Ont. Mar. 17, 1933					
1951-52 Toronto	1	0	0	0	2
SAMIS, PHILIP L. D					
1949-50 Toronto	2	0	0	0	0
SANDFORD, EDWARD M. LW-SR					
1947-48 Boston	59	10	15	25	25
1948-49 "	56	16	20	36	57
1949-50 "	19	1	4	5	6
1950-51 "	51	10	13	23	33
1951-52 "	65	13	12	25	54
1952-53 "	61	14	21	35	44
1953-54 "	70	16	31	47	42
1954-55 "	61	14	20	34	38
1955-56 Detroit-Chicago	61	12	9	21	56
9 Years	503	106	145	251	355
1953-54 2nd All-Star Team					
SANDS, CHARLES H. C&RW-SR					
Born: Fort William, Ont. Mar. 23, 1911					
1932-33 Toronto		0	3	3	0
1933-34 "		8	8	16	2
1934-35 Boston		15	12	27	0
1935-36 "		6	4	10	8
1936-37 "		18	5	23	6
1937-38 "		17	12	29	12
1938-39 "		7	5	12	10
1939-40 Montreal		9	20	29	10
1940-41 "		5	13	18	4
1941-42 "		11	16	27	6
1942-43 "	31	3	9	12	0
1943-44 New York	9	0	2	2	0
12 Years		99	109	208	58
SASAKAMOOSE, FRED C					
1953-54 Chicago	11	0	0	0	6
SAUNDERS, THEODORE RW					
Born: Ottawa, Ont.					
1933-34 Ottawa		1	3	4	4
SAVAGE, GORDON D					
Born: Calgary, Alb.					
1934-35 Boston-Mont. Canadiens		1	5	6	6
SCHAEFFER, PAUL					
Born: U. S. A.					
1936-37 Chicago		0	0	0	6
SCHERZA, CHARLES C					
1943-44 Boston-New York	14	4	3	7	17
1944-45 New York	22	2	3	5	18
2 Years	36	6	6	12	35
SCHMIDT, CLARENCE F					
1943-44 Boston	7	1	0	1	2
SCHMIDT, JOHN R. RW					
1942-43 Boston	45	6	7	13	6

Sea.	Club	Ga.	Go.	A.	P.	PM.

SCHMIDT, JOSEPH F

Sea. Club	Ga.	Go.	A.	P.	PM.
1943-44 Boston	2	0	0	0	0

SCHMIDT, MILTON CONRAD C-SL
Born: Kitchener, Ont. Mar. 5, 1918

Sea. Club	Ga.	Go.	A.	P.	PM.
1936-37 Boston		2	8	10	15
1937-38 "		13	14	27	15
1938-39 "		15	17	32	13
1939-40 "	48	22	*30	*52	37
1940-41 "	45	13	25	38	23
1941-42 "	36	14	21	35	34
1942-45 in Military Service					
1945-46 Boston	48	13	18	31	21
1946-47 "	59	27	35	62	40
1947-48 "	33	9	17	26	28
1948-49 "	44	10	22	32	25
1949-50 "	68	19	22	41	41
1950-51 "	62	22	39	61	33
1951-52 "	69	21	29	50	57
1952-53 "	68	11	23	34	30
1953-54 "	62	14	18	32	28
1954-55 "	23	4	8	12	26
16 Years		229	346	575	466

*League Leader
1939-40 1st All-Star Team
1946-47 " " " "
1950-51 " " " " & Hart Trophy
1951-52 2nd " " " "
1961 Hall of Fame

SCHNARR, WERNER

Sea. Club	Ga.	Go.	A.	P.	PM.
1924-25 Boston	24	0	0	0	0
1925-26 "	1	0	0	0	0
2 Years	25	0	0	0	0

SCHRINER, DAVID LW-SL
Born: Calgary, Alb. Nov. 30, 1911

Sea. Club	Ga.	Go.	A.	P.	PM.
1934-35 N. Y. Americans		18	22	40	6
1935-36 " " "		19	26	*45	8
1936-37 " ' "		21	25	*46	17
1937-38 " " "		21	17	38	22
1938-39 " " "		13	31	44	20
1939-40 Toronto		11	15	26	10
1940-41 "		24	14	38	6
1941-42 "		20	16	36	21
1942-43 "	37	19	17	36	13
1943-44 in Military Service					
1944-45 Toronto	26	22	15	37	10
1945-46 "	47	13	6	19	15
11 Years		201	204	405	148

*League Leader
1934-35 Rookie of the Year
1935-36 1st All-Star Team
1936-37 2nd " " "
1940-41 1st " " "
1962 Hall of Fame

SCLISIZZI, JAMES ENIO LW-SL

Sea. Club	Ga.	Go.	A.	P.	PM.
1947-48 Detroit	4	1	0	1	0
1948-49 "	50	9	8	17	24
1949-50 "	4	0	0	0	2
1951-52 "	9	2	1	3	0
1952-53 Chicago	14	0	2	2	0
5 Years	81	12	11	23	26

SCOTT, GANTON

Sea. Club	Ga.	Go.	A.	P.	PM.
1922-23 Toronto St. Patricks	17	0	0	0	0
1923-24 "	8	0	0	0	0
1924-25 Montreal Maroons	28	1	1	2	2
1926-27 Toronto St. Patricks	1	0	0	0	0
4 Years	54	1	1	2	2

SCOTT, LAWRENCE LW

Sea. Club	Ga.	Go.	A.	P.	PM.
1926-27 N. Y. Americans		6	2	8	22
1927-28 " " Rangers		0	1	1	6
2 Years		6	3	9	28

SEIBERT, EARL WALTER D-SR
Born: Kitchener, Ont. Dec. 7, 1911

Sea. Club	Ga.	Go.	A.	P.	PM.
1931-32 N. Y. Rangers		4	6	10	88
1932-33 " " "		2	3	5	92
1933-34 " " "		13	10	23	66
1934-35 " " "		6	19	25	86
1935-36 N. Y. Rangers-Chicago		5	9	14	27
1936-37 Chicago		9	6	15	46
1937-38 "		8	13	21	38
1938-39 "		4	11	15	57

(continued)

Sea. Club	Ga.	Go.	A.	P.	PM.
1939-40 "		3	7	10	35
1940-41 "		3	17	20	52
1941-42 "		7	14	21	52
1942-43 "	44	5	27	32	48
1943-44 "	50	8	25	33	40
1944-45 Chicago-Detroit	47	12	17	29	23
1945-46 Detroit	18	0	3	3	18
15 Years		89	187	276	768

1934-35 1st All-Star Team
1935-36 2nd All-Star Team
1936-37 " " " "
1937-38 " " " "
1938-39 " " " "
1939-40 " " " "
1940-41 " " " "
1941-42 1st All-Star Team
1942-43 " " " "
1943-44 " " " "
1963 Hall of Fame

SENICK, GEORGE Lw
Born: Saskatoon, Sask.

Sea. Club	Ga.	Go.	A.	P.	PM.
1952-53 New York	13	2	3	5	8

SHACK, JOSEPH LW

Sea. Club	Ga.	Go.	A.	P.	PM.
1942-43 New York	20	5	9	14	6
1944-45 " "	50	4	18	22	14
2 Years	70	9	27	36	20

SHANNON, CHARLES KITCHENER D-SL
Born: Campbellford, Ont. Mar. 22, 1916

Sea. Club	Ga.	Go.	A.	P.	PM.
1939-40 N. Y. Americans		0	0	0	2

SHANNON, GERALD LW
Born: Campbellford, Ont.

Sea. Club	Ga.	Go.	A.	P.	PM.
1933-34 Ottawa		11	15	26	26
1934-35 St. Louis-Boston		3	3	6	15
1935-36 Boston		0	1	1	6
1936-37 Mont. Maroons		9	7	16	13
1937-38 " "		0	3	3	20
5 Years		23	29	52	80

SHAY, NORMAN LW
Born: Huntsville, Ont.

Sea. Club	Ga.	Go.	A.	P.	PM.
1924-25 Boston	18	1	1	2	14
1925-26 Boston-Toronto	35	4	1	5	20
2 Years	53	5	2	7	34

SHEA, FRANCIS PATRICK

Sea. Club	Ga.	Go.	A.	P.	PM.
1931-32 Chicago		0	1	1	0

SHELTON, WAYNE DOUGLAS RW-SR
Born: Woodstock, Ont. June 27, 1945

Sea. Club	Ga.	Go.	A.	P.	PM.
1967-68 Chicago	5	0	1	1	2

SHEPPARD, FRANK

Sea. Club	Ga.	Go.	A.	P.	PM.
1927-28 Detroit		1	1	2	0

SHEPPARD, JAKE O. C
Born: Selkirk, Man.

Sea. Club	Ga.	Go.	A.	P.	PM.
1926-27 Detroit		13	8	21	60
1927-28 "		10	10	20	40
1928-29 N. Y. Americans		5	4	9	38
1929-30 " " "		14	15	29	32
1930-31 " " "		5	8	13	16
1931-32 " " "		1	0	1	2
1932-33 " " "		17	9	26	32
1933-34 Boston-Chicago		3	4	7	4
8 Years		68	58	126	224

SHERF, JOHN LW-SL
Born: Calumet, Mich. Apr. 8, 1914

Sea. Club	Ga.	Go.	A.	P.	PM.
1937-38 Detroit		0	0	0	2
1943-44 "	8	0	0	0	6
2 Years		0	0	0	8

SHERO, FREDERICK ALEXANDER D-SL
Born: Winnipeg, Man October 23, 1925

Sea. Club	Ga.	Go.	A.	P.	PM.
1947-48 New York	19	1	0	1	2
1948-49 " "	59	3	6	9	64
1949-50 " "	67	2	8	10	71
3 Years	145	6	14	20	137

SHERRITT, GORDON E. D
Born: Oakville, Man.

Sea. Club	Ga.	Go.	A.	P.	PM.
1943-44 Detroit	8	0	0	0	12

Sea. Club	Ga.	Go.	A.	P.	PM.
SHEWCHUK, JOHN MICHAEL D-SL					
Born: Brantford, Ont. June 19, 1917					
1938-39 Boston		0	0	0	2
1939-40 "		2	4	6	55
1940-41 "		2	2	4	8
1941-42 "	22	2	0	2	14
1942-43 "	48	2	6	8	50
1944-45 "	47	1	7	8	31
6 Years		9	19	28	160
SHIBICKY, ALEXANDER DIMITRI LW-SR					
Born: Winnipeg, Man. May 19, 1914					
1935-36 N. Y. Rangers		4	2	6	6
1936-37 " " "		14	8	22	30
1937-38 " " "		17	18	35	26
1938-39 " " "		24	9	33	22
1939-40 " " "		11	21	32	33
1940-41 " " "		10	14	24	14
1941-42 " " "	45	20	14	34	16
1942-45 in Military Service					
1945-46 N. Y. Rangers	33	10	5	15	12
8 Years		110	91	201	159
SHIELDS, ALLAN D-SL					
Born: Ottawa, Ont. May 10, 1907					
1927-28 Ottawa		0	1	1	2
1928-29 "		0	1	1	10
1929-30 "		6	3	9	32
1930-31 Philadelphia		7	3	10	98
1931-32 N. Y. Americans		4	1	5	45
1932-33 Ottawa		7	4	11	119
1933-34 "		4	7	11	44
1934-35 Mont. Maroons		4	8	12	45
1935-36 "		2	7	9	81
1936-37 N. Y. Americans-Boston		3	4	7	94
1937-38 Mont. Maroons		5	7	12	67
11 Years		42	46	88	637
SHILL, JOHN W. LW&C-SL					
Born: Toronto, Ont. 1912					
1933-34 Toronto		0	1	1	0
1934-35 Boston		4	4	8	22
1935-36 Toronto		0	1	1	0
1936-37 "		4	4	8	26
1937-38 N. Y. Americans-Chicago		5	6	11	18
1938-39 Chicago		2	4	6	4
6 Years		15	20	35	70
SHILL, WILLIAM R. RW					
1942-43 Boston	7	4	1	5	4
1945-46 "	45	15	12	27	12
1946-47 "	27	2	0	2	2
3 Years	79	21	13	34	18
SHORE, EDWARD WILLIAM D-SR					
Born: Fort Qu'Appele, Sask. Nov. 26, 1902					
1926-27 Boston		12	6	18	130
1927-28 "		11	6	17	*166
1928-29 "		12	7	19	96
1929-30 "		12	19	31	105
1930-31 "		15	16	31	105
1931-32 "		9	13	22	80
1932-33 "		8	27	35	102
1933-34 "		2	10	12	57
1934-35 "		7	26	33	32
1935-36 "		3	16	19	61
1936-37 "		3	1	4	12
1937-38 "		3	14	17	42
1938-39 "		4	14	18	47
1939-40 Boston-N. Y. Americans		4	4	8	13
14 Years		105	179	284	1048
*League Leader					
1930-31 1st All-Star Team					
1931-32 " " " "					
1932-33 " " " " & Hart Trophy					
1933-34 2nd " " "					
1934-35 1st " " " & Hart Trophy					
1935-36 " " " " & Hart Trophy					
1937-38 " " " " & Hart Trophy					
1938-39 " " " "					
1945 Hall of Fame					
SHORE, HAMBY D					
1917-18 Ottawa	18	3		3	
SIEBERT (Sebert), ALBERT CHARLES LW&D-SL					
Born: Plattsville, Ont. Jan. 14, 1904					
1925-26 Mont. Maroons		16	8	24	108

(continued)

Sea. Club	Ga.	Go.	A.	P.	PM.
1926-27 " "		5	3	8	116
1927-28 " "		8	9	17	109
1928-29 " "		3	5	8	52
1929-30 " "		14	19	33	94
1930-31 " "		16	12	28	76
1931-32 " "		21	18	39	64
1932-33 N. Y. Rangers		9	10	19	38
1933-34 N. Y. Rangers-Boston		5	7	12	49
1934-35 Boston		6	18	24	80
1934-35 "		6	18	24	80
1935-36 "		12	9	21	66
1936-37 Mont. Canadiens		8	20	28	38
1937-38 " "		8	11	19	56
1938-39 Montreal		9	7	16	36
14 Years		140	156	296	982
1935-36 1st All-Star Team					
1936-37 " " " " & Hart Trophy					
1937-38 " " " "					
1964 Hall of Fame					
SIMON, JOHN C. D					
1942-43 Detroit	34	1	1	2	34
1943-44 "	46	3	7	10	52
1944-45 Detroit-Chicago	50	0	3	3	35
3 Years	130	4	11	15	121
SIMON, THAIN A. C					
1946-47 Detroit	3	0	0	0	0
SIMPSON, CLIFFORD V. C					
1946-47 Detroit	6	0	1	1	0
SIMPSON, HAROLD EDWARD D-SR					
Born: Selkirk, Man. Aug. 13, 1893					
1925-26 N. Y. Americans		2	2	4	22
1926-27 " " "		4	2	6	39
1927-28 " " "		2	0	2	32
1928-29 " " "		3	2	5	29
1929-30 " " "		8	13	21	41
1930-31 " " "		2	0	2	13
6 Years		21	19	40	176
1962 Hall of Fame					
SINCLAIR, REGINALD A. RW-SR					
Born: Lachine, Quebec					
1950-51 New York	70	18	21	39	70
1951-52 " "	69	20	10	30	33
1952-53 Detroit	69	11	12	23	36
3 Years	208	49	43	92	139
SINGBUSH, ALEXANDER D					
Born: Winnipeg, Man.					
1940-41 Montreal		0	5	5	15
SKILTON, RAYMOND					
1917-18 Montreal Wanderers	1	0		0	
SKINNER, ALFRED RW-SR					
1917-18 Toronto	19	13		13	
1918-19 "	17	12	3	15	26
1924-25 Boston-Mont. Maroons	27	1	1	2	31
1925-26 Pittsburgh	7	0	0	0	2
4 Years	70	26	4	30	59
SKOV, GLEN FREDERICK C-SL					
Born: Wheatley, Ont. Jan. 26, 1931					
1949-50 Detroit	2	0	0	0	0
1950-51 "	19	7	6	13	13
1951-52 "	70	12	14	26	48
1952-53 "	70	12	15	27	54
1953-54 "	70	17	10	27	95
1954-55 "	70	14	16	30	53
1955-56 Chicago	70	7	20	27	26
1956-57 "	67	14	28	42	69
1957-58 "	70	17	18	35	35
1958-59 "	70	3	5	8	4
1959-60 "	69	3	4	7	16
1960-61 Montreal	3	0	0	0	0
12 Years	650	106	136	242	413
SLEAVER, JOHN C-SR					
Born: Copper Cliff, Ont. Aug. 18, 1934					
1953-54 Chicago	1	0	0	0	2
1956-57 "	12	1	0	1	4
2 Years	13	1	0	1	6
SLOAN, ALOYSIUS MARTIN C-SR					
Born: Vinton, Que. Nov. 30, 1927					
1947-48 Toronto	1	0	0	0	0

(continued)

Sea.	Club	Ga.	Go.	A.	P.	PM.
1948-49	"	29	3	4	7	0
1950-51	"	70	31	25	56	105
1951-52	"	68	25	23	48	89
1952-53	"	70	15	10	25	76
1953-54	"	67	11	32	43	100
1954-55	"	63	13	15	28	89
1955-56	"	70	37	29	66	100
1956-57	"	52	14	21	35	33
1957-58	"	59	13	25	38	58
1958-59	Chicago	59	27	35	62	79
1959-60	"	70	20	20	40	54
1960-61	"	67	11	23	34	48
13 Years		745	220	262	482	831

1955-56 2nd All-Star Team

SLOBODZIAN, PETER P. D
Born: Dauphin, Man.

Sea.	Club	Ga.	Go.	A.	P.	PM.
1940-41	N. Y. Americans		3	2	5	54

SLOWINSKI, EDWARD S. RW-SR

Sea.	Club	Ga.	Go.	A.	P.	PM.
1947-48	New York	38	6	5	11	2
1948-49	" "	20	1	1	2	2
1949-50	" "	63	14	23	37	12
1950-51	" "	69	14	18	32	15
1951-52	" "	64	21	22	43	18
1952-53	" "	37	2	5	7	14
6 Years		291	58	74	132	63

SMART, ALEXANDER LW-SR
Born: Winnipeg, Man.

Sea.	Club	Ga.	Go.	A.	P.	PM.
1942-43	Montreal	8	5	2	7	0

SMILLIE, DONALD

Sea.	Club	Ga.	Go.	A.	P.	PM.
1933-34	Boston		2	2	4	4

SMITH, ALEXANDER D-SL
Born: Bootle, England

Sea.	Club	Ga.	Go.	A.	P.	PM.
1924-25	Ottawa		0	0	0	2
1925-26	"		0	0	0	36
1926-27	"		4	1	5	58
1927-28	"		9	4	13	90
1928-29	"		1	7	8	96
1929-30	"		2	6	8	91
1930-31	"		5	6	11	73
1931-32	Detroit		6	8	14	47
1932-33	Ottawa-Boston		7	4	11	72
1933-34	Boston		4	6	10	32
1934-35	N. Y. Americans		3	8	11	46
11 Years			41	50	91	643

SMITH, ARTHUR D

Sea.	Club	Ga.	Go.	A.	P.	PM.
1927-28	Toronto		5	3	8	22
1928-29	"		5	0	5	91
1929-30	"		3	3	6	75
1930-31	Ottawa		2	4	6	61
4 Years			15	10	25	249

SMITH, BRIAN STUART LW-SL
Born: Creighton Mine, Ont. Dec. 6, 1937

Sea.	Club	Ga.	Go.	A.	P.	PM.
1957-58	Detroit	4	0	1	1	0
1959-60	"	31	2	5	7	2
1960-61	"	26	0	2	2	10
3 Years		61	2	8	10	12

SMITH, CARL D. RW

Sea.	Club	Ga.	Go.	A.	P.	PM.
1943-44	Detroit	7	1	1	2	2

SMITH, CLINTON J. C&LW-SL
Born: Assiniboia, Sask. Dec. 12, 1913

Sea.	Club	Ga.	Go.	A.	P.	PM.
1936-37	N. Y. Rangers	1	1	0	1	0
1937-38	" " "		14	23	37	0
1938-39	" " "		21	20	41	2
1939-40	" " "		8	16	24	2
1940-41	" " "		14	11	25	0
1941-42	" " "	47	10	24	34	4
1942-43	" " "	47	12	21	33	4
1943-44	Chicago	50	23	*49	72	4
1944-45	"	50	23	31	54	0
1945-46	"	50	26	24	50	2
1946-47	"	52	9	17	26	6
11 Years			161	236	397	24

*League Leader
1938-39 Lady Byng Trophy
1943-44 " " "

SMITH, DALTON J. C

Sea.	Club	Ga.	Go.	A.	P.	PM.
1943-44	Detroit	10	1	2	3	0

SMITH, DESMOND PATRICK D-SL
Born: Ottawa, Ont. Feb. 22, 1914

Sea.	Club	Ga.	Go.	A.	P.	PM.
1937-38	Mont. Maroons		3	1	4	47
1938-39	Montreal Canadiens		3	3	6	8
1939-40	Chicago-Boston		3	6	9	50
1940-41	Boston		6	8	14	61
1941-42	"		7	7	14	70
5 Years			22	25	47	236

SMITH, DONALD

Sea.	Club	Ga.	Go.	A.	P.	PM.
1919-20	Montreal	10	1	0	1	4

SMITH, DONALD A. RW

Sea.	Club	Ga.	Go.	A.	P.	PM.
1949-50	New York	11	1	1	2	0

SMITH, GLEN RW

Sea.	Club	Ga.	Go.	A.	P.	PM.
1950-51	Chicago	2	0	0	0	0

SMITH, GLENN

Sea.	Club	Ga.	Go.	A.	P.	PM.
1921-22	Toronto	9	0	0	0	0

SMITH, KENNETH A. LW

Sea.	Club	Ga.	Go.	A.	P.	PM.
1944-45	Boston	49	20	14	34	2
1945-46	"	23	2	6	8	0
1946-47	"	60	14	7	21	4
1947-48	"	60	11	12	23	14
1948-49	"	59	20	20	40	6
1949-50	"	66	10	31	41	12
1950-51	"	14	1	3	4	11
7 Years		331	78	93	171	49

SMITH, REGINALD J. C-SR
Born: Toronto, Ont. Jan. 7, 1905

Sea.	Club	Ga.	Go.	A.	P.	PM.
1924-25	Ottawa		10	3	13	81
1925-26	"		16	9	25	53
1926-27	"		9	6	15	125
1927-28	Mont. Maroons		14	5	19	72
1928-29	" "		10	9	19	120
1929-30	" "		21	9	30	83
1930-31	" "		12	14	26	68
1931-32	" "		11	33	44	49
1932-33	" "		20	21	41	66
1933-34	" "		18	19	37	58
1934-35	" "		5	22	27	41
1935-36	" "		19	19	38	75
1936-37	Boston		8	10	18	36
1937-38	N. Y. Americans		10	10	20	23
1938-39	" " "		8	11	19	18
1939-40	" " "		7	8	15	41
1940-41	" " "		2	7	9	4
17 Years			200	215	415	1013

1931-32 2nd All-Star Team
1935-36 1st " " "
Hall of Fame

SMITH, RODGER D

Sea.	Club	Ga.	Go.	A.	P.	PM.
1925-26	Pittsburgh		9	1	10	22
1926-27	"		4	0	4	6
1927-28	"		1	0	1	30
1928-29	"		4	2	6	49
1929-30	"		2	1	3	65
1930-31	Philadelphia		0	0	0	0
6 Years			20	4	24	172

SMITH, SIDNEY J. LW-SL
Born: Toronto, Ont.

Sea.	Club	Ga.	Go.	A.	P.	PM.
1946-47	Toronto	14	2	1	3	0
1947-48	"	31	7	10	17	10
1948-49	"	1	0	0	0	0
1949-50	"	68	22	23	45	6
1950-51	"	70	30	21	51	10
1951-52	"	70	27	30	57	6
1952-53	"	70	20	19	39	6
1953-54	"	70	22	16	38	28
1954-55	"	70	33	21	54	14
1955-56	"	55	4	17	21	8
1956-57	"	70	17	24	41	4
1957-58	"	12	2	1	3	2
12 Years		601	186	183	369	94

1950-51 2nd All-Star Team
1951-52 " " " & Lady Byng Trophy
1954-55 1st " " " & Lady Byng Trophy

SMITH, STANFORD G. LW&C
Born: Coal Creek, B. C.

Sea.	Club	Ga.	Go.	A.	P.	PM.
1939-40	N. Y. Rangers		0	0	0	0
1940-41	" " "		2	1	3	0
2 Years			2	1	3	0

Sea. Club	Ga.	Go.	A.	P.	PM.
SMITH, STUART RW					
1940-41 Montreal		2	1	3	0
1941-42 "	1	0	1	1	0
2 Years		2	2	4	0
SMITH, THOMAS C					
1919-20 Quebec	10	0	0	0	9
SMITH, WAYNE CLIFFORD D-SL					
Born: Kamsack, Sask. Feb. 12, 1943					
1966-67 Chicago	2	1	1	2	2
SMRKE, STANLEY LW-SL					
Born: Belgrade, Yugoslavia, Sept. 2, 1928					
1956-57 Montreal	4	0	0	0	0
1957-58 "	5	0	3	3	0
2 Years	9	0	3	3	0
SMYLIE, RODERICK LW					
1920-21 Toronto St. Patricks	23	2	0	2	2
1921-22 " " "	21	0	0	0	2
1922-23 " " "	2	0	0	0	0
1923-24 Ottawa Senators	14	1	1	2	6
1924-25 Toronto St. Patricks	11	0	0	0	2
1925-26 " " "	5	0	0	0	0
6 Years	76	3	1	4	12
SOLINGER, ROBERT EDWARD LW-SL					
Born: Star City, Sask. Dec. 23, 1925					
1951-52 Toronto	24	5	3	8	4
1952-53 "	18	1	1	2	2
1953-54 "	39	3	2	5	2
1954-55 "	17	1	5	6	11
1959-60 Detroit	1	0	0	0	0
5 Years	99	10	11	21	19
SOMERS, ARTHUR E. C-SL					
1929-30 Chicago		11	13	24	74
1930-31 "		3	6	9	33
1931-32 N. Y. Rangers		11	15	26	45
1932-33 " " "		7	15	22	28
1933-34 " " "		1	2	3	5
1934-35 " " "		0	5	5	4
6 Years		33	56	89	189
SONMOR, GLEN R. D					
Born: Hamilton, Ont.					
1953-54 New York	15	2	0	2	17
1954-55 " "	13	0	0	0	4
2 Years	28	2	0	2	21
SORRELL, JOHN ARTHUR LW-SL					
Born: Chesterville, Ont. Jan. 16, 1906					
1930-31 Detroit		9	7	16	10
1931-32 "		8	5	13	22
1932-33 "		14	10	24	11
1933-34 "		21	10	31	8
1934-35 "		20	16	36	12
1935-36 "		13	15	28	8
1936-37 "		8	16	24	4
1937-38 Detroit-N. Y. Americans		11	9	20	9
1938-39 N. Y. Americans		13	9	22	10
1939-40 " " "		8	16	24	4
1940-41 " " "		2	6	8	2
11 Years		127	119	246	100
SOUMI, AL					
Born: U. S. A.					
1936-37 Chicago		0	0	0	0
SPARROW, EMORY RW					
1924-25 Boston	6	0	0	0	4
SPENCER, JAMES IRVIN D-SL					
Born: Sudbury, Ont. Dec. 4, 1937					
1959-60 New York	32	1	2	3	20
1960-61 " "	56	1	8	9	30
1961-62 " "	43	2	10	12	31
1962-63 Boston	69	5	17	22	34
1963-64 Detroit	25	3	0	3	8
1967-68 "	5	0	1	1	4
6 Years	230	12	38	50	127
SPEYER, CHRISTOPHER D					
1923-24 Toronto	3	0	0	0	0
1924-25 "	2	0	0	0	0
2 Years	5	0	0	0	0

Sea. Club	Ga.	Go.	A.	P.	PM.
SPRING, JESSE RW					
1923-24 Hamilton		3	2	5	8
1924-25 "		2	0	2	11
1925-26 Pittsburg		5	0	5	23
1926-27 Toronto St. Patricks		0	0	0	0
1928-29 N. Y. Americans-Pittsburg		0	0	0	2
1929-30 " " "		1	0	1	18
6 Years		11	2	13	62
ST. LAURENT, DOLLARD HERVE D-SL					
Born: Verdun, Que. May 12, 1929					
1950-51 Montreal	3	0	0	0	0
1951-52 "	40	3	10	13	30
1952-53 "	54	2	6	8	34
1953-54 "	53	3	12	15	43
1954-55 "	58	3	14	17	24
1955-56 "	46	4	9	13	58
1956-57 "	64	1	11	12	49
1957-58 "	65	3	20	23	68
1958-59 Chicago	70	4	8	12	28
1959-60 "	68	4	13	17	60
1960-61 "	67	2	17	19	58
1961-62 "	64	0	13	13	44
12 Years	652	29	133	162	496
STACKHOUSE, THEODORE					
1921-22 Toronto	12	0	0	0	2
STALEY, ALLAN					
1948-49 New York	1	0	1	1	0
STANDING, GEORGE MICHAEL RW-SR					
Born: Toronto, Ont. Aug. 3, 1941					
1967-68 Minnesota	2	0	0	0	0
STANKIEWICZ, EDWARD RW-SR					
Born: Kitchener, Ont. Dec. 1, 1929					
1953-54 Detroit	1	0	0	0	2
1955-56 "	5	0	0	0	0
2 Years	6	0	0	0	2
STANLEY, RUSSELL RW-SL					
Born: Paisley, Ont. June 1, 1893					
1927-28 Chicago	2	0	0	0	0
1962 Hall of Fame					
STANOWSKI, WALTER P. D-SL					
Born: Winnipeg, Man. Apr. 28, 1919					
1939-40 Toronto		2	7	9	11
1940-41 "		7	14	21	35
1941-42 "	23	1	7	8	10
1944-45 "	34	2	9	11	16
1945-46 "	45	3	10	13	10
1946-47 "	51	3	16	19	12
1947-48 "	54	2	11	13	12
1948-49 New York	60	1	8	9	16
1949-50 " "	37	1	1	2	10
1950-51 " "	49	1	5	6	28
10 Years		23	88	111	160
1940-41 1st All-Star Team					
STARR, HAROLD D					
1929-30 Ottawa		2	1	3	12
1930-31 "		2	1	3	48
1931-32 Mont. Maroons		1	2	3	47
1932-33 Ottawa-Mont. Canadiens		0	0	0	36
1934-35 N. Y. Rangers		1	1	2	31
1935-36 " " "		0	0	0	12
6 Years		6	5	11	186
STARR, WILFRID P. LW					
1932-33 N. Y. Americans		4	3	7	8
1933-34 Detroit		2	2	4	17
1934-35 "		1	1	2	0
1935-36 "		1	0	1	0
4 Years		8	6	14	25
STASIUK, VICTOR JOHN LW&RW-SL					
Born: Lethbridge, Alb. May 23, 1929					
1949-50 Chicago	17	1	1	2	2
1950-51 Chicago-Detroit	70	8	13	21	18
1951-52 Detroit	58	5	9	14	19
1952-53 "	3	0	0	0	0
1953-54 "	42	5	2	7	4
1954-55 "	59	8	11	19	67
1955-56 Boston	59	19	18	37	118
1956-57 "	64	24	16	40	69

(continued)

Sea. Club	Ga.	Go.	A.	P.	PM.
1957-58 "	70	21	35	56	55
1958-59 "	70	27	33	60	63
1959-60 "	69	29	39	68	121
1960-61 Boston-Detroit	69	15	38	53	51
1961-62 Detroit	59	15	28	43	45
1962-63 "	36	6	11	17	37
14 Years	745	183	254	437	669

STEELE, FRANK F

Sea. Club	Ga.	Go.	A.	P.	PM.
1930-31 Detroit	1	0	0	0	2

STERNER, ULF C-SL
Born: Deje, Sweden Feb. 11, 1941

Sea. Club	Ga.	Go.	A.	P.	PM.
1964-65 New York	4	0	0	0	0

STEVENS, PHILIP D

Sea. Club	Ga.	Go.	A.	P.	PM.
1917-18 Mont. Wanderers	4	1		1	
1921-22 Mont. Canadiens	4	0	0	0	0
1925-26 Boston	17	0	0	0	0
3 Years	25	1	0	1	6

STEWART, JAMES GAYE LW-SL
Born: Fort William, Ont.

Sea. Club	Ga.	Go.	A.	P.	PM.
1942-43 Toronto	48	24	23	47	30
1945-46 "	50	*37	15	52	8
1946-47 "	60	19	14	33	15
1947-48 Toronto-Chicago	61	27	29	56	83
1948-49 Chicago	54	20	18	38	57
1949-50 "	70	24	19	43	43
1950-51 Detroit	67	18	13	31	18
1951-52 New York	69	15	25	40	22
1952-53 New York-Montreal	23	1	3	4	8
9 Years	502	185	159	344	284

*League Leader
1942-43 Calder Trophy
1945-46 1st All-Star Team
1947-48 2nd " " "

STEWART, JOHN SHERRATT D-SL
Born: Pilot Mound, Man. May 6, 1917

Sea. Club	Ga.	Go.	A.	P.	PM.
1938-39 Detroit	33	0	1	1	18
1939-40 "	47	1	0	1	40
1940-41 "	47	2	6	8	56
1941-42 "	44	4	7	11	93
1942-43 "	44	2	9	11	68
1945-46 "	47	4	11	15	*73
1946-47 "	55	5	9	14	83
1947-48 "	60	5	14	19	91
1948-49 "	60	4	11	15	96
1949-50 "	65	3	11	14	86
1950-51 Chicago	26	0	2	2	49
1951-52 "	37	1	3	4	12
12 Years	565	31	84	115	765

*League Leader
1942-43 1st All-Star Team
1945-46 2nd " " "
1946-47 " " " "
1947-48 1st " " "
1948-49 " " " "
1964 Hall of Fame

STEWART, KENNETH C
Born: Port Arthur, Ont.

Sea. Club	Ga.	Go.	A.	P.	PM.
1941-42 Chicago		1	1	2	0

STEWART, NELSON ROBERT C-SL
Born: Montreal, Que. Dec. 29, 1902

Sea. Club	Ga.	Go.	A.	P.	PM.
1925-26 Mont. Maroons		*34	8	*42	119
1926-27 " "		17	4	21	*133
1927-28 " "		27	7	34	104
1928-29 " "		21	8	29	74
1929-30 " "		39	16	55	81
1930-31 " "		25	14	39	75
1931-32 " "		22	11	33	61
1932-33 Boston		18	18	36	62
1933-34 "		22	17	39	68
1934-35 "		21	18	39	45
1935-36 N. Y. Americans		14	15	29	16
1936-37 Boston-N. Y. Americans		*23	12	35	37
1937-38 N. Y. Americans		19	17	36	29
1938-39 " " "		16	19	35	43
1939-40 " " "		6	7	13	6
15 Years		324	191	515	953

*League Leader
1925-26 Hart Trophy
1929-30 " "
1962 Hall of Fame

STODDARD, JOHN E. RW

Sea. Club	Ga.	Go.	A.	P.	PM.
1951-52 New York	20	4	2	6	2
1952-53 " "	60	12	13	25	29
2 Years	80	16	15	31	31

STRAIN, NEIL G. LW-SL

Sea. Club	Ga.	Go.	A.	P.	PM.
1952-53 New York	52	11	13	24	12

STRATE, GORDON LYNN D-SL
Born: Edmonton, Alb. May 28, 1935

Sea. Club	Ga.	Go.	A.	P.	PM.
1956-57 Detroit	5	0	0	0	4
1957-58 "	45	0	0	0	24
1958-59 "	11	0	0	0	6
3 Years	61	0	0	0	34

STRATTON, ARTHUR C-SL
Born: Winnipeg, Man. Oct. 8, 1935

Sea. Club	Ga.	Go.	A.	P.	PM.
1959-60 New York	18	2	5	7	2
1963-64 Detroit	5	0	3	3	2
1965-66 Chicago	2	0	0	0	0
1967-68 Pittsburgh-Phila.	70	16	25	41	20
4 Years	95	18	33	51	24

STUART, WILLIAM D

Sea. Club	Ga.	Go.	A.	P.	PM.
1920-21 Toronto		2	1	3	4
1921-22 "		3	6	9	16
1922-23 "		7	3	10	16
1923-24 "		4	3	7	16
1924-25 Toronto-Boston		5	2	7	32
1925-26 Boston		6	1	7	41
1926-27 "		3	1	4	20
7 Years		30	17	47	145

SULLIVAN, BARRY C. RW

Sea. Club	Ga.	Go.	A.	P.	PM.
1947-48 Detroit	1	0	0	0	0

SULLIVAN, FRANK T. D

Sea. Club	Ga.	Go.	A.	P.	PM.
1949-50 Toronto	1	0	0	0	0
1952-53 "	5	0	0	0	2
1954-55 Chicago	1	0	0	0	0
1955-56 "	1	0	0	0	0
4 Years	8	0	0	0	2

SULLIVAN, GEORGE JAMES C-SL
Born: Peterborough, Ont. Dec. 24, 1929

Sea. Club	Ga.	Go.	A.	P.	PM.
1949-50 Boston	3	0	1	1	0
1951-52 "	67	12	12	24	24
1952-53 "	32	3	8	11	8
1954-55 Chicago	70	19	42	61	51
1955-56 "	63	14	26	40	58
1956-57 New York	42	6	17	23	36
1957-58 " "	70	11	35	46	61
1958-59 " "	70	21	42	63	56
1959-60 " "	70	12	25	37	81
1960-61 " "	70	9	31	40	66
10 Years	557	107	239	346	441

SUMMERHILL, WILLIAM ARTHUR RW-SR
Born: Toronto, Ont. July 9, 1915

Sea. Club	Ga.	Go.	A.	P.	PM.
1938-39 Montreal		6	10	16	28
1939-40 "		3	2	5	24
1941-42 Brooklyn	16	5	5	10	18
3 Years		14	17	31	70

SUTHERLAND, RONALD D
Born: Eston, Sask.

Sea. Club	Ga.	Go.	A.	P.	PM.
1931-32 Boston		0	0	0	0

SWEENEY, WILLIAM C-SL
Born: Guelph, Ont. Jan. 30, 1937

Sea. Club	Ga.	Go.	A.	P.	PM.
1959-60 New York	4	1	0	1	0

TATCHELL, SPENCER H. D

Sea. Club	Ga.	Go.	A.	P.	PM.
1942-43 New York	1	0	0	0	0

TAYLOR, GORDON WILLIAM C-SL
Born: Kincaid, Sask. Oct. 14, 1942

Sea. Club	Ga.	Go.	A.	P.	PM.
1964-65 New York	2	0	0	0	0

Sea. Club	Ga.	Go.	A.	P.	PM.
TAYLOR, HARRY RW					
Born: Mar. 28, 1926					
1946-47 Toronto	9	0	2	2	0
1948-49 "	42	4	7	11	30
1951-52 Chicago	15	1	1	2	0
3 Years	66	5	10	15	30
TAYLOR, RALPH F. RW					
1927-28 Chicago		1	1	2	39
1928-29 "		0	0	0	56
1929-30 Chicago-N. Y. Rangers		3	0	3	74
3 Years		4	1	5	169
TAYLOR, ROBERT					
1929-30 Boston		0	0	0	6
TAYLOR, WILLIAM C-SR					
Born: Winnipeg, Man. May 3, 1919					
1939-40 Toronto		4	6	10	9
1940-41 "		9	26	35	15
1941-42 "	48	12	26	38	20
1942-43 "	50	18	42	60	2
1943-45 in Military Service					
1945-46 Toronto	48	23	18	41	14
1946-47 Detroit	60	17	*46	63	35
1947-48 Boston-New York	41	4	16	20	25
7 Years		87	180	267	120
*League Leader					
TEAL, ALLAN LESLIE C-SL					
Born: Ridgeway, Ont. July 17, 1933					
1954-55 Boston	1	0	0	0	0
TESSIER, ORVAL ROY C-SL					
Born: Cornwall, Ont. June 30, 1933					
1954-55 Montreal	4	0	0	0	0
1955-56 Boston	23	2	3	5	6
1960-61 "	32	3	4	7	0
3 Years	59	5	7	12	6
THIBEAULT, LAURENCE LORRAIN LW					
Born: Charleston, Ont.					
1944-45 Detroit	4	0	2	2	2
1945-46 Montreal	1	0	0	0	0
2 Years	5	0	2	2	2
THOMAS, CYRIL J. LW					
1947-48 Chicago-Toronto	14	2	2	4	12
THOMPSON, CLIFFORD D					
Born: Stoneham, Mass.					
1941-42 Boston	3	0	0	0	2
1948-49 "	10	0	1	1	0
2 Years	13	0	1	1	2
THOMPSON, KENNETH					
1917-18 Montreal Wanderers	1	0		0	
THOMPSON, PAUL I. LW-SL					
Born: Calgary, Alb. Nov. 2, 1907					
1926-27 N. Y. Rangers		7	3	10	12
1927-28 " " "		4	4	8	22
1928-29 " " "		10	7	17	38
1929-30 " " "		7	12	19	36
1930-31 " " "		7	7	14	36
1931-32 Chicago		8	14	22	34
1932-33 "		13	20	33	27
1933-34 "		20	16	36	17
1934-35 "		16	23	39	20
1935-36 "		17	23	40	19
1936-37 "		17	18	35	28
1937-38 "		22	22	44	14
1938-39 "		5	10	15	33
13 Years		153	179	332	336
1935-36 2nd All-Star Team					
1937-38 1st " " "					
THOMS, WILLIAM D. C-SL					
Born: Newmarket, Ont. Mar. 5, 1910					
1932-33 Toronto		3	9	12	15
1933-34 "		8	18	26	24
1934-35 "		9	13	22	15
1935-36 "		*23	15	38	29

(continued)

Sea. Club	Ga.	Go.	A.	P.	PM.
1936-37 "		10	9	19	14
1937-38 "		14	24	38	14
1938-39 Toronto-Chicago		7	15	22	20
1939-40 Chicago		9	13	22	4
1940-41 "		13	19	32	8
1941-42 "		15	30	45	8
1942-43 "	47	15	28	43	11
1943-44 "	7	3	5	8	2
1944-45 Chicago-Boston	38	6	8	14	8
13 Years		135	206	341	172
*League Leader					
1935-36 2nd All-Star Team					
THOMSON, JAMES R. D-SR					
Born: Winnipeg, Man. 1927					
1945-46 Toronto	5	0	1	1	4
1946-47 "	60	2	14	16	97
1947-48 "	59	0	29	29	82
1948-49 "	60	4	16	20	56
1949-50 "	70	0	13	13	76
1950-51 "	69	3	33	36	76
1951-52 "	70	0	25	25	86
1952-53 "	69	0	22	22	73
1953-54 "	61	2	24	26	86
1954-55 "	70	4	12	16	63
1955-56 "	62	0	7	7	96
1956-57 "	62	0	12	12	50
1957-58 Chicago	70	4	7	11	75
13 Years	787	19	215	234	920
1950-51 2nd All-Star Team					
1951-52 " " " "					
THOMSON, RHYS G. D-SL					
Born: Toronto, Ont. August 9, 1918					
1939-40 Montreal		0	0	0	16
1940-41 N. Y. Americans		0	0	0	0
1942-43 Toronto	17	0	2	2	22
3 Years		0	2	2	38
THOMSON, WILLIAM F. RW					
Born: Ayrshire, Scot.					
1943-44 Detroit	5	2	2	4	0
THORSTEINSON, JOSEPH					
1932-33 N. Y. Americans		0	0	0	0
THURIER, ALFRED M. C-SR					
Born: Granby, Que.					
1940-41 N. Y. Americans	3	2	1	3	0
1941-42 Brooklyn	27	7	7	14	4
1944-45 New York	50	16	19	35	14
3 Years	80	25	27	52	18
THURLBY, THOMAS NEWMAN D&LW-SL					
Born: Kingston, Ont. Nov. 9, 1938					
1967-68 Oakland	20	1	1	2	4
TIMGREN, RAYMOND C. LW-SL					
Born: Windsor, Ont.					
1948-49 Toronto	36	3	12	15	9
1949-50 "	68	7	18	25	22
1950-51 "	70	1	9	10	20
1951-52 "	50	2	4	6	11
1952-53 "	12	0	0	0	4
1954-55 Chicago-Toronto	15	1	1	2	4
6 Years	251	14	44	58	70
TOMSON, JOHN F. D-SR					
Born: Uxbridge, Eng. Jan. 31, 1918					
1939-40 N. Y. Americans	8	1	1	2	0
TOPPAZZINI, GERALD "Topper" RW-SR					
Born: Copper Cliff, Ont. July 29, 1931					
1952-53 Boston	69	10	13	23	36
1953-54 Boston-Chicago	51	5	8	13	42
1954-55 Chicago	70	9	18	27	59
1955-56 Detroit-Boston	68	8	14	22	53
1956-57 Boston	55	15	23	38	26
1957-58 "	64	25	24	49	51
1958-59 "	70	21	23	44	61
1959-60 "	69	12	33	45	26
1960-61 "	67	15	35	50	35
1961-62 "	70	19	31	50	26
1962-63 "	65	17	18	35	6
1963-64 "	65	7	4	11	15
12 Years	783	163	244	407	436

TOPPAZZINI, ZELLIO LOUIS PETER
Born: Copper Cliff, Ont. Jan. 5, 1930

Sea. Club	Ga.	Go.	A.	P.	PM.
1948-49 Boston	5	1	1	2	0
1949-50 "	36	5	5	10	18
1950-51 Boston-New York	59	14	14	28	27
1951-52 New York	16	1	1	2	4
1956-57 Chicago	7	0	0	0	0
5 Years	123	21	21	42	49

TOUHEY, WILLIAM LW&C
Born: Ottawa, Ont. Mar. 23, 1906

Sea. Club	Ga.	Go.	A.	P.	PM.
1927-28 Mont. Maroons		2	0	2	2
1928-29 Ottawa		9	3	12	28
1929-30 "		10	3	13	24
1930-31 "		15	15	30	8
1931-32 Boston		5	4	9	12
1932-33 Ottawa		12	7	19	12
1933-34 "		12	8	20	9
7 Years		65	40	105	95

TOUPIN, JACQUES C
Born: Three Rivers, Que.

Sea. Club	Ga.	Go.	A.	P.	PM.
1943-44 Chicago	8	1	2	3	0

TOWNSEND, ARTHUR D-SL

Sea. Club	Ga.	Go.	A.	P.	PM.
1926-27 Chicago	1	0	0	0	0

TRAINOR, THOMAS W. RW-SR
Born: Charlottetown, Prince Edward Island

Sea. Club	Ga.	Go.	A.	P.	PM.
1948-49 New York	17	1	2	3	6

TRAPP, ROBERT D

Sea. Club	Ga.	Go.	A.	P.	PM.
1926-27 Chicago		4	2	6	92
1927-28 "		0	2	2	37
2 Years		4	4	8	129

TRAUB, PERCY D

Sea. Club	Ga.	Go.	A.	P.	PM.
1926-27 Chicago		0	2	2	93
1927-28 Detroit		3	1	4	78
1928-29 "		0	0	0	46
3 Years		3	3	6	217

TREMBLAY, MARCEL BERNARD RW-SR
Born: St. Boniface, Man. July 4, 1915

Sea. Club	Ga.	Go.	A.	P.	PM.
1938-39 Montreal		0	2	2	0

TREMBLAY, NILS F

Sea. Club	Ga.	Go.	A.	P.	PM.
1944-45 Montreal	1	0	1	1	0

TROTTIER, DAVID T. LW-SL
Born: Pembroke, Ont. June 25, 1906

Sea. Club	Ga.	Go.	A.	P.	PM.
1928-29 Mont. Maroons		2	4	6	69
1929-30 " "		17	10	27	73
1930-31 " "		9	8	17	58
1931-32 " "		26	18	44	94
1932-33 " "		16	15	31	38
1933-34 " "		9	17	26	47
1934-35 " "		10	9	19	22
1935-36 " "		10	10	20	25
1936-37 " "		12	11	23	33
1937-38 " "		9	10	19	42
1938-39 Detroit		1	1	2	16
11 Years		121	113	234	517

TRUDEL, LOUIS NAPOLEON LW-SL
Born: Salem, Mass. July 21, 1913

Sea. Club	Ga.	Go.	A.	P.	PM.
1933-34 Chicago		1	3	4	13
1934-35 "		11	11	22	28
1935-36 "		3	4	7	27
1936-37 "		6	12	18	11
1937-38 "		6	16	22	15
1938-39 Montreal		8	13	21	2
1939-40 "		12	7	19	24
1940-41 "		2	3	5	2
8 Years		49	69	118	122

TRUDELL, RENE J. RW-SR
Born: Mariepolis, Man.

Sea. Club	Ga.	Go.	A.	P.	PM.
1945-46 New York	16	3	5	8	4
1946-47 " "	59	8	16	24	38
1947-48 " "	54	13	7	20	30
3 Years	129	24	28	52	72

TUDIN, CONNY C

Sea. Club	Ga.	Go.	A.	P.	PM.
1941-42 Montreal		0	1	1	4

TURLIK, GORDON C

Sea. Club	Ga.	Go.	A.	P.	PM.
1959-60 Boston	2	0	0	0	2

TURNER, ROBERT GEORGE D-SL
Born: Regina, Sask. Jan. 31, 1934

Sea. Club	Ga.	Go.	A.	P.	PM.
1955-56 Montreal	33	1	4	5	35
1956-57 "	58	1	4	5	48
1957-58 "	66	0	3	3	30
1958-59 "	68	4	24	28	66
1959-60 "	54	0	9	9	40
1960-61 "	60	2	2	4	16
1961-62 Chicago	69	8	2	10	52
1962-63 "	70	3	3	6	20
8 Years	478	19	51	70	307

TUSTIN, NORMAN R. LW
Born: Regina, Sask.

Sea. Club	Ga.	Go.	A.	P.	PM.
1941-42 New York	18	2	4	6	0

TUTEN, AUDLEY K. D
Born: Enterprize, Ala.

Sea. Club	Ga.	Go.	A.	P.	PM.
1941-42 Chicago	5	1	1	2	10
1942-43 "	34	3	7	10	38
2 Years	39	4	8	12	48

VAIL, MELVILLE D

Sea. Club	Ga.	Go.	A.	P.	PM.
1928-29 N. Y. Rangers		3	0	3	16
1929-30 " " "		1	1	2	10
2 Years		4	1	5	26

VOKES, –

Sea. Club	Ga.	Go.	A.	P.	PM.
1930-31 Chicago	4	0	0	0	0

VOSS, CARL C-SL
Born: Chelsea, Mass. Jan. 6, 1907

Sea. Club	Ga.	Go.	A.	P.	PM.
1926-27 Toronto St. Patricks		0	0	0	0
1932-33 N. Y. Rangers-Detroit		8	15	23	10
1933-34 Detroit-Ottawa		7	18	25	12
1934-35 St. Louis		13	18	31	14
1935-36 N. Y. Americans		3	9	12	10
1936-37 Mont. Maroons		0	2	2	4
1937-38 Chicago		3	8	11	0
7 Years		34	70	104	50

1932-33 Rookie of the Year

WAITE, FRANK E.

Sea. Club	Ga.	Go.	A.	P.	PM.
1930-31 N. Y. Rangers	18	1	3	4	4

WALKER, JOHN PHILLIP C-SL
Born: Silver Mountain, Ont. Nov. 28, 1888

Sea. Club	Ga.	Go.	A.	P.	PM.
1926-27 Detroit		3	4	7	6
1927-28 "		2	4	6	12
2 Years		5	8	13	18

1960 Hall of Fame

WALTON, ROBERT C. RW

Sea. Club	Ga.	Go.	A.	P.	PM.
1943-44 Montreal	4	0	0	0	0

WARD, DONALD D-SL
Born: Sarnia, Ont. Oct. 19, 1935

Sea. Club	Ga.	Go.	A.	P.	PM.
1957-58 Chicago	3	0	0	0	0
1959-60 Boston	31	0	1	1	16
2 Years	34	0	1	1	16

WARD, JAMES WILLIAM RW-SR
Born: Fort William, Ont. Sept. 1, 1906

Sea. Club	Ga.	Go.	A.	P.	PM.
1927-28 Mont. Maroons		10	2	12	44
1928-29 " "		14	8	22	46
1929-30 " "		10	7	17	54
1930-31 " "		14	8	22	52
1931-32 " "		19	19	38	39
1932-33 " "		16	17	33	52
1933-34 " "		14	9	23	46
1934-35 " "		9	6	15	24
1935-36 " "		12	19	31	30
1936-37 " "		14	14	28	34
1937-38 " "		11	15	26	34
1938-39 Montreal Canadiens		4	3	7	0
12 Years		147	127	274	455

WARES, EDWARD RW-SR
Born: Calgary, Alta. Mar. 19, 1915

Sea. Club	Ga.	Go.	A.	P.	PM.
1936-37 N. Y. Rangers	-	2	0	2	0
1937-38 Detroit	-	9	7	16	2
1938-39 "	-	8	8	16	10
1939-40 "	-	2	6	8	19

(continued)

Sea. Club	Ga.	Go.	A.	P.	PM.
1940-41 "	-	10	16	26	34
1941-42 "	43	9	29	38	31
1942-43 "	47	12	18	30	10
1945-46 Chicago	45	4	11	15	34
1946-47 "	60	4	7	11	21
9 Years	-	60	102	162	161

WARWICK, GRANT D. RW&C-SR
Born: Regina, Sask. Oct. 11, 1921

1941-42 New York	44	16	17	33	36
1942-43 " "	50	17	18	35	31
1943-44 " "	18	8	9	17	14
1944-45 " "	42	20	22	42	25
1945-46 " "	45	19	18	37	19
1946-47 " "	54	20	20	40	24
1947-48 New York-Boston	58	23	17	40	38
1948-49 Boston	58	22	15	37	14
1949-50 Montreal	26	2	6	8	19
9 Years	395	147	142	289	220
1941-42 Calder Trophy					

WARWICK, WILLIAM H. LW

1942-43 New York	1	0	1	1	4
1943-44 " "	13	3	2	5	12
2 Years	14	3	3	6	16

WASNIE, NICHOLAS RW-SR
Born: Winnipeg, Man.

1927-28 Chicago	-	1	0	1	22
1929-30 Mont. Canadiens	-	12	11	23	64
1930-31 " "	-	9	2	11	26
1931-32 " "	-	10	2	12	16
1932-33 N. Y. Americans	-	11	12	23	36
1933-34 Ottawa	-	11	6	17	10
1934-35 St. Louis	-	3	1	4	2
7 Years	-	57	34	91	176

WATSON, HARRY P. LW&C-SL
Born: Saskatoon, Sask.

1941-42 Brooklyn	43	10	8	18	6
1942-43 Detroit	50	13	18	31	10
1945-46 "	44	14	10	24	4
1946-47 Toronto	44	19	15	34	10
1947-48 "	57	21	20	41	16
1948-49 "	60	26	19	45	0
1949-50 "	60	19	16	35	11
1950-51 "	68	18	19	37	18
1951-52 "	70	22	17	39	18
1952-53 "	63	16	8	24	8
1953-54 "	70	21	7	28	30
1954-55 Toronto-Chicago	51	15	17	32	4
1955-56 Chicago	55	11	14	25	6
1956-57 "	70	11	19	30	9
14 Years	805	236	207	443	150

WATSON, PHILLIPE HENRI C-SR
Born: Montreal, Que. Oct. 24, 1914

1935-36 N. Y. Rangers	-	0	2	2	24
1936-37 " " "	-	11	17	28	22
1937-38 " " "	-	7	25	32	52
1938-39 " " "	-	15	22	37	42
1939-40 " " "	-	7	28	35	52
1940-41 " " "	-	11	25	36	49
1941-42 " " "	48	15	*37	52	58
1942-43 " " "	46	14	28	42	44
1943-44 Montreal	44	17	32	49	61
1944-45 New York	45	11	8	19	24
1945-46 " "	49	12	14	26	43
1946-47 " "	48	6	12	18	17
1947-48 " "	54	18	15	33	54
13 Years	-	144	265	409	542
*League Leader					
1941-42 2nd All-Star Team					

WEBSTER, DONALD LW

1943-44 Toronto	27	7	6	13	28

WEBSTER, JOHN R. RW

1949-50 New York	14	0	0	0	4

WEILAND, RALPH C. SL
Born: Egmondville, Ont. Nov. 5, 1905

1928-29 Boston	-	11	7	18	16
1929-30 "	-	*43	30	*73	27
1930-31 "	-	25	13	38	14
1931-32 "	-	14	12	26	20
1932-33 Ottawa	-	16	11	27	4

(continued)

Sea. Club	Ga.	Go.	A.	P.	PM.
1933-34 Ottawa-Detroit	-	13	19	32	10
1934-35 Detroit	-	13	25	38	10
1935-36 Boston	-	14	13	27	15
1936-37 "	-	6	9	15	6
1937-38 "	-	11	12	23	16
1938-39 "	-	7	9	16	9
11 Years	-	173	160	333	147
*League Leader					
1934-35 2nd All-Star Team					
Hall of Fame					

WELLINGTON, DUKE

1919-20 Quebec	1	0	0	0	0

WENTWORTH, MARVIN P. D-SR
Born: Grimsby, Ont. Jan. 24, 1905

1927-28 Chicago		5	5	10	31
1928-29 "		2	1	3	44
1929-30 "		3	4	7	28
1930-31 "		4	4	8	12
1931-32 "		3	10	13	30
1932-33 Mont. Maroons		4	10	14	48
1933-34 " "		2	5	7	31
1934-35 " "		4	9	13	28
1935-36 " "		4	5	9	24
1936-37 " "		3	4	7	29
1937-38 " "		4	5	9	32
1938-39 Montreal Canadiens		0	3	3	12
1939-40 " "		1	3	4	6
13 Years		39	68	107	355
1934-35 2nd All-Star Team					

WHARTON, THOMAS D
Born: Winnipeg, Man. December 13, 1927

1944-45 New York	1	0	0	0	0

WHITE, LEONARD A. F

1945-46 Montreal	4	0	1	1	2

WHITE, SHERMAN C

1946-47 New York	1	0	0	0	0
1949-50 " "	3	0	2	2	0
2 Years	4	0	2	2	0

WHITE, WILFRED RW

1925-26 Pittsburgh		7	1	8	22
1926-27 "		5	4	9	21
1927-28 "		5	1	6	54
1928-29 Pittsburgh-N. Y. Amer.		5	5	10	26
1929-30 Pittsburgh		8	1	9	16
1930-31 Philadelphia		3	0	3	2
6 Years		33	12	45	141

WHITELAW, ROBERT D
Born: Motherwell, Scot.

1940-41 Detroit		0	2	2	2
1941-42 "		0	0	0	0
2 Years		0	2	2	2

WIEBE, ARTHUR WALTER RONALD D-SL
Born: Rosthern, Sask. Sept. 28, 1913

1934-35 Chicago		2	1	3	27
1935-36 "		1	0	1	25
1936-37 "		0	2	2	6
1937-38 "		0	3	3	24
1938-39 "		1	2	3	24
1939-40 "		2	2	4	20
1940-41 "		3	2	5	28
1941-42 "		2	4	6	20
1942-43 "	33	1	7.	8	25
1943-44 "	21	2	4	6	2
10 Years		14	27	41	201

WILCOX, ARCHIBALD D

1929-30 Mont. Maroons		3	5	8	38
1930-31 " "		2	2	4	42
1931-32 " "		3	3	6	37
1932-33 " "		0	3	3	37
1933-34 Mont. Maroons-Boston		0	1	1	4
5 Years		8	14	22	158

WILDER, ARCHIBALD LW
Born: Melville, Sask.

1940-41 Detroit		0	2	2	2

WILKINSON, JOHN D-SL

1943-44 Boston	9	0	0	0	6

Sea. Club | Ga. | Go. | A. | P. | PM.

WILLIAMS, BURR D
Born: Okemah, Okla.

Sea. Club	Ga.	Go.	A.	P.	PM.
1933-34 Detroit		0	1	1	12
1934-35 St. Louis-Boston		0	0	0	12
1936-37 Detroit		0	0	0	4
3 Years		0	1	1	28

WILLSON, DONALD A. C
Born: Chatham, Ont.

1937-38 Mont. Canadiens		2	7	9	0

WILSON, CAROL RW-SR

1919-20 Toronto		21	5	26	*79
1920-21 Toronto-Montreal		8	2	10	46
1921-22 Hamilton		7	9	16	21
1922-23 "		16	3	19	46
1926-27 Chicago		8	4	12	40
5 Years		60	23	83	232

*League Leader

WILSON, GERALD C

1956-57 Montreal	3	0	0	0	2

WILSON, JOHN EDWARD LW-SL
Born: Kincardine, Ont. June 14, 1929

1949-50 Detroit	1	0	0	0	0
1951-52 "	28	4	5	9	18
1952-53 "	70	23	19	42	22
1953-54 "	70	17	17	34	22
1954-55 "	70	12	15	27	14
1955-56 Chicago	70	24	9	33	12
1956-57 "	70	18	30	48	24
1957-58 Detroit	70	12	27	39	14
1958-59 "	70	11	17	28	18
1959-60 Toronto	70	15	16	31	8
1960-61 Toronto-New York	59	14	13	27	24
1961-62 New York	40	11	3	14	14
12 Years	688	161	171	332	190

WILSON, LAWRENCE C-SL
Born: Kincardine, Ont. Oct. 23, 1930

1949-50 Detroit	1	0	0	0	2
1951-52 "	5	0	0	0	4
1952-53 "	15	0	4	4	6
1953-54 Chicago	66	9	33	42	22
1954-55 "	63	12	11	23	39
1955-56 "	2	0	0		2
6 Years	152	21	48	69	75

WILSON, ROBERT WAYNE D-SL
Born: Sudbury, Ont. Feb. 18, 1934

1953-54 Chicago	1	0	0	0	0

WILSON, WALLACE L. C

1947-48 Boston	53	11	8	19	18

WISEMAN, EDWARD RANDALL RW-SR
Born: Newcastle, N. Bruns. Dec. 28, 1912

1932-33 Detroit		8	8	16	16
1933-34 "		5	9	14	13
1934-35 "		11	13	24	14
1935-36 N. Y. Americans		12	16	28	15
1936-37 " " "		14	19	33	12
1937-38 " " "		18	14	32	32
1938-39 " " "		12	21	33	8
1939-40 N. Y. Americans-Boston		7	19	26	8
1940-41 Boston		16	24	40	10
1941-42 "		12	22	34	8
10 Years		115	165	280	136

WITIUK, STEPHEN RW-SR
Born: Winnipeg, Man. Jan. 8, 1929

Sea. Club	Ga.	Go.	A.	P.	PM.
1951-52 Chicago	33	3	8	11	14

WOCHY, (Wojciechowski) STEPHEN RW

1944-45 Detroit	49	19	20	39	17
1946-47 "	5	0	0	0	0
2 Years	54	19	20	39	17

WOIT, BENEDICT FRANCIS D-SR
Born: Fort William, Ont. Jan. 7, 1928

1950-51 Detroit	2	0	0	0	2
1951-52 "	58	3	8	11	20
1952-53 "	70	1	5	6	40
1953-54 "	70	0	2	2	38
1954-55 "	62	2	3	5	22
1955-56 Chicago	63	1	8	9	46
1956-57 "	9	0	0	0	2
7 Years	334	7	26	33	170

WOOD, ROBERT F

1950-51 New York	1	0	0	0	0

WRIGHT, KEITH EDWARD LW-SL
Born: Newmarket, Ont. Apr. 13, 1944

1967-68 Philadelphia	1	0	0	0	0

WYCHERLEY, RALPH LW
Born: Saskatoon, Sask.

1940-41 N. Y. Americans		4	5	9	4
1941-42 Brooklyn	2	0	2	2	2
2 Years		4	7	11	6

WYLIE, WILLIAM V. C

1950-51 New York	1	0	0	0	0

YACKEL, KENNETH JAMES RW-SR
Born: St. Paul, Minn. Mar. 5, 1932

1958-59 Boston	6	0	0	0	2

YOUNG, DOUGLAS C. D-SR
Born: Gleichen, Alb. Oct. 1, 1908

1931-32 Detroit		10	2	12	45
1932-33 "		5	6	11	59
1933-34 "		4	0	4	36
1934-35 "		4	6	10	37
1935-36 "		5	12	17	54
1936-37 "		0	0	0	6
1937-38 "		3	5	8	24
1938-39 "		1	5	6	16
1939-40 Montreal		3	9	12	22
1940-41 "		0	0	0	4
10 Years		35	45	80	303

ZENIUK, EDWARD D

1954-55 Detroit	2	0	0	0	0

ZOBROSKY, MARTIN D

1944-45 Chicago	1	0	0	0	2

ZUNICH, RALPH D

1943-44 Detroit	2	0	0	0	2

Sid Abel

Lawrence Aurie

Doug Bentley

Walter Broda

ACTIVE PLAYERS

The following players played in the National Hockey League after the 1967-68 season (1968-69 through 1971-72). For players whose careers ended prior to 1968-69 - - see page 171

Sea.	Club	Ga.	Go.	A.	P.	PM.
ACOMB, DOUGLAS RAYMOND C-SL						
Born: Toronto, Ont., May 15, 1949						
1969-70 Toronto		2	0	1	1	0
AMADIO, DAVID A. D-SR						
Born: Glace Bay, N. S., Apr. 23, 1939						
1957-58 Detroit		2	0	0	0	2
1967-68 Los Angeles		58	4	6	10	101
1968-69 ” ”		65	1	5	6	60
3 Years		125	5	11	16	163
ANDERSON, RONALD CHESTER GOINGS RW-SR						
Born: Red Deer, Alta., July 29, 1945						
1967-68 Detroit		18	2	0	2	13
1968-69 ” – Los Angeles		63	3	5	8	34
1969-70 St. Louis		59	9	9	18	36
1970-71 Buffalo		74	14	12	26	44
1971-72 ”		37	0	4	4	19
5 Years		251	28	30	58	146
ANDREA, PAUL LAWRENCE RW-SL						
Born: North Sydney, Nova Scotia, July 31, 1941						
1965-66 New York Rangers		4	1	1	2	0
1967-68 Pittsburgh		65	11	21	32	2
1968-69 ”		25	7	6	13	2
1970-71 Oakland-Buffalo		56	12	21	33	6
4 Years		150	31	49	80	10
ANGOTTI, LOUIS FREDERICK RW&C-SR						
Born: Toronto, Ont., Jan. 16, 1938						
1964-65 New York Rangers		70	9	8	17	20
1965-66 ” ” ” –Chicago		51	6	12	18	14
1966-67 Chicago		63	6	12	18	21
1967-68 Philadelphia		70	12	37	49	35
1968-69 Pittsburgh		71	17	20	37	36
1969-70 Chicago		70	12	26	38	25
1970-71 ”		65	9	16	25	19
1971-72 ”		65	5	10	15	23
8 Years		525	76	141	217	193
APPS, SYLVANUS MARSHALL C-SR						
Born: Toronto, Ont., Aug. 1, 1947						
1970-71 New York Rangers – Pittsburgh		62	10	18	28	32
1971-72 Pittsburgh		72	15	44	59	78
2 Years		134	25	62	87	110
ARBOUR, ALGER JOSEPH D-SL						
Born: Sudbury, Ont., Nov. 1, 1932						
1953-54 Detroit		36	0	1	1	18
1956-57 ”		44	1	6	7	38
1957-58 ”		69	1	6	7	104
1958-59 Chicago		70	2	10	12	86
1959-60 ”		57	1	5	6	66
1960-61 ”		53	3	2	5	40
1961-62 Toronto		52	1	5	6	68
1962-63 ”		4	1	0	1	4
1963-64 ”		6	0	1	1	0
1965-66 ”		4	0	1	1	2
1967-68 St. Louis		74	1	10	11	50
1968-69 ” ”		67	1	6	7	50
1969-70 ” ”		68	0	3	3	85
1970-71 ” ”		22	0	2	2	6
14 Years		626	12	58	70	617
ARBOUR, JOHN GILBERT D-SL						
Born: Niagara Falls, Ont., Sept. 28, 1945						
1965-66 Boston		2	0	0	0	0
1967-68 ”		4	0	1	1	11
1968-69 Pittsburgh		17	0	2	2	35
1970-71 Vancouver-St. Louis		66	1	6	7	93
1971-72 St. Louis		17	0	0	0	10
5 Years		106	1	9	10	149
ARMSTRONG, GEORGE EDWARD C&RW-SR						
Born: Skead, Ont., July 6, 1930						
1949-50 Toronto		2	0	0	0	0
1951-52 ”		20	3	3	6	30
1952-53 ”		52	14	11	25	54
1953-54 ”		63	17	15	32	60
1954-55 ”		66	10	18	28	80
1955-56 ”		67	16	32	48	97
1956-57 ”		54	18	26	44	37
1957-58 ”		59	17	25	42	93

(continued)

Sea.	Club	Ga.	Go.	A.	P.	PM.
1958-59 ”		59	20	16	36	37
1959-60 ”		70	23	28	51	60
1960-61 ”		47	14	19	33	21
1961-62 ”		70	21	32	53	27
1962-63 ”		70	19	24	43	27
1963-64 ”		67	20	17	37	14
1964-65 ”		59	15	22	37	14
1965-66 ”		70	16	35	51	12
1966-67 ”		70	9	24	33	26
1967-68 ”		62	13	21	34	4
1968-69 ”		53	11	16	27	10
1969-70 ”		49	13	15	28	12
1970-71 ”		59	7	18	25	6
21 Years		1188	296	417	713	721
ARNASON, CHARLES “CHUCK” RW-SR						
Born: Dauphin, Man., July 15, 1951						
1971-72 Montreal		17	3	0	3	4
ASHBEE, WILLIAM BARRY D-SR						
Born: Weston, Ont., July 28, 1939						
1965-66 Boston		14	0	3	3	14
1970-71 Philadelphia		64	4	23	27	44
1971-72 ”		73	6	14	20	75
3 Years		151	10	40	50	133
ATKINSON, STEVEN JOHN RW-SR						
Born: Toronto, Ont., Oct., 16, 1948						
1968-69 Boston		1	0	0	0	0
1970-71 Buffalo		57	20	18	38	12
1971-72 ”		67	14	10	24	26
3 Years		125	34	28	62	38
AWREY, DONALD WILLIAM D-SL						
Born: Kitchener, Ont., July 18, 1943						
1963-64 Boston		16	1	0	1	4
1964-65 ”		47	2	3	5	41
1965-66 ”		70	4	3	7	74
1966-67 ”		4	1	0	1	6
1967-68 ”		74	3	12	15	150
1968-69 ”		73	0	13	13	149
1969-70 ”		73	3	10	13	120
1970-71 ”		74	4	21	25	141
1971-72 ”		34	1	8	9	52
9 Years:		465	19	70	89	737
BACKSTROM, RALPH GERALD C-SL						
Born: Kirkland Lake, Ont., Sept. 18, 1937						
1956-57 Montreal		3	0	0	0	0
1957-58 ”		2	0	1	1	0
1958-59 ”		64	18	22	40	19
1959-60 ”		64	13	15	28	24
1960-61 ”		69	12	20	32	44
1961-62 ”		66	27	38	65	29
1962-63 ”		70	23	12	35	51
1963-64 ”		70	8	21	29	41
1964-65 ”		70	25	30	55	41
1965-66 ”		67	22	20	42	10
1966-67 ”		69	14	27	41	39
1967-68 ”		70	20	25	45	14
1968-69 ”		72	13	28	41	16
1969-70 ”		72	19	24	43	20
1970-71 ” – Los Angeles		49	15	17	32	8
1971-72 Los Angeles		76	23	29	52	22
16 Years		953	252	329	581	378
1958-59 Frank Calder Memorial Trophy						
BAILEY, GARNET EDWARD LW-SL						
Born: Lloydminster, Sask., June 13, 1948						
1968-69 Boston		8	3	3	6	10
1969-70 ”		58	11	11	22	82
1970-71 ”		36	0	6	6	44
1971-72 ”		73	9	13	22	64
4 Years		175	23	33	56	200
BAIRD, KENNETH STEWART “KEN” D-SL						
Born: Flin Flon, Man., Feb. 1, 1951						
1971-72 Oakland		10	0	2	2	15
BALL, TERRY JAMES D-SR						
Born: Selkirk, Man., Nov. 29, 1944						
1967-68 Philadelphia		1	0	0	0	0
1969-70 ”		61	7	18	25	20

(continued)

Sea.	Club	Ga.	Go.	A.	P.	PM.
1970-71	Buffalo	2	0	0	0	0
1971-72	”	10	0	1	1	6
4 Years		74	7	19	26	26

BALON, DAVID ALEXANDER LW-SL
Born: Wakaw, Sask., Aug. 2, 1938

1959-60	New York Rangers	3	0	0	0	0
1960-61	” ” ”	13	1	2	3	8
1961-62	” ” ”	30	4	11	15	11
1962-63	” ” ”	70	11	13	24	72
1963-64	Montreal	70	24	18	42	80
1964-65	”	63	18	23	41	61
1965-66	”	45	3	7	10	24
1966-67	”	48	11	8	19	31
1967-68	Minnesota	73	15	32	47	84
1968-69	New York Rangers	75	10	21	31	57
1969-70	” ” ”	76	33	37	70	100
1970-71	” ” ”	78	36	24	60	34
1971-72	” ” ” – Vancouver	75	23	24	47	23
13 Years		719	189	220	409	585

BARLOW, ROBERT GEORGE LW-SL
Born: Hamilton, Ont., June 17, 1935

1969-70	Minnesota	70	16	17	33	10
1970-71	”	7	0	0	0	0
2 Years		77	16	17	33	10

BARRETT, FREDERICK WILLIAM D-SL
Born: Ottawa, Ont., Jan. 26, 1950

1970-71	Minnesota	57	0	13	13	75

BARRIE, DOUGLAS ROBERT D-SR
Born: Edmonton, Alta., Oct. 2, 1946

1968-69	Pittsburgh	8	1	1	2	8
1970-71	Buffalo	75	4	23	27	168
1971-72	” – Los Angeles	75	5	18	23	92
3 Years		158	10	42	52	268

BATHGATE, ANDREW JAMES RW-SR
Born: Winnipeg, Man., Aug. 28, 1932

1952-53	New York Rangers	18	0	1	1	6
1953-54	” ” ”	20	2	2	4	18
1954-55	” ” ”	70	20	20	40	37
1955-56	” ” ”	70	19	47	66	59
1956-57	” ” ”	70	27	50	77	60
1957-58	” ” ”	65	30	48	78	42
1958-59	” ” ”	70	40	48	88	48
1959-60	” ” ”	70	26	48	74	28
1960-61	” ” ”	70	29	48	77	22
1961-62	” ” ”	70	28	*56	*84	44
1962-63	” ” ”	70	35	46	81	54
1963-64	” ” ” – Toronto	71	19	*58	77	34
1964-65	Toronto	55	16	29	45	34
1965-66	Detroit	70	15	32	47	25
1966-67	”	60	8	23	31	24
1967-68	Pittsburgh	74	20	39	59	55
1970-71	”	76	15	29	44	34
17 Years		1069	349	624	973	624

*league leader
1957-58 2nd All-Star Team at Right Wing
1958-59 1st All-Star Team at Right Wing and Dr. David A. Hart Trophy
1961-62 1st All-Star Team at Right Wing
1962-63 2nd All-Star Team at Right Wing

BAUN, ROBERT NEIL D-SR
Born: Lanigan, Sask., Sept. 9, 1936

1956-57	Toronto	20	0	5	5	37
1957-58	”	67	1	9	10	91
1958-59	”	51	1	8	9	87
1959-60	”	61	8	9	17	59
1960-61	”	70	1	14	15	70
1961-62	”	65	4	11	15	94
1962-63	”	48	4	8	12	65
1963-64	”	52	4	14	18	113
1964-65	”	70	0	18	18	160
1965-66	”	44	0	6	6	68
1966-67	”	54	2	8	10	83
1967-68	Oakland	67	3	10	13	81
1968-69	Detroit	76	4	16	20	121
1969-70	”	71	1	18	19	110
1970-71	” – Toronto	69	1	20	21	147
1971-72	Toronto	74	2	12	14	101
16 Years		959	36	186	222	1487

BEAUDIN, NORMAN JOSEPH ANDREW RW-SR
Born: Montmartre, Sask., Nov. 28, 1941

1967-68	St. Louis	13	1	1	2	4
1970-71	Minnesota	12	0	1	1	0
2 Years		25	1	2	3	4

Sea.	Club	Ga.	Go.	A.	P.	PM.

BELIVEAU, JEAN ARTHUR C-SL
Born: Trois Rivieres, Que., Aug. 31, 1931

1950-51	Montreal	2	1	1	2	0
1952-53	”	3	5	0	5	0
1953-54	”	44	13	21	34	22
1954-55	”	70	37	36	73	58
1955-56	”	70	*47	41	*88	143
1956-57	”	69	33	51	84	105
1957-58	”	55	27	32	59	93
1958-59	”	64	*45	46	91	67
1959-60	”	60	34	40	74	57
1960-61	”	69	32	*58	90	57
1961-62	”	43	18	23	41	36
1962-63	”	69	18	49	67	68
1963-64	”	68	28	50	78	42
1964-65	”	58	20	23	43	76
1965-66	”	67	29	*48	77	50
1966-67	”	53	12	26	38	22
1967-68	”	59	31	37	68	28
1968-69	”	69	33	49	82	55
1969-70	”	63	19	30	49	10
1970-71	”	70	25	51	76	40
20 Years		1125	507	712	1219	1029

*league leader
1954-55 1st All-Star Team at Centre
1955-56 ” ” ” ” ”, David A. Hart and Arthur Ross Trophies
1956-57 ” ” ” ” ”
1957-58 2nd ” ” ” ”
1958-59 1st ” ” ” ”
1959-60 ” ” ” ” ”
1960-61 ” ” ” ” ”
1963-64 2nd ” ” ” ” and Dr. David A. Hart Memorial Trophy
1965-66 ” ” ” ” ”
1968-69 ” ” ” ” ”

HALL OF FAME

BENNETT, CURT ALEXANDER C-SL
Born: Regina, Sask., March 27, 1948

1970-71	St. Louis	4	1	0	2	0
1971-72	” ”	31	3	5	8	30
2 Years		35	5	5	10	30

BERENSON, GORDON ARTHUR C-SL
Born: Regina, Sask., Dec. 8, 1939

1961-62	Montreal	4	1	2	3	4
1962-63	”	37	2	6	8	15
1963-64	”	69	7	9	16	12
1964-65	”	3	1	2	3	0
1965-66	”	23	3	4	7	12
1966-67	New York Rangers	30	0	5	5	2
1967-68	” ” ” – St. Louis	74	24	30	54	24
1968-69	St. Louis	76	35	47	82	43
1969-70	” ”	67	33	39	72	38
1970-71	” ” – Detroit	69	21	38	59	16
1971-72	Detroit	78	28	41	69	16
11 Years		530	155	223	378	182

BERGMAN, GARY GUNNAR D-SL
Born: Kenora, Ont., Oct. 7, 1938

1964-65	Detroit	58	4	7	11	85
1965-66	”	61	3	16	19	96
1966-67	”	70	5	30	35	129
1967-68	”	74	13	28	41	109
1968-69	”	76	7	30	37	80
1969-70	”	69	6	17	23	122
1970-71	”	68	8	25	33	149
1971-72	”	75	6	31	37	138
8 Years		551	52	184	236	908

BERNIER, SERGE JOSEPH C-SR
Born: Padoue, Que., April 29, 1947

1968-69	Philadelphia	1	0	0	0	2
1969-70	”	1	0	1	1	0
1970-71	”	77	23	28	51	77
1971-72	” – Los Angeles	70	23	22	45	63
4 Years		149	46	51	97	142

BERRY, ROBERT VICTOR LW-SL
Born: Montreal, Que., Nov. 29, 1943

1968-69	Montreal	2	0	0	0	0
1970-71	Los Angeles	77	25	38	63	52
1971-72	” ”	78	17	22	39	44
3 Years		157	42	60	102	96

Sea. Club	Ga.	Go.	A.	P.	PM.
BEVERLY, NICHOLAS GERALD D-SR					
Born: Toronto, Ont., April 21, 1947					
1966-67 Boston	2	0	0	0	0
1969-70 "	2	0	0	0	2
1971-72 "	1	0	0	0	0
3 Years	5	0	0	0	2
BLACKBURN, JOHN DONALD LW-SL					
Born: Kirkland Lake, Ont., May 14, 1938					
1962-63 Boston	6	0	5	5	4
1967-68 Philadelphia	67	9	20	29	23
1968-69 "	48	7	9	16	36
1969-70 New York Rangers	3	0	0	0	0
1970-71 " " "	1	0	0	0	0
5 Years	125	16	34	50	63
BLACKBURN, ROBERT JOHN D-SL					
Born: Rouyn, Que., Feb. 1, 1938					
1968-69 New York Rangers	11	0	0	0	0
1969-70 Pittsburgh	60	4	7	11	51
1970-71 "	64	4	5	9	54
3 Years	135	8	12	20	105
BLOCK, KENNETH RITCHARD D-SL					
Born: Grunthal, Man., March 18, 1944					
1970-71 Vancouver	1	0	0	0	0
BODDY, GREG ALLEN D-SL					
Born: Ponoka, Alta., March 19, 1949					
1971-72 Vancouver	40	2	5	7	45
BOIVIN, LEO JOSEPH D-SL					
Born: Prescott, Ont., Aug. 2, 1932					
1951-52 Toronto	2	0	1	1	0
1952-53 "	70	2	13	15	97
1953-54 "	58	1	6	7	81
1954-55 " – Boston	66	6	11	17	113
1955-56 Boston	68	4	16	20	80
1956-57 "	55	2	8	10	55
1957-58 "	33	0	4	4	54
1958-59 "	70	5	16	21	94
1959-60 "	70	4	21	25	66
1960-61 "	57	6	17	23	50
1961-62 "	65	5	18	23	70
1962-63 "	62	2	24	26	48
1963-64 "	65	10	14	24	42
1964-65 "	67	3	10	13	68
1965-66 " – Detroit	62	0	10	10	50
1966-67 Detroit	69	4	17	21	78
1967-68 Pittsburgh	73	9	13	22	74
1968-69 " – Minnesota	69	6	19	25	42
1969-70 Minnesota	69	3	12	15	30
19 Years	1150	72	250	322	1192
BOLDIREV, IVAN C-SL					
Born: Zranjanin, Yugoslavia, Aug. 15, 1949					
1970-71 Boston	2	0	0	0	0
1971-72 " – Oakland	68	16	25	41	60
2 Years	70	16	25	41	60
BORDELEAU, CHRISTIAN GERARD C					
Born: Noranda, Que., Sept. 23, 1947					
1968-69 Montreal	13	1	3	4	4
1969-70 "	48	2	13	15	18
1970-71 St. Louis	78	21	32	53	48
1971-72 " " – Chicago	66	14	17	31	12
4 Years	205	38	65	103	82
BORDELEAU, JEAN-PIERRE RW-SR					
Born: Noranda, Que., June 13, 1949					
1971-72 Chicago	3	0	2	2	2
BOUCHA, HENRY CHARLES C-SR					
Born: Warroad, Minn., June 1, 1951					
1971-72 Detroit	16	1	0	1	2
BOUCHARD, PIERRE D-SL					
Born: Montreal, Que., Feb. 20, 1948					
1970-71 Montreal	51	0	3	3	50
1971-72 "	60	3	5	8	39
2 Years	111	3	8	11	89
BOUDRIAS, ANDRE G. C&LW-SL					
Born: Montreal, Que., Sept. 19, 1943					
1963-64 Montreal	4	1	4	5	2
1964-65 "	1	0	0	0	2
1966-67 "	2	0	1	1	0
1967-68 Minnesota	74	18	35	53	42
1968-69 " – Chicago	73	8	19	27	10

(continued)

Sea. Club	Ga.	Go.	A.	P.	PM.
1969-70 St. Louis	50	3	14	17	20
1970-71 Vancouver	77	25	41	66	16
1971-72 "	78	27	34	61	26
8 Years	359	82	148	230	118
BOUGHNER, BARRY MICHAEL LW-SL					
Born: Delhi, Ont., Jan. 29, 1948					
1969-70 Oakland	4	0	0	0	2
1970-71 "	16	0	0	0	9
2 Years	20	0	0	0	11
BOYER, WALTER C-SL					
Born: Cowan, Man., Sept. 27, 1937					
1965-66 Toronto	46	4	17	21	23
1966-67 Chicago	42	5	6	11	15
1967-68 Oakland	74	13	20	33	44
1968-69 Pittsburgh	62	10	19	29	17
1969-70 "	72	11	12	23	34
1970-71 "	68	11	30	41	30
1971-72 "	1	0	1	1	0
7 Years	365	54	105	159	163
BRENNEMAN, JOHN GARY LW-SL					
Born: Fort Erie, Ont., Jan. 5, 1943					
1964-65 Chicago – New York	39	4	3	7	8
1965-66 New York	11	0	0	0	14
1966-67 Toronto	41	6	4	10	4
1967-68 Detroit – Oakland	40	10	10	20	14
1968-69 Oakland	21	1	2	3	6
5 Years	152	21	19	40	46
BREWER, CARL THOMAS D-SL					
Born: Toronto, Ont., Oct. 21, 1938					
1957-58 Toronto	2	0	0	0	0
1958-59 "	69	3	21	24	125
1959-60 "	67	4	19	23	*150
1960-61 "	51	1	14	15	92
1961-62 "	67	1	22	23	89
1962-63 "	70	2	23	25	168
1963-64 "	57	4	9	13	114
1964-65 "	70	4	23	27	*177
1969-70 Detroit	70	2	37	39	51
1970-71 St. Louis	19	2	9	11	29
1971-72 " "	42	2	16	18	40
11 Years	584	25	193	218	1035

*league leader
1961-62 2nd All-Star Team on Defence
1962-63 1st " " " " "
1964-65 2nd " " " " "
1969-70 " " " " " "

Sea. Club	Ga.	Go.	A.	P.	PM.
BRIERE, MICHEL EDOUARD C-SL					
Born: Malartic, Que., Oct. 21, 1949					
1969-70 Pittsburgh	76	12	32	44	20
BRINDLEY, DOUGLAS ALLEN C-SL					
Born: Walkerton, Ont., June 8, 1949					
1970-71 Toronto	3	0	0	0	0
BROOKS, GORDON JOHN RW-SR					
Born: Cobourg, Ont., Sept. 11, 1950					
1971-72 St. Louis	2	0	0	0	0
BROSSART, WILLIAM D-SL					
Born: Allan, Sask., May 29, 1949					
1970-71 Philadelphia	11	0	0	0	0
1971-72 "	42	0	4	4	12
2 Years	43	0	4	4	12
BROWN, LARRY WAYNE D-SL					
Born: Brandon, Man., April 14, 1947					
1969-70 New York Rangers	15	0	3	3	8
1970-71 " " " – Detroit	64	2	5	7	18
1971-72 Philadelphia	12	0	0	0	2
3 Years	91	2	8	10	28
BROWN, STEWART ARNOLD D-SL					
Born: Apsley, Ont., Jan. 28, 1942					
1961-62 Toronto	2	0	0	0	0
1963-64 "	4	0	0	0	6
1964-65 New York Rangers	58	1	11	12	145
1965-66 " " "	64	1	7	8	106
1966-67 " " "	69	2	10	12	61
1967-68 " " "	74	1	25	26	83
1968-69 " " "	74	10	12	22	48
1969-70 " " "	73	15	21	36	78
1970-71 " " " – Detroit	75	5	18	23	54
1971-72 Detroit	77	2	23	25	84
10 Years	570	37	127	164	665

Sea.	Club	Ga.	Go.	A.	P.	PM
BUCHANAN, RONALD LEONARD C-SL						
Born: Montreal, Que., Nov. 15, 1944						
1966-67	Boston	3	0	0	0	0
1969-70	St. Louis	2	0	0	0	0
2 Years		5	0	0	0	0
BUCYK, JOHN PAUL LW-SL						
Born: Edmonton, Alta., May 12, 1935						
1955-56	Detroit	38	1	8	9	20
1956-57	"	66	10	11	21	41
1957-58	Boston	68	21	31	52	57
1958-59	"	69	24	36	60	36
1959-60	"	56	16	36	52	26
1960-61	"	70	19	20	39	48
1961-62	"	67	20	40	60	32
1962-63	"	69	27	39	66	36
1963-64	"	62	18	36	54	36
1964-65	"	68	26	29	55	24
1965-66	"	63	27	30	57	12
1966-67	"	59	18	30	48	12
1967-68	"	72	30	39	69	8
1968-69	"	70	24	42	66	18
1969-70	"	76	31	38	69	13
1970-71	"	78	51	65	116	8
1971-72	"	78	32	51	83	4
17 Years		1129	395	581	976	431

1967-68 2nd All-Star Team at Left Wing
1970-71 lst   "   "   "   "   " and Lady Byng Memorial Trophy

Sea.	Club	Ga.	Go.	A.	P.	PM
BURNS, CHARLES FREDERICK C-SL						
Born: Detroit, Mich., Feb. 14, 1936						
1958-59	Detroit	70	9	11	20	32
1959-60	Boston	62	10	17	27	46
1960-61	"	62	15	26	41	16
1961-62	"	70	11	17	28	43
1962-63	"	68	12	10	22	13
1967-68	Oakland	73	9	26	35	20
1968-69	Pittsburgh	76	13	38	51	22
1969-70	Minnesota	50	3	13	16	10
1970-71	"	76	9	19	28	13
1971-72	"	77	11	14	25	24
10 Years		684	102	191	293	239

Sea.	Club	Ga.	Go.	A.	P.	PM
BURNS, ROBERT ARTHUR LW-SL						
Born: Montreal, Que., Aug. 27, 1946						
1970-71	Pittsburgh	10	0	3	3	4
1971-72	"	5	0	0	0	8
2 Years		15	0	3	3	12

Sea.	Club	Ga.	Go.	A.	P.	PM
BURROWS, DAVID JAMES D-SL						
Born: Toronto, Ont., Jan. 11, 1949						
1971-72	Pittsburgh	77	2	10	12	48

Sea.	Club	Ga.	Go.	A.	P.	PM
BYERS, MICHAEL ARTHUR RW-SR						
Born: Toronto, Ont. Sept. 11, 1946						
1967-68	Toronto	10	2	2	4	0
1968-69	" — Philadelphia	10	0	2	2	2
1970-71	Los Angeles	72	27	18	45	14
1971-72	" — Buffalo	74	13	12	25	23
4 Years		166	42	34	76	39

Sea.	Club	Ga.	Go.	A.	P.	PM
CAFFERY, TERRANCE MICHAEL C-SR						
Born: Toronto, Ont., April 1, 1949						
1969-70	Chicago	6	0	0	0	0
1970-71	Minnesota	8	0	0	0	0
2 Years		14	0	0	0	0

Sea.	Club	Ga.	Go.	A.	P.	PM
CAHAN, LAWRENCE LOUIS D-SR						
Born: Fort William, Ont. Dec. 25, 1933						
1954-55	Toronto	59	0	6	6	64
1955-56	"	21	0	2	2	46
1956-57	New York Rangers	61	5	4	9	65
1957-58	" " "	34	1	1	2	20
1958-59	" " "	16	1	0	1	8
1961-62	" " "	57	2	7	9	85
1962-63	" " "	56	6	14	20	47
1963-64	" " "	53	4	8	12	80
1964-65	" " "	26	0	5	5	32
1967-68	Oakland	74	9	15	24	80
1968-69	Los Angeles	72	3	11	14	76
1969-70	"	70	4	8	12	52
1970-71	" "	67	3	11	14	45
13 Years		666	38	92	130	700

Sea.	Club	Ga.	Go.	A.	P.	PM
CAMERON, CRAIG LAUDER RW-SR						
Born: Edmonton, Alta. July 19, 1945						
1966-67	Detroit	1	0	0	0	0
1967-68	St. Louis	32	7	2	9	8
1968-69	" "	72	11	5	16	40
1970-71	" "	78	14	6	20	32
1971-72	Minnesota	64	2	1	3	11
5 Years		247	34	14	48	91

Sea.	Club	Ga.	Go.	A.	P.	PM
CAMPBELL, BRYAN ALBERT C-SL						
Born: Sudbury, Ont., March 27, 1944						
1967-68	Los Angeles	44	6	15	21	16
1968-69	" "	18	2	1	3	4
1969-70	" " — Chicago	45	5	5	10	6
1970-71	Chicago	78	17	37	54	26
1971-72	"	75	5	13	18	22
5 Years		260	35	71	106	74

Sea.	Club	Ga.	Go.	A.	P.	PM
CARDWELL, STEPHEN MICHAEL LW-SL						
Born: Toronto, Ont., Aug. 13, 1950						
1970-71	Pittsburgh	5	0	1	1	15
1971-72	"	28	7	8	15	18
2 Years		33	7	9	16	33

Sea.	Club	Ga.	Go.	A.	P.	PM
CARLETON, KENNETH WAYNE LW-SL						
Born: Sudbury, Ont., Aug. 4, 1946						
1965-66	Toronto	2	0	1	1	0
1966-67	"	5	1	0	1	14
1967-68	"	65	8	11	19	34
1968-69	"	12	1	3	4	6
1969-70	" — Boston	49	6	20	26	29
1970-71	Boston	69	22	24	46	44
1971-72	Oakland	76	17	14	31	45
7 Years		278	55	73	128	172

Sea.	Club	Ga.	Go.	A.	P.	PM
CARLIN, BRIAN JOHN LW-SL						
Born: Gleichen, Alta., June 13, 1950						
1971-72	Los Angeles	5	1	0	1	0

Sea.	Club	Ga.	Go.	A.	P.	PM
CARON, ALAIN LUC RW-SR						
Born: Dolbeau, Que., Apr. 27, 1938						
1967-68	Oakland	58	9	13	22	18
1968-69	Montreal	2	0	0	0	0
2 Years		60	9	13	22	18

Sea.	Club	Ga.	Go.	A.	P.	PM
CARR, EUGENE WILLIAM C&LW-SL						
Born: Nanaimo, British Columbia, Sept. 17, 1951						
1971-72	St. Louis — New York Rangers	74	11	10	21	34

Sea.	Club	Ga.	Go.	A.	P.	PM
CASHMAN, WAYNE JOHN RW&LW-SR						
Born:						
1964-65	Boston	1	0	0	0	0
1967-68	"	12	0	4	4	2
1968-69	"	51	8	23	31	49
1969-70	"	70	9	26	35	79
1970-71	"	77	21	58	79	100
1971-72	"	74	23	29	52	103
6 Years		285	61	140	201	333

Sea.	Club	Ga.	Go.	A.	P.	PM
CHARRON, GUY JOSEPH JEAN C-SL						
Born: Verdun, Que., Jan. 24, 1949						
1969-70	Montreal	5	0	0	0	0
1970-71	" — Detroit	39	10	6	16	6
1971-72	Detroit	64	9	16	25	14
3 Years		108	19	22	41	20

Sea.	Club	Ga.	Go.	A.	P.	PM
CHERNOFF, MICHAEL TERANCE LW-SL						
Born: Yorkton, Sask., May 13, 1946						
1968-69	Minnesota	1	0	0	0	0

Sea.	Club	Ga.	Go.	A.	P.	PM
CHERRY, RICHARD JOHN D-SL						
Born: Kingston, Ont, March 28, 1937						
1956-57	Boston	6	0	0	0	4
1968-69	Philadelphia	71	9	6	15	18
1969-70	"	68	3	4	7	23
3 Years		145	12	10	22	45

Sea.	Club	Ga.	Go.	A.	P.	PM
CLANCY, TERRANCE JOHN RW-SL						
Born: Ottawa, Ont., April 2, 1943						
1967-68	Oakland	7	0	0	0	2
1968-69	Toronto	2	0	0	0	0
1969-70	"	52	6	5	11	31
3 Years		61	6	5	11	33

Sea.	Club	Ga.	Go.	A.	P.	PM
CLARKE, ROBERT EARLE C-SL						
Born: Flin Flon, Man., Aug. 13, 1949						
1969-70	Philadelphia	76	15	31	46	68
1970-71	"	77	27	36	63	78
1971-72	"	78	35	46	81	87
3 Years		231	77	113	190	233

1971-72 Bill Masterton Memorial Trophy

Sea. Club	Ga.	Go.	A.	P.	PM.
CLEMENT, BILL C-SL					
Born: Buckingham, Que., Dec. 20, 1950					
1971-72 Philadelphia	49	9	14	23	39
COLLINS, WILLIAM EARL RW-SR					
Born: Ottawa, Ont., July 13, 1943					
1967-68 Minnesota	71	9	11	20	41
1968-69 "	75	9	10	19	24
1969-70 "	74	29	9	38	48
1970-71 Montreal-Detroit	76	11	18	29	49
1971-72 Detroit	71	15	25	40	38
5 Years	367	73	73	146	200
COMEAU, REYNALD C-SL					
Born: Montreal, Que. Oct. 25, 1948					
1971-72 Montreal	4	0	0	0	0
CONACHER, BRIAN KENNEDY LW-SL					
Born: Toronto, Ont., Aug. 31, 1941					
1961-62 Toronto	1	0	0	0	0
1965-66 "	2	0	0	0	2
1966-67 "	66	14	13	27	47
1967-68 "	64	11	14	25	31
1971-72 Detroit	22	3	1	4	4
5 Years	155	28	28	56	84
CONNELLY, WAYNE FRANCIS RW-SR					
Born: Rouyn, Que., Dec. 16, 1939					
1960-61 Montreal	3	0	0	0	0
1961-62 Boston	61	8	12	20	34
1962-63 "	18	2	6	8	2
1963-64 "	26	2	3	5	12
1966-67 "	64	13	17	30	12
1967-68 Minnesota	74	35	21	56	40
1968-69 " – Detroit	74	18	25	43	11
1969-70 Detroit	76	23	36	59	10
1970-71 " – St. Louis	79	13	29	42	21
1971-72 St. Louis – Vancouver	68	19	25	44	14
10 Years	543	133	174	307	156
COOK, ROBERT ARTHUR RW-SR					
Born: Sudbury, Ont., Jan. 6, 1946					
1970-71 Vancouver	2	0	0	0	0
CORRIGAN, MICHAEL DOUGLAS LW-SL					
Born: Ottawa, Ont., Jan. 11, 1946					
1967-68 Los Angeles	5	0	0	0	2
1969-70 "	36	6	4	10	30
1970-71 Vancouver	76	21	28	49	103
1971-72 " – Los Angeles	75	15	26	41	120
4 Years	192	42	58	100	255
COURNOYER, YVAN SERGE RW-SL					
Born: Drummondville, Que. Nov. 22, 1943					
1963-64 Montreal	5	4	0	4	0
1964-65 "	55	7	10	17	10
1965-66 "	65	18	11	29	8
1966-67 "	69	25	15	40	14
1967-68 "	64	28	32	60	23
1968-69 "	76	43	44	87	31
1969-70 "	72	27	36	63	23
1970-71 "	65	37	36	73	21
1971-72 "	73	47	36	83	15
9 Years	544	236	220	456	145

1968-69 2nd All-Star Team at Right Wing
1970-71 " " " " " " "
1971-72 " " " " " " "

Sea. Club	Ga.	Go.	A.	P.	PM.
CRASHLEY, WILLIAM BARTON D-SR					
Born: Toronto, Ont., June 15, 1946					
1965-66 Detroit	1	0	0	0	0
1966-67 "	2	0	0	0	2
1967-68 "	57	2	14	16	18
1968-69 "	1	0	0	0	0
4 Years	61	2	14	16	20
CRISP, TERRANCE ARTHUR C-SL					
Born: Parry Sound, Ont., May 28, 1943					
1965-66 Boston	3	0	0	0	0
1967-68 St. Louis	73	9	20	29	10
1968-69 " "	57	6	9	15	14
1969-70 " "	26	5	6	11	2
1970-71 " "	54	5	11	16	13
1971-72 " "	75	13	18	31	12
6 Years	288	38	64	102	51
CROTEAU, GARY PAUL LW-SL					
Born: Sudbury, Ont. June 20, 1946					
1968-69 Los Angeles	11	5	1	6	6

(continued)

Sea. Club	Ga.	Go.	A.	P.	PM.
1969-70 " " – Detroit	13	0	2	2	2
1970-71 Oakland	74	15	28	43	82
1971-72 "	73	12	12	24	11
4 Years	171	32	43	75	31
CULLEN, RAYMOND MURRAY C-SR					
Born: Ottawa, Ont. Sept. 20, 1941					
1965-66 New York Rangers	8	1	3	4	0
1966-67 Detroit	27	8	8	16	8
1967-68 Minnesota	67	28	25	53	18
1968-69 "	67	26	38	64	44
1969-70 "	74	17	28	45	9
1970-71 Vancouver	70	12	21	33	42
6 Years	313	92	123	215	120
CURTIS, PAUL EDWIN D-SL					
Born: Peterborough, Ont., Sept. 29, 1947					
1969-70 Montreal	1	0	0	0	0
1970-71 Los Angeles	64	1	13	14	82
1971-72 " "	64	1	12	13	57
3 Years	129	2	25	27	139
DEA, WILLIAM FRASER LW-SL					
Born: Edmonton, Alta., April 3, 1933					
1953-54 New York Rangers	14	1	1	2	2
1956-57 Detroit	69	15	15	30	14
1957-58 " – Chicago	63	9	12	21	10
1967-68 Pittsburgh	73	16	12	28	6
1968-69 "	66	10	8	18	4
1969-70 Detroit	70	10	3	13	6
1970-71 "	42	6	3	9	2
7 Years	397	67	54	121	44
DEADMARSH, ERNEST CHARLES LW-SL					
Born: Trail, British Columbia, April 5, 1950					
1970-71 Buffalo	10	0	0	0	9
1971-72 "	12	1	1	2	4
2 Years	22	1	1	2	13
DELVECCHIO, ALEXANDER PETER C&LW-SL					
Born: Fort William, Ont., Dec. 4, 1931					
1950-51 Detroit	1	0	0	0	0
1951-52 "	65	15	22	37	22
1952-53 "	70	16	43	59	28
1953-54 "	69	11	18	29	34
1954-55 "	69	17	31	48	37
1955-56 "	70	25	26	51	24
1956-57 "	48	16	25	41	8
1957-58 "	70	21	38	59	22
1958-59 "	70	19	35	54	6
1959-60 "	70	19	28	47	8
1960-61 "	70	27	35	62	26
1961-62 "	70	26	43	69	18
1962-63 "	70	20	44	64	8
1963-64 "	70	23	30	53	11
1964-65 "	68	25	42	67	16
1965-66 "	70	31	38	69	16
1966-67 "	70	17	38	55	10
1967-68 "	74	22	48	70	14
1968-69 "	72	25	58	83	8
1969-70 "	73	21	47	68	24
1970-71 "	77	21	34	55	6
1971-72 "	75	20	45	65	22
22 Years	1461	437	768	1205	368

1952-53 2nd All-Star Team at Centre
1958-59 " " " " " Left Wing and Lady Byng Memorial Trophy
1965-66 Lady Byng Memorial Trophy
1968-69 " " " "

Sea. Club	Ga.	Go.	A.	P.	PM.
DeMARCO, ALBERT THOMAS D-SR					
Born: North Bay, Ont., Feb. 27, 1949					
1969-70 New York Rangers	3	0	0	0	0
1970-71 " " "	2	0	1	1	0
1971-72 " "	48	4	7	11	4
3 Years	53	4	8	12	4
DENNIS, NORMAN MARSHALL RW-SL					
Born: Aurora, Ont., Dec. 10, 1942					
1968-69 St. Louis	2	0	0	0	2
1969-70 " "	5	3	0	3	5
1970-71 " "	4	0	0	0	0
1971-72 " "	1	0	0	0	4
4 Years	12	3	0	3	11
DILLABOUGH, ROBERT WELLINGTON LW&C-SL					
Born: Belleville, Ont., April 24, 1941					
1961-62 Detroit	5	0	0	0	2
1964-65 "	4	0	0	0	2
1965-66 Boston	53	7	13	20	18
1966-67 "	60	6	12	18	14

(continued)

Sea.	Club	Ga.	Go.	A.	P.	PM.
ʃ67-68	Pittsburgh	47	7	12	19	18
1968-69	" — Oakland	62	7	12	19	6
1969-70	Oakland	52	5	5	10	16
7 Years		283	32	54	86	76

DINEEN, GARY DANIEL PATRICK C-SL
Born: Montreal, Que., Dec. 24, 1943

1968-69	Minnesota	4	0	1	1	0

DIONNE, MARCEL ELPHEGE C-SR
Born: Drummondville, Que. Aug. 3, 1951

1971-72	Detroit	78	28	49	77	14

DOAK, GARY WALTER D-SR
Born: Goderich, Ont., Feb. 25, 1946

1965-66	Detroit-Boston	24	0	8	8	40
1966-67	Boston	29	0	1	1	50
1967-68	"	59	2	10	12	100
1968-69	"	22	3	3	6	37
1969-70	"	44	1	7	8	63
1970-71	Vancouver	77	2	10	12	112
1971-72	" — New York Rangers	55	1	11	12	77
7 Years		310	9	50	59	479

DOREY, ROBERT JAMES D-SL
Born: Kingston, Ont., Aug. 17, 1947

1968-69	Toronto	61	8	22	30	200
1969-70	"	46	6	11	17	99
1970-71	"	74	7	22	29	198
1971-72	" — New York Rangers	51	4	19	23	56
4 Years		232	25	74	99	553

DORNHOEFER, GERHARDT OTTO RW-
Born: Kitchener, Ont., Feb. 2, 1943

1963-64	Boston	32	12	10	22	20
1964-65	"	20	0	1	1	13
1965-66	"	10	0	1	1	2
1967-68	Philadelphia	65	13	30	43	134
1968-69	"	60	8	16	24	80
1969-70	"	65	26	29	55	96
1970-71	"	57	20	20	40	93
1971-72	"	75	17	32	49	183
8 Years		384	96	139	235	621

DOUGLAS, KENT GEMMELL D-SL
Born: Cobalt, Ont. Feb. 6, 1936

1962-63	Toronto	70	7	15	22	105
1963-64	"	43	0	1	1	29
1964-65	"	67	5	23	28	129
1965-66	"	64	6	14	20	97
1966-67	"	39	2	12	14	48
1967-68	Oakland — Detroit	76	11	21	32	126
1968-69	Detroit	69	2	29	31	97
7 Years		428	33	115	148	631
1962-63	Calder Trophy					

DROLET, RENE GEORGES RW-SR
Born: Quebec City, Que., Nov. 13, 1944

1971-72	Philadelphia	1	0	0	0	0

DROUIN, JUDE C-SR
Born: Mont Louis, Que., Oct. 28, 1948

1968-69	Montreal	9	0	1	1	0
1969-70	"	3	0	0	0	2
1970-71	Minnesota	75	16	52	68	49
1971-72	"	63	13	43	56	31
4 Years		150	29	96	125	82

DUFF, TERRANCE RICHARD LW-SL
Born: Kirkland Lake, Ont., Feb. 18, 1936

1954-55	Toronto	3	0	0	0	2
1955-56	"	69	18	19	37	74
1956-57	"	70	26	14	40	50
1957-58	"	65	26	23	49	79
1958-59	"	69	29	24	53	73
1959-60	"	67	19	22	41	51
1960-61	"	67	16	17	33	54
1961-62	"	51	17	20	37	37
1962-63	"	69	16	19	35	56
1963-64	" — New York Rangers	66	11	14	25	61
1964-65	New York Rangers — Montreal	69	12	16	28	36
1965-66	Montreal	63	21	24	45	78
1966-67	"	51	12	11	23	23
1967-68	"	66	25	21	46	21
1968-69	"	68	19	21	40	24
1969-70	" — Los Angeles	49	6	9	15	12
1970-71	Los Angeles — Buffalo	60	8	13	21	12
1971-72	Buffalo	8	2	2	4	0
18 Years		1030	283	289	572	743

Sea.	Club	Ga.	Go.	A.	P.	PM.

DUFOUR, MARC CAROL RW-SR
Born: Trois Rivieres, Que., Sept. 11, 1941

1963-64	New York	10	1	0	1	2
1964-65	" "	2	0	0	0	0
1968-69	Los Angeles	2	0	0	0	0
3 Years		14	1	0	1	2

DUPERE, DENIS GILLES LW-SL
Born: Jonquiere, Que., June 21, 1948

1970-71	Toronto	20	1	2	3	4
1971-72	"	77	7	10	17	4
2 Years		97	8	12	20	8

DUPONT, ANDRE D-SL
Born: Trois Rivieres, Que., July 27, 1949

1970-71	New York Rangers	7	1	2	3	21
1971-72	St. Louis	60	3	10	13	147
2 Years		67	4	12	16	168

ECCLESTONE, TIMOTHY JAMES RW-SR
Born: Toronto, Ont., Sept. 24, 1947

1967-68	St. Louis	50	6	8	14	16
1968-69	" "	68	11	23	34	31
1969-70	" "	65	16	21	37	59
1970-71	" " — Detroit	74	19	34	53	47
1971-72	Detroit	72	18	35	53	33
5 Years		329	70	121	191	186

EDESTRAND, DARRYL D-SL
Born: Strathroy, Ont., Nov. 6, 1945

1967-68	St. Louis	12	0	0	0	2
1969-70	Philadelphia	2	0	0	0	6
1971-72	Pittsburgh	77	10	23	33	52
3 Years		91	10	23	33	60

EGERS, JOHN RICHARD LW-SL
Born: Sudbury, Ont., Jan. 28, 1949

1969-70	New York Rangers	6	3	0	3	2
1970-71	" " "	60	7	10	17	50
1971-72	" " " — St. Louis	80	23	26	49	48
3 Years		146	33	36	69	100

EHMAN, GERALD JOSEPH RW&LW-SR
Born: Cudworth, Sask., Nov. 3, 1932

1957-58	Boston	1	1	0	1	0
1958-59	Detroit — Toronto	44	12	14	26	16
1959-60	Toronto	69	12	16	28	26
1960-61	"	14	1	1	2	2
1963-64	"	4	1	1	2	0
1967-68	Oakland	73	19	25	44	20
1968-69	"	70	21	24	45	12
1969-70	"	76	11	19	30	8
1970-71	"	78	18	18	36	16
9 Years		429	96	118	214	100

ELLIS, RONALD JOHN EDWARD RW-SR
Born: Lindsay, Ont., Jan. 8, 1945

1963-64	Toronto	1	0	0	0	0
1964-65	"	62	23	16	39	14
1965-66	"	70	19	23	42	24
1966-67	"	67	22	23	45	14
1967-68	"	74	28	20	48	8
1968-69	"	72	25	21	46	12
1969-70	"	76	35	19	54	14
1970-71	"	78	24	29	53	10
1971-72	"	78	23	24	47	17
9 Years		578	199	175	374	113

ERICKSON, AUTRY RAYMOND D-SL
Born: Lethbridge, Alta., Jan. 25, 1938

1959-60	Boston	58	1	6	7	29
1960-61	"	68	2	6	8	65
1962-63	Chicago	3	0	0	0	8
1963-64	"	31	0	1	1	34
1967-68	Oakland	65	4	11	15	46
1969-70	"	1	0	0	0	0
6 Years		226	7	24	31	182

ERICKSON, GRANT CHARLES LW-SL
Born: Pierceland, Sask. April 28, 1947

1968-69	Boston	2	1	0	1	0
1969-70	Minnesota	4	0	0	0	0
2 Years		6	1	0	1	0

ESPOSITO, PHILIP ANTHONY C-SL
Born: Sault Ste. Marie, Ont. Feb. 20, 1942

1963-64	Chicago	27	3	2	5	2
1964-65	"	70	23	32	55	44
1965-66	"	69	27	26	53	49
1966-67	"	69	21	40	61	40

(continued)

Sea.	Club	Ga.	Go.	A.	P.	PM.
1967-68	Boston	74	35	*49	84	21
1968-69	"	74	49	*77	*126	79
1969-70	"	76	*43	56	99	50
1970-71	"	78	*76	76	*152	71
1971-72	"	76	*66	67	*133	76
9 Years		613	343	425	768	432

*league leader
1967-68 2nd All-Star Team at Centre
1968-69 1st " " " " David A. Hart and Arthur Ross Trophies
1969-70 " " " "
1970-71 " " " " " and Arthur H. Ross Trophy
1971-72 " " " " " " " "

EVANS, CHRISTOPHER BRUCE D-SL
Born: Toronto, Ont., Sept. 14, 1946

1969-70	Toronto	2	0	0	0	0
1971-72	Buffalo – St. Louis	63	6	18	24	98
2 Years		65	6	18	24	98

FAIRBAIRN, WILLIAM JOHN RW-SR
Born: Brandon, Man. Jan. 7, 1947

1968-69	New York Rangers	1	0	0	0	0
1969-70	" " "	76	23	33	56	23
1970-71	" " "	56	7	23	30	32
1971-72	" " "	78	22	37	59	53
4 Years		211	52	93	145	108

FALKENBERG, ROBERT ARTHUR D-SL
Born: Stettler, Alta., Jan. 1, 1946

1966-67	Detroit	16	1	1	2	10
1967-68	"	20	0	3	3	10
1968-69	"	5	0	0	0	0
1970-71	"	9	0	1	1	6
1971-72	"	4	0	0	0	0
5 Years		54	1	5	6	26

FEATHERSTONE, ANTHONY JAMES RW
Born: Toronto, Ont., July 31, 1949

1969-70	Oakland	9	0	1	1	17
1970-71	"	67	8	8	16	44
2 Years		76	8	9	17	61

FERGUSON, JOHN BOWIE LW-SL
Born: Vancouver, British Columbia. Sept. 5, 1938

1963-64	Montreal	59	18	27	45	125
1964-65	"	69	17	27	44	156
1965-66	"	65	11	14	25	153
1966-67	"	67	20	22	42	*177
1967-68	"	61	15	18	33	117
1968-69	"	71	29	23	52	185
1969-70	"	48	19	13	32	139
1970-71	"	60	16	14	30	162
8 Years		500	145	158	303	1214

*league leader

FERGUSON, NORMAN GERALD RW-SR
Born: Sydney, Nova Scotia. Oct. 16, 1945

1968-69	Oakland	76	34	20	54	31
1969-70	"	72	11	9	20	19
1970-71	"	54	14	17	31	9
1971-72	"	77	14	20	34	13
4 Years		279	73	66	139	72

FLEMING, REGINALD STEPHEN LW-SL
Born: Montreal, Que. April 21, 1936

1959-60	Montreal	3	0	0	0	2
1960-61	Chicago	66	4	4	8	145
1961-62	"	70	7	9	16	71
1962-63	"	64	7	7	14	99
1963-64	"	61	3	6	9	140
1964-65	Boston	67	18	23	41	136
1965-66	" – New York Rangers	69	14	20	34	*166
1966-67	New York Rangers	61	15	16	31	146
1967-68	" " "	73	17	7	24	132
1968-69	" " "	72	8	12	20	138
1969-70	Philadelphia	65	9	18	27	134
1970-71	Buffalo	78	6	10	16	159
12 Years		749	108	132	240	1468

*league leader

FLETT, WILLIAM MAYER RW-SR
Born: Vermilion, Alta. July 21, 1943

1967-68	Los Angeles	73	26	20	46	97
1968-69	" "	72	24	25	49	53
1969-70	" "	69	14	18	32	70
1970-71	" "	64	13	24	37	57
1971-72	" " – Philadelphia	76	18	22	40	44
5 Years		354	95	109	204	321

FOLEY, GERALD JAMES RW-SR
Born: Ware, Mass. Sept. 22, 1932

1954-55	Toronto	4	0	0	0	8
1956-57	New York	69	7	9	16	48
1957-58	"	68	2	5	7	43
1968-69	Los Angeles	1	0	0	0	0
4 Years		142	9	14	23	99

FOLEY, GILBERT ANTHONY D-SL
Born: Niagara Falls, Ont. Sept. 22, 1945

1970-71	Chicago	2	0	1	1	8
1971-72	Philadelphia	58	11	25	36	168
2 Years		60	11	26	37	176

FONTEYNE, VALERE RONALD LW-SL
Born: Wetaskiwin, Alta. Dec. 2, 1933

1959-60	Detroit	69	4	7	11	2
1960-61	"	66	6	11	17	4
1961-62	"	70	5	5	10	4
1962-63	"	67	6	14	20	2
1963-64	New York Rangers	69	7	18	25	4
1964-65	" " " – Detroit	43	2	6	8	6
1965-66	Detroit	59	5	10	15	0
1966-67	"	28	1	1	2	0
1967-68	Pittsburgh	69	6	28	34	0
1968-69	"	74	12	17	29	2
1969-70	"	68	11	15	26	2
1970-71	"	70	4	9	13	0
1971-72	"	68	6	13	19	0
13 Years		820	75	154	229	26

FORTIN, RAYMOND HENRI D-SL
Born: Drummondville, Que. March 11, 1941

1967-68	St. Louis	24	0	2	2	8
1968-69	" "	11	1	0	1	6
1969-70	" "	57	1	4	5	19
3 Years		92	2	6	8	33

GAGNON, GERMAIN LW-SL
Born: Chicoutimi, Que. Dec. 9, 1942

1971-72	Montreal	4	0	0	0	0

GAMBUCCI, GARY ALLAN LW-SL
Born: Virginia, Minn. Sept. 22, 1946

1971-72	Minnesota	9	1	0	1	0

GAUTHIER, JEAN PHILLIPE D-SR
Born: Montreal, Que. April 29, 1937

1960-61	Montreal	4	0	1	1	8
1961-62	"	12	0	1	1	10
1962-63	"	65	1	17	18	46
1963-64	"	1	0	0	0	2
1965-66	"	2	0	0	0	0
1966-67	"	2	0	0	0	2
1967-68	Philadelphia	65	5	7	12	74
1968-69	Boston	11	0	2	2	8
1969-70	Montreal	4	0	1	1	0
9 Years		166	6	29	35	150

GELDART, GARY DANIEL D-SL
Born: Moncton, New Brunswick. June 14,

1970-71	Minnesota	4	0	0	0	5

GENDRON, JEAN-GUY LW-SL
Born: Montreal, Que. Aug. 30, 1934

1955-56	New York Rangers	63	5	7	12	38
1956-57	" " "	70	9	6	15	40
1957-58	" " "	70	10	17	27	68
1958-59	Boston	60	15	9	24	57
1959-60	"	67	24	11	35	64
1960-61	" – Montreal	66	10	19	29	75
1961-62	New York Rangers	69	14	11	25	71
1962-63	Boston	66	21	22	43	42
1963-64	"	54	5	13	18	43
1967-68	Philadelphia	1	0	1	1	2
1968-69	"	74	20	35	55	65
1969-70	"	71	23	21	44	54
1970-71	"	76	20	16	36	46
1971-72	"	56	6	13	19	36
14 Years		863	182	201	383	701

GIBBS, BARRY PAUL D-SR
Born: Lloydminster, Sask. Sept. 28, 1948

1967-68	Boston	16	0	0	0	2
1968-69	"	8	0	0	0	2
1969-70	Minnesota	56	3	13	16	182
1970-71	"	68	5	15	20	132
1971-72	"	75	4	20	24	128
5 Years		223	12	48	60	446

Sea.	Club	Ga.	Go.	A.	P.	PM.

GILBERT, RODRIGUE GABRIEL RW-SR
Born: Montreal, Que. July 1, 1941

Sea.	Club	Ga.	Go.	A.	P.	PM.
1960-61	New York Rangers	1	0	1	1	2
1961-62	" " "	1	0	0	0	0
1962-63	" " "	70	11	20	31	20
1963-64	" " "	70	24	40	64	62
1964-65	" " "	70	25	36	61	52
1965-66	" " "	34	10	15	25	20
1966-67	" " "	64	28	18	46	12
1967-68	" " "	73	29	48	77	12
1968-69	" " "	66	28	49	77	22
1969-70	" " "	72	16	37	53	22
1970-71	" " "	78	30	31	61	65
1971-72	" " "	73	43	54	97	64
12 Years		672	244	349	593	353

1967-68 2nd All-Star Team at Right Wing
1971-72 1st " " " " "

GILBERTSON, STANLEY LW-SL
Born: Duluth, Minn. Oct. 29, 1944

1971-72	Oakland	78	16	16	32	47

GLENNIE, BRIAN ALEXANDER D-SL
Born: Toronto, Ont. Aug. 29, 1946

1969-70	Toronto	52	1	14	15	50
1970-71	"	54	0	8	8	31
1971-72	"	61	2	8	10	44
3 Years		167	3	30	33	125

GLOVER, HOWARD EDWARD RW-SR
Born: Toronto, Ont. Feb. 14, 1935

1958-59	Chicago	13	0	1	1	2
1960-61	Detroit	66	21	8	29	46
1961-62	"	39	7	8	15	44
1963-64	New York	25	1	0	1	9
1968-69	Montreal	1	0	0	0	0
5 Years		144	29	17	46	101

GOLDSWORTHY, WILLIAM ALFRED RW-SR
Born: Waterloo, Ont. Aug. 24, 1944

1964-65	Boston	2	0	0	0	0
1965-66	"	13	3	1	4	6
1966-67	"	18	3	5	8	21
1967-68	Minnesota	68	14	19	33	68
1968-69	"	68	14	10	24	110
1969-70	"	75	36	29	65	89
1970-71	"	77	34	31	65	85
1971-72	"	78	31	31	62	59
8 Years		399	135	126	261	438

GORING, ROBERT THOMAS C-SL
Born: St. Boniface, Man. Oct. 22, 1949

1969-70	Los Angeles	59	13	23	36	8
1970-71	" "	19	2	5	7	2
1971-72	" "	74	21	29	50	2
3 Years		152	36	57	93	12

GOULD, JOHN MILTON LW-SL
Born: Alliston, Ont. April 11,1949

1971-72	Buffalo	2	1	0	1	0

GOYETTE, JOSEPH GEORGES PHILLIPE C-SL
Born: Lachine, Que. Oct. 31, 1933

1956-57	Montreal	14	3	4	7	0
1957-58	"	70	9	37	46	8
1958-59	"	63	10	18	28	8
1959-60	"	65	21	22	43	4
1960-61	"	62	7	4	11	4
1961-62	"	69	7	27	34	18
1962-63	"	32	5	8	13	2
1963-64	New York Rangers	67	24	41	65	15
1964-65	" " "	52	12	34	46	6
1965-66	" " "	60	11	31	42	6
1966-67	" " "	70	12	49	61	6
1967-68	" " "	73	25	40	65	10
1968-69	" " "	67	13	32	45	8
1969-70	St. Louis	72	29	49	78	16
1970-71	Buffalo	60	15	46	61	6
1971-72	" – New York Rangers	45	4	25	29	14
16 Years		941	207	467	674	131

1969-70 Lady Byng Memorial Trophy

GRANT, DANIEL FREDERICK LW-SL
Born: Fredericton, New Brunswick. Feb. 21, 1946

1965-66	Montreal	1	0	0	0	0
1967-68	"	22	3	4	7	10
1968-69	Minnesota	75	34	31	65	46
1969-70	"	76	29	28	57	23
1970-71	"	78	34	23	57	46
1971-72	"	78	18	25	43	18
6 Years		330	118	111	229	143

1968-69 Frank Calder Memorial Trophy

GRATTON, NORMAND LIONEL RW-SL
Born: LaSalle, Que. Dec. 22, 1950

1971-72	New York Rangers	3	0	1	1	0

GRAVES, HILLIARD RW-SR
Born: St. John, New Brunswick. Oct. 18, 1950

1970-71	Oakland	14	0	0	0	0

GRAY, TERRENCE STANLEY RW-SR
Born: Montreal, Que. March 21, 1938

1961-62	Boston	42	8	7	15	15
1963-64	Montreal	4	0	0	0	6
1967-68	Los Angeles	65	12	16	28	22
1968-69	St. Louis	8	4	0	4	4
1969-70	" "	28	2	5	7	17
5 Years		147	26	28	54	64

GREEN, EDWARD JOSEPH D-SR
Born: St. Boniface, Man. March 23, 1940

1960-61	Boston	1	0	0	0	2
1961-62	"	66	3	8	11	116
1962-63	"	70	1	11	12	117
1963-64	"	70	4	10	14	145
1964-65	"	70	8	27	35	156
1965-66	"	27	5	13	18	113
1966-67	"	47	6	10	16	67
1967-68	"	72	7	36	43	133
1968-69	"	65	8	38	46	99
1970-71	"	78	5	37	42	60
1971-72	"	54	1	16	17	21
11 Years		620	48	206	254	1029

1968-69 2nd All-Star Team on Defence

GRENIER, LUCIEN S. J. RW-SL
Born: Malartic, Que. Nov. 3, 1946

1969-70	Montreal	23	2	3	5	2
1970-71	Los Angeles	68	9	7	16	12
1971-72	" "	60	3	4	7	4
3 Years		151	14	14	28	18

GUEVREMONT, JOCELYN MARCEL D-SR
Born: Montreal, Que. March 1, 1951

1971-72	Vancouver	75	13	38	51	44

HADFIELD, VICTOR EDWARD LW-SL
Born: Oakville, Ont. Oct. 4, 1940

1961-62	New York Rangers	44	3	1	4	22
1962-63	" " "	36	5	6	11	32
1963-64	" " "	69	14	11	25	*151
1964-65	" " "	70	18	20	38	102
1965-66	" " "	67	16	19	35	112
1966-67	" " "	69	13	20	33	80
1967-68	" " "	59	20	19	39	45
1968-69	" " "	73	26	40	66	108
1969-70	" " "	71	20	34	54	69
1970-71	" " "	63	22	22	44	38
1971-72	" " "	78	50	56	106	142
11 Years		699	207	248	455	901

*league leader
1971-72 2nd All-Star Team at Left Wing

HALE, LARRY JAMES D-SL
Born: Summerland, British Columbia. Oct. 9, 1941

1968-69	Philadelphia	67	3	16	19	28
1969-70	"	53	1	9	10	28
1970-71	"	70	1	11	12	34
1971-72	"	6	0	1	1	0
4 Years		196	5	37	42	90

HALL, DEL LW-SL
Born: Peterborough, Ont. May 7, 1949

1971-72	Oakland	1	0	0	0	0

HALL, MURRAY WINSTON RW&C-SR
Born: Kirkland Lake, Ont. Nov. 24, 1940

1961-62	Chicago	2	0	0	0	0
1963-64	"	23	2	0	2	4
1965-66	Detroit	1	0	0	0	0
1966-67	"	12	4	3	7	4
1967-68	Minnesota	17	2	1	3	10
1970-71	Vancouver	77	21	38	59	22
1971-72	"	32	6	6	12	6
7 Years		164	35	48	83	46

HAMILTON, ALLAN GUY D-SR
Born: Flin Flon, Man. Aug. 20, 1946

1965-66	New York Rangers	4	0	0	0	0
1967-68	" " "	2	0	0	0	0
1968-69	" " "	16	0	0	0	8
1969-70	" " "	59	0	5	5	54
1970-71	Buffalo	69	2	28	30	71
1971-72	"	76	4	30	34	105
6 Years		226	6	63	69	238

Sea. Club	Ga.	Go.	A.	P.	PM.
HAMPSON, EDWARD GEORGE C-SL					
Born: Togo, Sask. Dec. 11, 1936					
1959-60 Toronto	41	2	8	10	17
1960-61 New York Rangers	69	6	14	20	4
1961-62 " " "	68	4	24	28	10
1962-63 " " "	46	4	2	6	2
1963-64 Detroit	7	0	1	1	0
1964-65 "	1	0	0	0	0
1965-67 "	65	13	35	48	4
1967-68 " – Oakland	71	17	37	54	14
1968-69 Oakland	76	26	49	75	6
1969-70 "	76	17	35	52	13
1970-71 " – Minnesota	78	14	26	40	18
1971-72 Minnesota	78	5	14	19	6
12 Years	676	108	245	353	94
1968-69 Bill Masterton Memorial Trophy					
HANNIGAN, PATRICK EDWARD RW-SR					
Born: Timmins, Ont. Mar. 5, 1936					
1959-60 Toronto	1	0	0	0	0
1960-61 New York	53	11	9	20	24
1961-62 " "	56	8	14	22	34
1967-68 Philadelphia	65	11	15	26	36
1968-69 "	7	0	1	1	22
5 Years	182	30	39	69	116
HARBARUK, MIKOLAJ NICKOLAS RW-SR					
Born: Drohiczyn, Poland. Aug. 16, 1943					
1969-70 Pittsburgh	74	5	17	22	56
1970-71 "	78	13	12	25	108
1971-72 "	78	12	17	29	46
3 Years	230	30	46	76	210
HARDY, JOCELYN JOSEPH C-SL					
Born: Kenogami, Que. Dec. 5, 1944					
1969-70 Oakland	23	5	4	9	20
1970-71 "	40	4	10	14	31
2 Years	63	9	14	23	51
HARGREAVES, JAMES D-SR					
Born: Winnipeg, Man. May 2, 1950					
1970-71 Vancouver	7	0	1	1	33
HARPER, TERRANCE VICTOR D-SR					
Born: Regina, Sask. Jan. 27, 1940					
1962-63 Montreal	14	1	1	2	10
1963-64 "	70	2	15	17	149
1964-65 "	62	0	7	7	93
1965-66 "	69	1	11	12	91
1966-67 "	56	0	16	16	99
1967-68 "	57	3	8	11	66
1968-69 "	21	0	3	3	37
1969-70 "	75	4	18	22	109
1970-71 "	78	1	21	22	116
1971-72 "	52	2	12	14	35
10 Years	554	14	112	126	805
HARRIS, EDWARD ALEXANDER D-SL					
Born: Winnipeg, Man. July 18, 1936					
1963-64 Montreal	4	0	1	1	0
1964-65 "	68	1	14	15	107
1965-66 "	53	0	13	13	87
1966-67 "	65	2	16	18	86
1967-68 "	67	5	16	21	78
1968-69 "	76	7	18	25	102
1969-70 "	74	3	17	20	116
1970-71 Minnesota	78	2	13	15	130
1971-72 "	78	2	15	17	77
9 Years	563	22	123	145	783
1968-69 2nd All-Star Team on Defence					
HARRIS, RONALD THOMAS D-SR					
Born: Verdun, Que. June 30, 1942					
1962-63 Detroit	1	0	1	1	0
1963-64 "	3	0	0	0	7
1967-68 Oakland	54	4	6	10	60
1968-69 Detroit	73	3	13	16	91
1969-70 "	72	2	19	21	99
1970-71 "	42	2	8	10	65
1971-72 "	61	1	10	11	80
7 Years	306	12	57	69	402
HARRIS, WILLIAM EDWARD C-SL					
Born: Toronto, Ont. July 29, 1935					
1955-56 Toronto	70	9	13	22	8
1956-57 "	23	4	6	10	6
1957-58 "	68	16	28	44	32
1958-59 "	70	22	30	52	29
1959-60 "	70	13	25	38	29
1960-61 "	66	12	27	39	30

(continued)

Sea. Club	Ga.	Go.	A.	P.	PM.
1961-62 "	67	15	10	25	14
1962-63 "	65	8	24	32	22
1963-64 "	63	6	12	18	17
1964-65 "	48	1	6	7	0
1965-66 Detroit	24	1	4	5	6
1967-68 Oakland	62	12	17	29	2
1968-69 " – Pittsburgh	73	7	17	24	10
13 Years	769	126	219	345	205
HARRISON, JAMES DAVID C-SR					
Born: Bonnyville, Alta. July 9, 1947					
1968-69 Boston	16	1	2	3	21
1969-70 " – Toronto	54	10	11	21	52
1970-71 Toronto	78	13	20	33	108
1971-72 "	66	19	17	36	104
4 Years	214	43	50	93	285
HART, GERALD WILLIAM D-SL					
Born: Flin Flon, Man. Jan. 1, 1948					
1968-69 Detroit	1	0	0	0	2
1969-70 "	3	0	0	0	2
1970-71 "	64	2	7	9	148
1971-72 "	3	0	0	0	0
4 Years	71	2	7	9	152
HARVEY, DOUGLAS NORMAN D-SL					
Born: Montreal, Que. Dec. 19, 1924					
1947-48 Montreal	35	4	4	8	32
1948-49 "	55	3	13	16	87
1949-50 "	70	4	20	24	76
1950-51 "	70	5	24	29	93
1951-52 "	68	6	23	29	82
1952-53 "	69	4	30	34	67
1953-54 "	68	8	29	37	110
1954-55 "	70	6	43	49	58
1955-56 "	62	5	39	44	60
1956-57 "	70	6	44	50	92
1957-58 "	68	9	32	41	131
1958-59 "	61	4	16	20	61
1959-60 "	66	6	21	27	45
1960-61 "	58	6	33	39	48
1961-62 New York	69	6	24	30	42
1962-63 " "	68	4	35	39	92
1963-64 "	14	0	2	2	10
1966-67 Detroit	2	0	0	0	0
1968-69 St. Louis	70	2	20	22	30
19 Years	1113	88	452	540	1216
1951-52 1st All-Star Team					
1952-53 " " " "					
1953-54 " " " "					
1954-55 " " " " & Norris Trophy					
1955-56 " " " " " "					
1956-57 " " " "					
1957-58 " " " " & Norris Trophy					
1958-59 2nd " " "					
1959-60 1st " " " & Norris Trophy					
1960-61 " " " " " "					
1961-62 " " " " " "					
HARVEY, FREDERICK JOHN CHARLES RW-SR					
Born: Fredericton, New Brunswick. April 2, 1950					
1970-71 Minnesota	59	12	8	20	36
HATOUM, EDWARD RW-SR					
Born: Beirut, Lebanon. Dec. 7, 1947					
1968-69 Detroit	16	2	1	3	2
1969-70 "	5	0	2	2	2
1970-71 Vancouver	26	1	3	4	21
3 Years	47	3	6	9	25
HEINDL, WILLIAM WAYNE LW-SL					
Born: Sherbrooke, Que. May 13, 1946					
1970-71 Minnesota	12	1	1	2	0
1971-72 "	2	0	0	0	0
2 Years	14	1	1	2	0
HEISKALA, EARL WALDEMAR LW-SL					
Born: Kirkland Lake, Ont. Nov. 30, 1942					
1968-69 Philadelphia	21	3	3	6	51
1969-70 "	65	8	7	15	171
1970-71 "	41	2	1	3	72
3 Years	127	13	11	24	294
HENDERSON, PAUL GARNET LW-SR					
Born: Kincardine, Ont. Jan. 28, 1943					
1962-63 Detroit	2	0	0	0	9
1963-64 "	32	3	3	6	14
1964-65 "	70	8	13	21	30
1965-66 "	69	22	24	46	10
1966-67 "	46	21	19	40	10
1967-68 " – Toronto	63	18	26	44	43

(continued)

Sea. Club	Ga.	Go.	A.	P.	PM.
1968-69 Toronto	74	27	32	59	16
1969-70 "	67	20	22	42	18
1970-71 "	72	30	30	60	34
1971-71 "	73	38	19	57	32
10 Years	568	187	188	375	240

HENRY, CAMILLE JOSEPH WILFRID LW-SL
Born: Quebec City, Que. Jan. 31, 1933

Sea. Club	Ga.	Go.	A.	P.	PM.
1953-54 New York Rangers	66	24	15	39	10
1954-55 " " "	21	5	2	7	4
1956-57 " " "	36	14	15	29	2
1957-58 " " "	70	32	24	56	2
1958-59 " " "	70	23	35	58	2
1959-60 " " "	49	12	15	27	6
1960-61 " " "	53	28	25	53	8
1961-62 " " "	60	23	15	38	8
1962-63 " " "	60	37	23	60	8
1963-64 " " "	68	29	26	55	8
1964-65 " " " – Chicago	70	26	18	44	22
1967-68 " " " – Rangers	36	8	12	20	0
1968-69 St. Louis	64	17	22	39	8
1969-70 " "	4	1	2	3	0
14 Years	727	279	249	528	88

1953-54 Frank Calder Memorial Trophy
1957-58 2nd All-Star Team at Left Wing & Lady Byng Memorial Trophy

HEXTALL, BRYAN LEE C-SL
Born: Winnipeg, Man. May 23, 1941

Sea. Club	Ga.	Go.	A.	P.	PM.
1962-63 New York Rangers	21	0	2	2	10
1969-70 Pittsburgh	66	12	19	31	87
1970-71 "	76	16	32	48	133
1971-72 "	78	20	24	44	126
4 Years	241	48	77	125	356

HEXTALL, DENNIS HAROLD C-SL
Born: Winnipeg, Man. April 17, 1943

Sea. Club	Ga.	Go.	A.	P.	PM.
1968-69 New York Rangers	13	1	4	5	25
1969-70 Los Angeles	28	5	7	12	40
1970-71 Oakland	78	21	31	52	217
1971-72 Minnesota	33	6	10	16	49
4 Years	152	33	52	85	331

HICKE, ERNEST ALLEN LW-SL
Born: Regina, Sask. Nov. 7, 1947

Sea. Club	Ga.	Go.	A.	P.	PM.
1970-71 Oakland	78	22	25	47	62
1971-72 "	68	11	12	23	55
2 Years	146	33	37	70	117

HICKE, WILLIAM LAWRENCE RW-SL
Born: Regina, Sask. March 31, 1938

Sea. Club	Ga.	Go.	A.	P.	PM.
1959-60 Montreal	43	3	10	13	17
1960-61 "	70	18	27	45	31
1961-62 "	70	20	31	51	42
1962-63 "	70	17	22	39	39
1963-64 "	48	11	9	20	41
1964-65 " – New York Rangers	57	6	12	18	32
1965-66 New York Rangers	49	9	18	27	21
1966-67 " " "	48	3	4	7	11
1967-68 Oakland	52	21	19	40	32
1968-69 "	67	25	36	61	68
1969-70 "	69	15	29	44	14
1970-71 "	74	18	17	35	41
1971-72 Pittsburgh	12	2	0	2	6
13 Years	729	168	234	402	395

HILLMAN, LAWRENCE MORLEY D-SL
Born: Kirkland Lake, Ont. Feb. 5, 1937

Sea. Club	Ga.	Go.	A.	P.	PM.
1954-55 Detroit	6	0	0	0	2
1955-56 "	47	0	3	3	53
1956-57 "	16	1	2	3	4
1957-58 Boston	70	3	19	22	60
1958-59 "	55	3	10	13	19
1959-60 "	2	0	1	1	2
1960-61 Toronto	62	3	10	13	59
1961-62 "	5	0	0	0	4
1962-63 "	5	0	0	0	2
1963-64 "	33	0	4	4	31
1964-65 "	2	0	0	0	2
1965-66 "	48	3	25	28	34
1966-67 "	55	4	19	23	40
1967-68 "	55	3	17	20	13
1968-69 Minnesota – Montreal	37	1	10	11	17
1969-70 Philadelphia	76	5	26	31	73
1970-71 "	73	3	13	16	39
1971-72 Los Angeles – Buffalo	65	2	13	15	69
18 Years	712	31	172	203	523

HILLMAN, WAYNE JAMES D-SL
Born: Kirkland Lake, Ont. Nov. 13, 1938

Sea. Club	Ga.	Go.	A.	P.	PM.
1961-62 Chicago	19	0	2	2	14

(continued)

Sea. Club	Ga.	Go.	A.	P.	PM.
1962-63 "	67	3	5	8	74
1963-64 "	59	1	4	5	51
1964-65 " – New York Rangers	41	1	8	9	34
1965-66 New York Rangers	68	3	17	20	70
1966-67 " " "	67	2	12	14	43
1967-68 "	62	0	5	5	46
1968-69 Minnesota	50	0	8	8	32
1969-70 Philadelphia	68	3	5	8	69
1970-71 "	69	5	7	12	47
1971-72 "	47	0	3	3	21
11 Years	617	18	76	94	501

HODGE, KENNETH RAYMOND RW-SR
Born: Birmingham, England. June 25, 1944

Sea. Club	Ga.	Go.	A.	P.	PM.
1964-65 Chicago	1	0	0	0	2
1965-66 "	63	6	17	23	47
1966-67 "	68	10	25	35	59
1967-68 Boston	74	25	31	56	31
1968-69 "	75	45	45	90	75
1969-70 "	72	25	29	54	87
1970-71 "	78	43	62	105	113
1971-72 "	60	16	40	56	81
8 Years	491	170	249	419	495

1970-71 1st All-Star Team at Right Wing

HOGANSON, DALE GORDON D-SL
Born: North Battleford, Sask. July 8, 1949

Sea. Club	Ga.	Go.	A.	P.	PM.
1969-70 Los Angeles	49	1	7	8	37
1970-71 " "	70	4	10	14	52
1971-72 " " – Montreal	31	1	2	3	16
3 Years	150	6	19	25	105

HORNUNG, LARRY JOHN D-SL
Born: Gravelbourg, Sask. Nov. 10, 1945

Sea. Club	Ga.	Go.	A.	P.	PM.
1970-71 St. Louis	1	0	0	0	0
1971-72 " "	47	2	9	11	10
2 Years	48	2	9	11	10

HORTON, MYLES GILBERT D-SR
Born: Cochrane, Ont. Jan. 12, 1930

Sea. Club	Ga.	Go.	A.	P.	PM.
1949-50 Toronto	1	0	0	0	2
1951-52 "	4	0	0	0	8
1952-53 "	70	2	14	16	85
1953-54 "	70	7	24	31	94
1954-55 "	67	5	9	14	84
1955-56 "	35	0	5	5	36
1956-57 "	66	6	19	25	72
1957-58 "	53	6	20	26	39
1958-59 "	70	5	21	26	76
1959-60 "	70	3	29	32	69
1960-61 "	57	6	15	21	75
1961-62 "	70	10	28	38	88
1962-63 "	70	6	19	25	69
1963-64 "	70	9	20	29	71
1964-65 "	70	12	16	28	95
1965-66 "	70	6	22	28	76
1966-67 "	70	8	17	25	70
1967-68 "	69	4	23	27	82
1968-69 "	74	11	29	40	107
1969-70 " – New York Rangers	74	4	24	28	107
1970-71 New York Rangers	78	2	18	20	57
1971-72 Pittsburgh	44	2	9	11	40
22 Years	1322	114	381	495	1502

1953-54 2nd All-Star Team on Defence
1962-63 " " " " "
1963-64 1st " " " "
1966-67 2nd " " " "
1967-68 1st " " " "
1968-69 " " " " "

HOULE, REJEAN RW-SL
Born: Rouyn, Que. Oct. 25, 1949

Sea. Club	Ga.	Go.	A.	P.	PM.
1969-70 Montreal	9	0	1	1	0
1970-71 "	66	10	9	19	28
1971-72 "	77	11	17	28	21
3 Years	152	21	27	48	49

HOWE, GORDON RW-SR
Born: Floral, Sask. March 31, 1928

Sea. Club	Ga.	Go.	A.	P.	PM.
1946-47 Detroit	58	7	15	22	52
1947-48 "	60	16	28	44	63
1948-49 "	40	12	25	37	57
1949-50 "	70	35	33	68	69
1950-51 "	70	*43	*43	*86	74
1951-52 "	70	*47	39	*86	78
1952-53 "	70	*49	*46	*95	57
1953-54 "	70	33	*48	*81	109
1954-55 "	64	29	33	62	68
1955-56 "	70	38	41	79	100

(continued)

Sea.	Club	Ga.	Go.	A.	P.	PM.
1956-57	"	70	*44	45	*89	72
1957-58	"	64	33	44	77	40
1958-59	"	70	32	46	78	57
1959-60	"	70	28	45	73	46
1960-61	"	64	23	49	72	30
1961-62	"	70	33	44	77	54
1962-63	"	70	*38	48	*86	100
1963-64	"	69	26	47	73	70
1964-65	"	70	29	47	76	104
1965-66	"	70	29	46	75	83
1966-67	"	69	25	40	65	53
1967-68	"	74	39	43	82	53
1968-69	"	76	44	59	103	58
1969-70	"	76	31	40	71	58
1970-71	"	63	23	29	52	38
25 Years		1687	786	1023	1809	1643

*league leader
1948-49 2nd All-Star Team at Right Wing
1949-50 " " " " " "
1950-51 1st " " " " " " & Arthur H. Ross Trophy
1951-52 " " " " " " " & David Hart & Arthur Ross Trophies
1952-53 " " " " " " " " " " "
1953-54 " " " " " " " & Arthur H. Ross Trophy
1955-56 2nd " " " " " "
1956-57 1st " " " " " " " & David Hart & Arthur Ross Trophies
1957-58 " " " " " " " & Dr. David A. Hart Trophy
1958-59 2nd " " " " " "
1959-60 1st " " " " " " & Dr. David A. Hart Memorial Trophy
1960-61 2nd " " " " " "
1961-62 " " " " " "
1962-63 1st " " " " " " & David Hart & Arthur Ross Trophies
1963-64 2nd " " " " " "
1964-65 " " " " " "
1965-66 1st " " " " " "
1966-67 2nd " " " " " "
1967-68 1st " " " " " "
1968-69 " " " " " "
1969-70 " " " " " "
Hall of Fame

HOWELL, HENRY VERNON D-SL
Born: Hamilton, Ont. Dec. 28, 1932

Sea.	Club	Ga.	Go.	A.	P.	PM.
1952-53	New York Rangers	67	3	8	11	46
1953-54	" " "	67	7	9	16	58
1954-55	" " "	70	2	14	16	87
1955-56	" " "	70	3	15	18	77
1956-57	" " "	65	2	10	12	70
1957-58	" " "	70	4	7	11	62
1958-59	" " "	70	4	10	14	101
1959-60	" " "	67	7	6	13	58
1960-61	" " "	70	7	10	17	62
1961-62	" " "	66	6	15	21	89
1962-63	" " "	70	5	20	25	55
1963-64	" " "	70	5	31	36	75
1964-65	" " "	68	2	20	22	63
1965-66	" " "	70	4	29	33	92
1966-67	" " "	70	12	28	40	54
1967-68	" " "	74	5	24	29	62
1968-69	" " "	56	4	7	11	36
1969-70	Oakland	55	4	16	20	52
1970-71	" — Los Angeles	46	3	17	20	18
1971-72	Los Angeles	77	1	17	18	53
20 Years		1338	90	313	403	1270

1966-67 1st All-Star Team on Defence & James Norris Memorial Trophy

HUCK, ANTHONY FRANCIS C-SR
Born: Regina, Sask. Dec. 4, 1945

Sea.	Club	Ga.	Go.	A.	P.	PM.
1969-70	Montreal	2	0	0	0	0
1970-71	" — St. Louis	34	8	10	18	18
2 Years		36	8	10	18	18

HUGHES, BRENTON ALEXANDER D-SL
Born: Bowmanville, Ont. June 17, 1943

Sea.	Club	Ga.	Go.	A.	P.	PM.
1967-68	Los Angeles	44	4	10	14	36
1968-69	" "	72	2	19	21	73
1969-70	" "	52	1	7	8	108
1970-71	Philadelphia	30	1	10	11	21
1971-72	"	63	2	20	22	35
5 Years		261	10	66	76	273

HUGHES, FRANK RW-SR
Born: Fernie, British Columbia. Oct. 1, 1949

Sea.	Club	Ga.	Go.	A.	P.	PM.
1971-72	Oakland	5	0	0	0	0

HUGHES, HOWARD DUNCAN RW-SL
Born: St. Boniface, Man. April 4, 1939

Sea.	Club	Ga.	Go.	A.	P.	PM.
1967-68	Los Angeles	74	9	14	23	20
1968-69	" "	73	16	14	30	10
1969-70	" "	21	0	4	4	0
3 Years		168	25	32	57	30

HULL, DENNIS WILLIAM LW-SL
Born: Pointe Anne, Ont. Nov. 19, 1944

Sea.	Club	Ga.	Go.	A.	P.	PM.
1964-65	Chicago	55	10	4	14	18
1965-66	"	25	1	5	6	6
1966-67	"	70	25	17	42	33
1967-68	"	74	18	15	33	34
1968-69	"	72	30	34	64	25
1969-70	"	76	17	35	52	31
1970-71	"	78	40	26	66	16
1971-72	"	78	30	39	69	10
8 Years		528	171	175	346	173

HULL, ROBERT MARVIN LW-SL
Born: Pointe Anne, Ont. Jan. 3, 1939

Sea.	Club	Ga.	Go.	A.	P.	PM.
1957-58	Chicago	70	13	34	47	62
1958-59	"	70	18	32	50	50
1959-60	"	70	*39	42	*81	68
1960-61	"	67	31	25	56	43
1961-62	"	70	*50	34	*84	35
1962-63	"	65	31	31	62	27
1963-64	"	70	*43	44	87	50
1964-65	"	61	39	32	71	32
1965-66	"	65	*54	43	*97	70
1966-67	"	66	*52	28	80	52
1967-68	"	71	*44	31	75	39
1968-69	"	74	*58	49	107	48
1969-70	"	61	38	29	67	8
1970-71	"	78	44	52	96	32
1971-72	"	78	50	43	93	24
15 Years		1036	604	549	1153	640

*league leader
1959-60 1st All-Star Team at Left Wing & Arthur H. Ross Trophy
1961-62 " " " " " """ "
1962-63 2nd " " " " " "
1963-64 1st " " " " " "
1964-65 " " " " " " , Lady Byng & David A. Hart Trophies
1965-66 " " " " " " & Arthur H. Ross Trophy
1966-67 " " " " " "
1967-68 " " " " " "
1968-69 " " " " " "
1969-70 " " " " " "
1970-71 2nd " " " " " "
1971-72 1st " " " " " "

HURLEY, PAUL MICHAEL D-SR
Born: Melrose, Mass. July 12, 1946

Sea.	Club	Ga.	Go.	A.	P.	PM.
1968-69	Boston	1	0	1	1	0

INGARFIELD, EARL THOMPSON C-SL
Born: Lethbridge, Alta. Oct. 25, 1934

Sea.	Club	Ga.	Go.	A.	P.	PM.
1958-59	New York Rangers	35	1	2	3	10
1959-60	"	20	1	2	3	2
1960-61	" " "	66	13	21	34	18
1961-62	"	70	26	31	57	18
1962-63	" " "	69	19	24	43	40
1963-64	" " "	63	15	11	26	26
1964-65	" " "	69	15	13	28	40
1965-66	" " "	68	20	16	36	35
1966-67	" " "	67	12	22	34	12
1967-68	Pittsburgh	50	15	22	37	12
1968-69	" — Oakland	66	16	30	46	12
1969-70	Oakland	54	21	24	45	10
1970-71	"	49	5	8	13	4
13 Years		746	179	226	405	239

INGLIS, WILLIAM JOHN C-SL
Born: Ottawa, Ont. May 11, 1943

Sea.	Club	Ga.	Go.	A.	P.	PM.
1967-68	Los Angeles	12	1	1	2	0
1968-69	"	10	0	1	1	0
1970-71	Buffalo	14	0	1	1	4
3 Years		36	1	3	4	4

IRVINE, EDWARD AMOS LW-SL
Born: Winnipeg, Man. Dec. 8, 1944

Sea.	Club	Ga.	Go.	A.	P.	PM.
1963-64	Boston	1	0	0	0	0
1967-68	Los Angeles	73	18	22	40	26
1968-69	"	76	15	24	39	47
1969-70	" " — New York Rangers	75	11	16	27	38
1970-71	New York Rangers	76	20	18	38	137
1971-72	" "	78	15	21	36	66
6 Years		379	79	101	180	314

JARRETT, DOUGLAS WILLIAM D-SL
Born: London, Ont. April 22, 1944

Sea.	Club	Ga.	Go.	A.	P.	PM.
1964-65	Chicago	46	2	15	17	34
1965-66	"	66	4	12	16	71
1966-67	"	70	5	21	26	76
1967-68	"	74	4	19	23	48
1968-69	"	69	0	13	13	58
1969-70	"	72	4	20	24	78
1970-71	"	51	1	12	13	46
1971-72	"	78	6	23	29	68
8 Years		526	26	135	161	479

Sea. Club	Ga.	Go.	A.	P.	PM.
JARRETT, GARY WALTER LW-SL					
Born: Toronto, Ont. Sept. 3, 1942					
1960-61 Toronto	1	0	0	0	0
1966-67 Detroit	4	0	0	0	0
1967-68 "	68	18	21	39	20
1968-69 Oakland	63	22	23	45	22
1969-70 "	75	12	19	31	31
1970-71 "	75	15	19	34	40
1971-72 "	55	5	10	15	18
7 Years	341	72	92	164	131
JARRY, PIERRE JOSEPH REYNALD RW-SL					
Born: Montreal Que. March 30, 1949					
1971-72 New York Rangers – Toronto	52	6	7	13	33
JEFFREY, LAWRENCE JOSEPH C&LW-S					
Born: Zurich, Ont. Oct. 12, 1940					
1961-62 Detroit	18	5	3	8	20
1962-63 "	53	5	11	16	62
1963-64 "	58	10	18	28	87
1964-65 "	41	4	2	6	48
1965-66 Toronto	20	1	1	2	22
1966-67 "	56	11	17	28	27
1967-68 New York	47	2	4	6	15
1968-69 " "	75	1	6	7	12
8 Years	368	39	62	101	293
JIRIK, JAROSLAV LW-SL					
Born: Vojnuv, Mestac, Czechoslovakia, Dec. 10, 1939					
1969-70 St. Louis	3	0	0	0	0
JOHNSON, DANIEL DOUGLAS C&LW-SL					
Born: Winnipegosis, Man. Oct. 1, 1944					
1969-70 Toronto	1	0	0	0	0
1970-71 Vancouver	66	15	11	26	16
1971-72 " – Detroit	54	3	8	11	8
3 Years	121	18	19	37	24
JOHNSON, NORMAN JAMES LW&C-SL					
Born: Winnipeg, Man. Nov. 7, 1942					
1964-65 New York Rangers	1	0	0	0	0
1965-66 " " "	5	1	0	1	0
1966-67 " " "	2	0	0	0	0
1967-68 Philadelphia	13	2	1	3	2
1968-69 "	69	17	27	44	20
1969-70 "	72	18	30	48	17
1970-71 "	66	16	29	45	16
1971-72 " – Los Angeles	74	21	24	45	18
8 Years	302	75	111	186	73
JOHNSTON, JOSEPH JOHN LW-SL					
Born: Peterborough, Ont. March 3, 1949					
1968-69 Minnesota	11	1	0	1	6
1971-72 Oakland	77	15	17	32	107
2 Years	88	16	17	33	113
JOHNSTON, LAWRENCE ROY D-SR					
Born: Kitchener, Ont. July 20, 1943					
1967-68 Los Angeles	4	0	0	0	4
1971-72 Detroit	65	4	20	24	111
2 Years	69	4	20	24	115
JOHNSTON, MARSHALL D-SR					
Born: Birch Hills, Sask. June 6, 1941					
1967-68 Minnesota	7	0	0	0	0
1968-69 "	13	0	0	0	2
1969-70 "	28	0	5	5	14
1970-71 "	1	0	0	0	0
1971-72 Oakland	74	2	11	13	4
5 Years	123	2	16	18	20
JONES, JAMES WILLIAM D-SL					
Born: Espanola, Ont. July 27, 1949					
1971-72 Oakland	2	0	0	0	0
JONES, ROBERT CHARLES LW-SL					
Born: Espanola, Ont. Nov. 27, 1945					
1968-69 New York	2	0	0	0	0
JONES, RONALD PERRY D-SL					
Born: Vermilion, Alta. April 11, 1951					
1971-72 Boston	1	0	0	0	0
JOYAL, EDWARD ABEL C-SL					
Born: St Albert, Alta. May 8, 1940					
1962-63 Detroit	14	2	8	10	0
1963-64 "	47	10	7	17	6
1964-65 "	46	8	14	22	4
1965-66 Toronto	14	0	2	2	2
1967-68 Los Angeles	74	23	34	57	20

Sea. Club	Ga.	Go.	A.	P.	PM.
1968-69 " "	73	33	19	52	24
1969-70 " "	59	18	22	40	8
1970-71 " "	69	20	21	41	14
1971-72 " " – Philadelphia	70	14	7	21	25
9 Years	466	128	134	262	103
KANNEGIESSER, GORDON CAMERON D-SL					
Born: North Bay, Ont. Dec. 21, 1945					
1967-68 St. Louis	19	0	1	1	13
1971-72 " "	4	0	0	0	2
2 Years	23	0	1	1	15
KANNEGIESSER, SHELDON BRUCE D-SL					
Born: North Bay, Ont. Aug. 15, 1947					
1970-71 Pittsburgh	18	0	2	2	29
1971-72 "	54	2	4	6	47
2 Years	72	2	6	8	76
KARLANDER, ALLAN DAVID C-SL					
Born: Lac la Hache, British Columbia. Nov. 5, 1946					
1969-70 Detroit	41	5	10	15	6
1970-71 "	23	1	4	5	10
1971-72 "	71	15	20	35	29
3 Years	135	21	34	55	45
KEARNS, DENNIS McALEER D-SL					
Born: Kingston, Ont. Sept. 27, 1945					
1971-72 Vancouver	73	3	26	29	59
KEENAN, LAWRENCE CHRISTOPHER LW-SL					
Born: North Bay, Ont. Oct. 1, 1940					
1961-62 Toronto	2	0	0	0	0
1967-68 St. Louis	40	12	8	20	4
1968-69 " "	47	5	9	14	6
1969-70 " "	56	10	23	33	8
1970-71 " " – Buffalo	61	8	23	31	6
1971-72 Buffalo – Philadelphia	28	3	1	4	4
6 Years	234	38	64	102	28
KEHOE, RICKY THOMAS "RICK" RW-SR					
Born: Windsor, Ont. July 15, 1951					
1971-72 Toronto	38	8	8	16	4
KELLY, ROBERT JAMES LW-SL					
Born: Oakville, Ont. Nov. 25, 1950					
1970-71 Philadelphia	76	14	18	32	70
1971-72 "	78	14	15	29	157
2 Years	154	28	33	61	227
KENNEDY, FORBES TAYLOR C-SL					
Born: Dorchester, N. Bruns. Aug. 18, 1935					
1956-57 Chicago	69	8	13	21	102
1957-58 Detroit	70	11	16	27	135
1958-59 "	67	1	4	5	49
1959-60 "	17	1	2	3	8
1961-62 "	14	1	0	1	8
1962-63 Boston	49	12	18	30	46
1963-64 "	70	8	17	25	95
1964-65 "	52	6	4	10	41
1965-66 "	50	4	6	10	55
1967-68 Philadelphia	73	10	18	28	130
1968-69 " – Toronto	72	8	10	18	*219
11 Years	603	70	108	178	888
*League Leader					
KEON, DAVID MICHAEL C-SL					
Born: Noranda, Que. March 22, 1940					
1960-61 Toronto	70	20	25	45	6
1961-62 "	64	26	35	61	2
1962-63 "	68	28	28	56	2
1963-64 "	70	23	37	60	6
1964-65 "	65	21	29	50	10
1965-66 "	69	24	30	54	4
1966-67 "	66	19	33	52	2
1967-68 "	67	11	37	48	4
1968-69 "	75	27	34	61	12
1969-70 "	72	32	30	62	6
1970-71 "	76	38	38	76	4
1971-72 "	72	18	30	48	4
12 Years	834	287	386	673	62
1960-61 Frank Calder Memorial Trophy					
1961-62 2nd All-Star Team at Centre & Lady Byng Memorial Trophy					
1962-63 Lady Byng Memorial Trophy					
1970-71 2nd All-Star Team at Centre					
KESSELL, RICHARD JOHN LW&C-SL					
Born: Toronto, Ont. July 27, 1949					
1969-70 Pittsburgh	8	1	2	3	2
1970-71 "	6	0	2	2	2
1971-72 "	3	0	1	1	0
3 Years	17	1	5	6	4

Sea. Club	Ga.	Go.	A.	P.	PM.
KORAB, GERALD JOSEPH "JERRY" D-SL					
Born: Sault Ste. Marie, Ont. Sept. 15, 1948					
1970-71 Chicago	46	4	14	18	152
1971-72 "	73	9	5	14	95
2 Years	119	13	19	32	247
KOROLL, CLIFFORD EUGENE RW-SR					
Born: Canora, Sask. Oct. 1, 1946					
1969-70 Chicago	73	18	19	37	44
1970-71 "	72	16	34	50	85
1971-72 "	76	22	23	45	51
3 Years	221	56	76	132	180
KRAKE, PHILIP GORDON C-SR					
Born: North Battleford, Sask. Oct. 14, 1943					
1963-64 Boston	2	0	0	0	0
1965-66 "	2	0	0	0	0
1966-67 "	15	6	2	8	4
1967-68 "	68	5	7	12	13
1968-69 Los Angeles	30	3	9	12	11
1969-70 " "	58	5	17	22	86
1970-71 Buffalo	74	4	5	9	68
7 Years	249	23	40	63	182
KRULICKI, JAMES JOHN RW-SL					
Born: Kitchener, Ont. March 9, 1948					
1970-71 New York Rangers – Detroit	41	0	3	3	6
KURTENBACH, ORLAND JOHN C-SL					
Born: Cudworth, Sask. Sept. 7, 1936					
1960-61 New York Rangers	10	0	6	6	2
1961-62 Boston	8	0	0	0	6
1963-64 "	70	12	25	37	91
1964-65 "	64	6	20	26	86
1965-66 Toronto	70	9	6	15	54
1966-67 New York Rangers	60	11	25	36	58
1967-68 " " "	73	15	20	35	82
1968-69 " " "	2	0	0	0	2
1969-70 " " "	53	4	10	14	47
1970-71 Vancouver	52	21	32	53	84
1971-72 "	78	24	37	61	48
11 Years	540	102	181	283	560
LABOSSIERE, WILLIAM GORDON C-SR					
Born: St. Boniface, Man. Jan. 2, 1940					
1963-64 New York Rangers	15	0	0	0	12
1964-65 " " "	1	0	0	0	0
1967-68 Los Angeles	68	13	27	40	31
1968-69 " "	48	10	18	28	12
1970-71 " – Minnesota	74	19	14	33	20
1971-72 Minnesota	9	2	3	5	0
6 Years	215	44	62	106	75
LABRE, YVON JULES D-SL					
Born: Sudbury, Ont. Nov. 29, 1949					
1970-71 Pittsburgh	21	1	1	2	19
LACOMBE, FRANCOIS D-SL					
Born: Lachine, Que. Feb. 24, 1948					
1968-69 Oakland	72	2	16	18	50
1969-70 "	2	0	0	0	0
1970-71 Buffalo	1	0	1	1	2
3 Years	75	2	17	19	52
LACROIX, ANDRE JOSEPH C-SL					
Born: Lauzon, Que. June 5, 1945					
1967-68 Philadelphia	18	6	8	14	6
1968-69 "	75	24	32	56	4
1969-70 "	74	22	36	58	14
1970-71 "	78	20	22	42	12
1971-72 Chicago	51	4	7	11	6
5 Years	296	76	105	181	42
LAFLEUR, GUY DAMIEN RW-SR					
Born: Thurso, Que. Sept. 20, 1951					
1971-72 Montreal	73	29	35	64	48
LaFORGE, CLAUDE ROGER LW-SL					
Born: Sorel, Que. July 1, 1936					
1957-58 Montreal	5	0	0	0	0
1958-59 Detroit	57	2	5	7	18
1960-61 "	10	1	0	1	2

(continued)

Sea. Club	Ga.	Go.	A.	P.	PM.
1961-62 "	38	10	9	19	20
1963-64 "	17	2	3	5	4
1964-65 "	1	0	0	0	2
1967-68 Philadelphia	63	9	16	25	36
1968-69 "	2	0	0	0	0
8 Years	193	24	33	57	82
LAFRAMBOISE, PETER C-SL					
Born: Ottawa, Ont. Jan. 18, 1950					
1971-72 Oakland	5	0	0	0	0
LAGACE, JEAN-GUY D-SR					
Born: L'Abord a Plouffe, Que. Feb. 5, 1945					
1968-69 Pittsburgh	17	0	1	1	14
1970-71 Buffalo	3	0	0	0	2
2 Years	20	0	1	1	16
LAJEUNESSE, SERGE D-SR					
Born: Montreal, Que. June 11, 1950					
1970-71 Detroit	62	1	3	4	55
1971-72 "	7	0	0	0	20
2 Years	69	1	3	4	75
LALONDE, ROBERT PATRICK C&LW-SL					
Born: Montreal, Que. March 27, 1951					
1971-72 Vancouver	27	1	5	6	2
LAPERRIER, JOSEPH JACQUES HUGUES D-SL					
Born: Rouyn, Que. Nov. 22, 1941					
1962-63 Montreal	6	0	2	2	2
1963-64 "	65	2	28	30	102
1964-65 "	67	5	22	27	92
1965-66 "	57	6	25	31	85
1966-67 "	61	0	20	20	48
1967-68 "	72	4	21	25	84
1968-69 "	69	5	25	31	45
1969-70 "	73	6	31	37	98
1970-71 "	49	0	16	16	20
1971-72 "	73	3	25	28	50
10 Years	592	31	216	247	626
1963-64 2nd All-Star Team on Defence & Frank Calder Memorial Trophy					
1964-65 1st " " " " "					
1965-66 " " " " " & James Norris Memorial Trophy					
1969-70 2nd " " " " "					
LAPOINTE, GUY GERARD D-SL					
Born: Montreal, Que. March 18, 1948					
1968-69 Montreal	1	0	0	0	2
1969-70 "	5	0	0	0	4
1970-71 "	78	15	29	44	107
1971-72 "	69	11	38	49	58
4 Years	153	26	67	93	171
LAROSE, CLAUDE DAVID RW-SR					
Born: Hearst, Ont. March 2, 1942					
1962-63 Montreal	4	0	0	0	0
1963-64 "	21	1	1	2	43
1964-65 "	68	21	16	37	82
1965-66 "	64	15	18	33	67
1966-67 "	69	19	16	35	82
1967-68 "	42	2	9	11	28
1968-69 Minnesota	67	25	37	62	106
1969-70 "	75	24	23	47	109
1970-71 Montreal	64	10	13	23	90
1971-72 "	77	20	18	38	64
10 Years	551	137	151	288	671
LAUGHTON, MICHAEL FREDERIC C-SL					
Born: Nelson, British Columbia. Feb. 21, 1944					
1967-68 Oakland	35	2	6	8	38
1968-69 "	53	20	23	43	22
1969-70 "	76	16	19	35	39
1970-71 "	25	1	0	1	2
4 Years	189	39	48	87	101

Sea. Club	Ga.	Go.	A.	P.	PM
LAVENDER, BRIAN JAMES LW-SL					
Born: Edmonton, Alta. April 20, 1947					
1971-72 St. Louis	46	5	11	16	54
LAWSON, DANIEL MICHAEL RW-SR					
Born: Toronto, Ont. Oct. 30, 1947					
1967-68 Detroit	1	0	0	0	0
1968-69 " – Minnesota	62	8	10	18	25
1969-70 Minnesota	45	9	8	17	19
1970-71 "	33	1	5	6	2
1971-72 Buffalo	78	10	6	16	15
5 Years	219	28	29	57	61
LEACH, REGINALD JOSEPH RW-SR					
Born: Riverton, Man. April 23, 1950					
1970-71 Boston	23	2	4	6	0
1971-72 " – Oakland	73	13	20	33	19
2 Years	96	15	24	39	19
LEBLANC, JEAN-PAUL C-SL					
Born: South Durham, Que. Oct. 20, 1946					
1968-69 Chicago	6	1	2	3	0
LeCAINE, WILLIAM JOSEPH LW-SR					
Born: Moose Jaw, Sask. Mar. 11, 1940					
1968-69 Pittsburgh	4	0	0	0	0
LeCLERC, RENALD RW-SR					
Born: Ville de Vanier, Que. Nov. 12, 1947					
1968-69 Detroit	43	2	3	5	62
1970-71 "	44	8	8	16	43
2 Years	87	10	11	21	105
LEFLEY, CHARLES THOMAS C-SL					
Born: Winnipeg, Man. Jan. 20, 1950					
1970-71 Montreal	1	0	0	0	0
1971-72 "	16	0	2	2	0
2 Years	17	0	2	2	0
LEITER, ROBERT EDWARD C-SL					
Born: Winnipeg, Man. March 22, 1941					
1962-63 Boston	51	9	13	22	34
1963-64 "	56	6	13	19	43
1964-65 "	18	3	1	4	6
1965-66 "	9	2	1	3	2
1968-69 "	1	0	0	0	0
1971-72 Pittsburgh	78	14	17	31	18
6 Years	213	34	45	79	103
LEMAIRE, JACQUES GERARD LW-SL					
Born: Ville LaSalle, Que. Sept. 7, 1945					
1967-68 Montreal	69	22	20	42	16
1968-69 "	75	29	34	63	29
1969-70 "	69	32	28	60	16
1970-71 "	78	28	28	56	18
1971-72 "	77	32	49	81	26
5 Years	368	143	159	302	105
LEMIEUX, JACQUES LEONARD D-SR					
Born: Matane, Que. April 8, 1943					
1967-68 Los Angeles	16	0	3	3	8
1969-70 " "	3	0	1	1	0
2 Years	19	0	4	4	8
LEMIEUX, REAL GASTON LW-SL					
Born: Victoriaville, Que. Jan. 3, 1945					
1966-67 Detroit	1	0	0	0	0
1967-68 Los Angeles	74	12	23	35	60
1968-69 " "	75	11	29	40	68
1969-70 New York Rangers – Los Angeles	73	6	10	16	61
1970-71 Los Angeles	43	3	6	9	22
1971-72 " "	78	13	25	38	28
6 Years	344	45	93	138	239
LEMIEUX, RICHARD BERNARD C-SL					
Born: Temiscamingue, Que. April 19, 1951					
1971-72 Vancouver	42	7	9	16	4
LESUK, WILLIAM ANTON LW-SL					
Born: Moose Jaw, Sask. Nov. 1, 1946					
1968-69 Boston	5	0	1	1	0
1969-70 "	3	0	0	0	0
1970-71 Philadelphia	78	17	19	36	81
1971-72 " – Los Angeles	72	11	16	27	45
4 Years	158	28	36	64	126

Sea. Club	Ga.	Go.	A.	P.	PM
LEY, RICHARD NORMAN D-SL					
Born: Orillia, Ont. Nov. 2, 1948					
1968-69 Toronto	38	1	11	12	39
1969-70 "	48	2	13	15	102
1970-71 "	76	4	16	20	151
1971-72 "	67	1	14	15	124
4 Years	229	8	54	62	416
LIBETT, LYNN NICHOLAS LW-SL					
Born: Stratford, Ont. Dec. 9, 1945					
1967-68 Detroit	22	2	1	3	12
1968-69 "	75	10	14	24	34
1969-70 "	76	20	20	40	39
1970-71 "	78	16	13	29	25
1971-72 "	77	31	22	53	50
5 Years	328	79	70	149	160
LIDDINGTON, ROBERT ALLEN LW-SL					
Born: Calgary, Alta. Sept. 15, 1948					
1970-71 Toronto	11	0	1	1	2
LONSBERRY, DAVID ROSS LW-SL					
Born: Watson, Sask. Feb. 7, 1947					
1966-67 Boston	8	0	1	1	2
1967-68 "	19	2	2	4	12
1968-69 "	6	0	0	0	2
1969-70 Los Angeles	76	20	22	42	118
1970-71 "	76	25	28	53	80
1971-72 " " – Philadelphia	82	16	21	37	61
6 Years	267	63	74	137	275
LORENTZ, JAMES PETER C-SL					
Born: Waterloo, Ont. May 1, 1947					
1968-69 Boston	11	1	3	4	6
1969-70 "	68	7	16	23	30
1970-71 St. Louis	76	19	21	40	34
1971-72 " " – N. Y. Rangers – Buffalo	52	10	15	25	24
4 Years	207	37	55	92	94
LUCE, DONALD HAROLD C-SL					
Born: London, Ont. Oct. 2, 1948					
1969-70 New York Rangers	12	1	2	3	8
1970-71 " " – Detroit	67	3	12	15	18
1971-72 Buffalo	78	11	8	19	38
3 Years	157	15	22	37	64
LUNDE, LEONARD MELVIN C-SR					
Born: Campbell River, British Columbia. Nov. 13, 1936					
1958-59 Detroit	68	14	12	26	15
1959-60 "	66	6	17	23	10
1960-61 "	53	6	12	18	10
1961-62 "	23	2	9	11	4
1962-63 Chicago	60	6	22	28	30
1965-66 "	24	4	7	11	4
1967-68 Minnesota	7	0	1	1	0
1970-71 Vancouver	20	1	3	4	2
8 Years	321	39	83	122	75
MacDONALD, CALVIN PARKER LW-SL					
Born: Sydney, Nova Scotia June 14, 1933					
1952-53 Toronto	1	0	0	0	0
1954-55 "	62	8	3	11	36
1956-57 New York	45	7	8	15	24
1957-58 " "	70	8	10	18	30
1959-60 "	4	0	0	0	0
1960-61 Detroit	70	14	12	26	6
1961-62 "	32	5	7	12	8
1962-63 "	69	33	28	61	32
1963-64 "	68	21	25	46	25
1964-65 "	69	13	33	46	38
1965-66 Boston – Detroit	66	11	16	27	30
1966-67 Detroit	16	3	5	8	2
1967-68 Minnesota	69	19	23	42	22
1968-69 "	35	2	9	11	0
14 Years	676	144	179	323	253
MacDONALD, LOWELL WILSON RW-SR					
Born: New Glasgow, Pictou County, Nova Scotia. Aug. 30, 1941					
1961-62 Detroit	1	0	0	0	2
1962-63 "	26	2	1	3	8
1963-64 "	10	1	4	5	0
1964-65 "	9	2	1	3	0
1967-68 Los Angeles	74	21	24	45	12
1968-69 " "	58	14	14	28	10
1970-71 Pittsburgh	10	0	1	1	0
7 Years	188	40	45	85	32

Sea.	Club	Ga.	Go.	A.	P.	PM.
MacGREGOR, BRUCE CAMERON RW-SR						
Born: Edmonton, Alta. April 26, 1941						
1960-61	Detroit	12	0	1	1	0
1961-62	"	65	6	12	18	16
1962-63	"	67	11	11	22	12
1963-64	"	63	11	21	32	15
1964-65	"	66	21	20	41	19
1965-66	"	70	20	14	34	28
1966-67	"	70	28	19	47	14
1967-68	"	71	15	24	39	13
1968-69	"	69	18	23	41	14
1969-70	"	73	15	23	38	24
1970-71	" – New York Rangers	74	18	29	47	22
1971-72	New York Rangers	75	19	21	40	22
12 Years		775	182	218	400	199
MacKENZIE, JOHN BARRY D-SL						
Born: Toronto, Ont. Aug. 16, 1941						
1968-69	Minnesota	6	0	1	1	6
MacLEISH, RICHARD GEORGE LW&C-SL						
Born: Lindsay, Ont. Jan. 3, 1950						
1970-71	Philadelphia	26	2	4	6	19
1971-72	"	17	1	2	3	9
2 Years		43	3	6	9	28
MacMILLAN, WILLIAM STEWART RW-SL						
Born: Charlottetown, Prince Edward Island. March 7, 1943						
1970-71	Toronto	76	22	19	41	42
1971-72	"	61	10	7	17	39
2 Years		137	32	26	58	81
MacSWEYN, DONALD RALPH D-SR						
Born: Hawkesbury, Ont. Sept. 8, 1942						
1967-68	Philadelphia	4	0	0	0	0
1968-69	"	24	0	4	4	6
1969-70	"	17	0	0	0	4
1971-72	"	2	0	1	1	0
4 Years		47	0	5	5	10
MAGGS, DARRYL JOHN RW-SR						
Born: Victoria, British Columbia. April 6, 1949						
1971-72	Chicago	59	7	4	11	4
MAGNUSON, KEITH ARLEN D-SR						
Born: Saskatoon, Sask. April 27, 1947						
1969-70	Chicago	76	0	24	24	*213
1970-71	"	76	3	20	23	*291
1971-72	"	74	2	19	21	201
3 Years		226	5	63	68	705
*league leader						
MAHOVLICH, FRANCIS WILLIAM LW-SL						
Born: Timmins, Ont. Jan. 10, 1938						
1956-57	Toronto	3	1	0	1	2
1957-58	"	67	20	16	36	67
1958-59	"	63	22	27	49	94
1959-60	"	70	18	21	39	61
1960-61	"	70	48	36	84	131
1961-62	"	70	33	38	71	87
1962-63	"	67	36	37	73	56
1963-64	"	70	26	29	55	66
1964-65	"	59	23	28	51	76
1965-66	"	68	32	24	56	68
1966-67	"	63	18	28	46	44
1967-68	" – Detroit	63	26	26	52	32
1968-69	Detroit	76	49	29	78	38
1969-70	"	74	38	32	70	59
1970-71	" – Montreal	73	31	42	73	41
1971-72	Montreal	76	43	53	96	36
16 Years		1032	464	466	930	958

1957-58 Frank Calder Memorial Trophy
1960-61 1st All-Star Team at Left Wing
1961-62 2nd" " " " "
1962-63 1st" " " " "
1963-64 2nd" " " " "
1964-65 " " " " "
1965-66 " " " " "
1968-69 " " " " "
1969-70 " " " " "

Sea.	Club	Ga.	Go.	A.	P.	PM.
MAHOVLICH, PETER JOSEPH C&LW-SL						
Born: Timmins, Ont. Oct. 10, 1946						
1965-66	Detroit	3	0	1	1	0
1966-67	"	34	1	3	4	16
1967-68	"	15	6	4	10	13
1968-69	"	30	2	2	4	21
1969-70	Montreal	36	9	8	17	51
1970-71	"	78	35	26	61	181
1971-72	"	75	35	32	67	103
7 Years		271	88	76	164	385

Sea.	Club	Ga.	Go.	A.	P.	PM.
MAIR, JAMES McKAY D-SR						
Born: Schumacher, Ont. May 15, 1946						
1970-71	Philadelphia	2	0	0	0	0
1971-72	"	2	0	0	0	0
2 Years		4	0	0	0	0
MAKI, RONALD PATRICK "CHICO" RW-SR						
Born: Sault Ste. Marie, Ont. Aug. 17, 1939						
1961-62	Chicago	16	4	6	10	2
1962-63	"	65	7	17	24	35
1963-64	"	68	8	14	22	70
1964-65	"	65	16	24	40	58
1965-66	"	68	17	31	48	41
1966-67	"	56	9	29	38	14
1967-68	"	60	8	16	24	4
1968-69	"	66	7	21	28	30
1969-70	"	75	10	24	34	27
1970-71	"	72	22	26	48	18
1971-72	"	62	13	34	47	22
11 Years		673	121	242	363	321
MAKI, WAYNE LW-SL						
Born: Sault Ste. Marie, Ont. Nov. 10, 1944						
1967-68	Chicago	49	5	5	10	32
1968-69	"	1	0	0	0	0
1969-70	St. Louis	16	2	1	3	4
1970-71	Vancouver	78	25	38	63	99
1971-72	"	76	22	25	47	43
5 Years		220	54	69	123	178
MALONEY, DANIEL CHARLES LW-SL						
Born: Barrie, Ont. Sept. 24, 1950						
1970-71	Chicago	74	12	14	26	174
MANERY, RANDY NEAL D-SR						
Born: Leamington, Ont. Jan. 10, 1949						
1970-71	Detroit	2	0	0	0	0
1971-72	"	1	0	0	0	0
2 Years		3	0	0	0	0
MARCETTA, MILAN C-SL						
Born: Cadomin, Alb. Sept. 19, 1936						
1967-68	Minnesota	36	4	13	17	6
1968-69	"	18	3	2	5	4
2 Years		54	7	15	22	10
MARCHINKO, BRIAN NICHOLAS WAYNE C-SR						
Born: Weyburn, Sask. Aug. 2, 1948						
1970-71	Toronto	2	0	0	0	0
1971-72	"	3	0	0	0	0
2 Years		5	0	0	0	0
MARCOTTE, DONALD MICHEL LW-SL						
Born: Arthabaska, Que. April 15, 1947						
1965-66	Boston	1	0	0	0	0
1968-69	"	7	1	0	1	2
1969-70	"	35	9	3	12	14
1970-71	"	75	15	13	28	30
1971-72	"	47	6	4	10	12
5 Years		165	31	20	51	58
MAROTTE, JEAN GILLES D-SL						
Born: Verdun, Que. June 7, 1945						
1965-66	Boston	51	3	17	20	52
1966-67	"	67	7	8	15	112
1967-68	Chicago	73	0	21	21	122
1968-69	"	68	5	29	34	120
1969-70	" – Los Angeles	72	5	19	24	84
1970-71	Los Angeles	78	6	27	33	96
1971-72	"	72	10	24	34	83
7 Years		481	36	145	181	669
MARSH, GARY ARTHUR LW-SL						
Born: Toronto, Ont. Mar. 9, 1946						
1967-68	Detroit	6	1	3	4	4
1968-69	Toronto	1	0	0	0	0
2 Years		7	1	3	4	4
MARSHALL, ALBERT LEROY D-SL						
Born: Kamloops, British Columbia. Nov. 22, 1943						
1965-66	Detroit	61	0	19	19	45
1966-67	"	57	0	10	10	68
1967-68	" – Oakland	57	1	9	10	74
1968-69	Oakland	68	3	15	18	81
1969-70	"	72	1	15	16	109
1970-71	"	32	2	6	8	48
1971-72	"	66	0	14	14	68
7 Years		413	7	88	95	493

Sea.	Club	Ga.	Go.	A.	P.	PM.
MARSHALL, DONALD ROBERT LW-SL						
Born: Verdun, Que. March 23, 1932						
1951-52	Montreal	1	0	0	0	0
1954-55	"	39	5	3	8	9
1955-56	"	66	4	1	5	10
1956-57	"	70	12	8	20	6
1957-58	"	68	22	19	41	14
1958-59	"	70	10	22	32	12
1959-60	"	70	16	22	38	4
1960-61	"	70	14	17	31	8
1961-62	"	66	18	28	46	12
1962-63	"	65	13	20	33	6
1963-64	New York Rangers	70	11	12	23	8
1964-65	" " "	69	20	15	35	2
1965-66	" " "	69	26	28	54	6
1966-67	" " "	70	24	22	46	4
1967-68	" " "	70	19	30	49	2
1968-69	" " "	74	20	19	39	12
1969-70	" " "	57	9	15	24	6
1970-71	Buffalo	62	20	29	49	6
1971-72	Toronto	50	2	14	16	0
19 Years		1176	265	324	589	127
1966-67 2nd All-Star Team at Left Wing						
MARTIN, HUBERT JACQUES C-SR						
Born: Noranda, Que. Dec. 9, 1943						
1961-62	Detroit	1	0	1	1	0
1963-64	"	50	9	12	21	28
1964-65	"	58	8	9	17	32
1965-66	" – Boston	51	17	12	29	10
1966-67	Boston	70	20	22	42	40
1967-68	Chicago	63	16	19	35	36
1968-69	"	76	23	38	61	73
1969-70	"	73	30	33	63	61
1970-71	"	62	22	33	55	40
1971-72	"	78	24	51	75	56
10 Years		582	169	230	399	376
1969-70 Bill Masterton Memorial Trophy						
MARTIN, RICHARD LIONEL LW-SL						
Born: Verdun, Que. July 26, 1951						
1971-72	Buffalo	73	44	30	74	36
MATTIUSSI, RICHARD ARTHUR D-SL						
Born: Smooth Rock Falls, Ont. May 1, 1938						
1967-68	Pittsburgh	32	0	2	2	18
1968-69	" – Oakland	36	1	11	12	30
1969-70	Oakland	65	4	10	14	38
1970-71	"	67	3	8	11	38
4 Years		200	8	31	39	124
McCALLUM, DUNCAN SELBY D-SR						
Born: Flin Flon, Man. March 29, 1940						
1965-66	New York Rangers	2	0	0	0	2
1967-68	Pittsburgh	32	0	2	2	36
1968-69	"	62	5	13	18	81
1969-70	"	14	0	0	0	16
1970-71	"	77	9	20	29	95
5 Years		187	14	35	49	230
McCANN, RICHARD LEO C-SL						
Born: Hamilton, Ont. May 27, 1944						
1967-68	Detroit	3	0	0	0	0
1968-69	"	3	0	0	0	0
1969-70	"	18	0	1	1	4
1970-71	"	5	0	0	0	0
1971-72	"	1	0	0	0	0
5 Years		30	0	1	1	4
McCORD, ROBERT LOMER D-SR						
Born: Matheson, Ont. Mar. 20, 1934						
1963-64	Boston	65	1	9	10	49
1964-65	"	43	0	6	6	26
1965-66	Detroit	9	0	2	2	16
1966-67	"	14	1	2	3	27
1967-68	Detroit – Minnesota	73	3	9	12	41
1968-69	Minnesota	69	4	17	21	70
6 Years		273	9	45	54	229
McCREARY, VERNON KEITH LW-SL						
Born: Sundridge, Ont. June 19, 1940						
1964-65	Montreal	9	0	3	3	4
1967-68	Pittsburgh	70	14	12	26	44
1968-69	"	70	25	23	48	42
1969-70	"	60	18	8	26	67
1970-71	"	59	21	12	33	24
1971-72	"	33	4	4	8	22
6 Years		301	82	62	144	203
McCREARY, WILLIAM EDWARD LW-SL						
Born: Sundridge, Ont. Dec. 2, 1934						
1953-54	New York Rangers	2	0	0	0	2
1954-55	" "	8	0	2	2	0
1957-58	Detroit	3	1	0	1	2
1962-63	Montreal	14	2	3	5	0
1967-68	St. Louis	70	13	13	26	22
1968-69	"	71	13	17	30	50
1969-70	"	73	15	17	32	16
1970-71	"	68	9	10	19	16
8 Years		309	53	62	115	108
McDONALD, ALVIN BRIAN LW-SL						
Born: Winnipeg, Man. Feb. 18, 1936						
1958-59	Montreal	69	13	23	36	35
1959-60	"	68	9	13	22	26
1960-61	Chicago	61	17	16	33	22
1961-62	"	65	22	18	40	8
1962-63	"	69	20	41	61	12
1963-64	"	70	14	32	46	19
1964-65	Boston	60	9	9	18	6
1965-66	Detroit	43	6	16	22	6
1966-67	"	12	2	0	2	2
1967-68	Pittsburgh	74	22	21	43	38
1968-69	St. Louis	68	21	21	42	12
1969-70	" "	64	25	30	55	8
1970-71	" "	20	0	5	5	6
1971-72	Detroit	19	2	3	5	0
14 Years		762	182	248	430	200
McDONALD, BRIAN HAROLD C-SR						
Born: Toronto, Ont. March 23, 1945						
1970-71	Buffalo	12	0	0	0	29
McDONOUGH, JAMES ALLISON RW-SR						
Born: Hamilton, Ont. June 6, 1950						
1970-71	Los Angeles	6	2	1	3	0
1971-72	" – Pittsburgh	68	10	13	23	16
2 Years		74	12	14	26	16
McINTYRE, LAWRENCE ALBERT D-SL						
Born: Moose Jaw, Sask. July 13, 1949						
1969-70	Toronto	1	0	0	0	0
McKAY, RAY OWEN D-SL						
Born: Edmonton, Alta. Aug. 22, 1946						
1968-69	Chicago	9	0	1	1	12
1969-70	"	17	0	0	0	23
1970-71	"	2	0	0	0	0
1971-72	Buffalo	39	0	3	3	18
4 Years		67	0	4	4	53
McKECHNIE, WALTER THOMAS JOHN C-SL						
Born: London, Ont. June 19, 1947						
1967-68	Minnesota	4	0	0	0	0
1968-69	"	58	5	9	14	22
1969-70	"	20	1	3	4	21
1970-71	"	30	3	1	4	34
1971-72	Oakland	56	11	20	31	40
5 Years		168	20	33	53	117
McKENNY, JAMES CLAUDE D-SR						
Born: Ottawa, Ont. Dec. 1, 1946						
1965-66	Toronto	2	0	0	0	2
1966-67	"	6	1	0	1	0
1967-68	"	5	1	0	1	0
1968-69	"	7	0	0	0	2
1969-70	"	73	11	33	44	34
1970-71	"	68	4	26	30	42
1971-72	"	76	5	31	36	27
7 Years		237	22	90	112	107
McKENZIE, BRIAN STEWART LW-SL						
Born: St. Catharines, Ont. March 16, 1951						
1971-72	Pittsburgh	6	1	1	2	4
McKENZIE, JOHN ALBERT RW-SR						
Born: High River, Alta. Dec. 12, 1937						
1958-59	Chicago	32	3	4	7	22
1959-60	Detroit	59	8	12	20	50
1960-61	"	16	3	1	4	13
1963-64	Chicago	45	9	9	18	50
1964-65	"	51	8	10	18	46
1965-66	New York Rangers – Boston	71	19	14	33	72
1966-67	Boston	69	17	19	36	98
1967-68	"	74	28	38	66	107
1968-69	"	60	29	27	56	99
1969-70	"	72	29	41	70	114
1970-71	"	65	31	46	77	120
1971-72	"	77	22	47	69	126
12 Years		691	206	268	474	917
1969-70 2nd All-Star Team at Right Wing						

Sea.	Club	Ga.	Go.	A.	P.	PM.

McMAHON, MICHAEL WILLIAM D-SL
Born: Quebec City, Que. Aug. 30, 1941

Sea.	Club	Ga.	Go.	A.	P.	PM.
1963-64	New York Rangers	18	0	1	1	16
1964-65	" " "	1	0	0	0	0
1965-66	" " "	41	0	12	12	34
1967-68	Minnesota	74	14	33	47	71
1968-69	" – Chicago	63	0	19	19	27
1969-70	Detroit – Pittsburgh	14	1	3	4	19
1970-71	Buffalo	12	0	0	0	4
1971-72	New York Rangers	1	0	0	0	0
8 Years		224	15	68	83	171

MEEHAN, GERALD MARCUS C-SL
Born: Toronto, Ont. Sept. 3, 1946

Sea.	Club	Ga.	Go.	A.	P.	PM.
1968-69	Toronto – Philadelphia	37	0	5	5	6
1970-71	Buffalo	77	24	31	55	8
1971-72	"	77	19	27	46	12
3 Years		191	43	63	106	26

MEISSNER, BARRIE MICHAEL LW-SL
Born: Unity, Sask. July 26, 1946

Sea.	Club	Ga.	Go.	A.	P.	PM.
1967-68	Minnesota	1	0	0	0	2
1968-69	"	5	0	1	1	2
2 Years		6	0	1	1	4

MENARD, HOWARD HUBERT C-SR
Born: Timmins, Ont. April 28, 1942

Sea.	Club	Ga.	Go.	A.	P.	PM.
1963-64	Detroit	3	0	0	0	0
1967-68	Los Angeles	35	9	15	24	32
1968-69	"	56	10	17	27	31
1969-70	Chicago – Oakland	57	4	10	14	24
4 Years		151	23	42	65	87

MICKEY, ROBERT LARRY RW-SR
Born: Lacombe, Alta. Oct. 21, 1943

Sea.	Club	Ga.	Go.	A.	P.	PM.
1964-65	Chicago	1	0	0	0	0
1965-66	New York Rangers	7	0	0	0	2
1966-67	" "	8	0	0	0	0
1967-68	" "	4	0	2	2	0
1968-69	Toronto	55	8	19	27	43
1969-70	Montreal	21	4	4	8	4
1970-71	Los Angeles	65	6	12	18	46
1971-72	Philadelphia – Buffalo	18	1	3	4	8
8 Years		179	19	40	59	103

MIKITA (GVOTHOVA), STANISLAUS C-SR
Born: Sokolce, Czechoslovakia. May 20, 1940

Sea.	Club	Ga.	Go.	A.	P.	PM.
1958-59	Chicago	3	0	1	1	4
1959-60	"	67	8	18	26	119
1960-61	"	66	19	34	53	100
1961-62	"	70	25	52	77	97
1962-63	"	65	31	45	76	69
1963-64	"	70	39	50	*89	146
1964-65	"	70	28	*59	*87	154
1965-66	"	68	30	*48	78	58
1966-67	"	70	35	*62	*97	12
1967-68	"	72	40	47	*87	14
1968-69	"	74	30	67	97	52
1969-70	"	76	39	47	86	50
1970-71	"	74	24	48	72	85
1971-72	"	74	26	39	65	46
14 Years		919	374	617	991	1006

*league leader
1961-62 1st All-Star Team at Centre
1962-63 " " " " " "
1963-64 " " " " " " & Arthur H. Ross Trophy
1964-65 2nd " " " " " " "
1965-66 1st " " " " "
1966-67 " " " " Lady Byng, David Hart & Ross Trophies
1967-68 " " " " Lady Byng, David Hart & Ross Trophies
1969-70 2nd " " "

MIKKELSON, WILLIAM ROBERT D-SL
Born: Neepawa, Man. May 21, 1948

Sea.	Club	Ga.	Go.	A.	P.	PM.
1971-72	Los Angeles	15	0	1	1	6

MILLER, THOMAS WILLIAM C-SL
Born: Kitchener, Ont. March 31, 1947

Sea.	Club	Ga.	Go.	A.	P.	PM.
1970-71	Detroit	29	1	7	8	9

MISZUK, JOHN STANLEY D-SL
Born: Naliboki, Poland. Sept. 29, 1940

Sea.	Club	Ga.	Go.	A.	P.	PM.
1963-64	Detroit	42	0	2	2	30
1965-66	Chicago	2	1	1	2	2
1966-67	"	3	0	0	0	0
1967-68	Philadelphia	74	5	17	22	79
1968-69	"	66	1	13	14	70
1969-70	Minnesota	50	0	6	6	51
6 Years		237	7	39	46	232

MOHNS, DOUGLAS ALLEN D&LW-SL
Born: Capreol, Ont. Dec. 13, 1933

Sea.	Club	Ga.	Go.	A.	P.	PM.
1953-54	Boston	70	13	14	27	27
1954-55	"	70	14	18	32	82
1955-56	"	64	10	8	18	48
1956-57	"	68	6	34	40	89
1957-58	"	54	5	16	21	28
1958-59	"	47	6	24	30	40
1959-60	"	65	20	25	45	62
1960-61	"	65	12	21	33	63
1961-62	"	69	16	29	45	74
1962-63	"	68	7	23	30	63
1963-64	"	70	9	17	26	95
1964-65	Chicago	49	13	20	33	84
1965-66	"	70	22	27	49	63
1966-67	"	61	25	35	60	58
1967-68	"	65	24	29	53	53
1968-69	"	65	22	19	41	47
1969-70	"	66	6	27	33	46
1970-71	" – Minnesota	56	6	11	17	30
1971-72	Minnesota	78	6	30	36	82
19 Years		1220	242	427	669	1134

MONAHAN, GARRY MICHAEL LW&C-SL
Born: Barrie, Ont. Oct. 20, 1946

Sea.	Club	Ga.	Go.	A.	P.	PM.
1967-68	Montreal	11	0	0	0	8
1968-69	"	3	0	0	0	0
1969-70	Detroit – Los Angeles	72	3	7	10	36
1970-71	Toronto	78	15	22	37	79
1971-72	"	78	14	17	31	47
5 Years		242	32	46	78	170

MONTEITH, HENRY GEORGE LW-SL
Born: Stratford, Ont. Oct. 2, 1945

Sea.	Club	Ga.	Go.	A.	P.	PM.
1968-69	Detroit	34	1	9	10	6
1969-70	"	9	0	0	0	0
1970-71	"	34	4	3	7	0
3 Years		77	5	12	17	6

MORRISON, GEORGE HAROLD LW-SL
Born: Toronto, Ont. Dec. 24, 1948

Sea.	Club	Ga.	Go.	A.	P.	PM.
1970-71	St. Louis	73	15	10	25	6
1971-72	" "	42	2	11	13	7
2 Years		115	17	21	38	13

MORRISON, JAMES STUART HUNTER D-SL
Born: Montreal, Que. Oct. 11, 1931

Sea.	Club	Ga.	Go.	A.	P.	PM.
1951-52	Boston – Toronto	31	0	0	3	6
1952-53	Toronto	56	1	8	9	36
1953-54	"	60	9	11	20	51
1954-55	"	70	5	12	17	84
1955-56	"	63	2	17	19	77
1956-57	"	63	3	17	20	44
1957-58	"	70	3	21	24	62
1958-59	Boston	70	8	17	25	42
1959-60	Detroit	70	3	23	26	62
1960-61	New York Rangers	19	1	6	7	6
1969-70	Pittsburgh	59	5	15	20	40
1970-71	"	73	0	10	10	32
12 Years		704	40	160	200	542

MORRISON, LEWIS RW-SR
Born: Gainsborough, Sask. Feb. 11, 1948

Sea.	Club	Ga.	Go.	A.	P.	PM.
1969-70	Philadelphia	66	9	10	19	19
1970-71	"	78	5	7	12	25
1971-72	"	58	5	5	10	26
3 Years		202	19	22	41	70

MULOIN, JOHN WAYNE D-SL
Born: Dryden, Ont. Dec. 24, 1941

Sea.	Club	Ga.	Go.	A.	P.	PM.
1963-64	Detroit	3	0	1	1	2
1969-70	Oakland	71	3	6	9	53
1970-71	" – Minnesota	73	0	14	14	38
3 Years		147	3	21	24	93

MURDOCH, ROBERT JOHN D-SR
Born: Kirkland Lake, Ont. Nov. 20, 1946

Sea.	Club	Ga.	Go.	A.	P.	PM.
1970-71	Montreal	1	0	2	2	2
1971-72	"	11	1	1	2	8
2 Years		12	1	3	4	10

MURPHY, MICHAEL JOHN RW-SR
Born: Toronto, Ont. Sept. 12, 1950

Sea.	Club	Ga.	Go.	A.	P.	PM.
1971-72	St. Louis	63	20	23	43	19

MURPHY, ROBERT RONALD LW-SL
Born: Hamilton, Ont. April 10, 1933

Sea.	Club	Ga.	Go.	A.	P.	PM.
1952-53	New York Rangers	15	3	1	4	0
1953-54	" " "	27	1	3	4	20
1954-55	" " "	66	14	16	30	36

(continued)

Sea.	Club	Ga.	Go.	A.	P.	PM.
1955-56	" " "	66	16	28	44	71
1956-57	" " "	33	7	12	19	14
1957-58	Chicago	69	11	17	28	32
1958-59	"	59	17	30	47	52
1959-60	"	63	15	21	36	18
1960-61	"	70	21	19	40	30
1961-62	"	60	12	16	28	41
1962-63	"	68	18	16	34	28
1963-64	"	70	11	8	19	32
1964-65	Detroit	58	20	19	39	32
1965-66	" – Boston	34	10	8	18	10
1966-67	Boston	39	11	16	27	6
1967-68	"	12	0	1	1	4
1968-69	"	60	16	38	54	26
1969-70	"	20	2	5	7	8
18 Years		889	205	274	479	460

MURRAY, KENNETH R. D-SR
Born: Toronto, Ont. Jan. 22, 1948

Sea.	Club	Ga.	Go.	A.	P.	PM.
1969-70	Toronto	1	0	1	1	2
1970-71	"	4	0	0	0	0
2 Years		5	0	1	1	2

MURRAY, RANDALL D-SR
Born: Chatham, Ont. Aug. 24, 1945

Sea.	Club	Ga.	Go.	A.	P.	PM.
1969-70	Toronto	3	0	0	0	2

MYERS, HAROLD ROBERT LW-SL
Born: Edmonton, Alta. July 28, 1947

Sea.	Club	Ga.	Go.	A.	P.	PM.
1970-71	Buffalo	13	0	0	0	6

NANNE, LOUIS VINCENT D&RW-SR
Born: Sault Ste. Marie, Ont. June 2, 1941

Sea.	Club	Ga.	Go.	A.	P.	PM.
1967-68	Minnesota	2	0	1	1	0
1968-69	"	41	2	12	14	47
1969-70	"	74	3	20	23	75
1970-71	"	68	5	11	16	22
1971-72	"	78	21	28	49	27
5 Years		263	31	72	103	171

NEILSON, JAMES ANTHONY D-SL
Born: Big River, Sask. Nov. 28, 1940

Sea.	Club	Ga.	Go.	A.	P.	PM.
1962-63	New York Rangers	69	5	11	16	38
1963-64	" " "	69	5	24	29	93
1964-65	" " "	62	0	13	13	58
1965-66	" " "	65	4	19	23	84
1966-67	" " "	61	4	11	15	65
1967-68	" " "	67	6	29	35	60
1968-69	" " "	76	10	34	44	95
1969-70	" " "	62	3	20	23	75
1970-71	" " "	77	8	24	32	69
1971-72	" " "	78	7	30	37	56
10 Years		686	52	215	267	693

1967-68 2nd All-Star Team on Defence

NELSON, GORDON WILLIAM D-SL
Born: Kinistino, Sask. May 10, 1947

Sea.	Club	Ga.	Go.	A.	P.	PM.
1969-70	Toronto	3	0	0	0	11

NESTERENKO, ERIC PAUL RW-SR
Born: Flin Flon, Man. Oct. 31, 1933

Sea.	Club	Ga.	Go.	A.	P.	PM.
1951-52	Toronto	1	0	0	0	0
1952-53	"	35	10	6	16	27
1953-54	"	68	14	9	23	70
1954-55	"	62	15	15	30	99
1955-56	"	40	4	6	10	65
1956-57	Chicago	24	8	15	23	32
1957-58	"	70	20	18	38	104
1958-59	"	61	13	23	36	81
1959-60	"	68	16	18	34	71
1960-61	"	68	19	19	38	125
1961-62	"	68	15	14	29	97
1962-63	"	67	12	15	27	103
1963-64	"	70	7	19	26	93
1964-65	"	56	14	16	30	63
1965-66	"	67	15	25	40	58
1966-67	"	68	14	23	37	38
1967-68	"	71	11	25	36	37
1968-69	"	72	15	17	32	29
1969-70	"	67	16	18	34	26
1970-71	"	76	8	15	23	28
1971-72	"	38	4	8	12	27
21 Years		1219	250	324	574	1273

NEVIN, ROBERT FRANK RW-SR
Born: South Porcupine, Ont. March 18, 1938

Sea.	Club	Ga.	Go.	A.	P.	PM.
1957-58	Toronto	4	0	0	0	0
1958-59	"	2	0	0	0	2
1960-61	"	68	21	37	58	13
1961-62	"	69	15	30	45	10

(continued)

Sea.	Club	Ga.	Go.	A.	P.	PM.
1962-63	"	58	12	21	33	4
1963-64	" – New York Rangers	63	12	16	28	35
1964-65	New York Rangers	64	16	14	30	28
1965-66	" " "	69	29	33	62	10
1966-67	" " "	67	20	24	44	6
1967-68	" " "	74	28	30	58	20
1968-69	" " "	71	31	25	56	14
1969-70	" " "	68	18	19	37	8
1970-71	" " "	78	21	25	46	10
1971-72	Minnesota	72	15	19	34	6
14 Years		827	238	293	531	166

NIEKAMP, JAMES LAWRENCE D-SR
Born: Detroit, Mich. March 11, 1946

Sea.	Club	Ga.	Go.	A.	P.	PM.
1970-71	Detroit	24	0	2	2	27
1971-72	"	4	0	0	0	10
2 Years		28	0	2	2	37

NOLET, SIMON LAURENT RW-SR
Born: St. Odilon, Que. Nov. 23, 1941

Sea.	Club	Ga.	Go.	A.	P.	PM.
1967-68	Philadelphia	4	0	0	0	2
1968-69	"	35	4	10	14	8
1969-70	"	56	22	22	44	36
1970-71	"	74	9	19	28	42
1971-72	"	67	23	20	43	22
5 Years		236	58	71	129	110

NORIS, JOSEPH S. D-SR
Born: Denver, Col. Oct. 26, 1951

Sea.	Club	Ga.	Go.	A.	P.	PM.
1971-72	Pittsburgh	35	2	5	7	20

O'BRIEN, DENNIS FRANCIS D-SL
Born: Port Hope, Ont. June 10, 1949

Sea.	Club	Ga.	Go.	A.	P.	PM.
1970-71	Minnesota	27	3	2	5	29
1971-72	"	70	3	6	9	108
2 Years		97	6	8	14	137

O'DONOGHUE, DONALD FRANCIS RW-SL
Born: Kingston, Ont. Aug. 27, 1949

Sea.	Club	Ga.	Go.	A.	P.	PM.
1969-70	Oakland	68	5	6	11	21
1970-71	"	43	11	9	20	10
1971-72	"	14	2	2	4	4
3 Years		125	18	17	35	35

ODROWSKI, GERALD BERNARD D-SL
Born: Trout Creek, Ont. Oct. 4, 1938

Sea.	Club	Ga.	Go.	A.	P.	PM.
1960-61	Detroit	68	1	4	5	45
1961-62	"	69	1	6	7	24
1962-63	"	1	0	0	0	0
1967-68	Oakland	42	4	6	10	10
1968-69	"	74	5	1	6	24
1971-72	St. Louis	55	1	2	3	8
6 Years		309	12	19	31	111

O'FLAHERTY, GERARD JOSEPH RW-SL
Born: Pittsburgh, Penna. Aug. 31, 1950

Sea.	Club	Ga.	Go.	A.	P.	PM.
1971-72	Toronto	2	0	0	0	0

OLIVER, MURRAY CLIFFORD C-SL
Born: Hamilton, Ont. Nov. 14, 1937

Sea.	Club	Ga.	Go.	A.	P.	PM.
1957-58	Detroit	1	0	1	1	0
1959-60	"	54	20	19	39	16
1960-61	" – Boston	70	17	22	39	16
1961-62	Boston	70	17	29	46	20
1962-63	"	65	22	40	62	38
1963-64	"	70	24	44	68	41
1964-65	"	65	20	23	43	30
1965-66	"	70	18	42	60	30
1966-67	"	65	9	26	35	16
1967-68	Toronto	74	16	21	37	18
1968-69	"	76	14	36	50	16
1969-70	"	76	14	33	47	16
1970-71	Minnesota	61	9	23	32	8
1971-72	"	77	27	29	56	16
14 Years		894	227	388	615	281

ORBAN, WILLIAM TERRANCE LW-SL
Born: Regina, Sask. Feb. 20, 1944

Sea.	Club	Ga.	Go.	A.	P.	PM.
1967-68	Chicago	39	3	2	5	17
1968-69	" – Minnesota	66	5	11	16	43
1969-70	Minnesota	9	0	2	2	7
3 Years		114	8	15	23	67

O'REILLY, TERRY RW-SR
Born: Niagara Falls, Ont. June 7, 1951

Sea.	Club	Ga.	Go.	A.	P.	PM.
1971-72	Boston	1	1	0	1	0

ORR, ROBERT GORDON D-SL
Born: Parry Sound, Ont. March 20, 1948

Sea.	Club	Ga.	Go.	A.	P.	PM.
1966-67	Boston	61	13	28	41	102

(continued)

Sea.	Club	Ga.	Go.	A.	P.	PM.
1967-68	"	46	11	20	31	63
1968-69	"	67	21	43	64	133
1969-70	"	76	33	*87	*120	125
1970-71	"	78	37	*102	139	91
1971-72	"	76	37	*80	117	106
6 Years		404	152	360	512	620

*league leader
1966-67 2nd All-Star Team on Defence & Frank Calder Memorial Trophy
1967-68 1st " " " " & James Norris "
1968-69 " " " " " "
1969-70 " " " " " David A. Hart, Norris & Ross Trophies
1970-71 " " " " " " " " & James Norris "
1971-72 " " " " " " " " " "

O'SHEA, DANIEL PATRICK C-SL
Born: Toronto, Ont. June 15, 1945

1968-69	Minnesota	74	15	34	49	88
1969-70	"	75	10	24	34	82
1970-71	" – Chicago	77	18	19	37	26
1971-72	Chicago – St. Louis	68	9	12	21	39
4 Years		294	52	89	141	235

O'SHEA, KEVIN WILLIAM RW-SR
Born: Toronto, Ont. May 28, 1947

1970-71	Buffalo	41	4	4	8	8
1971-72	" – St. Louis	56	6	9	15	46
2 Years		97	10	13	23	54

PAIEMENT, JOSEPH WILFRID ROSAIRE RW-SR
Born: Earlton, Ont. Aug. 12, 1945

1967-68	Philadelphia	7	1	0	1	11
1968-69	"	27	2	4	6	52
1969-70	"	9	1	1	2	11
1970-71	Vancouver	78	34	28	62	152
1971-72	"	69	10	19	29	117
5 Years		190	48	52	100	343

PAPPIN, JAMES JOSEPH RW-SR
Born: Sudbury, Ont. Sept. 10, 1939

1963-64	Toronto	50	11	8	19	33
1964-65	"	44	9	9	18	33
1965-66	"	7	0	3	3	8
1966-67	"	64	21	11	32	89
1967-68	"	58	13	15	28	37
1968-69	Chicago	75	30	40	70	49
1969-70	"	66	28	25	53	68
1970-71	"	58	22	23	45	40
1971-72	"	64	27	21	48	38
9 Years		486	161	155	316	395

PARADISE, ROBERT H. D-SL
Born: St. Paul, Minn. April 22, 1944

1971-72	Minnesota	6	0	0	0	6

PARISE, JEAN-PAUL LW-SL
Born: Smooth Rock Falls, Ont. Dec. 11, 1941

1965-66	Boston	3	0	0	0	0
1966-67	"	18	2	2	4	10
1967-68	Toronto – Minnesota	44	11	17	28	27
1968-69	Minnesota	76	22	27	49	57
1969-70	"	74	24	48	72	72
1970-71	"	73	11	23	34	60
1971-72	"	71	19	18	37	70
7 Years		359	89	135	224	296

PARIZEAU, MICHEL GERARD LW-SL
Born: Montreal, Que. April 9, 1948

1971-72	St. Louis – Philadelphia	58	3	14	17	18

PARK, DOUGLAS BRADFORD D-SL
Born: Toronto, Ont. July 6, 1948

1968-69	New York Rangers	54	3	23	26	70
1969-70	" " "	60	11	26	37	98
1970-71	" " "	68	7	37	44	114
1971-72	" " "	75	24	49	73	130
4 Years		257	45	135	180	412

1969-70 1st All-Star Team on Defence
1970-71 2nd " " " "
1971-72 1st " " " "

PATRICK, CRAIG C&LW-SL
Born: Detroit, Mich. May 20, 1946

1971-72	Oakland	59	8	3	11	12

PELYK, MICHAEL JOSEPH D-SL
Born: Toronto, Ont. Sept. 29, 1947

1967-68	Toronto	24	0	3	3	55
1968-69	"	65	3	9	12	146
1969-70	"	36	1	3	4	37

(continued)

Sea.	Club	Ga.	Go.	A.	P.	PM.
1970-71	"	73	5	21	26	54
1971-72	"	46	1	4	5	44
5 Years		244	10	40	50	336

PERREAULT, GILBERT C-SL
Born: Victoriaville, Que. Nov. 13, 1950

1970-71	Buffalo	78	38	34	72	19
1971-72	"	76	26	48	74	24
2 Years		154	64	82	146	43

1970-71 Frank Calder Memorial Trophy

PERRY, BRIAN THOMAS LW-SL
Born: Aldershot, England. April 6, 1944

1968-69	Oakland	61	10	21	31	10
1969-70	"	34	6	8	14	14
1970-71	Buffalo	1	0	0	0	0
3 Years		96	16	29	45	24

PETERS, GARRY LORNE C-SL
Born: Regina, Sask. Oct. 9, 1942

1964-65	Montreal	13	0	2	2	6
1965-66	New York Rangers	63	7	3	10	42
1966-67	Montreal	4	0	1	1	2
1967-68	Philadelphia	31	7	5	12	22
1968-69	"	66	8	6	14	49
1969-70	"	59	6	10	16	69
1970-71	"	73	6	7	13	69
1971-72	Boston	2	0	0	0	2
8 Years		311	34	34	68	261

PETERS, JAMES STEPHEN C-SL
Born: Montreal, Que. June 20, 1944

1964-65	Detroit	1	0	0	0	0
1965-66	"	6	1	1	2	2
1966-67	"	2	0	0	0	0
1967-68	"	45	5	6	11	8
1968-69	Los Angeles	76	10	15	25	28
1969-70	"	74	15	9	24	10
6 Years		204	31	31	62	48

PICARD, JEAN-NOEL YVES D-SR
Born: Montreal, Que. Dec. 25, 1938

1964-65	Montreal	16	0	7	7	33
1967-68	St. Louis	66	1	10	10	142
1968-69	" "	67	5	19	24	131
1969-70	" "	39	1	4	5	88
1970-71	" "	75	3	8	11	119
1971-72	" "	15	1	5	6	50
6 Years		278	11	53	64	563

PINDER, ALLEN GERALD LW-SR
Born: Saskatoon, Sask. Sept. 15, 1948

1969-70	Chicago	75	19	20	39	41
1970-71	"	74	13	18	31	35
1971-72	Oakland	74	23	31	54	59
3 Years		223	55	69	124	135

PILOTE, PIERRE PAUL D-SL
Born: Kenogami, Que. Dec. 11, 1931

1955-56	Chicago	20	3	5	8	34
1956-57	"	70	3	14	17	117
1957-58	"	70	6	24	30	91
1958-59	"	70	7	30	37	79
1959-60	"	70	7	38	45	100
1960-61	"	70	6	29	35	*165
1961-62	"	59	7	35	42	97
1962-63	"	59	8	18	26	57
1963-64	"	70	7	46	53	84
1964-65	"	68	14	45	59	162
1965-66	"	51	2	34	36	60
1966-67	"	70	6	46	52	90
1967-68	"	74	1	36	37	69
1968-69	Toronto	69	3	18	21	46
14 Years		890	80	418	498	1251

*league leader
1959-60 2nd All-Star Team
1960-61 " " " "
1961-62 " " " "
1962-63 1st " " " & Norris Trophy
1963-64 " " " " " "
1964-65 " " " " "
1965-66 " " " "
1966-67 " " " "

PLAGER, BARCLAY GRAHAM D-SL
Born: Kirkland Lake, Ont. March 26, 1941

1967-68	St. Louis	49	5	15	20	*153
1968-69	" "	61	4	26	30	120
1969-70	" "	75	6	26	32	128
1970-71	" "	69	4	20	24	172

(continued)

Sea.	Club	Ga.	Go.	A.	P.	PM.
1971-72	" "	78	7	22	29	176
5 Years		332	26	109	135	749
*league leader						

PLAGER, ROBERT BRYAN D-SL
Born: Kirkland Lake, Ont. March 11, 1943

Sea.	Club	Ga.	Go.	A.	P.	PM.
1964-65	New York Rangers	10	0	0	0	18
1965-66	" " "	18	0	5	5	22
1966-67	" " "	1	0	0	0	0
1967-68	St. Louis	53	2	5	7	86
1968-69	" "	32	0	7	7	43
1969-70	" "	64	3	11	14	113
1970-71	" "	70	1	19	20	114
1971-72	" "	50	4	7	11	81
8 Years		298	10	54	64	477

PLAGER, WILLIAM RONALD D-SR
Born: Kirkland Lake, Ont. July 6, 1945

Sea.	Club	Ga.	Go.	A.	P.	PM.
1967-68	Minnesota	32	0	2	2	30
1968-69	St. Louis	2	0	0	0	2
1969-70	" "	24	1	4	5	30
1970-71	" "	36	0	3	3	45
1971-72	" "	65	1	11	12	64
5 Years		159	2	20	22	171

PLANTE, PIERRE RENALD RW-SR
Born: Valleyfield, Que. May 14, 1951

Sea.	Club	Ga.	Go.	A.	P.	PM.
1971-72	Philadelphia	24	1	0	1	15

PLEAU, LAWRENCE WINSLOW C&LW-SL
Born: Lynn, Mass. June 29, 1947

Sea.	Club	Ga.	Go.	A.	P.	PM.
1969-70	Montreal	20	1	0	1	0
1970-71	"	19	1	5	6	8
1971-72	"	55	7	10	17	14
3 Years		94	9	15	24	22

POLANIC, THOMAS JOSEPH D-SL
Born: Toronto, Ont. April 2, 1943

Sea.	Club	Ga.	Go.	A.	P.	PM.
1969-70	Minnesota	16	0	2	2	53
1970-71	"	3	0	0	0	0
2 Years		19	0	2	2	53

POLIS, GREGORY LINN LW-SL
Born: Westlock, Alta. Aug. 8, 1950

Sea.	Club	Ga.	Go.	A.	P.	PM.
1970-71	Pittsburgh	61	18	15	33	40
1971-72	"	76	30	19	49	38
2 Years		137	48	34	82	78

POPIEL, POUL PETER "PAUL" D-SL
Born: Sollested, Denmark, Feb. 28, 1943

Sea.	Club	Ga.	Go.	A.	P.	PM.
1965-66	Boston	3	0	1	1	2
1967-68	Los Angeles	1	0	0	0	0
1968-69	Detroit	62	2	13	15	82
1969-70	"	32	0	4	4	31
1970-71	Vancouver	78	10	22	32	61
1971-72	"	38	1	1	2	36
6 Years		214	13	41	54	212

POTVIN, JEAN RENE D-SR
Born: Ottawa, Ont. March 25, 1949

Sea.	Club	Ga.	Go.	A.	P.	PM.
1970-71	Los Angeles	4	1	3	4	2
1971-72	" " – Philadelphia	68	5	15	20	41
2 Years		72	6	18	24	43

PRATT, TRACY ARNOLD D-SL
Born: New York City, N.Y. March 8, 1943

Sea.	Club	Ga.	Go.	A.	P.	PM.
1967-68	Oakland	34	0	5	5	90
1968-69	Pittsburgh	18	0	5	5	34
1969-70	"	65	5	7	12	124
1970-71	Buffalo	76	1	7	8	179
1971-72	"	27	0	10	10	52
5 Years		220	6	34	40	479

PRENTICE, DEAN SUTHERLAND LW-SL
Born: Schumacher, Ont. Oct. 5, 1932

Sea.	Club	Ga.	Go.	A.	P.	PM.
1952-53	New York Rangers	55	6	3	9	20
1953-54	" " "	52	4	13	17	18
1954-55	" " "	70	16	15	31	20
1955-56	" " "	70	24	18	42	44
1956-57	" " "	68	19	23	42	38
1957-58	" " "	38	13	9	22	14
1958-59	" " "	70	17	33	50	11
1959-60	" " "	70	32	34	66	43
1960-61	" " "	56	20	25	45	17
1961-62	" " "	68	22	38	60	20
1962-63	" " " – Boston	68	19	34	53	22
1963-64	Boston	70	23	16	39	37
1964-65	"	31	14	9	23	12
1965-66	" – Detroit	69	13	31	44	18
1966-67	Detroit	68	23	22	45	18

Sea.	Club	Ga.	Go.	A.	P.	PM.
1967-68	"	69	17	38	55	42
1968-69	"	74	14	20	34	18
1969-70	Pittsburgh	75	26	25	51	14
1970-71	"	69	21	17	38	18
1971-72	Minnesota	71	20	27	47	14
20 Years		1281	363	450	813	458
1959-60	2nd All-Star Team at Left Wing					

PRICE, GARRY NOEL D-SL
Born: Brockville, Ont. Dec. 9, 1935

Sea.	Club	Ga.	Go.	A.	P.	PM.
1957-58	Toronto	1	0	0	0	5
1958-59	"	28	0	0	0	4
1959-60	New York Rangers	6	0	0	0	2
1960-61	" " "	1	0	0	0	2
1961-62	Detroit	20	0	1	1	6
1965-66	Montreal	15	0	6	6	8
1966-67	"	24	0	3	3	8
1967-68	Pittsburgh	70	6	27	33	48
1968-69	"	73	2	18	20	61
1970-71	Los Angeles	62	1	19	20	29
10 Years		300	9	74	83	173

PRONOVOST, JOSEPH JEAN DENIS RW-SR
Born: Shawinigan Falls, Que. Dec. 18, 1945

Sea.	Club	Ga.	Go.	A.	P.	PM.
1968-69	Pittsburgh	76	16	25	41	41
1969-70	"	72	20	21	41	45
1970-71	"	78	21	24	45	35
1971-72	"	68	30	23	53	12
4 Years		294	87	93	180	133

PRONOVOST, JOSEPH RENE MARCEL D-SL
Born: Lac a la Tortue (Turtle Lake), Que. June 15, 1930

Sea.	Club	Ga.	Go.	A.	P.	PM.
1950-51	Detroit	37	1	6	7	20
1951-52	"	69	7	11	18	50
1952-53	"	68	8	19	27	72
1953-54	"	57	6	12	18	50
1954-55	"	70	9	25	34	90
1955-56	"	68	4	13	17	46
1956-57	"	70	7	9	16	38
1957-58	"	62	2	18	20	52
1958-59	"	69	11	21	32	44
1959-60	"	69	7	17	24	38
1960-61	"	70	6	11	17	44
1961-62	"	70	4	14	18	38
1962-63	"	69	4	9	13	48
1963-64	"	67	3	17	20	42
1964-65	"	68	1	15	16	45
1965-66	Toronto	54	2	8	10	34
1966-67	"	58	2	12	14	28
1967-68	"	70	3	17	20	48
1968-69	"	34	1	2	3	20
1969-70	"	7	0	1	1	4
20 Years		1206	88	257	345	851
1957-58	2nd All-Star Team on Defence					
1958-59	" " " " " "					
1959-60	1st " " " " " "					
1960-61	" " " " " "					

PROVOST, JOSEPH ANTOINE CLAUDE RW-SR
Born: Montreal, Que. Sept. 17, 1933

Sea.	Club	Ga.	Go.	A.	P.	PM.
1955-56	Montreal	60	13	16	29	30
1956-57	"	67	16	14	30	24
1957-58	"	70	19	32	51	71
1958-59	"	69	16	22	38	37
1959-60	"	70	17	29	46	42
1960-61	"	49	11	4	15	32
1961-62	"	70	33	29	62	22
1962-63	"	67	20	30	50	26
1963-64	"	68	15	17	32	37
1964-65	"	70	27	37	64	28
1965-66	"	70	19	36	55	38
1966-67	"	64	11	13	24	16
1967-68	"	73	14	30	44	26
1968-69	"	73	13	15	28	18
1969-70	"	65	10	11	21	22
15 Years		1005	254	335	589	469
1964-65	1st All-Star Team at Right Wing					
1967-68	Bill Masterton Memorial Trophy					

PULFORD, ROBERT JESSE LW&C-SL
Born: Newton Robinson, Simcoe County, Ont. March 31, 1936

Sea.	Club	Ga.	Go.	A.	P.	PM.
1956-57	Toronto	65	11	11	22	32
1957-58	"	70	14	17	31	48
1958-59	"	70	23	14	37	53
1959-60	"	70	24	28	52	81
1960-61	"	40	11	18	29	41
1961-62	"	70	18	21	39	98
1962-63	"	70	19	25	44	49

(continued)

(continued)

Sea.	Club	Ga.	Go.	A.	P.	PM.
1963-64	"	70	18	30	48	73
1964-65	"	65	19	20	39	46
1965-66	"	70	28	28	56	51
1966-67	"	67	17	28	45	28
1967-68	"	74	20	30	50	40
1968-69	"	72	11	23	34	20
1969-70	"	74	18	19	37	31
1970-71	Los Angeles	59	17	26	43	53
1971-72	"	73	13	24	37	48
16 Years		1079	281	362	643	792

QUINN, JOHN BRIAN PATRICK D-SL
Born: Hamilton, Ont. Jan. 29, 1943

1968-69	Toronto	40	2	7	9	95
1969-70	"	59	0	5	5	88
1970-71	Vancouver	76	2	11	13	149
1971-72	"	57	2	3	5	63
4 Years		232	6	26	32	395

RAMSAY, CRAIG E. LW-SL
Born: Toronto, Ont. March 17, 1951

1971-72	Buffalo	57	6	10	16	0

RATELLE, JOSEPH GILBERT YVON JEAN C-SL
Born: Lac St. Jean, Que. Oct. 3, 1940

1960-61	New York Rangers	3	2	1	3	0
1961-62	" " "	31	4	8	12	4
1962-63	" " "	48	11	9	20	8
1963-64	" " "	15	0	7	7	6
1964-65	" " "	54	14	21	35	14
1965-66	" " "	67	21	30	51	10
1966-67	" " "	41	6	5	11	4
1967-68	" " "	74	32	46	78	18
1968-69	" " "	75	32	46	78	26
1969-70	" " "	75	32	42	74	28
1970-71	" " "	78	26	46	72	14
1971-72	" " "	63	46	63	109	4
12 Years		624	226	324	550	136

1970-71 Bill Masterton Memorial Trophy
1971-72 2nd All-Star Team at Centre & Lady Byng Memorial Trophy

RAVLICH, MATTHEW JOSEPH D-SL
Born: Sault Ste. Marie, Ont. July 12, 1938

1962-63	Boston	2	1	0	1	0
1964-65	Chicago	61	3	16	19	80
1965-66	"	62	0	16	16	78
1966-67	"	62	0	3	3	39
1968-69	"	60	2	12	14	57
1969-70	Detroit — Los Angeles	67	3	13	16	67
1970-71	Los Angeles	66	3	16	19	41
1971-72	Boston	25	0	1	1	2
8 Years		405	12	77	89	364

REAUME, MARC AVELLIN D-SL
Born: LaSalle, Ont. Feb. 7, 1934

1954-55	Toronto	1	0	0	0	4
1955-56	"	48	0	12	12	50
1956-57	"	63	6	14	20	81
1957-58	"	68	1	7	8	49
1958-59	"	51	1	5	6	67
1959-60	" — Detroit	45	0	2	2	8
1960-61	Detroit	38	0	1	1	8
1963-64	Montreal	3	0	0	0	2
1970-71	Vancouver	27	0	2	2	4
9 Years		344	8	43	51	273

REDMOND, MICHAEL EDWARD RW-SR
Born: Kirkland Lake, Ont. Dec. 27, 1947

1967-68	Montreal	41	6	5	11	4
1968-69	"	65	9	15	24	12
1969-70	"	75	27	27	54	61
1970-71	" — Detroit	61	20	23	43	42
1971-72	Detroit	78	42	29	71	34
5 Years		320	104	99	203	153

REDMOND, RICHARD D-SL
Born: Kirkland Lake, Ont. Aug. 14, 1949

1969-70	Minnesota	7	0	1	1	4
1970-71	" — Oakland	20	2	6	8	28
1971-72	Oakland	74	10	35	45	76
3 Years		101	12	42	54	108

REID, ALLAN THOMAS D-SL
Born: Fort Erie, Ont. June 24, 1946

1967-68	Chicago	56	0	4	4	25
1968-69	" — Minnesota	48	0	7	7	50
1969-70	Minnesota	66	1	7	8	51
1970-71	"	73	3	14	17	62
1971-72	"	78	6	15	21	107
5 Years		321	10	47	57	295

Sea.	Club	Ga.	Go.	A.	P.	PM.
	RICHARD, JOSEPH HENRI C-SR					
	Born: Montreal, Que. Feb. 29, 1936					
1955-56	Montreal	64	19	21	40	46
1956-57	"	63	18	36	54	71
1957-58	"	67	28	*52	80	56
1958-59	"	63	21	30	51	33
1959-60	"	70	30	43	73	66
1960-61	"	70	24	44	68	91
1961-62	"	54	21	29	50	48
1962-63	"	67	23	*50	73	57
1963-64	"	66	14	39	53	73
1964-65	"	53	23	29	52	43
1965-66	"	62	22	39	61	47
1966-67	"	65	21	34	55	28
1967-68	"	54	9	19	28	16
1968-69	"	64	15	37	52	45
1969-70	"	62	16	36	52	61
1970-71	"	75	12	37	49	46
1971-72	"	78	12	32	44	48
17 Years		1097	328	607	935	875

*league leader
1957-58 1st All-Star Team at Centre
1958-59 2nd " " " "
1960-61 " " " " "
1962-63 " " " " "

RIVERS, JOHN WAYNE RW-SR
Born: Hamilton, Ont. Feb. 1, 1942

1961-62	Detroit	2	0	0	0	0
1963-64	Boston	12	2	7	9	6
1964-65	"	58	6	17	23	72
1965-66	"	2	1	1	2	2
1966-67	"	8	2	1	3	6
1967-68	St. Louis	22	4	4	8	8
1968-69	New York	4	0	0	0	0
7 Years		108	15	30	45	94

RIZZUTO, GARTH ALEXANDER C-SL
Born: Trail, British Columbia. Sept. 11, 1947

1970-71	Vancouver	37	3	4	7	16

ROBERT, RENE PAUL RW-SR
Born: Trois Rivieres, Que. Dec. 31, 1948

1970-71	Toronto	5	0	0	0	0
1971-72	Pittsburgh — Buffalo	61	13	14	27	44
2 Years		66	13	14	27	44

ROBERTO, PHILLIP RW-SR
Born: Niagara Falls, Ont. Jan. 1, 1949

1969-70	Montreal	8	0	1	1	8
1970-71	"	39	14	7	21	76
1971-72	" — St. Louis	76	15	15	30	98
3 Years		123	29	23	52	182

ROBERTS, DOUGLAS WILLIAM D-SR
Born: Detroit, Mich. Oct. 28, 1942

1965-66	Detroit	1	0	0	0	0
1966-67	"	13	3	1	4	0
1967-68	"	37	8	9	17	12
1968-69	Oakland	76	1	19	20	79
1969-70	"	76	6	25	31	107
1970-71	"	78	4	13	17	94
1971-72	Boston	3	1	0	1	0
7 Years		284	23	67	90	292

ROBERTS, JAMES WILFRED RW-SR
Born: Toronto, Ont. April 9, 1940

1963-64	Montreal	15	0	1	1	2
1964-65	"	70	3	10	13	40
1965-66	"	70	5	5	10	20
1966-67	"	63	3	0	3	16
1967-68	St. Louis	74	14	23	37	66
1968-69	"	72	14	19	33	81
1969-70	"	76	13	17	30	51
1970-71	"	72	13	18	31	77
1971-72	" —Montreal	77	12	22	34	57
9 Years		589	77	115	192	410

ROBINSON, DOUGLAS GARNET LW-SL
Born: St. Catharines, Ont. Aug. 27, 1940

1964-65	Chicago — New York Rangers	61	10	23	33	10
1965-66	New York Rangers	51	8	12	20	8
1966-67	" "	1	0	0	0	0
1967-68	Los Angeles	34	9	9	18	6
1968-69	"	31	2	10	12	2
1970-71	" "	61	15	13	28	8
6 Years		239	44	67	111	34

Sea. Club	Ga.	Go.	A.	P.	PM.
ROBITAILLE, MICHAEL JAMES DAVID D-SR					
Born: Midland, Ont. Feb. 12, 1948					
1969-70 New York Rangers	4	0	0	0	8
1970-71 ” ” ” - Detroit	34	5	9	14	29
1971-72 Buffalo	31	2	10	12	22
3 Years	69	7	19	26	59
ROCHEFORT, LEON JOSEPH FERNAND RW-SR					
Born: Cap de la Madeleine, Que. May 4, 1939					
1960-61 New York Rangers	1	0	0	0	0
1962-63 ” ” ”	23	5	4	9	6
1963-64 Montreal	3	0	0	0	0
1964-65 ”	9	2	0	2	0
1965-66 ”	1	0	1	1	0
1966-67 ”	27	9	7	16	6
1967-68 Philadelphia	74	21	21	42	16
1968-69 ”	65	14	21	35	10
1969-70 Los Angeles	76	9	23	32	14
1970-71 Montreal	57	5	10	15	4
1971-72 Detroit	64	17	12	29	10
11 Years	400	82	99	181	66
ROLFE, DALE D-SL					
Born: Timmins, Ont. April 30, 1940					
1959-60 Boston	3	0	0	0	0
1967-68 Los Angeles	68	3	13	16	84
1968-69 ” ”	75	3	19	22	85
1969-70 ” ” – Detroit	75	3	18	21	89
1970-71 Detroit – New York Rangers	58	3	16	19	71
1971-72 New York Rangers	68	2	14	16	67
6 Years	347	14	80	94	396
ROMANCHYCH, LARRY BRIAN C-SR					
Born: Vancouver, British Columbia. Sept. 7, 1949					
1970-71 Chicago	10	0	2	2	2
RONSON, LEONARD KEITH LW-SL					
Born: Brantford, Ont. July 8, 1936					
1960-61 New York	13	2	1	3	10
1968-69 Oakland	5	0	0	0	0
2 Years	18	2	1	3	10
ROUSSEAU, JOSEPH JEAN-PAUL ROBERT RW-SR					
Born: St. Hyacinthe, Que. July 26, 1940					
1960-61 Montreal	15	1	2	3	4
1961-62 ”	70	21	24	45	26
1962-63 ”	62	19	18	37	15
1963-64 ”	70	25	31	56	32
1964-65 ”	66	12	35	47	26
1965-66 ”	70	30	*48	78	20
1966-67 ”	68	19	44	63	58
1967-68 ”	74	19	46	65	47
1968-69 ”	76	30	40	70	59
1969-70 ”	72	24	34	58	30
1970-71 Minnesota	63	4	20	24	12
1971-72 New York Rangers	78	21	36	57	12
12 Years	784	225	378	603	341
*league leader					
1961-62 Frank Calder Memorial Trophy					
1965-66 2nd All-Star Team at Right Wing					
RUPP, DUANE EDWARD FRANKLIN D-SL					
Born: MacNutt, Sask. March 29, 1938					
1962-63 New York Rangers	2	0	0	0	0
1964-65 Toronto	2	0	0	0	0
1965-66 ”	2	0	1	1	0
1966-67 ”	3	0	0	0	0
1967-68 ”	71	1	8	9	42
1968-69 Minnesota – Pittsburgh	59	5	11	16	32
1969-70 Pittsburgh	64	2	14	16	18
1970-71 ”	59	5	28	33	34
1971-72 ”	34	4	18	22	32
9 Years	296	17	80	97	158
SABOURIN, GARY BRUCE RW-SR					
Born: Parry Sound, Ont. Dec. 4, 1943					
1967-68 St. Louis	50	13	10	23	50
1968-69 ” ”	75	25	23	48	58
1969-70 ” ”	72	28	14	42	61
1970-71 ” ”	59	14	17	31	56
1971-72 ” ”	77	28	17	45	52
5 Years	333	108	81	189	277

Sea. Club	Ga.	Go.	A.	P.	PM.
ST. MARSEILLE, FRANCIS LEO RW-SR					
Born: Levack, Ont. Dec. 14, 1939					
1967-68 St. Louis	57	16	16	32	12
1968-69 ” ”	72	12	26	38	22
1969-70 ” ”	74	16	43	59	18
1970-71 ” ”	77	19	32	51	26
1971-72 ” ”	78	16	36	52	32
5 Years	358	79	153	232	110
SALESKI, DONALD RW-SR					
Born: Moose Jaw, Sask. Nov. 10, 1949					
1971-72 Philadelphia	1	0	0	0	0
SANDERSON, DEREK MICHAEL C-SL					
Born: Niagara Falls, Ont. June 16, 1946					
1965-66 Boston	2	0	0	0	0
1966-67 ”	2	0	0	0	0
1967-68 ”	71	24	25	49	98
1968-69 ”	61	26	22	48	146
1969-70 ”	50	18	23	41	118
1970-71 ”	71	29	34	63	130
1971-72 ”	78	25	33	58	108
7 Years	335	122	137	259	600
1967-68 Frank Calder Memorial Trophy					
SARRAZIN, RICHARD RW-SR					
Born: St. Gabriel de Brandon, Que. Jan. 22, 1946					
1968-69 Philadelphia	54	16	30	46	14
1969-70 ”	18	1	1	2	4
1971-72 ”	28	3	4	7	4
3 Years	100	20	35	55	22
SATHER, GLEN CAMERON LW-SL					
Born: High River, Alta. Sept. 2, 1943					
1966-67 Boston	5	0	0	0	0
1967-68 ”	65	8	12	20	34
1968-69 ”	76	4	11	15	67
1969-70 Pittsburgh	76	12	14	26	114
1970-71 ” – New York Rangers	77	10	3	13	148
1971-72 New York Rangers	76	5	9	14	77
6 Years	375	39	49	88	440
SAVARD, SERGE A. D-SL					
Born: Montreal, Que. Jan. 22, 1946					
1966-67 Montreal	2	0	0	0	0
1967-68 ”	67	2	13	15	34
1968-69 ”	74	8	23	31	73
1969-70 ”	64	12	19	31	38
1970-71 ”	37	5	10	15	30
1971-72 ”	23	1	8	9	16
6 Years	267	28	73	101	191
SCHELLA, JOHN EDWARD D-SR					
Born: Port Arthur, Ont. May 9, 1947					
1970-71 Vancouver	38	0	5	5	58
1971-72 ”	77	2	13	15	166
2 Years	115	2	18	20	224
SCHINKEL, KENNETH CALVIN RW-SR					
Born: Jansen, Sask. Nov. 27, 1932					
1959-60 New York Rangers	69	13	16	29	27
1960-61 ” ” ”	38	2	6	8	18
1961-62 ” ” ”	65	7	21	28	17
1962-63 ” ” ”	69	6	9	15	15
1963-64 ” ” ”	4	0	0	0	0
1966-67 ” ” ”	20	6	3	9	0
1967-68 Pittsburgh	57	14	25	39	19
1968-69 ”	76	18	34	52	18
1969-70 ”	72	20	25	45	19
1970-71 ”	50	15	19	34	6
1971-72 ”	74	15	30	45	8
11 Years	594	116	188	304	147
SCHMAUTZ, CLIFFORD HARVEY RW-SR					
Born: Saskatoon, Sask. March 17, 1939					
1970-71 Buffalo – Philadelphia	56	13	19	32	33
SCHMAUTZ, ROBERT JAMES RW-SR					
Born: Saskatoon, Sask. March 28, 1945					
1967-68 Chicago	13	3	2	5	6

(continued)

Sea.	Club	Ga.	Go.	A.	P.	PM.
1968-69	"	63	9	7	16	37
1970-71	Vancouver	26	5	5	10	14
1971-72	"	60	12	13	25	82
4 Years		162	29	27	56	139

SCHOCK, DANIEL PATRICK LW-SL
Born: Terrace Bay, Ont. Dec. 30, 1948

1970-71	Boston – Philadelphia	20	1	2	3	0

SCHOCK, RONALD LAWRENCE C-SL
Born: Chapleau, Ont. Dec. 19, 1943

1963-64	Boston	5	1	2	3	0
1964-65	"	33	4	7	11	14
1965-66	"	24	2	2	4	6
1966-67	"	66	10	20	30	8
1967-68	St. Louis	55	9	9	18	17
1968-69	" "	67	12	27	39	14
1969-70	Pittsburgh	76	8	21	29	40
1970-71	"	71	14	26	40	20
1971-72	"	77	17	29	46	22
9 Years		474	77	143	220	141

SCHULTZ, DAVID LW-SL
Born: Waldheim, Sask. Oct. 14, 1949

1971-72	Philadelphia	1	0	0	0	0

SEGUIN, DANIEL G. LW-SL
Born: Sudbury, Ont. June 7, 1948

1970-71	Minnesota – Vancouver	36	1	6	7	50

SEILING, RODNEY ALBERT D-SL
Born: Elmira, Ont. Nov. 14, 1944

1962-63	Toronto	1	0	1	1	0
1963-64	New York Rangers	2	0	1	1	0
1964-65	" " "	68	4	22	26	44
1965-66	" " "	52	5	10	15	24
1966-67	" " "	12	1	1	2	6
1967-68	" " "	71	5	11	16	44
1968-69	" " "	73	4	17	21	75
1969-70	" " "	76	5	21	26	68
1970-71	" " "	68	5	22	27	34
1971-72	" " "	78	5	36	41	62
10 Years		501	34	142	176	357

SELBY, ROBERT BRITON LW-SL
Born: Kingston, Ont. March 27, 1945

1964-65	Toronto	3	2	0	2	2
1965-66	"	61	14	13	27	26
1966-67	"	6	1	1	2	0
1967-68	Philadelphia	56	15	15	30	24
1968-69	" – Toronto	77	12	15	27	42
1969-70	Toronto	74	10	13	23	40
1970-71	" – St. Louis	64	1	5	6	29
1971-72	St. Louis	6	0	0	0	8
8 Years		347	55	62	117	171
1965-66 Frank Calder Memorial Trophy						

SELWOOD, BRADLEY WAYNE D-SL
Born: Leamington, Ont. March 18, 1948

1970-71	Toronto	28	2	10	12	13
1971-72	"	72	4	17	21	58
2 Years		100	6	27	33	71

SHACK, EDWARD STEVEN PHILLIP LW&RW-SL
Born: Sudbury, Ont. Feb. 11, 1937

1958-59	New York Rangers	67	7	14	21	109
1959-60	" " "	62	8	10	18	110
1960-61	" " " – Toronto	67	15	16	31	107
1961-62	Toronto	44	7	14	21	62
1962-63	"	63	16	9	25	97
1963-64	"	64	11	10	21	128
1964-65	"	67	5	9	14	68
1965-66	"	63	26	17	43	88
1966-67	"	63	11	14	25	58
1967-68	Boston	70	23	19	42	107
1968-69	"	50	11	11	22	74
1969-70	Los Angeles	73	22	12	34	113
1970-71	" " – Buffalo	67	27	19	46	101
1971-72	Buffalo – Pittsburgh	68	16	23	39	46
14 Years		888	205	197	402	1268

Sea.	Club	Ga.	Go.	A.	P.	PM.

SHEEHAN, ROBERT RICHARD C-SL
Born: Weymouth, Mass. Jan. 11, 1949

1969-70	Montreal	16	2	1	3	2
1970-71	"	29	6	5	11	2
1971-72	Oakland	78	20	26	46	12
3 Years		123	28	32	60	16

SHIRES, JAMES ARTHUR LW-SL
Born: Edmonton, Alta. Nov. 15, 1945

1970-71	Detroit	20	2	1	3	22
1971-72	St. Louis	18	0	3	3	8
2 Years		38	2	4	6	30

SHMYR, PAUL D-SL
Born: Cudworth, Sask. Jan. 28, 1946

1968-69	Chicago	3	1	0	1	8
1969-70	"	24	0	4	4	26
1970-71	"	57	1	12	13	41
1971-72	Oakland	69	6	21	27	156
4 Years		153	8	37	45	231

SIMMONS, AL D-SL
Born: Winnipeg, Man. Sept. 25, 1951

1971-72	Oakland	1	0	0	0	0

SITTLER, DARRYL GLEN C-SL
Born: Kitchener, Ont. Sept. 18, 1950

1970-71	Toronto	49	10	8	18	37
1971-72	"	74	15	17	32	44
2 Years		123	25	25	50	81

SLY, DARRYL HAYWARD D-SR
Born: Collingwood, Ont. April 3, 1939

1965-66	Toronto	2	0	0	0	0
1967-68	"	17	0	0	0	4
1969-70	Minnesota	29	1	0	1	6
1970-71	Vancouver	31	0	2	2	10
4 Years		79	1	2	3	20

SMITH, BRIAN DESMOND LW-SL
Born: Ottawa, Ont. Sept. 6, 1940

1967-68	Los Angeles	58	10	9	19	33
1968-69	Minnesota	9	0	1	1	0
2 Years		67	10	10	20	33

SMITH, DALLAS EARL D-SL
Born: Hamiota, Man. Oct. 10, 1941

1959-60	Boston	5	1	1	2	0
1960-61	"	70	1	9	10	79
1961-62	"	7	0	0	0	10
1965-66	"	2	0	0	0	2
1966-67	"	33	0	1	1	24
1967-68	"	74	4	23	27	65
1968-69	"	75	4	24	28	74
1969-70	"	75	7	17	24	119
1970-71	"	73	7	38	45	68
1971-72	"	78	8	22	30	132
10 Years		492	32	135	167	573

SMITH, FLOYD ROBERT DONALD RW-SR
Born: Perth, Ont. May 16, 1935

1954-55	Boston	3	0	1	1	0
1956-57	"	23	0	0	0	6
1960-61	New York Rangers	29	5	9	14	0
1962-63	Detroit	51	9	17	26	10
1963-64	"	52	18	13	31	22
1964-65	"	67	16	29	45	44
1965-66	"	66	21	28	49	20
1966-67	"	54	11	14	25	8
1967-68	" – Toronto	63	24	22	46	14
1968-69	Toronto	64	15	19	34	22
1969-70	"	61	4	14	18	13
1970-71	Buffalo	77	6	11	17	46
1971-72	"	6	0	1	1	2
13 Years		616	129	178	307	207

SMITH, RICHARD ALLAN D-SL
Born: Hamilton, Ont. June 29, 1948

1968-69	Boston	48	0	5	5	29
1969-70	"	69	2	8	10	65
1970-71	"	67	4	19	23	44
1971-72	" – Oakland	78	3	16	19	72
4 Years		262	9	48	57	210

Sea.	Club	Ga.	Go.	A.	P.	PM.
SNELL, RONALD WAYNE RW-SR						
Born: Regina, Sask. Aug. 11, 1948						
1968-69	Pittsburgh	4	3	1	4	6
1969-70	"	3	0	1	1	0
2 Years		7	3	2	5	6
SNOW, WILLIAM ALEXANDER RW-SR						
Born: Glace Bay, N.S. Nov. 11, 1946						
1968-69	Detroit	3	0	0	0	2
SPECK, FREDERICK EDMONDSTONE C-SL						
Born: Thorold, Ont. July 22, 1947						
1968-69	Detroit	5	0	0	0	2
1969-70	"	5	0	0	0	0
1971-72	Vancouver	18	1	2	3	0
3 Years		28	1	2	3	2
SPEER, FRANCIS WILLIAM D-SL						
Born: Lindsay, Ont. March 20, 1942						
1967-68	Pittsburgh	68	3	13	16	44
1968-69	"	34	1	4	5	27
1969-70	Boston	27	1	3	4	4
1970-71	"	1	0	0	0	4
4 Years		130	5	20	25	79
SPENCER, BRIAN ROY LW-SL						
Born: Fort St. James, British Columbia. Sept. 3, 1949						
1969-70	Toronto	9	0	0	0	12
1970-71	"	50	9	15	24	115
1971-72	"	36	1	5	6	65
3 Years		95	10	20	30	192
SPRING, FRANKLIN PATRICK RW-SR						
Born: Cranbrook, British Columbia. Oct. 19, 1949						
1969-70	Boston	1	0	0	0	0
STACKHOUSE, RONALD LORNE D-SR						
Born: Haliburton, Ont. Aug. 26, 1949						
1970-71	Oakland	78	8	24	32	73
1971-72	" – Detroit	79	6	28	34	89
2 Years		157	14	52	66	162
STANFIELD, FREDERIC WILLIAM C-SL						
Born: Toronto, Ont. May 4, 1944						
1964-65	Chicago	58	7	10	17	14
1965-66	"	39	2	2	4	2
1966-67	"	10	1	0	1	0
1967-68	Boston	73	20	44	64	10
1968-69	"	71	25	29	54	22
1969-70	"	73	23	35	58	14
1970-71	"	75	24	52	76	12
1971-72	"	78	23	56	79	12
8 Years		477	125	228	353	86
STANFIELD, JAMES BOVIARD C-SL						
Born: Toronto, Ont. Jan. 1, 1947						
1969-70	Los Angeles	1	0	0	0	0
1970-71	" "	2	0	0	0	0
1971-72	" "	4	0	1	1	0
3 Years		7	0	1	1	0
STANKIEWICZ, MYRON LW-SL						
Born: Kitchener, Ont. Dec. 4, 1935						
1968-69	St. Louis – Philadelphia	35	0	7	7	36
STANLEY, ALLAN HERBERT D-SL						
Born: Timmins, Ont. Mar. 1, 1926						
1948-49	New York	40	2	8	10	22
1949-50	" "	55	4	4	8	58
1950-51	" "	70	7	14	21	75
1951-52	" "	50	5	14	19	52
1952-53	" "	70	5	12	17	52
1953-54	" "	10	0	2	2	11
1954-55	New York – Chicago	64	10	16	26	24
1955-56	Chicago	59	4	14	18	70
1956-57	Boston	60	6	25	31	45
1957-58	"	69	6	25	31	37
1958-59	Toronto	70	1	22	23	47
1959-60	"	64	10	23	33	22
1960-61	"	68	9	25	34	42
1961-62	"	60	9	26	35	24

(continued)

Sea.	Club	Ga.	Go.	A.	P.	PM.
1962-63	"	61	4	15	19	22
1963-64	"	70	6	21	27	60
1964-65	"	64	2	15	17	30
1965-66	"	59	4	14	18	35
1966-67	"	53	1	12	13	20
1967-68	"	64	1	13	14	16
1968-69	Philadelphia	64	4	13	17	28
21 Years		1244	100	333	433	792
1959-60 2nd All-Star Team on Defence						
1960-61	" " " " " "					
1965-66	" " " " " "					
STAPLETON, PATRICK JAMES D-SL						
Born: Sarnia, Ont. July 4, 1940						
1961-62	Boston	69	2	5	7	42
1962-63	"	21	0	3	3	8
1965-66	Chicago	55	4	30	34	52
1966-67	"	70	3	31	34	54
1967-68	"	67	4	34	38	34
1968-69	"	75	6	50	56	44
1969-70	"	49	4	38	42	28
1970-71	"	76	7	44	51	30
1971-72	"	78	3	38	41	47
9 Years		560	33	273	306	339
1965-66 2nd All-Star Team on Defence						
1970-71	" " " " " "					
1971-72	" " " " " "					
STEMKOWSKI, PETER DAVID C-SL						
Born: Winnipeg, Man. Aug. 25, 1943						
1963-64	Toronto	1	0	0	0	2
1964-65	"	36	5	15	20	33
1965-66	"	56	4	12	16	55
1966-67	"	68	13	22	35	75
1967-68	" – Detroit	73	10	21	31	86
1968-69	Detroit	71	21	31	52	81
1969-70	"	76	25	24	49	114
1970-71	" – New York Rangers	78	18	31	49	69
1971-72	New York Rangers	59	11	17	28	53
9 Years		518	107	173	280	568
STEWART, JOHN ALEXANDER LW-SL						
Born: Eriksdale, Man. May 16, 1950						
1970-71	Pittsburgh	15	2	1	3	9
1971-72	"	25	2	8	10	23
2 Years		40	4	9	13	32
STEWART, RALPH DONALD C-SL						
Born: Fort William, Ont. Feb. 12, 1948						
1970-71	Vancouver	3	0	1	1	0
STEWART, ROBERT HAROLD D-SL						
Born: Charlottetown, Prince Edward Island. Nov. 10, 1950						
1971-72	Boston – Oakland	24	1	2	3	59
STEWART, RONALD GEORGE RW-SR						
Born: Calgary, Alta. July 11, 1932						
1952-53	Toronto	70	13	22	35	29
1953-54	"	70	14	11	25	72
1954-55	"	53	14	5	19	20
1955-56	"	69	13	14	27	35
1956-57	"	65	15	20	35	28
1957-58	"	70	15	24	39	51
1958-59	"	70	21	13	34	23
1959-60	"	67	14	20	34	28
1960-61	"	51	13	12	25	8
1961-62	"	60	8	9	17	14
1962-63	"	63	16	16	32	26
1963-64	"	65	14	5	19	46
1964-65	"	65	16	11	27	33
1965-66	Boston	70	20	16	36	19
1966-67	"	56	14	10	24	31
1967-68	St. Louis – New York Rangers	74	14	12	26	30
1968-69	New York Rangers	75	18	11	29	20
1969-70	" " "	76	14	10	24	14
1970-71	" " "	76	5	6	11	19
1971-72	Vancouver – New York Rangers	55	3	3	6	12
20 Years		1320	274	250	524	558
SUTHERLAND, WILLIAM FRASER C&LW-SL						
Born: Regina, Sask. Nov. 10, 1934						
1967-68	Philadelphia	60	20	9	29	6
1968-69	Toronto – Philadelphia	56	14	8	22	18
1969-70	Philadelphia	51	15	17	32	30
1970-71	" – St. Louis	69	19	20	39	41
1971-72	St. Louis – Detroit	14	2	4	6	4
5 Years		250	70	58	128	99
SWAIN, GARTH FREDERICK ARTHUR C-SL						
Born: Welland, Ont. Sept. 11, 1947						
1968-69	Pittsburgh	9	1	1	2	0

Sea.	Club	Ga.	Go.	A.	P.	PM.

SWARBRICK, GEORGE RAYMOND RW-SR
Born: Moose Jaw, Sask. Feb. 16, 1942

Sea.	Club	Ga.	Go.	A.	P.	PM.
1967-68	Oakland	49	13	5	18	62
1968-69	" – Pittsburgh	69	4	19	23	103
1969-70	Pittsburgh	12	0	1	1	8
1970-71	Philadelphia	2	0	0	0	0
4 Years		132	17	25	42	173

SZURA, JOSEPH BOLESLAW C-SL
Born: Ft. William, Ont. Dec. 18, 1938

Sea.	Club	Ga.	Go.	A.	P.	PM.
1967-68	Oakland	20	1	3	4	10
1968-69	"	70	9	12	21	20
2 Years		90	10	15	25	30

TALBOT, JEAN-GUY D-SL
Born: Cap de la Madeleine, Que. July 11, 1954-55

Sea.	Club	Ga.	Go.	A.	P.	PM.
1954-55	Montreal	3	0	1	1	0
1955-56	"	66	1	13	14	80
1956-57	"	59	0	13	13	70
1957-58	"	55	4	15	19	65
1958-59	"	69	4	17	21	77
1959-60	"	69	1	14	15	60
1960-61	"	70	5	26	31	143
1961-62	"	70	5	42	47	90
1962-63	"	70	3	22	25	51
1963-64	"	66	1	13	14	83
1964-65	"	67	8	14	22	64
1965-66	"	59	1	14	15	50
1966-67	"	68	3	5	8	51
1967-68	Minnesota – Detroit – St. Louis	59	0	7	7	16
1968-69	St. Louis	69	5	4	9	24
1969-70	"	75	2	15	17	40
1970-71	" – Buffalo	62	0	7	7	42
17 Years		1056	43	242	285	1006

1961-62 1st All-Star Team on Defence

TALLON, MICHAEL DALE LEE D-SL
Born: Noranda, Que. Oct. 19, 1950

Sea.	Club	Ga.	Go.	A.	P.	PM.
1970-71	Vancouver	78	14	42	56	58
1971-72	"	69	17	27	44	78
2 Years		147	31	69	100	136

TARDIF, MARC LW-SL
Born: Granby, Que. June 12, 1949

Sea.	Club	Ga.	Go.	A.	P.	PM.
1969-70	Montreal	18	3	2	5	27
1970-71	"	76	19	30	49	133
1971-72	"	75	31	22	53	81
3 Years		169	53	54	107	241

TAYLOR, EDWARD WRAY LW-SL
Born: Oak Lake, Man. Feb. 25, 1942

Sea.	Club	Ga.	Go.	A.	P.	PM.
1964-65	New York Rangers	4	0	0	0	4
1965-66	" " "	4	0	1	1	2
1966-67	Detroit	2	0	0	0	0
1967-68	Minnesota	31	3	5	8	34
1970-71	Vancouver	56	11	16	27	53
1971-72	"	69	9	13	22	88
6 Years		166	23	35	58	181

TERBENCHE, PAUL FREDERICK C-SL
Born: Cobourg, Ont. Sept. 16, 1945

Sea.	Club	Ga.	Go.	A.	P.	PM.
1967-68	Chicago	68	3	7	10	8
1970-71	Buffalo	3	0	0	0	2
1971-72	"	9	0	0	0	2
3 Years		80	3	7	10	12

THOMPSON, LORAN ERROL LW-SL
Born: Summerside, Prince Edward Island. May 28, 1950

Sea.	Club	Ga.	Go.	A.	P.	PM.
1970-71	Toronto	1	0	0	0	0

THOMSON, FLOYD HARVEY LW-SL
Born: Sudbury, Ont. June 14, 1949

Sea.	Club	Ga.	Go.	A.	P.	PM.
1971-72	St. Louis	49	4	6	10	48

TKACZUK, WALTER BOGDON C-SL
Born: Emsdetten, Germany. Sept. 29, 1947

Sea.	Club	Ga.	Go.	A.	P.	PM.
1967-68	New York Rangers	2	0	0	0	0
1968-69	" " "	71	12	24	36	28
1969-70	" " "	76	27	50	77	38
1970-71	" " "	77	26	49	75	48
1971-72	" " "	76	24	42	66	65
5 Years		302	89	165	254	179

TREMBLAY, JEAN-CLAUDE D-SL
Born: Bagotville, Que. Jan. 22, 1939

Sea.	Club	Ga.	Go.	A.	P.	PM.
1959-60	Montreal	11	0	1	1	0
1960-61	"	29	1	3	4	18
1961-62	"	70	3	17	20	18
1962-63	"	69	1	17	18	10
1963-64	"	70	5	16	21	24

(continued)

Sea.	Club	Ga.	Go.	A.	P.	PM.
1964-65	"	68	3	17	20	22
1965-66	"	59	6	29	35	8
1966-67	"	60	8	26	34	14
1967-68	"	73	4	26	30	18
1968-69	"	75	7	32	39	18
1969-70	"	58	2	19	21	7
1970-71	"	76	11	52	63	23
1971-72	"	76	6	51	57	24
13 Years		794	57	306	363	204

1967-68 2nd All-Star Team on Defence
1970-71 1st " " " " "

TREMBLAY, JOSEPH JEAN-GILLES LW-SL
Born: Montmorency, Que. Dec. 17, 1938

Sea.	Club	Ga.	Go.	A.	P.	PM.
1960-61	Montreal	45	7	11	18	4
1961-62	"	70	32	22	54	28
1962-63	"	60	25	24	49	42
1963-64	"	61	22	15	37	21
1964-65	"	26	9	7	16	16
1965-66	"	70	27	21	48	24
1966-67	"	62	13	19	32	16
1967-68	"	71	23	28	51	8
1968-69	"	44	10	15	25	2
9 Years		509	168	162	330	161

TROTTIER, GUY RW-SR
Born: Hull, Que. April 1, 1941

Sea.	Club	Ga.	Go.	A.	P.	PM.
1968-69	New York Rangers	2	0	0	0	0
1970-71	Toronto	61	19	5	24	21
1971-72	"	52	9	12	21	16
3 Years		115	28	17	45	37

UBRIACO, EUGENE STEPHEN LW&C-SL
Born: Sault Ste. Marie, Ont. Dec. 26, 1937

Sea.	Club	Ga.	Go.	A.	P.	PM.
1967-68	Pittsburgh	65	18	15	33	16
1968-69	" – Oakland	75	19	18	37	28
1969-70	Oakland – Chicago	37	2	2	4	6
3 Years		177	39	35	74	50

ULLMAN, NORMAN VICTOR ALEXANDER C-SL
Born: Provost, Alta. Dec. 26, 1935

Sea.	Club	Ga.	Go.	A.	P.	PM.
1955-56	Detroit	66	9	9	18	26
1956-57	"	64	16	36	52	47
1957-58	"	69	23	28	51	38
1958-59	"	69	22	36	58	42
1959-60	"	70	24	34	58	46
1960-61	"	70	28	42	70	34
1961-62	"	70	26	38	64	54
1962-63	"	70	26	30	56	53
1963-64	"	61	21	30	51	55
1964-65	"	70	*42	41	83	70
1965-66	"	70	31	41	72	35
1966-67	"	68	26	44	70	26
1967-68	" – Toronto	71	35	37	72	28
1968-69	Toronto	75	35	42	77	41
1969-70	"	74	18	42	60	37
1970-71	"	73	34	51	85	24
1971-72	"	77	23	50	73	26
17 Years		1187	439	631	1070	682

*league leader
1964-65 1st All-Star Team at Centre
1966-67 2nd " " " " "

UNGER, GARRY DOUGLAS C-SL
Born: Edmonton, Alta. Dec. 7, 1947

Sea.	Club	Ga.	Go.	A.	P.	PM.
1967-68	Toronto – Detroit	28	6	11	17	6
1968-69	Detroit	76	24	20	44	33
1969-70	"	76	42	24	66	67
1970-71	" – St. Louis	79	28	28	56	104
1971-72	St. Louis	78	36	34	70	104
5 Years		337	136	117	253	314

VAN IMPE, EDWARD CHARLES D-SL
Born: Montreal, Que. Sept. 25, 1945

Sea.	Club	Ga.	Go.	A.	P.	PM.
1966-67	Montreal	11	0	3	3	35
1967-68	"	31	1	1	2	31
1968-69	Oakland	76	15	27	42	151
1969-70	"	76	24	20	44	212
1970-71	"	42	10	16	26	91
1971-72	" – Boston	68	18	26	44	143
6 Years		304	68	93	161	663

VAN IMPE, EDWARD CHARLES C-SL
Born: Saskatoon, Sask. May 27, 1940

Sea.	Club	Ga.	Go.	A.	P.	PM.
1966-67	Chicago	61	8	11	19	111
1967-68	Philadelphia	67	4	13	17	141
1968-69	"	68	7	12	19	112
1969-70	"	65	0	10	10	117
1970-71	"	77	0	11	11	80
1971-72	"	73	4	9	13	78
6 Years		411	23	66	89	639

Sea. Club	Ga.	Go.	A.	P.	PM.
VASKO, ELMER D-SL					
Born: Duparquet, Que. Dec. 11, 1935					
1956-57 Chicago	64	3	12	15	31
1957-58 "	59	6	20	26	51
1958-59 "	63	6	10	16	52
1959-60 "	69	3	27	30	110
1960-61 "	63	4	18	22	40
1961-62 "	64	2	22	24	87
1962-63 "	64	4	9	13	70
1963-64 "	70	2	18	20	65
1964-65 "	69	1	10	11	56
1965-66 "	56	1	7	8	44
1967-68 Minnesota	70	1	6	7	45
1968-69 "	72	1	7	8	68
1969-70 "	3	0	0	0	0
13 Years	786	34	166	200	719
1962-63 2nd All-Star Team on Defence					
1963-64 " " " " " "					
VENERUZZO, GARY RAYMOND LW-SL					
Born: Fort William, Ont. June 28, 1943					
1967-68 St. Louis	5	1	1	2	0
1971-72 " "	2	0	0	0	0
2 Years	7	1	1	2	0
VOLMAR, DOUGLAS STEVEN RW-SR					
Born: Cleveland Heights, Ohio. Jan. 9, 1945					
1970-71 Detroit	2	0	1	1	2
1971-72 "	39	9	5	14	8
2 Years	41	9	6	15	10
WALL, ROBERT JAMES ALBERT D-SL					
Born: Elgin Mills, Ont. Dec. 1, 1942					
1964-65 Detroit	1	0	0	0	0
1965-66 "	8	1	1	2	8
1966-67 "	31	2	2	4	26
1967-68 Los Angeles	71	5	18	23	66
1968-69 " "	71	13	13	26	16
1969-70 " "	70	5	13	18	26
1970-71 St. Louis	25	2	4	6	4
1971-72 Detroit	45	2	4	6	9
8 Years	322	30	55	85	155
WALTON, MICHAEL ROBERT C-SL					
Born: Kirkland Lake, Ont. Jan. 3, 1945					
1965-66 Toronto	6	1	3	4	0
1966-67 "	31	7	10	17	13
1967-68 "	73	30	29	59	48
1968-69 "	66	22	21	43	34
1969-70 "	58	21	34	55	68
1970-71 " — Boston	45	6	15	21	31
1971-72 Boston	76	28	28	56	45
7 Years	355	115	140	255	239
WARD, RONALD LEON C-SR					
Born: Cornwall, Ont. Sept. 12, 1944					
1969-70 Toronto	18	0	1	1	2
1971-72 Vancouver	71	2	4	6	4
2 Years	89	2	5	7	6
WATSON, BRYAN JOSEPH D-SR					
Born: Bancroft, Ont. Nov. 14, 1942					
1963-64 Montreal	39	0	2	2	18
1964-65 "	5	0	1	1	7
1965-66 Detroit	70	2	7	9	133
1966-67 "	48	0	1	1	66
1967-68 Montreal	12	0	1	1	9
1968-69 Oakland — Pittsburgh	68	2	7	9	132
1969-70 Pittsburgh	61	1	9	10	189
1970-71 "	43	2	6	8	119
1971-72 "	75	3	17	20	*212
9 Years	421	10	51	61	885
*league leader					
WATSON, JAMES ARTHUR D-SL					
Born: Malartic, Que. June 28, 1943					
1963-64 Detroit	1	0	0	0	0
1964-65 "	1	0	0	0	2
1965-66 "	2	0	0	0	4
1967-68 "	61	0	3	3	87
1968-69 "	8	0	1	1	4
1969-70 "	4	0	0	0	0
1970-71 Buffalo	78	2	9	11	147
1971-72 "	66	2	6	8	101
8 Years	221	4	19	23	345
WATSON, JOSEPH JOHN D-SL					
Born: Smithers, British Columbia. July 6, 1943					
1964-65 Boston	4	0	1	1	0
1966-67 "	69	2	13	15	38

(continued)

Sea. Club	Ga.	Go.	A.	P.	PM.
1967-68 Philadelphia	73	5	14	19	56
1968-69 "	60	2	8	10	14
1969-70 "	54	3	11	14	28
1970-71 "	57	3	7	10	50
1971-72 "	65	3	7	10	38
7 Years	382	18	61	79	224
WEBSTER, THOMAS RONALD RW-SR					
Born: Kirkland Lake, Ont. Oct. 4, 1948					
1968-69 Boston	9	0	2	2	9
1969-70 "	2	0	1	1	2
1970-71 Detroit	78	30	37	67	40
1971-72 " — Oakland	12	3	2	5	10
4 Years	101	33	42	75	61
WESTFALL, VERNON EDWIN D&RW-SR					
Born: Belleville, Ont. Sept. 19, 1940					
1961-62 Boston	63	2	9	11	53
1962-63 "	48	1	11	12	34
1963-64 "	55	1	5	6	35
1964-65 "	68	12	15	27	65
1965-66 "	59	9	21	30	42
1966-67 "	70	12	24	36	26
1967-68 "	73	14	22	36	38
1968-69 "	70	18	24	42	22
1969-70 "	72	14	22	36	28
1970-71 "	78	25	34	59	48
1971-72 "	77	18	26	44	19
11 Years	733	126	213	339	410
WHARRAM, KENNETH MALCOLM RW-SR					
Born: Ferris, Ont. July 2, 1933					
1951-52 Chicago	1	0	0	0	0
1953-54 "	29	1	7	8	8
1955-56 "	3	0	0	0	0
1958-59 "	66	10	9	19	14
1959-60 "	59	14	11	25	16
1960-61 "	64	16	29	45	12
1961-62 "	62	14	23	37	24
1962-63 "	55	20	18	38	17
1963-64 "	70	39	32	71	18
1964-65 "	68	24	20	44	27
1965-66 "	69	26	17	43	28
1966-67 "	70	31	34	65	21
1967-68 "	74	27	42	69	18
1968-69 "	76	30	39	69	19
14 Years	766	252	281	533	222
1963-64 1st All-Star Team & Lady Byng Trophy					
1966-67 " " " "					
WHITE, WILLIAM EARL D-SR					
Born: Toronto, Ont. Aug. 26, 1939					
1967-68 Los Angeles	74	11	27	38	100
1968-69 " "	75	5	28	33	38
1969-70 " " — Chicago	61	4	16	20	39
1970-71 Chicago	67	4	21	25	64
1971-72 "	76	7	22	29	58
5 Years	353	31	114	145	299
1971-72 2nd All-Star Team on Defence					
WHITLOCK, ROBERT ANGUS C-SL					
Born: Charlottetown, Prince Edward Island. July 16, 1949					
1969-70 Minnesota	1	0	0	0	0
WIDING, JUHA MARKKU C-SL					
Born: Uleaborg, Finland. July 4, 1947					
1969-70 New York Rangers — Los Ange	48	7	9	16	12
1970-71 Los Angeles	78	25	40	65	24
1971-72 "	78	27	28	55	26
3 Years	204	59	77	136	62
WILKINS, BARRY JAMES D-SL					
Born: Toronto, Ont. Feb. 28, 1947					
1966-67 Boston	1	0	0	0	0
1968-69 "	1	1	0	1	0
1969-70 "	6	0	0	0	2
1970-71 Vancouver	70	5	18	23	131
1971-72 "	45	2	5	7	65
5 Years	123	8	23	31	198
WILLIAMS, THOMAS CHARLES "TOM" LW-SR					
Born: Windsor, Ont. Feb. 7, 1951					
1971-72 New York Rangers	3	0	0	0	2
WILLIAMS, THOMAS MARK C&RW-SR					
Born: Duluth, Minn. April 17, 1940					
1961-62 Boston	26	6	6	12	2
1962-63 "	69	23	20	43	11
1963-64 "	37	8	15	23	8
1964-65 "	65	13	21	34	28

(continued)

Sea.	Club	Ga.	Go.	A.	P.	PM.
1965-66	"	70	16	22	38	31
1966-67	"	29	8	13	21	2
1967-68	"	68	18	32	50	14
1968-69	"	26	4	7	11	19
1969-70	Minnesota	75	15	52	67	18
1970-71	" — Oakland	59	17	23	40	24
1971-72	Oakland	32	3	9	12	2
11 Years		556	131	220	351	159

WISTE, JAMES ANDREW C-SL
Born: Moose Jaw, Sask. Feb. 18, 1946

Sea.	Club	Ga.	Go.	A.	P.	PM.
1968-69	Chicago	3	0	0	0	0
1969-70	"	26	0	8	8	8
1970-71	Vancouver	23	1	2	3	0
3 Years		52	1	10	11	8

WOYTOWICH, ROBERT IVAN D-SR
Born: Winnipeg, Man. Aug. 18, 1941

Sea.	Club	Ga.	Go.	A.	P.	PM.
1964-65	Boston	21	2	10	12	16
1965-66	"	68	2	17	19	75
1966-67	"	64	2	7	9	43
1967-68	Minnesota	66	4	17	21	63
1968-69	Pittsburgh	71	9	20	29	62
1969-70	"	68	8	25	33	49
1970-71	"	78	4	22	26	30
1971-72	" — Los Angeles	67	1	8	9	14
8 Years		503	32	126	158	352

WRIGHT, LARRY C-SL
Born: Regina, Sask. Oct. 8, 1951

Sea.	Club	Ga.	Go.	A.	P.	PM.
1971-72	Philadelphia	27	0	1	1	2

WYROZUB, WILLIAM RANDALL C-SL
Born: Lacombe, Alta. April 8, 1950

Sea.	Club	Ga.	Go.	A.	P.	PM.
1970-71	Buffalo	16	2	2	4	6
1971-72	"	34	3	4	7	0
2 Years		50	5	6	11	6

YOUNG, HOWARD JOHN EDWARD D-SR
Born: Toronto, Ont. Aug. 2, 1937

Sea.	Club	Ga.	Go.	A.	P.	PM.
1960-61	Detroit	29	0	8	8	108
1961-62	"	30	0	2	2	67
1962-63	"	64	4	5	9	*273
1963-64	Chicago	39	0	7	7	99
1966-67	Detroit	44	3	14	17	100
1967-68	"	62	2	17	19	112
1968-69	Chicago	57	3	7	10	67
1970-71	Vancouver	11	0	2	2	25
8 Years		336	12	62	74	851

*league leader

ZAINE, RODNEY CARL C-SL
Born: Ottawa, Ont. May 18, 1946

Sea.	Club	Ga.	Go.	A.	P.	PM.
1970-71	Pittsburgh	37	8	5	13	21
1971-72	Buffalo	24	2	1	3	4
2 Years		61	10	6	16	25

ZEIDEL, LAZARUS D-SL
Born: Montreal, Que. June 1, 1928

Sea.	Club	Ga.	Go.	A.	P.	PM.
1951-52	Detroit	19	1	0	1	14
1952-53	"	9	0	0	0	8
1953-54	Chicago	64	1	6	7	102
1967-68	Philadelphia	57	1	10	11	68
1968-69	"	9	0	0	0	6
5 Years		158	3	16	19	198

League Leader (Goals)

Year	Player	Team	Goals
1971–72	Philip Esposito	Boston Bruins	66
1970–71	Philip Esposito	Boston Bruins	76
1969–70	Philip Esposito	Boston Bruins	43
1968–69	Robert Hull	Chicago	58
1967–68	Robert Hull	Chicago	44
1966–67	Robert Hull	Chicago	52
1965–66	Robert Hull	Chicago	54
1964–65	Norman Ullman	Detroit	42
1963–64	Robert Hull	Chicago	43
1962–63	Gordon Howe	Detroit	38
1961–62	Robert Hull	Chicago	50
1960–61	Bernard Geoffrion	Montreal	50
1959–60	Bronco Horvath,	Boston	
	Robert Hull	Chicago (tie)	39
1958–59	Jean Beliveau	Montreal	45
1957–58	Richard Moore	Montreal	36
1956–57	Gordon Howe	Detroit	44
1955–56	Jean Beliveau	Montreal	47
1954–55	Bernard Geoffrion	Montreal	
	Maurice Richard	Montreal (tie)	38
1953–54	Maurice Richard	Montreal	37
1952–53	Gordon Howe	Detroit	49
1951–52	Gordon Howe	Detroit	47
1950–51	Gordon Howe	Detroit	43
1949–50	Maurice Richard	Montreal	43
1948–49	Sidney Abel	Detroit	28

Year	Player	Team	Goals
1947–48	Robert Lindsay	Detroit	33
1946–47	Maurice Richard	Montreal	45
1945–46	James Stewart	Toronto	37
1944–45	Maurice Richard	Montreal	50
1943–44	Douglas Bentley	Chicago	38
1942–43	Douglas Bentley	Chicago	33
1941–42	Lynn Patrick	New York	32
1940–41	Bryan Hextall	N. Y. Rangers	26
1939–40	Bryan Hextall	N. Y. Rangers	24
1938–39	Roy Conacher	Boston	26
1937–38	Gordon Drillon	Toronto	26
1936–37	Lawrence Aurie	Detroit	
	Nelson Stewart	Boston—N. Y. Americans (tie)	23
1935–36	Charles Conacher	Toronto	
	William Thoms	Toronto (tie)	23
1934–35	Charles Conacher	Toronto	36
1933–34	Charles Conacher	Toronto	32
1932–33	William Cook	N. Y. Rangers	28
1931–32	Charles Conacher	Toronto	34
1930–31	Charles Conacher	Toronto	31
1929–30	Ralph Weiland	Boston	43
1928–29	Irvin Bailey	Toronto	22
1927–28	Howarth Morenz	Mont. Canadiens	33
1926–27	William Cook	N. Y. Rangers	33
1925–26	Nelson Stewart	Mont. Maroons	34
1924–25	Cecil Dye	Toronto	38
1923–24	Cyril Denneny	Ottawa	22
1922–23	Cecil Dye	Toronto	26
1921–22	Harry Broadbent	Ottawa	32
1920–21	Cecil Dye	Hamilton-Toronto	35
1919–20	Joseph Malone	Quebec	39
1918–19	Ogilvie Cleghorn	Montreal	
	Edouard Lalonde	Montreal (tie)	23
1917–18	Joseph Malone	Montreal	44

League Leader (Assists)

Year	Player	Team	Assists
1971–72	Robert Orr	Boston Bruins	80
1970–71	Robert Orr	Boston Bruins	102
1969–70	Robert Orr	Boston Bruins	87
1968–69	Philip Esposito	Boston	77
1967–68	Philip Esposito	Boston	49
1966–67	Stanley Mikita	Chicago	62
1965–66	Jean Beliveau	Montreal	
	Stanley Mikita	Chicago	
	Robert Rousseau	Montreal (tie)	48
1964–65	Stanley Mikita	Chicago	59
1963–64	Andrew Bathgate	New York—Toronto	58
1962–63	Henri Richard	Montreal	50

League Leader (Assists) (continued)

Year	Player	Team	Assists
1961–62	Andrew Bathgate	New York	56
1960–61	Jean Beliveau	Montreal	58
1959–60	Donald McKenney	Boston	49
1958–59	Richard Moore	Montreal	55
1957–58	Henri Richard	Montreal	52
1956–57	Robert Lindsay	Detroit	55
1955–56	Murray Olmstead	Montreal	56
1954–55	Murray Olmstead	Montreal	48
1953–54	Gordon Howe	Detroit	48
1952–53	Gordon Howe	Detroit	46
1951–52	Elmer Lach	Montreal	50
1950–51	Gordon Howe	Detroit	
	Theodore Kennedy	Toronto (tie)	43
1949–50	Robert Lindsay	Detroit	55
1948–49	Douglas Bentley	Chicago	43
1947–48	Douglas Bentley	Chicago	37
1946–47	William Taylor	Detroit	46
1945–46	Elmer Lach	Montreal	34
1944–45	Elmer Lach	Montreal	54
1943–44	Clinton Smith	Chicago	49
1942–43	William Cowley	Boston	45
1941–42	Phillipe Watson	New York	37
1940–41	William Cowley	Boston	45
1939–40	Milton Schmidt	Boston	30
1938–39	William Cowley	Boston	34
1937–38	Charles Apps	Toronto	29
1936–37	Charles Apps	Toronto	29
1935–36	Arthur Chapman	N. Y. Americans	28
1934–35	Arthur Chapman	N. Y. Americans	34
1933–34	A. Joseph Primeau	Toronto	32
1932–33	Frank Boucher	N. Y. Rangers	28
1931–32	A. Joseph Primeau	Toronto	37
1930–31	A. Joseph Primeau	Toronto	32
1929–30	Frank Boucher	N. Y. Rangers	36
1928–29	Frank Boucher	N. Y. Rangers	16
1927–28	Howarth Morenz	Mont. Canadiens	18
1926–27	James Irvin	Chicago	18
1925–26	Frank Nighbor	Ottawa	13
1924–25	Cyril Denneny	Ottawa	15
1923–24	Francis Clancy	Ottawa	8
1922–23	Edmond Bouchard	Hamilton	12
1921–22	Harry Broadbent	Ottawa	
	Leo Reise, Sr.	Hamilton (tie)	14
1920–21	Louis Berlinquette	Montreal	
	Harold Cameron	Toronto	
	Joseph Matte	Hamilton (tie)	9
1919–20	Corbett Denneny	Toronto	12
1918–19	Edouard Lalonde	Montreal	9
1917–18			*—

* Assists were not recorded in 1917-18.

League Leader (Points)

Year	Player	Team	Goals	Assists	Points
1971–72	Philip Esposito	Boston Bruins	66	67	133
1970–71	Philip Esposito	Boston Bruins	76	76	152
1969–70	Robert Orr	Boston Bruins	33	87	120
1968–69	Philip Esposito	Boston	49	77	126
1967–68	Stanley Mikita	Chicago	40	47	87
1966–67	Stanley Mikita	Chicago	35	62	97
1965–66	Robert Hull	Chicago	54	43	97
1964–65	Stanley Mikita	Chicago	28	59	87
1963–64	Stanley Mikita	Chicago	39	50	89
1962–63	Gordon Howe	Detroit	38	48	86
1961–62	Andrew Bathgate	New York	28	56	
	Robert Hull	Chicago (tie)	50	34	84
1960–61	Bernard Geoffrion	Montreal	50	45	95
1959–60	Robert Hull	Chicago	39	42	81
1958–59	Richard Moore	Montreal	41	55	96
1957–58	Richard Moore	Montreal	36	48	84
1956–57	Gordon Howe	Detroit	44	45	89
1955–56	Jean Beliveau	Montreal	47	41	88
1954–55	Bernard Geoffrion	Montreal	38	37	75
1953–54	Gordon Howe	Detroit	33	48	81
1952–53	Gordon Howe	Detroit	49	46	95
1951–52	Gordon Howe	Detroit	47	39	86
1950–51	Gordon Howe	Detroit	43	43	86
1949–50	Robert Lindsay	Detroit	23	55	78
1948–49	Roy Conacher	Chicago	26	42	68
1947–48	Elmer Lach	Montreal	30	31	61
1946–47	Maxwell Bentley	Chicago	29	43	72
1945–46	Maxwell Bentley	Chicago	31	30	61
1944–45	Elmer Lach	Montreal	26	54	80
1943–44	Herbert Cain	Boston	36	46	82
1942–43	Douglas Bentley	Chicago	33	40	73
1941–42	Bryan Hextall	New York	24	32	56
1940–41	William Cowley	Boston	17	45	62
1939–40	Milton Schmidt	Boston	22	30	52
1938–39	Hector Blake	Montreal	24	23	47
1937–38	Gordon Drillon	Toronto	26	26	52
1936–37	David Schriner	N.Y. Americans	21	25	46
1935–36	David Schriner	N.Y. Americans	19	26	45
1934–35	Charles Conacher	Toronto	36	21	57
1933–34	Charles Conacher	Toronto	32	20	52
1932–33	William Cook	N.Y. Rangers	28	22	50
1931–32	Harvey Jackson	Toronto	28	25	53
1930–31	Howarth Morenz	Mont. Canadiens	28	23	51
1929–30	Ralph Weiland	Boston	43	30	73
1928–29	Irvin Bailey	Toronto	22	10	32
1927–28	Howarth Morenz	Mont. Canadiens	33	18	51
1926–27	William Cook	N.Y. Rangers	33	4	37
1925–26	Nelson Stewart	Mont. Maroons	34	8	32
1924–25	Cecil Dye	Toronto	38	6	44
1923–24	Cyril Denneny	Ottawa	22	1	23
1922–23	Cecil Dye	Toronto	26	11	37
1921–22	Harry Broadbent	Ottawa	32	14	46
1920–21	Edouard Lalonde	Montreal	33	8	41
1919–20	Joseph Malone	Quebec	39	6	45
1918–19	Edouard Lalonde	Montreal	23	9	32
1917–18	Joseph Malone	Montreal	44	*—	44

* No assists recorded

League Leader (Penalties)

Year	Player	Team	Penalty Time In Minutes
1971–72	Bryan Watson	Pittsburgh Penguins	212
1970–71	Keith Magnuson	Chicago Black Hawks	291
1969–70	Keith Magnuson	Chicago Black Hawks	213
1968–69	Forbes Kennedy	Philadelphia–Toronto	219
1967–68	Barclay Plager	St. Louis	153
1966–67	John Ferguson	Montreal	177
1965–66	Reginald Fleming	Boston–New York	166
1964–65	Carl Brewer	Toronto	177
1963–64	Victor Hadfield	New York	151
1962–63	Howard Young	Detroit	273
1961–62	Louis Fontinato	Montreal	167
1960–61	Pierre Pilote	Chicago	165
1959–60	Carl Brewer	Toronto	150
1958–59	Robert Lindsay	Chicago	184
1957–58	Louis Fontinato	New York	152
1956–57	James Mortson	Chicago	147
1955–56	Louis Fontinato	New York	202
1954–55	Ferdinand Flaman	Boston	150
1953–54	James Mortson	Chicago	132
1952–53	Maurice Richard	Montreal	112
1951–52	Walter Kyle	Boston	127
1950–51	James Mortson	Toronto	142
1949–50	William Ezinicki	Toronto	144
1948–49	William Ezinicki	Toronto	145
1947–48	William Barilko	Toronto	147
1946–47	James Mortson	Toronto	133
1945–46	John Stewart	Detroit	73
1944–45	Martin Egan	Boston	86
1943–44	Michael McMahon	Montreal	98
1942–43	James Orlando	Detroit	99
1941–42	Martin Egan	Brooklyn	124
1940–41	James Orlando	Detroit	99
1939–40	George Horner	Toronto	87
1938–39	George Horner	Toronto	85
1937–38	George Horner	Toronto	92
1936–37	George Horner	Toronto	124
1935–36	George Horner	Toronto	167
1934–35	George Horner	Toronto	125
1933–34	George Horner	Toronto	146
1932–33	George Horner	Toronto	144
1931–32	Mervyn Dutton	N.Y. Americans	107
1930–31	Harvey Rockburn	Detroit	118
1929–30	Joseph Lamb	Ottawa	119
1928–29	Mervyn Dutton	Mont. Maroons	139
1927–28	Edward Shore	Boston	166
1926–27	Nelson Stewart	Mont. Maroons	133
1925–26	Bert Corbeau	Toronto	121
1924–25	William Boucher	Montreal	92
1923–24	Bert Corbeau	Toronto	55
1922–23	William Boucher	Montreal	52
1921–22	Sprague Cleghorn	Montreal	63
1920–21	Bert Corbeau	Montreal	86
1919–20	Carol Wilson	Toronto	79
1918–19	Joseph Hall	Montreal	85
1917–18			*—

* Penalties were not recorded in 1917-18.

Player Records

Career

Most Seasons

Gordon Howe	25	Donald Marshall	19
Myles Horton	22	Douglas Mohns	19
Alexander Delvecchio	22	J. H. Maurice Richard	18
Allan Stanley	21	R. Ronald Murphy	18
George Armstrong	21	T. Richard Duff	18
Eric Nesterenko	21	Lawrence Hillman	18
Aubrey Clapper	20	Reginald Smith	17
William Gadsby	20	Harold March	17
Leonard Kelly	20	Ferdinand Flaman	17
J. R. Marcel Pronovost	20	R. B. Theodore Lindsay	17
Jean Béliveau	20	Andrew Bathgate	17
Henry Howell	20	Jean-Guy Talbot	17
Dean Prentice	20	John Bucyk	17
Ronald Stewart	20	J. Henri Richard	17
Douglas Harvey	19	Norman Ullman	17
Leo Boivin	19		

Most Games

Gordon Howe	1687	Donald Marshall	1176
Alexander Delvecchio	1461	Leo Boivin	1150
Henry Howell	1338	John Bucyk	1129
Myles Horton	1322	Jean Béliveau	1125
Ronald Stewart	1320	Douglas Harvey	1113
Leonard Kelly	1316	J. Henri Richard	1097
Dean Prentice	1281	Robert Pulford	1079
William Gadsby	1248	Andrew Bathgate	1069
Allan Stanley	1244	R. B. Theodore Lindsay	1968
Douglas Mohns	1220	Jean-Guy Talbot	1056
Eric Nesterenko	1219	Robert Hull	1036
J. R. Marcel Pronovost	1206	Francis Mahovlich	1032
George Armstrong	1188	T. Richard Duff	1030
Norman Ullman	1187	J. R. Marcel Pronovost	1005

Most Goals

Gordon Howe	786	George Armstrong	296
Robert Hull	604	David Keon	287
J. H. Maurice Richard	544	T. Richard Duff	283
Jean Béliveau	507	Leonard Kelly	281
Francis Mahovlich	464	Robert Pulford	281
Norman Ullman	439	Camille Henry	279
Alexander Delvecchio	437	Ronald Stewart	274
John Bucyk	395	Howarth Morenz	270
Bernard Geoffrion	393	Aurèle Joliat	270
R. B. Theodore Lindsay	379	Donald Marshall	265
Stanley Mikita	374	Richard Moore	261
Dean Prentice	363	William Mosienko	258
Andrew Bathgate	349	J. A. Claude Provost	254
Philip Esposito	343	Kenneth Wharram	252
J. Henri Richard	328	Ralph Backstrom	252
Nelson Stewart	324	Eric Nesterenko	250

Most Assists

Gordon Howe	1023	Bernard Geoffrion	429
Alexander Delvecchio	768	Douglas Mohns	427
Jean Béliveau	712	Philip Esposito	425
Norman Ullman	631	J. H. Maurice Richard	421
Andrew Bathgate	624	M. Bert Olmstead	421
Stanley Mikita	617	Pierre Pilote	418
J. Henri Richard	607	George Armstrong	417
John Bucyk	581	Elmer Lach	408
Robert Hull	549	Murray Oliver	388
Leonard Kelly	542	David Keon	386
R. B. Theodore Lindsay	472	Myles Horton	381
J. G. Phillipe Goyette	467	J. J. Robert Rousseau	378
Francis Mahovlich	466	Robert Pulford	362
Douglas Harvey	452	Robert Orr	360
Dean Prentice	450	William Cowley	353
William Gadsby	437		

Most Points

Gordon Howe	(786 goals—1023 assists)	1809
Jean Béliveau	(507 goals— 712 assists)	1219
Alexander Delvecchio	(437 goals— 768 assists)	1205
Robert Hull	(604 goals— 549 assists)	1153
Norman Ullman	(439 goals— 631 assists)	1070
Stanley Mikita	(374 goals— 617 assists)	991
John Bucyk	(395 goals— 581 assists)	976
Andrew Bathgate	(349 goals— 624 assists)	973
J. H. Maurice Richard	(544 goals— 421 assists)	965
J. Henri Richard	(328 goals— 607 assists)	935
Francis Mahovlich	(464 goals— 466 assists)	930
R. B. Theodore Lindsay	(379 goals— 472 assists)	851
Leonard Kelly	(281 goals— 542 assists)	823
Bernard Geoffrion	(393 goals— 429 assists)	822
Dean Prentice	(363 goals— 450 assists)	813
Philip Esposito	(343 goals— 425 assists)	768
George Armstrong	(296 goals— 417 assists)	713
J. G. Phillipe Goyette	(207 goals— 467 assists)	674
David Keon	(287 goals— 386 assists)	673
Douglas Mohns	(242 goals— 427 assists)	669

Most Penalties in Minutes

R. B. Theodore Lindsay	1808	Pierre Pilote	1251
Gordon Howe	1643	Louis Fontinato	1247
William Gadsby	1539	Douglas Harvey	1216
Myles Horton	1502	John Ferguson	1214
Robert Baun	1487	Leo Boivin	1192
Reginald Fleming	1468	Douglas Mohns	1134
J. Angus Mortson	1380	Edward Shore	1048
Ferdinand Flaman	1370	Carl Brewer	1035
J. H. Maurice Richard	1285	Jean Béliveau	1029
Eric Nesterenko	1273	Edward Green	1029
Henry Howell	1270	Reginald Smith	1013
Edward Shack	1268	Jean-Guy Talbot	1006
G. Reginald Horner	1264	Stanley Mikita	1006

Season

Most Goals

1970–71	Philip Esposito	Boston Bruins	76
1971–72	Philip Esposito	Boston Bruins	66
1968–69	Robert Hull	Chicago Black Hawks	58
1965–66	Robert Hull	Chicago Black Hawks	54
1966–67	Robert Hull	Chicago Black Hawks	52
1970–71	John Bucyk	Boston Bruins	51
1944–45	J. H. Maurice Richard	Montreal Canadiens	50
1960–61	Bernard Geoffrion	Montreal Canadiens	50
1961–62	Robert Hull	Chicago Black Hawks	50
1971–72	Robert Hull	Chicago Black Hawks	50
1971–72	Victor Hadfield	New York Rangers	50

Most Assists

1970–71	Robert Orr	Boston Bruins	102
1969–70	Robert Orr	Boston Bruins	87
1971–72	Robert Orr	Boston Bruins	80
1968–69	Philip Esposito	Boston Bruins	77
1970–71	Philip Esposito	Boston Bruins	76
1968–69	Stanley Mikita	Chicago Black Hawks	67
1971–72	Philip Esposito	Boston Bruins	67
1970–71	John Bucyk	Boston Bruins	65
1971–72	J. G. Y. Jean Ratelle	New York Rangers	63
1966–67	Stanley Mikita	Chicago Black Hawks	62
1970–71	Kenneth Hodge	Boston Bruins	62

Most Points

1970–71	Philip Esposito	Boston Bruins	(76 goals— 76 assists)	152
1970–71	Robert Orr	Boston Bruins	(37 goals—102 assists)	139
1971–72	Philip Esposito	Boston Bruins	(66 goals— 67 assists)	133
1968–69	Philip Esposito	Boston Bruins	(49 goals— 77 assists)	126
1969–70	Robert Orr	Boston Bruins	(33 goals— 87 assists)	120
1971–72	Robert Orr	Boston Bruins	(37 goals— 80 assists)	117
1970–71	John Bucyk	Boston Bruins	(51 goals— 65 assists)	116
1971–72	J. G. Y. Jean Ratelle	N.Y. Rangers	(46 goals— 63 assists)	109
1968–69	Robert Hull	Chi. Black Hawks	(58 goals— 49 assists)	107
1971–72	Victor Hadfield	N.Y. Rangers	(50 goals— 56 assists)	106
1970–71	Kenneth Hodge	Boston Bruins	(43 goals— 62 assists)	105
1968–69	Gordon Howe	Det. Red Wings	(44 goals— 59 assists)	103

Most Penalties in Minutes

1970–71	Keith Magnuson	Chicago Black Hawks	291
1962–63	Howard Young	Detroit Red Wings	273
1968–69	Forbes Kennedy	Philadelphia Flyers-Toronto Maple Leafs	219
1970–71	Dennis Hextall	California Golden Seals	217
1969–70	Keith Magnuson	Chicago Black Hawks	213
1969–70	Carol Vadnais	Oakland Seals	212
1971–72	Bryan Watson	Pittsburgh Penguins	212
1955–56	Louis Fontinato	New York Rangers	202
1971–72	Keith Magnuson	Chicago Black Hawks	201
1968–69	R. James Dorey	Toronto Maple Leafs	200

Game

Most Goals

Jan. 31, 1920	M. Joseph Malone	Quebec Bulldogs	7
Jan. 10, 1920	Edouard Lalonde	Montreal Canadiens	6
Mar. 10, 1920	M. Joseph Malone	Quebec Bulldogs	6
Jan. 26, 1921	Corbett Denneny	Toronto St. Patricks	6
Mar. 7, 1921	Cyril Denneny	Ottawa Senators	6
Feb. 3, 1944	Sydney Howe	Detroit Red Wings	6
Nov. 7, 1968	Gordon Berenson	St. Louis Blues	6

Most Assists

Mar. 16, 1947	William Taylor	Detroit Red Wings	7
Feb. 6, 1943	Elmer Lach	Montreal Canadiens	6
Jan. 8, 1944	Walter Pratt	Toronto Maple Leafs	6
Feb. 3, 1944	Donald Grosso	Detroit Red Wings	6
Mar. 30, 1969	Patrick Stapleton	Chicago Black Hawks	6
Feb. 9, 1971	Kenneth Hodge	Boston Bruins	6

Most Points

Dec. 28, 1944	J. H. Maurice Richard	Montreal Canadiens (5 goals—3 assists)	8
Jan. 9, 1954	M. Bert Olmstead	Montreal Canadiens (4 goals—4 assists)	8

Most Penalties

Oct. 16, 1968	R. James Dorey	Toronto Maple Leafs	(3 misc.—2 maj.—4 min.)	9
Jan. 29, 1927	George Boucher	Ottawa Senators	(7 min.)	7
Dec. 26, 1965	Edward Green	Boston Bruins	(2 misc.—2 maj.—3 min.)	7
Feb. 15, 1970	Edward Shack	Los Angeles Kings	(1 misc.—2 maj.—4 min.)	7
Feb. 2, 1928	Irvin Bailey	Toronto Maple Leafs	(6 min.)	6
Dec. 21, 1929	Edward Shore	Boston Bruins	(6 min.)	6
Nov. 12, 1931	Ivan Johnson	New York Rangers	(6 min.)	6
Feb. 28, 1943	John Stewart	Detroit Red Wings	(6 min.)	6
Jan. 17, 1953	J. H. Maurice Richard	Montreal Canadiens	(1 misc.—1 maj.—4 min.)	6
Oct. 19, 1960	Reginald Fleming	Chicago Black Hawks	(2 misc.—3 maj.—1 min.)	6
Jan. 1, 1961	James Bartlett	Boston Bruins	(1 misc.—1 maj.—4 min.)	6
Mar. 24, 1962	Reginald Fleming	Chicago Black Hawks	(1 maj.—5 min.)	6
Jan. 24, 1965	J. Wayne Rivers	Boston Bruins	(1 misc.——————5 min.)	6
Jan. 22, 1966	Reginald Fleming	New York Rangers	(2 misc.——————4 min.)	6
Mar. 8, 1967	Gary Doak	Boston Bruins	(6 min.)	6

Dec.   3, 1967   Donald Awrey   Boston Bruins
                                                    (2 misc.—3 maj.—1 min.) 6
Jan.   25, 1968   Forbes Kennedy   Philadelphia Flyers
                                                    (2 misc.—2 maj.—2 min.) 6
Nov.   1, 1969   Thomas Polanic   Minnesota North Stars
                                                    (3 misc.————————3 min.) 6
Oct.   18, 1970   Reginald Fleming   Buffalo Sabres
                                                    (3 misc.—1 maj.—2 min.) 6
Jan.   10, 1971   Ronald Anderson   Buffalo Sabres
                                                    (1 misc.————————5 min.) 6

Most Penalties in Minutes

Oct.   16, 1968   R. James Dorey   Toronto Maple Leafs
                                                    (3 misc.—2 maj.—4 min.) 48
Oct.   18, 1970   Reginald Fleming   Buffalo Sabres
                                                    (3 misc.—1 maj.—2 min.) 39
Oct.   19, 1960   Reginald Fleming   Chicago Black Hawks
                                                    (2 misc.—3 maj.—1 min.) 37
Dec.   3, 1967   Donald Awrey   Boston Bruins
                                                    (2 misc.—3 maj.—1 min.) 37
Dec.   26, 1965   Edward Green   Boston Bruins
                                                    (2 misc.—2 maj.—3 min.) 36
Nov.   1, 1969   Thomas Polanic   Minnesota North Stars
                                                    (3 misc.————————3 min.) 36
Jan.   25, 1968   Forbes Kennedy   Philadelphia Flyers
                                                    (2 misc.—2 maj.—2 min.) 34

Period

Most Goals

Nov. 20, 1934	Harvey Jackson	Toronto Maple Leafs	3rd period 4
Jan. 28, 1943	Maxwell Bentley	Chicago Black Hawks	3rd period 4
Mar. 4, 1945	Clinton Smith	Chicago Black Hawks	3rd period 4
Nov. 7, 1968	Gordon Berenson	St. Louis Blues	2nd period 4

Most Assists

Nov. 8, 1942	Herbert O'Connor	Montreal Canadiens	3rd period 4
Jan. 28, 1943	Douglas Bentley	Chicago Black Hawks	3rd period 4
Jan. 23, 1944	Joseph Carveth	Detroit Red Wings	3rd period 4
Mar. 18, 1944	Phillipe Watson	Montreal Canadiens	3rd period 4
Mar. 4, 1945	William Mosienko	Chicago Black Hawks	3rd period 4
Dec. 29, 1962	Jean-Claude Tremblay	Montreal Canadiens	2nd period 4
Oct. 20, 1963	J. G. Phillipe Goyette	New York Rangers	1st period 4
Nov. 9, 1969	James Wiste	Chicago Black Hawks	3rd period 4
Dec. 16, 1970	Clifford Koroll	Chicago Black Hawks	2nd period 4
Mar. 24, 1971	Sylvanus M. Apps	Pittsburgh Penguins	3rd period 4
Feb. 15, 1972	Robert Orr	Boston Bruins	1st period 4

Most Points

Jan. 28, 1940	Leslie Cunningham	Chicago Black Hawks
		3rd period (2 go.—3 ass.) 5
Jan. 28, 1943	Maxwell Bentley	Chicago Black Hawks
		3rd period (4 go.—1 ass.) 5
Nov. 28, 1954	Leo LaBine	Boston Bruins
		2nd period (3 go.—2 ass.) 5

Most Penalties

Oct. 16, 1968	R. James Dorey	Toronto
		2nd period (3 misc.—2 maj.—2 min.) 7
Oct. 18, 1970	Reginald Fleming	Buffalo
		1st period (3 misc.—1 maj.—2 min.) 6
Oct. 19, 1960	Reginald Fleming	Chicago
		3rd period (2 misc.—2 maj.—1 min.) 5
Dec. 1, 1960	J. Henri Richard	Montreal
		3rd period (2 misc.—1 maj.—2 min.) 5
Dec. 7, 1963	Reginald Fleming	Chicago
		3rd period (2 misc.—2 maj.—1 min.) 5
Jan. 22, 1966	Reginald Fleming	New York
		2nd period (2 misc.————3 min.) 5
Nov. 1, 1969	Thomas Polanic	Minnesota
		2nd period (3 misc.————2 min.) 5
Feb. 15, 1970	Edward Shack	Los Angeles
		2nd period (1 misc.—1 maj.—3 min.) 5

Most Penalties in Minutes

Oct. 16, 1968	R. James Dorey	Toronto
		2nd period (3 misc.—2 maj.—2 min.) 44
Oct. 18, 1970	Reginald Fleming	Buffalo
		1st period (3 misc.—1 maj.—2 min.) 39
Nov. 1, 1969	Thomas Polanic	Minnesota
		2nd period (3 misc.————2 min.) 34
Oct. 19, 1960	Reginald Fleming	Chicago
		3rd period (2 misc.—2 maj.—1 min.) 32
Dec. 7, 1963	Reginald Fleming	Chicago
		3rd period (2 misc.—2 maj.—1 min.) 32
Nov. 15, 1970	Wayne Maki	Vancouver
		2nd period (2 misc.—2 maj.) 30
Nov. 15, 1970	Daniel Maloney	Chicago
		2nd period (2 misc.—2 maj.) 30
Mar. 21, 1971	Floyd Smith	Buffalo
		2nd period (3 misc.) 30
Dec. 1, 1960	J. Henri Richard	Montreal
		3rd period (2 misc.—1 maj.—2 min.) 29
Feb. 27, 1963	Reginald Fleming	Chicago
		2nd period (2 misc.—1 maj.—1 min.) 27
Feb. 5, 1967	John Ferguson	Montreal
		3rd period (2 misc.—1 maj.—1 min.) 27
Mar. 1, 1970	R. James Dorey	Toronto
		3rd period (2 misc.—1 maj.—1 min.) 27
Nov. 16, 1971	Barry Gibbs	Minnesota
		3rd period (2 misc.—1 maj.—1 min.) 27
Jan. 22, 1966	Reginald Fleming	New York
		2nd period (2 misc.————3 min.) 26

Consecutive Games

Played

Oct. 7, 1955—thru Mar. 22, 1964	Andrew Hebenton	630
Feb. 10, 1952—thru Mar. 20, 1960	John Wilson	580
Dec. 13, 1956—thru Nov. 11, 1964	Alexander Delvecchio	548
Nov. 16, 1926—thru Mar. 21, 1937	J. Murray Murdoch	508

Scored Goal

1921–22	Harry Broadbent	Ottawa Senators	16
1917–18	Joseph Malone	Montreal Canadiens	14
1920–21	Edouard Lalonde	Montreal Canadiens	13
1917–18	Cyril Denneny	Ottawa Senators	12
1920–21	Cecil Dye	Hamilton Tigers-Toronto St. Patricks	11
1921–22	Cecil Dye	Toronto St. Patricks	11
1962–63	Andrew Bathgate	New York Rangers	10
1968–69	Robert Hull	Chicago Black Hawks	10
1944–45	J. H. Maurice Richard	Montreal Canadiens	9
1960–61	Bernard Geoffrion	Montreal Canadiens	9
1961–62	Robert Hull	Chicago Black Hawks	9
1970–71	Philip Esposito	Boston Bruins	9
1960–61	Stanley Mikita	Chicago Black Hawks	8
1971–72	J. G. Y. Jean Ratelle	New York Rangers	8
1944–45	J. H. Maurice Richard	Montreal Canadiens	7
1959–60	Jean Béliveau	Montreal Canadiens	7
1965–66	John Bucyk	Boston Bruins	7
1970–71	William Goldsworthy	Minnesota North Stars	7

6
Register of Goaltenders

Abbreviations

The following appear after names of goaltenders:

SL—Shoots left
SR—Shoots right

The following appear as headings:

Sea.—Season
Ga.—Games
Go.—Goals
GA—Goals-Against
SO—Shut-Outs
Ave.—Average
A.—Assists
PM.—Penalties in Minutes

Numbers in parentheses following games indicates games played in.

A blank column indicates that information is unavailable.

Numbers in parentheses following games indicates games played in.
- - Assists and Penalties were not recorded in 1917-18.

Sea. Club	Ga.	GA	SO	Ave.	A.	PM.
ABBOTT, GEORGE						
1943-44 Boston Bruins	1	7		7.00	0	0
AIKEN, JOHN						
Born: Arlington, Mass., Jan. 1, 1932						
1957-58 Montreal Canadiens	3/5	6		10.00	0	0
AITKENHEAD, ANDREW G-SL						
Born: Glasgow, Scotland, Mar. 6, 1904						
1932-33 New York Rangers	48	107	3	2.23	0	0
1933-34 " " "	48	113	7	2.35	0	0
1934-35 " " "	10	37	1	3.70	0	0
3 Years	106	257	11	2.42	0	0
ALMAS, RALPH CLAYTON "RED" G-SR						
Born: Saskatoon, Sask., Apr. 26, 1924						
1946-47 Detroit Red Wings	1	5		5.00	0	0
1950-51 Chicago Black Hawks	1	5		5.00	0	0
1952-53 Detroit Red Wings	1	3		3.00	0	0
3 Years	3	13	0	4.33	0	0
ANDERSON, LORNE						
Born: Renfrew, Ont., July 26, 1931						
1951-52 New York Rangers	3	18	0	6.00	0	0
BASSEN, HENRY "HANK" G-SL						
Born: Calgary, Alta., Dec. 6, 1932						
1954-55 Chicago Black Hawks	21	63	0	3.00	0	0
1955-56 " " "	12	42	1	3.50	0	2
1960-61 Detroit Red Wings	34 1/6	102	0	2.99	1	6
1961-62 " " "	27	76	3	2.81	0	8
1962-63 " " "	16 1/3	53	0	3.24	1	14
1963-64 " " "	1	4		4.00	0	0
1965-66 " " "	6 3/4(11)	18	0	2.67	0	0
1966-67 " " "	6 1/3(8)	22	0	3.47	0	0
1967-68 Pittsburgh Penguins	21 2/3(25)	64	1	2.95	0	8
9 Years	146¼(157)	444	5	3.04	2	38
BASTIEN, ALDEGE "BAZ" G-SL						
Born: Timmins, Ont., Aug. 29, 1920						
1945-46 Toronto Maple Leafs	5	20	0	4.00	0	0
BAUMAN, GARRY GLENWOOD G-SL						
Born: Innisfail, Alta., July 21, 1940						
1966-67 Montreal Canadiens	2	5	0	2.50	0	0
1967-68 Minnesota North Stars	21 1/2(26)	75	0	3.49	0	2
1968-69 " " "	5 (7)	22	0	4.40	0	0
3 Years	28 1/2(35)	102	0	3.58	0	2
BELL, GORDON G-SL						
Born: Portage la Prairie, Man., Mar. 13, 1925						
1945-46 Toronto Maple Leafs	8	31	0	3.87	0	0

Sea.	Club	Ga.	GA	SO	Ave.	A.	PM.
BENEDICT, CLINTON S. "BENNY" G-SL							
Born: Ottawa, Ont., 1894							
1917-18	Ottawa Senators	22	114	*1	5.18	–	--
1918-19	” ”	18	54	*2	3.00	0	3
1919-20	” ”	24	64	*5	2.67	0	0
1920-21	” ”	24	75	*2	3.125	0	0
1921-22	” ”	24	84	*2	3.50	0	0
1922-23	” ”	24	54	*4	2.25	0	2
1923-24	” ”	22	45	*3	2.05	0	0
1924-25	Montreal Maroons	30	65	2	2.17	0	2
1925-26	” ”	36	73	6	2.03	0	0
1926-27	” ”	43	65	13	1.51	0	0
1927-28	” ”	43 1/3	76	6	1.75	0	0
1928-29	” ”	37	57	11	1.54	0	0
1929-30	” ”	12 1/6	38	0	3.12	0	0
13 Years		359½(361)	864	57	2.40	0	7

* league leader

Hall of Frame

BENNETT, HARVEY A. G-SR							
Born: Edington, Sask., July 23, 1925							
1944-45 Boston Bruins		24	103	0	4.29	0	0
BEVERIDGE, WILLIAM S. G-SL							
Born: Ottawa, Ont., July 1, 1909							
1929-30 Detroit Cougars		39	109	2	2.79	0	0
1930-31 Ottawa Senators		8 2/3	32	0	3.69	0	0
1932-33 ” ”		34 2/5	95	5	2.76	0	0
1933-34 ” ”		48	143	3	2.98	0	0
1934-35 St. Louis Eagles		48	144	3	3.00	0	0
1935-36 Montreal Maroons		32	71	1	2.22	0	0
1936-37 ” ”		21	47	1	2.24	0	0
1937-38 ” ”		48	149	2	3.10	0	0
1942-43 New York Rangers		17	89	1	5.24	0	0
9 Years		296(297)	879	18	2.97	0	0
BIBEAULT, PAUL G-SL							
Born: Montreal, Que., April 13, 1919							
1940-41 Montreal Canadiens		3 1/2	15	†0	4.29	0	0
1941-42 ” ”		38	131	1	3.45	0	0
1942-43 ” ”		50	191	1	3.82	0	0
1943-44 Toronto Maple Leafs		29	87	*5	3.00	0	0
1944-45 Boston Bruins		26	116	0	4.46	0	0
1945-46 ” - Montreal Canadiens		26	75	2	2.88	0	0
1946-47 Chicago Black Hawks		41	170	1	4.14	0	2
7 Years		213 1/2	785	10	3.68	0	2

*   league leader
†   also shared shut-out with Wilbert Gardiner on March 15, 1941 against New York Americans
    1943-44 2nd All-Star Team

BINETTE, ANDRE							
Born: Montreal, Que., Dec. 2, 1933							
1954-55 Montreal Canadiens		1	4		4.00	0	0
BINKLEY, LESLIE JOHN G-SR							
Born: Owen Sound, Ont., June 6, 1936							
1967-68 Pittsburgh Penguins		52 1/3(54)	152	6	2.91	0	0
1968-69 ” ”		48 (50)	160	0	3.33	0	0
1969-70 ” ”		24 3/5(27)	79	3	3.21	1	0
1970-71 ” ”		31 1/6(34)	89	2	2.86	0	0
1971-72 ” ”		27 5/6(31)	102	0	3.66	0	2
5 Years		184(196)	582	11	3.16	1	2
BITTNER, RICHARD J.							
Born: New Haven, Conn., Jan. 12, 1922							
1949-50 Boston Bruins		1	3		3.00	0	0
BOISVERT, GILLES G-SL							
Born: Trois Rivieres, Que., Feb. 15, 1933							
1959-60 Detroit Red Wings		3	9	0	3.00	0	0

Sea.	Club	Ga.	GA	SO	Ave.	A.	PM.
BOURQUE, CLAUDE HENNESSEY G-SL							
Born: Oxford, Nova Scotia, Mar. 31, 1915							
1938-39 Montreal Candiens		25	69	2	2.76	0	0
1939-40 " " - Detroit		37	123	3	3.32	0	0
2 Years		62	192	5	3.10	0	0
BOUVRETTE, LIONEL							
Born: Hawkesbury, Ont., June 10, 1914							
1942-43 New York Rangers		1	6		6.00	0	0
BOWER, JOHN WILLIAM G-SL							
Born: Prince Albert, Sask., Nov. 8, 1924							
1953-54 New York Rangers		70	182	5	2.60	0	0
1954-55 " "		5	13	0	2.60	0	0
1956-57 " " "		2	7	0	3.50	0	0
1958-59 Toronto Maple Leafs		40	109	3	2.725	0	2
1959-60 " " "		66	180	5	2.73	0	4
1960-61 " " "		58	145	2	2.50	0	0
1961-62 " " "		59	152	2	2.58	1	4
1962-63 " " "		42	110	1	2.62	0	2
1963-64 " " "		50 1/6	107	5	2.13	0	4
1964-65 " " "		34	81	3	2.38	0	6
1965-66 " " "		33 1/3(35)	76	3	2.28	1	0
1966-67 " " "		23 3/4(27)	65	2	2.74	0	0
1967-68 " " "		37 1/3(42)	88	4	2.36	1	14
1968-69 " " "		13(20)	37	2	2.85	0	0
1969-70 " " "		1	6		6.00	0	0
15 Years		534 2/3(552)	1358	37	2.54	3	36

1960-61 1st All-Star Team & Georges Vezina Memorial Trophy
1964-65 Georges Vezina Memorial Trophy (with Terrance Sawchuk)

BRANIGAN, ANDREW JOHN
Tended goal for New York Americans from 12:47 of 3rd period as they lost to Detroit Red Wings 5-4 on February 28, 1941 at Detroit (0 goals scored against him).

Sea.	Club	Ga.	GA	SO	Ave.	A.	PM.
BRIMSEK, FRANCIS CHARLES "MR. ZERO" G-SL							
Born: Eveleth, Minn., Sept. 26, 1915							
1938-39 Boston Bruins		43	68	*10	1.58	0	0
1939-40 " "		48	98	6	2.04	0	0
1940-41 " "		48	102	*6	2.125	0	0
1941-42 " "		47	115	3	2.47	0	0
1942-43 " "		50	176	1	3.52	0	0
in United States Coast Guard							
1945-46 Boston Bruins		34	111	2	3.26	0	0
1946-47 " "		60	175	3	2.91	0	2
1947-48 " "		60	168	3	2.82	0	0
1948-49 " "		54	147	1	2.72	0	2
1949-50 Chicago Black Hawks		70	244	5	3.49	0	2
10 Years		514	1404	40	2.73	0	6

* league leader
1938-39 1st All-Star Team, Frank Calder & Georges Vezina Memorial Trophies
1939-40 2nd " " "
1940-41 " " "
1941-42 1st " " " & Georges Vezina Memorial Trophy
1942-43 2nd " " "
1945-46 " " "
1946-47 " " "
1947-48 " " "

Hall of Fame

Sea.	Club	Ga.	GA	SO	Ave.	A.	PM.
BRODA, WALTER EDWARD "TURK" G-SL							
Born: Brandon, Man., May 15, 1914							
1936-37 Toronto Maple Leafs		45	106	3	2.36	0	0
1937-38 " " "		48	127	5	2.65	0	0
1938-39 " " "		48	107	8	2.23	0	0
1939-40 " " "		47	108	4	2.30	0	0
1940-41 " " "		48	99	5	2.06	0	0
1941-42 " " "		48	136	*6	2.83	0	0
1942-43 " " "		50	159	1	3.18	0	0
in Canadian Army							
1945-46 Toronto Maple Leafs		15	53	0	3.53	0	0
1946-47 " " "		60	172	4	2.86	0	0
1947-48 " " "		60	143	5	2.38	0	2

(continued)

Sea.	Club			Ga.	GA	SO	Ave.	A.	PM.
1948-49	,,	,,	,,	60	161	5	2.68	0	0
1949-50	,,	,,	,,	67 1/3	167	*9	2.48	0	2
1950-51	"	,,	,,	30 3/5	68	†5	2.22	0	4
1951-52	,,	,,	,,	1/2	3		6.00	0	0
14 Years				627 2/5(629)	1609	60	2.56	0	8

* league leader
† also shared shut-out with Elwin Rollins on December 2, 1950 against Chicago
1940-41 1st All-Star Team & Georges Vezina Memorial Trophy
1941-42 2nd " " "
1947-48 1st " " " & Georges Vezina Memorial Trophy

Hall of Fame

BRODERICK, KENNETH LORNE G-SR
Born: Toronto, Ont., Feb. 16, 1942

1969-70 Minnesota North Stars	6 (7)	26	0	4.33	0	0

BRODERICK, LEONARD G-SL
Born: Toronto, Ont., Oct. 11, 1930

1957-58 Montreal Canadiens	1	2		2.00	0	0

BROOKS, ARTHUR

1917-18 Toronto Areanas	3	18	0	6.00	- -	- -

BROPHY, FRANK

1919-20 Quebec Bulldogs	21	151	0	7.19	0	0

BROWN, ANDREW CONRAD G-SL
Born: Hamilton, Ont., Feb. 15, 1944

1971-72 Detroit Red Wings	9 1/3	37	0	3.96	1	0

BROWN, KENNETH MURRAY G-SL
Born: Port Arthur, Ont., Dec. 19, 1948

1970-71 Chicago Black Hawks	1/3	1		3.00	0	0

BUZINSKI, STEPHEN G-SL
Born: Swift Current, Sask., Oct. 15, 1917

1942-43 New York Rangers	9	55	0	6.11	0	0

CALEY, DONALD THOMAS G-SL
Born: Dauphin, Man. Oct. 9, 1945

1967-68 St. Louis Blues	1/2	3		6.00	0	0

CARON, JACQUES JOSEPH G-SL
Born: Noranda, Que. April 21, 1940

1967-68 Los Angeles Kings	1	4		4.00	0	0
1968-69 " " "	2 1/3	10	0	4.29	0	0
1971-72 St. Louis Blues	27 (28)	70	1	2.59	1	0
3 Years	30 1/3 (32)	84	1	2.80	1	0

CARTER, LYLE DWIGHT "CAT" G-SL
Born: Truro, Nova Scotia. April 29, 1945

1971-72 Oakland Seals	12(15)	51	0	4.25	0	2

CHABOT, LORNE G-SL
Born: Montreal, Que. Oct. 5, 1900

1926-27 New York Rangers	36 2/3	59	10	1.61	0	0
1927-28 " " "	44	79	11	1.80	0	0
1928-29 Toronto Maple Leafs	42 5/6(44)	67	†11	1.56	0	2
1929-30 " " "	42	113	*6	2.69	0	0
1930-31 " " "	37	80	6	2.16	0	0
1931-32 " " "	43	109	4	2.53	0	2
1932-33 " " "	48	111	5	2.35	0	2
1933-34 Montreal Canadiens	47	101	8	2.15	0	2
1934-35 Chicago Black Hawks	48	88	8	1.83	0	0
1935-36 Montreal Maroons	16	35	2	2.19	0	0
1936-37 New York Americans	6	25	1	4.17	0	0
11 Years	410 1/2(412)	867	72	2.11	0	8

*league leader
†also shared shut-out with Benjamin Grant on March 14, 1929 against New York Americans
1934-35 1st All-Star Team & Georges Vezina Memorial Trophy
Note: On March 15, 1932 Chabot drew minor penalty and was ordered to penalty-box. Toronto defencemen
    Homer, Levinsky and Clancy, in turn, attempted to guard net and each had a goal scored on him. These 3
    goals are charged against Chabot.

Sea.	Club	Ga.	GA	SO	Ave.	A.	PM.
CHADWICK, EDWIN WALTER G-SL							
Born: Fergus, Ont. May 8, 1933							
1955-56 Toronto Maple Leafs		5	3	2	0.60	0	0
1956-57 " " "		70	192	5	2.74	0	0
1957-58 " " "		70	226	4	3.23	0	0
1958-59 " " "		30	92	3	3.07	0	0
1959-60 " " "		4	15	0	3.75	0	0
1961-62 Boston Bruins		4	22	0	5.50	0	0
6 Years		183	550	14	3.01	0	0
CHEEVERS, GERALD MICHAEL "CHEESY" G-SL							
Born: St. Catharines, Ont. Dec. 2, 1940							
1961-62 Toronto Maple Leafs		2	7	0	3.50	0	0
1965-66 Boston Bruins		5 2/3(7)	34	0	6.00	0	0
1966-67 " "		21 2/3	72	1	3.32	0	12
1967-68 " "		44 1/6(47)	128	3	2.90	2	8
1968-69 " "		51 5/6	146	3	2.82	0	14
1969-70 " "		39 3/4(41)	108	4	2.72	0	4
1970-71 " "		40	109	3	2.725	0	4
1971-72 " "		40 1/3	101	2	2.50	2	25
8 Years		245 1/3(252)	705	16	2.87	4	67

CLEGHORN, J. OGILVIE
Tended goal for Pittsburgh Pirates as they defeated Montreal Canadiens 3-2 on February 23, 1926 at Pittsburgh.

Sea.	Club	Ga.	GA	SO	Ave.	A.	PM.
COLVIN, LESTER							
Born: Oshawa, Ont. Feb. 8, 1921							
1948-49 Boston Bruins		1	4		4.00	0	0
CONNELL, ALEXANDER "OTTAWA FIREMAN" G-SL							
Born: Ottawa, Ont. 1901							
1924-25 Ottawa Senators		30	66	*7	2.20	0	2
1925-26 " "		36	42	*15	1.17	0	0
1926-27 " "		44	69	13	1.57	0	2
1927-28 " "		44	57	*15	1.30	0	0
1928-29 " "		44	67	7	1.52	0	0
1929-30 " "		44	118	3	2.68	0	0
1930-31 " "		35 1/3	110	3	3.11	0	0
1931-32 Detroit Falcons		48	108	6	2.25	0	0
1932-33 Ottawa Senators		13 3/5	36	1	2.65	0	0
1933-34 New York Americans		2/3	2		3.00	0	0
1934-35 Montreal Maroons		48	92	*9	1.92	0	0
1936-37 " "		27	63	2	2.33	0	0
12 Years		414 3/5(416)	830	81	2.00	0	4

*league leader

Hall of Fame

Connell's great consecutive games shut-out record

Jan. 28, 1928	Ottawa	2	Canadiens	1	Mantha (Canadiens) scored at 14:21 of 2nd Period - -		
					time left	25 min. 39 sec.	
Jan. 31, 1928	"	4	Toronto	0		60 "	
Feb. 2,	"	1	Maroons	0	Kilrea scored at 9:20 of overtime		
					(game over when goal scored)	69 "	20 "
Feb. 7,	"	0	Rangers	0	10 minutes overtime played	70 "	
Feb. 9,	"	0	"	0	10 " " "	70 "	
Feb. 16,	"	0	Pittsburgh	0	10 " " "	70 "	
Feb. 18,	"	1	Canadiens	0		60 "	
Feb. 22,	"	3	Chicago	2	Keats (Chicago) scored at 18:30 of		
					2nd period	38 "	30 "
						463 min. 29 sec.	

Sea.	Club	Ga.	GA	SO	Ave.	A.	PM.
COURTEAU, MAURICE LAURENT							
Born: Quebec City, Que. Feb. 18, 1918							
1943-44 Boston Bruins		6	33	0	5.50	0	0
COX, ABBIE							
1929-30 Montreal Maroons		1	2		2.00	0	0
1933-34 New York Americans-Detroit		1 1/2	7	0	4.67	0	0
1935-36 Montreal Canadiens		1	1		1.00	0	0
3 Years		3 1/2	10	0	2.86	0	0

Sea.	Club	Ga.	GA	SO	Ave.	A.	PM.
CROZIER, ROGER ALLAN G-SR							
Born: Bracebridge, Ont. March 16, 1942							
1963-64	Detroit Red Wings	15	51	2	3.40	0	0
1964-65	" " "	69 1/2	171	*6	2.46	0	10
1965-66	" " "	62 1/4 (64)	175	*7	2.81	0	4
1966-67	" " "	54 1/3 (58)	183	4	3.37	0	2
1967-68	" " "	28 3/4 (34)	97	1	3.37	0	2
1968-69	" " "	30 1/3 (38)	103	0	3.40	0	0
1969-70	" " "	31 1/4 (34)	83	0	2.66	0	0
1970-71	Buffalo Sabres	36 2/3 (44)	136	1	3.71	0	0
1971-72	" "	60 5/6 (63)	221	2	3.63	0	10
9 Years		389(420)	1220	23	3.14	0	28
*league leader							
1964-65 1st All-Star Team & Frank Calder Memorial Trophy							
CUDE, WILFRED REGINALD G-SL							
Born: Barry, South Wales. July 4, 1910							
1930-31	Philadelphia Quakers	28 1/6	127	1	4.51	0	0
1931-32	Boston Bruins – Chicago	2 1/2	10	1	4.00	0	0
1933-34	Montreal Canadiens–Detroit	30	47	5	1.57	0	0
1934-35	" "	48	145	1	3.02	0	0
1935-36	" "	47	122	6	2.60	0	0
1936-37	" "	44	99	5	2.25	0	0
1937-38	" "	47	126	3	2.68	0	0
1938-39	" "	23	77	2	3.35	0	0
1939-40	" "	7	29	0	4.14	0	0
1940-41	" "	3	13	0	4.33	0	0
10 Years		279 2/3(281)	795	24	2.84	0	0
1935-36 2nd All-Star Team							
1936-37 " " " "							
CYR, CLAUDE							
Born: Montreal, Que. March 27, 1939							
1958-59	Montreal Canadiens	1/3	1		3.00	0	0
DALEY, THOMAS JOSEPH "JOE" G-SL							
Born: Winnipeg, Man. Feb. 20, 1943							
1968-69	Pittsburgh Penguins	27(29)	89	2	3.30	0	2
1969-70	"	8 4/5	27	0	3.07	0	0
1970-71	Buffalo Sabres	34 1/2(38)	130	1	3.77	1	12
1971-72	Detroit Red Wings	27 (29)	86	0	3.19	0	2
4 Years		97 2/5(105)	332	3	3.41	1	16
DAMORE, NICHOLAS J.							
Born: Niagara Falls, Ont. July 10, 1916							
1941-42	Boston Bruins	1	3		3.00	0	0
DeCOURCY, ROBERT PHILIP G-SL							
Born: Toronto, Ont. June 12, 1927							
1947-48	New York Rangers	1/2	6		12.00	0	0
DeFELICE, NORMAN G-SL							
Born: Schumacher, Ont. Jan. 19, 1933							
1956-57	Boston Bruins	10	30	0	3.00	0	2
DeJORDY, DENIS EMILE G-SL							
Born: St. Hyacinthe, Que. Nov. 12, 1938							
1962-63	Chicago Black Hawks	4 5/6	12	0	2.48	0	0
1963-64	" " "	5 2/3	19	0	3.35	0	0
1964-65	" " "	29 1/3	76	3	2.59	1	0
1965-67	" " "	42 1/4(44)	104	4	2.46	0	0
1967-68	" " "	47 1/3(50)	128	4	2.70	0	0
1968-69	" " "	49 2/3(53)	156	2	3.14	1	2
1969-70	" – Los Angeles Kings	28 1/2(31)	87	0	3.05	0	0
1970-71	Los Angeles Kings	56 1/4(60)	217	1	3.86	0	0
1971-72	" " " –Montreal	10 1/3(12)	48	0	4.65	1	0
9 Years		274 1/6(291)	847	14	3.09	3	2
1966-67 Georges Vezina Memorial Trophy (with Glenn Hall)							
DESJARDINS, GERARD FERDINAND "BIGGER" G-SL							
Born: Sudbury, Ont. July 22, 1944							
1968-69	Los Angeles Kings	58 1/3(60)	194	4	3.33	1	6
1969-70	" " –Chicago	44 5/6(47)	168	3	3.75	1	14
1970-71	Chicago Black Hawks	20 1/3(22)	51	0	2.51	0	6
1971-72	" " "	6	22	0	3.67	0	0
4 Years		129 1/2(135)	435	7	3.36	2	26

Sea. Club	Ga.	GA	SO	Ave.	A.	PM.
DICKIE, WILLIAM G-SR						
1941-42 Chicago Black Hawks	1	3		3.00	0	0
DION, CONRAD G-SR						
Born: St. Remi, Que. Aug. 11, 1918						
1943-44 Detroit Red Wings	26	80	1	3.08	0	0
1944-45 " " "	12	39	0	3.25	0	0
2 Years	38	119	1	3.13	0	0
DOLSON, CLARENCE "DOLLY"						
1928-29 Detroit Cougars	44	63	10	1.43	0	0
1929-30 " "	5	24	0	4.80	0	0
1930-31 " – Falcons	44	105	6	2.39	0	0
3 Years	93	192	16	2.06	0	0
DRYDEN, DAVID MURRAY G-SL						
Born: Hamilton, Ont. Sept. 5, 1941						
1961-62 New York Rangers	2/3	3		4.50	0	0
1965-66 Chicago Black Hawks	7 3/5(11)	23	0	3.03	1	0
1967-68 " " "	21 1/6(27)	72	1	3.40	0	0
1968-69 " " "	24 2/3(30)	80	3	3.29	1	0
1970-71 Buffalo Sabres	6 5/6(10)	25	1	3.66	1	0
1971-72 " "	17 1/6(20)	68	0	3.96	0	0
6 Years	78(99)	271	5	3.47	3	0
DRYDEN, KENNETH WAYNE G-SL						
Born: Hamilton, Ont. Aug. 8, 1947						
1970-71 Montreal Canadiens	5 2/5	9	0	1.67	0	0
1971-72 " "	63 1/3	144	8	2.27	3	4
2 Years	68 4/5(70)	153	8	2.22	3	4
1971-72 2nd All-Star Team & Frank Calder Memorial Trophy						
DURNAN, WILLIAM G-SR or L						
Born: Toronto, Ont. Jan. 22, 1915						
1943-44 Montreal Canadiens	50	109	2	2.18	0	0
1944-45 " "	50	121	1	2.42	0	0
1945-46 " "	40 40	104	4	2.60	0	0
1946-47 " "	60	138	4	2.30	0	0
1947-48 " "	58 2/5	162	5	2.77	0	5
1948-49 " "	60	126	10	2.10	0	0
1949-50 " "	64	141	8	2.20	1	2
7 Years	382 2/5	901	34	2.36	1	7
league leader						
1943-44 1st All-Star Team & Georges Vezina Memorial Trophy						
1944-45 " " " " " " " " "						
1945-46 " " " " " " " "						
1946-47 " " " " " " " "						
1948-49 " " " " " " " "						
1949-50 " " " " " " " "						
Hall of Fame						
DYCK, EDWARD G-SL						
Born: Warman, Sask. Oct. 29, 1950						
1972-72 Vancouver Canucks	9 1/2(12)	36	0	3.79	0	0
EDWARDS, ALLAN ROY G-SR						
Born: Seneca, Ont. March 12, 1937						
1967-68 Detroit Red Wings	36 1/4(41)	128	0	3.53	0	0
1968-69 " " "	35 (40)	90	4	2.57	0	0
1969-70 " " "	44 3/4(47)	116	2	2.59	1	0
1970-71 " " "	35 (37)	119	0	3.40	0	2
1971-72 Pittsburgh Penguins	14 1/6	38	0	2.68	1	0
5 Years	165 1/6(180)	491	6	2.97	2	2
EDWARDS, GARY WILLIAM G-SL						
Born: Toronto, Ont. Oct. 5, 1947						
1968-69 St. Louis Blues	4 min.(Dec.11th)	0			0	0
1969-70 " " "	1	4		4.00	0	0
1971-72 Los Angeles Kings	41 2/3(44)	152	2	3.65	0	0
3 Years	42 2/3(46)	156	2	3.66	0	0
EDWARDS, MARVIN WAYNE G-SL						
Born: St. Catharines, Ont. Aug. 15, 1935						
1968-69 Pittsburgh Penguins	1	3		3.00	0	0
1969-70 Toronto Maple Leafs	23 2/3(25)	78	1	3.30	1	24
2 Years	24 2/3(26)	81	1	3.28	1	24

Sea.	Club	Ga.	GA	SO	Ave.	A.	PM.

ESPOSITO, ANTHONY JAMES "TONY" G-SR
Born: Sault Ste. Marie, Ont. April 23, 1943

Sea.	Club	Ga.	GA	SO	Ave.	A.	PM.
1968-69	Montreal Canadiens	12 1/2	36	2	2.88	0	0
1969-70	Chicago Black Hawks	62 2/3	137	*15	2.19	2	2
1970-71	" " "	55 1/3(57)	126	6	2.28	1	4
1971-72	" " "	46 1/3(48)	82	*9	1.77	1	2
4 Years		176 5/6(181)	381	32	2.15	4	8

*league leader
1969-70 1st All-Star Team, Frank Calder & Georges Vezina Memorial Trophies
1971-72 " " " " & Georges Vezina Memorial Trophy (with Gary Smith)

EVANS, CLAUDE G-SL
Born: Longueuil, Que. April 28, 1933

Sea.	Club	Ga.	GA	SO	Ave.	A.	PM.
1954-55	Montreal Canadiens	3 1/3	12	0	3.60	0	0
1957-58	Boston Bruins	1	4		4.00	0	0
2 Years		4 1/3	16	0	3.69	0	0

FAVELL, DOUGLAS ROBERT G-SL
Born: St. Catharines, Ont. April 5, 1945

Sea.	Club	Ga.	GA	SO	Ave.	A.	PM.
1967-68	Philadelphia Flyers	36 1/2	85	4	2.33	0	37
1968-69	" "	20 (21)	71	1	3.55	0	4
1969-70	" "	13 2/3(15)	44	1	3.22	0	2
1970-71	" "	40 1/2(44)	111	2	2.74	1	9
1971-72	.. ..	49 5/6(54)	145	5	2,91	1	32
5 Years		160 1/2(171)	456	13	2.84	2	84

FORBES, VERNON "JAKIE"
Born: Toronto, Ont.

Sea.	Club	Ga.	GA	SO	Ave.	A.	PM.
1919-20	Toronto St. Patricks	5	21	0	4.20	0	0
1920-21	" " "	20	78	0	3.90	0	0
1922-23	Hamilton Tigers	24	110	0	4.58	0	0
1923-24	" "	24	68	1	2.83	0	0
1924-25	" "	30	60	6	2.00	0	2
1925-26	New York Americans	35 1/3	86	2	2.43	0	0
1926-27	" " "	44	91	8	2.07	0	0
1927-28	" " "	16	51	2	3.19	0	0
1928-29	" " "	1	3		3.00	0	0
1929-30	" " "	1	1		1.00	0	0
1930-31	Philadelphia Quakers	2	7	0	3.50	0	0
1931-32	New York Americans	6	16	0	2.67	0	0
1932-33	" " "	1	2		2.00	0	0
13 Years		209 1/3	594	19	2.84	0	

FOWLER, NORMAN BOSTOCK "HEC" G-SL
Born: Saskatoon, Sask.

Sea.	Club	Ga.	GA	SO	Ave.	A.	PM.
1924-25	Boston Bruins	7	43	0	6.14	0	0

FRANCIS, EMILE PERCY "THE CAT" G-SL
Born: North Battleford, Sask. Sept. 13, 1926

Sea.	Club	Ga.	GA	SO	Ave.	A.	PM.
1946-47	Chicago Black Hawks	19	104	0	5.47	0	0
1947-48	" " "	54	183	1	3.39	0	6
1948-49	New York Rangers	2	4	0	2.00	0	0
1949-50	" " "	1	8		8.00	0	0
1950-51	" " "	4 1/3	14	0	3.23	0	0
1951-52	" " "	14	42	0	3.00	0	0
6 Years		94 1/3	355	1	3.76	0	6

FRANKS, JAMES REGINALD G-SL
Born: Melville, Sask. Nov. 8, 1914

Sea.	Club	Ga.	GA	SO	Ave.	A.	PM.
1937-38	Detroit Red Wings	1	3		3.00	0	0
1942-43	New York Rangers	23	103	0	4.48	0	0
1943-44	Detroit Red Wings – Boston	18	75	1	4.17	0	0
3 Years		42	181	1	4.31	0	0

FREDERICK, RAYMOND G-SL
Born: Fort Francis, Ont. July 31, 1929

Sea.	Club	Ga.	GA	SO	Ave.	A.	PM.
1954-55	Chicago Black Hawks	5	22	0	4.40	0	0

GAMBLE, BRUCE GEORGE G-SL
Born: Port Arthur, Ont. May 24, 1938

Sea.	Club	Ga.	GA	SO	Ave.	A.	PM.
1958-59	New York Rangers	2	6	0	3.00	0	0
1960-61	Boston Bruins	52	195	0	3.75	0	14
1961-62	" "	28	123	1	4.39	0	4
1965-66	Toronto Maple Leafs	8 1/3(10)	21	4	2.52	0	0

(continued)

Sea.	Club			Ga.	GA	SO	Ave.	A.	PM.
1966-67	”	”	”	19 3/4(23)	68	0	3.44	0	0
1967-68	”	”	”	36 2/3(41)	88	5	2.40	0	2
1968-69	”	”	”	57 2/5(61)	164	3	2.86	0	2
1969-70	”	”	”	51(52)	156	5	3.06	1	0
1970-71	” —Philadelphia Flyers			32 1/2(34)	123	†2	3.78	0	0
1971-72	Philadelphia Flyers			19 5/6(24)	60	2	3.03	0	2
10 Years				307 1/2(327)	1004	22	3.27	1	24

†also shared shut-out with J. Jacques Plante on January 2, 1971 against Detroit

GARDINER, CHARLES ROBERT "CHUCK" G-SR
Born: Edinburgh, Scotland. December 31, 1904

1927-28	Chicago Black Hawks			40	114	3	2.85	0	0
1928-29	”	”	”	44	85	5	1.93	0	2
1929-30	”	”	”	44	111	3	2.52	0	0
1930-31	”	”	”	44	78	*12	1.77	0	0
1931-32	”	”	”	47 1/2	97	4	2.04	0	0
1932-33	”	”	”	48	101	5	2.10	0	0
1933-34	”	”	”	48	83	*10	1.73	0	0
7 Years				315 1/2	669	42	2.12	0	2

*league leader
1930-31 1st All-Star Team
1931-32 ” ” ” ” & Georges Vezina Memorial Trophy
1932-33 2nd ” ” ”
1933-34 1st ” ” ” & Georges Vezina Memorial Trophy
Hall of Fame

GARDINER, WILBERT "BERT" G-SL
Born: Saskatoon, Sask. March 25, 1913

1935-36	New York Rangers	1	1		1.00	0	0
1940-41	Montreal Canadiens	41 1/2	119	†1	2.87	0	0
1941-42	” ”	10	42	0	4.20	0	0
1942-43	Chicago Black Hawks	50	180	1	3.60	0	0
1943-44	Boston Bruins	41	212	1	5.17	1	0
5 Years		143 1/2	554	3	3.86	1	0

†also shared shut-out with Paul Bibeault on March 15, 1941 against New York Americans

GARDNER, GEORGE EDWARD "BUD" G-SL
Born: Lachine, Que. Oct. 8, 1942

1965-66	Detroit Red Wings			1	1		1.00	0	0
1966-67	”	”	”	9 1/3(11)	36	0	3.86	0	0
1967-68	”	”	”	9 (12)	32	0	3.56	0	0
1970-71	Vancouver Canucks			15 1/3(18)	53	0	3.46	0	0
1971-72	” ”			20 2/3(24)	87	0	4.21	0	0
5 Years				55 1/3(66)	209	0	3.78	0	0

GATHERUM, DAVID L. G-SL
Born: Fort William, Ont. March 28, 1932

1953-54	Detroit Red Wings	3	3	1	1.00	0	0

GAUTHIER, PAUL G-SR
Born: Winnipeg, Man.

1937-38	Montreal Canadiens	1	2		2.00	0	0

GELINEAU, JOHN EDWARD "JACK" G-SL
Born: Montreal, Que. Nov. 11, 1924

1948-49	Boston Bruins	4	12	0	3.00	0	0
1949-50	” ”	67	220	3	3.28	0	0
1950-51	” ”	70	197	4	2.81	0	4
1953-54	Chicago Black Hawks	2	18	0	9.00	0	0
4 Years		143	447	7	3.13	0	4

1949-50 Frank Calder Memorial Trophy

GIACOMIN, EDWARD "GO GO" G-SL
Born: Sudbury, Ont. June 6, 1939

1965-66	New York Rangers			35(36)	130	0	3.71	0	8
1966-67	”	”	”	66 1/3(68)	175	*9	2.64	0	8
1967-68	”	”	”	65 2/3	162	*8	2.47	0	4
1968-69	”	”	”	68 3/5(70)	178	7	2.59	0	2
1969-70	”	”	”	69 1/6	169	6	2.44	2	2
1970-71	”	”	”	44(45)	98	*8	2.23	0	4
1971-72	”	”	”	42 1/2(44)	117	1	2.75	3	4
7 Years				391 1/5(399)	1029	39	2.63	5	32

*league leader
1966-67 1st All-Star Team

(continued)

Sea.	Club	Ga.	GA	SO	Ave.	A.	PM.
1967-68 2nd " " " "							
1968-69 " " " "							
1969-70 " " " "							
1970-71 1st " " " & Georges Vezina Memorial Trophy (with Gilles Villemure)							

GILBERT, GILLES JOSEPH G-SL
Born: St. Esprit, Que. March 31, 1949

Sea.	Club	Ga.	GA	SO	Ave.	A.	PM.
1969-70 Minnesota North Stars		1	6		6.00	0	0
1970-71 " " "		15 1/2(17)	59	0	3.81	0	2
1971-72 " " "		3 2/3	11	0	3.00	0	0
3 Years		20 1/6(22)	76	0	3.77	0	2

GILL, ANDRE G-SL
Born: Sorel, Que. Sept. 19, 1941

Sea.	Club	Ga.	GA	SO	Ave.	A.	PM.
1967-68 Boston Bruins		4 1/2	13	1	2.89	0	0

GOODMAN, PAUL G-SL
Born: Selkirk, Man. Nov. 4, 1909

Sea.	Club	Ga.	GA	SO	Ave.	A.	PM.
1939-40 Chicago Black Hawks		31	62	4	2.00	0	0
1940-41 " " "		21	55	2	2.62	0	0
2 Years		52	117	6	2.25	0	0

GRANT, BENJAMIN CAMERON
Born: Owen Sound, Ont. July 14, 1908

Sea.	Club	Ga.	GA	SO	Ave.	A.	PM.
1929-29 Toronto Maple Leafs		1 1/6	2	†0	1.71	0	0
1929-30 " – New York Americans		9	36	0	4.00	0	0
1930-31 " Maple Leafs		7	19	2	2.71	0	0
1931-32 " " "		5	18	1	3.60	0	0
1933-34 New York Americans		5	18	1	3.60	0	0
1943-44 Toronto Maple Leafs – Boston		21	93	0	4.43	0	0
6 Years		48 1/6	186	4	3.86	0	0

†also shared shut-out with Lorne Chabot on March 14, 1929 against New York Americans

GRAY, GERALD ROBERT G-SR
Born: Brantford, Ont. Jan. 28, 1948

Sea.	Club	Ga.	GA	SO	Ave.	A.	PM.
1970-71 Detroit Red Wings		6 1/3	30	0	4.74	0	0

GRAY, HARRISON LEROY G-SL
Born: Calgary, Alta. Sept. 5, 1941

Sea.	Club	Ga.	GA	SO	Ave.	A.	PM.
1963-64 Detroit Red Wings		2/3	5		7.50	0	0

HAINSWORTH, GEORGE G-SL
Born: Toronto, Ont. June 26, 1895

Sea.	Club	Ga.	GA	SO	Ave.	A.	PM.
1926-27 Montreal Canadiens		44	67	*14	1.52	0	0
1927-28 " "		44	48	13	1.09	0	0
1928-29 " "		44	43	*22	0.98	0	0
1929-30 " "		42	108	4	2.57	0	0
1930-31 " "		44	89	8	2.02	0	0
1931-32 " "		48	111	6	2.31	0	2
1932-33 " "		48	115	8	2.40	0	0
1933-34 Toronto Maple Leafs		48	119	3	2.48	0	0
1934-35 " " "		48	111	8	2.31	0	0
1935-36 " " "		48	106	8	2.21	0	0
1936-37 " –Montreal Canadiens		7	21	0	3.00	0	0
11 Years		465	938	94	2.02	0	2

*league leader
1926-27 Georges Vezina Memorial Trophy
1927-28 " " " "
1928-29 " " " "

Note: On December 2, 1931 Hainsworth drew minor penalty and was ordered to penalty-box. Canadiens' defenceman Leduc attempted to guard net and had a goal scored on him. This goal is charged against Hainsworth.

Hall of Fame

HALL, GLENN HENRY "MR. GOALIE" G-SL
Born: Humboldt, Sask. Oct. 3, 1931

Sea.	Club	Ga.	GA	SO	Ave.	A.	PM.
1952-53 Detroit Red Wings		6	10	1	1.67	0	0
1954-55 " " "		2	2	0	1.00	0	0
1955-56 " " "		70	148	*12	2.11	0	14
1956-57 " " "		70	157	4	2.24	0	2
1957-58 Chicago Black Hawks		70	202	7	2.89	0	10
1958-59 " " "		70	208	1	2.97	0	0
1959-60 " " "		70	180	*6	2.57	1	2
1960-61 " " "		70	180	*6	2.57	1	0

(continued)

Sea.	Club			Ga.	GA	SO	Ave.	A.	PM.
1961-62	"	"	"	70	186	*9	2.66	0	12
1962-63	"	"	"	65 1/6	166	*5	2.55	0	0
1963-64	"	"	"	64 1/3	150	7	2.33	2	2
1964-65	"	"	"	40 2/3	100	4	2.46	0	2
1965-66	"	"	"	62 2/5(64)	164	4	2.63	2	14
1966-67	"	"	"	27 3/4(32)	66	2	2.38	0	10
1967-68 St. Louis Blues				47 2/3(49)	120	5	2.52	0	0
1968-69	"	"	"	39 1/4(41)	85	*8	2.17	2	20
1969-70	"	"	"	16 5/6(18)	49	1	2.91	0	0
1970-71	"	"	"	19 1/3(32)	72	†2	2.45	1	0
18 Years				891 2/5(906)	2245	84	2.52	9	88

*league leader
†also shared shut-out with Ernest Wakely on November 5, 1970 against Boston
1955-56 2nd All-Star Team & Frank Calder Memorial Trophy
1956-57 1st " "
1957-58 " " " "
1959-60 " " " "
1960-61 2nd " " "
1961-62 " " " "
1962-63 1st " " " & Georges Vezina Memorial Trophy
1963-64 " " " "
1965-66 " " " "
1966-67 2nd " " " & Georges Vezina Memorial Trophy (with Denis DeJordy)
1968-69 1st " " " " " " " " (with J. Jacques Plante)

HEAD, DONALD CHARLES G-SL
Born: Mount Dennis, Ont. June 30, 1933

1961-62 Boston Bruins	38	161	2	4.24	0	14

HEBERT, SAMUEL
Born: 1894

1917-18 Toronto Arenas	3	15	0	5.00		
1923-24 Ottawa Senators	2	9	0	4.50	0	0
2 Years	5	24	0	4.80	0	0

HENDERSON, JOHN DUNCAN "LONG JOHN" G-SL
Born: Toronto, Ont. March 25, 1933

1954-55 Boston Bruins	43 2/3	109	5	2.50	0	0
1955-56 " "	1	4		4.00	0	0
2 Years	44 2/3	113	5	2.53	0	0

HENRY, GORDON DAVID "RED"
Born: Owen Sound, Ont. Aug. 17, 1926

1948-49 Boston Bruins	1	0	1	0.00	0	0
1949-50 " "	2	5	0	2.50	0	0
2 Years	3	5	1	1.67	0	0

HENRY, SAMUEL JAMES "SUGAR JIM" G-SL
Born: Winnipeg, Man. Oct. 24, 1920

1941-42 New York Rangers	48	143	1	2.98	0	0
in Canadian Army						
1945-46 New York Rangers	10	42	1	4.20	0	0
1946-47 " " "	2	9	0	4.50	0	0
1947-48 " " "	48	153	2	3.19	0	0
1948-49 Chicago Black Hawks	60	211	0	3.52	0	0
1951-52 Boston Bruins	70	176	7	2.51	0	0
1952-53 " "	70	172	8	2.46	0	0
1953-54 " "	70	181	8	2.58	0	0
1954-55 " "	26 1/3	79	1	3.00	0	0
9 Years	404 1/3	1166	28	2.88	0	0

1951-52 2nd All-Star Team

HIGHTON, HECTOR SALISBURY G-SR
Born: Medicine Hat, Alta. Dec. 10, 1923

1943-44 Chicago Black Hawks	24	108	0	4.50	0	0

HIMES, NORMAN
Tended goal for New York Americans from early in 3rd period as they lost to Montreal Canadiens 4 - 0 on December 3, 1927 at Montreal (0 goals scored against him).
Tended goal for New York Americans as they lost to Toronto Maple Leafs 3 - 0 on December 1, 1928 at Toronto.

Sea.	Club	Ga.	GA	SO	Ave.	A.	PM.

HODGE, CHARLES EDWARD G-SL
Born: Lachine, Que. July 28, 1933

Sea.	Club	Ga.	GA	SO	Ave.	A.	PM.
1954-55	Montreal Canadiens	13 2/3	31	1	2.27	0	0
1957-58	" "	12	31	1	2.58	0	0
1958-59	" "	2	6	0	3.00	0	0
1959-60	" "	1	3		3.00	0	0
1960-61	" "	30	76	4	2.53	0	0
1963-64	" "	62	141	*8	2.27	0	2
1964-65	" "	52(53)	135	3	2.60	0	2
1965-66	" "	21 2/3(26)	56	1	2.58	0	0
1966-67	" "	34 1/4(37)	88	3	2.57	0	2
1967-68	Oakland Seals	55 1/6(58)	158	†3	2.86	0	4
1968-69	" "	13 (14)	48	0	3.69	0	0
1969-70	" "	12 1/3(14)	43	0	3.49	0	0
1970-71	Vancouver Canucks	32 2/3(35)	112	0	3.43	0	0
13 Years		341 3/4(358)	928	24	2.72	0	10

*league leader
†also shared shut-out with Gary Smith on February 14, 1968 against Philadelphia
1963-64 2nd All-Star Team & Georges Vezina Memorial Trophy
1964-65 " " " "
1965-66 Georges Vezina Memorial Trophy (with Lorne Worsley)

HOGANSON, PAUL EDWARD G-SR
Born: Toronto, Ont. Nov. 12, 1949

Sea.	Club	Ga.	GA	SO	Ave.	A.	PM.
1970-71	Pittsburgh Penguins	1(2)	7		7.00	0	0

HOLMES, HARRY "HAP" G-SL
Born: Aurora, Ont. Feb. 21, 1889

Sea.	Club	Ga.	GA	SO	Ave.	A.	PM.
1917-18	Montreal Wanderers–Toronto	21	111	0	5.29	- -	- -
1918-19	Toronto Arenas	2	9	0	4.50	0	0
1926-27	Detroit Cougars	41	100	6	2.44	0	0
1927-28	" "	44	79	11	1.80	0	0
4 Years		108	299	17	2.77	0	0

Hall of Fame

IRONS, ROBERT RICHARD "ROBBIE" G-SL
Born: Toronto, Ont. Nov. 19, 1946

Sea.	Club	Ga.	GA	SO	Ave.	A.	PM.
1968-69	St. Louis Blues	3 min. (Nov. 13th)	0			0	0

IRONSTONE, JOSEPH

Sea.	Club	Ga.	GA	SO	Ave.	A.	PM.
1925-26	New York Americans	2/3	3		4.50	0	0
1927-28	Toronto Maple Leafs	1	0	1	0.00	0	0
2 Years		1 2/3	3	1	1.80	0	0

JACKSON, DOUGLAS
Born: Winnipeg, Man. Dec. 12, 1924

Sea.	Club	Ga.	GA	SO	Ave.	A.	PM.
1947-48	Chicago Black Hawks	6	42	0	7.00	0	0

JACKSON, PERCY G-SL
Born: Canmore, Alta. Sept. 21, 1907

Sea.	Club	Ga.	GA	SO	Ave.	A.	PM.
1931-32	Boston Bruins	3 2/3	8	0	2.18	0	0
1933-34	New York Americans	1	9		9.00	0	0
1934-35	" " Rangers	1	8		8.00	0	0
1935-36	Boston Bruins	2/3	1		1.50	0	0
4 Years		6 1/3	26	0	4.11	0	0

JENKINS, ROGER
Tended goal for New York Americans from midway in 2nd period as they lost to New York Rangers 11-5 on March 16, 1939 at New York (7 goals scored against him).

JOHNSTON, EDWARD JOSEPH G-SL
Born: Montreal, Que. Nov. 23, 1935

Sea.	Club	Ga.	GA	SO	Ave.	A.	PM.
1962-63	Boston Bruins	48 1/2(50)	196	1	4.04	0	10
1963-64	" "	70	212	6	3.03	0	0
1964-65	" "	47	167	3	3.55	0	4
1965-66	" "	29(33)	109	1	3.76	0	2
1966-67	" "	31 1/3(34)	117	0	3.73	1	0
1967-68	" "	25 1/3(28)	75	0	2.96	0	0
1968-69	" "	24	75	2	3.125	1	0
1969-70	" "	36 1/4	108	3	2.98	2	2
1970-71	" "	38	98	4	2.58	1	6
1971-72	" "	37 2/3	103	2	2.73	4	0
10 Years		387 1/6(399)	1260	22	3.25	9	24

Sea. Club	Ga.	GA	SO	Ave.	A.	PM.
JUNKIN, JOSEPH BRIAN G-SL						
Born: Lindsay, Ont. Sept. 8, 1946						
1968-69 Boston Bruins	1/6	0		0.00	0	0
KARAKAS, MICHAEL "IRON MIKE" G-SL						
Born: Aurora, Minn. Dec. 12, 1911						
1935-36 Chicago Black Hawks	48	92	9	1.92	0	0
1936-37 ” ” ”	48	131	5	2.73	0	2
1937-38 ” ” ”	48	139	1	2.90	0	0
1938-39 ” ” ”	48	132	5	2.75	0	2
1939-40 ” –Montreal Canadiens	22	76	0	3.45	0	0
1943-44 ” Black Hawks	26	79	3	3.04	0	0
1944-45 ” ” ”	48	187	*4	3.90	1	0
1945-46 ” ” ”	48	166	1	3.46	0	5
8 Years	336	1002	28	2.98	1	9
*league leader						
1935-36 Rookie of the Year						
1944-45 2nd All-Star Team						
KEENAN, DONALD						
1958-59 Boston Bruins	1	4		4.00	0	0
KERR, DAVID ALEXANDER G-SR						
Born: Toronto, Ont. Jan. 11, 1910						
1930-31 Montreal Maroons	30 2/3(32)	76	1	2.48	0	0
1931-32 New York Americans	1	6		6.00	0	0
1932-33 Montreal Maroons	26	58	4	2.23	0	0
1933-34 ” ”	48	122	6	2.54	0	0
1934-35 New York Rangers	37	94	4	2.54	0	0
1935-36 ” ” ”	47	95	8	2.02	0	0
1936-37 ” ” ”	48	106	4	2.21	0	0
1937-38 ” ” ”	48	96	*8	2.00	0	0
1938-39 ” ” ”	48	105	6	2.19	0	0
1939-40 ” ” ”	48	77	*8	1.60	0	0
1940-41 ” ” ”	48	125	2	2.60	0	0
11 Years	429 2/3(431)	960	51	2.23	0	0
*league leader						
1937-38 2nd All-Star Team						
1939-40 1st ” ” ” & Georges Vezina Memorial Trophy						
KLYMKIW, JULIAN						
Born: Winnipeg, Man. July 16, 1933						
1958-59 New York Rangers	1/3	2		6.00	0	0
KURT, GARY DAVID G-SR						
Born: Kitchener, Ont. March 9, 1947						
1971-72 Oakland Seals	14(16)	61	0	4.36	0	0
LACROIX, ALPHONSE A.						
Born: Boston, Mass.						
1925-26 Montreal Canadiens	4 2/3	15	0	3.21	0	0
LEHMAN, FREDERICK HUGH (OLD EAGLE EYE) G-SL						
Born: Pembroke, Ont. Oct. 27, 1885						
1926-27 Chicago Black Hawks	44	116	5	2.64	0	0
1927-28 ” ” ”	4	20	1	5.00	0	0
2 Years	48	136	6	2.83	0	0
			Hall of Fame			
LINDSAY, BERT						
1918-19 Toronto Arenas	16	83	0	5.19	0	0
LOCKHART, HOWARD "HOLES"						
1919-20 Toronto St. Patricks-Quebec	6	28	0	4.67	0	0
1920-21 Hamilton Tigers	24	132	1	5.50	0	0
1921-22 ” ”	24	105	0	4.375	0	0
1923-24 Toronto St. Patricks	1	5		5.00	0	0
1924-25 Boston Bruins	2	11	0	5.50	0	0
5 Years	57	281	1	4.93	0	0
LoPRESTI, SAMUEL G-SL						
Born: Elcor, Minn. Jah. 30, 1917						
1940-41 Chicago Black Hawks	27	84	1	5.11	0	0
1941-42 ” ” ”	47	152	3	3.23	0	0
2 Years	74	236	4	3.19	0	0

Sea.	Club	Ga.	GA	SO	Ave.	A.	PM.

LUMLEY, HARRY G-SL
Born: Owen Sound, Ont. Nov. 11, 1926

Sea.	Club	Ga.	GA	SO	Ave.	A.	PM.
1943-44	Detroit Red Wings—New York	2 1/3	13	0	5.57	0	0
1944-45	" " "	37	119	1	3.22	0	0
1945-46	" " "	50	159	2	3.18	0	6
1946-47	" " "	52	159	3	3.05	0	4
1947-48	" " "	59 5/6	147	*7	2.46	0	8
1948-49	" " "	60	145	6	2.42	0	12
1949-50	" " "	63	148	7	2.35	0	10
1950-51	Chicago Black Hawks	63 (64)	246	3	3.90	0	4
1951-52	" " "	69 2/3	241	2	3.46	0	2
1952-53	Toronto Maple Leafs	70	167	*10	2.38	0	18
1953-54	" " "	69	128	*13	1.85	0	6
1954-55	" " "	69	134	8	1.94	0	9
1955-56	" " "	58 4/5	159	3	2.70	0	2
1957-58	Boston Bruins	25	71	3	2.84	0	2
1958-59	" "	11	27	1	2.45	0	0
1959-60	" "	42	147	2	3.50	0	12
16 Years		801 2/3 (804)	2210	71	2.76	0	95

*league leader
1953-54 1st All-Star Team & Georges Vezina Memorial Trophy
1954-55 " " " "

MANIAGO, CESARE G-SL
Born: Trail, British Columbia. Jan. 13, 1939

Sea.	Club	Ga.	GA	SO	Ave.	A.	PM.
1960-61	Toronto Maple Leafs	7	18	0	2.57	0	2
1962-63	Montreal Canadiens	13 2/3	42	0	3.07	0	2
1965-66	New York Rangers	26 5/6(28)	94	2	3.50	2	2
1966-67	" " "	3 2/3(6)	14	0	3.82	0	0
1967-68	Minnesota North Stars	48(52)	133	6	2.77	0	12
1968-69	"	60(64)	200	1	3.33	0	12
1969-70	" " "	48 1/6(50)	163	2	3.38	0	0
1970-71	" " "	39 2/3	107	5	2.70	1	2
1971-72	" "	42 1/3	112	3	2.65	0	4
9 Years		289 1/3(304)	883	19	3.05	3	36

MAROIS, JEAN

Sea.	Club	Ga.	GA	SO	Ave.	A.	PM.
1943-44	Toronto Maple Leafs	1	4		4.00	0	0
1953-54	Chicago Black Hawks	2	11	0	5.50	0	0
2 Years		3	15	0	5.00	0	0

MARTIN, SETH G-SL
Born: Rossland, British Columbia. May 4, 1933

Sea.	Club	Ga.	GA	SO	Ave.	A.	PM.
1967-68	St. Louis Blues	25 5/6(30)	68	1	2.63	1	0

MAYER, GILLES G-SL
Born: Ottawa, Ont. Aug. 24, 1930

Sea.	Club	Ga.	GA	SO	Ave.	A.	PM.
1949-50	Toronto Maple Leafs	1	2		2.00	0	0
1953-54	" " "	1	3		3.00	0	0
1954-55	" " "	1	1		1.00	0	0
1955-56	" " "	6	19	0	3.17	0	0
4 Years		9	25	0	2.78	0	0

McAULEY, KENNETH LESLIE G-SR
Born: Edmonton, Alta. Jan. 9, 1921

Sea.	Club	Ga.	GA	SO	Ave.	A.	PM.
1943-44	New York Rangers	49 2/3	310	0	6.25	0	0
1944-45	" " "	46	227	1	4.93	0	0
2 Years		95 2/3	537	1	5.61	0	0

McCARTAN, JOHN WILLIAM "JACK" G-SL
Born: St. Paul, Minn. Aug. 5, 1935

Sea.	Club	Ga.	GA	SO	Ave.	A.	PM.
1959-60	New York Rangers	4	7	0	1.75	0	0
1960-61	" " "	7 1/3	36	1	4.91	0	0
2 Years		11 1/3	43	1	3.79	0	0

McCOOL, FRANK G-SL
Born: Calgary, Alta. Oct. 27, 1918

Sea.	Club	Ga.	GA	SO	Ave.	A.	PM.
1944-45	Toronto Maple Leafs	50	161	*4	3.22	0	0
1945-46	" " "	22	81	0	3.68	0	5
2 Years		72	242	4	3.36	0	5

*league leader
1944-45 Frank Calder Memorial Trophy

Sea.	Club	Ga.	GA	SO	Ave.	A.	PM.

McDUFFE, PETER ARNOLD G-SL
Born: Milton, Ont. Feb. 16, 1945

1971-72 St. Louis Blues		7 5/6(10)	29	0	3.70	0	0

McGRATTON, THOMAS
Born: Brantford, Ont. Oct. 19, 1927

1947-48 Detroit Red Wings		1/6	1		6.00	0	0

McLACHLAN, MURRAY G-SL
Born: London, Ont. Oct. 20, 1948

1970-71 Toronto Maple Leafs		1/2(2)	4		8.00	0	0

McLEOD, DONALD MARTIN G-SL
Born: Trail, British Columbia. Aug. 24, 1946

1970-71 Detroit Red Wings		11 2/3(14)	62	0	5.31	0	0
1971-72 Philadelphia Flyers		3(4)	15	0	5.00	0	0
2 Years		14 2/3(18)	77	0	5.25	0	0

McLEOD, JAMES BRADLEY G-SL
Born: Port Arthur, Ont. April 7, 1937

1971-72 St. Louis Blues		14 2/3(16)	45	0	3.07	1	0

McNAMARA, GERALD LIONEL G-SL
Born: Turgeon Falls, Ont. Sept. 22, 1934

1960-61 Toronto Maple Leafs		5	13	0	2.60	0	2
1969-70 ” ” ”		1/3 (2)	2		6.00	0	0
2 Years		5 1/3(7)	15	0	2.81	0	2

McNEIL, GERARD GEORGE G-SL
Born: Quebec City, Que. April 17, 1926

1947-48 Montreal Canadiens		1 3/5	7	0	4.375	0	0
1949-50 ” ”		6	9	1	1.50	0	0
1950-51 ” ”		70	184	6	2.63	0	0
1951-52 ” ”		70	164	5	2.34	0	0
1952-53 ” ”		66	140	*10	2.12	0	0
1953-54 ” ”		53	114	6	2.15	0	0
1956-57 ” ”		9	32	0	3.56	0	2
7 Years		275 3/5	650	28	2.36	0	2

*league leader
1952-53 2nd All-Star Team

MELOCHE, GILLES G-SL
Born: Montreal, Que. July 12, 1950

1970-71 Chicago Black Hawks		2	6	0	3.00	0	0
1971-72 Oakland Seals		52(56)	176	4	3.38	2	6
2 Years		54(58)	182	4	3.37	2	6

MILLAR, FRANKLIN ALLAN "AL" G-SL
Born: Winnipeg, Man. Sept. 18, 1929

1957-58 Boston Bruins		6	25	0	4.17	0	0

MILLER, JOSEPH G-SL
Born: Morrisburg, Ont. Oct. 6, 1900

1927-28 New York Americans		27 2/3	77	5	2.78	0	0
1928-29 Pittsburgh Pirates		44	80	11	1.82	0	0
1929-30 ” ”		43 1/3	181	0	4.18	0	0
1930-31 Philadelphia Quakers		13 5/6(15)	50	0	3.61	0	0
4 Years		128 5/6(131)	388	16	3.01	0	0

MITCHELL, IVAN

1919-20 Toronto St. Patricks		14	68	0	4.86	0	0
1920-21 ” ” ”		4	22	0	5.50	0	0
1921-22 ” ” ”		2	6	0	3.00	0	0
3 Years		20	96	0	4.80	0	0

MOORE, ALFRED ERNEST G-SR
Born: Toronto, Ont. Dec. 1, 1906

1936-37 New York Americans		18	64	1	3.56	0	0
1938-39 ” ”		2	14	0	7.00	0	0
1939-40 Detroit Red Wings		1	3		3.00	0	0
3 Years		21	81	1	3.86	0	0

MORISSETTE, JEAN-GUY G-SL
Born: Causapscal, Que. Dec. 16, 1937

1963-64 Montreal Canadiens		3/5	4		6.67	0	0

Sea. Club	Ga.	GA	SO	Ave.	A.	PM.
MOWERS, JOHN THOMAS G-SL						
Born: Niagara Falls, Ont. Oct. 29, 1916						
1940-41 Detroit Red Wings	48	102	4	2.13	0	0
1941-42 ” ” ”	47	144	5	3.06	1	0
1942-43 ” ” ”	50	124	*6	2.48	0	0
in Armed Forces						
1946-47 Detroit Red Wings	7	29	0	4.14	0	2
4 Years	152	399	15	2.63	1	2
*league leader						
1942-43 1st All-Star Team & Georges Vezina Memorial Trophy						

MUMMERY, HARRY
Tended goal for Quebec Bulldogs through 2 games in 1919-20 (15 goals - against—0 shut-outs—7.50 average).

MURPHY, HAL						
Born: Montreal, Que. July 6, 1927						
1952-53 Montreal Canadiens	1	4		4.00	0	0
MURRAY, THOMAS						
1929-30 Montreal Canadiens	1	4		4.00	0	0
MYRE, LOUIS PHILIPPE G-SL						
Born: Ste. Anne de Bellevue, Que. Nov. 1, 1947						
1969-70 Montreal Canadiens	8 2/5(10)	19	0	2.26	0	2
1970-71 ” ”	28 (30)	88	1	3.14	1	17
1971-72 ” ”	8 5/6	32	0	3.62	0	4
3 Years	45 1/5(49)	139	1	3.08	1	23
NEWTON, CAMERON CHARLES G-SR						
Born: Peterborough, Ont. Feb. 25, 1950						
1970-71 Pittsburgh Penguins	4 2/3	16	0	3.43	0	4
NORRIS, JACK WAYNE G-SL						
Born: Saskatoon, Sask. Aug. 5, 1942						
1964-65 Boston Bruins	23	86	1	3.74	0	0
1967-68 Chicago Black Hawks	5 1/2(7)	22	1	4.00	0	0
1968-69 ” ”	1 2/3(3)	10	0	6.00	0	0
1970-71 Los Angeles Kings	21 3/4(25)	86	0	3.95	0	0
4 Years	52(58)	204	2	3.92	0	0
OLESEVICH, DANIEL JOHN						
Born: Port Colborne, Ont. Aug. 16, 1937						
1961-62 New York Rangers	1/2	2		4.00	0	0
OUIMET, EDWARD JOHN “TED” G-SL						
Born: Noranda, Que. July 6, 1947						
1968-69 St. Louis Blues	1	2		2.00	0	0
PAILLE, MARCEL G-SL						
Born: Shawinigan Falls, Que. Dec. 8, 1932						
1957-58 New York Rangers	33	102	1	3.09	0	0
1958-59 ” ” ”	1	4	0	4.00	0	0
1959-60 ” ” ”	17	67	1	3.94	0	0
1960-61 ” ” ”	4	16	0	4.00	0	0
1961-62 ” ” ”	10	28	0	2.80	0	0
1962-63 ” ” ”	3	10	0	3.33	0	0
1964-65 ” ” ”	37 2/3(39)	136	0	3.61	1	2
7 Years	105 2/3(107)	363	2	3.44	1	2
PARENT, BERNARD MARCEL G-SL						
Born: Montreal, Que. April 3, 1945						
1965-66 Boston Bruins	34 2/3(39)	128	1	3.69	0	4
1966-67 ” ”	17(18)	64	0	3.76	0	2
1967-68 Philadelphia Flyers	37 1/2	94	4	2.51	1	23
1968-69 ” ”	56(58)	154	1	2.75	0	4
1969-70 ” ”	61 1/3	178	3	2.90	3	14
1970-71 ” ”-Toronto	43 5/6(48	123	†2	2.81	2	5
1971-72 Toronto Maple Leafs	45 1/4(47)	119	3	2.63	1	6
7 Years	295 2/3(310)	860	14	2.91	7	58
†also shared shut-out with J. Jacques Plante on March 24, 1971 against Oakland.						
PELLETIER, MARCEL G-SR						
Born: Drummondville, Que. Dec. 6, 1927						
1950-51 Chicago Black Hawks	6	29	0	4.83	0	2
1962-63 New York Rangers	2/3(2)	4		6.00	0	0
2 Years	6 2/3(8)	33	0	4.95	0	2

Sea.	Club	Ga.	GA	SO	Ave.	A.	PM.

PERREAULT, ROBERT MICHEL G-SL
Born: Trois Rivieres, Que. Jan. 28, 1931

Sea.	Club	Ga.	GA	SO	Ave.	A.	PM.
1955-56	Montreal Canadiens	6	12	1	2.00	0	0
1958-59	Detroit Red Wings	3	9	1	3.00	0	0
1962-63	Boston Bruins	21 1/2	85	1	3.95	0	0
3 Years		30 1/2	106	3	3.48	0	0

PLANTE, JOSEPH JACQUES OMER "JAKE THE SNAKE" G-SL
Born: Mount Carmel, Que. Jan. 17, 1929

Sea.	Club	Ga.	GA	SO	Ave.	A.	PM.
1952-53	Montreal Canadiens	3	4	0	1.33	0	0
1953-54	" "	17	27	5	1.59	0	0
1954-55	" "	52	110	5	2.11	0	2
1955-56	" "	64	119	7	1.86	0	10
1956-57	" "	61	123	*9	2.02	0	16
1957=58	" "	56 2/5	119	*9	2.11	0	13
1958-59	" "	66 2/3	144	*9	2.16	1	11
1959-60	" "	69	175	3	2.54	0	2
1960-61	" "	40	112	2	2.80	0	2
1961-62	" "	70	166	4	2.37	0	14
1962-63	" "	55 1/3	138	*5	2.49	1	2
1963-64	New York Rangers	65	224	3	3.45	1	6
1964-65	" " "	32 1/3	110	2	3.40	1	6
1968-69	St. Louis Blues	35 2/3(37)	70	5	1.96	0	2
1969-70	" "	30 2/3(32)	68	5	2.22	2	0
1970-71	Toronto Maple Leafs	38 2/3(40)	75	†4	1.94	0	2
1971-72	" " "	32 3/4(34)	89	2	2.72	0	2
17 Years		789 1/2(797)	1873	79	2.37	6	90

*league leader
†also shared shut-out with Bruce Gamble on January 2, 1971 against Detroit
" " " " " Bernard Parent on March 24, 1971 against Oakland
1955-56 1st All-Star Team & Georges Vezina Memorial Trophy
1956-57 2nd " " " " " " " " "
1957-58 " " " " " " " " " "
1958-59 1st " " " " " " " " "
1959-60 2nd " " " " " " " "
1961-62 1st " " " " David A. Hart & Georges Vezina Memorial Trophies
1968-69 Georges Vezina Memorial Trophy (with Glenn Hall)
1970-71 2nd All-Star Team

PLASSE, MICHEL G-SL
Born: Montreal, Que. June 1, 1948

Sea.	Club	Ga.	GA	SO	Ave.	A.	PM.
1970-71	St. Louis Blues	1	3		3.00	0	0

PRONOVOST, CLAUDE G-SL
Born: Shawinigan Falls, Que. July 22, 1935

Sea.	Club	Ga.	GA	SO	Ave.	A.	PM.
1955-57	Boston Bruins	1	0	1	0.00	0	2
1958-59	Montreal Canadiens	1 (2)	7		7.00	0	0
2 Years		2 (3)	7	1	3.50	0	2

RAYNER, CLAUDE EARL "CHUCK" G-SL
Born: Sutherland, Sask. Aug. 11, 1920

Sea.	Club	Ga.	GA	SO	Ave.	A.	PM.
1940-41	New York Americans	11 5/6	44	0	3.72	0	0
1941-42	Brooklyn "	36	129	1	3.58	0	0
in Royal Canadian Navy							
1945-46	New York Rangers	40	149	1	3.72	0	6
1946-47	" " "	58	177	*5	3.05	0	0
1947-48	" " "	11 1/2	42	0	3.65	0	0
1948-49	" " "	58	168	7	2.90	0	2
1949-50	" " "	69	181	6	2.62	0	6
1950-51	" " "	65 2/3	187	2	2.85	0	6
1951-52	" " "	53	159	2	3.00	0	4
1952-53	" " "	20	58	1	2.90	0	2
10 Years		423(424)	1294	25	3.06	0	26

*league leader
1948-49 2nd All-Star Team
1949-50 " " " " & Dr. David A. Hart Trophy
1950-51 " " " "

RHEAUME, HERBERT

Sea.	Club	Ga.	GA	SO	Ave.	A.	PM.
1925-26	Montreal Canadiens	30	89	0	2.97	0	0

Sea.	Club	Ga.	GA	SO	Ave.	A.	PM.
RIGGIN, DENNIS MELVILLE G-SL							
Born: Kincardine, Ont. April 11, 1936							
1959-60 Detroit Red Wings		9	32	1	3.56	0	0
1962-63 " " "		7 2/3(9)	22	0	2.87	0	0
2 Years		16 2/3(18)	54	1	3.24	0	0
RING, ROBERT							
1965-66 Boston Bruins		2/3	4		6.00	0	0
RIVARD, FERNAND JOSEPH G-SL							
Born: Grand Mere, Que. Jan. 18, 1946							
1968-69 Minnesota North Stars		11 (13)	48	0	4.36	0	0
1969-70 " " "		13 1/3	42	1	3.15	0	6
2 Years		24 1/3(26)	90	1	3.70	0	6
ROACH, JOHN ROSS G-SL							
Born: Port Perry, Ont. June 23, 1900							
1921-22 Toronto St. Patricks		22	91	0	4.14	0	0
1922-23 " " "		24	88	1	3.66	0	0
1923-24 " " "		23	80	1	3.48	0	0
1924-25 " " "		30	84	1	2.80	0	0
1925-26 " " "		36	114	2	3.17	0	0
1926-27 " " "		44	94	4	2.14	0	0
1927-28 " Maple Leafs		43	88	4	2.05	0	0
1928-29 New York Rangers		44	65	13	1.48	0	0
1929-30 " " "		44	143	1	3.25	0	0
1930-31 " " "		44	87	7	1.98	0	0
1931-32 " " "		48	112	9	2.33	0	0
1932-33 Detroit Red Wings		48	93	10	1.94	0	0
1933-34 " " "		18	47	1	2.61	0	0
1934-35 " " "		23	62	4	2.70	0	0
14 Years		491	1248	58	2.54	0	0
1932-33 1st All-Star Team							
ROBERTS, MORRIS "MOE" SR							
Born: Waterbury, Conn. Dec. 13, 1907							
1925-26 Boston Bruins		1 1/2	5	0	3.33	0	0
1931-32 New York Americans		1	1		1.00	0	0
1933-34 " " "		5 1/2	25	0	4.55	0	0
1951-52 Chicago Black Hawks		1/3	0		0.00	0	0
4 Years		8 1/3(10)	31	0	3.72	0	0

Note: Roberts played in his first game on December 8, 1925 when he replaced the injured Charles Stewart in the 2nd period. He played in his final game on November 25, 1951 when he replaced Harry Lumley for the 3rd period - - a span of 26 years.

Sea.	Club	Ga.	GA	SO	Ave.	A.	PM.
ROBERTSON, EARL COOPER G-SL							
Born: Bengough, Sask. Nov. 24, 1911							
1937-38 New York Americans		48	111	6	2.31	0	0
1938-39 " " "		45 1/2	136	3	2.99	0	0
1939-40 " " "		48	140	6	2.92	0	0
1940-41 " " "		36	142	1	3.94	0	0
1941-42 Brooklyn		12	46	0	3.83	0	0
5 Years		189 1/2	575	16	3.03	0	0
1938-39 2nd All-Star Team							
ROLLINS, ELWIN IRA "AL" G-SL							
Born: Vanguard, Sask. Oct. 9, 1926							
1949-50 Toronto Maple Leafs		1 2/3	4	1	2.40	0	0
1950-51 " " "		39 2/5	70	†5	1.78	0	0
1951-52 " " "		69 1/2	154	5	2.22	0	4
1952-53 Chicago Black Hawks		70	175	6	2.50	0	0
1953-54 " " "		66	213	5	3.23	0	20
1954-55 " " "		44	150	0	3.41	0	0
1955-56 " " "		58	174	3	3.00	0	10
1956-57 " " "		70	225	3	3.21	1	9
1959-60 New York Rangers		10	31	0	3.10	0	0
9 Years		428 3/5(430)	1196	28	2.79	1	43

†also shared shut-out with Walter Broda on December 2, 1950 against Chicago
1950-51 Georges Vezina Memorial Trophy
1953-54 Dr. David A. Hart Trophy

Sea.	Club	Ga.	GA	SO	Ave.	A.	PM.
RUPP, PATRICK LLOYD G-SL							
Born: Detroit, Mich. Aug. 12, 1942							
1963-64 Detroit Red Wings		1	4		4.00	0	0

Sea.	Club	Ga.	GA	SO	Ave.	A.	PM.

RUTHERFORD, JAMES EARL G-SL
Born: Beeton, Ont. Feb. 17, 1949

Sea.	Club	Ga.	GA	SO	Ave.	A.	PM.
1970-71	Detroit Red Wings	25(29)	97	1	3.88	0	0
1971-72	Pittsburgh Penguins	36(40)	118	1	3.28	0	16
2 Years		61(69)	215	2	3.52	0	16

RUTLEDGE, WAYNE ALVIN G-SL
Born: Barrie, Ont. Jan. 5, 1942

Sea.	Club	Ga.	GA	SO	Ave.	A.	PM.
1967-68	Los Angeles Kings	40 3/4(45)	119	2	2.92	0	4
1968-69	" " "	15 1/3(17)	56	0	3.65	0	2
1969-70	" " "	16(20)	68	0	4.25	0	5
3 Years		72(82)	243	2	3.375	0	11

SAWCHUK, TERRANCE GORDON "UKEY" G-SL
Born: Winnipeg, Man. Dec. 28, 1929

Sea.	Club	Ga.	GA	SO	Ave.	A.	PM.
1945-50	Detroit Red Wings	7	16	1	2.29	0	0
1950-51	" " "	70	139	*11	1.99	0	2
1951-52	" " "	70	133	*12	1.90	0	2
1952-53	" " "	63	120	9	1.90	0	5
1953-54	" " "	66 3/4	129	12	1.93	1	31
1954-55	" " "	68	132	*12	1.94	1	10
1955-56	Boston Bruins	68	181	9	2.66	0	20
1956-57	" "	34	81	2	2.38	0	14
1957-58	Detroit Red Wings	70	207	3	2.96	0	39
1958-59	" " "	67	209	5	3.12	0	12
1959-60	" " "	58	156	5	2.69	0	22
1960-61	" " "	35 5/6(37)	113	2	3.15	1	8
1961-62	" " "	43	143	5	3.33	0	12
1962-63	" " "	46(48)	119	3	2.59	0	14
1963-64	" " "	52 1/3	140	5	2.68	0	0
1964-65	Toronto Maple Leafs	36	92	1	2.56	2	24
1965-66	" " "	25 1/3(27)	81	1	3.20	1	12
1966-67	" " "	23 1/2(28)	66	2	2.81	0	2
1967-68	Los Angeles Kings	32 1/4(36)	101	2	3.13	0	0
1968-69	Detroit Red Wings	10 2/3(13)	28	0	2.625	0	0
1969-70	New York Rangers	6 5/6(8)	20	1	2.93	1	0
21 Years		953 1/2(971)	2406	103	2.52	7	229

*league leader
1950-51 1st All-Star Team & Frank Calder Memorial Trophy
1951-52 " " " " & Georges Vezina Memorial Trophy
1952-53 " " " " " " " " "
1953-54 2nd " " "
1954-55 " " " " & Georges Vezina Memorial Trophy
1958-59 " " " "
1962-63 " " " "
1964-65 Georges Vezina Memorial Trophy (with John Bower)
                                        Hall of Fame

SCHAEFER, JOSEPH P. G-SL
Born: Long Island City, N. Y. Dec. 21, 1924

Sea.	Club	Ga.	GA	SO	Ave.	A.	PM.
1959-60	New York Rangers	2/3	5		7.50	0	0
1960-61	" " "	5/6	3		3.60	0	0
2 Years		1 1/2	8		5.33	0	0

SHIELDS, ALLAN
Tended goal for New York Americans from 3:43 of 2nd period as they lost to Toronto Maple Leafs 11-3 on January 19, 1932 at Toronto (7 goals scored against him).

SIMMONS, DONALD WILLIAM "DIPPY" G-SR
Born: Port Colborne, Ont. Sept. 13, 1931

Sea.	Club	Ga.	GA	SO	Ave.	A.	PM.
1956-57	Boston Bruins	26	63	4	2.42	0	0
1957-58	" "	37 1/6	93	5	2.50	0	0
1958-59	" "	58	184	3	3.17	0	4
1959-60	" "	28	94	2	3.36	0	4
1960-61	" "	18	59	1	3.28	0	6
1961-62	Toronto Maple Leafs	9	21	1	2.33	0	0
1962-63	" " "	28	70	1	2.50	0	0
1963-64	" " "	19 5/6(21)	65	3	3.28	0	0
1965-66	New York Rangers	8 1/6(11)	37	0	4.53	0	0
1967-68	" " "	5	13	0	2.60	0	0
1968-69	" " "	3 2/5(5)	9	0	2.65	0	0
11 Years		240 1/2(247)	708	20	2.94	0	14

Sea. Club	Ga.	GA	SO	Ave.	A.	PM.

SMITH, ALLAN ROBERT "AL" G-SL
Born: Toronto, Ont. Nov. 10, 1945

Sea. Club	Ga.	GA	SO	Ave.	A.	PM.
1965-66 Toronto Maple Leafs	1(2)	2		2.00	0	0
1966-67 ” ” ”	1	5		5.00	0	0
1968-69 ” ” ”	5 3/5(7)	16	0	2.86	0	0
1969-70 Pittsburgh Penguins	42 3/5(46)	132	2	3.10	0	20
1970-71 ” ”	41 1/6(46)	128	2	3.11	0	41
1971-72 Detroit Red Wings	41 2/3(43)	139	4	3.34	4	23
6 Years	133(145)	422	8	3.17	4	84

SMITH, GARY EDWARD G-SL
Born: Ottawa, Ont. Feb. 4, 1944

Sea. Club	Ga.	GA	SO	Ave.	A.	PM.
1965-66 Toronto Maple Leafs	2(3)	7	0	3.50	0	0
1966-67 ” ” ”	2	7	0	3.50	0	0
1967-68 Oakland Seals	18 5/6(21)	61	†1	3.24	1	4
1968-69 ” ”	49 5/6(54)	149	4	2.99	2	7
1969-70 ” ”	62 2/3(65)	195	2	3.11	1	18
1970-71 ” ”	66 1/4(71)	259	2	3.91	1	6
1971-72 Chicago Black Hawks	25 2/3(28)	62	5	2.42	0	0
7 Years	227 1/4(244)	740	14	3.26	5	35

†also shared shut-out with Charles Hodge on February 14, 1968 against Philadelphia
1971-72 Georges Vezina Memorial Trophy (with Anthony Esposito)

SMITH, NORMAN E. G-SL
Born: Toronto, Ont. March 18, 1908

Sea. Club	Ga.	GA	SO	Ave.	A.	PM.
1931-32 Montreal Maroons	19 5/6	62	0	3.13	0	0
1934-35 Detroit Red Wings	25	52	2	2.08	0	0
1935-36 ” ” ”	48	103	6	2.15	0	0
1936-37 ” ” ”	48	102	*6	2.125	0	0
1937-38 ” ” ”	47	130	3	2.77	0	0
1938-39 ” ” ”	4	12	0	3.00	0	0
1943-44 ” ” ”	5	15	0	3.00	0	0
1944-45 ” ” ”	1	3		3.00	0	0
8 Years	197 5/6	479	17	2.42	0	0

*league leader
1936-37 1st All-Star Team & Georges Vezina Memorial Trophy

SMITH, WILLIAM JOHN G-SR
Born: Perth, Ont. Dec. 12, 1950

Sea. Club	Ga.	GA	SO	Ave.	A.	PM.
1971-72 Los Angeles Kings	5	23	0	4.60	0	5

SNEDDON, ROBERT ALLAN G-SR
Born: Montreal, Que. May 31, 1944

Sea. Club	Ga.	GA	SO	Ave.	A.	PM.
1970-71 Oakland Seals	3 3/4(5)	21	0	5.60	0	0

SPOONER, "RED"

Sea. Club	Ga.	GA	SO	Ave.	A.	PM.
1929-30 Pittsburgh Pirates	2/3	4		6.00	0	0

STARR, HAROLD
Tended goal for Montreal Maroons after Norman Smith was injured in 3rd period as they lost to Montreal Canadiens 5-1 on January 2, 1932 at Montreal (0 goals scored against him).

STEIN, PHILIP J.
Born: Toronto, Ont. Sept. 13, 1913

Sea. Club	Ga.	GA	SO	Ave.	A.	PM.
1939-40 Toronto Maple Leafs	1	2		2.00	0	0

STEPHANSON, FREDERICK WAYNE G-SL
Born: Fort William, Ont. Jan. 29, 1945

Sea. Club	Ga.	GA	SO	Ave.	A.	PM.
1971-72 St. Louis Blues	1 2/3	9	0	5.40	0	0

STEVENSON, DOUGLAS G-SL
Born: Regina, Sask. April 6, 1924

Sea. Club	Ga.	GA	SO	Ave.	A.	PM.
1944-45 New York Rangers–Chicago	6	27	0	4.50	0	0
1945-46 Chicago Black Hawks	2	12	0	6.00	0	0
2 Years	8	39	0	4.875	0	0

STEWART, CHARLES "DOC"

Sea. Club	Ga.	GA	SO	Ave.	A.	PM.
1924-25 Boston Bruins	21	65	2	3.10	0	0
1925-26 ” ”	34 1/2	80	6	2.32	0	0
1926-27 ” ”	21	49	2	2.33	0	0
3 Years	76 1/2	194	10	2.54	0	0

STUART, HERBERT

Sea. Club	Ga.	GA	SO	Ave.	A.	PM.
1926-27 Detroit Cougars	3	5	0	1.67	0	0

Sea. Club	Ga.	GA	SO	Ave.	A.	PM.
TAUGHER, WILLIAM						
1925-26 Montreal Canadiens	1	3		3.00	0	0
TAYLOR, ROBERT IAN G-SL						
Born: Calgary, Alta. Jan. 24, 1945						
1971-72 Philadelphia Flyers	5 1/3	16	0	3.00	0	0
TENO, HARVEY						
Born: Windsor, Ont.						
1938-39 Detroit Red Wings	5	15	0	3.00	0	0
THOMPSON, CECIL RALPH "TINY" G-SL						
Born: Sandon, British Columbia. May 31, 1905						
1928-29 Boston Bruins	44	52	12	1.18	0	0
1929-30 ” ”	44	98	3	2.23	0	0
1930-31 ” ”	44	90	3	2.05	0	0
1931-32 ” ”	42 1/3	103	*9	2.43	0	0
1932-33 ” ”	48	88	*11	1.83	0	0
1933-34 ” ”	48	130	5	2.71	0	0
1934-35 ” ”	48	112	8	2.33	0	0
1935-36 ” ”	47 1/3	82	*10	1.73	1	0
1936-37 ” ”	48	110	*6	2.29	0	0
1937-38 ” ”	48	89	7	1.85	0	0
1938-39 ” ” — Detroit	44	109	4	2.48	0	0
1939-40 Detroit Red Wings	46	120	3	2.61	0	0
12 Years	551 2/3(553)	1183	81	2.14	1	0

*league leader
1929-30 Georges Vezina Memorial Trophy
1930-31 2nd All-Star Team
1932-33 Georges Vezina Memorial Trophy
1934-35 2nd All-Star Team
1935-36 1st ”   ” ” & Georges Vezina Memorial Trophy
1937-38 ” ”   ” ” ” ”   ”   ”   ”

Hall of Fame

Sea. Club	Ga.	GA	SO	Ave.	A.	PM.
TURNER, JOSEPH						
Born: Windsor, Ont.						
1941-42 Detroit Red Wings	1	3		3.00	0	0
VACHON, ROGATIEN ROSAIRE "THE ROGUE" G-SL						
Born: Palmarolle, Que. Sept. 8, 1945						
1966-67 Montreal Canadiens	19	48	1	2.53	1	0
1967-68 ” ”	37 1/6(39)	93	4	2.50	0	2
1968-69 ” ”	34 1/6(36)	98	2	2.87	0	2
1969-70 ” ”	61 3/5(64)	168	4	2.73	0	0
1970-71 ” ”	44 3/5(47)	119	2	2.67	0	0
1971-72 ” —Los Angeles Kings	26 5/6(29)	111	0	4.14	0	0
6 Years	223 1/3(234)	637	13	2.85	1	4

1967-68 Georges Vezina Memorial Trophy (with Lorne Worsley)

Sea. Club	Ga.	GA	SO	Ave.	A.	PM.
VEZINA, GEORGES "CHICOUTIMI CUCUMBER" G-SL						
Born: Chicoutimi, Que. Jan. 1887						
1917-18 Montreal Canadiens	21	84	*1	4.00	- -	- -
1918-19 ” ”	18	78	1	4.33	0	0
1919-20 ” ”	24	113	0	4.71	0	0
1920-21 ” ”	24	99	1	4.13	0	0
1921-22 ” ”	24	94	0	3.92	0	2
1922-23 ” ”	24	61	2	2.54	0	0
1923-24 ” ”	24	48	*3	2.00	0	0
1924-25 ” ”	30	56	5	1.87	0	0
1925-26 ”	1/3	1		3.00	0	0
9 Years	189 1/3	634	13	3.35	0	2

*league leader

Hall of Fame

Sea. Club	Ga.	GA	SO	Ave.	A.	PM.
VILLEMURE, GILLES G-SR						
Born: Trois Rivieres, Que. May 30, 1940						
1963-64 New York Rangers	5	18	0	3.60	0	0
1967-68 ” ” ”	3 1/3	8	1	2.40	0	0
1968-69 ” ” ”	4	9	0	2.25	0	0
1970-71 ” ” ”	34	79	4	2.32	0	0
1971-72 ” ” ”	35 1/2(37)	75	3	2.11	2	6
5 Years	81 5/6(84)	189	8	2.31	2	6

1970-71 Georges Vezina Memorial Trophy (with Edward Giacomin)

Sea.	Club	Ga.	GA	SO	Ave.	A.	PM.
WAKELY, ERNEST ALFRED LINTON G-SL							
Born: Flin Flon, Man. Nov. 27, 1940							
1962-63	Montreal Canadiens	1	3		3.00	0	0
1968-69	"	1	4		4.00	0	0
1969-70	St. Louis Blues	27 1/2(30)	58	4	2.11	0	0
1970-71	" "	47 2/3(51)	133	†3	2.79	2	0
1971-72	" "	26 5/6(30)	94	1	3.50	1	2
5 Years		104(113)	292	8	2.81	3	2

†also shared shut-out with Glenn Hall on November 5, 1970 against Boston

WALSH, JAMES PATRICK "FLAT"							
Born: Kingston, Ont. March 23, 1897							
1926-27	Montreal Maroons	1	3		3.00	0	0
1927-28	" "	2/3	1		1.50	0	0
1928-29	New York Americans –Maroons	11	9	4	0.82	0	0
1929-30	Montreal Maroons	30 5/6	74	2	2.40	0	0
1930-31	" "	13 1/3(15)	30	2	2.25	0	0
1931-32	"	28	77	2	2.75	0	0
1932-33	"	22	61	2	2.77	0	0
7 Years		106 5/6(109)	255	12	2.39	0	0

WETZEL, CARL DAVID G-SL							
Born: Detroit, Mich. Dec. 12, 1938							
1964-65	Detroit Red Wings	1/2(2)	4		8.00	0	0
1967-68	Minnesota North Stars	4 1/2	18	0	4.00	0	0
2 Years		5(7)	22	0	4.40	0	0

WILSON, DUNCAN SHEPHERD G-SL							
Born: Toronto, Ont. March 22, 1948							
1969-70	Philadelphia Flyers	1	3		3.00	0	0
1970-71	Vancouver Canucks	30(35)	131	0	4.37	0	18
1971-72	" "	47 5/6(53)	174	1	3.64	0	17
3 Years		78 5/6(89)	308	1	3.91	0	35

WILSON, ROSS INGRAM "LEFTY"							
Born: Toronto, Ont. Oct. 15, 1919							
1953-54	Detroit Red Wings	1/4	0		0.00	0	0
1955-56	" "	1/5	0		0.00	0	0
1957-58	Boston Bruins	5/6	1		1.20	0	0
3 Years		1 1/4(3)	1		0.80	0	0

WINKLER, HAROLD LANG G-SL							
Born: Gretna, Man. March 20, 1892							
1926-27	New York Rangers–Boston	30 1/3	53	6	1.75	0	0
1927-28	Boston Bruins	44	70	*15	1.59	0	0
2 Years		74 1/3	123	21	1.65	0	0

*league leader

WOODS, ALEC							
Born: Falkirk, Scotland							
1936-37	New York Americans	1	3		3.00	0	0

WORSLEY, LORNE JOHN "GUMP" G-SL							
Born: Montreal, Que. May 14, 1929							
1952-53	New York Rangers	50	153	2	3.06	0	2
1954-55	" "	65	197	4	3.03	0	2
1955-56	" "	70	203	4	2.90	0	2
1956-57	" "	68	220	3	3.24	0	19
1957-58	" "	37	86	4	2.32	0	10
1958-59	" "	66 2/3	205	2	3.075	0	10
1959-60	" "	38 1/3	137	0	3.57	0	12
1960-61	" "	57 5/6(59)	193	1	3.34	0	10
1961-62	" "	58 5/6(60)	174	2	2.96	0	12
1962-63	" "	66 1/3	219	2	3.30	0	14
1963-64	Montreal Canadiens	7 2/5	22	1	2.97	0	0
1964-65	"	18(19)	50	1	2.78	0	0
1965-66	"	48 1/3(51)	117	2	2.42	1	4
1966-67	"	14 3/4(18)	47	1	3.19	0	4
1967-68	"	36 5/6(40)	74	6	2.01	0	10
1968-69	"	28 1/3(30)	64	5	2.26	0	0
1969-70	" – Minnesota	13 1/2	34	1	2.52	0	0
1970-71	Minnesota North Stars	22 5/6(24)	57	0	2.50	0	10
1971-72	" "	32(34)	68	2	2.125	1	2
19 Years		800(820)	2320	43	2.90	2	123

(continued)

Sea.	Club	Ga.	GA	SO	Ave.	A.	PM.
1952-53 Frank Calder Memorial Trophy							
1965-66 2nd All-Star Team & Georges Vezina Memorial Trophy (with Charles Hodge)							
1967-68 1st " " " " " " " Rogatien Vachon)							

WORTERS, ROY "SHRIMP" G-SL
Born: Toronto, Ont. Oct. 19, 1900

Sea.	Club	Ga.	GA	SO	Ave.	A.	PM.
1925-26	Pittsburgh Pirates	35	68	7	1.94	0	0
1926-27	" "	44	108	4	2.45	0	0
1927-28	" "	44	76	11	1.73	0	0
1928-29	New York Americans	38	46	13	1.21	0	0
1929-30	" " "—Canadiens	37	137	2	3.70	0	0
1930-31	" " "	44	74	8	1.68	0	0
1931-32	" " "	39 2/5	112	5	2.84	0	0
1932-33	" " "	47	116	5	2.47	0	0
1933-34	" " "	35 1/3	75	4	2.12	0	0
1934-35	" " "	48	142	3	2.96	0	0
1935-36	" " "	48	122	3	2.54	0	0
1936-37	" " "	23	69	2	3.00	0	0
12 Years		482 2/3(484)	1145	67	2.37	0	0

1928-29 Dr. David A. Hart Trophy
1930-31 Georges Vezina Memorial Trophy
1931-32 2nd All-Star Team
1933-34 " " " "

Hall of Fame

WORTHY, CHRISTOPHER JOHN G-SL
Born: Bristol, England. Oct. 23, 1947

Sea.	Club	Ga.	GA	SO	Ave.	A.	PM.
1968-69	Oakland Seals	13 1/6	54	0	4.10	0	2
1969-70	" "	1	5		5.00	0	2
1970-71	" "	8(11)	40	0	5.00	0	2
3 Years		22 1/6(26)	99	0	4.47	0	6

League Leader

Shut-Outs

Season	Player	Team	SO
1917–18	Clinton Benedict / Georges Vezina	Ottawa Senators / Montreal Canadiens	1
1918–19	Clinton Benedict	Ottawa Senators	2
1919–20	Clinton Benedict	Ottawa Senators	5
1920–21	Clinton Benedict	Ottawa Senators	2
1921–22	Clinton Benedict	Ottawa Senators	2
1922–23	Clinton Benedict	Ottawa Senators	4
1923–24	Clinton Benedict / Georges Vezina	Ottawa Senators / Montreal Canadiens	3
1924–25	Alexander Connell	Ottawa Senators	7
1925–26	Alexander Connell	Ottawa Senators	15
1926–27	George Hainsworth	Montreal Canadiens	14
1927–28	Alexander Connell / Harold Winkler	Ottawa Senators / Boston Bruins	15
1928–29	George Hainsworth	Montreal Canadiens	22
1929–30	Lorne Chabot	Toronto Maple Leafs	6
1930–31	Charles Gardiner	Chicago Black Hawks	12
1931–32	Cecil Thompson	Boston Bruins	9
1932–33	Cecil Thompson	Boston Bruins	11
1933–34	Charles Gardiner	Chicago Black Hawks	10
1934–35	Alexander Connell	Montreal Maroons	9
1935–36	Cecil Thompson	Boston Bruins	10
1936–37	Cecil Thompson / Norman Smith	Boston Bruins / Detroit Red Wings	6
1937–38	David Kerr	New York Rangers	8
1938–39	Francis Brimsek	Boston Bruins	10

1939–40	David Kerr	New York Rangers	8
1940–41	Francis Brimsek	Boston Bruins	6
1941–42	Walter Broda	Toronto Maple Leafs	6
1942–43	John Mowers	Detroit Red Wings	6
1943–44	Paul Bibeault	Toronto Maple Leafs	5
1944–45	{ Frank McCool { Michael Karakas	Toronto Maple Leafs Chicago Black Hawks	4
1945–46	William Durnan	Montreal Canadiens	4
1946–47	Claude Rayner	New York Rangers	5
1947–48	Harry Lumley	Detroit Red Wings	7
1948–49	William Durnan	Montreal Canadiens	10
1949–50	Walter Broda	Toronto Maple Leafs	9
1950–51	Terrance Sawchuk	Detroit Red Wings	11
1951–52	Terrance Sawchuk	Detroit Red Wings	12
1952–53	{ Harry Lumley { Gerard McNeil	Toronto Maple Leafs Montreal Canadiens	10
1953–54	Harry Lumley	Toronto Maple Leafs	13
1954–55	Terrance Sawchuk	Detroit Red Wings	12
1955–56	Glenn Hall	Detroit Red Wings	12
1956–57	J. Jacques Plante	Montreal Canadiens	9
1957–58	J. Jacques Plante	Montreal Canadiens	9
1958–59	J. Jacques Plante	Montreal Canadiens	9
1959–60	Glenn Hall	Chicago Black Hawks	6
1960–61	Glenn Hall	Chicago Black Hawks	6
1961–62	Glenn Hall	Chicago Black Hawks	9
1962–63	{ Glenn Hall { J. Jacques Plante	Chicago Black Hawks Montreal Canadiens	5
1963–64	Charles Hodge	Montreal Canadiens	8
1964–65	Roger Crozier	Detroit Red Wings	6
1965–66	Roger Crozier	Detroit Red Wings	7
1966–67	Edward Giacomin	New York Rangers	9
1967–68	Edward Giacomin	New York Rangers	8
1968–69	Glenn Hall	St. Louis Blues	8
1969–70	Anthony Esposito	Chicago Black Hawks	15
1970–71	Edward Giacomin	New York Rangers	8
1971–72	Anthony Esposito	Chicago Black Hawks	9

Goaltenders Records

Career

Most Seasons			*Most Games*	
Terrance Sawchuk	21	Terrance Sawchuk	953½	(971)
Lorne Worsley	19	Glenn Hall	891⅔	(906)
Glenn Hall	18	Harry Lumley	801⅓	(804)
J. Jacques Plante	17	Lorne Worsley	800	(820)
Harry Lumley	16	J. Jacques Plante	789½	(797)
John Bower	15	Walter Broda	627⅔	(629)
John Roach	14	Cecil Thompson	551⅔	(553)
Walter Broda	14	John Bower	534⅔	(552)
Clinton Benedict	13	Francis Brimsek	514	
Vernon Forbes	13	John Roach	491	
Charles Hodge	13	Roy Worters	482⅔	(484)
Alexander Connell	12	George Hainsworth	465	
Roy Worters	12	David Kerr	429⅓	(431)
Cecil Thompson	12	Elwin Rollins	428⅔	(430)

Numbers in parentheses indicates games played in.

Most Shut-Outs			*Average (200 or more games)*	
Terrance Sawchuk	103	Alexander Connell		2.00
George Hainsworth	94	George Hainsworth		2.02
Glenn Hall	84	Lorne Chabot		2.11
Alexander Connell	81	Charles Gardiner		2.12
Cecil Thompson	81	Cecil Thompson		2.14
J. Jacques Plante	79	David Kerr		2.23
Lorne Chabot	72	William Durnan		2.36
Harry Lumley	71	Gerard McNeil		2.36
Roy Worters	67	Roy Worters		2.37
Walter Broda	60	J. Jacques Plante		2.37
John Roach	58	Clinton Benedict		2.40
Clinton Benedict	57	Terrance Sawchuk		2.52
David Kerr	51	Glenn Hall		2.52
Lorne Worsley	43	John Roach		2.54
Charles Gardiner	42	John Bower		2.54
Francis Brimsek	40	Walter Broda		2.56

Most Assists			*Most Penalties in Minutes*	
Glenn Hall	9	Terrance Sawchuk		229
Edward Johnston	9	Lorne Worsley		123
Terrance Sawchuk	7	Harry Lumley		95
Bernard Parent	7	J. Jacques Plante		90
J. Jacques Plante	6	Glenn Hall		88
Gary Smith	5	Allan Smith		84
Edward Giacomin	5	Douglas Favell		84

Season

Most Shut-Outs

1928–29	George Hainsworth	Montreal Canadiens	22
1925–26	Alexander Connell	Ottawa Senators	15
1927–28	Alexander Connell	Ottawa Senators	15
1927–28	Harold Winkler	Boston Bruins	15
1969–70	Anthony Esposito	Chicago Black Hawks	15
1926–27	George Hainsworth	Montreal Canadiens	14
1926–27	Clinton Benedict	Montreal Maroons	13
1926–27	Alexander Connell	Ottawa Senators	13
1927–28	George Hainsworth	Montreal Canadiens	13
1928–29	John Roach	New York Rangers	13
1928–29	Roy Worters	New York Americans	13
1953–54	Harry Lumley	Toronto Maple Leafs	13

Average (35 or more games)

1928–29	George Hainsworth	Montreal Canadiens	0.98
1927–28	George Hainsworth	Montreal Canadiens	1.09
1925–26	Alexander Connell	Ottawa Senators	1.17
1928–29	Cecil Thompson	Boston Bruins	1.18
1928–29	Roy Worters	New York Americans	1.21
1927–28	Alexander Connell	Ottawa Senators	1.30
1928–29	Clarence Dolson	Detroit Cougars	1.43
1928–29	John Roach	New York Rangers	1.48
1926–27	Clinton Benedict	Montreal Maroons	1.51
1926–27	George Hainsworth	Montreal Canadiens	1.52
1928–29	Alexander Connell	Ottawa Senators	1.52
1928–29	Clinton Benedict	Montreal Maroons	1.54

Most Assists

1971–72	Edward Johnston	Boston Bruins	4
1971–72	Allan Smith	Detroit Red Wings	4
1969–70	Bernard Parent	Philadelphia Flyers	3
1971–72	Kenneth Dryden	Montreal Canadiens	3
1971–72	Edward Giacomin	New York Rangers	3

Most Penalties in Minutes

1970–71	Allan Smith	Pittsburgh Penguins	41
1957–58	Terrance Sawchuk	Detroit Red Wings	39
1967–68	Douglas Favell	Philadelphia Flyers	37
1971–72	Douglas Favell	Philadelphia Flyers	32
1953–54	Terrance Sawchuk	Detroit Red Wings	31
1971–72	Gerald Cheevers	Boston Bruins	25
1964–65	Terrance Sawchuk	Toronto Maple Leafs	24
1969–70	Marvin Edwards	Toronto Maple Leafs	24
1967–68	Bernard Parent	Philadelphia Flyers	23
1971–72	Allan Smith	Detroit Red Wings	23
1959–60	Terrance Sawchuk	Detroit Red Wings	22
1953–54	Elwin Rollins	Chicago Black Hawks	20
1955–56	Terrance Sawchuk	Boston Bruins	20
1968–69	Glenn Hall	St. Louis Blues	20
1969–70	Allan Smith	Pittsburgh Penguins	20

Consecutive Games

Oct. 6, 1955—thru Nov. 7, 1962   Glenn Hall   503

Consecutive Shut-Outs

1927–28	Alexander Connell	Ottawa Senators	(463 minutes—29 seconds)	6
1930–31	Roy Worters	N.Y. Americans	(324 minutes—40 seconds)	4
1948–49	William Durnan	Mont. Canadiens	(309 minutes—21 seconds)	4
1927–28	Lorne Chabot	N.Y. Rangers	(297 minutes—42 seconds)	4
1930–31	Charles Gardiner	Chi. Black Hawks	(290 minutes—12 seconds)	4

Most Shots Stopped (1 game)

March 4, 1941   Samuel LoPresti   Chicago Blacks Hawks   80
(Boston Bruins shot 83 times—defeated Chicago 3–2)

Gordon Drillon

Bill Durnan

Cecil Dye

Chuck Gardiner

Ed Giacomin

Rod Gilbert

George Hainsworth

Douglas Norman Harvey

Bryan Hextall

Gordon Howe

Harry Howell

"Dick" Irvin

"Newsy" Lalonde

Ted Lindsay

Harry Lumley

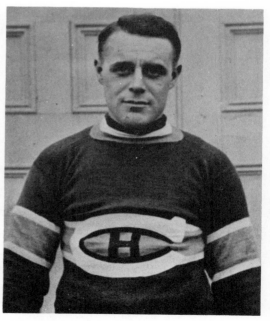

Joseph Malone

Frank McGee

"Dickie" Moore

Lynn Patrick

Howarth W. Morenz

7
Trophies

Clarence S. Campbell Bowl

This trophy is given to the club finishing first in the Western Division of the National Hockey League.

1971–72	Chicago Black Hawks
1970–71	Chicago Black Hawks
1969–70	St. Louis Blues
1968–69	St. Louis Blues
1967–68	Philadelphia Flyers

Kendall Memorial Trophy

This trophy was presented to the National Hockey League by the brothers of George W. Kennedy, to be competed for by the two Montreal clubs in the National Hockey League at that time—the Canadiens and Maroons. George W. Kennedy's real name was Kendall and he owned the Montreal Canadiens while they were in the National Hockey Association and later in the National Hockey League. He passed away in 1921.

1937–38	Mont. Canadiens
1936–37	Mont. Maroons
1935–36	Mont. Maroons
1934–35	Mont. Canadiens
1933–34	Mont. Maroons
1932–33	Mont. Maroons
1931–32	Mont. Canadiens
1930–31	Mont. Canadiens
1929–30	Mont. Maroons
1928–29	Mont. Canadiens
1927–28	Mont. Canadiens

William J. MacBeth Trophy

In 1938 the Hockey Writers Association of New York presented this trophy in memory of William J. MacBeth. A native of Canada, he was one of the pioneer hockey writers in New York. It was competed for by the two New York clubs, the Rangers and Americans, based on the games played with each other in the regular National Hockey League schedule.

1941–42	N.Y. Rangers
1940–41	N.Y. Rangers
1939–40	N.Y. Rangers
1938–39	N.Y. Rangers
1937–38	N.Y. Rangers

Prince of Wales Trophy

This trophy was presented to the National Hockey League by His Royal Highness, the Prince of Wales, in 1924. For the first three seasons it was given to the league champions. From 1927–28 through 1937–38, this trophy was given to the club that finished first in the American Division of the National Hockey League. With the abandonment of the two division system this trophy was then given to the club that finished first in the regular National Hockey League schedule. With the National Hockey League expanded to two divisions again in 1967–68 this trophy is presented to the Eastern Division champion.

1971–72	Boston Bruins	1947–48	Toronto
1970–71	Boston Bruins	1946–47	Montreal
1969–70	Chicago Black Hawks	1945–46	Montreal
1968–69	Montreal	1944–45	Montreal
1967–68	Montreal	1943–44	Montreal
1966–67	Chicago	1942–43	Detroit
1965–66	Montreal	1941–42	New York
1964–65	Detroit	1940–41	Boston
1963–64	Montreal	1939–40	Boston
1962–63	Toronto	1938–39	Boston
1961–62	Montreal	1937–38	Boston
1960–61	Montreal	1936–37	Detroit
1959–60	Montreal	1935–36	Detroit
1958–59	Montreal	1934–35	Boston
1957–58	Montreal	1933–34	Detroit
1956–57	Detroit	1932–33	Boston
1955–56	Montreal	1931–32	N.Y. Rangers
1954–55	Detroit	1930–31	Boston
1953–54	Detroit	1929–30	Boston
1952–53	Detroit	1928–29	Boston
1951–52	Detroit	1927–28	Boston
1950–51	Detroit	1926–27	Ottawa
1949–50	Detroit	1925–26	Mont. Maroons
1948–49	Detroit	1924–25	Mont. Canadiens

Frank Calder Trophy

1942–43	James Stewart	Toronto
1941–42	Grant Warwick	New York
1940–41	John Quilty	Montreal
1939–40	James MacDonald	N.Y. Rangers
1938–39	Francis Brimsek	Boston
1937–38	Carl Dahlstrom	Chicago
1936–37	Charles Apps	Toronto
1935–36	*Michael Karakas	Chicago
1934–35	*David Schriner	N.Y. Americans
1933–34	*Russell Blinco	Mont. Maroons
1932–33	*Carl Voss	N.Y. Rangers—Detroit

* These players were chosen by a group of sports writers. They received no trophy.

Frank Calder Memorial Trophy

Starting with the 1936–37 season Frank Calder, then President of the National Hockey League, bought the Frank Calder Trophy. Each season it was to be given to the outstanding rookie to keep permanently. After the death of Frank Calder in 1943, the League presented this trophy in his memory. It is given to the player who is chosen as the most proficient in his first season of competition. To be eligible a player cannot have played more than 25 games in any preceding season nor to have played six or more games in each of two preceding seasons.

1971–72	Kenneth Dryden	Montreal
1970–71	Gilbert Perreault	Buffalo
1969–70	Anthony Esposito	Chicago
1968–69	Daniel Grant	Minnesota
1967–68	Derek Sanderson	Boston
1966–67	Robert G. Orr	Boston
1965–66	Briton Selby	Toronto
1964–65	Roger Crozier	Detroit
1963–64	Jacques Laperriére	Montreal
1962–63	Kent Douglas	Toronto
1961–62	Joseph Rousseau	Montreal
1960–61	David Keon	Toronto
1959–60	William Hay	Chicago
1958–59	Ralph Backstrom	Montreal
1957–58	Francis Mahovlich	Toronto
1956–57	Lawrence Regan	Boston
1955–56	Glenn Hall	Detroit
1954–55	Edward Litzenberger	Montreal—Chicago
1953–54	Camille Henry	New York
1952–53	Lorne Worsley	New York
1951–52	Bernard Geoffrion	Montreal
1950–51	Terrance Sawchuk	Detroit
1949–50	John Gelineau	Boston
1948–49	Pentti Lund	New York
1947–48	James McFadden	Detroit
1946–47	Howard Meeker	Toronto

1945–46	Edgar Laprade	New York
1944–45	Frank McCool	Toronto
1943–44	August Bodnar	Toronto

Dr. David A. Hart Memorial Trophy

This trophy was presented by the National Hockey League after the original trophy was given to the Hockey Hall of Fame.

1971–72	Robert Orr	Boston
1970–71	Robert Orr	Boston
1969–70	Robert Orr	Boston
1968–69	Philip Esposito	Boston
1967–68	Stanley Mikita	Chicago
1966–67	Stanley Mikita	Chicago
1965–66	Robert Hull	Chicago
1964–65	Robert Hull	Chicago
1963–64	Jean Béliveau	Montreal
1962–63	Gordon Howe	Detroit
1961–62	Jacques Plante	Montreal
1960–61	Bernard Geoffrion	Montreal
1959–60	Gordon Howe	Detroit

Dr. David A. Hart Trophy

This trophy was presented to the National Hockey League by Dr. David A. Hart, father of Cecil M. Hart, a former coach of the Montreal Canadiens. It is awarded to the player adjudged to be most valuable to his club.

1958–59	Andrew Bathgate	New York
1957–58	Gordon Howe	Detroit
1956–57	Gordon Howe	Detroit
1955–56	Jean Béliveau	Montreal
1954–55	Theodore Kennedy	Toronto
1953–54	Edwin Rollins	Chicago
1952–53	Gordon Howe	Detroit
1951–52	Gordon Howe	Detroit
1950–51	Milton Schmidt	Boston
1949–50	Claude Rayner	New York
1948–49	Sidney Abel	Detroit
1947–48	Herbert O'Connor	New York
1946–47	Maurice Richard	Montreal
1945–46	Maxwell Bentley	Chicago
1944–45	Elmer Lach	Montreal
1943–44	Walter Pratt	Toronto
1942–43	William Cowley	Boston
1941–42	Thomas Anderson	Brooklyn
1940–41	William Cowley	Boston

1939–40	Ebenezer Goodfellow	Detroit
1938–39	Hector Blake	Montreal
1937–38	Edward Shore	Boston
1936–37	Albert Siebert	Mont. Canadiens
1935–36	Edward Shore	Boston
1934–35	Edward Shore	Boston
1933–34	Aurèle Joliat	Mont. Canadiens
1932–33	Edward Shore	Boston
1931–32	Howarth Morenz	Mont. Canadiens
1930–31	Howarth Morenz	Mont. Canadiens
1929–30	Nelson Stewart	Mont. Maroons
1928–29	Roy Worters	N.Y. Americans
1927–28	Howarth Morenz	Mont. Canadiens
1926–27	Herbert Gardiner	Mont. Canadiens
1925–26	Nelson Stewart	Mont. Maroons
1924–25	William Burch	Hamilton
1923–24	Frank Nighbor	Ottawa

Lady Byng Trophy

In 1925 Lady Byng, wife of a former Governor-General of Canada, presented this trophy to the National Hockey League. It is awarded to the player adjudged to have exhibited the best type of sportsmanship and gentlemanly conduct combined with a high standard of playing ability. Frank Boucher, after winning this trophy 7 times, was given permanent possession of it and Lady Byng presented another in 1936. After 1950, the trophy became the Lady Byng Memorial Trophy.

1971–72	J. G. Y. Jean Ratelle	New York
1970–71	John Bucyk	Boston
1969–70	J. G. Phillipe Goyette	St. Louis
1968–69	Alexander Delvecchio	Detroit
1967–68	Stanley Mikita	Chicago
1966–67	Stanley Mikita	Chicago
1965–66	Alexander Delvecchio	Detroit
1964–65	Robert Hull	Chicago
1963–64	Kenneth Wharram	Chicago
1962–63	David Keon	Toronto
1961–62	David Keon	Toronto
1960–61	Leonard Kelly	Toronto
1959–60	Donald McKenney	Boston
1958–59	Alexander Delvecchio	Detroit
1957–58	Camille Henry	New York
1956–57	Andrew Hebenton	New York
1955–56	Earl Reibel	Detroit
1954–55	Sidney Smith	Toronto
1953–54	Leonard Kelly	Detroit
1952–53	Leonard Kelly	Detroit
1951–52	Sidney Smith	Toronto
1950–51	Leonard Kelly	Detroit

1949–50	Edgar Laprade	New York
1948–49	Hubert Quackenbush	Detroit
1947–48	Herbert O'Connor	New York
1946–47	Robert Bauer	Boston
1945–46	Hector Blake	Montreal
1944–45	William Mosienko	Chicago
1943–44	Clinton Smith	Chicago
1942–43	Maxwell Bentley	Chicago
1941–42	Charles Apps	Toronto
1940–41	Robert Bauer	Boston
1939–40	Robert Bauer	Boston
1938–39	Clinton Smith	N.Y. Rangers
1937–38	Gordon Drillon	Toronto
1936–87	Martin Barry	Detroit
1935–36	Elwin Romnes	Chicago
1934–35	Frank Boucher	N.Y. Rangers
1933–34	Frank Boucher	N.Y. Rangers
1932–33	Frank Boucher	N.Y. Rangers
1931–32	A. Joseph Primeau	Toronto
1930–31	Frank Boucher	N.Y. Rangers
1929–30	Frank Boucher	N.Y. Rangers
1928–29	Frank Boucher	N.Y. Rangers
1927–28	Frank Boucher	N.Y. Rangers
1926–27	William Burch	N.Y. Americans
1925–26	Frank Nighbor	Ottawa
1924–25	Frank Nighbor	Ottawa

Bill Masterton Memorial Trophy

This trophy was named in honor of Bill Masterton of the Minnesota North Stars who was fatally injured while playing in 1968. The recipient of this award is selected by the National Hockey League Writers Association for demonstrating the finest qualities of sportsmanship, dedication and perseverance.

1971–72—Robert Clarke (Philadelphia)
1970–71—J. G. Y. Jean Ratelle (New York)
1969–70—Hubert Martin (Chicago)
1968–1969—Ted Hampson (Oakland)
1967–1968—Claude Provost (Montreal)

James Norris Memorial Trophy

In 1953, the children of James D. Norris, Sr., former owner of the Detroit Red Wings, presented this trophy to the National Hockey League. It is awarded to the defenseman who demonstrates the greatest all-around ability at that position.

1971–72	Robert Orr	Boston
1970–71	Robert Orr	Boston .
1969–70	Robert Orr	Boston
1968–69	Robert Orr	Boston
1967–68	Robert Orr	Boston
1966–67	Henry Howell	New York
1965–66	Jacques Laperriére	Montreal
1964–65	Pierre Pilote	Chicago
1963–64	Pierre Pilote	Chicago
1962–63	Pierre Pilote	Chicago
1961–62	Douglas Harvey	New York
1960–61	Douglas Harvey	Montreal
1959–60	Douglas Harvey	Montreal
1958–59	Thomas Johnson	Montreal
1957–58	Douglas Harvey	Montreal
1956–57	Douglas Harvey	Montreal
1955–56	Douglas Harvey	Montreal
1954–55	Douglas Harvey	Montreal
1953–54	Leonard Kelly	Detroit

Lester Patrick Trophy

This trophy was presented to the National Hockey League by the New York Rangers in 1966 to honor Lester Patrick, their former General-manager and coach. It is awarded for outstanding service to hockey in the United States and players, officials, coaches, executives and referees are all eligible for it.

1972	Clarence Sutherland Campbell
1971	William M. Jennings
1970	Edward William Shore
1969	Robert Hull
1968	Thomas F. Lockhart
1967	Gordon Howe
1966	John Adams

Arthur H. Ross Trophy

Arthur H. Ross, former General-manager and coach of the Boston Bruins, presented this trophy to the National Hockey League in 1947. It is awarded to the player who leads the league in scoring. If there is a tie it is given to the player who has scored the most goals. Should a tie still result it is then given to the player who has played the least number of games.

1971–72	Philip Esposito	Boston
1970–71	Philip Esposito	Boston
1969–70	Robert Orr	Boston

1968–69	Philip Esposito	Boston
1967–68	Stanley Mikita	Chicago
1966–67	Stanley Mikita	Chicago
1965–66	Robert Hull	Chicago
1964–65	Stanley Mikita	Chicago
1963–64	Stanley Mikita	Chicago
1962–63	Gordon Howe	Detroit
1961–62	Robert Hull	Chicago
1960–61	Bernard Geoffrion	Montreal
1959–60	Robert Hull	Chicago
1958–59	Richard Moore	Montreal
1957–58	Richard Moore	Montreal
1956–57	Gordon Howe	Detroit
1955–56	Jean Béliveau	Montreal
1954–55	Bernard Geoffrion	Montreal
1953–54	Gordon Howe	Detroit
1952–53	Gordon Howe	Detroit
1951–52	Gordon Howe	Detroit
1950–51	Gordon Howe	Detroit
1949–50	Robert Lindsay	Detroit
1948–49	Roy Conacher	Chicago
1947–48	Elmer Lach	Montreal

Conn Smythe Trophy

Maple Leaf Gardens Limited presented this trophy in 1964 to honor Conn Smythe, former owner, General-manager and coach of the Toronto Maple Leafs. It is awarded to the player selected by the National Hockey League Governors who has been the most valuable to his club during the playoffs for the Stanley Cup.

1972	Robert Orr	Boston
1971	Kenneth Dryden	Montreal
1970	Robert Orr	Boston
1969	Serge Savard	Montreal
1968	Glenn Hall	St. Louis
1967	David Keon	Toronto
1966	Roger Crozier	Detroit
1965	Jean Béliveau	Montreal

Georges Vézina Memorial Trophy

Joseph Catarinich, Joseph Viateur "Léo" Dandurand and Louis Letourneau, former owners of the Montreal Canadiens, presented this trophy to the National Hockey League in memory of Georges Vézina, Montreal Canadien goaltender, who collapsed at the end of the 1st period in the Canadiens' first game of the season on November 28, 1925 and died four months later. It is awarded to the goaltender(s) who have played a minimum of 25 games for the club with the fewest goals scored against it.

1971–72	Anthony Esposito, Gary Smith	Chicago
1970–71	Edward Giacomin, Gilles Villemure	New York
1969–70	Anthony Esposito	Chicago
1968–69	Glenn Hall, Jacques Plante	St. Louis
1967–68	Rogatien Vachon, Lorne Worsley	Montreal
1966–67	Denis DeJordy, Glenn Hall	Chicago
1965–66	Charles Hodge, Lorne Worsley	Montreal
1964–65	John Bower, Terrance Sawchuk	Toronto
1963–64	Charles Hodge	Montreal
1962–63	Glenn Hall	Chicago
1961–62	Jacques Plante	Montreal
1960–61	John Bower	Toronto
1959–60	Jacques Plante	Montreal
1958–59	Jacques Plante	Montreal
1957–58	Jacques Plante	Montreal
1956–57	Jacques Plante	Montreal
1955–56	Jacques Plante	Montreal
1954–55	Terrance Sawchuk	Detroit
1953–54	Harry Lumley	Toronto
1952–53	Terrance Sawchuk	Detroit
1951–52	Terrance Sawchuk	Detroit
1950–51	Elwin Rollins	Toronto
1949–50	William Durnan	Montreal
1948–49	William Durnan	Montreal
1947–48	Walter Broda	Toronto
1946–47	William Durnan	Montreal
1945–46	William Durnan	Montreal
1944–45	William Durnan	Montreal
1943–44	William Durnan	Montreal
1942–43	John Mowers	Detroit
1941–42	Francis Brimsek	Boston
1940–41	Walter Broda	Toronto
1939–40	David Kerr	N. Y. Rangers
1938–39	Francis Brimsek	Boston
1937–38	Cecil Thompson	Boston
1936–37	Norman Smith	Detroit
1935–36	Cecil Thompson	Boston
1934–35	Lorne Chabot	Chicago
1933–34	Charles Gardiner	Chicago
1932–33	Cecil Thompson	Boston
1931–32	Charles Gardiner	Chicago
1930–31	Roy Worters	N. Y. Americans
1929–30	Cecil Thompson	Boston
1928–29	George Hainsworth	Mont. Canadiens
1927–28	George Hainsworth	Mont. Canadiens
1926–27	George Hainsworth	Mont. Canadiens

8
All-Star Teams

These teams were chosen by a poll of hockey writers conducted by the Canadian Press through the 1945–46 season. From 1946 through the 1949–50 season the National Hockey League coaches selected the teams but discontinued the All-Star coaches. From 1950 through 1966–67 the All-Star Teams were selected by the hockey writers and broadcasters of the National Hockey League cities. In 1967–68 the teams were again selected by the coaches. In 1968–69 the National Hockey League Writers' Association (3 from each city) began making the selections.

1971–72

1st Team		2nd Team
Anthony Esposito, Chicago	goal	Kenneth Dryden, Mont. Canadiens
Robert Orr, Boston	defence	Patrick Stapleton, Chicago
D. Bradford Park, N.Y. Rangers	defence	William White, Chicago
Philip Esposito, Boston	centre	J. G. Y. Jean Ratelle, N.Y. Rangers
Rodrigue Gilbert, N.Y. Rangers	right wing	Yvan Cournoyer, Mont. Canadiens
Robert Hull, Chicago	left wing	Victor Hadfield, N.Y. Rangers

1970–71

1st Team		2nd Team
Edward Giacomin, N.Y. Rangers	goal	J. Jacques Plante, Toronto
Robert Orr, Boston	defence	D. Bradford Park, N.Y. Rangers
Jean-Claude Tremblay, Mont. Canadiens	defence	Patrick Stapleton, Chicago
Philip Esposito, Boston	centre	David Keon, Toronto
Kenneth Hodge, Boston	right wing	Yvan Cournoyer, Mont. Canadiens
John Bucyk, Boston	left wing	Robert Hull, Chicago

1969–70

1st Team		2nd Team
Anthony Esposito, Chicago	goal	Edward Giacomin, N.Y. Rangers
Robert Orr, Boston	defence	Carl Brewer, Detroit
D. Bradford Park, N.Y. Rangers	defence	J. Jacques Laperriére, Mont. Canadiens
Philip Esposito, Boston	centre	Stanley Mikita, Chicago
Gordon Howe, Detroit	right wing	John McKenzie, Boston
Robert Hull, Chicago	left wing	Francis Mahovlich, Detroit

1968–69

FIRST TEAM
G—Glenn Hall, St. Louis
D—Robert G. Orr, Boston
D—Myles Horton, Toronto
F—Philip Esposito, Boston
F—Gordon Howe, Detroit
F—Robert Hull, Chicago

SECOND TEAM
G—Edward Giacomin, New York
D—Edward Green, Boston
D—Edward Harris, Montreal
F—Jean Béliveau, Montreal
F—Yvan Cournoyer, Montreal
F—Francis Mahovlich, Detroit

1967–68

FIRST TEAM
G—Lorne Worsley, Montreal
D—Robert G. Orr, Boston
D—Tim Horton, Toronto
F—Stanley Mikita, Chicago
F—Gordon Howe, Detroit
F—Robert Hull, Chicago

SECOND TEAM
G—Edward Giacomin, New York
D—Jim Neilson, New York
D—Jean-Claude Tremblay, Montreal
F—Phil Esposito, Boston
F—Rod Gilbert, New York
F—John Bucyk, Boston

1966–67

FIRST TEAM
G—Edward Giacomin, New York
D—Henry Howell, New York
D—Pierre Pilote, Chicago
F—Stanley Mikita, Chicago
F—Kenneth Wharram, Chicago
F—Robert Hull, Chicago
SECOND TEAM
G—Glenn Hall, Chicago
D—Myles Horton, Toronto
D—Robert G. Orr, Boston
F—Norman Ullman, Detroit
F—Gordon Howe, Detroit
F—Donald Marshall, New York

1965–66

FIRST TEAM
G—Glenn Hall, Chicago
D—Jacques Laperriére, Montreal
D—Pierre Pilote, Chicago
F—Stanley Mikita, Chicago
F—Gordon Howe, Detroit
F—Robert Hull, Chicago
SECOND TEAM
G—Lorne Worsley, Montreal
D—Allan Stanley, Toronto
D—Patrick Stapleton, Chicago
F—Jean Béliveau, Montreal
F—Joseph Rousseau, Montreal
F—Francis Mahovlich, Toronto

1964–65
FIRST TEAM
G—Roger Crozier, Detroit
D—Pierre Pilote, Chicago
D—Jacques Laperriére, Montreal
F—Norman Ullman, Detroit
F—Claude Provost, Montreal
F—Robert Hull, Chicago
SECOND TEAM
G—Charles Hodge, Montreal
D—William Gadsby, Detroit
D—Carl Brewer, Toronto
F—Stanley Mikita, Chicago
F—Gordon Howe, Detroit
F—Francis Mahovlich, Toronto

1963–64
FIRST TEAM
G—Glenn Hall, Chicago
D—Pierre Pilote, Chicago
D—Myles Horton, Toronto
F—Stanley Mikita, Chicago
F—Kenneth Wharram, Chicago
F—Robert Hull, Chicago
SECOND TEAM
G—Charles Hodge, Montreal
D—Elmer Vasko, Chicago
D—Jacques Laperriére, Montreal
F—Jean Béliveau, Montreal
F—Gordon Howe, Detroit
F—Francis Mahovlich, Toronto

1962–63
FIRST TEAM
G—Glenn Hall, Chicago
D—Pierre Pilote, Chicago
D—Carl Brewer, Toronto
F—Stanley Mikita, Chicago
F—Gordon Howe, Detroit
F—Francis Mahovlich, Toronto
SECOND TEAM
G—Terrance Sawchuk, Detroit
D—Myles Horton, Toronto
D—Elmer Vasko, Chicago
F—Henri Richard, Montreal
F—Andrew Bathgate, New York
F—Robert Hull, Chicago

1961–62
FIRST TEAM
G—Jacques Plante, Montreal
D—Douglas Harvey, New York
D—Jean-Guy Talbot, Montreal
F—Stanley Mikita, Chicago
F—Andrew Bathgate, New York
F—Robert Hull, Chicago
SECOND TEAM
G—Glenn Hall, Chicago
D—Carl Brewer, Toronto
D—Pierre Pilote, Chicago
F—David Keon, Toronto
F—Gordon Howe, Detroit
F—Francis Mahovlich, Toronto

1960–61
FIRST TEAM
G—John Bower, Toronto
D—Douglas Harvey, Montreal
D—Joseph Pronovost, Detroit
F—Jean Beliveau, Montreal
F—Bernard Geoffrion, Montreal
F—Francis Mahovlich, Toronto
SECOND TEAM
G—Glenn Hall, Chicago
D—Allan Stanley, Toronto
D—Pierre Pilote, Chicago
F—Henri Richard, Montreal
F—Gordon Howe, Detroit
F—Richard Moore, Montreal

1959–60
FIRST TEAM
G—Glenn Hall, Chicago
D—Douglas Harvey, Montreal
D—Joseph Pronovost, Detroit
F—Jean Béliveau, Montreal
F—Gordon Howe, Detroit
F—Robert Hull, Chicago
SECOND TEAM
G—Jacques Plante, Montreal
D—Allan Stanley, Toronto
D—Pierre Pilote, Chicago
F—Bronco Horvath, Boston
F—Bernard Geoffrion, Montreal
F—Dean Prentice, New York

1958–59
FIRST TEAM
G—Jacques Plante, Montreal
D—Thomas Johnson, Montreal
D—William Gadsby, New York
F—Jean Béliveau, Montreal
F—Andrew Bathgate, New York
F—Richard Moore, Montreal
SECOND TEAM
G—Terrance Sawchuk, Detroit
D—Joseph Pronovost, Detroit
D—Douglas Harvey, Montreal
F—Henri Richard, Montreal
F—Gordon Howe, Detroit
F—Alexander Delvecchio, Detroit

1957–58
FIRST TEAM
G—Glenn Hall, Chicago
D—Douglas Harvey, Montreal
D—William Gadsby, New York
F—Henry Richard, Montreal
F—Gordon Howe, Detroit
F—Richard Moore, Montreal
SECOND TEAM
G—Jacques Plante, Montreal
D—Ferdinand Flaman, Boston
D—Joseph Pronovost, Detroit
R—Jean Béliveau, Montreal
F—Andrew Bathgate, New York
F—Camille Henry, New York

1956–57
FIRST TEAM
G—Glenn Hall, Detroit
D—Douglas Harvey, Montreal
D—Leonard Kelly, Detroit
F—Jean Béliveau, Montreal
F—Gordon Howe, Detroit
F—Robert Lindsay, Detroit
SECOND TEAM
G—Jacques Plante, Montreal
D—William Gadsby, New York
D—Ferdinand Flaman, Boston
F—Edward Litzenberger, Chicago
F—Joseph Richard, Montreal
F—Réal Chevrefils, Boston

1955–56
FIRST TEAM
G—Jacques Plante, Montreal
D—Douglas Harvey, Montreal
D—William Gadsby, New York
F—Jean Béliveau, Montreal
F—Joseph Richard, Montreal
F—Robert Lindsay, Detroit
SECOND TEAM
G—Glenn Hall, Detroit
D—Leonard Kelly, Detroit
D—Thomas Johnson, Montreal
F—Aloysius Sloan, Toronto
F—Gordon Howe, Detroit
F—Murray Olmstead, Montreal

1954–55
FIRST TEAM
G—Harry Lumley, Toronto
D—Douglas Harvey, Montreal
D—Leonard Kelly, Detroit
F—Jean Béliveau, Montreal
F—Joseph Richard, Montreal
F—Sidney Smith, Toronto
SECOND TEAM
G—Terrance Sawchuk, Detroit
D—Robert Goldham, Detroit
D—Ferdinand Flaman, Boston
F—Kenneth Mosdell, Montreal
F—Bernard Geoffrion, Montreal
F—Daniel Lewicki, New York

1953–54
FIRST TEAM
G—Harry Lumley, Toronto
D—Leonard Kelly, Detroit
D—Douglas Harvey, Montreal
F—Kenneth Mosdell, Montreal
F—Gordon Howe, Detroit
F—Robert Lindsay, Detroit
SECOND TEAM
G—Terrance Sawchuk, Detroit
D—William Gadsby, Chicago
D—Myles Horton, Toronto
F—Theodore Kennedy, Toronto
F—Joseph Richard, Montreal
F—Edward Sandford, Boston

1952-53
FIRST TEAM
G—Terrance Sawchuk, Detroit
D—Leonard Kelly, Detroit
D—Douglas Harvey, Montreal
F—Fleming Mackell, Boston
F—Gordon Howe, Detroit
F—Robert Lindsay, Detroit
SECOND TEAM
G—Gerard McNeil, Montreal
D—Hubert Quackenbush, Boston
D—William Gadsby, Chicago
F—Alexander Delvecchio, Detroit
F—Joseph Richard, Montreal
F—Murray Olmstead, Montreal

1951-52
FIRST TEAM
G—Terrance Sawchuk, Detroit
D—Leonard Kelly, Detroit
D—Douglas Harvey, Montreal
F—Elmer Lach, Montreal
F—Gordon Howe, Detroit
F—Robert Lindsay, Detroit
SECOND TEAM
G—Samuel Henry, Boston
D—Hyman Buller, New York
D—James Thomson, Toronto
F—Milton Schmidt, Boston
F—Joseph Richard, Montreal
F—Sidney Smith, Toronto

1950-51
FIRST TEAM
G—Terrance Sawchuk, Detroit
D—Leonard Kelly, Detroit
D—Hubert Quackenbush, Boston
F—Milton Schmidt, Boston
F—Gordon Howe, Detroit
F—Robert Lindsay, Detroit
SECOND TEAM
G—Claude Rayner, New York
D—James Thomson, Toronto
D—Leo Reise, Jr., Detroit
F—Sidney Abel, Detroit;
   Theodore Kennedy, Toronto (tie)
F—Henri Richard, Montreal
F—Sidney Smith, Toronto

1949-50
FIRST TEAM
G—William Durnan, Montreal
D—James Mortson, Toronto
D—Kenneth Reardon, Montreal
F—Sidney Abel, Detroit
F—Joseph Richard, Montreal
F—Robert Lindsay, Detroit
SECOND TEAM
G—Claude Rayner, New York
D—Leo Reise, Jr., Detroit
D—Leonard Kelly, Detroit
F—Theodore Kennedy, Toronto
F—Gordon Howe, Detroit
F—Anthony Leswick, New York

1948-49
FIRST TEAM
G—William Durnan, Montreal
D—Hubert Quackenbush, Detroit
D—John Stewart, Detroit
F—Sidney Abel, Detroit
F—Joseph Richard, Montreal
F—Roy Conacher, Chicago
SECOND TEAM
G—Claude Rayner, New York
D—Glen Harmon, Montreal
D—Kenneth Reardon, Montreal
F—Douglas Bentley, Chicago
F—Gordon Howe, Detroit
F—Robert Lindsay, Detroit

1947-48
FIRST TEAM
G—Walter Broda, Toronto
D—Hubert Quackenbush, Detroit
D—John Stewart, Detroit
F—Elmer Lach, Montreal
F—Joseph Richard, Montreal
F—Robert Lindsay, Detroit
SECOND TEAM
G—Francis Brimsek, Boston
D—Kenneth Reardon, Montreal
D—Neil Colville, New York
F—Herbert O'Connor, New York
F—Norman Poile, Toronto—Chicago
F—James Stewart, Toronto—Chicago

1946-47
FIRST TEAM
G—William Durnan, Montreal
D—Kenneth Reardon, Montreal
D—Emile Bouchard, Montreal
F—Milton Schmidt, Boston
F—Joseph Richard, Montreal
F—Douglas Bentley, Chicago
SECOND TEAM
G—Francis Brimsek, Boston
D—John Stewart, Detroit
D—Hubert Quackenbush, Detroit
F—Maxwell Bentley, Chicago
F—Robert Bauer, Boston
F—Woodrow Dumart, Boston

1945-46
FIRST TEAM
G—William Durnan, Montreal
D—John Crawford, Boston
D—Emile Bouchard, Montreal
F—Maxwell Bentley, Chicago
F—Joseph Richard, Montreal
F—James Stewart, Toronto
Co—James Irvin, Montreal
SECOND TEAM
G—Francis Brimsek, Boston
D—Kenneth Reardon, Montreal
D—John Stewart, Detroit
F—Elmer Lach, Montreal
F—William Mosienko, Chicago
F—Hector Blake, Montreal
Co—John Gottselig, Chicago

1944-45
FIRST TEAM
G—William Durnan; Montreal
D—Emile Bouchard, Montreal
D—William Hollett, Detroit
F—Elmer Lach, Montreal
F—Joseph Richard, Montreal
F—Hector Blake, Montreal
Co—James Irvin, Montreal
SECOND TEAM
G—Micheal Karakas, Chicago
D—Glen Harmon, Montreal
D—Walter Pratt, Toronto
F—William Cowley, Boston
F—William Mosienko, Chicago
F—Sydney Howe, Detroit
Co—John Adams, Detroit

1943-44
FIRST TEAM
G—William Durnan, Montreal
D—Earl Seibert, Chicago
D—Walter Pratt, Toronto
F—William Cowley, Boston
F—Lorne Carr, Toronto
F—Douglas Bentley, Chicago
Co—James Irvin, Montreal
SECOND TEAM
G—Paul Bibeault, Toronto
D—Emile Bouchard, Montreal
D—Aubrey Clapper, Boston
F—Elmer Lach, Montreal
F—Joseph Richard, Montreal
F—Herbert Cain, Boston
Co—Clarence Day, Toronto

1942-43
FIRST TEAM
G—John Mowers, Detroit
D—Earl Seibert, Chicago
D—John Stewart, Detroit
F—William Cowley, Boston
F—Lorne Carr, Toronto
F—Douglas Bentley, Chicago
Co—John Adams, Detroit
SECOND TEAM
G—Francis Brimsek, Boston
D—John Crawford, Boston
D—William Hollett, Boston
F—Charles Apps, Toronto
F—Bryan Hextall, New York
F—Joseph Patrick, New York
Co—Arthur Ross, Boston

1941-42
FIRST TEAM
G—Francis Brimsek, Boston
D—Earl Seibert, Chicago
D—Thomas Anderson, Brooklyn
F—Charles Apps, Toronto
F—Bryan Hextall, New York
F—Joseph Patrick, New York
Co—Frank Boucher, New York
SECOND TEAM
G—Walter Broda, Toronto
D—Martin Egan, Brooklyn
D—Wilfred McDonald, Toronto
F—Phillipe Watson, New York
F—Gordon Drillon, Toronto
F—Sidney Abel, Detroit
Co—Paul Thompson, Chicago

1940-41

FIRST TEAM
G—Walter Broda, Toronto
D—Aubrey Clapper, Boston
D—Walter Stanowski, Toronto
F—William Cowley, Boston
F—Bryan Hextall, N.Y. Rangers
F—David Schriner, Toronto
Co—Ralph Weiland, Boston

SECOND TEAM
G—Francis Brimsek, Boston
D—Earl Seibert, Chicago
D—Ehrhardt Heller, N.Y. Rangers
F—Charles Apps, Toronto
F—Robert Bauer, Boston
F—Woodrow Dumart, Boston
Co—James Irvin, Montreal

1939-40

FIRST TEAM
G—David Kerr, N.Y. Rangers
D—Aubrey Clapper, Boston
D—Ebenezer Goodfellow, Detroit
F—Milton Conrad Schmidt, Boston
F—Bryan Hextall, N.Y. Rangers
F—Hector Blake, Montreal
Co—Paul Thompson, Chicago

SECOND TEAM
G—Francis Brimsek, Boston
D—Arthur Coulter, N.Y. Rangers
D—Earl Seibert, Chicago
F—Neil Colville, N.Y. Rangers
F—Robert Bauer, Boston
F—Woodrow Dumart, Boston
Co—Frank Boucher, N.Y. Rangers

1938-39

FIRST TEAM
G—Francis Brimsek, Boston
D—Edward Shore, Boston
D—Aubrey Clapper, Boston
F—Charles Apps, Toronto
F—Gordon Drillon, Toronto
F—Hector Blake, Montreal
Co—Arthur Ross, Boston

SECOND TEAM
G—Earl Robertson, N.Y. Americans
D—Earl Seibert, Chicago
D—Arthur Coulter, N.Y. Rangers
F—Neil Colville, N.Y. Rangers
F—Robert Bauer, Boston
F—John Gottselig, Chicago
Co—Mervyn Dutton, N.Y. Americans

1937-38

FIRST TEAM
G—Cecil Thompson, Boston
D—Edward Shore, Boston
D—Albert Siebert, Mont. Canadiens
F—William Cowley, Boston
F—Cecil Dillon, N.Y. Rangers;
  Gordon Drillon, Toronto (tie)
F—Paul Thompson, Chicago
Co—Lester Patrick, N.Y. Rangers

SECOND TEAM
G—David Kerr, N.Y. Rangers
D—Arthur Coulter, N.Y. Rangers
D—Earl Seibert, Chicago
F—Charles Apps, Toronto
F—Hector Blake, Mont. Canadiens
Co—Arthur Ross, Boston

1936-37

FIRST TEAM
G—Norman Smith, Detroit
'D—Albert Siebert, Mont. Canadiens
D—Ebenezer Goodfellow, Detroit
F—Martin Barry, Detroit
F—Lawrence Aurie, Detroit
F—Harvey Jackson, Toronto
Co—John Adams, Detroit

SECOND TEAM
G—Wilfred Cude, Mont. Canadiens
D—Earl Seibert, Chicago
D—Lionel Conacher, Mont. Maroons
F—Arthur Chapman, N.Y. Americans
F—Cecil Dillon, N.Y. Rangers
F—David Schriner, N.Y. Americans
Co—Cecil Hart, Mont. Canadiens

1935-36

FIRST TEAM
G—Cecil Thompson, Boston
D—Edward Shore, Boston
D—Albert Siebert, Boston
F—Reginald Smith, Mont. Maroons
F—Charles Conacher, Toronto
F—David Schriner, N.Y. Americans
Co—Lester Patrick, N.Y. Rangers

SECOND TEAM
G—Wilfred Cude, Mont. Canadiens
D—Earl Seibert, N.Y. Rangers—Chi.
D—Ebenezer Goodfellow, Detroit
F—William Thoms, Toronto
F—Cecil Dillon, N.Y. Rangers
F—Paul Thompson, Chicago
Co—Thomas Gorman, Mont. Maroons

1934–35
FIRST TEAM
G—Lorne Chabot, Chicago
D—Edward Shore, Boston
D—Earl Seibert, N.Y. Rangers
F—Frank Boucher, N.Y. Rangers
F—Charles Conacher, Toronto
F—Harvey Jackson, Toronto
Co—Lester Patrick, N.Y. Rangers
SECOND TEAM
G—Cecil Thompson, Boston
D—Marvin Wentworth, Mont, Maroons
D—Arthur Coulter, Chicago
F—Ralph Weiland, Detroit
F—Aubrey Clapper, Boston
F—Aurèle Joliat, Mont. Canadiens
Co—James Irvin, Toronto

1933–34
FIRST TEAM
G—Charles Gardiner, Chicago
D—Francis Clancy, Toronto
D—Lionel Conacher, Chicago
F—Frank Boucher, N.Y. Rangers
F—Charles Conacher, Toronto
F—Harvey Jackson, Toronto
Co—Lester Patrick, N.Y. Rangers
SECOND TEAM
G—Roy Worters, N.Y. Americans
D—Edward Shore, Boston
D—Ivan Johnson, N.Y. Rangers
F—A. Joseph Primeau, Toronto
F—William Cook, N.Y. Rangers
F—Aurèle Joliat, Mont. Canadiens
Co—James Irvin, Toronto

1932–33
FIRST TEAM
G—John Roach, Detroit
D—Edward Shore, Boston
D—Ivan Johnson, N.Y. Rangers
F—Frank Boucher, N.Y. Rangers
F—William Cook, N.Y. Rangers
F—Lawrence Northcott, Mont.
Maroons
Co—Lester Patrick, N.Y. Rangers
SECOND TEAM
G—Charles Gardiner, Chicago
D—Francis Clancy, Toronto
D—Lionel Conacher, Mont. Maroons
F—Howarth Morenz, Mont. Canadiens
F—Charles Conacher, Toronto
F—Harvey Jackson, Toronto
Co—James Irvin, Toronto

1931–32
FIRST TEAM
G—Charles Gardiner, Chicago
D—Edward Shore, Boston
D—Ivan Johnson, N.Y. Rangers
F—Howarth Horenz, Mont. Canadiens
F—William Cook, N.Y. Rangers
F—Harvey Jackson, Toronto
Co—Lester Patrick, N.Y. Rangers
SECOND TEAM
G—Roy Worters, N.Y. Americans
D—Sylvio Mantha, Mont. Canadiens
D—Francis Clancy, Toronto
F—Reginald Smith, Mont. Maroons
F—Charles Conacher, Toronto
F—Aurèle Joliat, Mont. Canadiens
Co—James Irvin, Toronto

1930–31
FIRST TEAM
G—Charles Gardiner, Chicago
D—Edward Shore, Boston
D—Francis Clancy, Toronto
F—Howarth Morenz, Mont. Canadiens
F—William Cook, N.Y. Rangers
F—Aurèle Joliat, Mont. Canadiens
Co—Lester Patrick, N.Y. Rangers
SECOND TEAM
G—Cecil Thompson, Boston
D—Sylvio Mantha, Mont. Canadiens
D—Ivan Johnson, N.Y. Rangers
F—Frank Boucher, N.Y. Rangers
F—Aubrey Clapper, Boston
F—Frederick Cook, N.Y. Rangers
Co—James Irvin, Chicago

9
All-Star Games

All-Star Games

These games originated in 1947 to augment the players' pension fund. The first 19 games were played before the start of the regular season between the club holding the Stanley Cup and the players who were voted to the 1st and 2nd All-Star Teams at the end of the previous season (except 5th and 6th games). The All-Star club was coached by the coach of the defeated Stanley Cup finalists, who selected the rest of his players from the other clubs in the league. Any All-Stars on the club holding the Stanley Cup remained with that club. All of these games have been played in the city of the club holding the Stanley Cup except the 2nd game, which was played at Chicago.

The 5th and 6th games were played between the 1st and 2nd All-Star Teams. The 1st All-Star Team was coached by the coach of the club that had won the Stanley Cup and he selected the rest of his players from the clubs in the United States cities (Boston, Chicago, Detroit and New York). The 2nd All-Star Team was coached by the coach of the defeated Stanley Cup finalists and he selected the rest of his players from the clubs in the Canadian cities (Montreal and Toronto).

The 20th and 21st games were played in mid-season (January) under the original format (Stanley Cup winner vs. 1st and 2nd All-Star Teams of previous season).

In the 22nd, 23rd, 24th and 25th games the East Division opposed the West Division, with the players selected by the National Hockey League Writers' Association. The writers in the East Division cities selected two players at each position (12) from the East Division clubs and the writers in the West Division cities did likewise. The coaches in the Stanley Cup final series of the previous season coached the clubs and they selected the rest of their players from clubs in their own division (if the writers had not selected a player from each club then the coaches must—each club had at least one player in game).

Since 1970 the games have been rotated in the National Hockey League cities (all prior games—except 2nd game—were played in city of club holding Stanley Cup).

Since the 22nd game players on the 1st and 2nd All-Star Teams of the previous season are not automatically eligible to play in these games. The players selected by the National Hockey League Writers' Association for these games should not be confused with the players they later select for the 1st and 2nd All-Star Teams at the end of the season.

1st game Oct. 13, 1947 at Toronto	All-Stars 4	Tor. Maple Leafs 3
2nd game Nov. 3, 1948 at Chicago	All-Stars 3	Tor. Maple Leafs 1
3rd game Oct. 10, 1949 at Toronto	All-Stars 3	Tor. Maple Leafs 1
4th game Oct. 8, 1950 at Detroit	All-Stars 1	Det. Red Wings 7
5th game Oct. 9, 1951 at Toronto	1st All-Star Team 2	2nd All-Star Tm. 2
6th game Oct. 5, 1952 at Detroit	1st All-Star Team 1	2nd All-Star Tm. 1
7th game Oct. 3, 1953 at Montreal	All-Stars 3	Mont. Canadiens 1
8th game Oct. 2, 1954 at Detroit	All-Stars 2	Det. Red Wings 2
9th game Oct. 2, 1955 at Detroit	All-Stars 1	Det. Red Wings 3
10th game Oct. 9, 1956 at Montreal	All-Stars 1	Mont. Canadiens 1
11th game Oct. 5, 1957 at Montreal	All-Stars 5	Mont. Canadiens 3
12th game Oct. 4, 1958 at Montreal	All-Stars 3	Mont. Canadiens 6
13th game Oct. 3, 1959 at Montreal	All-Stars 1	Mont. Canadiens 6
14th game Oct. 1, 1960 at Montreal	All-Stars 2	Mont. Canadiens 1
15th game Oct. 7, 1961 at Chicago	All-Stars 3	Chi. Blk. Hawks 1
16th game Oct. 6, 1962 at Toronto	All-Stars 1	Tor. Maple Leafs 4
17th game Oct. 5, 1963 at Toronto	All-Stars 3	Tor. Maple Leafs 3
18th game Oct. 10, 1964 at Toronto	All-Stars 3	Tor. Maple Leafs 2
19th game Oct. 20, 1965 at Montreal	All-Stars 5	Mont. Canadiens 2
20th game Jan. 18, 1967 at Montreal	All-Stars 0	Mont. Canadiens 3
21st game Jan. 16, 1968 at Toronto	All-Stars 3	Tor. Maple Leafs 4
22nd game Jan. 21, 1969 at Montreal	East Division 3	West Division 3
23rd game Jan. 20, 1970 at St. Louis	East Division 4	West Division 1
24th game Jan. 19, 1971 at Boston	East Division 1	West Division 2
25th game Jan. 25, 1972 at Bloomington	East Division 3	West Division 2

10
Stanley Cup

Stanley Cup Winners

1894	Montreal Amateur Athletic Association	1932	Toronto Maple Leafs
1895	Montreal Victorias	1933	New York Rangers
1896	Winnipeg Victorias	1934	Chicago Black Hawks
1897	Montreal Victorias	1935	Montreal Maroons
1898	Montreal Victorias	1936	Detroit Red Wings
1899	(February) Montreal Victorias (March) Montreal Shamrocks	1937	Detroit Red Wings
		1938	Chicago Black Hawks
1900	Montreal Shamrocks	1939	Boston Bruins
1901	Winnipeg Victorias	1940	New York Rangers
1902	Montreal Amateur Athletic Association	1941	Boston Bruins
		1942	Toronto Maple Leafs
1903	Ottawa Silver Seven	1943	Detroit Red Wings
1904	Ottawa Silver Seven	1944	Montreal Canadiens
1905	Ottawa Silver Seven	1945	Toronto Maple Leafs
1906	Montreal Wanderers	1946	Montreal Canadiens
1907	(January) Kenora Thistles (March) Montreal Wanderers	1947	Toronto Maple Leafs
		1948	Toronto Maple Leafs
		1949	Toronto Maple Leafs
1908	Montreal Wanderers	1950	Detroit Red Wings
1909	Ottawa Senators	1951	Toronto Maple Leafs
1910	Montreal Wanderers	1952	Detroit Red Wings
1911	Ottawa Senators	1953	Montreal Canadiens
1912	Quebec Bulldogs	1954	Detroit Red Wings
1913	Quebec Bulldogs	1955	Detroit Red Wings
1914	Toronto Blueshirts	1956	Montreal Canadiens
1915	Vancouver Millionaires	1957	Montreal Canadiens
1916	Montreal Canadiens	1958	Montreal Canadiens
1917	Seattle Metropolitans	1959	Montreal Canadiens
1918	Toronto Arenas	1960	Montreal Canadiens
1919	none	1961	Chicago Black Hawks
1920	Ottawa Senators	1962	Toronto Maple Leafs
1921	Ottawa Senators	1963	Toronto Maple Leafs
1922	Toronto St. Patricks	1964	Toronto Maple Leafs
1923	Ottawa Senators	1965	Montreal Canadiens
1924	Montreal Canadiens	1966	Montreal Canadiens
1925	Victoria Cougars	1967	Toronto Maple Leafs
1926	Montreal Maroons	1968	Montreal Canadiens
1927	Ottawa Senators	1969	Montreal Canadiens
1928	New York Rangers	1970	Boston Bruins
1929	Boston Bruins	1971	Montreal Canadiens
1930	Montreal Canadiens	1972	Boston Bruins
1931	Montreal Canadiens		

Most Times Stanley Cup Winner

Montreal Canadiens	17
Toronto Maple Leafs	11
Detroit Red Wings	7
Ottawa Senators	6
Boston Bruins	5
Montreal Victorias	4
Montreal Wanderers	4
Ottawa Silver Seven	3
New York Rangers	3
Chicago Black Hawks	3

Club Records

Game

Most Goals (both clubs)

Jan. 16, 1905	Ottawa Silver Seven (23) & Dawson City Klondikers (2)	25
Feb. 27, 1906	Ottawa Silver Seven (16) & Queen's University (7)	23
Jan. 20, 1910	Edmonton (7) & Ottawa Senators (13)	20
Feb. 28, 1906	Ottawa Silver Seven (12) & Queen's University (7)	19
Dec. 27, 1897	Montreal Victorias (15) & Ottawa Capitals (2)	17
Mar. 16, 1911	Ottawa Senators (13) & Port Arthur (4)	17
Mar. 8, 1913	Quebec Bulldogs (14) & Sydney Millionaires (3)	17

Most Goals (1 club)

Jan. 16, 1905 at Ottawa	Ottawa Silver Seven	23
Feb. 27, 1906 at Ottawa	Ottawa Silver Seven	16
Dec. 27, 1897 at Montreal	Montreal Victorias	15
Mar. 8, 1913 at Quebec City	Quebec Bulldogs	14
Jan. 13, 1908 at Montreal	Montreal Wanderers	13
Jan. 20, 1910 at Ottawa	Ottawa Senators	13
Mar. 16, 1911 at Ottawa	Ottawa Senators	13

Most Assists (both clubs)

Apr. 18, 1968	Los Angeles Kings (6) & Minnesota North Stars (16)	22
Apr. 19, 1962	Chicago Black Hawks (7) & Toronto Maple Leafs (14)	21
Apr. 6, 1972	Minnesota North Stars (12) & St. Louis Blues (9)	21
Mar. 30, 1957	Montreal Canadiens (14) & New York Rangers (6)	20
Apr. 18, 1968	Chicago Black Hawks (3) & Montreal Canadiens (17)	20
Apr. 7, 1936	Detroit Red Wings (13) & Toronto Maple Leafs (6)	19
Apr. 9, 1972	Chicago Black Hawks (10) & Pittsburgh Penguins (9)	19

Most Assists (1 club)

Mar. 30, 1944 at Montreal	Montreal Canadiens	17
Apr. 18, 1968 at Montreal	Montreal Canadiens	17
Mar. 29, 1947 at Toronto	Detroit Red Wings	16
Apr. 18, 1968 at Inglewood, Calif.	Minnesota North Stars	16
Apr. 20, 1972 at Boston	Boston Bruins	16
Apr. 2, 1969 at Boston	Boston Bruins	15

Most Points (both clubs)

Apr. 18, 1968	Los Angeles Kings	(10)	& Minnesota North Stars (25)	35
Apr. 19, 1962	Chicago Black Hawks	(11)	& Toronto Maple Leafs (22)	33
Apr. 7, 1936	Detroit Red Wings	(22)	& Toronto Maple Leafs (10)	32
Apr. 6, 1972	Minnesota North Stars	(18)	& St. Louis Blues (14)	32
Mar. 30, 1957	Montreal Canadiens	(22)	& New York Rangers (9)	31
Apr. 18, 1968	Chicago Black Hawks	(5)	& Montreal Canadiens (26)	31
Apr. 9, 1972	Chicago Black Hawks	(16)	& Pittsburgh Penguins (14)	30
Apr. 20, 1972	Boston Bruins	(26)	& St. Louis Blues (4)	30

Most Points (1 club)

Mar. 30, 1944	at Montreal	Montreal Canadiens	(11 goals—17 assists)	28
Apr. 18, 1968	at Montreal	Montreal Canadiens	(9 goals—17 assists)	26
Apr. 20, 1972	at Boston	Boston Bruins	(10 goals—16 assists)	26
Mar. 29, 1947	at Toronto	Detroit Red Wings	(9 goals—16 assists)	25
Apr. 18, 1968	at Inglewood	Minnesota North Stars	(9 goals—16 assists)	25
Apr. 2, 1969	at Boston	Boston Bruins	(10 goals—15 assists)	25

Most Penalties (both clubs)

Apr. 2, 1969	Boston Bruins	(18)	& Toronto Maple Leafs (20)	38
Apr. 11, 1970	Boston Bruins	(20)	& New York Rangers (18)	38
Apr. 14, 1966	Montreal Canadiens	(16)	& Toronto Maple Leafs (19)	35
Apr. 8, 1971	New York Rangers	(16)	& Toronto Maple Leafs (18)	34
Mar. 26, 1964	Montreal Canadiens	(16)	& Toronto Maple Leafs (15)	31
Apr. 2, 1964	Montreal Canadiens	(15)	& Toronto Maple Leafs (15)	30
Apr. 19, 1970	Pittsburgh Penguins	(18)	& St. Louis Blues (12)	30
Mar. 25, 1952	Detroit Red Wings	(13)	& Toronto Maple Leafs (16)	29
May 7, 1972	Boston Bruins	(18)	& New York Rangers (11)	29
Mar. 28, 1930	Montreal Canadiens	(12)	& New York Rangers (16)	28
Apr. 4, 1927	Boston Bruins	(16)	& New York Rangers (11)	27
Mar. 23, 1929	Boston Bruins	(14)	& Montreal Canadiens (12)	26
Apr. 9, 1966	Montreal Canadiens	(12)	& Toronto Maple Leafs (14)	26
Apr. 13, 1968	Philadelphia Flyers	(12)	& St. Louis Blues (14)	26
May 11, 1971	Chicago Black Hawks	(14)	& Montreal Canadiens (12)	26
Apr. 8, 1970	Boston Bruins	(14)	& New York Rangers (11)	25
Apr. 18, 1972	Boston Bruins	(12)	& St. Louis Blues (13)	25
Apr. 5, 1972	Minnesota North Stars	(11)	& St. Louis Blues (13)	24

Most Penalties (1 club)

Apr. 2, 1969	at Boston	Toronto Maple Leafs	20
Apr. 11, 1970	at New York	Boston Bruins	20
Apr. 14, 1966	at Toronto	Toronto Maple Leafs	19
Apr. 2, 1969	at Boston	Boston Bruins	18
Apr. 11, 1970	at New York	New York Rangers	18
Apr. 19, 1970	at St. Louis	Pittsburgh Penguins	18
Apr. 8, 1971	at New York	Toronto Maple Leafs	18
May 7, 1972	at New York	Boston Bruins	18

Most Penalties in Minutes (both clubs)

Apr. 11, 1970	Boston Bruins (93) & New York Rangers (81)	174
Apr. 8, 1971	New York Rangers (87) & Toronto Maple Leafs (83)	170
Apr. 14, 1966	Montreal Canadiens (74) & Toronto Maple Leafs (80)	154
Apr. 19, 1970	Pittsburgh Penguins (83) & St. Louis Blues (66)	149
Apr. 2, 1969	Boston Bruins (56) & Toronto Maple Leafs (79)	135
May 11, 1971	Chicago Black Hawks (61) & Montreal Canadiens (49)	110

Most Penalties in Minutes (1 club)

Apr. 11, 1970 at New York	Boston Bruins	(4 misc.—7 maj.—9 min.)	93
Apr. 8, 1971 at New York	N.Y. Rangers	(5 misc.—5 maj.—6 min.)	87
Apr. 19, 1970 at St. Louis	Pitts. Penguins	(4 misc.—5 maj.—9 min.)	83
Apr. 8, 1971 at New York	Tor. Maple Leafs	(4 misc.—5 maj.—9 min.)	83
Apr. 11, 1970 at New York	N.Y. Rangers	(3 misc.—7 maj.—8 min.)	81
Apr. 14, 1966 at Toronto	Tor. Maple Leafs	(3 misc.—6 maj.—10 min.)	80
Apr. 2, 1969 at Boston	Tor. Maple Leafs	(3 misc.—5 maj.—12 min.)	79
Apr. 14, 1966 at Toronto	Mont. Canadiens	(3 misc.—6 maj.—7 min.)	74
May 7, 1972 at New York	Boston Bruins	(2 misc.—5 maj.—11 min.)	67

Most Goals-Against

Jan. 16, 1905 at Ottawa	Dawson City Klondikers	23
Feb. 27, 1906 at Ottawa	Queen's University	16
Dec. 27, 1897 at Montreal	Ottawa Capitals	15
Mar. 8, 1913 at Quebec City	Sydney Millionaires	14
Jan. 13, 1908 at Montreal	Ottawa Victorias	13
Jan. 20, 1910 at Ottawa	Edmonton	13
Mar. 16, 1911 at Ottawa	Port Arthur	13

Period

Most Goals (both clubs)

Mar. 26, 1915	Ottawa Senators (1) & Van. Millionaires (6)	3rd period 7
Mar. 26, 1936	Boston Bruins (1) & Tor. Maple Leafs (6)	2nd period 7
Mar. 22, 1940	Detroit Red Wings (3) & N.Y. Americans (4)	3rd period 7
Mar. 30, 1944	Mont. Canadiens (7) & Tor. Maple Leafs (0)	3rd period 7
Apr. 6, 1967	Mont. Canadiens (5) & N.Y. Rangers (2)	3rd period 7
Apr. 18, 1968	Chi. Black Hawks (2) & Mont. Canadiens (5)	3rd period 7
Apr. 18, 1968	Los Angeles Kings (2) & Minn. North Stars (5)	2nd period 7
Apr. 20, 1972	Boston Bruins (5) & St. Louis Blues (2)	3rd period 7

Most Goals (1 club)

Mar. 30, 1944 at Montreal	Montreal Canadiens	3rd period 7
Mar. 26, 1915 at Vancouver	Vancouver Millionaires	3rd period 6
Mar. 26, 1936 at Toronto	Toronto Maple Leafs	2nd period 6
Mar. 29, 1947 at Toronto	Detroit Red Wings	3rd period 6

Most Assists (both clubs)

Mar. 30, 1944 Mont. Canadiens (13) & Tor. Maple Leafs (0) 3rd period 13
Apr. 18, 1968 Chi. Black Hawks (3) & Mont. Canadiens (9) 3rd period 12
Mar. 26, 1936   Boston Bruins (1) & Tor. Maple Leafs (10) 2nd period 11
Mar. 22, 1940   Det. Red Wings (4) & N.Y. Americans (7) 3rd period 11
Apr. 11, 1968 Chi. Black Hawks (9) & N.Y. Rangers (2)   3rd period 11
Apr. 18, 1968 Los Angeles Kings (3) & Minn. North Stars (8) 2nd period 11

Most Assists (1 club)

Mar. 30, 1944 at Montreal	Montreal Canadiens	3rd period	13
Mar. 26, 1936 at Toronto	Toronto Maple Leafs	2nd period	10
Mar. 29, 1947 at Toronto	Detroit Red Wings	3rd period	10
Mar. 25, 1954 at Montreal	Montreal Canadiens	1st period	9
Apr. 11, 1968 at Chicago	Chicago Black Hawks	3rd period	9
Apr. 18, 1968 at Montreal	Montreal Canadiens	3rd period	9
Apr. 27, 1971 at Montreal	Montreal Canadiens	3rd period	9

Most Points (both clubs)

Mar. 30, 1944 Mont. Canadiens (20) & Tor. Maple Leafs (0) 3rd period 20
Apr. 18, 1968 Chi. Black Hawks (5) & Mont. Canadiens (14) 3rd period 19
Mar. 26, 1936   Boston Bruins (2) & Tor. Maple Leafs (16) 2nd period 18
Mar. 22, 1940 Detroit Red Wings (7) & N.Y. Americans (11) 3rd period 18
Apr. 18, 1968 Los Angeles Kings (5) & Minn. No. Stars (13) 2nd period 18
Apr. 11, 1968 Chi. Black Hawks (14) & N.Y. Rangers (3)   3rd period 17
Apr. 6, 1967 Mont. Canadiens (13) & N.Y. Rangers (3)   3rd period 16
Apr. 20, 1972   Boston Bruins (12) & St. Louis Blues (4)   3rd period 16

Most Points (1 club)

Mar. 30, 1944 at Montreal	Montreal Canadiens 3rd period	(7 goals—13 assists)	20
Mar. 26, 1936 at Toronto	Toronto Maple Leafs 2nd period	(6 goals—10 assists)	16
Mar. 29, 1947 at Toronto	Detroit Red Wings 3rd period	(6 goals—10 assists)	16
Mar. 25, 1954 at Montreal	Montreal Canadiens 1st period	(5 goals— 9 assists)	14
Apr. 11, 1968 at Chicago	Chicago Black Hawks 3rd period	(5 goals— 9 assists)	14
Apr. 18, 1968 at Montreal	Montreal Canadiens 3rd period	(5 goals— 9 assists)	14

Most Penalties (both clubs)

Apr. 11, 1970   Boston Bruins (12) & N.Y. Rangers (12)   1st period 24
Apr. 14, 1966 Mont. Canadiens (12) & Tor. Maple Leafs (11) 1st period 23
Apr. 2, 1969   Boston Bruins (9) & Tor. Maple Leafs (12) 3rd period 21
Apr. 8, 1971 New York Rangers (9) & Tor. Maple Leafs (10) 3rd period 19
May 11, 1971 Chi. Black Hawks (10) & Mont. Canadiens (8) 3rd period 18
May 7, 1972   Boston Bruins (11) & N.Y. Rangers (7)   1st period 18
Apr. 8, 1970   Boston Bruins (10) & N.Y. Rangers (7)   3rd period 17
Mar. 26, 1964 Mont. Canadiens (8) & Tor. Maple Leafs (8)   1st period 16
Apr. 19, 1970 Pitts. Penguins (10) & St. Louis Blues (6)   1st period 16
Apr. 1, 1951   Boston Bruins (7) & Tor. Maple Leafs (8)   1st period 15

Apr. 2, 1964 Mont. Canadiens (8) & Tor. Maple Leafs (7) 1st period 15
Apr. 13, 1971   Boston Bruins (7) & Mont. Canadiens (8) 1st period 15
Apr. 5, 1972 Minn. North Stars (8) & St. Louis Blues (7) 1st period 15

Most Penalties (1 club)

Apr. 14, 1966 at Toronto   Montreal Canadiens   1st period 12
Apr. 2, 1969 at Boston   Toronto Maple Leafs   3rd period 12
Apr. 11, 1970 at New York   Boston Bruins   1st period 12
Apr. 11, 1970 at New York   New York Rangers   1st period 12
Apr. 14, 1966 at Toronto   Toronto Maple Leafs   1st period 11
May 7, 1972 at New York   Boston Bruins   1st period 11
Apr. 8, 1970 at Boston   Boston Bruins   3rd period 10
Apr. 19, 1970 at St. Louis   Pittsburgh Pirates   1st period 10
Apr. 8, 1971 at New York   Toronto Maple Leafs   3rd period 10
May 11, 1971 at Montreal   Chicago Black Hawks   3rd period 10

Most Penalties in Minutes (both clubs)

Apr. 11, 1970   Boston Bruins (66) & N.Y. Rangers (66)   1st period 132
Apr. 14, 1966 Mont. Canadiens (66) & Tor. Maple Leafs (64) 1st period 130
Apr. 8, 1971   N.Y. Rangers (59) & Tor. Maple Leafs (53) 3rd period 112
May 11, 1971 Chi. Black Hawks (53) & Mont. Canadiens (41) 3rd period 94
Apr. 2, 1969   Boston Bruins (35) & Tor. Maple Leafs (57) 3rd period 92
Apr. 19, 1970   Pitts. Penguins (40) & St. Louis Blues (40) 3rd period 80

Most Penalties in Minutes (1 club)

Apr. 14, 1966 at Toronto   Montreal Canadiens
                    1st period (3 misc.—6 maj.—3 min.) 66
Apr. 11, 1970 at New York Boston Bruins
                    1st period (3 misc.—6 maj.—3 min.) 66
Apr. 11, 1970 at New York New York Rangers
                    1st period (3 misc.—6 maj.—3 min.) 66
Apr. 14, 1966 at Toronto   Toronto Maple Leafs
                    1st period (3 misc.—6 maj.—2 min.) 64
Apr. 8, 1971 at New York New York Rangers
                    3rd period (4 misc.—3 maj.—2 min.) 59
Apr. 2, 1969 at Boston   Toronto Maple Leafs
                    3rd period (3 misc.—3 maj.—6 min.) 57
Apr. 8, 1971 at New York Toronto Maple Leafs
                    3rd period (3 misc.—3 maj.—4 min.) 53
May 11, 1971 at Montreal   Chicago Black Hawks
                    3rd period (3 misc.—3 maj.—4 min.) 53
May 7, 1972 at New York Boston Bruins
                    1st period (2 misc.—4 maj.—5 min.) 50
May 11, 1971 at Montreal   Montreal Canadiens
                    3rd period (2 misc.—3 maj.—3 min.) 41
Apr. 8, 1970 at Boston   Boston Bruins
                    3rd period (1 misc.—4 maj.—5 min.) 40
Apr. 19, 1970 at St. Louis Pittsburgh Penguins
                    3rd period (3 misc.—2 maj.)   40
Apr. 19, 1970 at St. Louis St. Louis Blues
                    3rd period (3 misc.—2 maj.)   40

Most Goals-Against

Mar. 30, 1944 at Montreal	Toronto Maple Leafs	3rd period 7
Mar. 26, 1915 at Vancouver	Ottawa Senators	3rd period 6
Mar. 26, 1936 at Toronto	Boston Bruins	2nd period 6
Mar. 29, 1947 at Toronto	Toronto Maple Leafs	3rd period 6

11
Register of Players
(Stanley Cup)

Inactive players (excluding goaltenders)   326

Active players (excluding goaltenders)   352

Inactive Players (Excluding Goaltenders)

This section includes players whose careers ended prior to the 1968–69 season. For players active after 1968–69 see page 352.

Abbreviations

The following appear after names of players:

LW—Left Wing
RW—Right Wing
C—Center
D—Defense
SL—Shoots left
SR—Shoots right

The following appear as headings:

Sea.—Season
Ga.—Games
Go.—Goals
A.—Assists
P.—Points
PM.—Penalties in Minutes

A blank column indicates that information is unavailable.

Records begin with the formation of the National Hockey League. Capital letters in parentheses following the club indicate leagues other than the National Hockey League. An asterisk preceding club indicates Stanley Cup winner.

Other leagues:

PCHA—Pacific Coast Hockey Association
WCHL—Western Canada Hockey League

Sea. Club	Ga.	Go.	A.	P.	PM.
ABEL, CLARENCE					
1927 New York Rangers		0	1	1	8
1928 * "		1	0	1	14
1929 "		0	0	0	8
1930 Chicago		0	0	0	10
1931 "		0	0	0	8
1932 "		0	0	0	2
1934 * "		0	0	0	8
		1	1	2	58
ABEL, SIDNEY GERALD					
1939 Detroit	3	1	1	2	2
1940 "	5	0	3	3	21
1941 "	9	2	2	4	2
1942 "	12	4	2	6	6
1943 * "	10	5	8	13	4
1946 "	3	0	0	0	0
1947 "	3	1	1	2	2
1948 "	10	0	3	3	16
1949 "	11	3	3	6	6
1950 * "	14	6	2	8	6
1951 "	6	4	3	7	0
1952 * "	7	2	2	4	12
1953 Chicago	1	0	0		0
	94	28	30	58	77
ADAMS, JOHN JAMES					
1921 Vancouver (PCHA)		2	1	3	9
1922 " (PCHA)		6	0	6	28
1927 *Ottawa		0	0	0	2
		8	1	9	39
ADAMS, STEWART					
1930 Chicago	2	0	0	0	6
1931 "	9	3	3	6	8
	11	3	3	6	14
ADAMS, W. "BILL" SL					
1921 Vancouver (PCHA)		0	0	0	0
1922 Regina (WCHL)		0	0	0	3
		0	0	0	3
ALDCORN, GARY WILLIAM					
1960 Detroit	6	1	2	3	4
ALEXANDRE, ARTHUR					
1932 Mont. Canadiens	4	0	0	0	0
ALLEN, COURTNEY KEITH					
1954 *Detroit	5	0	0	0	0
ALLEN, GEORGE					
1939 New York Rangers		0	0	0	4
1940 Chicago	2	0	0	0	0
1941 "	5	2	2	4	10
1942 "	3	1	1	2	0
1944 "	9	5	4	9	8
1946 "	4	0	0	0	4
1947 Montreal	11	1	3	4	6
		9	10	19	32
ANDERSON, DALE NORMAN					
1957 Detroit	2	0	0	0	0
ANDERSON, DOUGLAS "ANDY" C-SL					
Born: Edmonton, Alta. Oct. 20, 1927					
1953 *Montreal	2	0	0	0	0
ANDERSON, ERNIE RW					
1922 Regina (WCHL)		1	0	1	0
1924 Calgary (WCHL)		0	0	0	2
		1	0	1	2
ANDERSON, "JOCKO" RW					
1925 *Victoria (WCHL)		1	0	1	10
1926 " "		0	0		0
		1	0	1	10
ANDERSON, THOMAS LINTON					
1936 N. Y. Americans	4	0	0	0	6
1938 " "	6	1	4	5	2
1939 " "		0	0	0	0
1940 " "	3	1	3	4	0
		2	7	9	8
ANDREWS, LLOYD					
1922 *Toronto		2	0	2	3

Sea. Club	Ga.	Go.	A.	P.	PM.
APPS, CHARLES JOSEPH SYLVANUS					
1937 Toronto	2	0	1	1	0
1938 "	7	1	4	5	0
1939 "	10	2	6	8	2
1940 "	10	5	2	7	2
1941 "	5	3	2	5	2
1942 * "	13	5	9	14	2
1947 * "	11	5	1	6	0
1948 * "	9	4	4	8	0
	67	25	29	54	8
ARBOUR, ERNEST					
1930 Chicago		1	0	1	0
1931 "		1	0	1	6
		2	0	2	6
ARMSTRONG, MURRAY A.					
1938 Toronto	3	0	0	0	0
1944 Detroit	5	0	2	2	0
1945 "	14	4	2	6	2
1946 "	5	0	2	2	0
	27	4	6	10	2
ARMSTRONG, ROBERT RICHARD					
1952 Boston	5	0	0	0	2
1953 "	11	1	1	2	10
1954 "	4	0	1	1	0
1955 "	5	0	0	0	2
1957 "	10	0	3	3	10
1959 "	7	0	2	2	4
	42	1	7	8	28
ASMUNDSON, OSCAR					
1933 *N. Y. Rangers		0	2	2	4
AUBUCHON, OSCAR					
1943 Boston	6	1	0	1	0
AURIE, LAWRENCE					
1929 Detroit		1	0	1	2
1932 "		0	0	0	0
1933 "		1	0	1	4
1934 "		3	7	10	2
1936 * "		1	2	3	2
		6	9	15	10
BABANDO, PETER JOSEPH					
1948 Boston	5	1	1	2	2
1949 "	4	0	0	0	2
1950 *Detroit	8	2	2	4	2
	17	3	3	6	6
BAILEY, IRVIN W.					
1929 Toronto		1	2	3	4
1931 "		1	1	2	0
1932 * "		1	0	1	4
1933 "		0	1	1	4
		3	4	7	12
BAILEY, ROBERT ALLEN					
1954 Toronto	5	0	2	2	4
1955 "	1	0	0	0	0
1957 Detroit	5	0	2	2	2
1958 "	4	0	0	0	16
	15	0	4	4	22
BALFOUR, EARL FREDERICK					
1952 Toronto	1	0	0	0	0
1956 "	3	0	1	1	2
1959 Chicago	6	0	2	2	0
1960 "	4	0	0	0	0
1961 * "	12	0	0	0	2
	26	0	3	3	4
BALFOUR, MURRAY LEWIS					
1960 Chicago	4	1	0	1	0
1961 * "	11	5	5	10	14
1962 "	12	1	1	2	15
1963 "	6	0	2	2	12
1964 "	7	2	2	4	4
	40	9	10	19	45
BARILKO, WILLIAM					
1947 *Toronto	11	0	3	3	18
1948 * "	9	1	0	1	17
1949 * "	9	0	1	1	20
1950 "	7	1	1	2	18
1951 * "	11	3	2	5	31
	47	5	7	12	104

Sea. Club	Ga.	Go.	A.	P.	PM.
BARKLEY, NORMAN DOUGLAS					
1963 Detroit	11	0	3	3	16
1964 "	14	0	5	5	33
1965 "	5	0	1	1	14
	30	0	9	9	63
BARRY, MARTIN J.					
1930 Boston	6	3	2	5	14
1931 "	5	1	1	2	4
1933 "	5	2	2	4	6
1935 "	4	0	0	0	2
1936 *Detroit	7	2	4	6	6
1937 *"	10	4	7	11	2
1939 "	6	3	1	4	0
	43	15	17	32	34
BARTLETT, JAMES BAKER					
1955 Montreal Canadiens	2	0	0	0	0
BATHGATE, ANDREW JAMES					
1956 New York Rangers	5	1	2	3	2
1957 " " "	5	2	0	2	7
1958 " " "	6	5	3	8	6
1962 " " "	6	1	2	3	4
1964 *Toronto Maple Leafs	14	5	4	9	25
1965 " " "	6	1	0	1	6
1966 Detroit Red Wings	12	6	3	9	6
	54	21	14	35	56
BATTELL, CARL W					
1922 Regina (WCHL)		0	0	0	0
BAUER, ROBERT T.					
1937 Boston	1	0	0		0
1938 Boston	3	0	0	0	2
1939 *Boston	12	3	2	5	0
1940 "	6	1	0	1	2
1941 *Boston	11	2	2	4	0
1946 "	10	4	3	7	2
1947 "	5	1	1	2	0
	48	11	8	19	6
BEATTIE, JOHN					
1931 Boston		0	0	0	0
1933 "		0	0	0	2
1935 "		1	0	1	2
1936 "		0	0	0	2
1937 "		1	0	1	0
1938 N. Y. Americans		2	2	4	2
		4	2	6	8
BENOIT, JOSEPH					
1941 Montreal		4	0	4	2
1942 "		1	0	1	5
1943 "	5	1	3	4	4
		6	3	9	11
BENTLEY, DOUGLAS WAGNER					
1940 Chicago	2	0	0	0	4
1941 "	5	1	1	2	4
1942 "	3	0	1	1	4
1944 "	9	8	4	12	4
1946 "	4	0	2	2	0
	23	9	8	17	16
BENTLEY, MAXWELL HERBERT LLOYD					
1941 Chicago	5	1	3	4	2
1942 "	3	2	0	2	0
1946 "	4	1	0	1	4
1948 *Toronto	9	4	7	11	0
1949 *"	9	4	3	7	2
1950 "	7	3	3	6	0
1951 *"	11	2	11	13	4
1952 "	4	1	0	1	2
	52	18	27	45	14
BERLINQUETTE, LOUIS					
1919 Montreal Canadiens	5	1	1	2	0
BIONDA, JACK ARTHUR					
1957 Boston	10	0	1	1	14
1959 "	1	0	0	0	0
	11	0	1	1	14

Sea. Club	Ga.	Go.	A.	P.	PM.
BLACK, STEPHEN					
1950 *Detroit	13	0	0	0	13
BLAIR, ANDREW					
1929 Toronto		3	0	3	2
1931 "		1	0	1	0
1932 *"		2	2	4	6
1933 "		0	2	2	4
1934 "		0	2	2	16
1935 "		0	0	0	2
1936 "		0	0	0	2
		6	6	12	32
BLAKE, HECTOR					
1937 Montreal	5	1	0	1	0
1938 "	3	3	1	4	2
1939 "	3	1	1	2	2
1941 "	3	0	3	3	5
1942 "	3	0	3	3	2
1943 Montreal	5	4	3	7	0
1944 *"	9	7	11	18	2
1945 "	6	0	2	2	5
1946 *"	9	7	6	13	5
1947 "	11	2	7	9	0
	57	25	37	62	23
BLINCO, RUSSELL PERCIVAL					
1934 Mont. Maroons		0	1	1	0
1935 *" "		2	2	4	2
1936 " "		0	0	0	0
1937 " "		1	0	1	2
		3	3	6	4
BODNAR, AUGUST					
1944 Toronto	5	0	0	0	0
1945 *"	13	3	1	4	4
1947 *"	1	0	0	0	0
1953 Chicago	7	1	1	2	2
1954 Boston	1	0	0	0	0
1955 "	5	0	1	1	4
	32	4	3	7	10
BOESCH, GARTH VERNON					
1947 *Toronto	11	0	2	2	6
1948 *"	8	2	1	3	2
1949 *"	9	0	2	2	6
1950 "	6	0	0	0	4
	34	2	5	7	18
BOLL, FRANK THORMAN					
1933 Toronto		0	0	0	0
1934 "		0	0	0	9
1935 "		0	0	0	0
1936 "		7	3	10	2
1937 "		0	0	0	0
1938 "		0	0	0	2
		7	3	10	13
BOLTON, HUGH E.					
1952 Toronto	3	0	0	0	4
1954 "	5	0	1	1	4
1955 "	4	0	3	3	6
1956 "	5	0	1	1	0
	17	0	5	5	14
BONIN, MARCEL					
1953 Detroit	5	0	1	1	0
1955 *"	11	0	2	2	4
1958 *Montreal	9	0	1	1	12
1959 *"	11	10	5	15	4
1960 *"	8	1	4	5	12
1961 "	6	0	1	1	29
	50	11	14	25	61
BOONE, CARL GEORGE					
1957 Boston	10	1	0	1	12
1958 "	12	1	1	2	13
	22	2	1	3	25
BOOTHMAN, GEORGE E.					
1944 Toronto	5	2	1	3	2
BOSTROM, HELGE					
1923 Edmonton (WCHL)		0	0	0	0
1924 Vancouver (PCHA)	1	0	1		2
1930 Chicago		0	0	0	0
1931 Chicago		0	0	0	16
1932 "		0	0	0	0
	1	0	1		18

Sea. Club	Ga.	Go.	A.	P.	PM.
BOUCHARD, EMILE JOSEPH					
1942 Montreal	3	1	1	2	0
1943 "	5	0	1	1	4
1944 *"	9	1	3	4	4
1945 "	6	3	4	7	4
1946 *"	9	2	1	3	17
1947 "	11	0	3	3	21
1949 "	7	0	0	0	6
1950 "	5	0	2	2	2
1951 "	11	1	1	2	2
1952 "	11	0	2	2	14
1953 *"	12	1	1	2	6
1954 "	11	2	1	3	4
1955 "	12	0	1	1	37
1956 *Montreal	1	0	0	0	0
	113	11	21	32	121
BOUCHER, FRANK XAVIER					
1923 Vancouver Maroons (PCHA)		2	0	2	2
1924 " "		1	0	1	2
1927 N. Y. Rangers		0	0	0	4
1928 *" "		7	3	10	2
1929 " "		1	0	1	0
1930 " "		1	1	2	0
1931 " "		0	2	2	0
1932 " "		3	6	9	0
1933 *" "		2	2	4	6
1934 " "		0	0	0	0
1935 " "		0	3	3	0
1937 " "		2	3	5	0
		19	20	39	16
BOUCHER, GEORGE					
1920 *Ottawa		2	0	2	3
1921 *"		3	0	3	12
1923 *"		2	1	3	6
1927 *"		0	0	0	17
1928 "		0	0	0	4
1930 Mont. Maroons		0	0	0	2
1932 Chicago		0	1	1	0
		7	2	9	44
BOUCHER, WILLIAM					
1924 *Mont. Canadiens		5	1	6	6
1925 " "		1	1	2	13
1927 Boston		0	0	0	2
		6	2	8	21
BOURGAULT, LEO A.					
1927 N. Y. Rangers		0	0	0	4
1928 *" "		0	0	0	10
1929 " "		0	0	0	0
1930 " "		1	1	2	6
1933 Mont. Canadiens		0	0	0	0
1934 Mont. Canadiens		0	0	0	0
		1	1	2	20
BOWMAN, RALPH					
1936 *Detroit		2	1	3	2
1937 *"		0	1	1	4
1939 "		0	0	0	0
		2	2	4	6
BOYD, IRVIN					
1943 Boston	5	0	1	1	4
BOYD, WILLIAM G.					
1928 *N. Y. Rangers		0	0	0	4
BRENNAN, DOUGLAS R.					
1932 N. Y. Rangers		1	0	1	10
1933 *"		0	0	0	11
1934 "		0	0	0	0
		1	0	1	21
BROADBENT, HARRY L.					
1920 *Ottawa		0	0	0	3
1921 *"		2	0	2	0
1923 *"		6	1	7	14
1926 *Mont. Maroons		1	0	1	20
1927 " "		0	0	0	0
1928 Ottawa Senators		0	0	0	0
1929 N. Y. Americans		0	0	0	2
		9	1	10	39
BRODEN, CONNELL					
1957 *Montreal	6	0	1	1	0
1958 *"	1	0	0	0	0
	7	0	1	1	0

Sea. Club	Ga.	Go.	A.	P.	PM.
BROPHY, BERNARD					
1929 Detroit Cougars		0	0	0	2
BROWN, ADAM					
1942 Detroit	10	0	2	2	4
1943 *"	6	1	1	2	2
1944 "	5	0	0	0	8
1946 "	5	1	1	2	0
	26	2	4	6	14
BROWN, FRED					
1928 Mont. Maroons	9	0	0	0	0
BROWN, GEORGE					
1938 Mont. Canadiens		0	0	0	2
BROWN, GERALD W. J.					
1942 Detroit	12	2	1	3	4
BROWN, PATRICK CONWAY					
1940 Detroit	5	2	1	3	0
1941 "	5	0	2	2	0
	10	2	3	5	0
BROWN, STANLEY					
1927 N. Y. Rangers	2	0	0	0	0
BROWN, WAYNE HEWETSON					
Born: Deloro, Ont. November 16, 1930					
1954 Boston	4	0	0	0	2
BRUCE, ARTHUR GORDON					
1942 Boston	5	2	3	5	4
BRUCE, MORLEY					
1920 *Ottawa		0	0	0	0
1921 *"		0	0	0	0
		0	0	0	0
BRUNETEAU, EDWARD E. H.					
1945 Detroit	14	5	2	7	0
1946 "	4	1	0	1	0
1947 "	4	1	4	5	0
1948 "	6	0	0	0	0
	28	7	6	13	0
BRUNETEAU, MODERE FERNAND					
1936 *Detroit	7	2	2	4	0
1937 *"	10	2	0	2	6
1939 "	1	0	0	0	0
1940 "	5	3	2	5	0
1941 "	9	2	1	3	2
1942 "	12	5	1	6	6
1943 *Detroit	9	5	4	9	0
1944 "	5	1	2	3	2
1945 "	14	3	2	5	2
	72	23	14	37	18
BRYDGE, WILLIAM HENRY					
1929 Detroit	2	0	0	0	4
BRYDSON, GLENN					
1931 Mont. Maroons		0	0	0	0
1932 " "		0	0	0	4
1933 Mont. Maroons		0	0	0	0
1934 " "		0	0	0	0
1936 Chicago		0	0	0	4
		0	0	0	8
BUKOVICH, ANTHONY J.					
1945 Detroit	6	0	1	1	0
BURCH, WILLIAM					
1929 New York Americans	2	0	0	0	0
BURKE, MARTIN					
1928 Pittsburgh	2	1	0	1	2
1929 Mont. Canadiens	3	0	0	0	8

(continued)

Sea. Club	Ga.	Go.	A.	P.	PM.
1930 *" "	6	0	1	1	6
1931 *" "	10	1	2	3	10
1932 " "	4	0	0	0	12
1934 " "	2	0	1	1	2
1935 Chicago	2	0	0	0	2
1936 "	2	0	0	0	2
	31	2	4	6	44

BURTON, CUMMING SCOTT

Sea. Club	Ga.	Go.	A.	P.	PM.
1956 Detroit	3	0	0	0	0

BUSH, EDWARD WEBSTER

Sea. Club	Ga.	Go.	A.	P.	PM.
1942 Detroit	11	1	6	7	23

BUSWELL, WALTER

Sea. Club	Ga.	Go.	A.	P.	PM.
1933 Detroit		0	0	0	4
1934 "		0	1	1	2
1937 Mont. Canadiens		0	0	0	2
1938 " "		0	0	0	0
1939 " "		2	0	2	2
		2	1	3	10

CAFFERY, JOHN

Sea. Club	Ga.	Go.	A.	P.	PM.
1957 Boston	10	1	0	1	4

CAIN, HERBERT J.

Sea. Club	Ga.	Go.	A.	P.	PM.
1934 Mont. Maroons		0	0	0	0
1935 *Mont. Maroons		1	0	1	2
1936 " "		0	1	1	0
1937 " "		1	1	2	0
1939 Montreal Canadiens		0	0	0	2
1940 Boston		1	3	4	2
1941 *"		3	2	5	5
1942 "		1	0	1	0
1943 "	7	4	2	6	0
1945 "	7	5	2	7	0
1946 "	9	0	2	2	2
	16	13	29	13	

CALLIGHEN, FRANCIS C. W.

Sea. Club	Ga.	Go.	A.	P.	PM.
1928 *N. Y. Rangers		0	0	0	0

CAMERON, HAROLD HUGH

Sea. Club	Ga.	Go.	A.	P.	PM.
1918 *Toronto		3	0	3	
1922 *"		0	0	0	16
		3	0	3	16

CAMPEAU, JEAN C.

Sea. Club	Ga.	Go.	A.	P.	PM.
1949 Montreal	1	0	0	0	0

CARR, LORNE

Sea. Club	Ga.	Go.	A.	P.	PM.
1936 N. Y. Americans		1	1	2	0
1938 " " "		3	1	4	2
1939 " " "		0	0	0	0
1940 " " "	3	0	0	0	0
1942 *Toronto		3	2	5	6
1943 "	6	1	2	3	0
1944 "	5	0	1	1	0
1945 *"	13	2	2	4	5
		10	9	19	13

CARRIGAN, EUGENE

Sea. Club	Ga.	Go.	A.	P.	PM.
1934 Detroit Red Wings	4	0	0	0	0

CARSE, ROBERT ALLISON

Sea. Club	Ga.	Go.	A.	P.	PM.
1940 Chicago	2	0	0	0	0
1941 "	5	0	0	0	2
1942 "	3	0	2	2	0
	10	0	2	2	2

CARSE, WILLIAM ALEXANDER

Sea. Club	Ga.	Go.	A.	P.	PM.
1939 New York Rangers		1	1	2	0
1940 Chicago Black Hawks		1	0	1	0
1941 " " "	2	0	0	0	0
1942 " " "	3	1	1	2	0
	3	2	5	0	

CARSON, FRANK

Sea. Club	Ga.	Go.	A.	P.	PM.
1926 *Mont. Maroons		0	0	0	0
1927 " "		0	0	0	2
1932 Detroit		0	0	0	0
1933 "		0	1	1	0
1934 "		0	1	1	5
		0	2	2	7

CARSON, GERALD GEORGE

Sea. Club	Ga.	Go.	A.	P.	PM.
1929 N. Y. Rangers		0	0	0	0
1930 *Mont. Canadiens		0	0	0	0
1933 " "		0	0	0	2

(continued)

Sea. Club	Ga.	Go.	A.	P.	PM.
1934 " "		0	0	0	2
1935 " "		0	0	0	4
1937 " Maroons		0	0	0	4
		0	0	0	12

CARSON, WILLIAM J.

Sea. Club	Ga.	Go.	A.	P.	PM.
1929 *Boston		2	0	2	8
1930 "		1	0	1	6
		3	0	3	14

CARVETH, JOSEPH G.

Sea. Club	Ga.	Go.	A.	P.	PM.
1942 Detroit	12	4	0	4	0
1943 *"	10	6	2	8	4
1944 "	5	2	1	3	8
1945 "	14	5	6	11	2
1946 "	5	0	1	1	0
1947 Boston	5	2	1	3	0
1949 Montreal	7	0	1	1	8
1950 *Detroit	14	2	4	6	6
	72	21	16	37	28

CHAD, JOHN

Sea. Club	Ga.	Go.	A.	P.	PM.
1940 Chicago	2	0	0	0	0
1941 "	5	0	0	0	2
1946 "	3	0	1	1	0
	10	0	1	1	2

CHAMBERLAIN, ERWIN GROVES

Sea. Club	Ga.	Go.	A.	P.	PM.
1938 Toronto	5	0	0	0	2
1939 "	10	2	5	7	4
1940 "	3	0	0	0	0
1941 Montreal	3	0	2	2	11
1943 Boston	6	1	1	2	12
1944 *Montreal	9	5	3	8	12
1945 "	6	1	1	2	10
1946 *"	9	4	2	6	18
1947 "	11	1	3	4	19
1949 "	4	0	0	0	8
	66	14	17	31	96

CHAPMAN, ARTHUR V.

Sea. Club	Ga.	Go.	A.	P.	PM.
1931 Boston		0	1	1	7
1933 "		0	0	0	2
1936 N. Y. Americans		0	3	3	0
1938 " " "		0	1	1	0
1939 " " "		0	0	0	0
1940 " " "		1	0	1	0
		1	5	6	9

CHERRY, DONALD STEWART D-SL
Born: Kingston, Ont. Feb. 5, 1934

Sea. Club	Ga.	Go.	A.	P.	PM.
1955 Boston	1	0	0	0	0

CHEVREFILS, REAL

Sea. Club	Ga.	Go.	A.	P.	PM.
1952 Boston	7	1	1	2	6
1953 "	7	0	1	1	6
1955 "	5	2	1	3	4
1957 "	10	2	1	3	4
1958 "	1	0	0	0	0
	30	5	4	9	20

CHISHOLM, ALEXANDER

Sea. Club	Ga.	Go.	A.	P.	PM.
1941 Toronto		1	0	1	0

CHURCH, JOHN

Sea. Club	Ga.	Go.	A.	P.	PM.
1939 Toronto	1	0	0	0	0
1940 "	7	1	1	2	6
1941 "		0	0	0	8
1946 Boston	9	0	0	0	4
	1	1	2	18	

CIESLA, HENRY EDWARD

Sea. Club	Ga.	Go.	A.	P.	PM.
1958 New York	6	0	2	2	0

CLANCY, FRANCIS MICHAEL

Sea. Club	Ga.	Go.	A.	P.	PM.
1923 *Ottawa		1	0	1	2
1927 *"		1	1	2	14
1928 "		0	0	0	6
1930 "		0	1	1	2
1931 Toronto		1	0	1	0
1932 *Toronto		2	1	3	14
1933 "		0	3	3	14
1934 "		0	0	0	8
1935 "		1	0	1	8
1936 "		2	2	4	10
		8	8	16	78

Sea. Club	Ga.	Go.	A.	P.	PM.
CLAPPER, AUBREY VICTOR					
1928 Boston		0	0	0	2
1929 *"		1	0	1	0
1930 "		4	0	4	4
1931 "		2	4	6	4
1933 "		1	1	2	2
1935 "		1	0	1	0
1936 "		0	1	1	0
1937 "		2	0	2	5
1938 "		0	0	0	12
1939 *"		0	1	1	6
1940 "	5	0	2	2	2
1941 *"	11	0	5	5	4
1943 "	9	2	3	5	9
1945 "	7	0	0	0	0
1946 "	4	0	0	0	0
		13	17	30	50
CLEGHORN, J. OGILVIE					
1919 Montreal Canadiens		2	0	2	9
1924 *" "		0	1	1	0
		2	1	3	9
CLEGHORN, SPRAGUE					
1920 *Ottawa		0	1	1	6
1921 *"		0	1	1	31
1924 *Montreal Canadiens		2	1	3	2
1925 "		0	0	0	2
1927 Boston		1	0	1	8
1928 "		0	0	0	0
		3	3	6	49
COLLINS, RANLEIGH GARY C-SL					
Born: Toronto, Ont. Sept. 27, 1935					
1959 Toronto	2	0	0	0	0
COLVILLE, MATTHEW L.					
1937 N. Y. Rangers	9	1	2	3	2
1938 " " "	3	0	2	2	0
1939 " " "	7	1	2	3	4
1940 *" " "	12	3	2	5	6
1941 " " "	3	1	1	2	2
1942 " " "	6	3	1	4	0
	40	9	10	19	14
COLVILLE, NEIL MacNEIL					
1937 N. Y. Rangers	9	3	3	6	0
1938 " " "	2	0	1	1	0
1939 " " "	7	0	2	2	2
1940 *" " "	12	2	7	9	18
1941 " " "	3	1	1	2	0
1942 " " "	6	0	6	6	6
1948 " " "	6	1	0	1	6
	45	7	20	27	32
CONACHER, BRIAN KENNEDY					
1967 *Toronto	12	3	2	5	21
CONACHER, CHARLES WILLIAM					
1931 Toronto		0	1	1	0
1932 *"		6	2	8	6
1933 "		1	1	2	10
1934 "		3	2	5	0
1935 "		1	4	5	6
1936 "		3	2	5	12
1937 "		0	0	0	5
1939 Detroit		2	5	7	2
1940 N. Y. Americans		1	1	2	8
		17	18	35	49
CONACHER, CHARLES WILLIAM Jr.					
1953 Chicago	2	0	0	0	0
1956 New York	5	0	0	0	0
	7	0	0	0	0
CONACHER, JAMES					
1946 Detroit	5	1	1	2	0
1947 "	5	2	1	3	2
1948 "	9	2	0	2	2
	19	5	2	7	4
CONACHER, LIONEL PRETORIA					
1929 N. Y. Americans		0	0	0	10
1931 Mont. Maroons		0	0	0	2
1932 " "		0	0	0	8

(continued)

Sea. Club	Ga.	Go.	A.	P.	PM.
1933 " "		0	1	1	0
1934 *Chicago		2	0	2	4
1935 *Mont. Maroons		0	0	0	14
1937 " "		0	1	1	2
		2	2	4	40
CONACHER, ROY G.					
1939 *Boston	12	6	4	10	12
1940 "	6	2	1	3	0
1941 *"	11	1	5	6	4
1942 "	5	2	1	3	0
1946 "	3	0	0	0	0
1947 Detroit	5	4	4	8	2
	42	15	15	30	18
CONNOLLY, ALBERT P.					
1935 N. Y. Rangers		1	0	1	0
1938 *Chicago		0	0	0	0
		1	0	1	0
CONNOR, HARRY					
1928 Boston	2	0	0	0	0
1929 N. Y. Americans	2	0	0	0	6
1930 Boston	5	0	0	0	0
	9	0	0	0	6
CONNORS, ROBERT					
1929 Detroit	2	0	0	0	10
COOK, FREDERICK JOSEPH					
1927 N. Y. Rangers		0	0	0	6
1928 *" " "		2	1	3	10
1929 " " "		1	0	1	12
1930 " " "		2	0	2	2
1931 " " "		0	0	0	2
1932 " " "		6	2	8	12
1933 *" " "		2	0	2	4
1934 " " "		0	0	0	2
1935 " " "		2	0	2	0
		15	3	18	50
COOK, LLOYD					
1918 Vancouver (PCHA)		2	0	2	
1921 " "		2	0	2	10
1922 " "		2	1	3	7
1923 " "		0	0	0	6
1924 " "		0	0	0	4
		6	1	7	27
COOK, THOMAS JOHN					
1930 Chicago		0	1	1	4
1931 "		1	3	4	11
1932 "		0	0	0	2
1934 *"		1	0	1	0
1935 "		0	0	0	2
		2	4	6	19
COOK, WILLIAM OSSER					
1927 N. Y. Rangers	2	1	0	1	10
1928 *" " "	9	2	3	5	26
1929 " " "	6	0	0	0	6
1930 " " "	4	0	1	1	11
1931 " " "	4	3	0	3	4
1932 " " "	7	3	4	7	2
1933 *" " "	8	3	2	5	4
1934 " " "	2	0	0	0	2
1935 " " "	4	1	2	3	7
	46	13	12	25	72
COOPER, CARSON					
1927 Mont. Canadiens	3	0	0	0	0
1929 Detroit Cougars	2	0	0	0	2
1932 " Falcons	2	0	0	0	0
	7	0	0	0	2
COOPER, JOSEPH					
1937 N. Y. Rangers	9	1	1	2	12
1938 " " "	3	0	0	0	4
1940 Chicago	2	0	0	0	6
1941 "	5	1	0	1	8
1942 "	3	0	2	2	2
1944 "	9	1	1	2	18
1946 "	4	0	1	1	14
	35	3	5	8	64
CORBEAU, BERT					
1919 Montreal Canadiens	5	0	1	1	3
CORBETT, MICHAEL CHARLES RW-SL SL					
Born: Toronto, Ont. Oct. 4, 1942					
1968 Los Angeles	2	0	1	1	2

Sea. Club	Ga.	Go.	A.	P.	PM.
CORCORAN, NORMAN					
1955 Boston	4	0	0	0	6
COSTELLO, J. MURRAY					
1955 Boston	1	0	0	0	2
1956 Detroit	4	0	0	0	0
	5	0	0	0	2
COSTELLO, LESTER JOHN THOMAS					
1948 *Toronto	5	2	2	4	2
1950 "	1	0	0	0	0
	6	2	2	4	2
COTTON, E. HAROLD					
1928 Pittsburgh		1	1	2	2
1929 Toronto		0	0	0	2
1931 "		0	0	0	2
1932 *"		2	2	4	8
1933 "		0	3	3	6
1934 "		0	2	2	0
1935 "		0	0	0	17
1936 N. Y. Americans		0	1	1	9
		3	9	12	46
COULTER, ARTHUR EDMUND					
1932 Chicago		1	0	1	0
1934 *"		1	0	1	10
1935 "		0	0	0	5
1937 N. Y. Rangers		0	3	3	15
1939 " " "		1	1	2	6
1940 *" " "		1	0	1	21
1941 " " "	3	0	0	0	14
1942 " " "	6	0	1	1	4
		4	5	9	75
COUTU, WILLIAM					
1919 Montreal Canadiens		0	1	1	0
1924 *" "		0	0	0	0
1925 " "		1	0	1	10
1927 Boston		1	0	1	4
		2	1	3	14
COUTURE, GERALD J. W. A.					
1945 Detroit	2	0	0	0	0
1946 "	1	0	2	2	0
1947 "	1	0	0	0	0
1949 "	10	2	0	2	2
1950 *"	14	5	4	9	2
1951 "	6	1	1	2	0
1953 Chicago	7	1	0	1	0
	45	9	7	16	4
COUTURE, ROSARIO					
1930 Chicago		0	0	0	2
1931 "		0	3	3	2
1932 "		0	0	0	2
1934 *"		1	2	3	4
1935 "		0	0	0	5
		1	5	6	15
COWLEY, WILLIAM MAILES					
1936 Boston	2	2	1	3	2
1937 "	3	0	3	3	0
1938 "	3	2	0	2	0
1939 *"	12	3	11	14	2
1940 "	6	0	1	1	7
1941 * "	2	0	0		0
1942 "	5	0	3	3	5
1943 "	9	1	7	8	4
1945 "	7	3	3	6	0
1946 "	10	1	3	4	2
1947 "	5	0	2	2	0
	64	12	34	46	22
COX, DANIEL S.					
1929 Toronto	4	0	1	1	4
1930 Ottawa	2	0	0	0	0
1932 Detroit	2	0	0	0	2
1934 N. Y. Rangers	2	0	0	0	0
	10	0	1	1	6
CRAWFORD, JOHN SHEA					
1939 *Boston	12	1	1	2	9
1940 "	6	0	0	0	0
1941 *"	11	0	2	2	7
1942 "	5	0	1	1	4
1943 "	6	1	1	2	10

(continued)

Sea. Club	Ga.	Go.	A.	P.	PM.
1945 "	7	0	5	5	0
1946 "	10	1	2	3	4
1947 "	2	0	0	0	0
1948 "	4	0	1	1	2
1949 "	3	0	0	0	0
	66	3	13	16	36
CREIGHTON, DAVID THEODORE					
1949 Boston	3	0	0	0	0
1951 "	5	0	1	1	0
1952 "	7	2	1	3	2
1953 "	11	4	5	9	10
1954 "	4	0	0	0	0
1956 New York	5	0	0	0	4
1957 " "	5	2	2	4	2
1958 " "	6	3	3	6	2
1959 Toronto	5	0	1	1	0
	51	11	13	24	20
CRUTCHFIELD, NELSON					
1935 Mont. Canadiens	2	0	1	1	22
CULLEN, BRIAN JOSEPH					
1955 Toronto	4	1	0	1	0
1956 "	5	1	0	1	2
1959 "	10	1	0	1	0
	19	3	0	3	2
CULLEN, CHARLES FRANCIS					
1959 Toronto	2	0	0	0	0
1960 Detroit	4	0	0	0	2
	6	0	0	0	2
CUNNINGHAM, LESLIE ROY					
1940 Chicago	1	0	0	0	2
CUPOLO, WILLIAM D.					
1945 Boston	7	1	2	3	0
CURRY, FLOYD JAMES					
1949 Montreal	2	0	0	0	2
1950 "	5	1	0	1	2
1951 "	11	0	2	2	2
1952 "	11	4	3	7	6
1953 *"	12	2	1	3	2
1954 "	11	4	0	4	4
1955 "	12	8	4	12	4
1956 *"	10	1	5	6	12
1957 *"	10	3	2	5	2
1958 *"	7	0	0	0	2
	91	23	17	40	38
DAHLSTROM, CARL					
1938 *Chicago	-	3	1	4	2
1940 "	2	0	0	0	0
1941 "	-	3	3	6	2
1944 "	9	0	4	4	6
		6	8	14	10
DALEY, FRANK PATRICK					
1929 Detroit Cougars	2	0	0	0	0
DARRAGH, HAROLD					
1928 Pittsburgh		0	1	1	0
1931 Boston		0	1	1	2
1932 *Toronto		0	1	1	2
		0	3	3	4
DARRAGH, JOHN PROCTOR					
1920 *Ottawa	5	5	2	7	3
1921 *"	5	5	0	5	13
	10	10	2	12	16
DAVIDSON, ROBERT					
1936 Toronto		1	3	4	2
1937 "		0	0	0	5
1938 "		0	2	2	10
1939 "		1	1	2	6
1940 "		0	3	3	16
1941 "		0	2	2	7
1942 *"		1	2	3	20
1943 "	6	1	2	3	7
1944 "	5	0	0	0	4
1945 *"	13	1	2	3	2
		5	17	22	79
DAVIES, KENNETH GEORGE "BUCK"					
Born: Bowmanville, Ont. August 10, 1922					
1948 New York	1	0	0	0	0

Sea. Club	Ga.	Go.	A.	P.	PM.
DAVIS, LORNE AUSTIN					
1953 *Montreal	7	1	1	2	2
1954 "	11	2	0	2	8
	18	3	1	4	10
DAWES, ROBERT J.					
1949 *Toronto	9	0	0	0	2
1951 Montreal	1	0	0	0	2
	10	0	0	0	4
DAY, CLARENCE HENRY					
1929 Toronto		1	0	1	4
1931 "		0	3	3	7
1932 *"		3	3	6	6
1933 "		0	1	1	21
1934 "		0	0	0	6
1935 "		0	0	0	4
1936 "		0	0	0	8
1937 "		0	0	0	0
1938 N. Y. Americans		0	0	0	0
		4	7	11	56
DEACON, DONALD					
1943 Boston	9	3	0	3	2
DeMARCO, ALBERT					
1939 Detroit	2	2	1	3	0
DENNENY, CORBETT					
1918 *Toronto		3	2	5	
1922 *"		3	2	5	2
1923 Vancouver (PCHA)		0	0	0	0
		6	4	10	2
DENNENY, CYRIL					
1920 *Ottawa		0	0	0	3
1921 *"		2	2	4	13
1923 *"		1	1	2	4
1927 *"		5	0	5	0
1928 "		0	0	0	0
1929 *Boston		0	0	0	0
		8	3	11	20
DESILETS, JOFFRE WILFRED					
1937 Mont. Canadiens	5	1	0	1	12
1938 " "	2	0	0	0	7
	7	1	0	1	19
DESIREAU, SID RW					
1921 Vancouver (PCHA)	2	0	0	0	6
DESJARDINS, VICTOR A.					
1931 Chicago	9	0	0	0	0
1932 N. Y. Rangers	7	0	0	0	0
	16	0	0	0	0
DEWSBURY, ALBERT P.					
1947 Detroit	2	0	0	0	4
1948 "	1	0	0	0	0
1950 *"	4	0	3	3	8
1953 Chicago	7	1	2	3	4
	14	1	5	6	16
DHEERE, MARCEL A.					
1943 Montreal	5	0	0	0	6
DICKENS, ERNEST L.					
1942 *Toronto	5	0	0	0	4
DILLON. CECIL GORDON					
1931 N. Y. Rangers		0	1	1	0
1932 " " "		2	1	3	4
1933 *" " "		8	2	10	6
1934 " " "		0	1	1	2
1935 " " "		2	1	3	0
1937 " " "		0	3	3	0
1938 " " "		1	0	1	0
1939 " " "		0	0	0	0
1940 Detroit		1	0	1	0
		14	9	23	12
DINEEN. WILLIAM PATRICK					
1954 *Detroit	12	0	0	0	2
1955 *"	11	0	1	1	8
1956 "	10	1	0	1	8
1957 "	4	0	0	0	0
	37	1	1	2	18
DINSMORE, CHARLES					
1926 *Mont. Maroons	4	0	0	0	0
1930 " "	4	0	0	0	0
	8	0	0	0	0

Sea. Club	Ga.	Go.	A.	P.	PM.
DONNELLY, "BABE"					
1927 Mont. Maroons	2	0	0	0	0
DORAN, JOHN M.					
1936 N. Y. Americans		0	0	0	0
DORATY, KENNETH					
1933 Toronto		5	0	5	4
1934 "		2	2	4	0
		7	2	9	4
DOUGLAS, KENT GEMMELL					
1963 *Toronto	10	1	1	2	2
1965 "	5	0	1	1	19
1966 "	4	0	1	1	12
	19	1	3	4	33
DOUGLAS, LESTER					
1943 *Detroit	10	3	2	5	2
DRILLON, GORDON					
1937 Toronto	2	0	0	0	0
1938 "	7	7	1	8	2
1939 "	10	7	6	13	4
1940 "	10	3	1	4	0
1941 "	7	3	2	5	2
1942 *"	9	2	3	5	0
1943 Mont. Canadiens	5	4	2	6	0
	50	26	15	41	10
DROUIN, PAUL EMILE					
1938 Mont. Canadiens		0	0	0	0
1939 " "		0	1	1	5
1941 " "		0	0	0	0
		0	1	1	5
DRURY, HERBERT J.					
1928 Pittsburgh		0	1	1	0
DUBE, JOSEPH GILLES					
1954 *Detroit	2	0	0	0	0
DUGUID, LORNE					
1933 Mont. Maroons		0	0	0	4
1936 Boston		1	0	1	2
		1	0	1	6
DUMART, WOODROW W. C.					
1937 Boston	3	0	0	0	0
1938 "	3	0	0	0	0
1939 *"	12	1	3	4	0
1940 "	6	1	0	1	0
1941 *"	11	1	3	4	9
1946 "	10	4	3	7	0
1947 "	5	1	1	2	8
1948 "	5	0	0	0	0
1949 "	5	3	0	3	0
1951 "	6	1	2	3	0
1952 "	7	0	1	1	0
1953 "	11	0	2	2	0
1954 "	4	0	0	0	0
	88	12	15	27	23
DUNCAN, ARTHUR					
1921 Vancouver (PCHA)		2	1	3	3
1922 " "		3	0	3	6
1923 " "		3	2	5	0
1924 " "		0	0	0	6
1929 Toronto		0	0	0	4
		8	3	11	19
DUSSAULT, JOSEPH NORMAND					
1949 Montreal	2	0	0	0	0
1950 "	5	3	1	4	0
	7	3	1	4	0
DUTKOWSKI, LAUDES JOSEPH					
1927 Chicago	2	0	0	0	0
1930 "	2	0	0	0	6
1934 N. Y. Rangers	2	0	0	0	0
	6	0	0	0	6
DUTTON, MERVYN A.					
1924 Calgary (WCHL)		0	0	0	9
1927 Mont. Maroons		0	0	0	4
1928 " "		1	0	1	29
1930 " "		0	0	0	4
		1	0	1	46
DYE, CECIL HENRY					
1922 *Toronto	5	9	2	11	3
1927 Chicago	2	0	0	0	2
1929 N. Y. Americans	2	0	0	0	0
	9	9	2	11	5

Sea. Club	Ga.	Go.	A.	P.	PM.
EDDOLLS, FRANK H.					
1945 Montreal	3	0	0	0	0
1946 *"	8	0	1	1	2
1947 "	7	0	0	0	4
1948 New York	2	0	0	0	0
1950 " "	11	0	1	1	4
	31	0	2	2	10
EDMUNDSON, GARRY FRANK					
1952 Montreal	2	0	0	0	4
1960 Toronto	9	0	1	1	4
	11	0	1	1	8
EGAN, MARTIN JOSEPH					
1945 Boston	7	2	0	2	6
1946 "	10	3	0	3	8
1947 "	5	0	2	2	6
1948 "	5	1	1	2	2
1949 "	5	0	0	0	16
1950 New York	12	3	1	4	6
	44	9	4	13	44
EMBERG, EDWARD					
Born: Montreal, Quebec Nov. 18, 1921					
1945 Montreal	2	1	0	1	0
EMMS, LEIGHTON					
1932 Detroit	2	0	0	0	2
1933 "	4	0	0	0	8
1934 "	8	0	0	0	2
	14	0	0	0	12
ERICKSON, AUTRY RAYMOND					
1964 Chicago	6	0	0	0	0
1967 *Toronto	1	0	0	0	2
	7	0	0	0	2
EVANS, STEWART					
1933 Detroit		0	0	0	6
1934 Mont. Maroons		0	0	0	4
1935 *Mont. Maroons		0	0	0	8
1936 " "		0	0	0	0
1937 " "		0	0	0	0
1939 Mont. Canadiens		0	0	0	2
		0	0	0	20
EVANS, WILLIAM JOHN					
1956 New York	5	1	0	1	18
1957 " "	5	0	1	1	4
1958 " "	6	0	0	0	17
1959 Chicago	6	0	0	0	10
1960 "	4	0	0	0	4
1961 *"	12	1	1	2	14
1962 "	12	0	0	0	26
1963 "	6	0	0	0	4
	56	2	2	4	97
EZINICKI, WILLIAM					
1947 *Toronto	11	0	2	2	30
1948 *"	9	3	1	4	6
1949 *"	9	1	4	5	20
1950 "	5	0	0	0	13
1951 Boston	6	1	1	2	18
	40	5	8	13	87
FAULKNER, SELM ALEXANDER					
1963 Detroit	8	5	0	5	2
1964 "	4	0	0	0	0
	12	5	0	5	2
FERGUSON, LORNE ROBERT					
1951 Boston	6	1	0	1	2
1955 "	4	1	0	1	2
1956 Detroit	10	1	2	3	12
1957 "	5	1	0	1	6
1959 Chicago	6	2	1	3	2
	31	6	3	9	24
FIELD, WILFRED S.					
1939 N. Y. Americans	2	0	0	0	2
	2	0	0	0	2
FIELDER, GUYLE ABNER					
1953 Detroit	4	0	0	0	0
1954 Boston	2	0	0	0	2
	6	0	0	0	2

Sea. Club	Ga.	Go.	A.	P.	PM.
FILLION, ROBERT L.					
1944 *Montreal	3	0	0	0	2
1945 "	1	3	0	3	0
1946 *"	9	4	3	7	6
1947 "	8	0	0	0	0
1949 "	7	0	1	1	4
1950 "	5	0	0	0	0
	33	7	4	11	12
FINNEY, JOSEPH SIDNEY					
1953 Chicago	7	0	2	2	0
FINNIGAN, FRANK					
1927 *Ottawa		3	0	3	0
1928 "		0	1	1	6
1930 "		0	0	0	4
1932 *Toronto		2	3	5	8
1935 "		1	2	3	2
1936 "		0	3	3	0
		6	9	15	20
FISHER, DUNCAN ROBERT					
1948 New York	1	0	1	1	0
1950 " "	12	3	3	6	14
1951 Boston	6	1	0	1	0
1952 "	2	0	0	0	0
	21	4	4	8	14
FISHER, JOSEPH					
1940 Detroit	5	1	1	2	0
1941 "	5	1	0	1	6
1943 *"	1	0	0	0	0
	11	2	1	3	6
FITZPATRICK, ALEXANDER STEWART					
1968 Minnesota	12	0	0	0	0
FLAMAN, FERDINAND CHARLES					
1947 Boston	5	0	0	0	8
1948 "	5	0	0	0	12
1949 "	5	0	1	1	8
1951 *Toronto	9	1	0	1	8
1952 "	4	0	2	2	18
1954 "	2	0	0	0	0
1955 Boston	4	1	0	1	2
1957 "	10	0	3	3	19
1958 "	12	2	2	4	10
1959 "	7	0	0	0	8
	63	4	8	12	93
FOGOLIN, LIDIO J.					
1948 Detroit	2	0	1	1	6
1949 "	9	0	0	0	4
1950 *"	10	0	0	0	16
1953 Chicago	7	0	1	1	4
	28	0	2	2	30
FOLEY, GERALD JAMES					
1957 New York	3	0	0	0	0
1958 " "	6	0	1	1	2
	9	0	1	1	2
FONTINATO, LOUIS					
1956 New York	4	0	0	0	6
1957 "	5	0	0	0	7
1958 " "	6	0	1	1	6
1962 Montreal	6	0	1	1	23
	21	0	2	2	42
FORSEY, JACK					
1943 Toronto	3	0	1	1	0
FOWLER, JAMES					
1937 Toronto		0	0	0	0
1938 "		0	2	2	0
1939 "		0	1	1	2
		0	3	3	2
FOYSTON, FRANK C.					
1919 Seattle (PCHA)		9	1	10	0
1920 " "		6	2	8	12
1925 *Victoria (WCHL)		1	0	1	0
1926 " "		0	0	0	2
		16	3	19	14
FRAMPTON, ROBERT P. J.					
1950 Montreal	3	0	0	0	0

Sea. Club	Ga.	Go.	A.	P.	PM.
FRASER, GORDON					
1925 *Victoria (WCHL)		2	1	3	6
1926 " "		0	0	0	16
1927 Chicago		1	0	1	6
		3	1	4	28
FREDRICKSON, FRANK					
1925 *Victoria (WCHL)	4	3	2	5	6
1926 " "	4	1	1	2	10
1927 Boston	8	2	4	6	20
1928 "	2	0	1	1	4
	18	6	8	14	40
FREW, IRVINE					
1934 Mont. Maroons	4	0	0	0	6
GADSBY, WILLIAM ALEXANDER					
1953 Chicago	7	0	1	1	4
1956 New York	5	1	3	4	4
1957 " "	5	1	2	3	2
1958 " "	6	0	3	3	4
1963 Detroit	11	1	4	5	36
1964 "	14	0	4	4	22
1965 "	7	0	3	3	8
1966 "	12	1	3	4	12
	67	4	23	27	92
GAGNE, ARTHUR					
1923 Edmonton (WCHL)		0	0	0	2
1927 Mont. Canadiens		0	0	0	0
1928 " "		1	1	2	4
1929 " "		0	0	0	12
1930 Ottawa		1	0	1	4
		2	1	3	22
GAGNON, JEAN					
1931 *Mont. Canadiens		6	2	8	8
1932 " "		1	1	2	4
1933 " "		0	2	2	0
1934 " "		1	0	1	2
1935 " "		0	1	1	2
1937 " "		2	1	3	7
1938 " "		1	3	4	2
1939 " "		0	2	2	20
1940 N. Y. Americans		1	0	1	0
		12	12	24	45
GAINOR, NORMAN					
1928 Boston		0	0	0	6
1929 *"		2	0	2	4
1930 "		0	0	0	0
1931 "		0	1	1	2
1932 N. Y. Rangers		0	0	0	2
		2	1	3	14
GALBRAITH, W. PERCIVAL					
1927 Boston		3	3	6	2
1928 "		0	1	1	6
1929 *"		0	0	0	2
1930 "		1	3	4	8
1931 "		0	0	0	6
1933 "		0	0	0	0
		4	7	11	24
GALLAGHER, JOHN					
1931 Mont. Maroons		0	0	0	0
1933 Detroit		1	1	2	4
1937 *"		1	0	1	17
1938 N. Y. Americans		0	2	2	6
		2	3	5	27
GALLINGER, DONALD C.					
1943 Boston	9	3	1	4	10
1946 "	10	2	4	6	2
1947 "	4	0	0	0	7
	23	5	5	10	19
GAMBLE, RICHARD FRANK					
1952 Montreal	7	0	2	2	0
1953 *"	5	1	0	1	2
1955 "	2	0	0	0	2
	14	1	2	3	4
GARDINER, HERBERT MARTIN					
1924 Calgary (WCHL)	2	1	0	1	0
1927 Mont. Canadiens	4	0	0	0	10
1928 " "	2	0	1	1	4
1929 " "	2	0	0	0	0
	10	1	1	2	14

Sea. Club	Ga.	Go.	A.	P.	PM.
GARDNER, CALVIN PEARLY					
1948 New York	5	0	0	0	0
1949 *Toronto	9	2	5	7	0
1950 "	7	1	0	1	4
1951 *"	11	1	1	2	4
1952 "	3	0	0	0	2
1953 Chicago	7	0	2	2	4
1954 Boston	4	1	1	2	0
1955 "	5	0	0	0	4
1957 "	10	2	1	3	2
	61	7	10	17	20
GAUDREAULT, ARMAND G.					
1945 Boston	7	0	2	2	8
GAUDREAULT, LEO					
1928 Mont. Canadiens	2	0	0	0	0
GAUTHIER, ARTHUR					
1927 Mont. Canadiens	2	0	0	0	0
GAUTHIER, RENE FERNAND					
1945 Montreal	4	0	0	0	0
1946 Detroit	5	3	0	3	2
1947 "	3	1	0	1	0
1948 "	10	1	1	2	5
	22	5	1	6	7
GEE, GEORGE					
1946 Chicago	4	1	1	2	4
1949 Detroit	10	1	3	4	22
1950 *"	14	3	6	9	0
1951 "	6	0	1	1	0
1953 Chicago	7	1	2	3	6
	41	6	13	19	32
GEOFFRION, BERNARD ANDRE					
1951 Montreal	11	1	1	2	6
1952 "	11	3	1	4	6
1953 *"	12	6	4	10	12
1954 "	11	6	5	11	18
1955 "	12	8	5	13	8
1956 *"	10	5	9	14	6
1957 *"	10	11	7	18	2
1958 *"	10	6	5	11	2
1959 *"	11	5	8	13	10
1960 *"	8	2	10	12	4
1961 "	4	2	1	3	0
1962 "	5	0	1	1	6
1963 "	5	0	1	1	4
1964 "	7	1	1	2	4
1967 New York	4	2	0	2	0
1968 " "	1	0	1	1	0
	132	58	60	118	88
GERARD, EDWARD GEORGE					
1920 *Ottawa	5	2	1	3	6
1921 *"	5	0	0	0	37
1922 *Toronto	1	0	0	0	0
1923 *Ottawa	4	1	0	1	4
	15	3	1	4	47
GETLIFFE, RAYMOND					
1937 Boston		2	1	3	2
1938 "		0	1	1	2
1939 *"		1	1	2	2
1941 Montreal		1	1	2	0
1942 "	3	0	0	0	0
1943 "	5	0	1	1	8
1944 *"	9	5	4	9	16
1945 "	6	0	1	1	2
		9	10	19	32
GIESEBRECHT, ROY GEORGE					
1939 Detroit	6	0	2	2	0
1941 "	9	2	1	3	0
1942 "		0	0	0	0
		2	3	5	0
GIROUX, ARTHUR					
1933 Mont. Canadiens	2	0	0	0	0
GLADU, JOSEPH JEAN-PAUL					
1945 Boston	7	2	2	4	0
GLOVER, FREDERICK AUSTIN					
1949 Detroit	2	0	0	0	0
1951 "	6	0	0	0	0
	8	0	0	0	0
GLOVER, HOWARD EDWARD					
1961 Detroit	11	1	2	3	2

Sea. Club	Ga.	Go.	A.	P.	PM.
GODFREY, WARREN EDWARD					
1953 Boston	11	0	1	1	2
1954 "	4	0	0	0	4
1955 "	3	0	0	0	0
1957 Detroit	5	0	0	0	6
1958 "	4	0	0	0	0
1960 "	6	1	0	1	10
1961 "	11	0	2	2	18
1965 "	4	0	1	1	2
1966 "	4	0	0	0	0
	52	1	4	5	42
GOEGAN, PETER JOHN					
1958 Detroit	4	0	0	0	18
1960 "	6	1	0	1	13
1961 "	11	0	1	1	18
1963 "	11	0	2	2	12
1966 "	1	0	0	0	0
	33	1	3	4	61
GOLDHAM, ROBERT J.					
1942 *Toronto	13	2	2	4	31
1951 "	6	0	1	1	2
1952 *"	8	0	1	1	8
1953 "	6	1	1	2	2
1954 *"	12	0	2	2	2
1955 *"	11	0	4	4	4
1956 Detroit	10	0	3	3	4
	66	3	14	17	53
GOLDSWORTHY, LEROY D.					
1930 N. Y. Rangers		0	0	0	2
1933 Detroit Red Wings		0	0	0	0
1934 *Chicago		0	0	0	0
1935 Mont. Canadiens		1	0	1	0
1937 Boston		0	0	0	0
1938 "		0	0	0	2
		1	0	1	4
GOLDUP, HENRY					
1940 Toronto	10	5	1	6	4
1941 "	2	0	0	0	0
1942 *"	9	0	0	0	2
	21	5	1	6	6
GOODFELLOW, EBENEZER R.					
1932 Detroit		0	0	0	0
1933 "		1	0	1	11
1934 "		4	3	7	12
1936 *"		1	0	1	4
1937 *"		2	2	4	12
1939 "		0	0	0	8
1940 "		0	2	2	9
1941 "		0	1	1	9
		8	8	16	65
GORDON, FRED					
1928 Boston Bruins	2	0	0	0	0
GORDON, JOHN					
1950 New York	9	1	1	2	7
GORMAN, EDWIN					
1927 *Ottawa		0	0	0	0
GOTTSELIG, JOHN P.					
1930 Chicago	2	0	0	0	4
1931 "	9	3	3	6	4
1932 "	2	0	0	0	2
1934 *"	8	4	3	7	4
1935 "		0	0	0	0
1936 "		0	2	2	0
1938 *"	10	5	3	8	4
1940 "		0	1	1	0
1944 "	6	1	1	2	2
		13	13	26	20
GOUPILLE, CLIFFORD					
1938 Mont. Canadiens		2	0	2	4
1941 " "		0	0	0	0
1942 " "		0	0	0	2
		2	0	2	6
GOYER, GERALD FRANCIS					
1968 Chicago	3	0	0	0	2
GRABOSKI, ANTHONY					
1941 Montreal		0	0		6

Sea. Club	Ga.	Go.	A.	P.	PM.
GRACIE, ROBERT J.					
1931 Toronto		0	0	0	0
1932 *Toronto		3	1	4	0
1933 "		0	1	1	0
1935 *Mont. Maroons		0	2	2	2
1936 " "		0	1	1	0
1937 " "		1	2	3	2
		4	7	11	4
GRAHAM, EDWARD DIXON					
1930 Chicago		0	0	0	8
1931 "		0	0	0	12
1932 "		0	0	0	2
1934 Detroit		1	1	2	8
		1	1	2	30
GRAVELLE, JOSEPH G. LEO					
1947 Montreal	6	2	0	2	2
1949 "	7	2	1	3	0
1950 "	4	0	0	0	0
	17	4	1	5	2
GRAY, ALEXANDER					
1928 *N. Y. Rangers		1	0	1	0
GRIFFIS, SILAS SETH D					
Born: Onaga, Kan. Sept. 1883					
1918 Vancouver (PCHA)		1	0	1	0
GRIGOR, GEORGE					
1944 Chicago	1	0	0	0	0
GROSS, LLOYD					
1934 Detroit Red Wings	1	0	0	0	0
GROSSO. DONALD JOSEPH					
1939 Detroit	3	1	2	3	7
1940 "	5	0	0	0	0
1941 "	9	1	4	5	0
1942 "	12	8	6	14	19
1943 *"	10	4	2	6	10
1944 "	5	1	0	1	0
1946 Chicago	4	0	0	0	17
	48	15	14	29	53
GROSVENOR, LEONARD					
1928 Ottawa	2	0	0	0	2
1933 Mont. Canadiens	2	0	0	0	0
	4	0	0	0	2
GUIDOLIN, ARMAND					
1943 Boston	9	0	4	4	12
1946 "	10	5	2	7	13
1947 "	3	0	1	1	6
1948 Detroit	2	0	0	0	4
	24	5	7	12	35
HADDON. LLOYD WARD					
1960 Detroit	1	0	0	0	0
HAGGARTY, JAMES					
1942 Montreal		2	1	3	2
HAIDY, GORDON ADAM RW					
Born: Winnipeg, Man. April 11, 1928					
1950 *Detroit	1	0	0	0	0
HALDERSON, HAROLD					
1925 *Victoria (WCHL)		2	1	3	8
1926 " "		1	0	1	8
		3	1	4	16
HALEY, LEONARD FRANK					
1960 Detroit	6	1	3	4	6
HALL, JOSEPH HENRY					
1919 Montreal Canadiens	5	0	0	0	6
HALL, MURRAY WINSTON					
1963 Chicago	4	0	0		0
1965 Detroit	1	0	0		0
1966 "	1	0	0		0
	6	0	0		0
HALLIDAY, MILTON					
1927 *Ottawa		0	0		0
1939 *Boston	11	0	0	0	0

Sea. Club	Ga.	Go.	A.	P.	PM.
HAMILL, ROBERT GEORGE					
1940 Boston	5	0	1	1	5
1942 Chicago	3	0	1	1	0
1946 "	4	1	0	1	7
	23	1	2	3	12
HAMILTON, JOHN M.					
1943 Toronto	6	1	1	2	0
1944 "	5	1	0	1	0
	11	2	1	3	0
HAMILTON, REGINALD					
1937 Toronto	2	0	1	1	2
1938 "	7	0	1	1	2
1939 "	10	0	2	2	4
1940 "	3	0	0	0	0
1941 "	7	1	2	3	13
1943 "	6	1	1	2	9
1944 "	5	1	0	1	8
1945 *"	13	0	0	0	6
1946 Chicago	4	0	1	1	2
	57	3	8	11	46
HANNIGAN, JOHN GORDON					
1954 Toronto	5	2	0	2	4
1956 "	4	0	0	0	4
	9	2	0	2	8
HARMON, GLEN DAVID					
1943 Montreal	5	0	1	1	2
1944 *"	9	1	2	3	4
1945 "	6	1	0	1	2
1946 *"	9	1	4	5	0
1947 "	11	1	1	2	4
1949 "	7	1	1	2	4
1950 "	5	0	1	1	21
1951 "	1	0	0	0	0
	53	5	10	15	37
HARMS, JOHN					
1944 Chicago	3	3	0	3	2
HARRINGTON, LELAND					
1928 Boston Bruins	2	0	0	0	0
1933 Mont. Canadiens	2	1	0	1	2
	4	1	0	1	2
HARRIS, FRED					
1921 Vancouver (PCHA)		2	1	3	9
1923 " "		0	1	1	8
		2	2	4	17
HARRIS, HENRY					
1931 Boston Bruins	3	0	0	0	0
HARRIS, WILLIAM EDWARD					
1956 Toronto	5	1	0	1	4
1959 "	12	3	4	7	16
1960 "	9	0	3	3	4
1961 "	5	1	0	1	0
1962 * "	12	2	1	3	2
1963 * "	10	0	1	1	0
1964 * "	9	1	1	2	4
	62	8	10	18	30
HARRISON, EDWARD F.					
1948 Boston	5	1	0	1	2
1949 "	4	0	0	0	0
	9	1	0	1	2
HART, WILFRED					
1925 *Victoria (WCHL)	4	2	1	3	0
1926 Victoria (WCHL)	4	0	0	0	4
1927 Mont. Canadiens	4	0	0	0	0
1928 " "	2	0	0	0	0
1933 " "	16	2	2	4	4
HAY, GEORGE					
1922 Regina (WCHL)		0	0	0	0
1927 Chicago		1	2	3	2
1929 Detroit		1	0	1	0
1933 "		0	1	1	0
		2	3	5	2
HAY, JAMES ALEXANDER					
1953 Detroit	4	0	0	0	0
1955 *"	5	1	0	1	0
	9	1	0	1	0

Sea. Club	Ga.	Go.	A.	P.	PM.
HAY, WILLIAM CHARLES					
1960 Chicago	4	1	2	3	2
1961 *"	12	2	5	7	20
1962 "	12	3	7	10	18
1963 "	6	3	2	5	6
1964 "	7	3	1	4	4
1965 "	14	3	1	4	4
1966 "	6	0	2	2	4
1967 "	6	0	1	1	4
	67	15	21	36	62
HAYNES, PAUL					
1932 Mont. Maroons		0	0	0	0
1933 Mont. Maroons		0	0	0	2
1934 " "		0	1	1	2
1935 Boston		0	0	0	0
1937 Mont. Canadiens		2	3	5	0
1938 " "		0	4	4	5
1939 " "		0	0	0	4
		2	8	10	13
HEADLEY, FERN					
1925 Mont. Canadiens		0	0	0	0
HEBENTON, ANDREW ALEX					
1956 New York	5	1	0	1	2
1957 " "	5	2	0	2	2
1958 " "	6	2	3	5	4
1962 " "	6	1	2	3	0
	22	6	5	11	8
HEFFERNAN, GERALD					
1942 Montreal	3	2	1	3	0
1943 "	2	0	0	0	0
1944 *"	7	1	2	3	8
	12	3	3	6	8
HELLER, EHRHARDT HENRY					
1932 N. Y. Rangers	7	3	1	4	8
1933 *" " "	8	3	0	3	10
1934 ,, ,, ,,	2	0	0	0	0
1935 ,, ,, ,,	4	0	1	1	4
1937 " " "	9	0	0	0	11
1938 " " "	3	0	1	1	2
1939 " " "	7	0	1	1	10
1940 *" " "	12	0	3	3	12
1941 " " "	3	0	1	1	4
1942 " " "	6	0	0	0	0
	61	6	8	14	61
HENDERSON, JOHN MURRAY					
1945 Boston	7	0	1	1	2
1946 "	10	1	1	2	4
1947 "	4	0	0	0	4
1948 "	3	1	0	1	5
1949 "	5	0	1	1	2
1951 "	5	0	0	0	2
1952 "	7	0	0	0	4
	41	2	3	5	23
HERBERTS, JAMES					
1927 Boston	8	3	0	3	11
1929 Detroit	1	0	0	0	2
	9	3	0	3	13
HERGESHEIMER, PHILIP					
1940 Chicago	1	0	0	0	0
1941 "	5	0	0	0	2
	6	0	0	0	2
HERGESHEIMER, WALTER E.					
1956 New York	5	1	0	1	0
HERON, ROBERT G.					
1939 Toronto	2	0	0	0	4
1940 "	9	2	0	2	2
1941 "	7	0	2	2	0
1942 Mont. Canadiens	3	0	0	0	0
	21	2	2	4	6
HEXIMER, ORVILLE R.					
1933 Boston		0	0	0	2
HEXTALL, BRYAN ALDWIN					
1938 N. Y. Rangers	3	2	0	2	0
1939 " " "	7	0	1	1	4
1940 *" " "	12	4	3	7	11
1941 " " "	3	0	1	1	0
1942 " " "	6	1	1	2	4
1948 " "	6	1	3	4	0
	37	8	9	17	19

Sea. Club	Ga.	Go.	A.	P.	PM.
HICKS, WAYNE WILSON					
1960 Chicago	1	0	1	1	0
1961 *"	1	0	0	0	2
	2	0	1	1	2
HILL, JOHN MELVIN					
1939 *Boston	12	6	3	9	12
1940	2	0	0	0	0
1941 *"	10	1	1	2	0
1943 Toronto	6	3	0	3	0
1945 *"	13	2	3	5	6
	43	12	7	19	18
HILLER, WILBERT CARL					
1938 N. Y. Rangers	1	0	0	0	0
1939 " " "	7	1	0	1	9
1940 *" " "	12	2	4	6	2
1941 " " "	3	0	0	0	0
1942 Boston	5	0	1	1	0
1943 Montreal	5	1	0	1	4
1945 "	6	1	1	2	4
1946 *"	9	4	2	6	2
	48	9	8	17	21
HIMES, NORMAN					
1929 N. Y. Americans	2	0	0	0	0
HIRSCHFELD, JOHN A.					
1950 Montreal	5	1	0	1	0
HITCHMAN, LIONEL					
1923 *Ottawa		1	0	1	4
1927 Boston		1	0	1	11
1928 "		0	0	0	2
1929 *"		0	1	1	22
1930 "		1	0	1	14
1931 "		0	0	0	0
1933 "		0	0	0	0
		3	1	4	53
HOEKSTRA, EDWARD ADRIAN					
1968 Philadelphia	7	0	1	1	0
HOLLETT, WILLIAM					
1935 Toronto	7	0	0	0	6
1937 Boston	3	0	0	0	2
1938 "	3	0	1	1	0
1939 *"	12	1	3	4	2
1940 "	5	1	2	3	2
1941 *"	11	3	4	7	8
1942 "	5	0	1	1	2
1943 "	9	0	9	9	4
1944 Detroit	5	0	0	0	6
1945 "	14	3	4	7	6
1946 "	5	0	2	2	0
	79	8	26	34	38
HOLLINGWORTH, GORDON					
1956 Detroit	3	0	0	0	2
HOLMES, LOUIS CHARLES CARTER					
1932 Chicago	2	0	0	0	2
HOLWAY, ALBERT R.					
1926 *Mont. Maroons		0	0	0	0
HORECK, PETER					
1946 Chicago	4	0	0	0	2
1947 Detroit	5	2	0	2	6
1948 "	10	3	7	10	12
1949 "	11	1	1	2	10
1951 Boston	4	0	0	0	13
	34	6	8	14	43
HORNE, GEORGE					
1929 Toronto		0	0	0	4
HORNER, GEORGE REGINALD					
1929 Toronto	4	1	0	1	2
1931 "	2	0	0	0	4
1932 *"	7	2	2	4	20
1933 "	9	1	0	1	10
1934 "	5	1	0	1	6
1935 "	7	0	1	1	4
1936 "	9	1	2	3	22
1937 "	2	0	0	0	7
1938 "	7	0	1	1	14
1939 "	10	1	2	3	26
1940 "	9	0	2	2	55
	71	7	10	17	170

Sea. Club	Ga.	Go.	A.	P.	PM.
HORVATH, BRONCO JOSEPH					
1956 New York	5	1	2	3	4
1958 Boston	12	5	3	8	8
1959 "	7	2	3	5	0
1962 Chicago	12	4	1	5	6
	36	12	9	21	18
HOWE, SYDNEY HARRIS					
1930 Ottawa Senators		0	0	0	0
1936 *Detroit		3	3	6	2
1937 *"		2	5	7	0
1939 "		3	1	4	4
1940 "		2	2	4	2
1941 "		1	7	8	0
1942 "		3	5	8	0
1943 *"	7	1	2	3	0
1944 "	5	2	2	4	0
1945 "	7	0	0	0	2
		17	27	44	10
HUTTON, WILLIAM DAVIS					
1930 Ottawa Senators	2	0	0	0	0
HRYMNAK, STEPHEN					
1953 Detroit	2	0	0	0	0
HUCUL, FREDERICK ALBERT					
1953 Chicago	6	1	0	1	10
HURST, RONALD					
1956 Toronto	3	0	2	2	4
INGRAM, FRANK					
1930 Chicago		0	0	0	0
1931 "		0	1	1	2
		0	1	1	2
INGRAM, RONALD WALTER					
1963 Chicago	2	0	0	0	0
IRVIN, JAMES DICKENSON					
1922 Regina (WCHL)	2	1	0	1	0
1927 Chicago	2	2	0	2	4
	4	3	0	3	4
IRWIN, IVAN DUANE					
1956 New York	5	0	0	0	8
JACKSON, ARTHUR					
1936 Toronto		0	3	3	2
1938 Boston		0	0	0	0
1939 N. Y. Americans		0	0	0	2
1940 Boston		1	2	3	0
1941 *"		1	3	4	16
1942 "		0	1	1	0
1943 "	9	6	3	9	7
1945 *Toronto	8	0	0	0	0
	8	12	20	27	
JACKSON, HAROLD R.					
1938 *Chicago		0	0	0	2
1941 Detroit		0	0	0	7
1943 *Detroit	6	0	1	1	4
1944 Detroit	5	0	0	0	11
1945 "	14	1	1	2	10
1946 "	5	0	0	0	6
		1	2	3	40
JACKSON, HARVEY					
1931 Toronto		0	0	0	2
1932 *"		5	2	7	13
1933 "		3	1	4	2
1934 "		1	0	1	8
1935 "		3	2	5	4
1936 "		3	2	5	4
1937 "		1	0	1	2
1938 "		1	0	1	8
1939 "		0	1	1	2
1940 N. Y. Americans		0	1	1	2
1942 Boston		0	1	1	0
1943 "	9	1	2	3	10
		18	12	30	57
JAMES, GERALD EDWIN					
1956 Toronto	5	1	0	1	8
1960 "	10	0	0	0	0
	15	1	0	1	8
JANKOWSKI, LOUIS CASIMER					
1953 Detroit	1	0	0	0	0

Sea. Club	Ga.	Go.	A.	P.	PM.
JENKINS, ROGER					
1931 Chicago		0	0	0	0
1934 *Chicago		0	0	0	4
1935 Mont. Canadiens		1	0	1	2
1936 Boston		0	1	1	2
1938 *Chicago		0	6	6	8
		1	7	8	16
JENNINGS, JOSEPH W.					
1941 Detroit	9	2	2	4	0
1944 ”	4	0	0	0	0
1945 Boston	7	2	2	4	6
	20	4	4	8	6
JERWA, JOSEPH					
1931 N. Y. Rangers		0	0	0	4
1936 N. Y. Americans		2	3	5	2
1938 ” ” ”		0	0	0	8
1939 ” ” ”		0	0	0	2
		2	3	5	16
JOHNSON, ALLAN EDMUND					
1961 Detroit	11	2	2	4	6
JOHNSON, IVAN W.					
1927 N. Y. Rangers		0	0	0	8
1928 *” ” ”		1	1	2	46
1929 ” ” ”		0	0	0	26
1930 ” ” ”		0	0	0	14
1931 ” ” ”		1	0	1	17
1932 ” ” ”		2	0	2	24
1933 *” ” ”		1	0	1	14
1934 ” ” ”		0	0	0	4
1935 ” ” ”		0	0	0	4
1937 ” ” ”		0	1	1	4
1938 N. Y. Americans		0	0	0	2
		5	2	7	161
JOHNSON, NORMAN BRUCE					
1958 Boston	12	4	0	4	6
1960 Chicago	2	0	0	0	0
	14	4	0	4	6
JOHNSON, THOMAS CHRISTIAN					
1950 Montreal	1	0	0	0	0
1951 ”	11	0	0	0	6
1952 ”	11	1	0	1	2
1953 *”	12	2	3	5	8
1954 ”	11	1	2	3	30
1955 ”	12	2	0	2	22
1956 *”	10	0	2	2	8
1957 *”	10	0	2	2	13
1958 *”	2	0	0	0	0
1959 *”	11	2	3	5	8
1960 *”	8	0	1	1	4
1961 ”	6	0	1	1	8
1962 ”	6	0	1	1	0
	111	8	15	23	109
JOHNSON, VIRGIL					
1938 *Chicago		0	0	0	0
1944 ”	9	0	3	3	4
		0	3	3	4
JOHNSTONE. ROBERT ROSS					
1944 Toronto	3	0	0	0	0
JOLIAT, AURELE					
1924 *Mont. Canadiens	4	3	3	6	6
1925 ” ”	4	2	1	3	16
1927 ” ”	4	1	0	1	10
1928 ” ”	2	0	0	0	4
1929 ” ”	3	1	1	2	i ɔ
1930 *” ”	6	0	2	2	6
1931 *” ”	10	0	4	4	12
1932 ” ”	3	2	0	2	4
1933 ” ”	2	2	1	3	2
1934 ” ”	2	0	1	1	0
1935 ” ”	2	1	0	1	0
1937 ” ”	5	0	3	3	2
	47	12	16	28	72
JONES, ALVIN B.					
1939 Detroit	6	0	1	1	10
1943 Toronto	6	0	0	0	8
	12	0	1	1	18
JUZDA, WILLIAM					
1942 New York	6	0	1	1	4
1948 ” ”	6	0	0	0	9
1949 *Toronto	9	0	2	2	8
1950 ”	7	0	0	0	16
1951 *”	11	0	0	0	7
1952 ”	3	0	0	0	2
	42	0	3	3	46

Sea. Club	Ga.	Go.	A.	P.	PM.
KAISER, VERNON C.					
1951 Montreal	2	0	0	0	0
KALBFLEISH, WALTER					
1936 N. Y. Americans		0	0	0	2
KALETA, ALEXANDER					
1942 Chicago	3	1	2	3	0
1946 ”	4	0	1	1	2
1950 New York	10	0	3	3	0
	17	1	6	7	2
KAMINSKY, MAX					
1935 Boston	4	0	0	0	0
KAMPMAN, RUDOLPH					
1938 Toronto	7	0	1	1	6
1939 ”	10	1	1	2	20
1940 ”	10	0	0	0	0
1941 ”	2	0	0	0	0
1942 *”	13	0	2	2	12
	42	1	4	5	38
KEATS, GORDON BLANCHARD					
1923 Edmonton (WCHL)	2	0	0	0	4
KEELING, MELVILLE SYDNEY					
1929 N. Y. Rangers		3	0	3	2
1930 ” ” ”		0	3	3	8
1931 ” ” ”		1	1	2	0
1932 ” ” ”		2	1	3	12
1933 *” ” ”		1	2	3	8
1934 ” ” ”		0	0	0	0
1935 ” ” ”		2	1	3	0
1937 ” ” ”		3	2	5	2
1938 ” ” ”		0	1	1	2
		12	11	23	34
KELLY, LEONARD PATRICK					
1948 Detroit	10	3	2	5	2
1949 ”	11	1	1	2	6
1950 *”	14	1	3	4	2
1951 ”	6	0	1	1	0
1952 *”	5	1	0	1	0
1953 ”	6	0	4	4	0
1954 *”	12	5	1	6	4
1955 *”	11	2	4	6	17
1956 ”	10	2	4	6	2
1957 ”	5	1	0	1	0
1958 ”	4	0	1	1	2
1960 Toronto	10	3	8	11	2
1961 ”	2	1	0	1	0
1962 *”	12	4	6	10	0
1963 *”	10	2	6	8	6
1964 *”	14	4	9	13	4
1965 ”	6	3	2	5	2
1966 ”	4	0	2	2	0
1967 *”	12	0	5	5	2
	164	33	59	92	51
KELLY, PETER					
1936 *Detroit		1	1	2	2
1937 *”		2	0	2	0
1939 ”		0	0	0	0
		3	1	4	2
KELLY, REGIS					
1935 Toronto		2	0	2	4
1936 ”		2	3	5	4
1938 ”		2	2	4	2
1939 ”		1	0	1	0
1940 ”		0	1	1	0
		7	6	13	10
KENDALL, WILLIAM					
1934 *Chicago		0	0	0	0
1936 ”		0	0	0	0
		0	0	0	0
KENNEDY, THEODORE S.					
1944 Toronto	5	1	1	2	2
1945 *”	13	7	2	9	2
1947 *”	11	4	5	9	4
1948 *”	9	8	6	14	0
1949 *”	9	2	6	8	2
1950 ”	7	1	2	3	8
1951 *”	11	4	5	9	4
1952 ”	4	0	0	0	4
1954 ”	5	1	1	2	2
1955 ”	4	1	3	4	0
	78	29	31	60	32

Sea. Club	Ga.	Go.	A.	P.	PM.
KILREA, HECTOR					
1927 *Ottawa		1	1	2	4
1928 "		1	0	1	2
1930 "		0	0	0	4
1932 Detroit		0	0	0	0
1934 Toronto		2	0	2	2
1935 "		0	0	0	4
1936 *Detroit		0	3	3	2
1937 *"		3	1	4	2
1939 "		1	2	3	0
		8	7	15	20
KILREA, KENNETH ARMSTRONG					
1939 Detroit	3	1	1	2	4
1940 "	5	1	1	2	0
1944 "	2	0	0	0	0
	10	2	2	4	4
KILREA, WALTER					
1930 Ottawa Senators		0	0	0	0
1933 Mont. Maroons		0	0	0	0
1934 " "		0	0	0	0
1936 *Detroit		2	0	4	2
1937 *"		0	2	2	4
		2	4	6	6
KLEIN, JAMES LLOYD					
1929 *Boston Bruins	3	0	0	0	0
1936 N. Y. Americans		0	0	0	2
	3	0	0	0	2
KLUKAY, JOSEPH FRANCIS					
1943 Toronto	1	0	0	0	0
1947 *"	11	1	0	1	0
1948 *"	9	1	1	2	2
1949 *"	9	2	3	5	4
1950 "	7	3	0	3	4
1951 *"	11	4	3	7	0
1952 "	4	1	1	2	0
1953 Boston	11	1	2	3	9
1954 "	4	0	0	0	0
1956 Toronto	4	0	0	0	4
	71	13	10	23	23
KRAFTCHECK, STEPHEN S.					
1951 Boston	6	0	0	0	7
KRYZANOWSKI, EDWARD L.					
1949 Boston	5	0	1	1	2
1951 "	6	0	0	0	2
1952 "	7	0	0	0	0
	18	0	1	1	4
KULLMAN, EDWARD G.					
1948 New York	6	1	0	1	2
KUNTZ, ALAN R.					
1942 New York	6	1	0	1	2
KURYLUK, MERVIN LW-SL					
Born: Yorkton, Sask. August 10, 1937					
1962 Chicago	2	0	0	0	0
KYLE, WALTER L.					
1950 New York	12	1	2	3	30
1952 Boston	2	0	0	0	4
	14	1	2	3	34
LaBINE, LEO GERALD					
1952 Boston	5	0	1	1	4
1953 "	7	2	1	3	19
1954 "	4	0	1	1	28
1955 "	5	2	1	3	11
1957 "	10	3	2	5	14
1958 "	11	0	2	2	10
1959 "	7	2	1	3	12
1961 Detroit	11	3	2	5	4
	60	12	11	23	102
LACH, ELMER JAMES					
1941 Montreal	1	1	0	1	0
1943 "	5	2	4	6	6
1944 *"	9	2	11	13	*4
1945 "	6	4	4	8	2
1946 *"	9	5	12	17	4
1949 "	1	0	0	0	4
1950 "	5	1	2	3	4
1951 "	11	2	2	4	2
1952 Montreal	11	1	2	3	4
1953 *Montreal	12	1	6	7	6
1954 Montreal	4	0	2	2	0
	74	19	45	64	36

Sea. Club	Ga.	Go.	A.	P.	PM.
LaFRANCE, ADELARD					
1934 Montreal Canadiens	2	0	0	0	0
LALONDE, EDOUARD CHARLES					
1919 Montreal Canadiens	5	6	0	6	3
LAMB, JOSEPH GORDON					
1928 Mont. Maroons		1	0	1	32
1930 Ottawa		0	0	0	11
1933 Boston		0	1	1	6
1936 Mont. Maroons		0	0	0	2
		1	1	2	51
LAMIRANDE JEAN-PAUL					
1948 New York	6	0	0	0	4
1950 " "	2	0	0	0	0
	8	0	0	0	4
LAMOUREUX, LEO P.					
1944 *Montreal	9	0	3	3	8
1945 "	6	1	1	2	2
1946 *"	9	0	2	2	2
1947 "	4	0	0	0	4
	28	1	6	7	16
LANCIEN, JOHN G.					
1948 New York	2	0	0	0	2
1950 " "	4	0	1	1	0
	6	0	1	1	2
LANE, MYLES J.					
1929 *Boston Bruins	2	0	0	0	0
1930 " "	4	0	0	0	0
	6	0	0	0	0
LANGELLE, PETER					
1939 Toronto	9	1	2	3	2
1940 "	10	0	3	3	0
1941 "	7	1	1	2	0
1942 *"	13	3	3	6	2
	39	5	9	14	4
LANGLOIS, ALBERT					
1958 *Montreal	7	0	1	1	4
1959 *"	7	0	0	0	4
1960 *"	8	0	3	3	18
1961 "	5	0	0	0	6
1962 New York	6	0	1	1	2
1964 Detroit	14	0	0	0	12
1965 "	6	1	0	1	4
	53	1	5	6	50
LANGLOIS, CHARLES					
1928 Montreal Canadiens	2	0	0	0	0
LAPRADE, EDGAR L.					
1948 New York	6	1	4	5	0
1950 " "	12	3	5	8	4
	18	4	9	13	4
LAROCHELLE, WILDORE					
1927 Mont. Canadiens		0	0	0	0
1928 " "		0	0	0	0
1930 *Mont. Canadiens		1	0	1	12
1931 *" "		1	2	3	8
1932 " "		2	1	3	4
1933 " "		1	0	1	0
1934 " "		1	1	2	0
1935 " "		0	0	0	0
		6	4	10	24
LAYCOE, HAROLD RICHARDSON					
1949 Montreal	7	0	1	1	13
1950 "	2	0	0	0	0
1951 Boston	6	0	1	1	5
1952 "	7	1	1	2	11
1953 "	11	0	2	2	10
1954 "	2	0	0	0	0
1955 "	5	1	0	1	0
	40	2	5	7	39
LEACH, LAWRENCE RAYMOND					
1959 Boston	7	1	1	2	8
LECLAIR, JOHN LOUIS					
1955 Montreal	12	5	0	5	2
1956 *"	8	1	1	2	4
	20	6	1	7	6

Sea. Club	Ga.	Go.	A.	P.	PM.
JUZDA, WILLIAM					
1942 New York	6	0	1	1	4
1948 " "	6	0	0	0	9
1949 *Toronto	9	0	2	2	8
1950 "	7	0	0	0	16
1951 *"	11	0	0	0	7
1952 "	3	0	0	0	2
	42	0	3	3	46
LEGER, ROGER					
1947 Montreal	11	0	6	6	10
1949 "	5	0	1	1	2
1950 "	4	0	0	0	2
	20	0	7	7	14
LEPINE, ALFRED					
1927 Mont. Canadiens		0	0	0	4
1928 " "		0	0	0	0
1929 " "		0	0	0	2
1930 *" "		2	2	4	6
1931 *" "		4	2	6	6
1932 Mont. Canadiens		1	0	1	4
1933 " "		0	0	0	2
1934 " "		0	0	0	0
1935 " "		0	0	0	2
1937 " "		0	1	1	0
1938 " "		0	0	0	0
		7	5	12	26
LESIEUR, ARTHUR J.					
1931 *Mont. Canadiens	10	0	0	0	4
1932 " "	4	0	0	0	0
	14	0	0	0	4
LESWICK, ANTHONY J.					
1948 New York	6	3	2	5	8
1950 " "	12	2	4	6	12
1952 *Detroit	8	3	1	4	22
1953 "	6	1	0	1	11
1954 *"	12	3	1	4	18
1955 *"	11	1	2	3	20
1958 "	4	0	0	0	0
	59	13	10	23	91
LEVINSKY, ALEXANDER					
1931 Toronto		0	0	0	0
1932 *Toronto		0	0	0	6
1933 "		1	0	1	14
1934 "		0	0	0	6
1936 Chicago		0	1	1	0
1938 *"		1	0	1	0
		2	1	3	26
LEWICKI, DANIEL					
1951 *Toronto	9	0	0	0	0
1956 New York	5	0	3	3	0
1957 " "	5	0	1	1	2
1958 " "	6	0	0	0	6
1959 Chicago	3	0	0	0	0
	28	0	4	4	8
LEWIS, HERBERT					
1932 Detroit Falcons		0	0	0	0
1933 Detroit		1	0	1	0
1934 "		6	2	8	2
1936 *"		2	3	5	0
1937 *"		4	3	7	4
1939 "		1	2	3	0
		14	10	24	6
LINDSAY, ROBERT BLAKE THEODORE					
1945 Detroit	14	2	0	2	6
1946 "	5	0	1	1	0
1947 "	5	2	2	4	10
1948 "	10	3	1	4	6
1949 "	11	2	6	8	31
1950 *"	13	4	4	8	16
1951 "	6	0	1	1	8
1952 *"	8	5	2	7	8
1953 "	6	4	4	8	6
1954 *"	12	4	4	8	14
1955 *"	11	7	12	19	12
1956 "	10	6	3	9	22
1957 "	5	2	4	6	8
1959 Chicago	6	2	4	6	13
1960 "	4	1	1	2	0
1965 Detroit	7	3	0	3	34
	133	47	49	96	194
LISCOMBE, HARRY CARL					
1939 Detroit	3	0	0	0	2
1941 "	9	4	3	7	12
1942 "	12	6	6	12	2
1943 *"	10	6	8	14	2
1944 "	5	1	0	1	2
1945 "	14	4	2	6	0
1946 "	4	1	0	1	0
	57	22	19	41	20
LITZENBERGER, EDWARD C. J.					
1959 Chicago	6	3	5	8	8
1960 "	4	0	1	1	4
1961 *"	10	1	3	4	2
1962 *Toronto	10	0	2	2	4
1963 *"	9	1	2	3	6
1964 *"	1	0	0	0	10
	40	5	13	18	34
LONG, STANLEY GORDON					
Born: Owen Sound, Ont. Nov. 6, 1929					
1952 Montreal	3	0	0	0	0
LORRAIN, RODRIGUE					
1937 Mont. Canadiens		0	0	0	0
1938 " "		0	0	0	0
1939 "		0	3	3	0
		0	3	3	0
LOUGHLIN, CLEMENT JOSEPH					
1925 *Victoria (WCHL)		1	0	1	4
1926 " "		1	0	1	8
		2	0	2	12
LOWE, ROSS R.					
1951 Montreal	2	0	0	0	0
LOWREY, GERALD					
1932 Chicago		1	0	1	2
LUND, PENTTI, A.					
1947 Boston	1	0	0	0	0
1948 "	2	0	0	0	0
1950 New York	12	6	5	11	0
1952 Boston	2	1	0	1	0
1953 "	2	0	0	0	0
	19	7	5	12	0
LUNDE, LEONARD MELVIN					
1960 Detroit	6	1	2	3	0
1961 "	10	2	0	2	0
1963 Chicago	4	0	0	0	2
	20	3	2	5	2
LUNDY, PATRICK A.					
1946 Detroit	2	1	0	1	0
1947 "	5	0	1	1	2
1948 "	5	1	1	2	0
1949 "	4	0	0	0	0
	16	2	2	4	2
LYNN, VICTOR I.					
1947 *Toronto	11	4	1	5	16
1948 *"	9	2	5	7	20
1949 *"	8	0	1	1	2
1950 "	7	0	2	2	2
1951 Boston	5	0	0	0	2
1953 Chicago	7	1	1	2	4
	47	7	10	17	46
LYON, RONALD					
1931 Boston		0	0	0	0
MacDONALD, JAMES ALLAN KILBY					
1940 *New York Rangers		0	2	2	4
1941 " " "		1	0	1	0
		1	2	3	4
MACEY, HUBERT					
1942 New York	1	0	0	0	0
1947 Montreal	7	0	0	0	0
	8	0	0	0	0
MacKAY, CALUM					
1950 Montreal	5	0	1	1	2
1951 "	11	1	0	1	0
1953 *"	7	1	3	4	10
1954 "	3	0	1	1	0
1955 "	12	3	8	11	8
	38	5	13	18	20
MacKAY, DAVID					
1941 Chicago		0	1	1	2

Sea. Club	Ga.	Go.	A.	P.	PM.

MacKAY, DUNCAN

Sea. Club	Ga.	Go.	A.	P.	PM.
1918 Vancouver (PCHA)		5	4	9	
1921 " "		0	1	1	0
1922 " "		1	0	1	6
1923 " "		1	0	1	4
1924 " "		0	1	1	2
1927 Chicago Black Hawks		0	0	0	0
1929 *Boston		0	0	0	2
1930 "		0	0	0	4
		7	6	13	18

MacKAY, MURDO J.

Sea. Club	Ga.	Go.	A.	P.	PM.
1947 Montreal	9	0	1	1	0
1949 "	6	1	1	2	0
	15	1	2	3	0

MACKELL, FLEMING DAVID

Sea. Club	Ga.	Go.	A.	P.	PM.
1949 *Toronto	9	2	4	6	4
1950 "	7	1	1	2	11
1951 *"	11	2	3	5	9
1952 Boston	5	2	1	3	12
1953 "	11	2	7	9	7
1954 "	4	1	1	2	8
1955 "	4	0	1	1	0
1957 "	10	5	3	8	4
1958 "	12	5	14	19	12
1959 "	7	2	6	8	8
	80	22	41	63	75

MacKENZIE, WILLIAM K.

Sea. Club	Ga.	Go.	A.	P.	PM.
1934 Mont. Maroons		0	0	0	0
1935 N. Y. Rangers		0	0	0	0
1937 Mont. Canadiens		1	0	1	0
1938 *Chicago		0	1	1	11
		1	1	2	11

MACKEY, REGINALD

Sea. Club	Ga.	Go.	A.	P.	PM.
1927 N. Y. Rangers	1	0	0	0	0

MACKIE, HOWARD

Sea. Club	Ga.	Go.	A.	P.	PM.
1937 *Detroit		0	0	0	0

MacMILLAN, JOHN STEWART

Sea. Club	Ga.	Go.	A.	P.	PM.
1961 Toronto	4	0	0	0	0
1962 *"	3	0	0	0	0
1963 *"	1	0	0	0	0
1964 Detroit	4	0	1	1	2
	12	0	1	1	2

MacNEIL, ALLISTER WENCES

Sea. Club	Ga.	Go.	A.	P.	PM.
1962 Montreal	5	0	0	0	2
1963 Chicago	4	0	1	1	4
1964 "	7	0	2	2	25
1965 "	14	0	1	1	34
1966 "	3	0	0	0	0
1967 New York	4	0	0	0	2
	37	0	4	4	67

MacPHERSON JAMES ALBERT

Sea. Club	Ga.	Go.	A.	P.	PM.
1951 Montreal	11	0	2	2	8
1952 "	11	0	0	0	0
1953 *"	4	0	1	1	9
1954 "	3	0	0	0	4
	29	0	3	3	21

MAHAFFY, JOHN

Sea. Club	Ga.	Go.	A.	P.	PM.
1945 Montreal	1	0	1	1	0

MAJEAU, FERNAND

Sea. Club	Ga.	Go.	A.	P.	PM.
1944 *Montreal	1	0	0	0	0

MALONEY, PHILIP FRANCIS

Sea. Club	Ga.	Go.	A.	P.	PM.
1959 Chicago	6	0	0	0	0

MANTHA, LEON-GEORGES

Sea. Club	Ga.	Go.	A.	P.	PM.
1929 Mont. Canadiens		0	0	0	0
1930 *Mont. Canadiens		0	0	0	8
1931 *" "		5	1	6	4
1932 " "		0	0	0	2
1935 " "		0	0	0	4
1937 " "		0	0	0	2
1938 " "		1	0	1	0
		6	1	7	20

MANTHA, SYLVIO

Sea. Club	Ga.	Go.	A.	P.	PM.
1924 *Mont. Canadiens		0	0	0	0
1925 " "		0	0	0	2
1927 " "		1	0	1	0
1928 " "		0	0	0	6
1929 " "		0	0	0	0
1930 *" "		2	1	3	18
1931 *" "		2	1	3	26
1932 " "		0	1	1	8
1933 " "		0	1	1	2
1934 " "		0	0	0	2
1935 " "		0	0	0	2
		5	4	9	66

MARACLE, HENRY ELMER

Sea. Club	Ga.	Go.	A.	P.	PM.
1931 N. Y. Rangers		0	0	0	2

MARCH, HAROLD

Sea. Club	Ga.	Go.	A.	P.	PM.
1931 Chicago		3	1	4	11
1932 "		0	0	0	2
1934 *"		2	2	4	6
1935 "		0	0	0	0
1936 "		2	3	5	0
1938 "		2	4	6	12
1940 "		1	0	1	2
1941 "		2	3	5	0
1942 "	3	0	2	2	4
1944 "	5	0	0	0	4
		12	15	27	41

MARIUCCI, JOHN

Sea. Club	Ga.	Go.	A.	P.	PM.
1941 Chicago	4	0	2	2	16
1942 "	3	0	0	0	0
1946 "	4	0	1	1	10
	11	0	3	3	26

MARKER, AUGUST

Sea. Club	Ga.	Go.	A.	P.	PM.
1934 Detroit Red Wings		0	0	0	2
1935 *Mont. Maroons		1	1	2	4
1936 " "		1	0	1	2
1937 " "		0	1	1	0
1939 Toronto		2	2	4	0
1940 "		1	3	4	23
1941 "		0	0	0	5
		5	7	12	36

MARQUESS, CLARENCE E.

Sea. Club	Ga.	Go.	A.	P.	PM.
1947 Boston	4	0	0	0	0

MARTIN, FRANCIS WILLIAM

Sea. Club	Ga.	Go.	A.	P.	PM.
1953 Boston	6	0	1	1	2
1954 "	4	0	1	1	0
	10	0	2	2	2

MARTIN, GEORGE CLARE

Sea. Club	Ga.	Go.	A.	P.	PM.
1942 Boston	5	0	0	0	0
1947 "	5	0	1	1	0
1948 "	5	0	0	0	6
1950 *Detroit	10	0	1	1	0
1951 "	2	0	0	0	0
	27	0	2	2	6

MASNICK, PAUL ANDREW

Sea. Club	Ga.	Go.	A.	P.	PM.
1951 Montreal	11	2	1	3	4
1952 "	6	1	0	1	12
1953 *"	6	1	0	1	7
1954 "	10	0	4	4	4
	33	4	5	9	27

MASON, CHARLES C.

Sea. Club	Ga.	Go.	A.	P.	PM.
1935 N. Y. Rangers		0	1	1	0

MATTE, JOSEPH

Sea. Club	Ga.	Go.	A.	P.	PM.
1924 Vancouver (PCHA)	2	1	0	1	2

MATZ, JEAN

Sea. Club	Ga.	Go.	A.	P.	PM.
1925 Mont. Canadiens		0	0	0	2

MAZUR, EDWARD JOSEPH

Sea. Club	Ga.	Go.	A.	P.	PM.
1951 Montreal	2	0	0	0	0
1952 "	5	2	0	2	4
1953 *"	7	2	2	4	11
1954 "	11	0	3	3	7
	25	4	5	9	22

McATEE, JEROME

Sea. Club	Ga.	Go.	A.	P.	PM.
1945 Detroit	14	2	1	3	0

McAVOY, GEORGE D-SL
Born: Edmonton, Alb. June 21, 1931

Sea. Club	Ga.	Go.	A.	P.	PM.
1955 Montreal	4	0	0	0	0

(continued)

Sea. Club	Ga.	Go.	A.	P.	PM.
McCAFFREY, ALBERT					
1928 Pittsburgh		0	0	0	0
1930 *Mont. Canadiens		1	1	2	6
		1	1	2	6
McCAIG, DOUGLAS					
1942 Detroit	2	0	0	0	6
1947 "	5	0	1	1	4
	7	0	1	1	10
McCORMACK, JOHN R.					
1950 Toronto	6	1	0	1	0
1953 *Montreal	9	0	0	0	0
1954 "	7	0	1	1	0
	22	1	1	2	0
McCREEDY, JOHN					
1942 *Toronto		4	3	7	6
1945 *"	8	0	0	0	0
		4	3	7	6
McCURRY, DUKE					
1928 Pittsburgh		0	0	0	0
McDONALD, BYRON R.					
1940 Detroit	5	0	2	2	0
McDONALD, "JACK"					
1919 Montreal	5	1	1	2	3
McDONALD, "RAN" RW-SR					
1918 Vancouver (PCHA)		2	1	3	0
1919 Seattle (PCHA)		1	1	2	0
		3	2	5	0
McDONALD, WILFRED K.					
1936 *Detroit		3	0	3	10
1937 *"		0	0	0	2
1939 Toronto		0	0	0	4
1940 "		0	0	0	0
1941 "		2	0	2	2
1942 *"		0	1	1	2
1943 "	6	1	0	1	4
	6	1	7		24
McFADDEN, JAMES A.					
1947 Detroit	4	0	2	2	0
1948 "	10	5	3	8	10
1949 "	8	0	1	1	6
1950 *"	14	2	3	5	8
1951 "	6	0	0	0	2
1953 Chicago	7	3	0	3	4
	49	10	9	19	30
McFADYEN, DONALD					
1934 *Chicago	8	2	2	4	5
McGILL, JACK J.					
1935 Mont. Canadiens		2	0	2	0
1937 " "		0	0	0	0
		2	0	2	0
McGILL, JOHN G.					
1942 Boston	5	4	1	5	6
1945 "	7	3	3	6	0
1946 "	10	0	0	0	0
1947 "	5	0	0	0	11
	27	7	4	11	17
McINENLY, BERTRAM					
1935 Boston		0	0	0	2
McINTYRE, JOHN ARCHIBALD					
1951 Boston	2	0	0	0	0
1952 "	7	1	2	3	2
1953 "	10	4	2	6	2
1958 Detroit	4	1	1	2	0
1960 "	6	1	1	2	0
	29	7	6	13	4
McKAY, DOUGLAS A. LW					
Born: Hamilton, Ont. May 28, 1929					
1950 *Detroit	1	0	0	0	0
McKELL, JACK					
1920 *Ottawa		0	0	0	0
1921 *"		0	0	0	0
		0	0	0	0

Sea. Club	Ga.	Go.	A.	P.	PM.
McKENNEY, DONALD HAMILTON					
1955 Boston	5	1	2	3	4
1957 "	10	1	5	6	4
1958 "	12	9	8	17	0
1959 "	7	2	5	7	0
1964 *Toronto	12	4	8	12	0
1965 "	6	0	0	0	0
1968 St. Louis	6	1	1	2	2
	58	18	29	47	10
McKINNON, JOHN					
1928 Pittsburgh	2	0	0	0	4
McLEAN, JACK					
1943 Toronto	6	2	2	4	2
1944 "	3	0	0	0	6
1945 *"	4	0	0	0	0
	13	2	2	4	8
McLENAHAN, ROLAND J.					
1946 Detroit	2	0	0	0	0
McLEOD, ROBERT JOHN					
1950 New York	7	0	0	0	0
McMAHON, MICHAEL C.					
1943 Montreal	5	0	0	0	14
1944 *"	8	1	2	3	16
	13	1	2	3	30
McMANUS, SAMUEL					
1935 *Mont. Maroons		0	0	0	0
McNAB, MAXWELL D.					
1948 Detroit	3	0	0	0	2
1949 "	10	1	0	1	2
1950 *"	10	0	0	0	0
1951 "	2	0	0	0	0
	25	1	0	1	4
McNABNEY, SIDNEY C					
Born: Toronto, Ont. January 15, 1929					
1951 Montreal	5	0	1	1	2
McNEILL, WILLIAM RONALD					
1958 Detroit	4	1	1	2	4
McREAVY, PATRICK JOSEPH					
1941 *Boston		2	2	4	5
1942 Detroit	11	1	1	2	4
		3	3	6	9
McVEIGH, CHARLES					
1922 Regina (WCHL)		0	0	0	0
1927 Chicago		0	0	0	0
1929 N. Y. Americans		0	0	0	2
		0	0	0	2
McVICAR, JOHN					
1931 Mont. Maroons	2	0	0	0	2
1932 " "	4	0	0	0	0
	6	0	0	0	0
MEEKER, HOWARD WILLIAM					
1947 *Toronto	11	3	3	6	6
1948 *"	9	2	4	6	15
1950 "	7	0	1	1	4
1951 *"	11	1	1	2	14
1952 "	4	0	0	0	11
	42	6	9	15	50
MEEKING, HARRY					
1918 *Toronto		1	2	3	
1925 *Victoria (WCHL)		0	2	2	2
1926 Victoria (WCHL)		0	0	0	6
		1	4	5	8
MEGER, PAUL C.					
1950 Montreal	2	0	0	0	2
1951 "	11	1	3	4	4
1952 "	11	0	3	3	2
1953 *"	5	1	2	3	4
1954 "	6	1	0	1	4
	35	3	8	11	16
MELNYK, MICHAEL GERALD					
1956 Detroit	6	0	0	0	0
1960 "	6	3	0	3	0

(continued)

Sea. Club	Ga.	Go.	A.	P.	PM.
1961 "	11	1	0	1	2
1962 Chicago	7	0	0	0	2
1965 "	6	0	0	0	0
1968 St. Louis	17	2	6	8	2
	53	6	6	12	6

MERONEK, WILLIAM

Sea. Club	Ga.	Go.	A.	P.	PM.
1943 Montreal	1	0	0	0	0

METZ, DONALD MAURICE

Sea. Club	Ga.	Go.	A.	P.	PM.
1939 Toronto	2	0	0	0	0
1940 "	2	0	0	0	0
1941 "	5	1	1	2	2
1942 *"	4	4	3	7	0
1945 *"	11	0	1	1	4
1947 *"	11	2	3	5	4
1948 *"	2	0	0	0	2
1949 *"	3	0	0	0	0
	40	7	8	15	12

METZ, NICHOLAS J.

Sea. Club	Ga.	Go.	A.	P.	PM.
1935 Toronto	6	1	1	2	0
1937 "		0	0	0	0
1938 "		0	2	2	0
1939 "		3	3	6	6
1940 "		1	3	4	9
1941 "	7	3	4	7	0
1942 *"	13	4	4	8	12
1945 *"	7	1	1	2	2
1947 *"	6	4	2	6	0
1948 *"	9	2	0	2	2
		19	20	39	31

MICKOSKI, NICHOLAS

Sea. Club	Ga.	Go.	A.	P.	PM.
1948 New York	2	0	1	1	0
1950 " "	12	1	5	6	2
1958 Detroit	4	0	0	0	4
	18	1	6	7	6

MIGAY, RUDOLPH JOSEPH

Sea. Club	Ga.	Go.	A.	P.	PM.
1954 Toronto	5	1	0	1	4
1955 "	3	0	0	0	10
1956 "	5	0	0	0	6
1959 "	2	0	0	0	0
	15	1	0	1	20

MILKS, HIBBERT

Sea. Club	Ga.	Go.	A.	P.	PM.
1928 Pittsburgh	2	0	0	0	2
1932 N. Y. Rangers	7	0	0	0	0
	9	0	0	0	2

MILLAR, HUGH A.

Sea. Club	Ga.	Go.	A.	P.	PM.
1947 Detroit	1	0	0	0	0

MILLER, EARL

Sea. Club	Ga.	Go.	A.	P.	PM.
1930 Chicago	2	1	0	1	7
1932 *Toronto	7	0	0	0	0
	9	1	0	1	7

MILLER, WILLIAM

Sea. Club	Ga.	Go.	A.	P.	PM.
1935 *Mont. Maroons		0	0	0	0
1937 Mont. Canadiens		0	0	0	0
		0	0	0	0

MOE, WILLIAM C.

Sea. Club	Ga.	Go.	A.	P.	PM.
1948 New York	1	0	0	0	0

MOFFATT, RONALD

Sea. Club	Ga.	Go.	A.	P.	PM.
1933 Detroit	4	0	0	0	0
1934 Detroit	3	0	0	0	0
	7	0	0	0	0

MOLYNEAUX, LAWRENCE S.

Sea. Club	Ga.	Go.	A.	P.	PM.
1938 N. Y. Rangers		0	0	0	8

MONDOU, ARMAND

Sea. Club	Ga.	Go.	A.	P.	PM.
1929 Mont. Canadiens		0	0	0	2
1930 *" "		1	0	1	6
1931 *" "		0	0	0	0
1932 " "		1	2	3	2
1934 " "		0	1	1	0
1935 " "		0	1	1	0
1937 " "		0	0	0	0
1939 " "		1	0	1	2
		3	4	7	12

MOORE, RICHARD WINSTON

Sea. Club	Ga.	Go.	A.	P.	PM.
1952 Montreal	11	1	1	2	12
1953 *"	12	3	2	5	13
1954 "	11	5	8	13	8
1955 "	12	1	5	6	22
1956 *"	10	3	6	9	12
1957 *"	10	3	7	10	4
1958 *"	10	4	7	11	4
1959 *"	11	5	12	17	8
1960 *"	8	6	4	10	4
1961 "	6	3	1	4	4
1962 "	6	4	2	6	8
1963 "	5	0	1	1	2
1965 Toronto	5	1	1	2	6
1968 St. Louis	18	7	7	14	15
	135	46	64	110	122

MORAN, AMBROSE JASON

Sea. Club	Ga.	Go.	A.	P.	PM.
1922 Regina (WCHL)	2	0	0	0	10

MORENZ, HOWARTH W.

Sea. Club	Ga.	Go.	A.	P.	PM.
1924 *Mont. Canadiens		4	1	5	2
1925 " "		4	1	5	4
1927 " "		1	0	1	4
1928 " "		0	0	0	12
1929 " "		0	0	0	6
1930 *" "		3	0	3	10
1931 *" ".		1	4	5	10
1932 " "		1	0	1	4
1933 " "		0	3	3	2
1934 " "		1	1	2	0
1935 Chicago		0	0	0	0
		15	10	25	54

MORRIS, BERNARD PATRICK

Sea. Club	Ga.	Go.	A.	P.	PM.
1920 Seattle (PCHA)		0	2	2	0
1924 Calgary (WCHL)		0	0	0	2
		0	2	2	2

MORRIS, ELWYN

Sea. Club	Ga.	Go.	A.	P.	PM.
1944 Toronto	5	1	2	3	2
1945 *"	13	3	0	3	14
	18	4	2	6	16

MORRISON, DONALD M.

Sea. Club	Ga.	Go.	A.	P.	PM.
1948 Detroit	3	0	1	1	0

MORRISON, JOHN

Sea. Club	Ga.	Go.	A.	P.	PM.
1923 Edmonton (WCHL)		1	0	1	0

MORRISON, RODERICK F.

Sea. Club	Ga.	Go.	A.	P.	PM.
1948 Detroit	3	0	0	0	0

MORTSON, JAMES ANGUS GERALD

Sea. Club	Ga.	Go.	A.	P.	PM.
1947 *Toronto	11	1	3	4	22
1948 *"	5	1	2	3	2
1949 *"	9	2	1	3	8
1950 "	7	0	0	0	18
1951 *"	11	0	1	1	4
1952 "	4	0	0	0	6
1953 Chicago	7	1	1	2	6
	54	5	8	13	68

MOSDELL, KENNETH

Sea. Club	Ga.	Go.	A.	P.	PM.
1946 *Montreal	9	4	1	5	6
1947 "	4	2	0	2	4
1949 "	7	1	1	2	4
1950 "	5	0	0	0	12
1951 "	11	1	1	2	4
1952 "	2	1	0	1	0
1953 *"	7	3	2	5	4
1954 "	11	1	0	1	4
1955 "	12	2	7	9	8
1956 *"	9	1	1	2	2
1959 *"	2	0	0	0	0
	79	16	13	29	48

MOSIENKO, WILLIAM

Sea. Club	Ga.	Go.	A.	P.	PM.
1942 Chicago	3	2	0	2	0
1944 "	8	2	2	4	6
1946 "	4	2	0	2	2
1953 "	7	4	2	6	7
	22	10	4	14	15

Sea. Club	Ga.	Go.	A.	P.	PM.
MOTTER, ALEXANDER E.					
1935 Boston		0	0	0	0
1936 "		0	0	0	0
1939 Detroit		0	1	1	0
1940 "		1	1	2	15
1941 "		1	3	4	4
1942 "		1	3	4	12
1943 *"	5	0	1	1	2
		3	9	12	33
MOYNES, FRANK RW					
1918 Vancouver (PCHA)		0	0	0	
MUMMERY, HARRY					
1918 *Toronto		0	4	4	
MUNRO, DUNCAN B.					
1926 *Mont. Maroons		1	0	1	6
1927 " "		0	0	0	4
1928 " "		0	2	2	8
1930 " "		2	0	2	4
1932 Mont. Canadiens		0	0	0	2
		3	2	5	24
MURDOCH, JOHN MURRAY					
1927 N. Y. Rangers	2	0	0	0	0
1928 *" " "	9	2	1	3	12
1929 " " "	6	0	0	0	2
1930 " " "	4	3	0	3	6
1931 " " "	4	0	2	2	0
1932 " " "	7	0	2	2	2
1933 *" " "	8	2	4	6	2
1934 " " "	2	0	0	0	0
1935 " " "	4	0	2	2	4
1937 " " "	9	1	1	2	0
	55	8	12	20	28
MURRAY, ALLAN					
1936 N. Y. Americans	5	0	0	0	2
1938 " " "	6	0	0	0	6
	11	0	0	0	8
MURRAY, JACK "MUZZ"　C-SR					
1919 Seattle (PCHA)		3	0	3	6
1920 " (PCHA)		0	0	0	6
		3	0	3	12
NIGHBOR, FRANK J.					
1920 *Ottawa	5	6	1	7	3
1921 *"	5	0	1	1	0
1923 *"	6	1	1	2	10
1927 *"	6	1	1	2	2
1928 "	2	0	0	0	2
	24	8	4	12	17
NOBLE, EDWARD REGINALD					
1918 *Toronto		2	1	3	-
1922 *"		0	2	2	9
1926 *Mont. Maroons		0	0	0	6
1927 " "		0	0	0	2
1929 Detroit		0	0	0	2
1932 "		0	0	0	0
1933 Mont. Maroons		0	0	0	2
		2	3	5	21
NORTHCOTT, LAWRENCE					
1930 Mont. Maroons		0	0	0	4
1931 " "		0	1	1	0
1932 " "		1	2	3	4
1933 " "		0	0	0	4
1934 " "		2	0	2	0
1935 *" "		4	1	5	0
1936 " "		0	0	0	0
1937 " "		1	1	2	2
		8	5	13	14
OATMAN, EDWARD　C-SR					
Born: 1889					
1922 Vancouver (PCHA)		1	1	2	14
1924 Calgary (WCHL)		0	1	1	0
		1	2	3	14
OATMAN, WARREN RUSSELL					
1926 Victoria (WCHL)	4	0	0	0	8
1927 Mont. Maroons	2	0	0	0	0
1928 Mont. Maroons	9	1	0	1	18
1929 " "	6	0	0	0	0
	21	1	0	1	26

Sea. Club	Ga.	Go.	A.	P.	PM.
O'CONNOR, HERBERT W.					
1942 Montreal	3	0	1	1	0
1943 "	5	4	5	9	0
1944 *"	8	1	2	3	2
1945 "	2	0	0	0	0
1946 *"	9	2	3	5	0
1947 "	8	3	4	7	0
1948 New York	6	1	4	5	0
1950 " "	12	4	2	6	4
	53	15	21	36	6
OLIVER, HAROLD					
1924 Calgary (WCHL)		0	0	0	0
1927 Boston		4	2	6	4
1928 "		2	0	2	4
1929 *"		1	1	2	8
1930 "		2	1	3	6
1931 "		0	0	0	2
1933 "		0	0	0	0
1936 N. Y. Americans		1	2	3	0
		10	6	16	24
OLMSTEAD, MURRAY BERT					
1951 Montreal	11	2	3	5	9
1952 "	11	0	1	1	4
1953 *"	12	2	2	4	4
1954 "	11	0	1	1	19
1955 "	12	0	4	4	21
1956 *"	10	4	10	14	8
1957 *"	10	0	9	9	13
1958 *"	9	0	3	3	0
1959 Toronto	12	4	2	6	13
1960 "	10	3	4	7	0
1961 "	3	1	2	3	10
1962 *"	4	0	1	1	0
	115	16	42	58	101
O'NEIL, JAMES BEATON					
1935 Boston		0	0	0	9
1936 "		1	1	2	4
1941 Montreal		0	0	0	0
		1	1	2	13
O'NEILL, THOMAS B.					
1944 Toronto	4	0	0	0	6
ORLANDO, JAMES V.					
1940 Detroit	5	0	0	0	15
1941 "	9	0	2	2	31
1942 "	12	0	4	4	45
1943 *"	10	0	3	3	14
	36	0	9	9	105
OWEN, GEORGE					
1929 *Boston		0	0	0	0
1930 "		0	2	2	6
1931 "		2	3	5	13
1933 "		0	0	0	6
		2	5	7	25
PALANGIO, PETER					
1927 Mont. Canadiens		0	0	0	0
1938 *Chicago		0	0	0	0
		0	0	0	0
PAPIKE, JOSEPH					
1941 Chicago		0	2	2	0
PARKES, ERNEST					
1922 Vancouver (PCHA)		0	1	1	0
1923 " "		0	1	1	2
		0	2	2	2
PARSONS, GEORGE					
1938 Toronto		3	2	5	11
PATRICK, FREDERICK MURRAY					
1938 N. Y. Rangers	3	0	0	0	2
1939 " " "	7	1	0	1	17
1940 *" " "	12	3	0	3	13
1941 " " "	3	0	0	0	2
	25	4	0	4	34
PATRICK, JOSEPH LYNN					
1935 N. Y. Rangers	4	2	2	4	0
1937 " " "	9	3	0	3	2
1938 " " "	3	0	1	1	2

(continued)

Sea.	Club	Ga.	Go.	A.	P.	PM.
1939	" " "	7	1	1	2	0
1940	*" " "	12	2	2	4	4
1941	" " "	3	1	0	1	14
1942	New York	6	1	0	1	0
		44	10	6	16	22
PATTERSON, GEORGE						
1928	Mont. Canadiens	1	0	0	0	0
1929	" "	3	0	0	0	2
		4	0	0	0	2
PAVELICH, MARTIN N.						
1948	Detroit	10	2	2	4	6
1949	"	9	0	1	1	8
1950	*"	14	4	2	6	13
1951	"	6	0	1	1	2
1952	*"	8	2	2	4	2
1953	"	6	2	1	3	7
1954	*"	12	2	2	4	4
1955	*"	11	1	3	4	12
1956	"	10	0	1	1	14
1957	"	5	0	0	0	6
		91	13	15	28	74
PEIRSON, JOHN F.						
1948	Boston	5	3	2	5	0
1949	"	5	3	1	4	4
1951	"	2	1	1	2	2
1952	"	7	0	2	2	4
1953	"	11	3	6	9	2
1954	"	4	0	0	0	2
1957	"	10	0	3	3	12
1958	"	5	0	1	1	0
		49	10	16	26	26
PETERS, FRANK J.						
1931	N. Y. Rangers		0	0	0	2
PETERS, JAMES MELDRUM						
1946	*Montreal	9	3	1	4	6
1947	"	11	1	2	3	10
1948	Boston	5	1	2	3	2
1949	"	4	0	1	1	0
1950	*Detroit	8	0	2	2	0
1951	"	6	0	0	0	0
1953	Chicago	7	0	1	1	4
1954	*Detroit	10	0	0	0	0
		60	5	9	14	22
PETTINGER, ERIC						
1929	Toronto		1	0	1	8
PETTINGER, GORDON R.						
1933	*N. Y. Rangers		0	0	0	0
1934	Detroit		1	0	1	2
1936	*"		2	2	4	0
1937	*"		0	2	2	2
1938	Boston		0	0	0	0
1939	*"		1	1	2	7
		4	5	9	11	
PHILLIPS, MERLYN J.						
1926	*Mont. Maroons		1	1	2	0
1927	" "		0	0	0	0
1928	" "		2	1	3	9
1930	" "		0	0	0	2
1931	" "		0	0	0	2
1932	" "		0	0	0	2
		3	2	5	15	
PHILLIPS, W. J.						
1930	Mont. Maroons		0	0	0	2
PIKE, ALFRED G.						
1940	*N. Y. Rangers	12	3	1	4	6
1941	" " "	3	0	1	1	2
1942	" " "	6	1	0	1	4
		21	4	2	6	12
PITRE, DIDIER						
1919	Montreal Canadiens	5	0	3	3	0
PLAMONDON, GERARD R.						
1946	*Montreal	1	0	0	0	0
1949	"	7	5	1	6	0
1950	"	3	0	1	1	2
		11	5	2	7	2
PODOLSKY, NELSON						
1949	Detroit	7	0	0	0	4

Sea.	Club	Ga.	Go.	A.	P.	PM.
POILE, DONALD B.						
1958	Detroit	4	0	0	0	0
POILE, NORMAN ROBERT						
1943	Toronto	6	2	4	6	4
1947	*"	7	2	0	2	2
1949	Detroit	10	0	1	1	2
		23	4	5	9	8
POLIZIANI, DANIEL						
1959	Boston	3	0	0	0	0
POPEIN, LAWRENCE THOMAS						
1956	New York	5	0	1	1	2
1957	" "	5	0	3	3	0
1958	" "	6	1	0	1	4
		16	1	4	5	6
PORTLAND, JOHN FREDERICK						
1934	Mont. Canadiens	2	0	0	0	0
1937	Boston		0	0	0	4
1938	"		0	0	0	4
1939	*"		0	0	0	11
1940	Chicago	2	0	0	0	2
1941	Montreal		0	1	1	2
1942	"		0	0	0	0
1943	"	5	1	2	3	2
			1	3	4	25
PRATT, JACK						
1931	Boston Bruins	2	0	0	0	0
PRATT, WALTER						
1937	N. Y. Rangers	9	3	1	4	11
1938	" " "	2	0	0	0	2
1939	" " "	7	1	2	3	9
1940	*" " "	12	3	1	4	18
1941	" " "	3	1	1	2	6
1942	" " "	6	1	3	4	24
1943	Toronto	6	1	2	3	8
1944	"	5	0	3	3	4
1945	*"	13	2	4	6	8
		63	12	17	29	90
PRICE, GARRY NOEL						
1959	Toronto	5	0	0	0	2
1966	*Montreal	3	0	1	1	0
		8	0	1	1	2
PRICE, JOHN REES						
1953	Chicago	4	0	0	0	0
PRIMEAU, A. JOSEPH						
1931	Toronto		0	0	0	0
1932	*"		0	6	6	2
1933	"		0	1	1	4
1934	"		2	4	6	6
1935	"		0	3	3	0
1936	"		3	4	7	0
		5	18	23	12	
PRONOVOST, JOSEPH RENE MARCEL						
1950	*Detroit	9	0	1	1	10
1951	"	6	0	0	0	0
1952	* "	8	0	1	1	10
1953	"	6	0	0	0	6
1954	* "	12	2	3	5	12
1955	* "	11	1	2	3	6
1956	"	10	0	2	2	8
1957	"	5	0	0	0	6
1958	"	4	0	1	1	4
1960	"	6	1	1	2	2
1961	"	9	2	3	5	0
1963	"	11	1	4	5	8
1964	"	14	0	2	2	14
1965	"	7	0	3	3	4
1966	Toronto	4	0	0	0	6
1967	* "	12	1	0	1	8
		134	8	23	31	104
PRYSTAI, METRO						
1951	Detroit	3	1	0	1	0
1952	*"	8	2	5	7	0
1953	"	6	4	4	8	2
1954	*"	12	2	3	5	0
1956	"	9	1	2	3	6
1957	"	5	2	0	2	0
		43	12	14	26	8
PURPUR, CLIFFORD						
1944	Chicago	9	1	1	2	0
1945	Detroit	7	0	1	1	4
		16	1	2	3	4

Sea. Club	Ga.	Go.	A.	P.	PM.
PUSIE, JEAN BAPTISTE					
1931 *Mont. Canadiens	2	0	0	0	0
QUACKENBUSH, HUBERT G.					
1944 Detroit	2	1	0	1	0
1945 "	14	0	2	2	2
1946 "	5	0	1	1	0
1947 "	5	0	0	0	2
1948 Detroit	10	0	2	2	0
1949 "	11	1	1	2	0
1951 Boston	6	0	1	1	0
1952 "	7	0	3	3	0
1953 "	10	0	4	4	4
1954 "	4	0	0	0	0
1955 "	5	0	5	5	0
	79	2	19	21	8
QUACKENBUSH, MAXWELL J.					
1951 Boston	6	0	0	0	4
QUENNEVILLE, LEO					
1930 N. Y. Rangers	3	0	0	0	0
QUILTY, JOHN F.					
1941 Montreal	3	0	2	2	0
1942 "	3	0	1	1	0
1947 "	7	3	2	5	9
	13	3	5	8	9
RAGLAN, CLARENCE E.					
1953 Chicago	3	0	0	0	0
RALEIGH, JAMES DONALD					
1948 New York	6	2	0	2	2
1950 " "	12	4	5	9	4
	18	6	5	11	6
RANDALL, KENNETH					
1918 *Toronto		1	0	1	0
1922 *Toronto		1	0	1	9
		2	0	2	9
RAYMOND, ARMAND					
1938 Mont. Canadiens		0	0	0	2
RAYMOND, PAUL MARCEL					
1934 Mont. Canadiens	2	0	0	0	0
REARDON, KENNETH JOSEPH					
1941 Montreal	2	0	0	0	4
1942 "	3	0	0	0	4
1946 *Montreal	9	1	1	2	4
1947 Montreal	7	1	2	3	20
1949 "	7	0	0	0	18
1950 "	2	0	2	2	12
	30	2	5	7	62
REARDON, TERRENCE GEORGE					
1940 Boston	1	0	1	1	0
1941 *Boston	11	2	4	6	6
1942 Montreal	3	2	2	4	2
1946 Boston	10	4	0	4	2
1947 "	5	0	3	3	2
	30	8	10	18	12
REAUME, MARC AVELLIN					
1955 Toronto	4	0	0	0	2
1956 "	5	0	2	2	6
1959 "	10	0	0	0	0
1960 Detroit	2	0	0	0	0
	21	0	2	2	8
REAY, WILLIAM T.					
1946 *Montreal	9	1	2	3	4
1947 "	11	6	1	7	14
1949 "	7	1	5	6	4
1950 "	4	0	1	1	0
1951 "	11	3	3	6	10
1952 "	10	2	2	4	7
1953 *"	11	0	2	2	4
	63	13	16	29	43
REGAN, LAWRENCE EMMETT					
1957 Boston	8	0	2	2	10
1958 "	12	3	8	11	6
1959 Toronto	8	1	1	2	2
1960 "	10	3	3	6	0
1961 "	4	0	0	0	0
	42	7	14	21	18

Sea. Club	Ga.	Go.	A.	P.	PM.
REGAN, WILLIAM D.					
1930 N. Y. Rangers	4	0	0	0	0
1931 " " "	4	0	0	0	2
	8	0	0	0	2
REIBEL, EARL					
1954 *Detroit	9	1	3	4	0
1955 *"	11	5	7	12	2
1956 "	10	0	2	2	2
1957 "	5	0	2	2	0
1959 Boston	4	0	0	0	0
	39	6	14	20	4
REID, GERALD ROLAND					
Born: Owen Sound, Ont. October 13, 1928					
1949 Detroit	2	0	0	0	2
REISE, LEO C. Sr.					
1929 N. Y. Americans	2	0	0	0	0
1930 N. Y. Rangers	4	0	0	0	16
	6	0	0	0	16
REISE, LEO C. Jr.					
1947 Detroit	5	0	1	1	4
1948 "	10	2	1	3	12
1949 "	11	1	0	1	4
1950 *Detroit	14	2	0	2	19
1951 "	6	2	3	5	2
1952 *"	6	1	0	1	27
	52	8	5	13	68
RICHARD, JOSEPH HENRI MAURICE					
1944 *Montreal	9	12	5	17	10
1945 "	6	6	2	8	10
1946 *"	9	7	4	11	15
1947 "	10	6	5	11	44
1949 "	7	2	1	3	14
1950 "	5	1	1	2	6
1951 "	11	9	4	13	13
1952 "	11	4	2	6	6
1953 *Montreal	12	7	1	8	2
1954 "	11	3	0	3	22
1956 *"	10	5	9	14	24
1957 *"	10	8	3	11	8
1958 *"	10	11	4	15	10
1959 *"	4	0	0	0	2
1960 *"	8	1	3	4	2
	133	82	44	126	188
RICKEY, ROY A. D-SL					
1919 Seattle (PCHA)	5	1	2	3	0
1920 " "	5	2	0	2	9
	10	3	2	5	9
RILEY, JACK					
1934 Mont. Canadiens		0	1	1	0
1935 " "		0	2	2	0
		0	3	3	0
RILEY, JAMES NORMAN					
1920 Seattle (PCHA)	5	0	2	2	0
RIOPELLE, HOWARD J.					
1949 Montreal	7	1	1	2	2
1950 "	1	0	0	0	0
	8	1	1	2	2
RIPLEY, VICTOR M.					
1930 Chicago		0	0	0	2
1931 "		2	1	3	4
1932 "		0	0	0	0
1933 Boston		1	0	1	0
1934 N. Y. Rangers		1	0	1	4
		4	1	5	10
RIVERS, GUSTAVE					
1930 *Mont. Canadiens		1	0	1	2
1931 *" "		1	0	1	0
		2	0	2	2
ROBERTSON, FRED					
1932 *Toronto		0	0	0	0
ROBINSON, EARL					
1930 Mont. Maroons		0	0	0	0
1933 " "		0	0	0	0
1934 " "		2	0	2	0
1935 *" "		2	2	4	0

(continued)

Sea. Club	Ga.	Go.	A.	P.	PM.
1936 " "		0	0	0	0
1937 " "		1	2	3	0
		5	4	9	0
ROCHE, EARL					
1931 Mont. Maroons	2	0	0	0	0
RODDEN, EDMUND A.					
1927 Chicago		0	1	1	0
ROMNES, ELWIN NELSON					
1931 Chicago		1	1	2	0
1932 "		0	0	0	0
1934 •"		2	7	9	0
1935 "		0	0	0	0
1936 "		1	2	3	0
1938 •"		2	4	6	2
1939 Toronto		1	4	5	0
		7	18	25	2
RONTY, PAUL					
1948 Boston	5	0	4	4	0
1949 "	5	1	2	3	2
1951 "	6	0	1	1	2
1955 Montreal	5	0	0	0	2
	21	1	7	8	6
ROSSIGNOL, ROLAND					
1945 Montreal	1	0	0	0	2
ROTHSCHILD, SAMUEL					
1926 •Mont. Maroons		0	0	0	0
1927 " "		0	0	0	0
		0	0	0	0
ROWE, ROBERT					
1919 Seattle (PCHA)	5	1	0	1	6
1920 " "	5	2	0	2	19
	10	3	0	3	25
ROZZINI, GINO					
1945 Boston	6	1	2	3	6
RUNGE, PAUL					
1936 Boston		0	0	0	2
1937 Mont. Maroons		0	0	0	4
		0	0	0	6
ST. LAURENT, DOLLARD HERVE					
1952 Montreal	9	0	3	3	6
1953 •"	12	0	3	3	4
1954 "	10	1	2	3	8
1955 "	12	0	5	5	12
1956 •Montreal	4	0	0	0	2
1957 •"	7	0	1	1	13
1958 •"	5	0	0	0	10
1959 Chicago	6	0	1	1	2
1960 "	4	0	1	1	0
1961 •"	11	1	2	3	12
1962 "	12	0	4	4	18
	92	2	22	24	87
SAMIS. PHILIP L.					
1948 •Toronto	5	0	1	1	2
SANDFORD, EDWARD M.					
1948 Boston	5	1	0	1	0
1949 "	5	1	3	4	2
1951 "	6	0	1	1	4
1952 "	7	2	2	4	0
1953 "	11	8	3	11	11
1954 "	3	0	1	1	4
1955 "	5	1	1	2	6
	42	13	11	24	27
SANDS, CHARLES H.					
1933 Toronto		2	2	4	2
1934 "		1	0	1	0
1935 Boston		0	0	0	0
1936 "		0	0	0	0
1937 "		1	2	3	0
1938 "	3	1	1	2	0
1939 •"	1	0	0	0	0
1941 Montreal	2	1	0	1	0
1942 "	3	0	1	1	2
1943 "	2	0	0	0	0
		6	6	12	4
SCHMIDT, JOHN					
1943 Boston	5	0	0	0	0

Sea. Club	Ga.	Go.	A.	P.	PM.
SCHMIDT, MILTON CONRAD					
1937 Boston	3	0	0	0	0
1938 "	3	0	0	0	0
1939 •"	12	3	3	6	2
1940 "	6	0	0	0	0
1941 •"	11	5	6	11	9
1946 "	10	3	5	8	2
1947 "	5	3	1	4	4
1948 "	5	2	5	7	2
1949 "	4	0	2	2	8
1951 "	6	0	1	1	7
1952 "	7	2	1	3	0
1953 "	10	5	1	6	6
1954 "	4	1	0	1	20
	86	24	25	49	60
SCHRINER, DAVID					
1936 N. Y. Americans		3	1	4	2
1938 " " "		1	0	1	0
1939 " " "		0	0	0	30
1940 Toronto		1	3	4	4
1941 "		2	1	3	4
1942 •"		6	3	9	10
1943 "	4	2	2	4	0
1945 •"	13	3	1	4	4
		18	11	29	54
SCLISIZZI, JAMES ENIO					
1947 Detroit	1	0	0	0	0
1948 "	6	0	0	0	4
1949 "	6	0	0	0	2
	13	0	0	0	6
SEIBERT, EARL WALTER					
1932 N. Y. Rangers	7	1	2	3	14
1933 •" " "	8	1	0	1	14
1934 " " "	2	0	0	0	4
1935 " " "	4	0	0	0	6
1936 Chicago	2	2	0	2	0
1938 •"	10	5	2	7	12
1940 "	2	0	1	1	8
1941 "	5	0	0	0	12
1942 "	2	0	0	0	0
1944 "	9	0	2	2	2
1945 Detroit	14	2	1	3	4
	65	11	8	19	76
SHANNON, GERALD					
1935 Boston		0	0	0	2
1937 Mont. Maroons		0	1	1	0
		0	1	1	2
SHEPPARD. JAKE O.					
1929 N. Y. Americans		0	0	0	0
1934 •Chicago		0	0	0	0
		0	0	0	0
SHERF, JOHN					
1937 •Detroit		0	1	1	2
1939 "		0	0	0	0
		0	1	1	2
SHERO, FREDERICK A.					
1948 New York	6	0	1	1	6
1950 " "	7	0	1	1	2
	13	0	2	2	8
SHEWCHUK, JOHN MICHAEL					
1940 Boston	6	0	0	0	0
1942 "	5	0	1	1	7
1943 "	9	0	0	0	12
	20	0	1	1	19
SHIBICKY, ALEXANDER DIMITRI					
1937 N. Y. Rangers	9	1	4	5	0
1938 " " "	3	2	0	2	2
1939 " " "	7	3	1	4	2
1940 •" " "	12	2	5	7	4
1941 " " "	3	1	0	1	2
1942 " " "	6	3	2	5	2
	40	12	12	24	12
SHIELDS, ALLAN					
1928 Ottawa Senators		0	0	0	0
1930 " "		0	0	0	0
1935 •Mont. Maroons		0	1	1	6
1936 " "		0	0	0	6
1937 Boston		0	0	0	2
		0	1	1	14

Sea. Club	Ga.	Go.	A.	P.	PM.
SHILL, JOHN W.					
1934 Toronto		0	0	0	0
1935 Boston		0	0	0	0
1936 Toronto		0	3	3	8
1937 "		0	0	0	0
1938 *Chicago		1	3	4	15
		1	6	7	23
SHILL, WILLIAM R.					
1946 Boston	7	1	2	3	2
SHORE, EDWARD WILLIAM					
1927 Boston	8	1	1	2	42
1928 "	2	0	0	0	8
1929 *Boston	5	1	1	2	28
1930 Boston	6	1	0	1	26
1931 "	5	2	1	3	22
1933 "	5	1	1	2	14
1935 "	4	0	1	1	2
1936 "	2	1	1	2	12
1938 "	3	0	1	1	6
1939 *"	12	0	4	4	19
1940 N. Y. Americans	3	0	2	2	2
	55	7	13	20	181
SIEBERT, ALBERT CHARLES (SEBERT)					
1926 *Mont. Maroons		1	2	3	6
1927 " "		1	1	2	2
1928 " "		2	0	2	26
1930 " "		0	0	0	0
1931 " "		0	0	0	6
1932 " "		0	1	1	4
1933 *N. Y. Rangers		1	0	1	12
1935 Boston		0	0	0	6
1936 "		0	1	1	0
1937 Mont. Canadiens		1	2	3	2
1938 " "		1	1	2	0
		7	9	20	64
SIMON. JOHN C.					
1943 *Detroit	9	1	0	1	4
1944 "	5	0	0	0	2
	14	1	0	1	6
SIMPSON, CLIFFORD V.					
1947 Detroit	1	0	0	0	0
1948 "	1	0	0	0	2
	2	0	0	0	2
SIMPSON, HAROLD EDWARD					
1923 Edmonton (WCHL)	2	0	1	1	0
SINCLAIR, REGINALD A.					
1953 Detroit	3	1	0	1	0
SINGBUSH, ALEXANDER					
1941 Montreal		0	0	0	4
SKINNER, ALF.					
1918 *Toronto		8	0	8	0
1921 Vancouver (PCHA)		4	0	4	9
1922 " "		1	0	1	9
1923 " "		1	1	2	6
1924 " "		0	0	0	0
		14	1	15	24
SKOV, GLEN FREDERICK					
1951 Detroit	6	0	0	0	0
1952 *"	8	1	4	5	16
1953 "	6	1	0	1	2
1954 *"	12	1	2	3	16
1955 *"	11	2	0	2	8
1959 Chicago	6	2	1	3	4
1960 "	4	0	0	0	2
	53	7	7	14	48
SLOAN, ALOYSIUS MARTIN					
1951 *Toronto	11	4	5	9	18
1952 "	4	0	0	0	10
1954 "	5	1	1	2	24
1955 "	4	0	0	0	2
1956 "	2	0	0	0	5
1959 Chicago	6	3	5	8	0
1960 "	3	0	0	0	0
1961 *Chicago	12	1	1	2	8
	47	9	12	21	67
SLOWINSKI, EDWARD S.					
1948 New York	4	0	0	0	0
1950 " "	12	2	6	8	6
	16	2	6	8	6

Sea. Club	Ga.	Go.	A.	P.	PM.
SMITH, ALEXANDER					
1927 *Ottawa		0	0	0	8
1928 "		0	0	0	4
1930 "		0	0	0	4
1932 Detroit		0	0	0	4
1933 Boston		0	2	2	6
		0	2	2	26
SMITH, ARTHUR					
1929 Toronto	4	1	1	2	8
SMITH, BRIAN STUART					
1960 Detroit	5	0	0	0	0
SMITH, CLINTON J.					
1938 N. Y. Rangers	3	2	0	2	0
1939 " " "	7	1	2	3	0
1940 *" " "	12	1	3	4	2
1941 " " "	2	0	0	0	0
1942 " " "	5	0	0	0	0
1944 Chicago	9	4	8	12	0
1946 "	4	2	1	3	0
	42	10	14	24	2
SMITH, DESMOND PATRICK					
1939 Montreal	3	0	0	0	4
1940 Boston	4	0	0	0	0
1941 *"	11	0	2	2	12
1942 "	5	1	2	3	2
	23	1	4	5	18
SMITH, DONALD A.					
1950 New York	1	0	0	0	0
SMITH, KENNETH A.					
1945 Boston	7	3	4	7	0
1946 "	8	0	4	4	0
1947 "	5	3	0	3	2
1948 "	5	2	3	5	0
1949 "	5	0	2	2	4
	30	8	13	21	6
SMITH, REGINALD J.					
1927 *Ottawa		1	0	1	16
1928 Mont. Maroons		2	1	3	23
1930 " "		1	1	2	14
1932 " "		2	1	3	2
1933 " "		2	0	2	2
1934 " "		0	1	1	6
1935 *" "		0	0	0	14
1936 " "		0	0	0	2
1937 Boston		0	0	0	0
1938 N. Y. Americans		0	3	3	0
1939 " " "		0	0	0	14
1940 " " "		3	1	4	2
		11	8	19	95
SMITH, RODGER					
1928 Pittsburgh		2	0	2	0
SMITH, SIDNEY J					
1948 *Toronto	2	0	0	0	0
1949 *"	6	5	2	7	0
1950 *"	7	0	3	3	2
1951 *"	11	7	3	10	0
1952 "	4	0	0	0	0
1954 "	5	1	1	2	0
1955 "	4	3	1	4	0
1956 "	5	1	0	1	0
	44	17	10	27	2
SMITH, WAYNE CLIFFORD					
1967 Chicago	1	0	0	0	0
SMYLIE, RODERICK					
1922 *Toronto	4	1	2	3	0
SOMERS, ARTHUR E.					
1930 Chicago		0	0	0	4
1931 "		0	0	0	0
1932 N. Y. Rangers		0	1	1	8
1933 *" " "		1	4	5	8
1934 " " "		0	0	0	0
1935 " " "		0	0	0	2
		1	5	6	22
SORRELL, JOHN ARTHUR					
1932 Detroit		1	0	1	0
1933 "		2	2	4	4
1934 "		0	2	2	0

(continued)

Sea. Club	Ga.	Go.	A.	P.	PM.
1936 *"		3	4	7	0
1937 *"		2	4	6	2
1938 N. Y. Americans		4	0	4	2
1939 " " "		0	0	0	0
1940 " " "		0	3	3	2
		12	15	27	10

SPARROW, EMORY

1922 Regina (WCHL)	2	0	0	0	3

SPENCER, IRVIN JAMES

1962 New York	1	0	0	0	2
1964 Detroit	11	0	0	0	0
1965 "	1	0	0	0	4
1966 "	3	0	0	0	2
	16	0	0	0	8

STACKHOUSE, THEODORE

1922 *Toronto	1	0	0	0	0

STAHAN, FRANK RALPH "BUTCH" D
Born: Minnedosa, Man. October 29, 1915

1945 Montreal	3	0	1	1	2

STANFIELD, JOHN GORDON "JACK" LW-SL
Born: Toronto, Ont. May 30, 1942

1966 Chicago	1	0	0	0	0

STANLEY, RUSSELL

1918 Vancouver (PCHA)		2	0	2	

STANOWSKI, WALTER P.

1940 Toronto	10	1	0	1	2
1941 "	7	0	3	3	2
1942 *"	13	2	7	9	2
1945 *"	13	0	1	1	5
1947 *"	8	0	0	0	0
1948 *"	9	0	2	2	2
	60	3	13	16	13

STARR, HAROLD

1930 Ottawa		1	(	1	0
1932 Mont. Maroons		0	0	0	0
1933 Mont. Canadiens		0	0	0	2
1934 Mont. Maroons		0	0	0	0
1935 N. Y. Rangers		0	0	0	2
		1	0	1	4

STARR, WILFRID P.

1934 Detroit		0	2	2	2

STASIUK, VICTOR JOHN

1952 *Detroit	7	0	2	2	0
1955 *"	11	5	3	8	6
1957 Boston	10	2	1	3	2
1958 "	12	0	5	5	13
1959 "	7	4	2	6	11
1961 Detroit	11	2	5	7	4
1963 "	11	3	0	3	4
	69	16	18	34	40

STEWART, JAMES GAYE

1942 *Toronto	3	0	0	0	0
1943 "	4	0	2	2	4
1947 *"	11	2	5	7	8
1951 Detroit	6	0	2	2	4
1954 Montreal	3	0	0	0	0
	27	2	9	11	16

STEWART, JOHN SHERRATT

1940 Detroit	5	0	0	0	4
1941 "	9	1	2	3	8
1942 "	12	0	1	1	12
1943 *"	10	1	2	3	35
1946 "	5	0	0	0	14
1947 "	5	0	1	1	12
1948 "	9	1	3	4	6
1949 "	11	1	1	2	32
1950 *"	14	1	4	5	20
	80	5	14	19	143

STEWART, NELSON ROBERT

1926 *Mont. Maroons		6	1	7	14
1927 " "		0	0	0	4
1928 " "		2	0	2	13
1930 " "		1	1	2	2
1931 " "		1	0	1	6
1932 " "		0	1	1	2

(continued)

Sea. Club	Ga.	Go.	A.	P.	PM.
1933 Boston		2	0	2	4
1935 "		0	1	1	0
1936 N. Y. Americans		1	2	3	4
1938 " " "		2	3	5	2
1939 " " "		0	0	0	0
1940 " " "		0	0	0	0
		15	9	24	51

STRATTON, ARTHUR

1968 Philadelphia	5	0	0	0	0

STUART, WILLIAM

1922 *Toronto		0	0	0	9
1927 Boston		0	0	0	6
		0	0	0	15

SULLIVAN, GEORGE JAMES

1951 Boston	2	0	0	0	2
1952 "	7	0	0	0	0
1953 "	3	0	0	0	0
1957 New York	5	1	2	3	4
1958 " "	1	0	0	0	0
	18	1	2	3	6

SUMMERHILL, WILLIAM ARTHUR

1938 Mont. Canadiens	1	0	0	0	0
1939 " "	2	0	0	0	2
	3	0	0	0	2

TAYLOR, FREDERIC WELLINGTON "CYCLONE" C-SL
Born: Tara, Ont. June 23, 1885

1918 Vancouver (PCHA)	5	9	1	10	0
1921 " "	3	0	1	1	0
	8	9	2	11	0

TAYLOR, HARRY

1949 *Toronto	1	0	0	0	0

TAYLOR, RALPH F.

1930 N. Y. Rangers		0	0	0	10

TAYLOR, WILLIAM

1940 Toronto	2	1	0	1	0
1941 "	7	0	3	3	5
1942 *"	13	2	8	10	4
1943 "	6	2	2	4	0
1947 Detroit	5	1	5	6	4
	33	6	18	24	13

TERBENCHE, PAUL FREDERICK

1968 Chicago	6	0	0	0	0

THIFFAULT, LEO EDMOND LW-SL
Born: Drummondville, Que. Dec. 16, 1944

1968 Minnesota	5	0	0	0	0

THOMPSON, PAUL I.

1927 N. Y. Rangers		0	0	0	0
1928 *" " "		0	0	0	30
1929 " " "		0	2	2	6
1930 " " "		0	0	0	2
1931 " " "		3	0	3	0
1932 Chicago		0	0	0	2
1934 *"		4	3	7	6
1935 "		0	0	0	0
1936 "		0	3	3	0
1938 *"		4	3	7	6
		11	11	22	52

THOMS, WILLIAM D.

1933 Toronto		1	1	2	4
1934 "		0	2	2	0
1935 "		2	0	2	0
1936 "		3	5	8	0
1937 "		0	0	0	0
1938 "		0	1	1	0
1940 Chicago		0	0	0	0
1942 "	3	0	1	1	0
1945 Boston	1	0	0	0	2
		6	10	16	6

THOMSON, JAMES R.

1947 *Toronto	11	0	1	1	22
1948 *"	9	1	1	2	9
1949 *"	9	1	5	6	10
1950 "	7	0	2	2	7
1951 *"	11	0	1	1	34
1952 "	4	0	0	0	25

(continued)

Sea. Club	Ga.	Go.	A.	P.	PM.
1954 "	3	0	0	0	2
1955 "	4	0	0	0	16
1956 "	5	0	3	3	10
	63	2	13	15	135
THOMSON, WILLIAM F.					
1944 Detroit	2	0	0	0	0
TIMGREN, RAYMOND C.					
1949 *Toronto	9	3	3	6	2
1950 "	6	0	4	4	2
1951 *"	11	0	1	1	2
1952 "	4	0	1	1	0
	30	3	9	12	6
TOBIN, CHARLES RW-SR					
Born: Winnipeg, Manitoba, 1885					
1922 Vancouver (PCHA)	3	0	0	0	0
TOMSON, JOHN F.					
1939 N. Y. Americans		0	0	0	0
TOPPAZZINI, GERALD					
1953 Boston	11	0	3	3	9
1957 "	10	0	1	1	2
1958 "	12	9	3	12	2
1959 "	7	4	2	6	0
	40	13	9	22	13
TOPPAZZINI, ZELLIO LOUIS PETER					
1949 Boston	2	0	0	0	0
TOUHEY, WILLIAM					
1930 Ottawa		1	0	1	0
TOUPIN, JACQUES					
1944 Chicago	4	0	0	0	0
TRAPP, ROBERT					
1923 Edmonton (WCHL)	2	0	0	0	2
1927 Chicago	2	0	0	0	4
1929 Detroit Cougars	2	0	0	0	0
	6	0	0	0	6
TRAUB, PERCY					
1922 Regina (WCHL)	2	0	0	0	0
1927 Chicago	2	0	0	0	6
	4	0	0	0	6
TREMBLAY, NILS					
1945 Montreal	2	0	0	0	0
TROTTIER, DAVID T.					
1930 Mont. Maroons		0	2	2	8
1931 " "		0	0	0	6
1932 " "		1	0	1	2
1933 " "		0	0	0	6
1934 " "		0	0	0	6
1935 *" "		2	1	3	4
1936 " "		0	0	0	4
1937 " "		1	0	1	5
		4	3	7	41
TRUDEL, LOUIS NAPOLEON					
1934 *Chicago		0	0	0	2
1935 "		0	0	0	0
1936 "		0	0	0	2
1938 *"		0	3	3	2
1939 Montreal		1	0	1	0
		1	3	4	6
TRUDELL, RENE J.					
1948 New York	5	0	0	0	2
TURNER, ROBERT GEORGE					
1956 *Montreal	10	0	1	1	10
1957 *"	6	0	1	1	0
1958 *"	10	0	0	0	2
1959 *"	11	0	2	2	20
1960 *"	8	0	0	0	0
1961 "	5	0	0	0	0
1962 Chicago	12	1	0	1	6
1963 "	6	0	0	0	6
	68	1	4	5	44

Sea. Club	Ga.	Go.	A.	P.	PM
VAIL, MELVILLE					
1929 N. Y. Rangers		0	0	0	2
1930 " " "		0	0	0	0
		0	0	0	2
VENERUZZO, GARY RAYMOND					
1968 St. Louis	9	0	2	2	2
VOSS, CARL					
1933 Detroit		1	1	2	0
1936 N. Y. Americans		0	0	0	0
1937 Mont. Maroons		1	0	1	0
1938 *Chicago		3	2	5	0
		5	3	8	0
WALKER, JOHN PHILLIP					
1919 Seattle (PCHA)		3	0	3	12
1920 " "		1	2	3	0
1925 *Victoria (WCHL)		4	1	5	0
1926 " "		0	0	0	0
		8	3	11	12
WARD, JAMES WILLIAM					
1928 Mont. Maroons		1	1	2	0
1930 " "		0	1	1	12
1931 " "		0	0	0	2
1932 " "		2	1	3	0
1933 " "		0	0	0	0
1934 " "		0	0	0	0
1935 *" "		1	1	2	0
1936 " "		0	0	0	0
		4	4	8	26
WARES, EDWARD					
1939 Detroit		1	0	1	8
1940 "		0	0	0	0
1941 "	2	0	0	0	0
1942 "	12	1	3	4	22
1943 *"	10	3	3	6	0
1946 Chicago	3	0	1	1	0
		5	7	12	34
WARWICK, GRANT D.					
1942 New York	6	0	1	1	2
1948 Boston	5	0	3	3	4
1949 "	5	2	0	2	0
	16	2	4	6	6
WASNIE, NICHOLAS					
1930 *Mont. Canadiens	6	2	2	4	12
1931 *" "	10	3	1	4	8
1932 " "	3	0	0	0	0
	19	5	3	8	20
WATSON, HARRY P.					
1943 *Detroit	7	0	0	0	
1946 "	5	2	0	2	
1947 *Toronto	11	3	2	5	0
1948 *"	9	5	2	7	0
1949 *"	9	4	2	6	2
1950 "	7	0	0	0	0
1951 *"	5	1	2	3	4
1952 "	4	1	0	1	
1954 "	5	0	1	1	
	62	16	9	25	2
WATSON, PHILLIPE HENRI					
1937 N. Y. Rangers	9	0	2	2	2
1938 " " "	3	0	2	2	2
1939 " " "	7	1	1	2	7
1940 *" " "	12	3	6	9	16
1941 " " "	3	0	2	2	9
1942 " " "	6	1	4	5	9
1944 *Montreal	9	3	5	8	16
1948 New York	5	2	3	5	2
	54	10	25	35	67
WEBSTER, DONALD					
1944 Toronto	5	0	0	0	12
WEILAND, RALPH					
1929 *Boston		2	0	2	2
1930 "		1	5	6	2
1931 "		6	3	9	2
1934 Detroit		2	2	4	2
1936 Boston		1	0	1	0
1937 "		0	0	0	
1938 "		0	0	0	
1939 *"		0	0	0	
		12	10	22	12

Sea. Club	Ga.	Go.	A.	P.	PM.
WENTWORTH, MARVIN P.					
1931 Chicago		1	1	2	14
1932 "		0	0	0	0
1933 Mont. Maroons		0	1	1	0
1934 " "		0	2	2	2
1935 *" "		3	2	5	0
1936 " "		0	0	0	0
1937 " "		1	0	1	0
1939 Mont. Canadiens		0	0	0	4
		5	6	11	20
WHITE, WILFRED					
1928 Pittsburgh		0	0	0	0
1929 N. Y. Americans		0	0	0	2
		0	0	0	2
WIEBE, ARTHUR WALTER RONALD					
1935 Chicago		0	0	0	2
1936 "		0	0	0	0
1938 *"		0	1	1	2
1940 "		1	0	1	2
1941 "		0	0	0	0
1942 "		0	0	0	0
1944 "	8	0	2	2	4
		1	3	4	10
WILCOX, ARCHIBALD					
1930 Mont. Maroons	4	1	0	1	2
1931 " "	2	0	0	0	2
1932 " "	4	0	0	0	4
1933 " "	2	0	0	0	0
	12	1	0	1	8
WILLIAMS, BURR					
1934 Detroit		0	0	0	8
WILLSON, DONALD A.					
1938 Mont. Canadiens		0	0	0	0
WILSON, CAROL					
1919 Seattle (PCHA)		1	3	4	6
1922 Regina (WCHL)		0	0	0	0
1924 Calgary (WCHL)		0	0	0	2
1927 Chicago		1	0	1	6
		2	3	5	14
WILSON, GORDON ALLAN LW-SL					
Born: Port Arthur, Ont. Aug. 13, 1932					
1955 Boston	2	0	0	0	0
WILSON, JOHN EDWARD					
1950 *Detroit	8	0	1	1	0
1951 "	1	0	0	0	0
1952 *"	8	4	1	5	5
1953 "	6	2	5	7	0
1954 *"	12	3	0	3	0
1955 *"	11	0	1	1	0
1958 "	4	2	1	3	0
1960 Toronto	10	1	2	3	2
1962 New York	6	2	2	4	4
	66	14	13	27	11

Sea. Club	Ga.	Go.	A.	P.	PM.
WILSON, LAWRENCE					
1950 *Detroit	4	0	0	0	0
WILSON, WALLACE L.					
1948 Boston	1	0	0	0	0
WISEMAN, EDWARD RANDALL					
1933 Detroit		0	0	0	0
1934 "		0	1	1	4
1936 N. Y. Americans		2	1	3	0
1938 " " "		0	4	4	10
1939 " " "		0	0	0	0
1940 Boston		2	1	3	2
1941 *"		6	2	8	0
1942 "		0	1	1	0
		10	10	20	16
WOCHY, STEPHEN					
1945 Detroit	6	0	1	1	0
WOIT, BENEDICT FRANCIS					
1951 Detroit	4	0	0	0	2
1952 *"	8	1	1	2	2
1953 "	6	1	3	4	0
1954 *"	12	0	1	1	8
1955 *"	11	0	1	1	6
	41	2	6	8	18
YACKEL, KENNETH JAMES					
1959 Boston	2	0	0	0	2
YOUNG, DOUGLAS C.					
1932 Detroit		0	0	0	2
1933 "		1	1	2	0
1934 "		1	0	1	10
1936 *"		0	2	2	0
1939 "		0	2	2	4
		2	5	7	16
YOUNG, HOWARD JOHN EDWARD					
1961 Detroit	11	2	2	4	30
1963 "	8	0	2	2	16
	19	2	4	6	46

ACTIVE PLAYERS

The following players played in Stanley Cup games after 1967 (1968 through 1971). For players who played prior to 1968 - - see page 326
An asterisk preceding club indicates Stanley Cup Winner.

Sea.	Club	Ga.	Go.	A.	P.	PM.
AMADIO, DAVID A.						
1968	Los Angeles	7	0	2	2	8
1969	" "	.9	1	0	1	10
		16	1	2	3	18
ANDERSON, RONALD CHESTER GOINGS						
1969	Los Angeles	4	0	0	0	2
1970	St. Louis	1	0	0	0	2
		5	0	0	0	4
ANDRASCIK, STEVEN GEORGE RW-SR						
Born: Sherridon, Manitoba, Nov. 6, 1948						
1972	New York Rangers	1	0	0	0	0
ANGOTTI, LOUIS FREDERICK						
1966	Chicago	6	0	0	0	2
1967	"	6	2	1	3	2
1968	Philadelphia	7	0	0	0	2
1970	Chicago	8	0	0	0	0
1971	"	16	3	3	6	9
1972	"	6	0	0	0	0
		49	5	4	9	15
APPS, SYLVANUS MARSHALL						
1972	Pittsburgh	4	1	0	1	2
ARBOUR, ALGER JOSEPH						
1956	Detroit	4	0	1	1	0
1957	"	5	0	0	0	6
1958	"	4	0	1	1	4
1959	Chicago	6	1	2	3	26
1960	"	4	0	0	0	4
1961 *	"	7	0	0	0	2
1962 *	Toronto	8	0	0	0	6
1964 *	"	1	0	0	0	0
1965	"	1	0	0	0	2
1968	St. Louis	14	0	3	3	10
1969	" "	12	0	0	0	10
1970	" "	14	0	1	1	16
1971	" "	6	0	0	0	6
		86	1	8	9	92
ARBOUR, JOHN GILBERT						
1971	St. Louis	5	0	0	0	0
ARMSTRONG, GEORGE EDWARD						
1952	Toronto	4	0	0	0	2
1954	"	5	1	0	1	2
1955	"	4	1	0	1	4
1956	"	5	4	2	6	0
1959	"	12	0	4	4	10
1960	"	10	1	4	5	4
1961	"	5	1	1	2	0
1962 *	"	12	7	5	12	2
1963 *	"	10	3	6	9	4
1964 *	"	14	5	8	13	10
1965	"	6	1	0	1	4
1966	"	4	0	1	1	4
1967 *	"	9	2	1	3	6
1969	"	4	0	0	0	0
1971	"	6	0	2	2	0
		110	26	34	60	52
AWREY, DONALD WILLIAM						
1968	Boston	4	0	1	1	4
1969	"	10	0	1	1	28
1970 *	"	14	0	5	5	32
1971	"	7	0	0	0	17
1972 *	"	15	0	4	4	45
		50	0	11	11	126
BACKSTROM, RALPH GERALD						
1959 *	Montreal	11	3	5	8	12
1960 *	"	7	0	3	3	2
1961	"	5	0	0	0	4
1962	"	5	0	1	1	6
1963	"	5	0	0	0	2
1964	"	7	2	1	3	0
1965 *	"	13	2	3	5	10
1966 *	"	10	3	4	7	4
1967	"	10	5	2	7	6
1968 *	"	13	4	3	7	4
1969 *	"	14	3	4	7	10
		100	22	26	48	68

Sea.	Club	Ga.	Go.	A.	P.	PM.
BAILEY, GARNET EDWARD		1	0	0	0	2
1969	Boston	1	0	0	0	10
1971	"	13	2	4	6	16
1972 *	"	15	2	4	6	28
BALON, DAVID ALEXANDER		6	2	3	5	2
1962	New York Rangers	7	1	1	2	25
1964	Montreal	10	0	0	0	10
1965 *	"	9	2	3	5	16
1966 *	"	9	0	2	2	6
1967	"	14	4	9	13	14
1968	Minnesota	4	1	0	1	0
1969	New York Rangers	6	1	1	2	32
1970	" "	13	3	2	5	4
1971	" " "	78	14	21	35	109
BARLOW, ROBERT GEORGE		6	2	2	4	6
1970	Minnesota					
BAUN, ROBERT NEIL		12	0	0	0	24
1959	Toronto	10	1	0	1	17
1960	"	3	0	0	0	8
1961	"	12	0	3	3	19
1962 *	"	10	0	3	3	6
1963 *	"	14	2	3	5	42
1964 *	"	6	0	1	1	14
1965	"	4	0	1	1	8
1966	"	10	0	0	0	4
1967 *	"	4	0	0	0	6
1970	Detroit	6	0	1	1	19
1971	Toronto	5	0	0	0	4
1972	"	96	3	12	15	171
BELIVEAU, JEAN ARTHUR		10	2	8	10	4
1954	Montreal	12	6	7	13	18
1955	"	10	12	7	19	22
1956 *	"	10	6	6	12	15
1957 *	"	10	4	8	12	10
1958 *	"	3	1	4	5	4
1959 *	"	8	5	2	7	6
1960 *	"	6	0	5	5	0
1961	"	6	2	1	3	4
1962	"	5	2	1	3	2
1963	"	5	2	0	2	18
1964	"	13	8	8	16	34
1965 *	"	10	5	5	10	6
1966 *	"	10	6	5	11	26
1967	"	10	7	4	11	6
1968 *	"	14	5	10	15	8
1969 *	"	20	6	16	22	28
1971 *	"	162	79	97	176	211
1965 Conn Smythe Trophy						
BENNETT, CURT ALEXANDER		2	0	0	0	0
1971	St. Louis	10	0	0	0	12
1972	" "	12	0	0	0	12
BERENSON, GORDON ARTHUR		5	2	0	2	0
1962	Montreal	5	0	0	0	0
1963	"	7	0	0	0	4
1964	"	9	0	1	1	2
1965 *	"	4	0	1	1	2
1967	New York Rangers	18	5	2	7	9
1968	St. Louis	12	7	3	10	20
1969	" "	16	7	5	12	8
1970	" "	76	21	12	33	45
BERGMAN, GARY GUNNAR		5	0	1	1	4
1965	Detroit	12	0	3	3	14
1966	"	4	0	1	1	2
1970	"	21	0	5	5	20
BERNIER, SERGE JOSEPH		4	1	1	2	0
1971	Philadelphia					

Sea. Club	Ga.	Go.	A.	P.	PM.
BLACKBURN, JOHN DONALD					
1968 Philadelphia	7	3	0	3	8
1969 "	4	0	0	0	2
1970 New York Rangers	1	0	0	0	0
	12	3	0	3	10
BLACKBURN, ROBERT JOHN					
1970 Pittsburgh	6	0	0	0	4
BOIVIN, LEO JOSEPH					
1954 Toronto	5	0	0	0	2
1955 Boston	5	0	1	1	4
1957 "	10	2	3	5	12
1958 "	12	0	3	3	21
1959 "	7	1	2	3	4
1966 Detroit	12	0	1	1	16
1970 Minnesota	3	0	0	0	0
	54	3	10	13	59
BORDELEAU, CHRISTIAN GERARD					
1969 * Montreal	6	1	0	1	0
1971 St. Louis	5	0	1	1	17
1972 Chicago	8	3	6	9	0
	19	4	7	11	17
BORDELEAU, JEAN-PIERRE					
1970 Chicago	1	0	0	0	0
BOUCHARD, PIERRE					
1971 * Montreal	13	0	1	1	10
1972 "	1	0	0	0	0
	14	0	1	1	10
BOUDRIAS, ANDRE G.					
1968 Minnesota	14	3	6	9	8
1970 St. Louis	14	2	4	6	4
	28	5	10	15	12
BOYER, WALTER					
1966 Toronto	4	0	1	1	0
1967 Chicago	1	0	0	0	0
1970 Pittsburgh	10	1	2	3	0
	15	1	3	4	0
BREWER, CARL THOMAS					
1959 Toronto	12	0	6	6	40
1960 "	10	2	3	5	16
1961 "	5	0	0	0	4
1962 * "	8	0	2	2	22
1963 * "	10	0	1	1	12
1964 * "	12	0	1	1	30
1965 "	6	1	2	3	12
1970 Detroit	4	0	0	0	2
1971 St. Louis	5	0	2	2	8
	72	3	17	20	146
BRIERE, MICHEL EDOUARD					
1970 Pittsburgh	10	5	3	8	17
BROWN, LARRY WAYNE					
1971 New York Rangers	11	0	1	1	0
BROWN, STEWART ARNOLD					
1967 New York Rangers	4	0	0	0	6
1968 " " "	6	0	1	1	8
1969 " " "	4	0	1	1	0
1970 " " "	4	0	4	4	9
	18	0	6	6	23
BUCYK, JOHN PAUL					
1956 Detroit	10	1	1	2	8
1957 "	5	0	1	1	0
1958 Boston	12	0	4	4	16
1959 "	7	2	4	6	6
1968 "	3	0	2	2	0
1969 "	10	5	6	11	0
1970 * "	14	11	8	19	2
1971 "	7	2	5	7	0
1972 * "	15	9	11	20	6
	83	30	42	72	38
BURNS, CHARLES FREDERICK					
1970 Minnesota	6	1	0	1	2
1971 "	12	3	3	6	2
1972 "	7	1	1	2	2
	25	5	4	9	6
BURROWS, DAVID JAMES					
1972 Pittsburgh	4	0	0	0	4
BYERS, MICHAEL ARTHUR					
1969 Philadelphia	4	0		1	0
CAFFERY, TERRANCE MICHAEL					
1971 Minnesota	1	0	0	0	0
CAHAN, LAWRENCE LOUIS					
1955 Toronto	4	0	0	0	0
1957 New York Rangers	3	0	0	0	2
1958 " "	5	0	0	0	8
1962 " " "	6	0	0	0	10
1969 Los Angeles	11	1	1	2	22
	29	1	1	2	38
CAMERON, CRAIG LAUDER					
1968 St. Louis	14	1	0	1	11
1969 " "	2	0	0	0	0
1971 " "	6	2	0	2	4
1972 Minnesota	5	0	1	1	2
	27	3	1	4	17
CAMPBELL, BRYAN ALBERT					
1969 Los Angeles	6	2	1	3	0
1970 Chicago	8	1	2	3	0
1971 "	4	0	1	1	0
1972 "	4	0	0	0	2
	22	3	4	7	2
CARDWELL, STEPHEN MICHAEL					
1972 Pittsburgh	4	0	0	0	2
CARLETON, KENNETH WAYNE					
1970 * Boston	14	2	4	6	14
1971 "	4	0	0	0	0
	18	2	4	6	14
CARR, EUGENE WILLIAM					
1972 New York Rangers	16	1	3	4	21
CASHMAN, WAYNE JOHN					
1968 Boston	1	0	0	0	0
1969 "	6	0	1	1	0
1970 * "	14	5	4	9	50
1971 "	7	3	2	5	15
1972 * "	15	4	7	11	42
	43	12	14	26	107
CHERRY, RICHARD JOHN					
1969 Philadelphia	4	1	0	1	4
CLARKE, ROBERT EARLE					
1971 Philadelphia	4	0	0	0	2
COLLINS, WILLIAM EARL					
1968 Minnesota	10	2	4	6	4
1970 "	6	0	1	1	8
	16	2	5	7	12
CONNELLY, WAYNE FRANCIS					
1968 Minnesota	14	8	3	11	2
1970 Detroit	4	1	3	4	2
1971 St. Louis	6	2	1	3	0
	24	11	7	18	4
COURNOYER, YVAN SERGE					
1965 * Montreal	12	3	1	4	0
1966 * "	10	2	3	5	2
1967 "	10	2	3	5	6
1968 * "	13	6	8	14	4
1969 * "	14	4	7	11	5
1971 * "	20	10	12	22	6
1972 "	6	2	1	3	2
	85	29	35	64	25
CRISP, TERRANCE ARTHUR					
1968 St. Louis	18	1	5	6	6
1969 " "	12	3	4	7	20
1970 " "	16	2	3	5	2
1971 " "	6	1	0	1	2
1972 " "	11	1	3	4	2
	63	8	15	23	32
CROTEAU, GARY PAUL					
1969 Los Angeles	11	3	2	5	8
CULLEN, RAYMOND MURRAY					
1968 Minnesota	14	2	6	8	2
1970 "	6	1	4	5	0
	20	3	10	13	2
DEA, WILLIAM FRASER					
1957 Detroit	5	2	0	2	2
1967 Chicago	2	0	0	0	2
1970 Detroit	4	0	1	1	2
	11	2	1	3	6

Sea. Club	Ga.	Go.	A.	P.	PM.
DELVECCHIO, ALEXANDER PETER	8	0	3	3	4
1952 * Detroit	6	2	4	6	2
1953 "	12	2	7	9	7
1954 * "	11	7	8	15	2
1955 * "	10	7	3	10	2
1956 "	5	3	2	5	2
1957 "	4	0	1	1	0
1958 "	6	2	6	8	0
1960 "	11	4	5	9	0
1961 "	11	3	6	9	2
1963 "	14	3	8	11	0
1964 "	7	2	3	5	4
1965 "	12	0	11	11	4
1966 "	4	0	2	2	0
1970 "	121	35	69	104	29
DeMARCO, ALBERT THOMAS	5	0	0	0	2
1970 New York Rangers	4	0	1	1	0
1972 "	9	0	1	1	2
DENNIS, NORMAN MARSHALL	2	0	0	0	2
1970 St. Louis	3	0	0	0	0
1971 " "	5	0	0	0	2
DILLABOUGH, ROBERT WELLINGTON	1	0	0	0	0
1963 Detroit	1	0	0	0	0
1964 "	4	0	0	0	0
1965 "	7	3	0	3	0
1969 Oakland	4	0	0	0	0
1970 "	17	3	0	3	0
DOAK, GARY WALTER	4	0	0	0	4
1968 Boston	8	0	0	0	9
1970 * "	12	0	0	0	46
1972 New York Rangers	24	0	0	0	59
DOREY, ROBERT JAMES	4	0	1	1	21
1969 Toronto	6	0	1	1	19
1971 "	1	0	0	0	0
1972 New York Rangers	11	0	2	2	40
DORNHOEFER, GERHARDT OTTO	3	0	0	0	15
1968 Philadelphia	4	0	1	1	20
1969 "	2	0	0	0	4
1971 "	9	0	1	1	39
DROUIN, JUDE	12	5	7	12	10
1971 Minnesota	7	4	4	8	6
1972 "	19	9	11	20	16
DUFF, TERRANCE RICHARD	5	1	4	5	2
1956 Toronto	12	4	3	7	8
1959 "	10	2	4	6	6
1960 "	5	0	1	1	2
1961 "	12	3	10	13	20
1962 * "	10	4	1	5	2
1963 * "	13	3	6	9	17
1965 * Montreal	10	2	5	7	2
1966 * "	10	2	3	5	4
1967 "	13	3	4	7	4
1968 * "	14	6	8	14	11
1969 * "	114	30	49	79	78
DUPERE, DENIS GILLES	6	0	0	0	0
1971 Toronto	5	0	0	0	0
1972 "	11	0	0	0	0
DUPONT, ANDRE	11	1	0	1	20
1972 St. Louis					
ECCLESTONE, TIMOTHY JAMES	12	1	2	3	2
1968 St. Louis	12	2	2	4	20
1969 " "	16	3	4	7	48
1970 " "	40	6	8	14	70
EDESTRAND, DARRYL	4	0	2	2	0
1972 Pittsburgh					
EGERS, JOHN RICHARD	5	3	1	4	10
1970 New York Rangers •	3	0	0	0	2
1971 " " "	11	1	4	5	14
1972 St. Louis	19	4	5	9	26

Sea. Club	Ga.	Go.	A.	P.	PM.
EHMAN, GERALD JOSEPH	12	6	7	13	8
1959 Toronto	9	0	0	0	0
1960 "	9	1	0	1	4
1964 * "	7	2	2	4	0
1969 Oakland	4	1	1	2	0
1970 "	41	10	10	20	12
ELLIS, RONALD JOHN EDWARD	6	3	0	3	2
1965 Toronto	4	0	0	0	2
1966 "	12	2	1	3	4
1967 * "	4	2	1	3	2
1969 "	6	1	1	2	2
1971 "	5	1	1	2	2
1972 "	37	9	4	13	16
ESPOSITO, PHILIP ANTHONY	4	0	0	0	0
1964 Chicago	13	3	3	6	15
1965 "	6	1	1	2	2
1966 "	6	0	0	0	7
1967 "	4	0	3	3	0
1968 Boston	10	8	10	18	8
1969 "	14	13	14	27	16
1970 * "	7	3	7	10	6
1971 "	15	9	15	24	24
1972 * "	79	37	53	90	78
EVANS, CHRISTOPHER BRUCE	7	1	0	1	4
1972 St. Louis					
FAIRBAIRN, WILLIAM JOHN	6	0	1	1	10
1970 New York Rangers	4	0	0	0	0
1971 " "	16	5	7	12	11
1972 " " "	26	5	8	13	21
FEATHERSTONE, ANTHONY JAMES	2	0	0	0	0
1970 Oakland					
FERGUSON, JOHN BOWIE	7	0	1	1	25
1964 Montreal	13	3	1	4	28
1965 * "	10	2	0	2	44
1966 * "	10	4	2	6	22
1967 "	13	3	5	8	25
1968 * "	14	4	3	7	80
1969 * "	18	4	6	10	36
1971 * "	85	20	18	38	260
FERGUSON, NORMAN GERALD	7	1	4	5	7
1969 Oakland	3	0	0	0	0
1970 "	10	1	4	5	7
FLEMING, REGINALD STEPHEN	12	1	0	1	12
1961 * Chicago	12	2	2	4	27
1962 "	6	0	0	0	27
1963 "	7	0	0	0	18
1964 "	4	0	2	2	11
1967 New York Rangers	6	0	2	2	4
1968 "	3	0	0	0	7
1969 " " "	50	3	6	9	106
FLETT, WILLIAM MAYER	7	1	2	3	8
1968 Los Angeles	10	3	4	7	11
1969 " "	17	4	6	10	19
FOLEY, GILBERT ANTHONY	4	0	1	1	4
1971 Chicago					
FONTEYNE, VALERE RONALD	6	0	4	4	0
1960 Detroit	11	2	3	5	0
1961 "	11	0	0	0	0
1963 "	5	0	1	1	0
1965 "	12	1	0	1	4
1966 "	10	0	2	2	0
1970 Pittsburgh	4	0	0	0	2
1972 "	59	3	10	13	8
FORTIN, RAYMOND HENRI	3	0	0	0	2
1968 St. Louis	3	0	0	0	6
1970 " "	6	0	0	0	8
GAUTHIER, JEAN PHILLIPE	5	0	0	0	12
1963 Montreal	2	0	0	0	4
1965 * "	7	1	3	4	6
1968 Philadelphia	14	1	3	4	22

Sea. Club	Ga.	Go.	A.	P.	PM.
GENDRON, JEAN-GUY	5	2	1	3	2
1956 New York Rangers	5	0	1	1	6
1957 " "	6	1	0	1	11
1958 " "	7	1	0	1	18
1959 Boston	5	0	0	0	2
1961 Montreal	6	3	1	4	2
1962 New York Rangers	4	0	0	0	6
1969 Philadelphia	4	0	1	1	0
1971 "	42	7	4	11	47
GIBBS, BARRY PAUL	6	1	0	1	7
1970 Minnesota	12	0	1	1	47
1971 "	7	1	1	2	9
1972 "	25	2	2	4	63
GILBERT, RODRIGUE GABRIEL	4	2	3	5	4
1962 New York Rangers	4	2	2	4	6
1967 " " "	6	5	0	5	4
1968 " " "	4	1	0	1	2
1969 " " "	6	4	5	9	0
1970 " " "	13	4	6	10	8
1971 " " "	16	7	8	15	11
1972 " " "	53	25	24	49	35
GLENNIE, BRIAN ALEXANDER	3	0	0	0	0
1971 Toronto	5	0	0	0	25
1972 "	8	0	0	0	25
GOLDSWORTHY, WILLIAM ALFRED	14	8	7	15	12
1968 Minnesota	6	4	3	7	6
1970 "	7	2	4	6	6
1971 "	7	2	3	5	6
1972 "	34	16	17	33	30
GOYETTE, JOSEPH GEORGES PHILLIPE	10	2	1	3	4
1957 *Montreal	10	4	1	5	4
1958 * "	10	0	4	4	0
1959 * "	8	2	1	3	4
1960 * "	6	3	3	6	0
1961 "	6	1	4	5	2
1962 "	2	0	0	0	0
1963 "	4	1	0	1	0
1967 New York Rangers	6	0	1	1	4
1968 " "	3	0	0	0	0
1969 " " "	16	3	11	14	6
1970 St. Louis	13	1	3	4	2
1972 New York Rangers	94	17	29	46	26
GRANT, DANIEL FREDERICK	10	0	3	3	5
1968 * Montreal	6	0	2	2	4
1970 Minnesota	12	5	5	10	8
1971 "	7	2	1	3	0
1972 "	35	7	11	18	17
GRAY, TERRENCE STANLEY	7	0	2	2	10
1968 Los Angeles	11	3	2	5	8
1969 St. Louis	16	2	1	3	4
1970 " "	1	0	0	0	0
1971 " "	35	5	5	10	22
GREEN, EDWARD JOSEPH	4	1	1	2	11
1968 Boston	10	2	7	9	18
1969 "	7	1	0	1	25
1971 "	10	0	0	0	0
1972 * "	31	4	8	12	54
GRENIER, LUCIEN S. J.	2	0	0	0	0
1969 * Montreal					
HADFIELD, VICTOR EDWARD	4	0	0	0	2
1962 New York Rangers	4	1	0	1	17
1967 " " "	6	1	2	3	6
1968 " " "	4	2	1	3	2
1969 " " "	13	8	5	13	46
1971 " " "	16	7	9	16	22
1972 " " "	47	19	17	36	95
HALE, LARRY JAMES	4	0	0	0	10
1969 Philadelphia	4	0	0	0	2
1971 "	8	0	0	0	12

Sea. Club	Ga.	Go.	A.	P.	PM.
HAMILTON, ALLAN GUY	1	0	0	0	0
1969 New York Rangers	5	0	0	0	2
1970 " "	6	0	0	0	2
HAMPSON, EDWARD GEORGE	6	0	1	1	0
1962 New York Rangers	7	3	4	7	2
1969 Oakland	4	1	1	2	0
1970 "	11	3	3	6	0
1971 Minnesota	7	0	1	1	0
1972 "	35	7	10	17	2
HANNIGAN, PATRICK EDWARD	4	0	0	0	2
1962 New York	7	1	2	3	9
1968 Philadelphia	11	1	2	3	11
HARBARUK, MIKOLAJ NICKOLAS	10	3	0	3	20
1970 Pittsburgh	4	0	1	1	0
1972 "	14	3	1	4	20
HARDY, JOCELYN JOSEPH	4	0	0	0	0
1970 Oakland					
HARPER, TERRANCE VICTOR	5	1	0	1	8
1963 Montreal	7	0	0	0	6
1964 "	13	0	0	0	19
1965 * "	10	2	3	5	18
1966 * "	10	0	1	1	15
1967 "	13	0	1	1	8
1968 * "	11	0	0	0	8
1969 * "	20	0	6	6	28
1971 * "	5	1	1	2	6
1972 "	94	4	12	16	116
HARRIS, EDWARD ALEXANDER	13	0	5	5	45
1965 *Montreal	10	0	0	0	38
1966 * "	10	0	1	1	19
1967 "	13	0	4	4	22
1968 * "	14	1	2	3	34
1969 * "	12	0	4	4	36
1971 Minnesota	7	0	1	1	17
1972 "	79	1	17	18	211
HARRIS, RONALD THOMAS	4	0	0	0	8
1970 Detroit					
HARRISON, JAMES DAVID	6	0	1	1	33
1971 Toronto	5	1	0	1	10
1972 "	11	1	1	2	43
HARVEY, DOUGLAS NORMAN	7	0	1	1	10
1949 Montreal	5	0	2	2	10
1950 "	11	0	5	5	12
1951 "	11	0	3	3	8
1952 "	12	0	5	5	8
1953* "	10	0	2	2	12
1954 "	12	0	8	8	6
1955 "	10	2	5	7	10
1956* "	10	0	7	7	10
1957* "	10	2	9	11	16
1958* "	11	1	11	12	22
1959* "	8	3	0	3	6
1960* "	6	0	1	1	8
1961 "	6	0	1	1	8
1962 New York	8	0	4	4	12
1968 St. Louis	137	8	64	72	152
HARVEY, FREDERICK JOHN CHARLES	7	0	0	0	4
1971 Minnesota	1	0	0	0	0
1972 "	8	0	0	0	4
HAYES, CHRISTOPHER JOSEPH LW—SL					
Born: Rouyn, Que., Aug. 24, 1946					
1972 *Boston	1	0	0	0	0
HENDERSON, PAUL GARNET	14	2	3	5	6
1964 Detroit	7	0	2	2	0
1965 "	12	3	3	6	10
1966 "	4	0	1	1	0
1969 Toronto	6	5	1	6	4
1971 "	5	1	2	3	6
1972 "	48	11	12	23	26

Sea. Club	Ga.	Go.	A.	P.	PM.
HENRY, CAMILLE JOSEPH WILFRID					
1957 New York Rangers	5	2	3	5	0
1958 " " "	6	1	4	5	5
1962 " " "	5	0	0	0	0
1965 Chicago	14	1	0	1	2
1968 New York Rangers	6	0	0	0	0
1969 St. Louis	10	2	5	7	0
	46	6	12	18	7
HEXTALL, BRYAN LEE					
1970 Pittsburgh	10	0	1	1	34
1972 "	4	0	2	2	9
	14	0	3	3	43
HEXTALL, DENNIS HAROLD					
1968 New York Rangers	2	0	0	0	0
1972 Minnesota	7	0	2	2	19
	9	0	2	2	19
HICKE, WILLIAM LAWRENCE					
1959 *Montreal	1	0	0	0	0
1960 * "	7	1	2	3	0
1961 "	5	2	0	2	19
1962 "	6	0	2	2	14
1963 "	5	0	0	0	0
1964 "	7	0	2	2	2
1969 Oakland	7	0	3	3	4
1970 "	4	0	1	1	2
	42	3	10	13	41
HILLMAN, LAWRENCE MORLEY					
1955 *Detroit	3	0	0	0	0
1956 "	10	0	1	1	6
1958 Boston	11	0	2	2	6
1959 "	7	0	1	1	0
1961 Toronto	5	0	0	0	0
1964 * "	11	0	0	0	2
1966 "	4	1	1	2	6
1967 "	12	1	2	3	0
1969 *Montreal	1	0	0	0	0
1971 Philadelphia	4	0	2	2	2
	68	2	9	11	22
HILLMAN, WAYNE JAMES					
1961 *Chicago	1	0	0	0	0
1963 "	6	0	2	2	2
1964 "	7	0	1	1	15
1967 New York	4	0	0	0	2
1968 " "	2	0	0	0	0
	20	0	3	3	19
HODGE, KENNETH RAYMOND					
1966 Chicago	5	0	0	0	8
1967 "	6	0	0	0	4
1968 Boston	4	3	0	3	2
1969 "	10	5	7	12	4
1970 * "	14	3	10	13	17
1971 "	7	2	5	7	6
1972 * "	15	9	8	17	62
	61	22	30	52	103
HORNUNG, LARRY JOHN					
1972 St. Louis	11	0	2	2	2
HORTON, MYLES GILBERT					
1950 Toronto	1	0	0	0	2
1954 "	5	1	1	2	4
1956 "	2	0	0	0	4
1959 "	12	0	3	3	16
1960 "	10	0	1	1	5
1961 "	5	0	0	0	0
1962 * "	12	3	13	16	16
1963 * "	10	1	3	4	10
1964 * "	14	0	4	4	20
1965 "	6	0	2	2	13
1966 "	4	1	0	1	12
1967 * "	12	3	5	8	25
1969 "	4	0	0	0	7
1970 New York Rangers	6	1	1	2	28
1971 " " "	13	1	4	5	14
1972 Pittsburgh	4	0	1	1	2
	120	11	38	49	179
HOULE, REJEAN					
1971 *Montreal	20	2	5	7	20
1972 "	6	0	0	0	2
	26	2	5	7	22
HOWE, GORDON					
1947 Detroit	5	0	0	0	18
1948 "	10	1	1	2	11

(continued)

Sea. Club	Ga.	Go.	A.	P.	PM.
1949 "	11	8	3	11	19
1950 * "	1	0	0	0	7
1951 "	6	4	3	7	4
1952 * "	8	2	5	7	2
1953 "	6	2	5	7	2
1954 * "	12	4	5	9	31
1955 * "	11	9	11	20	24
1956 "	10	3	9	12	8
1957 "	5	2	5	7	6
1958 "	4	1	1	2	0
1960 "	6	1	5	6	4
1961 "	11	4	11	15	10
1963 "	11	7	9	16	22
1964 "	14	9	10	19	16
1965 "	7	4	2	6	20
1966 "	12	4	6	10	12
1970 "	4	2	0	2	2
	154	67	91	158	218
HOWELL, HENRY VERNON					
1956 New York Rangers	5	0	1	1	4
1957 " " "	5	1	0	1	6
1958 " " "	6	1	0	1	8
1962 " " "	6	0	1	1	8
1967 " " "	4	0	0	0	4
1968 " " "	6	1	0	1	0
1969 " " "	2	0	0	0	0
1970 Oakland	4	0	1	1	2
	38	3	3	6	32
HUCK, ANTHONY FRANCIS					
1971 St. Louis	6	1	2	3	2
HUGHES, BRENTON ALEXANDER					
1968 Los Angeles	7	0	0	0	10
1969 " "	11	1	3	4	37
1971 Philadelphia	4	0	0	0	6
	22	1	3	4	53
HUGHES, HOWARD DUNCAN					
1968 Los Angeles	7	2	0	2	0
1969 " "	7	0	0	0	2
	14	2	0	2	2
HULL, DENNIS WILLIAM					
1965 Chicago	6	0	0	0	0
1966 "	3	0	0	0	0
1967 "	6	0	1	1	12
1968 "	11	1	3	4	6
1970 "	8	5	2	7	0
1971 "	18	7	6	13	2
1972 "	8	4	2	6	4
	60	17	14	31	24
HULL, ROBERT MARVIN					
1959 Chicago	6	1	1	2	2
1960 "	3	1	0	1	2
1961 * "	12	4	10	14	4
1962 "	12	8	5	13	10
1963 "	5	8	2	10	4
1964 "	7	2	5	7	2
1965 "	14	10	7	17	27
1966 "	6	2	2	4	10
1967 "	6	4	2	6	0
1968 "	11	4	6	10	15
1970 "	8	3	8	11	2
1971 "	18	11	14	25	16
1972 "	8	4	4	8	6
	116	62	66	128	100
INGARFIELD, EARL THOMPSON					
1962 New York Rangers	6	3	2	5	2
1967 " " "	4	1	0	1	2
1969 Oakland	7	4	6	10	2
1970 "	4	1	0	1	4
	21	9	8	17	10
INGLIS, WILLIAM JOHN					
1969 Los Angeles	11	1	2	3	4
IRVINE, EDWARD AMOS					
1968 Los Angeles	6	1	3	4	2
1969 " "	11	5	1	6	7
1970 New York Rangers	6	1	2	3	8
1971 " " "	12	1	2	3	28
1972 " " "	16	4	5	9	19
	51	12	13	25	64

Sea. Club	Ga.	Go.	A.	P.	PM.
JARRETT, DOUGLAS WILLIAM					
1965 Chicago	11	1	0	1	10
1966 "	5	0	1	1	9
1967 "	6	0	3	3	8
1968 "	11	4	0	4	9
1970 "	8	1	0	1	4
1971 "	18	1	6	7	14
1972 "	8	0	2	2	16
	67	7	12	19	70
JARRETT, GARY WALTER					
1969 Oakland	7	2	1	3	4
1970 "	4	1	0	1	6
	11	3	1	4	10
JARRY, PIERRE JOSEPH REYNALD					
1972 Toronto	5	0	1	1	0
JEFFREY, LAWRENCE JOSEPH					
1963 Detroit	9	3	3	6	8
1964 "	14	1	6	7	28
1965 "	2	0	0	0	0
1967 *Toronto	6	0	1	1	4
1968 New York Rangers	3	0	0	0	0
1969 " " "	4	0	0	0	2
	38	4	10	14	42
JOHNSON, NORMAN JAMES					
1969 Philadelphia	3	0	0	0	2
1971 "	4	0	2	2	0
	7	0	2	2	2
JOHNSTON, MARSHALL					
1970 Minnesota	6	0	0	0	2
JOYAL, EDWARD ABEL					
1963 Detroit	11	1	0	1	2
1964 "	14	2	3	5	10
1965 "	7	1	1	2	4
1968 Los Angeles	7	4	1	5	2
1969 " "	11	3	3	6	0
	50	11	8	19	18
KARLANDER, ALLAN DAVID					
1970 Detroit	4	0	1	1	0
KEENAN, LAWRENCE CHRISTOPHER					
1968 St. Louis	18	4	5	9	4
1969 "	12	4	5	9	8
1970 " "	16	7	6	13	0
	46	15	16	31	12
KEHOE, RICK					
1972 Toronto	2	0	0	0	2
KELLY, ROBERT JAMES					
1971 Philadelphia	4	1	0	1	2
KENNEDY, FORBES TAYLOR					
1958 Detroit	4	1	0	1	12
1968 Philadelphia	7	1	4	5	14
1969 Toronto	1	0	0	0	38
	12	2	4	6	64
KEON, DAVID MICHAEL					
1961 Toronto	5	1	1	2	0
1962 * "	12	5	3	8	0
1963 * "	10	7	5	12	0
1964 * "	14	7	2	9	2
1965 "	6	2	2	4	2
1966 "	4	0	2	2	0
1967 * "	12	3	5	8	0
1969 "	4	1	3	4	2
1971 "	6	3	2	5	0
1972 "	5	2	3	5	0
	78	31	28	59	6
1967 Conn Smythe Trophy					
KORAB, GERALD JOSEPH					
1971 Chicago	7	1	0	1	20
1972 "	8	0	1	1	20
	15	1	1	2	40
KOROLL, CLIFFORD EUGENE					
1970 Chicago	8	1	4	5	9
1971 "	18	7	9	16	18
1972 "	8	0	0	0	11
	34	8	13	21	38

Sea. Club	Ga.	Go.	A.	P.	PM.
KRAKE, PHILIP GORDON					
1968 Boston	4	0	0	0	2
1969 Los Angeles	6	1	0	1	15
	10	1	0	1	17
KURTENBACH, ORLAND JOHN					
1966 Toronto	4	0	0	0	20
1967 New York Rangers	3	0	2	2	0
1968 " " "	6	1	0	1	26
1970 " " "	6	1	2	3	24
	19	2	4	6	70
LABOSSIERE, WILLIAM GORDON					
1968 Los Angeles	7	2	3	5	24
1971 Minnesota	3	0	0	0	4
	10	2	3	5	28
LACOMBE, FRANCOIS					
1969	3	1	0	1	0
LACROIX, ANDRE JOSEPH					
1968 Philadelphia	7	2	3	5	0
1969 "	4	0	0	0	0
1971 "	4	0	2	2	0
1972 Chicago	1	0	0	0	0
	16	2	5	7	0
LaFORGE, CLAUDE ROGER					
1968 Philadelphia	5	1	2	3	15
LAFLEUR, GUY DAMIEN					
1972 Montreal	6	1	4	5	2
LAPERRIERE, JOSEPH JACQUES HUGUES					
1963 Montreal	5	0	1	1	4
1964 "	7	1	1	2	8
1965 * "	6	1	1	2	16
1967 "	9	0	1	1	9
1968 * "	13	1	3	4	20
1969 * "	14	1	3	4	28
1971 * "	20	4	9	13	12
1972 "	4	0	0	0	2
	78	8	19	27	99
LAPOINTE, GUY GERARD					
1971 * Montreal	20	4	5	9	34
1972 "	6	0	1	1	0
	26	4	6	10	34
LAROSE, CLAUDE DAVID					
1964 Montreal	2	1	0	1	0
1965 * "	13	0	1	1	14
1966 * "	6	0	1	1	31
1967 "	10	1	5	6	15
1968 * "	12	3	2	5	8
1970 Minnesota	6	1	1	2	25
1971 *Montreal	11	1	0	1	10
1972 "	6	2	1	3	23
	66	9	11	20	126
LAUGHTON, MICHAEL FREDERIC					
1969 Oakland	7	3	2	5	0
1970 "	4	0	1	1	0
	11	3	3	6	0
LAVENDER, BRIAN JAMES					
1972 St. Louis	3	0	0	0	2
LAWSON, DANIEL MICHAEL					
1970 Minnesota	6	0	1	1	2
1971 "	10	0	0	0	0
	16	0	1	1	2
LEACH, REGINALD JOSEPH					
1971 Boston	3	0	0	0	0
LEFLEY, CHARLES THOMAS					
1971 *Montreal	1	0	0	0	0
LEITER, ROBERT EDWARD					
1972 Pittsburgh	4	3	0	3	0
LEMAIRE, JACQUES GERARD					
1968 *Montreal	13	7	6	13	6
1969 * "	14	4	2	6	6
1971 * "	20	9	10	19	17
1972 "	6	2	1	3	2
	53	22	19	41	31

Sea. Club	Ga.	Go.	A.	P.	PM.
LEMIEUX, JACQUES LEONARD					
1969 Los Angeles	1	0	0	0	0
LEMIEUX, REAL GASTON					
1968 Los Angeles	7	1	1	2	0
1969 "	11	1	3	4	10
	18	2	4	6	10
LESUK, WILLIAM ANTON					
1969 Boston	1	0	0	0	0
1970 * "	2	0	0	0	0
1971 Philadelphia	4	1	0	1	8
	7	1	0	1	8
LEY, RICHARD NORMAN					
1969 Toronto	3	0	0	0	9
1971 "	6	0	2	2	4
1972 "	5	0	0	0	7
	14	0	2	2	20
LIBETT, LYNN NICHOLAS					
1970 Detroit	4	2	0	2	2
LORENTZ, JAMES PETER					
1970 *Boston	11	1	0	1	4
1971 St. Louis	6	0	1	1	4
	17	1	1	2	8
LUCE, DONALD HAROLD					
1970 New York Rangers	5	0	1	1	4
MacDONALD, CALVIN PARKER					
1955 Toronto	4	0	0	0	4
1957 New York	1	1	1	2	0
1958 " "	6	1	2	3	2
1961 Detroit	9	1	0	1	0
1963 "	11	3	2	5	2
1964 "	14	3	3	6	2
1965 "	7	1	1	2	6
1966 "	9	0	0	0	2
1968 Minnesota	14	4	5	9	2
	75	14	14	28	20
MacDONALD, LOWELL WILSON					
1963 Detroit	1	0	0	0	2
1968 Los Angeles	7	3	4	7	2
1969 " "	7	2	3	5	0
	15	5	7	12	4
MacGREGOR, BRUCE CAMERO √					
1961 Detroit	8	1	2	3	6
1963 "	10	1	4	5	10
1964 "	14	5	2	7	12
1965 "	7	0	2	2	2
1966 "	12	1	4	5	2
1970 "	4	1	0	1	2
1971 New York Rangers	13	0	4	4	2
1972 " " "	16	2	6	8	4
	84	11	24	35	40
MacLEISH, RICHARD GEORGE					
1971 Philadelphia	4	1	0	1	0
MacMILLAN, WILLIAM STEWART					
1971 Toronto	6	0	3	3	2
1972 "	5	0	0	0	0
	11	0	3	3	2
MacSWEYN, DONALD RALPH					
1969 Philadelphia	4	0	0	0	4
1971 "	4	0	0	0	2
	8	0	0	0	6
MAGGS, DARRYL JOHN					
1972 Chicago	4	0	0	0	0
MAGNUSON, KEITH ARLEN					
1970 Chicago	8	1	2	3	17
1971 "	18	0	2	2	63
1972 "	8	0	1	1	29
	34	1	5	6	109
MAHOVLICH, FRANCIS WILLIAM					
1959 Toronto	12	6	5	11	18
1960 "	10	3	1	4	27
1961 "	5	1	1	2	6
1962 * "	12	6	6	12	29
1963 * "	9	0	2	2	8
1964 * "	14	4	11	15	20

(continued)

Sea. Club	Ga.	Go.	A.	P.	PM.
1965 "	6	0	3	3	9
1966 "	4	1	0	1	10
1967 * "	12	3	7	10	8
1970 Detroit	4	0	0	0	2
1971 *Montreal	20	14	13	27	18
1972 "	6	3	2	5	2
	114	41	51	92	157
MAHOVLICH, PETER JOSEPH					
1971 *Montreal	20	10	6	16	43
1972 "	6	0	2	2	12
	26	10	8	18	55
MAIR, JAMES McKAY					
1971 Philadelphia	4	1	2	3	4
MAKI, RONALD PATRICK					
1961 *Chicago	1	0	0	0	0
1963 "	6	0	1	1	2
1964 "	7	0	0	0	15
1965 "	14	3	9	12	8
1966 "	3	1	1	2	0
1967 "	6	0	0	0	0
1968 "	11	2	5	7	4
1970 "	8	2	2	4	2
1971 "	18	6	5	11	6
1972 "	8	1	4	5	4
	82	15	27	42	41
MAKI, WAYNE					
1968 Chicago	2	1	0	1	2
MALONEY, DANIEL CHARLES					
1971 Chicago	10	0	1	1	8
MARCETTA, MILAN					
1967 *Toronto	3	0	0	0	0
1968 Minnesota	14	7	7	14	4
	17	7	7	14	4
MARCOTTE, DONALD MICHEL					
1970 *Boston	14	2	0	2	11
1971 "	4	0	0	0	0
1972 * "	14	3	0	3	6
	32	5	0	5	17
MAROTTE, JEAN GILLES					
1968 Chicago	11	3	1	4	14
MARSHALL, ALBERT LEROY					
1966 Detroit	12	1	3	4	16
1969 Oakland	7	0	7	7	20
1970 "	4	0	1	1	12
	23	1	11	12	48
MARSHALL, DONALD ROBERT					
1955 Montreal	12	1	1	2	2
1956 * "	10	1	0	1	0
1957 * "	10	1	3	4	2
1958 * "	10	0	2	2	4
1959 * "	11	0	2	2	2
1960 * "	8	2	2	4	0
1961 "	6	0	2	2	0
1962 "	6	0	1	1	2
1963 "	5	0	0	0	0
1967 New York Rangers	4	0	1	1	2
1968 " " "	6	2	1	3	0
1969 " " "	4	1	0	1	0
1970 " " "	1	0	0	0	0
1972 Toronto	1	0	0	0	0
	94	8	15	23	14
MARTIN, HUBERT JACQUES					
1964 Detroit	14	1	4	5	14
1965 "	3	0	1	1	2
1968 Chicago	11	3	6	9	2
1970 "	8	3	3	6	4
1971 "	17	2	7	9	12
1972 "	8	4	2	6	4
	61	13	23	36	38
MATTIUSSI, RICHARD ARTHUR					
1969 Oakland	7	0	1	1	6
1970 "	1	0	0	0	0
	8	0	1	1	6
McCALLUM, DUNCAN SELBY					
1970 Pittsburgh	10	1	2	3	12
McCORD, ROBERT LOMER					
1968 Minnesota	14	2	5	7	10

Sea. Club	Ga.	Go.	A.	P.	PM.
McCREARY, VERNON KEITH					
1962 Montreal	1	0	0	0	0
1970 Pittsburgh	10	0	4	4	4
1972 "	1	0	0	0	2
	12	0	4	4	6
McCREARY, WILLIAM EDWARD					
1968 St. Louis	15	3	2	5	0
1969 " "	12	1	5	6	14
1970 " "	15	1	7	8	0
1971 " "	6	1	2	3	0
	48	6	16	22	14
McDONALD, ALVIN BRIAN					
1958 *Montreal	2	0	0	0	2
1959 *	11	1	1	2	6
1961 *Chicago	8	2	2	4	0
1962 "	12	6	6	12	0
1963 "	6	2	3	5	9
1964 "	7	2	2	4	0
1966 Detroit	10	1	4	5	4
1969 St. Louis	12	2	1	3	10
1970 " "	16	5	10	15	13
	84	21	29	50	44
McDONALD, BRIAN HAROLD					
1968 Chicago	8	0	0	0	2
McDONOUGH, JAMES ALLISON					
1972 Pittsburgh	4	0	1	1	0
McKAY, RAY OWEN					
1970 Chicago	1	0	0	0	0
McKECHNIE, WALTER THOMAS JOHN					
1968 Minnesota	9	3	2	5	0
McKENNY, JAMES CLAUDE					
1971 Toronto	6	2	1	3	2
1972 "	5	3	0	3	2
	11	5	1	6	4
McKENZIE, JOHN ALBERT					
1959 Chicago	2	0	0	0	2
1960 Detroit	2	0	0	0	0
1964 Chicago	4	0	1	1	6
1965 "	11	0	1	1	6
1968 Boston	4	1	1	2	8
1969 "	10	2	2	4	17
1970 * "	14	5	12	17	35
1971 "	7	2	3	5	22
1972 * "	15	5	12	17	37
	69	15	32	47	133
McMAHON, MICHAEL WILLIAM					
1968 Minnesota	14	3	7	10	4
MEEHAN, GERALD MARCUS					
1969 Philadelphia	4	0	0	0	0
MENARD, HOWARD HUBERT					
1968 Los Angeles	7	0	5	5	24
1969 " "	11	3	2	5	12
1970 Oakland	1	0	0	0	0
	19	3	7	10	36
MICKEY, ROBERT LARRY					
1969 Toronto	3	0	0	0	5
MIKITA, STANLEY					
1960 Chicago	3	0	1	1	2
1961 * "	12	6	5	11	21
1962 "	12	6	15	21	19
1963 "	6	3	2	5	2
1964 "	7	3	6	9	8
1965 "	14	3	7	10	53
1966 "	6	1	2	3	2
1967 "	6	2	2	4	2
1968 "	11	5	7	12	6
1970 "	8	4	6	10	2
1971 "	18	5	13	18	16
1972 "	8	3	1	4	14
	111	41	67	108	137
MISZUK, JOHN STANLEY					
1964 Detroit	3	0	0	0	2
1966 Chicago	3	0	0	0	4
1967 "	2	0	0	0	2
1968 Philadelphia	7	0	3	3	11
1969 "	4	0	0	0	4
	19	0	3	3	23

Sea. Club	Ga.	Go.	A.	P.	PM.
MOHNS, DOUGLAS ALLEN					
1954 Boston	4	1	0	1	4
1955 "	5	0	0	0	4
1957 "	10	2	3	5	2
1958 "	12	3	10	13	18
1959 "	4	0	2	2	12
1965 Chicago	14	3	4	7	21
1966 "	5	1	0	1	4
1967 "	5	0	5	5	8
1968 "	11	1	5	6	12
1970 "	8	0	2	2	15
1971 Minnesota	6	2	2	4	10
1972 "	4	1	2	3	10
	88	14	35	49	120
MONAHAN, GARRY MICHAEL					
1971 Toronto	6	2	0	2	2
1972 "	5	0	0	0	0
	11	2	0	2	2
MONTEITH, HENRY GEORGE					
1970 Detroit	4	0	0	0	0
MORRISON, GEORGE HAROLD					
1971 St. Louis	3	0	0	0	0
MORRISON, JAMES STUART HUNTER					
1952 Toronto	2	0	0	0	0
1954 "	5	0	0	0	4
1955 "	4	0	1	1	4
1956 "	5	0	0	0	4
1959 Boston	6	0	6	6	16
1960 Detroit	6	0	2	2	0
1970 Pittsburgh	8	0	3	3	10
	36	0	12	12	38
MORRISON, LEWIS					
1971 Philadelphia	4	0	0	0	2
MULOIN, JOHN WAYNE					
1970 Oakland	4	0	0	0	0
1971 Minnesota	7	0	0	0	2
	11	0	0	0	2
MURDOCH, ROBERT JOHN					
1971 *Montreal	2	0	0	0	0
1972 "	1	0	0	0	0
	3	0	0	0	0
MURPHY, MICHAEL JOHN					
1972 St. Louis	11	2	3	5	6
MURPHY, ROBERT RONALD					
1956 New York Rangers	5	0	1	1	2
1957 " " "	5	0	0	0	0
1960 Chicago	4	1	0	1	0
1961 * "	12	2	1	3	0
1963 "	1	0	0	0	0
1964 "	7	0	1	1	8
1965 Detroit	5	0	1	1	4
1968 Boston	4	0	0	0	0
1969 "	10	4	4	8	12
	53	7	8	15	26
NANNE, LOUIS VINCENT					
1970 Minnesota	5	0	2	2	2
1971 "	12	3	6	9	4
1972 "	7	0	0	0	0
	24	3	8	11	6
NEILSON, JAMES ANTHONY					
1967 New York Rangers	4	1	0	1	0
1968 " " "	6	0	1	1	4
1969 " " "	4	0	3	3	5
1970 " " "	6	0	1	1	8
1971 " " "	13	0	3	3	30
1972 " " "	10	0	3	3	8
	43	1	11	12	55
NESTERENKO, ERIC PAUL					
1954 Toronto	5	0	1	1	9
1955 "	4	0	1	1	6
1959 Chicago	6	2	2	4	8
1960 "	4	0	0	0	2
1961 * "	11	2	3	5	6
1962 "	12	0	5	5	22
1963 "	6	2	3	5	8
1964 "	7	2	1	3	8
1965 "	14	2	2	4	16
1966 "	6	1	0	1	4
1967 "	6	1	2	3	2
1968 "	10	0	1	1	2
1970 "	7	1	2	3	4
1971 "	18	0	1	1	19
1972 "	8	0	0	0	11
	124	13	24	37	127

Sea. Club	Ga.	Go.	A.	P.	PM.
NEVIN, ROBERT FRANK					
1961 Toronto	5	1	0	1	2
1962 * "	12	2	4	6	6
1963 * "	10	3	0	3	2
1967 New York Rangers	4	0	3	3	2
1968 " " "	6	0	3	3	4
1969 " " "	4	0	2	2	0
1970 " " "	6	1	1	2	2
1971 " " "	13	5	3	8	0
1972 Minnesota	7	1	1	2	0
	67	13	17	30	18
NICHOLSON, NEIL D-SR					
Born: St. John, New Brunswick, Sept. 12,					
1970 Oakland	2	0	0	0	0
NOLET, SIMON LAURENT					
1968 Philadelphia	1	0	0	0	0
1971 "	4	2	1	3	0
	5	2	1	3	0
O'BRIEN, DENNIS FRANCIS					
1971 Minnesota	9	0	0	0	20
1972 "	3	0	1	1	11
	12	0	1	1	31
O'DONOGHUE, DONALD FRANCIS					
1970 Oakland	3	0	0	0	0
ODROWSKI, GERALD BERNARD					
1961 Detroit	10	0	0	0	4
1963 "	2	0	0	0	2
1969 Oakland	7	0	1	1	2
1972 St. Louis	11	0	0	0	8
	30	0	1	1	16
OLIVER, MURRAY CLIFFORD					
1960 Detroit	6	1	0	1	4
1969 Toronto	4	1	2	3	0
1971 Minnesota	12	7	5	12	0
1972 "	7	0	6	6	4
	29	9	13	22	8
ORBAN, WILLIAM TERRANCE					
1968 Chicago	3	0	0	0	0
ORR, ROBERT GORDON					
1968 Boston	4	0	2	2	2
1969 "	10	1	7	8	10
1970 * "	14	9	11	20	14
1971 "	7	5	7	12	25
1972 * "	15	5	19	24	19
	50	20	46	66	70
1970 Conn Smythe Trophy					
1972 " "					
O'SHEA, DANIEL PATRICK					
1970 Minnesota	6	1	0	1	8
1971 Chicago	18	2	5	7	15
1972 St. Louis	10	0	2	2	36
	34	3	7	10	59
O'SHEA, KEVIN WILLIAM					
1972 St. Louis	11	2	1	3	10
PAIEMENT, JOSEPH WILFRID ROSAIRE					
1968 Philadelphia	3	3	0	3	0
PAPPIN, JAMES JOSEPH					
1964 *Toronto	11	0	0	0	0
1967 * "	12	7	8	15	12
1970 Chicago	8	3	2	5	6
1971 "	18	10	4	14	24
1972 "	8	2	5	7	4
	57	22	19	41	46
PARADISE, ROBERT H.					
1972 Minnesota	4	0	0	0	2
PARISE, JEAN-PAUL					
1968 Minnesota	14	2	5	7	10
1970 "	6	3	2	5	2
1971 "	12	3	3	6	22
1972 "	7	3	3	6	6
	39	11	13	24	40
PARK, DOUGLAS BRADFORD					
1969 New York Rangers	4	0	2	2	7
1970 " " "	5	1	2	3	11
1971 " " "	13	0	4	4	42
1972 " " "	16	4	7	11	21
	38	5	15	20	81

Sea. Club	Ga.	Go.	A.	P.	PM.
PELYK, MICHAEL JOSEPH					
1969 Toronto	4	0	0	0	8
1971 "	6	0	0	0	10
1972 "	5	0	0	0	8
	15	0	0	0	26
PERRY, BRIAN THOMAS					
1969 Oakland	6	1	1	2	4
1970 "	2	0	0	0	0
	8	1	1	2	4
PETERS, GARRY LORNE					
1969 Philadelphia	4	1	1	2	16
1971 "	4	1	1	2	15
1972 *Boston	1	0	0	0	0
	9	2	2	4	31
PETERS, JAMES STEPHEN					
1969 Los Angeles	11	0	2	2	4
PICARD, JEAN-NOEL YVES					
1965 *Montreal	3	0	1	1	0
1968 St. Louis	13	0	3	3	46
1969 " "	12	1	4	5	30
1970 " "	16	0	2	2	65
1971 " "	6	1	1	2	26
	50	2	11	13	167
PILOTE, PIERRE PAUL					
1959 Chicago	6	0	2	2	10
1960 "	4	0	1	1	8
1961 * "	12	3	12	15	8
1962 "	12	0	7	7	8
1963 "	6	0	8	8	8
1964 "	7	2	6	8	6
1965 "	12	0	7	7	22
1966 "	6	0	2	2	10
1967 "	6	2	4	6	6
1968 "	11	1	3	4	12
1969 Toronto	4	0	1	1	4
	86	8	53	61	102
PINDER, ALLEN GERALD					
1970 Chicago	8	0	4	4	4
1971 "	9	0	0	0	2
	17	0	4	4	6
PLAGER, BARCLAY GRAHAM					
1968 St. Louis	18	2	5	7	73
1969 " "	12	0	4	4	31
1970 " "	13	0	2	2	20
1971 " "	6	0	3	3	10
1972 " "	11	1	4	5	21
	60	3	18	21	155
PLAGER, ROBERT BRYAN					
1968 St. Louis	18	1	2	3	69
1969 " "	9	0	4	4	47
1970 " "	16	0	3	3	46
1971 " "	6	0	2	2	4
1972 " "	11	1	4	5	5
	60	2	15	17	171
PLAGER, WILLIAM RONALD					
1968 Minnesota	12	0	2	2	8
1969 St. Louis	4	0	0	0	4
1970 " "	3	0	0	0	0
1971 " "	1	0	0	0	2
1972 " "	11	0	0	0	12
	31	0	2	2	26
PLEAU, LAWRENCE WINSLOW					
1972 Montreal	4	0	0	0	0
POLANIC, THOMAS JOSEPH					
1970 Minnesota	5	1	1	2	4
POLIS, GREGORY LINN					
1972 Pittsburgh	4	0	2	2	0
POPIEL, POUL PETER					
1968 Los Angeles	3	1	0	1	4
1970 Detroit	1	0	0	0	0
	4	1	0	1	4
PRATT, TRACY ARNOLD					
1970 Pittsburgh	10	0	1	1	51

Sea.	Club	Ga.	Go.	A.	P.	PM.
PRENTICE, DEAN SUTHERLAND						
1956	New York Rangers	5	1	0	1	2
1957	" " "	5	0	2	2	4
1958	" " "	6	1	3	4	4
1962	" " "	3	0	2	2	0
1966	Detroit	12	5	5	10	4
1970	Pittsburgh	10	2	5	7	8
1972	Minnesota	7	3	0	3	0
		48	12	17	29	22
PRONOVOST, JOSEPH ARMAND ANDRE						
1957	*Montreal	8	1	0	1	4
1958 *	"	10	2	0	2	16
1959 *	"	11	2	1	3	6
1960 *	"	8	1	2	3	0
1963	Detroit	11	1	4	5	6
1964	"	14	4	3	7	26
1968	Minnesota	8	0	1	1	0
		70	11	11	22	58
PRONOVOST, JOSEPH JEAN DENIS						
1970	Pittsburgh	10	3	4	7	2
1972	"	4	1	1	2	0
		14	4	5	9	2
PROVOST, JOSEPH ANTOINE CLAUDE						
1956	*Montreal	10	3	3	6	12
1957 *	"	10	0	1	1	8
1958 *	"	10	1	3	4	8
1959 *	"	11	6	2	8	2
1960 *	"	8	1	1	2	0
1961	"	6	1	3	4	4
1962	"	6	2	2	4	2
1963	"	5	0	1	1	2
1964	"	7	2	2	4	22
1965 *	"	13	2	6	8	12
1966 *	"	10	2	3	5	2
1967	"	7	1	1	2	0
1968 *	"	13	2	8	10	10
1969 *	"	10	2	2	4	2
		126	25	38	63	86
PULFORD, ROBERT JESSE						
1959	Toronto	12	4	4	8	8
1960	"	10	4	1	5	10
1961	"	5	0	0	0	8
1962 *	"	12	7	1	8	24
1963 *	"	10	2	5	7	14
1964 *	"	14	5	3	8	20
1965	"	5	1	1	2	16
1966	"	4	1	1	2	12
1967 *	"	12	1	10	11	12
1969	"	4	0	0	0	2
		88	25	26	51	126
QUINN, JOHN BRIAN PATRICK						
1969	Toronto	4	0	0	0	13
RATELLE, JOSEPH GILBERT YVON JEAN						
1967	New York Rangers	4	0	0	0	2
1968	" " "	6	0	4	4	2
1969	" " "	4	1	0	1	0
1970	" " "	6	1	3	4	0
1971	" " "	13	2	9	11	8
1972	" " "	6	0	1	1	0
		39	4	17	21	12
RAVLICH, MATTHEW JOSEPH						
1965	Chicago	14	1	4	5	14
1966	"	6	0	1	1	2
1968	"	4	0	0	0	0
		24	1	5	6	16
REDMOND, MICHAEL EDWARD						
1968	*Montreal	2	0	0	0	0
1969 *	"	14	2	3	5	2
		16	2	3	5	2
REID, ALLAN THOMAS						
1968	Chicago	9	0	0	0	2
1970	Minnesota	6	0	1	1	4
1971	"	12	0	6	6	20
1972	"	7	1	4	5	17
		34	1	11	12	43
RICHARD, JOSEPH HENRI						
1956	*Montreal	10	4	4	8	21
1957 *	"	10	2	6	8	10
1958 *	"	10	1	7	8	11
1959 *	"	11	3	8	11	13

(continued)

Sea.	Club	Ga.	Go.	A.	P.	PM.
1960 *	"	8	3	9	12	9
1961	"	6	2	4	6	22
1963	"	5	1	1	2	2
1964	"	7	1	1	2	9
1965 *	"	13	7	4	11	24
1966 *	"	8	1	4	5	2
1967	"	10	4	6	10	2
1968 *	"	13	4	4	8	4
1969 *	"	14	2	4	6	8
1971 *	"	20	5	7	12	20
1972	"	6	0	3	3	4
		151	40	72	112	161
ROBERTO, PHILLIP						
1971	*Montreal	15	0	1	1	36
1972	St. Louis	11	7	6	13	29
		26	7	7	14	65
ROBERTS, DOUGLAS WILLIAM						
1969	Oakland	7	0	1	1	34
1970	"	4	0	2	2	6
		11	0	3	3	40
ROBERTS, JAMES WILFRED						
1964	Montreal	7	0	1	1	14
1965 *	"	13	0	0	0	30
1966 *	"	10	1	1	2	10
1967	"	4	1	0	1	0
1968	St. Louis	18	4	1	5	20
1969	" "	12	1	4	5	10
1970	" "	16	2	3	5	29
1971	" "	6	2	1	3	11
1972	Montreal	6	1	0	1	0
		92	12	11	23	124
ROBINSON, DOUGLAS GARNET						
1964	Chicago	4	0	0	0	0
1968	Los Angeles	7	4	3	7	0
		11	4	3	7	0
ROCHEFORT, LEON JOSEPH FERNAND						
1966	*Montreal	4	1	1	2	4
1967	"	10	1	1	2	4
1968	Philadelphia	7	2	0	2	2
1969	"	3	0	0	0	0
1971	*Montreal	10	0	0	0	6
		34	4	2	6	16
ROLFE, DALE						
1968	Los Angeles	7	0	1	1	14
1969	" "	10	0	4	4	8
1970	Detroit	4	0	2	2	8
1971	New York Rangers	13	0	1	1	14
1972	" " "	16	4	3	7	16
		50	4	11	15	60
ROUSSEAU, JOSEPH JEAN-PAUL ROBERT						
1962	Montreal	6	0	2	2	0
1963	"	5	0	1	1	2
1964	"	7	1	1	2	2
1965 *	"	13	5	8	13	24
1966 *	"	10	4	4	8	6
1967	"	10	1	7	8	4
1968 *	"	13	2	4	6	8
1969 *	"	14	3	2	5	8
1971	Minnesota	12	2	6	8	0
1972	New York Rangers	16	6	11	17	7
		106	24	46	70	61
RUPP, DUANE EDWARD FRANKLIN						
1970	Pittsburgh	6	2	2	4	2
1972	"	4	0	0	0	6
		10	2	2	4	8
SABOURIN, GARY BRUCE						
1968	St. Louis	18	4	2	6	30
1969	" "	12	6	5	11	12
1970	" "	16	5	0	5	10
1972	" "	11	3	3	6	6
		57	18	10	28	58
ST. MARSEILLE, FRANCIS LEO						
1968	St. Louis	18	5	8	13	0
1969	" "	12	3	3	6	0
1970	" "	15	6	7	13	4
1971	" "	6	2	1	3	4
1972	" "	11	3	5	8	6
		62	19	24	43	14

Sea. Club	Ga.	Go.	A.	P.	PM
SANDERSON, DEREK MICHAEL					
1968 Boston	4	0	2	2	9
1969 "	9	8	2	10	36
1970 * "	14	5	4	9	72
1971 "	7	2	1	3	13
1972 * "	11	1	1	2	44
	45	16	10	26	174
SARRAZIN, RICHARD					
1969 Philadelphia	4	0	0	0	0
SATHER, GLEN CAMERON					
1968 Boston	3	0	0	0	0
1969 "	10	0	0	0	18
1970 Pittsburgh	10	0	2	2	17
1971 New York Rangers	13	0	1	1	18
1972 " " "	16	0	1	1	22
	52	0	4	4	75
SAVARD, SERGE A.					
1968 *Montreal	6	2	0	2	0
1969 * "	14	4	6	10	24
1972 "	6	0	0	0	10
	26	6	6	12	34
1969 Conn Smythe Trophy					
SCHINKEL, KENNETH CALVIN					
1962 New York Rangers	2	1	0	1	0
1967 "	4	0	1	1	0
1970 Pittsburgh	10	4	1	5	4
1972 "	3	2	0	2	0
	19	7	2	9	4
SCHMAUTZ, ROBERT JAMES					
1968 Chicago	11	2	3	5	2
SCHOCK, DANIEL PATRICK					
1970 *Boston	1	0	0	0	0
SCHOCK, RONALD LAWRENCE					
1968 St. Louis	12	1	2	3	0
1969 " "	12	1	2	3	6
1970 Pittsburgh	10	1	6	7	7
1972 "	4	1	0	1	6
	38	4	10	14	19
SEILING, RODNEY ALBERT					
1968 New York Rangers	6	1	2	3	4
1969 " " "	4	1	0	1	2
1970 " " "	2	0	0	0	0
1971 " " "	13	1	0	1	12
1972 " " "	16	1	4	5	10
	41	4	6	10	28
SELBY, ROBERT BRITON					
1966 Toronto	4	0	0	0	0
1968 Philadelphia	7	1	1	2	4
1969 Toronto	4	0	0	0	4
1971 St. Louis	1	0	0	0	0
	16	1	1	2	8
SELWOOD, BRADLEY WAYNE					
1972 Toronto	5	0	0	0	4
SHACK, EDWARD STEVEN PHILLIP					
1961 Toronto	4	0	0	0	2
1962 * "	9	0	0	0	18
1963 * "	10	2	1	3	11
1964 * "	13	0	1	1	25
1965 "	5	1	0	1	8
1966 "	4	2	1	3	33
1967 * "	8	0	0	0	8
1968 Boston	4	0	1	1	6
1969 "	9	0	2	2	23
1972 Pittsburgh	4	0	1	1	15
	70	5	7	12	149
SHEEHAN, ROBERT RICHARD					
1971 *Montreal	6	0	0	0	0
SHMYR, PAUL					
1970 Chicago	7	0	0	0	8
1971 "	9	0	0	0	17
	16	0	0	0	25
SITTLER, DARRYL GLEN					
1971 Toronto	6	2	1	3	31
1972 "	3	0	0	0	2
	9	2	1	3	33
SMITH, BRIAN DESMOND					
1968 Los Angeles	7	0	0	0	0

Sea. Club	Ga.	Go.	A.	P.	PM
SMITH, DALLAS EARL					
1968 Boston	4	0	2	2	0
1969 "	10	0	3	3	16
1970 * "	14	0	3	3	19
1971 "	7	0	3	3	26
1972 * "	15	0	4	4	22
	50	0	15	15	83
SMITH, FLOYD ROBERT DONALD					
1963 Detroit	11	2	3	5	4
1964 "	14	4	3	7	4
1965 "	7	1	3	4	4
1966 "	12	5	2	7	4
1969 Toronto	4	0	0	0	0
	48	12	11	23	16
SMITH, RICHARD ALLAN					
1969 Boston	9	0	0	0	6
1970 * "	14	1	3	4	17
1971 "	6	0	0	0	0
	29	1	3	4	23
SPEER, FRANCIS WILLIAM					
1970 *Boston	8	1	0	1	4
SPENCER, BRIAN ROY					
1971 Toronto	6	0	1	1	17
STANFIELD, FREDERIC WILLIAM					
1965 Chicago	14	2	1	3	2
1966 "	5	0	0	0	2
1967 "	1	0	0	0	0
1968 Boston	4	0	1	1	0
1969 "	10	2	2	4	0
1970 * "	14	4	12	16	6
1971 "	7	3	4	7	0
1972 * "	15	7	9	16	0
	70	18	29	47	10
STANKIEWICZ, MYRON					
1969 Philadelphia	1	0	0	0	0
STANLEY, ALLAN HERBERT					
1950 New York Rangers	12	2	5	7	10
1958 Boston	12	1	3	4	6
1959 Toronto	12	0	3	3	2
1960 "	10	2	3	5	2
1961 "	5	0	3	3	0
1962 * "	12	0	3	3	6
1963 * "	10	1	6	7	8
1964 * "	14	1	6	7	20
1965 "	6	0	1	1	12
1966 "	1	0	0	0	0
1967 * "	12	0	2	2	10
1969 Philadelphia	3	0	1	1	4
	109	7	36	43	80
STAPLETON, PATRICK JAMES					
1966 Chicago	6	2	3	5	4
1967 "	6	1	1	2	12
1968 "	11	0	4	4	4
1971 "	18	3	14	17	4
1972 "	8	2	2	4	4
	49	8	24	32	28
STEMKOWSKI, PETER DAVID					
1965 Toronto	6	0	3	3	7
1966 "	4	0	0	0	26
1967 * "	12	5	7	12	20
1970 Detroit	4	1	1	2	6
1971 New York Rangers	13	3	2	5	6
1972 " " "	16	4	8	12	18
	55	13	21	34	83
STEWART, RONALD GEORGE					
1954 Toronto	5	0	1	1	10
1955 "	4	0	0	0	2
1956 "	5	1	1	2	2
1959 "	12	3	3	6	6
1960 "	10	0	2	2	2
1961 "	5	1	0	1	2
1962 * "	11	1	6	7	4
1963 * "	10	4	0	4	2
1964 * "	14	0	4	4	24
1965 "	6	0	1	1	2
1968 New York Rangers	6	1	1	2	2
1969 " " "	4	0	1	1	0
1970 " " "	6	0	0	0	2
1971 " " "	13	1	0	1	0
1972 " " "	8	2	1	3	0
	119	14	21	35	60

Sea. Club	Ga.	Go.	A.	P.	PM.
SUTHERLAND, WILLIAM FRASER					
1963 Montreal	2	0	0	0	0
1968 Philadelphia	7	1	3	4	0
1969 "	4	1	1	2	0
1971 St. Louis	1	0	0	0	0
	14	2	4	6	0
SZURA, JOSEPH BOLESLAW					
1969 Oakland	7	2	3	5	2
TALBOT, JEAN-GUY					
1956 *Montreal	9	0	2	2	4
1957 * "	10	0	2	2	10
1958 * "	10	0	3	3	12
1959 * "	11	0	1	1	10
1960 * "	8	1	1	2	8
1961 "	6	1	1	2	10
1962 "	6	1	1	2	10
1963 "	5	0	0	0	8
1964 "	7	0	2	2	10
1965 * "	13	0	1	1	22
1966 * "	10	0	2	2	8
1967 "	10	0	0	0	0
1968 St. Louis	17	0	2	2	8
1969 " "	12	0	2	2	6
1970 " "	16	1	6	7	16
	150	4	26	30	142
TARDIF, MARC					
1971 *Montreal	20	3	1	4	40
1972 "	6	2	3	5	9
	26	5	4	9	49
TKACZUK, WALTER ROBERT					
1969 New York Rangers	4	0	1	1	6
1970 " " "	6	2	1	3	17
1971 " " "	13	1	5	6	14
1972 " " "	16	4	6	10	35
	39	7	13	20	72
TREMBLAY, JEAN-CLAUDE					
1961 Montreal	5	0	0	0	2
1962 "	6	0	2	2	2
1963 "	5	0	0	0	0
1964 "	7	2	1	3	9
1965 * "	13	1	9	10	18
1966 * "	10	2	9	11	2
1967 "	10	2	4	6	2
1968 * "	13	3	6	9	2
1969 * "	13	1	4	5	6
1971 * "	20	3	14	17	15
1972 "	6	0	2	2	0
	108	14	51	65	58
TREMBLAY, JOSEPH JEAN-GILLES					
1961 Montreal	6	1	3	4	0
1962 "	6	1	0	1	2
1963 "	5	2	0	2	0
1964 "	2	0	0	0	0
1966 * "	10	4	5	9	0
1967 "	10	0	1	1	0
1968 * "	9	1	5	6	2
	48	9	14	23	4
TROTTIER, GUY					
1971 Toronto	5	0	0	0	0
1972 "	4	1	0	1	16
	9	1	0	1	16
UBRIACO, EUGENE STEPHEN					
1969 Oakland	7	2	0	2	2
1970 Chicago	4	0	0	0	2
	11	2	0	2	4
ULLMAN, NORMAN VICTOR ALEXANDER					
1956 Detroit	10	1	3	4	13
1957 "	5	1	1	2	6
1958 "	4	0	2	2	4
1960 "	6	2	2	4	0
1961 "	11	0	4	4	4
1963 "	11	4	12	16	14
1964 "	14	7	10	17	6
1965 "	7	6	4	10	2
1966 "	12	6	9	15	12
1969 Toronto	4	1	0	1	0
1971 "	6	0	2	2	2
1972 "	5	1	3	4	2
	95	29	52	81	65

Sea. Club	Ga.	Go.	A.	P.	PM.
UNGER, GARRY DOUGLAS					
1970 Detroit	4	0	1	1	6
1971 St. Louis	6	3	2	5	20
1972 " "	11	4	5	9	35
	21	7	8	15	61
VADNAIS, CAROL MARCEL					
1967 Montreal	1	0	0	0	2
1968 * "	1	0	0	0	2
1969 Oakland	7	1	4	5	10
1970 "	4	2	1	3	15
1972 *Boston	15	0	2	2	43
	28	3	7	10	72
VAN IMPE, EDWARD CHARLES					
1967 Chicago	6	0	0	0	8
1968 Philadelphia	7	0	4	4	11
1969 "	1	0	0	0	17
1971 "	4	0	1	1	8
	18	0	5	5	44
VASKO, ELMER					
1959 Chicago	6	0	1	1	4
1960 "	4	0	0	0	0
1961 * "	12	1	1	2	23
1962 "	12	0	0	0	4
1963 "	6	0	1	1	8
1964 "	7	0	0	0	4
1965 "	14	1	2	3	20
1966 "	3	0	0	0	4
1968 Minnesota	14	0	2	2	6
	78	2	7	9	73
VOLMAR, DOUGLAS STEVEN					
1970 Detroit	2	1	0	1	0
WALL, ROBERT JAMES ALBERT					
1965 Detroit	1	0	0	0	0
1966 "	6	0	0	0	2
1968 Los Angeles	7	0	1	1	0
1969 " "	8	0	2	2	0
	22	0	3	3	2
WALTON, MICHAEL ROBERT					
1967 *Toronto	12	4	3	7	2
1969 "	4	0	0	0	4
1971 Boston	5	2	0	2	19
1972 * "	15	6	6	12	13
	36	12	9	21	38
WATSON, BRYAN JOSEPH					
1964 Montreal	6	0	0	0	2
1966 Detroit	12	2	0	2	30
1970 Pittsburgh	10	0	0	0	17
1972 "	4	0	0	0	21
	32	2	0	2	70
WATSON, JOSEPH JOHN					
1968 Philadelphia	7	1	1	2	28
1969 "	4	0	0	0	0
1971 "	1	0	0	0	0
	12	1	1	2	28
WEBSTER, THOMAS RONALD					
1969 Boston	1	0	0	0	0
WESTFALL, VERNON EDWIN					
1968 Boston	4	2	0	2	2
1969 "	10	3	7	10	11
1970 * "	14	3	5	8	4
1971 "	7	1	2	3	2
1972 * "	15	4	3	7	10
	50	13	17	30	29
WHARRAM, KENNETH MALCOLM					
1959 Chicago	6	0	2	2	2
1960 "	4	1	1	2	0
1961 * "	12	3	5	8	12
1962 "	12	3	4	7	8
1963 "	6	1	5	6	0
1964 "	7	2	2	4	6
1965 "	12	2	3	5	4
1966 "	6	1	0	1	4
1967 "	6	2	2	4	2
1968 "	9	1	3	4	0
	80	16	27	43	38

Sea. Club	Ga.	Go.	A.	P.	PM.	Sea. Club	Ga.	Go.	A.	P.	PM.
WHITE, WILLIAM EARL						WOYTOWICH, ROBERT IVAN					
1968 Los Angeles	7	2	2	4	4	1968 Minnesota	14	0	1	1	18
1969 " "	11	1	4	5	8	1970 Pittsburgh	10	1	2	3	2
1970 Chicago	8	1	2	3	8		24	1	3	4	20
1971 "	18	1	4	5	20						
1972 "	8	0	3	3	6	ZEIDEL, LAZARUS					
	52	5	15	20	46	1952 *Detroit	5	0	0	0	0
						1968 Philadelphia	7	0	1	1	12
WILLIAMS, THOMAS MARK							12	0	1	1	12
1968 Boston	4	1	0	1	2						
1970 Minnesota	6	1	5	6	0						
	10	2	5	7	2						

Player Records

Career

Most Playoffs

Leonard Kelly	19	Eric Nesterenko	15
Gordon Howe	19	Ronald Stewart	15
Jean Béliveau	17	Emile Bouchard	14
R. B. Theodore Lindsay	16	Richard Moore	14
J. R. Marcel Pronovost	16	J. A. Claude Provost	14
Bernard Geoffrion	16	Alexander Delvecchio	14
Myles Horton	16	Donald Marshall	14
Aubrey Clapper	15	Sidney Abel	13
J. H. Maurice Richard	15	Woodrow Dumart	13
Douglas Harvey	15	Milton Schmidt	13
Jean-Guy Talbot	15	Thomas Johnson	13
George Armstrong	15	Alger Arbour	13
J. Henri Richard	15	Robert Hull	13

Most Games

Leonard Kelly	164	Myles Horton	120
Jean Béliveau	162	Ronald Stewart	119
Gordon Howe	154	Robert Hull	116
J. Henri Richard	151	M. Bert Olmstead	115
Jean-Guy Talbot	150	T. Richard Duff	114
Douglas Harvey	137	Francis Mahovlich	114
Richard Moore	135	Emile Bouchard	113
J. R. Marcel Pronovost	134	Thomas Johnson	111
J. H. Maurice Richard	133	Stanley Mikita	111
R. B. Theodore Lindsay	133	George Armstrong	110
Bernard Geoffrion	132	Allan Stanley	109
J. A. Claude Provost	126	Jean-Claude Tremblay	108
Eric Nesterenko	124	J. J. Robert Rousseau	106
Alexander Delvecchio	121	Ralph Backstrom	100

Most Goals

J. H. Maurice Richard	82	Theodore Kennedy	29
Jean Béliveau	79	Norman Ullman	29
Gordon Howe	67	Yvan Cournoyer	29
Francis McGee	63	Sidney Abel	28
Robert Hull	62	Gordon Drillon	26
Bernard Geoffrion	58	George Armstrong	26
R. B. Theodore Lindsay	47	Hector Blake	25
Richard Moore	46	C. J. Sylvanus Apps	25
Stanley Mikita	41	Robert Pulford	25
Francis Mahovlich	41	J. A. Claude Provost	25
J. Henri Richard	40	Rodrigue Gilbert	25
Philip Esposito	37	Milton Schmidt	24
Alexander Delvecchio	35	J. J. Robert Rousseau	24
Leonard Kelly	33	M. Joseph Malone	23
David Keon	31	Modere Bruneteau	23
T. Richard Duff	30	Floyd Curry	23
John Bucyk	30		

Most Assists

Jean Béliveau	97	Robert Orr	46
Gordon Howe	91	Elmer Lach	45
J. Henri Richard	72	J. H. Maurice Richard	44
Alexander Delvecchio	69	M. Bert Olmstead	42
Stanley Mikita	67	John Bucyk	42
Robert Hull	66	Fleming Mackell	41
Douglas Harvey	64	J. A. Claude Provost	38
Richard Moore	64	Myles Horton	38
Bernard Geoffrion	60	Hector Blake	37
Leonard Kelly	59	Allan Stanley	36
Pierre Pilote	53	Yvan Cournoyer	35
Philip Esposito	53	Douglas Mohns	35
Norman Ullman	52	William Cowley	34
Francis Mahovlich	51	George Armstrong	34
Jean-Claude Tremblay	51	John McKenzie	32
R. B. Theodore Lindsay	49	Theodore Kennedy	31
T. Richard Duff	49	Sidney Abel	30
J. J. Robert Rousseau	46	Kenneth Hodge	30

Most Points

Jean Béliveau	(79 goals—97 assists)	176
Gordon Howe	(67 goals—91 assists)	158
Robert Hull	(62 goals—66 assists)	128
J. H. Maurice Richard	(82 goals—44 assists)	126
Bernard Geoffrion	(58 goals—60 assists)	118
J. Henri Richard	(40 goals—72 assists)	112
Richard Moore	(46 goals—64 assists)	110
Stanley Mikita	(41 goals—67 assists)	108
Alexander Delvecchio	(35 goals—69 assists)	104
R. B. Theodore Lindsay	(47 goals—49 assists)	96
Leonard Kelly	(33 goals—59 assists)	92
Francis Mahovlich	(41 goals—51 assists)	92
Philip Esposito	(37 goals—53 assists)	90
Norman Ullman	(29 goals—52 assists)	81
T. Richard Duff	(30 goals—49 assists)	79
Douglas Harvey	(8 goals—64 assists)	72
John Bucyk	(30 goals—42 assists)	72
J. J. Robert Rousseau	(24 goals—46 assists)	70

Most Penalties in Minutes

John Ferguson	260	Ivan Johnson	161
Gordon Howe	218	J. Henri Richard	161
Jean Béliveau	211	Francis Mahovlich	157
Edward Harris	211	Barclay Plager	155
R. B. Theodore Lindsay	194	Douglas Harvey	152
J. H. Maurice Richard	188	Edward Shack	149
Edward Shore	181	Carl Brewer	146
Myles Horton	179	John Stewart	143
Derek Sanderson	174	Jean-Guy Talbot	142
Robert Baun	171	Stanley Mikita	137
Robert Plager	171	James Thomson	135
G. Reginald Horner	170	John McKenzie	133
Jean-Noël Picard	167	Eric Nesterenko	127

Game

Most Goals

Jan. 16, 1905	Francis McGee	Ottawa Silver Seven	14
Mar. 16, 1911	Martin Walsh	Ottawa Senators	10
Mar. 8, 1913	M. Joseph Malone	Quebec Bulldogs	9
Mar. 17, 1906	Harry Smith	Ottawa Silver Seven	6
Jan. 13, 1908	Ernest Russell	Montreal Wanderers	6
Jan. 5, 1910	Martin Walsh	Ottawa Senators	6
Feb. 25, 1904	Francis McGee	Ottawa Silver Seven	5
Mar. 9, 1904	Francis McGee	Ottawa Silver Seven	5
Jan. 16, 1905	Harry Westwick	Ottawa Silver Seven	5
Feb. 27, 1906	Alfred E. Smith	Ottawa Silver Seven	5
Feb. 28, 1906	Harry Smith	Ottawa Silver Seven	5
Mar. 6, 1906	Francis McGee	Ottawa Silver Seven	5
Dec. 28, 1908	Harry Smith	Montreal Wanderers	5
Jan. 20, 1910	Bruce Stuart	Ottawa Senators	5
Mar. 13, 1912	"Jack" McDonald	Quebec Bulldogs	5
Mar. 26, 1917	Bernard Morris	Seattle Metropolitans	5
Mar. 23, 1944	J. H. Maurice Richard	Montreal Canadiens	5

Most Assists

Mar. 23, 1944	Hector Blake	Montreal Canadiens	5
Mar. 27, 1956	J. H. Maurice Richard	Montreal Canadiens	5
Mar. 30, 1957	M. Bert Olmstead	Montreal Canadiens	5
Apr. 5, 1958	Donald McKenney	Boston Bruins	5

Most Points

Mar. 25, 1954	Richard Moore	Montreal Canadiens (2 goals—4 assists)	6
Apr. 2, 1969	Philip Esposito	Boston Bruins (4 goals—2 assists)	6

Most Penalties

Apr. 2, 1969	Forbes Kennedy	Toronto Maple Leafs (2 misc.—2 maj.—4 min.)	8
Apr. 4, 1927	Edward Shore	Boston Bruins (7 min.)	7
Apr. 4, 1921	Edward Gerard	Ottawa Senators (1 misc.————5 min.)	6
Mar. 28, 1940	G. Reginald Horner	Toronto Maple Leafs (2 misc.—1 maj.—3 min.)	6
Apr. 14, 1966	John Ferguson	Montreal Canadiens (1 misc.—2 maj.—3 min.)	6
Apr. 5, 1969	John Ferguson	Montreal Canadiens (2 misc.—3 maj.—1 min.)	6
Apr. 8, 1971	Victor Hadfield	New York Rangers (2 misc.—2 maj.—2 min.)	6

Most Penalties in Minutes

Apr. 2, 1969	Forbes Kennedy	Toronto Maple Leafs (2 misc.—2 maj.—4 min.)	38

Apr. 5, 1969	John Ferguson	Montreal Canadiens
		(2 misc.—3 maj.—1 min.) 37
Apr. 8, 1971	Victor Hadfield	New York Rangers
		(2 misc.—2 maj.—2 min.) 34
Apr. 11, 1970	Wayne Cashman	Boston Bruins
		(2 misc.—2 maj.—1 min.) 32
Apr. 19, 1970	Tracy Pratt	Pittsburgh Penguins
		(2 misc.—2 maj.—1 min.) 32
Mar. 28, 1940	G. Reginald Horner	Toronto Maple Leafs
		(2 misc.—1 maj.—3 min.) 31
Apr. 15, 1969	Robert Plager	St. Louis Blues
		(2 misc.—2 maj.) 30
Apr. 11, 1970	David Balon	New York Rangers
		(2 misc.—2 maj.) 30
Apr. 11, 1970	Derek Sanderson	Boston Bruins
		(2 misc.—2 maj.) 30

Period

Most Goals

Mar. 16, 1911	Martin Walsh	Ottawa Senators	3rd period 3
Mar. 26, 1917	Bernard Morris	Seattle Metropolitans	3rd period 3
Mar. 24, 1919	Frank Foyston	Seattle Metropolitans	1st period 3
Apr. 1, 1920	John Darragh	Ottawa Senators	3rd period 3
Apr. 5, 1932	Harvey Jackson	Toronto Maple Leafs	2nd period 3
Mar. 23, 1944	J. H. Maurice Richard	Montreal Canadiens	2nd period 3
Mar. 29, 1945	J. H. Maurice Richard	Montreal Canadiens	3rd period 3
Apr. 5, 1955	R. B. Theodore Lindsay	Detroit Red Wings	2nd period 3
Apr. 6, 1957	J. H. Maurice Richard	Montreal Canadiens	2nd period 3
Apr. 15, 1969	Gordon Berenson	St. Louis Blues	2nd period 3
Apr. 20, 1971	Jacques Lemaire	Montreal Canadiens	2nd period 3

Most Assists

Mar. 26, 1917	Robert Rowe	Seattle Metropolitans	3rd period 3
Mar. 25, 1941	Nicholas Metz	Toronto Maple Leafs	2nd period 3
Mar. 23, 1944	Hector Blake	Montreal Canadiens	2nd period 3
Mar. 30, 1944	Elmer Lach	Montreal Canadiens	3rd period 3
Apr. 13, 1944	Hector Blake	Montreal Canadiens	3rd period 3
Mar. 24, 1946	Robert Bauer	Boston Bruins	3rd period 3
Mar. 25, 1954	Jean Bèliveau	Montreal Canadiens	1st period 3
Mar. 27, 1956	J. H. Maurice Richard	Montreal Canadiens	2nd period 3
Apr. 6, 1957	Douglas Harvey	Montreal Canadiens	2nd period 3
Apr. 5, 1958	Donald McKenney	Boston Bruins	3rd period 3
Apr. 2, 1959	Douglas Harvey	Montreal Canadiens	1st period 3
Apr. 2, 1959	Richard Moore	Montreal Canadiens	1st period 3
Apr. 7, 1960	J. Henri Richard	Montreal Canadiens	1st period 3
May 1, 1965	J. J. Robert Rousseau	Montreal Canadiens	1st period 3
Apr. 14, 1966	Alexander Delvecchio	Detroit Red Wings	3rd period 3
Apr. 21, 1970	Alvin B. McDonald	St. Louis Blues	1st period 3
Apr. 8, 1971	Robert Orr	Boston Bruins	2nd period 3
Apr. 22, 1971	Daniel Grant	Minnesota North Stars	1st period 3
Apr. 22, 1971	J. G. Y. Jean Ratelle	New York Rangers	1st period 3
Apr. 27, 1971	Jean Bèliveau	Montreal Canadiens	3rd period 3
Apr. 9, 1972	Robert Orr	Boston Bruins	3rd period 3

Most Points

Mar. 24, 1919   Frank Foyston   Seattle
                                        1st period (3 goals—1 assists) 4
Mar. 29, 1945   J. H. Maurice Richard   Montreal
                                        3rd period (3 goals—1 assists) 4
Mar. 25, 1954   Richard Moore   Montreal
                                        1st period (2 goals—2 assists) 4

Most Penalties

Apr. 2, 1969   Forbes Kennedy   Toronto
                                        3rd period (2 misc.—2 maj.—2 min.) 6

Most Penalties in Minutes

Apr. 2, 1969   Forbes Kennedy   Toronto
                                        3rd period (2 misc.—2 maj.—2 min.) 34
Apr. 5, 1969   John Ferguson   Montreal
                                        3rd period (2 misc.—2 maj.)   30
Apr. 11, 1970   David Balon   New York
                                        1st period (2 misc.—2 maj.)   30
Apr. 11, 1970   Derek Sanderson   Boston
                                        1st period (2 misc.—2 maj.)   30
Apr. 7, 1971   Barry Gibbs   Minnesota
                                        2nd period (2 misc.—1 maj.—1 min.) 27
Apr. 8, 1971   D. Bradford Park   New York
                                        3rd period (2 misc.—1 maj.—1 min.) 27
Apr. 8, 1971   Darryl Sittler   Toronto
                                        3rd period (2 misc.—1 maj.—1 min.) 27

12
Register of Goaltenders
(Stanley Cup)

Abbreviations

The following appear after names of goaltenders:

SL—Shoots left
SR—Shoots right

The following appear as headings:

Sea.—Season
Ga.—Games
GA—Goals-Against
SO—Shut-Outs
Ave.—Average
A.—Assists
PM.—Penalties in Minutes

Numbers in parentheses following games indicates games played in.

A blank column indicates that information is unavailable.

Records begin with the formation of the National Hockey League. Capital letters in parentheses following the club indicate leagues other than the National Hockey League. An asterisk preceding club indicates Stanley Cup winner.

Other leagues:

PCHA—Pacific Coast Hockey Association
WCHL—Western Canada Hockey League

Sea.	Club	Ga.	GA	SO	Ave.	A.	PM.
AITKENHEAD, ANDREW							
1933	*New York Rangers	8	13	2	1.625	0	0
1934	" " "	2	2	1	1.00	0	0
		10	15	3	1.50	0	0
ALMAS, RALPH CLAYTON							
1947	Detroit Red Wings	4 1/4	13	0	3.06	0	0
BASSEN, HENRY							
1961	Detroit Red Wings	3 2/3	9	0	2.45	0	0
1966	" " "	1	2		2.00	0	0
		4 2/3	11	0	2.36	0	0
BELL, GORDON							
1956	New York Rangers	2	9	0	4.50	0	0
BENEDICT, CLINTON S.							
1920	*Ottawa Senators	5	11	1	2.20	0	0
1921 *	" "	5	12	0	2.40	0	0
1923 *	" "	6	8	2	1.33	0	2
1926 *	Montreal Maroons	4	3	3	0.75	0	0
1927	" "	2	2	0	1.00	0	0
1928	" "	9	8	4	0.89	0	0
		31	44	10	1.42	0	2
BEVERIDGE, WILLIAM S.							
1937	Montreal Maroons	5	11	0	2.20	0	0
BIBEAULT, PAUL •							
1942	Montreal Canadiens	3	8	1	2.67	0	0
1943	" "	5	18	1	3.60	0	0
1944	Toronto Maple Leafs	5	23	0	4.60	0	0
1945	Boston Bruins	7	22	0	3.14	0	0
		20	71	2	3.55	0	0
BINKLEY, LESLIE JOHN							
1970	Pittsburgh Penguins	7	15	0	2.14	0	0
BOURQUE, CLAUDE HENNESSEY							
1939	Montreal Canadiens	3	8	1	2.67	0	0
BOWER, JOHN WILLIAM							
1959	Toronto Maple Leafs	12	39	0	3.25	0	0
1960	" " "	10	31	0	3.10	0	0
1961	" " "	3	9	0	3.00	0	2
1962 *	" " "	9 1/4	22	0	2.38	0	0
1963 *	" " "	10	16	2	1.60	1	0
1964 *	" " "	14	31	2	2.21	0	0
1965	" " "	5	14	0	2.80	0	0
1966	" " "	2	9	0	4.50	0	0
1967 *	" " "	2 3/5(4)	5	1	1.92	0	2
1969	" " "	2 3/5(4)	11	0	4.23	0	0
		70 1/2(74)	187	5	2.65	1	4
BRIMSEK, FRANCIS CHARLES							
1939	*Boston Bruins	12	18	1	1.50	0	0
1940	" "	6	15	0	2.50	0	0
1941 *	" "	11	23	1	2.09	0	0
1942	" "	5	16	0	3.20	0	0
1943	" "	9	33	0	3.67	0	0
1946	" "	10	29	0	2.90	0	0
1947	" "	5	16	0	3.20	0	0
1948	" "	5	20	0	4.00	0	0
1949	" "	5	16	0	3.20	0	0
		68	186	2	2.74	0	0
BRODA, WALTER EDWARD							
1937	Toronto Maple Leafs	2	5	0	2.50	0	0
1938	" " "	7	13	1	1.86	0	0
1939	" " "	10	20	2	2.00	0	0
1940	" " "	10	19	1	1.90	0	0
1941	" " "	7	15	0	2.14	0	0
1942 *	" " "	13	31	1	2.38	0	0
1943	" " "	6	20	0	3.33	0	0

(continued)

Sea.	Club			Ga.	GA	SO	Ave.	A.	PM.
1947 *	”	”	”	11	27	1	2.45	0	0
1948 *	”	”	”	9	20	1	2.22	0	10
1949 *	”	”	”	9	15	1	1.67	0	2
1950	”	”	”	7	10	3	1.43	0	0
1951 *	”	”	”	7 3/4	9	2	1.16	0	0
1952	”	”	”	2	7	0	3.50	0	0
				100 3/4	211	13	2.09	0	12

CARON, JACQUES JOSEPH

1972 St. Louis Blues	8	27	0	3.31	0	2

CHABOT, LORNE

1927 New York Rangers	2	3	1	1.50	0	0
1928 * ” ”	5 2/5	8	1	1.48	0	0
1929 Toronto Maple Leafs	4	5	0	1.25	0	0
1931 ” ” ”	2	4	0	2.00	0	0
1932 ” ” ”	7	15	0	2.14	0	0
1933 ” ” ”	9	18	2	2.00	0	0
1934 Montreal Canadiens	2	4	0	2.00	0	0
1935 Chicago Black Hawks	2	1	1	0.50	0	0
1936 Montreal Maroons	3	6	0	2.00	0	0
	36 2/5	64	5	1.76	0	0

CHAMPOUX, ROBERT JOSEPH G-SL
Born: St. Hilaire, Quebec., Dec. 2, 1942

1964 Detroit Red Wings	5/6	4		4.80	0	0

CHEEVERS, GERALD MICHAEL

1968 Boston Bruins	4	15	0	3.75	0	4
1969 ” ”	9	16	3	1.78	0	17
1970 * ” ”	13	29	0	2.23	1	2
1971 ” ”	6	21	0	3.50	0	4
1972 * ” ”	8	21	2	2.625	0	0
	40	102	5	2.55	1	27

CONNELL, ALEXANDER

1927 * Ottawa Senators	6	4	2	0.67	0	0
1928 ” ”	2	3	0	1.50	0	0
1930 ” ”	2	6	0	3.00	0	0
1932 Detroit Falcons	2	3	0	1.50	0	0
1935 * Montreal Maroons	7	8	2	1.14	0	0
	19	24	4	1.26	0	0

CROZIER, ROGER ALLAN

1964 Detroit Red Wings	2 (3)	5	0	2.50	0	0
1965 ” ” ”	7	23	0	3.29	0	2
1966 ” ” ”	11 (12)	26	1	2.36	0	0
1970 ” ” ”	3/5	3		5.00	0	0
	20 3/5(23)	57	1	2.77	0	2

1966 Conn Smythe Trophy

CUDE, WILFRED REGINALD

1934 Detroit Red Wings	9	21	1	2.33	0	0
1935 Montreal Canadiens	2	6	0	3.00	0	0
1937 ” ”	5	13	0	2.60	0	0
1938 ” ”	3	11	0	3.67	0	0
	19	51	1	2.68	0	0

DE JORDY, DENIS EMILE

1964 Chicago Black Hawks	1/3	2		6.00	0	0
1965 ” ” ”	1 1/3	9	0	6.75	0	0
1967 ” ” ”	3 (4)	10	0	3.33	0	0
1968 ” ” ”	11	34	0	3.09	0	0
	15 2/3(18)	55	0	3.51	0	0

DESJARDINS, GERARD FERDINAND

1969 Los Angeles Kings	7 1/6(9)	28	0	3.91	1	0
1972 Chicago Black Hawks	1	5		5.00	0	4
	8 1/6(10)	33	0	4.04	1	4

DION, CONRAD

1944 Detroit Red Wings	5	17	0	3.40	0	0

DOLSON, CLARENCE

1929 Detroit Cougars	2	7	0	3.50	0	0

Sea. Club	Ga.	GA	SO	Ave.	A.	PM.
DRYDEN, DAVID MURRAY						
1966 Chicago Black Hawks	1/5	0		0.00	0	0
DRYDEN, KENNETH WAYNE						
1971 * Montreal Canadiens	20	63	0	3.15	1	0
1972 ” ”	6	19	0	3.17	0	0
	26	82	0	3.15	0	0
1971 Conn Smythe Trophy						
DURNAN, WILLIAM RONALD						
1944 * Montreal Canadiens	9	14	1	1.56	0	0
1945 ” ”	6	15	0	2.50	0	0
1946 * ” ”	9	20	0	2.22	0	0
1947 ” ”	11	23	1	2.09	0	0
1949 ” ”	7	17	0	2.43	0	0
1950 ” ”	3	10	0	3.33	0	0
	45	99	2	2.20	0	0
EDWARDS, ALLAN ROY						
1970 Detroit Red Wings	3 2/5	13	0	3.82	0	0
ESPOSITO, ANTHONY JAMES						
1970 Chicago Black Hawks	8	28	0	3.50	0	0
1971 ” ” ”	18	42	2	2.33	0	0
1972 ” ” ”	5	17	0	3.40	0	0
	31	87	2	2.81	0	0
FAVELL, DOUGLAS ROBERT						
1968 Philadelphia Flyers	2	8	0	4.00	0	5
1969 ” ”	1	5		5.00	0	0
1971 ” ”	2	8	0	4.00	0	0
	5	21	0	4.20	0	5
FRANKS, JAMES REGINALD						
1937 * Detroit Red Wings	1/2	2		4.00	0	0
GAMBLE, BRUCE GEORGE						
1969 Toronto Maple Leafs	1 2/5(3)	13	0	9.27	0	0
1971 Philadelphia Flyers	2	12	0	6.00	0	0
	3 2/5(5)	25	0	7.35	0	0
GARDINER, CHARLES ROBERT						
1930 Chicago Black Hawks	2	3	0	1.50	0	0
1931 ” ” ”	9	14	2	1.56	0	0
1932 ” ” ”	2	6	1	3.00	0	0
1934 * ” ” ”	8	12	2	1.50	0	0
	21	35	5	1.67	0	0
GARDINER, WILBERT						
1939 New York Rangers	6	12	0	2.00	0	0
1941 Montreal Canadiens	3	8	0	2.67	0	0
	9	20	0	2.22	0	0
GELINEAU, JOHN EDWARD						
1951 Boston Bruins	4	7	1	1.75	0	0
GIACOMIN, EDWARD						
1967 New York Rangers	4	14	0	3.50	0	0
1968 ” ” ”	6	18	0	3.00	0	0
1969 ” ” ”	3	12	0	4.00	0	5
1970 ” ” ”	4 2/3	19	0	4.07	0	0
1971 ” ” ”	11 2/3	30	0	2.57	0	2
1972 ” ” ”	10	27	0	2.70	0	2
	39 1/3	120	0	3.05	0	9
GOODMAN, PAUL						
1938 *Chicago Black Hawks	1	5		5.00	0	0
1940 ” ” ”	2	5	0	2.50	0	0
	3	10	0	3.33	0	0
HAINSWORTH, GEORGE						
1927 Montreal Canadiens	4	6	1	1.50	0	0
1928 ” ”	2	3	0	1.50	0	0
1929 ” ”	3	5	0	1.67	0	0
1930 * ” ”	6	6	3	1.00	0	0
1931 * ” ”	10	21	2	2.10	0	0

(continued)

Sea.	Club	Ga.	GA	SO	Ave.	A.	PM.
1932	,, ,,	4	13	0	3.25	0	0
1933	,, ,,	2	8	0	4.00	0	0
1934	Toronto Maple Leafs	5	11	0	2.20	0	0
1935	,, ,, ,,	7	12	2	1.71	0	0
1936	,, ,, ,,	9	27	0	3.00	0	0
		52	112	8	2.15	0	0

HALL, GLENN HENRY

Sea.	Club	Ga.	GA	SO	Ave.	A.	PM.
1956	Detroit Red Wings	10	28	0	2.80	0	0
1957	,, ,, ,,	5	15	0	3.00	0	10
1959	Chicago Black Hawks	6	21	0	3.50	0	0
1960	,, ,, ,,	4	14	0	3.50	0	0
1961 *	,, ,, ,,	12	27	2	2.25	0	0
1962	,, ,, ,,	12	31	2	2.58	0	2
1963	,, ,, ,,	6	25	0	4.17	0	0
1964	,, ,, ,,	6 2/3	22	0	3.30	0	0
1965	,, ,, ,,	12 2/3	28	1	2.21	0	0
1966	,, ,, ,,	5 4/5	22	0	3.79	0	0
1967	,, ,, ,,	3	8	0	2.67	0	0
1968	St. Louis Blues	16 4/5(18)	45	1	2.68	0	0
1969	,, ,, ,,	2 1/6	5	0	2.31	0	0
1970	,, ,, ,,	7	21	0	3.00	0	0
1971	,, ,, ,,	3	9	0	3.00	0	0
		112(115)	321	6	2.87	0	12

1968 Conn Smythe Trophy

HENDERSON, JOHN DUNCAN

Sea.	Club	Ga.	GA	SO	Ave.	A.	PM.
1955	Boston Bruins	2	8	0	4.00	0	0

HENRY, GORDON DAVID

Sea.	Club	Ga.	GA	SO	Ave.	A.	PM.
1951	Boston Bruins	2	10	0	5.00	0	0
1953	,, ,,	2 3/4	11	0	4.00	0	0
		4 3/4	21	0	4.42	0	0

HENRY, SAMUEL JAMES

Sea.	Club	Ga.	GA	SO	Ave.	A.	PM.
1942	New York Rangers	6	13	1	2.17	0	0
1952	Boston Bruins	7	18	1	2.57	0	0
1953	,, ,,	8 1/4	26	0	3.15	0	0
1954	,, ,,	4	16	0	4.00	0	0
1955	,, ,,	3	8	0	2.67	0	0
		28 1/4	81	2	2.87	0	0

HODGE, CHARLES EDWARD

Sea.	Club	Ga.	GA	SO	Ave.	A.	PM.
1955	Montreal Canadiens	1 1/2(4)	6	†0	4.00	0	0
1964	,, ,,	7	17	1	2.43	0	0
1965 *	,, ,,	5	10	1	2.00	0	0
		13 1/2(16)	33	2	2.44	0	0

†also shared shut-out with J. Jacques Plante on March 22, 1955 against Boston

HOLMES, HARRY

Sea.	Club	Ga.	GA	SO	Ave.	A.	PM.
1918 *	Toronto Arenas	5	21	0	4.20	0	0
1919	Seattle Metropolitans (PCHA)	5	10	2	2.00	0	0
1920	,, ,, ,,	5	15	0	3.00	0	0
1925 *	Victoria Cougars (WCHL)	4	8	0	2.00	0	0
1926	,, ,, ,,	4	10	0	2.50	0	0
		23	64	2	2.78	0	0

JOHNSTON, EDWARD JOSEPH

Sea.	Club	Ga.	GA	SO	Ave.	A.	PM.
1969	Boston Bruins	1	4		4.00	0	0
1970 *	,, ,,	1	4		4.00	0	2
1971	,, ,,	1	7		7.00	0	0
1972 *	,, ,,	7	13	1	1.86	0	0
		10	28	1	2.80	0	2

KARAKAS, MICHAEL

Sea.	Club	Ga.	GA	SO	Ave.	A.	PM.
1936	Chicago Black Hawks	2	7	0	3.50	0	0
1938 *	,, ,, ,,	8	15	2	1.875	0	0
1944	,, ,, ,,	9	24	1	2.67	0	0
1946	,, ,, ,,	4	26	0	6.50	0	0
		23	72	3	3.13	0	0

KERR, DAVID ALEXANDER

Sea.	Club	Ga.	GA	SO	Ave.	A.	PM.
1931	Montreal Maroons	2	8	0	4.00	0	0
1933	,, ,,	2	5	0	2.50		

(continued)

Sea.	Club	Ga.	GA	SO	Ave.	A.	PM.
1934	" "	4	7	1	1.75	0	0
1935	New York Rangers	4	10	0	2.50	0	0
1937	" " "	9	10	4	1.11	0	0
1938	" " "	3	8	0	2.67	0	0
1939	" " "	1	2		2.00	0	0
1940 *	" " "	12	20	3	1.67	0	0
1941	" " "	3	6	0	2.00	0	0
		40	76	8	1.90	0	0

LAIRD, BILL

1922	Regina Capitals (WCHL)	2	5	0	2.50	0	0

LEHMAN, FREDERICK HUGH

1918	Vancouver Millionaires (PCHA)	5	18	0	3.60	0	0
1921	" " "	5	12	0	2.40	0	0
1922	" " "	7	18	2	2.57	0	0
1923	Vancouver Maroons (PCHA)	4	10	0	2.50	0	0
1924	" " "	2	5	0	2.50	0	0
1927	Chicago Black Hawks	2	10	0	5.00	0	0
		25	73	2	2.92	0	0

LoPRESTI, SAMUEL

1941	Chicago Black Hawks	5	12	0	2.40	0	0
1942	" " "	3	5	1	1.67	0	0
		8	17	1	2.125	0	0

LUMLEY, HARRY

1945	Detroit Red Wings	14	31	2	2.21	0	0
1946	" " "	5	16	1	3.20	0	0
1948	" " "	10	30	0	3.00	0	10
1949	" " "	11	26	0	2.36	0	2
1950 *	" " "	14	28	3	2.00	0	0
1954	Toronto Maple Leafs	5	15	0	3.00	0	0
1955	" " "	4	14	0	3.50	0	0
1956	" " "	5	14	1	2.80	0	2
1958	Boston Bruins	1	5		5.00	0	0
1959	" "	7	20	0	2.86	0	4
		76	199	7	2.62	0	18

MANIAGO, CESARE

1961	Toronto Maple Leafs	2	6	0	3.00	0	0
1968	Minnesota North Stars	14	39	0	2.79	0	0
1970	" " "	3	6	1	2.00	0	0
1971	" " "	8	29	0	3.625	0	0
1972	" " "	3 3/4	12	0	3.20	0	0
		30 3/4	92	1	2.99	0	0

MARTIN, SETH

1968	St. Louis Blues	1 1/5	5	0	4.17	0	0

McCOOL, FRANK

1945 *	Toronto Maple Leafs	13	30	4	2.31	0	0

McDUFFE, PETER ARNOLD

1972	St. Louis Blues	1	7		7.00	0	0

McNEIL, GERARD GEORGE

1950	Montreal Canadiens	2	5	0	2.50	0	0
1951	" "	11	25	1	2.27	0	0
1952	" "	11	23	1	2.09	0	0
1953 *	" "	8	16	2	2.00	0	0
1954	" "	3	3	1	1.00	0	0
		35	72	5	2.06	0	0

MILLER, JOSEPH

1928	*New York Rangers	3	3	1	1.00	0	0

MOORE, ALFRED ERNEST

1938	*Chicago Black Hawks	1	1		1.00	0	0
1939	New York Americans	2	6	0	3.00	0	0
		3	7	0	2.33	0	0

MOWERS, JOHN THOMAS

1941	Detroit Red Wings	9	20	0	2.22	0	0
1942	" " "	12	38	0	3.17	0	0
1943 *	" " "	10	22	2	2.20	0	0
1947	" " "	3/4	5		6.67	0	0
		31 3/4	85	2	2.68	0	0

Sea. Club	Ga.	GA	SO	Ave.	A.	PM.
PARENT, BERNARD MARCEL						
1968 Philadelphia Flyers	5	9	0	1.80	0	0
1969 ” ”	3	12	0	4.00	0	0
1971 Toronto Maple Leafs	4	9	0	2.25	0	0
1972 ” ” ”	4	13	0	3.25	0	0
	16	43	0	2.69	0	0
PATRICK, LESTER						
1928 * New York Rangers	3/5	1		1.67	0	0
PLANTE, JOSEPH JACQUES OMER						
1953 *Montreal Canadiens	4	7	1	1.75	0	0
1954 ” ”	8	15	2	1.875	0	0
1955 ” ”	10 1/2(12)	30	†0	2.86	0	0
1956 * ” ”	10	18	2	1.80	0	2
1957 * ” ”	10	18	1	1.80	0	4
1958 * ” ”	10	20	1	2.00	0	2
1959 * ” ”	11	28	0	2.55	0	0
1960 * ” ”	8	11	3	1.375	0	0
1961 ” ”	6	16	0	2.67	0	2
1962 ” ”	6	19	0	3.17	0	2
1963 ” ”	5	14	0	2.80	0	0
1969 St. Louis Blues	9 5/6	15	3	1.53	1	0
1970 ” ” ”	5 2/5	8	1	1.48	0	2
1971 Toronto Maple Leafs	2 (3)	7	0	3.50	0	0
1972 ” ” ”	1	5		5.00	0	0
	106 2/3(110)	231	14	2.17	1	14

†also shared shut-out with Charles Hodge on March 22, 1955 against Boston

RAYNER, CLAUDE EARL						
1948 New York Rangers	6	17	0	2.83	0	0
1950 ” ” ”	12	29	1	2.42	0	0
	18	46	1	2.56	0	0
REID, CHARLES G-SR						
1924 Calgary Tigers (WCHL)	2	9	0	4.50	0	0
ROACH, JOHN ROSS						
1922 *Toronto St. Patricks	5	9	1	1.80	0	0
1929 New York Rangers	6	5	3	0.83	0	0
1930 ” ” ”	4	7	0	1.75	0	0
1931 ” ” ”	4	4	1	1.00	0	0
1932 ” ” ”	7	27	1	3.86	0	0
1933 Detroit Red Wings	4	8	1	2.00	0	0
	30	60	7	2.00	0	0
ROBERTSON, EARL COOPER						
1937 * Detroit Red Wings	5 2/3	8	2	1.41	0	0
1938 New York Americans	6	12	0	2.00	0	0
1940 ” ” ”	3	9	0	3.00	0	0
	14 2/3	29	2	1.98	0	0
ROLLINS, ELWIN IRA						
1951 *Toronto Maple Leafs	3 1/4	6	0	1.85	0	0
1952 ” ” ”	2	6	0	3.00	0	0
1953 Chicago Black Hawks	7	18	0	2.57	0	0
	12 1/4	30	0	2.45	0	0
RUTHERFORD, JAMES EARL						
1972 Pittsburgh Penguins	4	14	0	3.50	0	0
RUTLEDGE, WAYNE ALVIN						
1968 Los Angeles Kings	2 1/3	8	0	3.43	0	0
1969 ” ” ”	3 5/6(5)	13	0	3.39	0	4
	6 1/6(8)	21	0	3.41	0	4
SAWCHUK, TERRANCE GORDON						
1951 Detroit Red Wings	6	13	1	2.17	0	0
1952 * ” ” ”	8	5	4	0.625	0	0
1953 ” ” ”	6	21	1	3.50	0	10
1954 * ” ” ”	12	20	2	1.67	0	2
1955 * ” ” ”	11	26	1	2.36	0	12
1958 ” ” ”	4	19	0	4.75	0	0

(continued)

Sea.	Club	Ga.	GA	SO	Ave.	A.	PM.
1960	" " "	6	20	0	3.33	0	0
1961	" " "	7 1/3	18	1	2.45	0	0
1963	" " "	11	36	0	3.27	0	0
1964	" " "	11 1/6(13)	31	1	2.78	0	2
1965	Toronto Maple Leafs	1	3		3.00	0	0
1966	" "	2	6	0	3.00	0	0
1967 *	" " "	9 2/5	25	0	2.66	0	0
1968	Los Angeles Kings	4 2/3	18	1	3.86	0	0
1970	New York Rangers	1 1/3(3)	6	0	4.50	0	0
		100 4/5(106)	267	12	2.65	0	26

SIMMONS, DONALD WILLIAM

1957	Boston Bruins	10	29	2	2.90	0	0
1958	" "	11	27	1	2.45	0	0
1962	*Toronto Maple Leafs	2 3/4	8	0	2.91	0	0
		23 3/4	64	3	2.69	0	0

SMITH, ALLAN ROBERT

1970	Pittsburgh Penguins	3	10	0	3.33	0	0

SMITH, GARY EDWARD

1969	Oakland Seals	7	23	0	3.29	0	0
1970	" "	4	13	0	3.25	0	4
1972	Chicago Black Hawks	2	3	1	1.50	0	0
		13	39	1	3.00	0	4

SMITH, NORMAN E.

1936	*Detroit Red Wings	7	12	2	1.71	0	0
1937 *	" " "	3 5/6(5)	6	1	1.57	0	0
		10 5/6(12)	18	3	1.66	0	0

THOMPSON, CECIL RALPH

1929	*Boston Bruins	5	3	3	0.60	0	0
1930	" "	6	12	0	2.00	0	0
1931	" "	5	13	0	2.60	0	0
1933	" "	5	9	0	1.80	0	0
1935	" "	4	7	1	1.75	0	0
1936	" "	2	8	1	4.00	0	0
1937	" "	3	8	1	2.67	0	0
1938	" "	3	6	0	2.00	0	0
1939	Detroit Red Wings	6	15	1	2.50	0	0
1940	" " "	5	12	0	2.40	0	0
		44	93	7	2.11	0	0

VACHON, ROGATIEN ROSAIRE

1967	Montreal Canadiens	8 2/3	22	0	2.54	0	0
1968 *	" "	2	4	0	2.00	0	0
1969 *	" "	8	12	1	1.50	0	2
		18 2/3	38	1	2.04	0	2

VEZINA, GEORGES

1919	Montreal Canadiens	5	19	1	3.80	0	0
1924 *	" "	4	4	1	1.00	0	0
1925	" "	4	16	0	4.00	0	0
		13	39	2	3.00	0	0

VILLEMURE, GILLES

1969	New York Rangers	1	4		4.00	0	0
1971	" " "	1 1/3	6	0	4.50	0	0
1972	" " "	6	14	0	2.33	0	0
		8 1/3	24	0	2.88	0	0

WAKELY, ERNEST ALFRED LINTON

1970	St. Louis Blues	3 3/5	17	0	4.72	0	0
1971	" " "	3	7	1	2.33	0	0
1972	" " "	1 5/6(3)	13	0	7.09	0	0
		8 2/5(10)	37	1	4.40	0	0

WALSH, JAMES PATRICK

1930	Montreal Maroons	4	11	1	2.75	0	0
1932	" "	4	5	1	1.25	0	0
		8	16	2	2.00	0	0

WINKLER, HAROLD LANG

1923	Edmonton Eskimos (WCHL)	2	3	0	1.50	0	0
1927	Boston Bruins	8	13	2	1.625	0	0
1928	" "	2	5	0	2.50	0	0
		12	21	2	1.75	0	0

Sea.	Club	Ga.	GA	SO	Ave.	A.	PM.
WORSLEY, LORNE JOHN							
1956	New York Rangers	3	15	0	5.00	0	2
1957	" " "	5	22	0	4.40	0	0
1958	" " "	6	28	0	4.67	0	0
1962	" " "	6	22	0	3.67	0	0
1965	*Montreal Canadiens	8	16	2	2.00	0	0
1966	* " "	10	20	1	2.00	0	0
1967	" "	1 1/3	3	0	2.25	0	0
1968	* " "	11 (12)	21	1	1.91	0	10
1969	* " "	6 (7)	14	0	2.33	0	5
1970	Minnesota North Stars	3	14	0	4.67	0	0
1971	" " "	4	13	0	3.25	0	0
1972	" " "	3 1/4	7	1	2.15	0	0
		66 1/2 (70)	195	5	2.93	0	17
WORTERS, ROY							
1928	Pittsburgh Pirates	2	6	0	3.00	0	0
1929	New York Americans	2	1	1	0.50	0	0
1936	" " "	5	11	2	2.20	0	0
		9	18	3	2.00	0	0

Career Records

Most Playoffs

Terrance Sawchuk	15
Glenn Hall	15
J. Jacques Plante	15
Walter Broda	13
Lorne Worsley	12
George Hainsworth	10
Cecil Thompson	10
Harry Lumley	10
John Bower	10

Most Games

Glenn Hall	112	(115)
J. Jacques Plante	106⅔	(110)
Terrance Sawchuk	100⅘	(106)
Walter Broda	100¾	
Harry Lumley	76	
John Bower	70½	(74)
Francis Brimsek	68	
Lorne Worsley	66½	(70)

Numbers in parentheses indicates games played in.

Most Shut-outs

J. Jacques Plante	14
Walter Broda	13
Terrance Sawchuk	12
Clinton Benedict	10
George Hainsworth	8
David Kerr	8
John Roach	7
Cecil Thompson	7
Harry Lumley	7

Average (10 or more games)

Alexander Connell	1.26
Clinton Benedict	1.42
Andrew Aitkenhead	1.50
Norman Smith	1.66
Charles Gardiner	1.67
Harold Winkler	1.75
Lorne Chabot	1.76
David Kerr	1.90
Earl Robertson	1.98
John Roach	2.00

Frank Nighbor

Frank A. Patrick

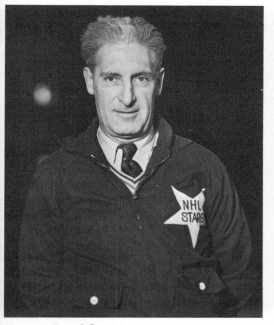

Lester Patrick

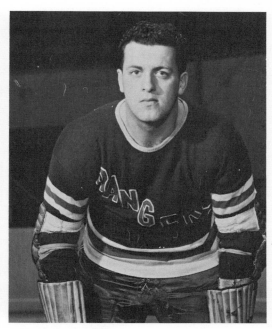

Murray Patrick

Maurice Richard

Terrance Gordon Sawchuk

Edward William Shore

Norman E. Smith

13
Officials

In the early days, hockey games were handled by a referee and a judge of play. Later, one referee officiated the games, and in 1927–28 the National Hockey League started using two referees in a game.

In 1938–39, a linesman began aiding the referee and in 1945–46 a second linesman was added. In 1946–47, the referee and linesmen began using a system of signals so that the reasons for calling penalties and other decisions (off-sides, delayed penalties, etc.) could be understood by the spectators.

Many of hockey's famous personalities have officiated in the National Hockey League. Among them have been Clarence Campbell, who was a referee for three seasons and later became the president of the league.

Francis Michael ("The King") Clancy, one of the all-time great defensemen, was a referee for eleven seasons. William L. "Bill" Chadwick, a native of New York City, officiated for 15 seasons and is honored in Hockey's Hall of Fame. William J. "Bald Bill" Stewart, who umpired in the National Baseball League for 22 years (1933–54), retired from refereeing in 1940–41. He also coached the Chicago Black Hawks to a Stanley Cup victory in 1938. Edward Powers, Jr., son of the former coach of the Toronto St. Patricks, refereed in the N.H.L. Douglas C. Young, former Detroit and Montreal defenseman, was a linesman for sixteen seasons.

At the end of the 1964–65 season, Carl Voss, who had been the N.H.L. Referee in Chief since 1950–51, retired and Ian (Scotty) Morrison, a native of Montreal, succeeded him. Frank Udvari, who had officiated in the N.H.L. since 1951–52, was made Supervisor of Officials before the start of the 1966–67 season. When the National Hockey League expanded to twelve clubs in 1967–68, Udvari became Eastern Supervisor of Officials and William (Dutch) van Deelen was named Western Supervisor of Officials.

All-Time List of Officials

- - - - - Alford
Neil Armstrong
Malcolm Ashford
George Ashley
John Ashley

Walter Atanas
Samuel Babcock
Dominic Baolto
Alex Barilko
E. T. Barry

Robert Barry
Harry Batstone
Bill Beagan
Joseph Claude Bechard
Bill Bell (1967–68)
William E. Bell
Turkey Bellingham
Clinton S. Benedict
Pean Bennett
Louis Berlinquette
George Berry
John Blake
Jim Boddy
Ken Bodendistel
George Boucher
Russell Bowie
William G. Boyd
John Brennan
Desse Brown
Vernon Buffey
Edward Burke
Robert Burns
Clarence Bush
Ed Butler
Ernest Butterworth
Harold Hugh Cameron
John Cameron
Clarence Sutherland Campbell
William Alexander Carse
Brent Casselman
Arthur Casterton
William L. "Bill" Chadwick
Jim Christison
Francis Michael Clancy
Jack Clancy
Pat Clark
William J. Cleary
J. Ogilvie Cleghorn
William Clements
David Clutsan
Bert Corbeau
Eusebe Daigneault
John D'Amico
Joseph Viateur "Léo" Dandurand
Douglas Davies
E. Davin
Clarence Henry Day
Cyril Denneny
Charles Dinsmore
Loring Doolittle
Ernest Dufresne
Arthur Duncan
Red Dunn
Jean Dussault
Cecil Henry Dye

James Edgeworth
Ron Ego
Edward Enright
Luigi Farelli
Gordon Fevreau
Ron Finn
Robert P. J. Frampton
Edward French
William Friday
Herbert Gallagher
Raymond Getliffe
Charles Ghedi
Lloyd Gilmour
Alan Glaspell
Charles Good
Gerald "Jerry" Goodman
Edward Dixon Graham
- - - - - Grant
Georges Gravel
James Haggarty
Wally Harris
Melvin Harwood (Larwell)
George Hayes
Bert Hedges
Leo Heffernan
William Milton "Riley" Hern
Robert W. "Bobby" Hewitson
Ron Hoggarth
William Holke
Bruce Hood
George Reginald Horner
Bill Hughes
Harry M. Hyland
Frederick James (Mickey) Ion
Harold R. Jackson
Auréle Emile Joliat
Melville Sydney Keeling
Bob Kilger
William E. Knott
Jerry LaFlamme
Edouard Charles Lalonde
Norman Lamport
Russell Larcelle
Elwood (Ace) Lee
Bernard LeMaitre
Hector Lepine
Percy LeSueur
Bryan Lewis
Russell Louelle
Redvers "Red" MacKenzie
Charles MacKinley
Kenneth MacLeod
George Mallinson
Sylvio Mantha
Harold March

Jack Marks
Louis Marsh
John C. "Jack" Marshall
Louis Maschio
Saul Maslow
Dalton McArthur
Stanley McCabe
Albert J. McCaffrey
John McCauley
Francis J. McCurry
"Jack" McDonald
Moylan J. McDonnell
Donald McFadyen
Bob McLaren
Hugh McLean
Archie McTier
Charles McVeigh
Jack Mehlenbacher
Melvin Meldrum
Robert Meldrum
Tom Melville
Edward Mepham
Steven Meuris
Morley Meyers
John Mitchell
Ian (Scotty) Morrison
William Morrison
Ken Mullins
Ernest Mundey
Sibby Mundey
Leo Murray
Bob Myers
Ralph W. Nattrass
Dave Newell
Sparky Nicholson
Edward Reginald Noble
Willard Norris
Frank (Obs) O'Brien
William O'Hara
Edward J. (Doc) O'Leary
Jerry Olinski
Harry Ornest
Edward Panczak
Frank A. Patrick
Jack M. Paterson
Matthew Pavelich
Reginald Percival
James Meldrum Peters
Terry Pierce
Edward Powers, Jr.
Stanley Pratt
James Primeau
E. Harvey Pulford
William Quenville

W. Beattie Ramsey
Bill Riley
David Ritchie
William Roberts
Fred Rocque
Michael J. "Mike" Rodden
Alex Romeril
Arthur Howey Ross
William Orville Roulston
Joseph Rys
Jean Sauve
Ray Scapinello
William Scherr
William Shaver
Norman Shay
Pat "Red" Shetler
Dave Shewchyk
Bill Sikes
Bruce Sims
Arthur Skov
Robert Sloan
Walter Smaill
J. Cooper Smeaton
A. G. Smith
David Smith
Donald Smith
Thomas Smith
Brian Sopp
Jack Sparrow
Jesse Spring
Joseph Springer
Harvey Sproule
Frederick Stevenson
James Gaye Stewart
A. C. Stewart
William J. "Bald Bill" Stewart
Leon Stickle
Roy Alvin (Red) Storey
Rodger Strong
William Stuart
Frank (Red) Synott
Yves Tessier
Clifford Thompson
Frank Udvari
Steven Vair
Bob Waddell
Victor Wagner
Maurice Walsh
Ronald Wicks
Gerry Wiggett
Archibald Wilcox
John Wilken
Douglas C. Young

14
Hall of Fame

Hockey Hall of Fame

The Hockey Hall of Fame was officially opened August 26, 1961, by the then Prime Minister of Canada, John F. Diefenbaker. The building is located in the center of the Canadian National Exhibition Park on the shore of Lake Ontario in Toronto.

The six Member Clubs of the N.H.L. then operating provided the necessary funds required to construct the building. The City of Toronto, as owners of the C.N.E. grounds, provided the site and has agreed to maintain the building and grounds for the purposes of the Hockey Hall of Fame.

The hockey exhibits are provided and financed by the N.H.L. and the Canadian Amateur Hockey Association. The cost of administration are shared by the N.H.L. and the C.N.E.

To be eligible, any person who is, or has been distinguished in hockey as a player, executive or as a referee, shall be qualified for election. Player and referee candidates will normally have completed their active careers five years prior to election, but in exceptional cases this period may be shortened by the Hockey Hall of Fame Committee. Only the Committee can nominate executives and referees for election, and they will be known as "Builders." The candidates for election shall be chosen on the basis of "playing ability, integrity, character and their contribution to their team and the game of hockey in general."

*Players**

Abel, Sidney Gerald (June/69)
Adams, John James "Jack" (Sept/59)
Apps, Charles Joseph Sylvanus "Syl" (June/61)

Bain, Donald H. "Dan" (April/45)
Baker, Hobart A. H. "Hobey" (April/45)
Barry, Martin J. "Marty" (June/65)
Béliveau, Jean Arthur "Le Gros Bill" (June/72)
Benedict, Clinton S. (June/65)
Bentley, Douglas Wagner (June/64)
Bentley, Maxwell Herbert Lloyd (June/66)
Blake, Hector "Toe" (June/66)
Boon, Richard R. "Dickie" (August/52)

Bouchard, Emile Joseph "Butch" (June/66)
Boucher, Frank Xavier (April/58)
Boucher, George "Buck" (Sept/60)
Bowie, Russell (April/45)
Brimsek, Francis Charles (June/66)
Broadbent, Harry L. "Punch" (June/62)
Broda, Walter Edward "Turk" (June/67)

Cameron, Harold Hugh "Harry" (August/62)
Clancy, Francis Michael "King" (April/58)
Clapper, Aubrey Victor "Dit" (April/45)
Cleghorn, Sprague (April/58)
Colville, Neil MacNeil (June/67)
Conacher, Charles William (June/61)

---

* The year of election is indicated in parentheses after the members' names.

Connell, Alexander (April/58)
Cook, William Osser (August/52)
Cowley, William Mailes (June/68)
Crawford, Samuel Russell "Rusty"
    (August/62)

Darragh, John Proctor "Jack" (August/62)
Davidson, Allan M. "Scotty" (June/50)
Day, Clarence Henry "Hap" (June/61)
Denneny, Cyril "Cy" (Sept/59)
Drinkwater, Charles Graham (June/50)
Durnan, William Ronald (June/64)
Dutton, Mervyn A. "Red" (April/58)
Dye, Cecil Henry "Babe" (June/70)

Farrell, Arthur F. (June/65)
Foyston, Frank C. (April/58)
Fredrickson, Frank (April/58)

Gadsby, William Alexander "The Great"
    (June/70)
Gardiner, Charles Robert "Chuck"
    (April/45)
Gardiner, Herbert Martin "Herb" (April/58)
Gardner, James Henry "Jimmy"
    (August/62)
Geoffrion, Joseph Bernard Andre "Boom-
    Boom" (June/72)
Gerard, Edward George (April/45)
Gilmour, Hamilton Livingstone "Billy"
    (August/62)
Goheen, Frank Xavier "Moose" (August/52)
Goodfellow, Ebenezer R. "Ebbie" (June/63)
Grant, Michael "Mike" (June/50)
Green, Wilfred "Shorty" (August/62)
Griffis, Silas Seth "Si" (June/50)

Hainsworth, George (June/61)
Hall, Joseph Henry (June/61)
Hay, George (April/58)
Hern, William Milton "Riley" (August/62)
Hextall, Brian Aldwin (June/69)
Holmes, Harry "Hap" (June/72)
Hooper, Charles Thomas "Tom"
    (August/62)
Horner, George Reginald "Red" (June/65)
Howe, Gordon "Gordie" (June/72)
Howe, Sydney Harris (June/65)
Hutton, John Bower "Bouse" (August/62)
Hyland, Harry M. (June/62)

Irvin, James Dickenson "Dick" (April/58)

Jackson, Harvey "Busher" (June/71)
Johnson, Ernest "Moose" (August/52)
Johnson, Ivan W. "Ching" (April/58)
Johnson, Thomas Christian "Tom"
    (June/70)
Joliat, Aurele (April/45)

Keats, Gordon Blanchard "Duke" (April/58)
Kelly, Leonard Patrick "Red" (June/69)
Kennedy, Theodore S. "Teeder" (June/66)

Lach, Elmer James (June/66)
Lalonde, Edouard Charles "Newsy"
    (June/50)
Laviolette, Jean Baptiste "Jack"
    (August/62)
Lehman, Hugh (April/58)
LeSueur, Percy (June/61)
Lindsay, Robert Blake Theodore "Ted"
    (June/66)

MacKay, Duncan "Mickey" (August/52)
Malone, Joseph "Joe" (June/50)
Mantha, Sylvio (Sept/60)
Marshall, John "Jack" (June/65)
Maxwell, Fred G. "Steamer" (June/62)
McGee, Frank (April/45)
McGimsie, William George "Billy"
    (August/62)
McNamara, George (April/58)
Moran, Patrick Joseph "Paddy" (April/58)
Morenz, Howarth W. (April/45)
Mosienko, William "Billy" (June/65)

Nighbor, Frank (April/45)
Noble, Edward Reginald "Reg" (June/62)

Oliver, Harold "Harry" (June/67)

Patrick, Lester (April/45)
Phillips, "Tom" (April/45)
Pitre, Didier "Pit" (August/62)
Pratt, Walter "Babe" (June/66)
Primeau, A. Joseph (June/63)
Pulford, E. Harvey (April/45)

Rankin, Frank (June/61)
Reardon, Kenneth Joseph (June/66)
Richard, Joseph Henri Maurice "Rocket"
    (June/61)
Richardson, George Taylor (June/50)
Roberts, Gordon (June/71)
Ross, Arthur Howey (April/45)
Russell, Blair (June/65)
Russell, Ernest (June/65)
Ruttan, J. D. "Jack" (August/62)

Sawchuk, Terrance Gordon "Ukey"
    (June/71)
Scanlan, Fred (June/65)
Schmidt, Milton Conrad "Milt" (June/61)
Schriner, David "Sweeney" (June/62)
Seibert, Earl Walter (June/63)
Seibert, Oliver Levi (June/61)
Shore, Edward William "Eddie" (April/45)
Siebert, Albert Charles "Babe" (June/64)
Simpson, Harold Edward "Bullet Joe"
    (August/62)
Smith, Alfred E. (June/62)
Smith, Reginald J. "Hooley" (June/72)
Stanley, Russell "Barney" (August/62)
Stewart, John Sherratt "Black Jack"
    (June/64)
Stewart, Nelson Robert "Nels" (August/62)

Stuart, Bruce (June/61)
Stuart, Hodgson "Hod" (April/45)

Taylor, Frederic Wellington "Cyclone"
    (April/45)
Thompson, Cecil Ralph "Tiny" (Sept./59)
Trihey, Harry J. (June/50)

Vezina, Georges (April/45)

Walker, John Phillip "Jack" (Sept./60)
Walsh, Martin "Marty" (August/62)
Watson, Harry E. (August/62)
Weiland, Ralph C. "Cooney" (June/71)
Westwick, Harry "Rat" (August/62)
Whitcroft, Fred (August/62)
Wilson, Gordon Allan "Phat" (August/62)
Worters, Roy (June/69)

Builders

Adams, Charles Francis (Sept./60)
Adams, Sr., Weston W. (June/72)
Ahearn, Thomas Franklin "Frank"
    (June/62)
Allan, Sir H. Montague (C.V.O.) (April/45)

Brown, George V. (June/61)
Brown, Walter A. (June/62)

Calder, Frank (April/45)
Campbell, Angus Daniel (June/64)
Campbell, Clarence Sutherland (June/66)

Dandurand, Joseph Viateur "Leo"
    (April/63)
Dilio, Francis Paul (June/64)
Dudley, George S. (April/58)
Dunn, James A. (June/68)

Gorman, Thomas Patrick "Tommy"
    (April/63)

Hendy, James Cecil V. "Jim" (June/68)
Hewitt, Foster William (Jan./65)
Hewitt, William Abraham (April/45)
Hume, Fred J. (June/62)

Kilpatrick, Gen. John Reed (Sept./60)

Leader, George A. "Al" (June/69)
LeBel, Robert "Bob" (June/70)

Lockhart, Thomas F. (Jan./65)
Loicq, Paul (June/61)

McLaughlin, Major Frederic W. (April/63)

Nelson, Francis (April/45)
Norris, Bruce A. (June/69)
Norris, Sr., James D. (April/58)
Norris Jr., James Dougan (June/62)
Northey, William M. (April/45)

O'Brien, John Ambrose (June/62)

Patrick, Frank A. (June/58)
Pickard, Allan W. "Al" (April/58)

Raymond, Sen. Donat (April/58)
Robertson, John Ross (April/45)
Robinson, Claude C. (April/45)

Selke, Frank J. (Sept./60)
Smith, Frank Donald (June/62)
Smythe, Conn (April/58)
Stanley of Preston, Lord (G.C.B.)
    (April/45)
Sutherland, Capt. James T. (April/45)

Turner, Lloyd (April/58)

Waghorne, Fred C. (June/61)
Wirtz, Sr., Arthur Michael (June/71)

Referees

Chadwick, William L "Bill" (June/64)
Elliott, Chaucer (June/61)
Hewitson, Robert W. "Bobby" (June/63)
Ion, Frederick James "Mickey" (June/61)

Rodden, Michael J. "Mike" (June/62)
Smeaton, J. Cooper (June/61)
Storey, Roy Alvin "Red" (June/67)

15
Playing Rule Changes

Since the first attempts at bringing some definite rules into hockey at McGill University in 1879, many changes have taken place. The rule-makers at McGill proposed nine players to a side; this was reduced to seven about 10 years later. A team then consisted of a goaltender, point, cover-point, rover, center, right wing and left wing. The point lined up behind the cover-point and in front of the goaltender, placing the three players in a straight line and behind the three forwards.

The rover played between the forwards and the cover-point and was just what his name implied. He roamed all over the ice helping the forwards on the attack and aiding the point and cover-point on defense. Hamilton "Billy" Gilmour, Edouard "Newsy" Lalonde, Bruce Stuart, Frederic "Cyclone" Taylor and Harry "Rat" Westwick were five of the great players at that position. When the rover position was abandoned, Lalonde and Taylor moved to center where they continued to star.

It was Lester Patrick, who played either defense or rover, who altered the positions of the point and cover-point. He placed them side by side and they became known as the right and left defensemen.

In 1911–12, the National Hockey Association eliminated the rover position but the Pacific Coast Hockey Association continued to play with seven players until 1922–23.

This caused a problem when eastern clubs played the Pacific Coast Hockey Association for the Stanley Cup. It was resolved by alternating the number of players for each game.

In 1919–20 the National Hockey League reduced the time of a minor penalty from 3 to 2 minutes. In 1922–23 the Pacific Coast Hockey Association reduced their minor penalty time from 3 to 2 minutes. During Stanley Cup play this difference was solved in the same manner as the number of players.

Other important rule changes concerned the length of the game. In the early days when a club scored three goals it was declared the victor. With this method a game could end abruptly or go on indefinitely. This was unsatisfactory so teams began to play two 30-minute periods. In 1910–11, this was changed to three 20-minute periods.

The first hockey was played with the "no-substitution" rule in effect. This rule prohibited an injured player from being replaced; the opposing club had to remove a player from the ice to equalize the teams. This rule persisted for many years and when a change did take place it concerned only the goaltender. In 1913, a goaltender could be replaced if he couldn't

continue. A goaltender wasn't permitted to drop to the ice until 1922. Previous to 1922 he was assessed a penalty if he didn't remain on his feet.

In the early days of hockey the clubs carried only nine or ten players and it was not uncommon for a player to play 50 or 55 minutes of a game. Even in the first years of the National Hockey League there were only 12 players on each club and players from the bench replaced those on the ice individually. It was Frank and Lester Patrick who began working the three forwards as a unit and started the practice of making line changes.

Lester Patrick was the first defenseman to carry the puck into the opposing club's area. This occurred in a 1904 Stanley Cup game at Ottawa when he was a member of the Brandon Wheat Kings. Before this, defensemen had never strayed far from their own area.

In 1918–19, the playing surface was divided into three areas by blue lines and forward passing, at the suggestion of Frank and Lester Patrick, was permitted in the center area. Previous to this no forward passing was allowed and the National Hockey League didn't permit it til the 1921–22 season. Another idea of Frank and Lester Patrick was adopted in 1918–19 when the kicking of the puck was permitted. Still another idea of these famous brothers was started in 1918–19 with the recording of assists, although the Pacific Coast Hockey Association had been recording assists since 1912–13.

In 1920–21, goaltenders were allowed to pass the puck forward as far as their own blue line.

In 1925–26, the delayed penalty rule came into effect. After this the referee did not blow his whistle if the club not being penalized had control of the puck. He blew his whistle only after the non-penalized club either scored or lost control to the club being penalized. This rule gave the non-penalized club a chance to complete its play. Another new rule in 1930–31 permitted a club to have four players on the ice no matter how many players they had in the penalty box.

In 1927–28, forward passing was permitted in a club's defending zone as well as the center ice area. The width of the goaltenders' pads was reduced from 12 to 10 inches and a hockey stick was limited to 53 inches in length.

In 1928–29, forward passing was allowed in all three zones.

In 1929–30, a rule was passed allowing players to precede the puck into the center and offensive zones. On entering the offensive zone the puck had to be carried over the blue line by a player but any number of teammates could have preceded him. If the defenders gained possession of the puck and either carried or shot it out of their zone, the attackers had to leave that area or be given a minor penalty. This rule was intended to increase the scoring opportunities, but with attackers lurking around the goal the goaltender had little chance. This rule didn't last through the season.

In 1934–35, the penalty shot was introduced. A player was permitted to skate to a line 28 feet from the goal before shooting.

In 1938–39, the player taking a penalty shot was allowed to skate right up to the goal if he so wished.

In 1940–41, the flooding of the ice between periods, as was done in England, began.

On November 21, 1942, the National Hockey League ceased to play any

overtime in regular season games.

In 1943–44, at the suggestion of Frank Boucher, former player and coach of the New York Rangers, the red line at center ice was added. This permitted players to pass to teammates over their own blue line and then over the red line.

In 1949–50, the clubs were allowed to dress 17 players, exclusive of the goaltender(s), for a game.

In 1951–52, the goal crease was enlarged from 3 by 7 to 4 by 8 feet, and the faceoff circles were enlarged from a 10- to a 15-foot radius.

In 1956–57, at the suggestion of John (Jack) Adams, former general manager of Detroit, a player serving a minor penalty was allowed to return to the ice if the opposing club scored.

In 1960–61, the number of players permitted to dress was reduced to 16.

In 1964–65, no bodily contact was allowed during faceoff.

In 1965–66, each club had to carry two goaltenders dressed and ready to play. If a goaltender was injured he was not to be treated on the ice, but replaced by the other. The practice of each club warming up in their zones at the same time was abandoned. The home club would now warm up for 15 minutes, starting 45 minutes before game time. The visiting club would then follow until 15 minutes before game time and then the ice would be resurfaced. Shots on goal would be recorded, when directed at the goal, whether on target or not.

In 1966–67, when a player from each club received a major penalty simultaneously, substitutes could replace them.

16
Amateur Champions

Olympics

Hockey first came to Europe in 1910 when Canadian students introduced it at Cambridge and Oxford Universities in England. It was soon being played in many European countries and in 1920 became an Olympic sport.

Canada had little opposition during the first four Olympic tournaments (1920, '24, '28, and '32). In the first Olympic tournament the Canadians scored 29 goals and had only one scored against them. In the second Olympic competition they dominated the games even more; defeating Czechoslovakia 30–0, Great Britain 19–2, Sweden 22–0, Switzerland 33–0 and the United States 6–1.

In the third Olympic tournament it was planned to divide the countries into three groups with the winners playing for the Olympic title. After watching the Canadians practice the Olympic officials made an unprecedented request—would the Canadians remain out of group competition and meet each group winner? The Canadians considered this odd, but flattering proposition and finally agreed. They dispatched the group winners easily; Sweden 11–0, Great Britain 14–0 and Switzerland 13–0.

The European hockey clubs began to improve as Canadians came to coach and play. Austria, Denmark, Germany, Sweden, Switzerland and other European countries hired Canadians to coach their clubs. In later years the pupil was to defeat the teacher. Russia was probably the only country that didn't import coaches or players. Instead they sent observers and took motion pictures of games and soon were entering clubs in the tournaments.

Canada's first defeat in Olympic hockey came in 1936 at Garmisch–Partenkirchen, Germany. Great Britain, using several Canadian players, including their goaltender, defeated the Canadians 2–1. Edgar "Chirp" Brenchley, who over 30 years later would become a scout for the Pittsburgh Penguins, scored the winning goal at 13:48 of the 3rd period.

The United States has won one Olympic championship—in 1960 at Squaw Valley, California in which two players performed outstandingly: John McCartan, a goaltender, who signed with the New York Rangers immediately afterward and Thomas Williams, a forward, who later became a Boston Bruin.

Year	Country	Played at
1920	Canada (Winnipeg Falcons)	Antwerp, Belgium
1924	Canada (Toronto Granites)	Chamonix, France
1928	Canada (U. of Toronto Varsity Grads)	St. Moritz, Switzerland
1932	Canada (Winnipeg 'Pegs)	Lake Placid, N.Y., U.S.A.
1936	Great Britain	Garmisch-Partenkirchen, Germany
1940	none	
1944	none	
1948	Canada (Royal C. Air Force Flyers)	St. Moritz, Switzerland
1952	Canada (Edmonton Mercurys)	Oslo, Norway
1956	Russia	Cortina d'Ampezza, Italy
1960	United States	Squaw Valley, Calif., U.S.A.
1964	Russia	Innsbruck, Austria
1968	Russia	Grenoble, France
1972	Russia	Sapporo, Japan

World's Amateur Champions

These tournaments began in 1930 and were played between Olympic years. The first one began at Chamonix, France but when unfavorable ice conditions occurred (they were playing on natural ice) midway in the tournament it was moved to the Sports Palace at Berlin, Germany. World War II brought them to a halt and they were not resumed until 1947. The United States has won once—1933 at Prague, Czechoslovakia. Starting in 1972 these tournaments are also held in Olympic years.

Year	Country	Played at
1930	Canada (Toronto CCM)	Chamonix, France & Berlin, Germany
1931	Canada (U. of Manitoba Grads)	Krynica, Poland
1932	see Olympics	
1933	United States	Prague, Czechoslovakia
1934	Canada (Saskatoon Quakers)	Milan, Italy
1935	Canada (Winnipeg Monarchs)	Davos, Switzerland
1936	see Olympics	
1937	Canada (Kimberley Dynamiters)	London, England
1938	Canada (Sudbury Wolves)	Prague, Czechoslovakia
1939	Canada (Trail Smoke-Eaters)	Basle, Switzerland
1947	Czechoslovakia	Prague, Czechoslovakia
1948	see Olympics	
1949	Czechoslovakia	Stockholm, Sweden
1950	Canada (Edmonton Mercurys)	London, England
1951	Canada (Lethbridge Maple Leafs)	Paris, France
1952	see Olympics	
1953	Sweden	Zurich, Switzerland
1954	Russia	Stockholm, Sweden
1955	Canada (Penticton V's)	Cologne, Dortmund, Duesseldorf & Krefeld, Germany
1956	see Olympics	
1957	Sweden	Moscow, Russia

1958 Canada (Whitby Dunlops)   Oslo, Norway
1959 Canada (Belleville McFarlands)   Prague, Czechoslovakia
1960 see Olympics
1961 Canada (Trail Smoke-Eaters)   Geneva & Lausanne, Switzerland
1962 Sweden   Colorado Springs, Colo., U.S.A.
1963 Russia   Stockholm, Sweden
1964 see Olympics
1965 Russia   Tampere, Finland
1966 Russia   Ljubljana, Yugoslavia
1967 Russia   Vienna, Austria
1968 see Olympics
1969 Russia   Stockholm, Sweden
1970 Russia   Stockholm, Sweden
1971 Russia   Bern & Geneva, Switzerland
1972 Czechoslovakia   Prague, Czechoslovakia

Note: Due to a disagreement over the eligibility of players Canada has not competed in any of these tournaments since 1969.

Allan Cup Champions

When Lord Stanley presented the Stanley Cup in 1892, all hockey clubs were amateur. Soon after the turn of the century many professional clubs were formed and began dominating the competition for the Stanley Cup. In 1908, Sir H. Montague Allan, C.V.O., Montreal financier and industrialist, presented the Allan Cup for competition between Canada's senior amateur hockey clubs. It was presented to the Montreal Victorias with the stipulation that when the league championship was decided, the winner would take possession. The league champions were the Ottawa Cliffsides.

1972	Spokane (Wash.) Jets	1952	Fort Francis Canadians
1971	Galt Hornets	1951	Owen Sound Mercurys
1970	Spokane (Wash.) Jets	1950	Toronto Marlboros
1969	Galt Hornets	1949	Ottawa Senators
1968	Victoriaville Tigers	1948	Edmonton Flyers
1967	Drummondville Eagles	1947	Montreal Royals
1966	Drumheller Miners	1946	Calgary Stampeders
1965	Sherbrooke Beavers	1945	None
1964	Winnipeg Maroons	1944	Quebec Aces
1963	Windsor Bulldogs	1943	Ottawa Commandos
1962	Trail Smoke-Eaters	1942	Ottawa RCAF Flyers
1961	Galt Terriers	1941	Regina Rangers
1960	Chatham Maroons	1940	Kirkland Lake Blue Devils
1959	Whitby Dunlops		
1958	Belleville McFarlands	1939	Port Arthur Bearcats
1957	Whitby Dunlops	1938	Trail Smoke-Eaters
1956	Vernon Canadians	1937	Sudbury Tigers
1955	Kitchener-Waterloo Dutchmen	1936	Kimberley Dynamiters
		1935	Halifax Wolverines
1954	Penticton V's	1934	Moncton Hawks
1953	Kitchener-Waterloo Dutchmen	1933	Moncton Hawks
		1932	Toronto Nationals

1931	Winnipeg 'Pegs	1918	Kitchener Hockey Club
1930	Montreal A.A.A.	1917	Toronto Dentals
1929	Port Arthur Bearcats	1916	61st Battalion, Winnipeg
1928	University of Manitoba–	1915	Melville Millionaires
	Winnipeg	1915	Winnipeg Monarchs
1927	Toronto Varsity Grads	1914	Regina Victorias
1926	Port Arthur Bearcats	1913	Winnipeg Hockey Club
1925	Port Arthur Bearcats	1912	Winnipeg Victorias
1924	Sault Ste. Marie Greyhounds	1911	Winnipeg Victorias
1923	Toronto Granites	1910	Toronto St. Michael's College
1922	Toronto Granites	1909	Queen's University—
1921	University of Toronto		Kingston
1920	Winnipeg Falcons	1908	Ottawa Cliffsides
1919	Hamilton Tigers		

Memorial Cup Champions

This cup is presented to the junior amateur hockey champions of Canada. Eastern Canada conducts a series of eliminations and the winner is awarded the George T. Richardson Memorial Cup. Western Canada conducts a series of eliminations and the winner is awarded the Abbott Memorial Cup. These winners then meet in a series for the Memorial Cup.

1972	Cornwall Royals	1946	Winnipeg Monarchs
1971	Quebec Remparts		(Regals)
1970	Montreal Jr. Canadiens	1945	Toronto St. Michael's
1969	Montreal Jr. Canadiens		College Majors
1968	Niagara Falls Flyers	1944	Oshawa Generals
1967	Toronto Marlboros	1943	Winnipeg Rangers
1966	Edmonton Oil Kings	1942	Portage la Prairie
1965	Niagara Falls Flyers		Terriers
1964	Toronto Marlboros	1941	Winnipeg Rangers
1963	Edmonton Oil Kings	1940	Oshawa Generals
1962	Hamilton Red Wings	1939	Oshawa Generals
1961	Toronto St. Michael's	1938	St. Boniface Seals
	College Majors	1937	Winnipeg Monarchs
1960	St. Catharines Teepees	1936	West Toronto Nationals
1959	Winnipeg Braves	1935	Winnipeg Monarchs
1958	Hull-Ottawa Canadiens	1934	Toronto St. Michael's
1957	Flin Flon Bombers		College
1956	Toronto Marlboros	1933	Newmarket Redmen
1955	Toronto Marlboros	1932	Sudbury Wolves
1954	St. Catharines Teepees	1931	Elmwood Millionaires
1953	Barrie Flyers		(Winnipeg)
1952	Guelph Biltmores	1930	Regina Patricias
1951	Barrie Flyers	1929	Toronto Marlboros
1950	Montreal Jr. Canadiens	1928	Regina Monarchs
1949	Montreal Royals	1927	Owen Sound Greys
1948	Port Arthur West End	1926	Calgary Canadians
	Bruins	1925	Regina Patricias
1947	Toronto St. Michael's	1924	Owen Sound Greys
	College Majors		

1923	University of Manitoba–Winnipeg	1921	Winnipeg Falcons
1922	Fort William G. War Veterans A.	1920	Toronto Canoe Club
		1919	Toronto Varsity

17
Father and Son(s)

ABEL	Sidney Gerald	Gerald Scott
ADAMS	Charles Francis	Weston W., Sr.
ADAMS	Weston W., Sr.	Weston W., Jr.
APPS	Charles Joseph Sylvanus	Sylvanus Marshall
BENNETT	Harvey A.	Curt Alexander
BOUCHARD	Emile Joseph	Pierre
BROWN	Adam	Andrew Conrad
BROWN	George V.	Walter A.
BUCHANAN	Ralph L.	Ronald Leonard
CARR	Alfred George	Eugene William
CLANCY	Francis Michael	Terrance John
CONACHER	Charles William, Sr.	Charles William, Jr.
CONACHER	Lionel Pretoria	Brian Kennedy
DeMARCO	Albert	Albert Thomas
GARDNER	Calvin Pearly	David
HART	Dr. David A.	Cecil M.
HEWITT	William Abraham	Foster William
HEXTALL	Bryan Aldwin	Bryan Lee & Dennis Harold
HOLMES	Louis Charles Carter	Charles Frank
IMLACH	George F.	Brent
LINDSAY	Bert	Robert Blake Theodore
McMAHON	Michael C.	Michael William
NORRIS	James D., Sr.	Bruce A. & James Dougan, Jr.
O'FLAHERTY	John B.	Gerard Joseph
PATRICK	Lester	Frederick Murray & Joseph Lynn
PATRICK	Joseph Lynn	Craig
PETERS	James Meldrum	James Stephen
POWERS	Edward, Sr.	Edward, Jr.
PRATT	Walter	Tracy Arnold
REISE	Leo C., Sr.	Leo C., Jr.
SEIBERT	Oliver Levi	Earl Walter
SELKE	Frank J.	Frank D.
SMITH	Desmond Patrick	Brian Desmond & Gary Edward
SMITH	Stuart	Brian Stuart
SMYTHE	Conn	C. Stafford
WALTON	Robert C.	Michael Robert

18
Brothers

Brothers

ADAMS—John James & W. "Bill"
ANDERSON—Ernie & "Jocko"
ARBOUR—Ernest & John A.
BARILKO—Alex & William
BATHGATE—Andrew James & Frank D.
BELL—Gordon & Joseph A.
BENTLEY—Douglas Wagner, Maxwell Herbert Lloyd & Reginald
BLAIR—Charles & George
BORDELEAU—Christian Gerard & Jean-Pierre
BOUCHER—Frank Xavier, George, Robert & William
BOURCIER—Conrad & Jean-Louis
BRODERICK—Kenneth Lorne & Leonard
BRUNETEAU—Edward E. H. & Modere Fernand
CAFFERY—John & Terrance Michael
CARSE—Robert Allison & William Alexander
CARSON—Francis, Gerald George & William J.
CHERRY—Donald Stewart & Richard John
CLEGHORN—J. Ogilvie & Sprague
COLVILLE—Matthew L. & Neil MacNeil
CONACHER—Charles William, Lionel Pretoria & Roy G.
COOK—Alexander, Frederick Joseph & William Osser
COSTELLO—J. Murray & Lester John Thomas
CULLEN—Brian Joseph, Charles Francis & Raymond Murray
DARRAGH—Harold & John Proctor
DENNENY—Corbett & Cyril Joseph
DRYDEN—David Murray & Kenneth Wayne
EDWARDS—Allan Roy & Marvin Wayne
ESPOSITO—Anthony James & Philip Anthony
GILMOUR—Dave J., Hamilton Livingstone & S. C.
GLOVER—Frederick Austin & Howard Edward
HANNIGAN—John Gordon, Patrick Edward & Raymond J.
HARRIS—Fred & Henry
HERGESHEIMER—Philip & Walter E.
HEXTALL—Bryan Lee & Dennis Harold
HICKE—Ernest Allen & William Lawrence
HILLMAN—Floyd Arthur, Lawrence Morley & Wayne James
HOEKSTRA—Cecil Thomas & Edward Adrian
HOWE—Gordon & Victor S.
HOWELL—Henry Vernon & Ronald
HULL—Dennis William & Robert Marvin
JACKSON—Arthur & Harvey

JERWA—Frank & Joseph
JOLIAT—Aurèle Emile & Rene
KANNEGIESSER—Gordon Cameron & Sheldon Bruce
KILREA—Hector, Kenneth Armstrong & Walter
KYLE—Walter L. & William
LEFLEY—Bryan Andrew & Charles Thomas
LOUGHLIN—Clement Joseph & Wilfred
MAHOVLICH—Francis William & Peter Joseph
MAKI—Ronald Patrick & Wayne
MANTHA—Leon-Georges & Sylvio
MATTE—Joseph & Roland
McCREARY—Vernon Keith & William Edward
McNAMARA—George & Howard
MEISSNER—Barrie Michael & Richard Donald
MENARD—Hillary & Howard Hubert
METZ—Donald Maurice & Nicholas J.
MORRISON—Donald M. & Roderick F.
NORRIS—Bruce A. & James Dougan
OATMAN—Edward & Warren Russell
O'SHEA—Daniel Patrick & Kevin William
PATRICK—Frank 'A. & Lester
PATRICK—Frederick Murray & Joseph Lynn
PAVELICH—Martin N. & Matthew
PICARD—Adrien Roger & Jean-Noël Yves
PLAGER—Barclay Graham, Robert Bryan & William Ronald
POILE—Donald B. & Norman Robert
PRENTICE—Dean Sutherland & Eric D.
PRONOVOST—Claude, Joseph Jean Denis & Joseph René Marcel
QUACKENBUSH—Hubert G. & Maxwell J.
REARDON—Kenneth Joseph & Terrence George
REDMOND—Michael Edward & Richard
RICHARD—Joseph Henri & Joseph Henri Maurice
ROCHE—Desmond & Earl
RODDEN—Edmund A. & Michael J.
ROUSSEAU—Guy Lucien, Joseph Jean-Paul Robert & Roland
SCHMAUTZ—Clifford Harvey & Robert James
SCHMIDT—John R. & Joseph
SCHOCK—Daniel Patrick & Ronald Lawrence
SIMON—John C. & Thain A.
SKOV—Arthur & Glen Frederick
SMITH—Brian Desmond & Gary Edward
SMITH—Harry & Thomas
STANFIELD—Frederic William, James Boviard & John Gordon
STANKIEWICZ—Edward & Myron
STUART—Bruce & William Hodgson
THOMPSON—Cecil Ralph & Paul I.
TOPPAZZINI—Gerald & Zellio Louis Peter
WARWICK—Grant D. & William H.
WILSON—John Edward & Lawrence

19
Pension Plan

1947—Plan started. Players contributed $900 each per year. The League contribution was variable, averaging $65,000 per year. Each player entitled to paid-up annual pension of $90 per year of service, payable commencing at age 45 and guaranteed for a minimum of 10 years.

1957—Ten years of plan completed. The League completed the past-service portion by contributing $400 per year of past service, including War years, on behalf of players already in NHL when plan started in 1947. A dividend of 34½ percent ($315 per year of service) of players' contributions declared for first 10 years of plan. The League began matching the players' contributions of $900 per year. Pension benefits increased to $180 annually per year of service.

1962—Five years of revised plan completed. A dividend of 61½ percent ($560) per year of service declared.

1964—Plan revised. Contributions of both players and the League increased to $1,500 per year. Pension benefits increased to $300 annually per year of service. Effective Oct. 1, 1964, these contributions will produce an annual pension of $985 for each year of service, payable at age 65.

1969—Plan revised. Owners agreed to fund the plan fully. Players' pension benefits continue to be $300 annually per year of service, payable at age 45 and $1,000 for each year of service at age 65.

20
Seating Diagrams

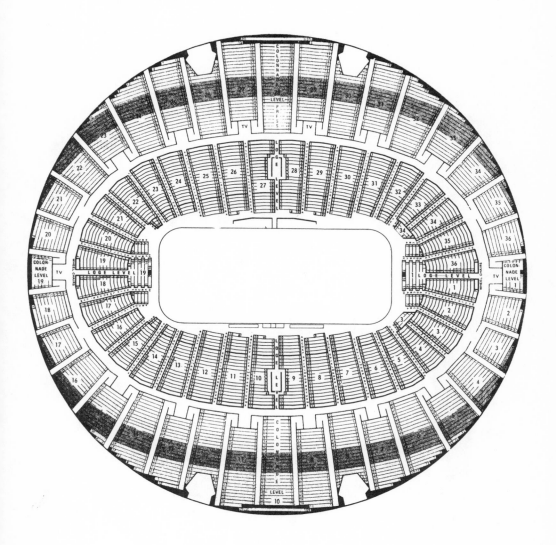

Los Angeles Kings (THE FORUM)

Montreal Canadiens (THE FORUM)

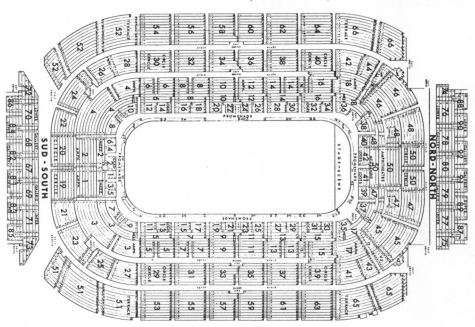

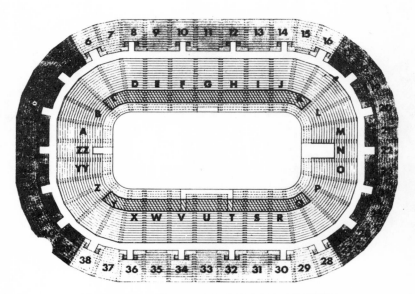

Minnesota North Stars (MET SPORTS CENTER)

New York Rangers (MADISON SQUARE GARDEN)

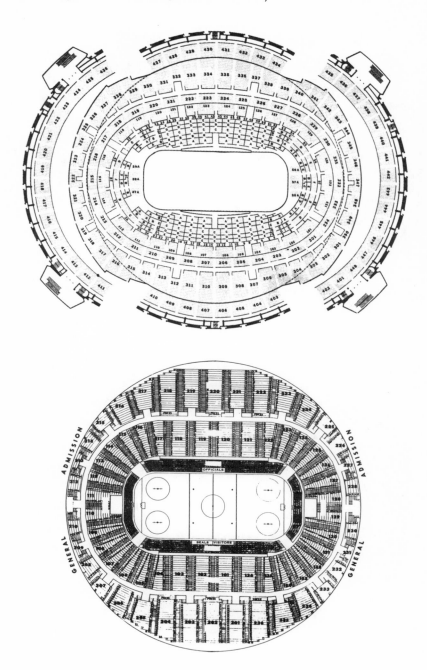

Oakland Seals (OAKLAND COLISEUM ARENA)

Philadelphia Flyers (THE SPECTRUM)

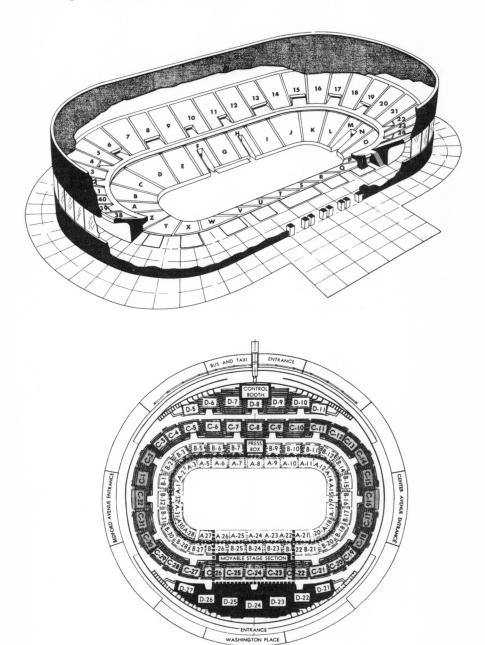

Pittsburgh Penguins (CIVIC ARENA)

St. Louis Blues (THE ARENA)

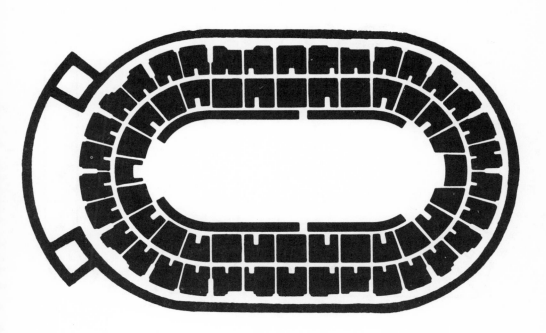

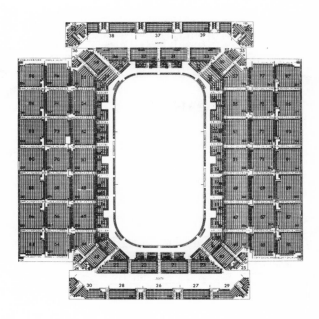

Toronto Maple Leafs (MAPLE LEAF GARDENS)

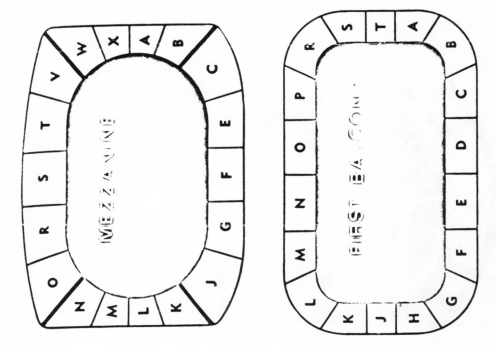

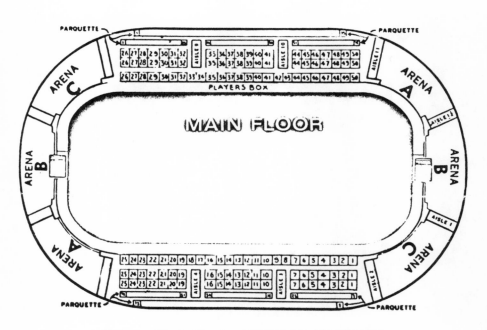

Chicago Black Hawks (CHICAGO STADIUM)

Lord Stanley

Nelson Stewart

Cyclone Taylor

Georges Vezina

Frank Calder

Lorne Chabot

Chuck Conacher

Roy Conacher

21
1972-1973 Season

League Standings

Each club played 6 games with 3 clubs and 5 games with 12 clubs.
Example—Los Angeles—played 6 games with California, Philadelphia and Pittsburgh
played 5 games with Atlanta, Boston, Buffalo, Chicago, Detroit,
Minnesota, Montreal, N.Y. Islanders, N.Y. Rangers, St. Louis,
Toronto and Vancouver

East Division

Clubs	Games	Won	Lost	Tied	Points	Goals for	Goals against	Shut-outs
Mont. Canadiens	78	52	10	16	120	329	184	7
Boston Bruins	78	51	22	5	107	330	235	9
N.Y. Rangers	78	47	23	8	102	297	208	7
Buffalo Sabres	78	37	27	14	88	257	219	6
Det. Red Wings	78	37	29	12	86	265	243	7
Tor. Maple Leafs	78	27	41	10	64	247	279	4
Van. Canucks	78	22	47	9	53	233	339	2
N.Y. Islanders	78	12	60	6	30	170	347	0
						2128		42

	General-Mgr.	Asst. General-Mgr.	Coach
Boston	Harry Sinden	none	T. C. Johnson
Buffalo	George F. Imlach	Frederick T. Hunt	J. R. Crozier
Detroit	Nevin D. Harkness	Aldege Bastien	John E. Wilson
Montreal	Samuel Pollock	Ronald Caron	W. S. Bowman
N.Y. Islanders	William A. Torrey	none	J. P. Goyette
N.Y. Rangers	Emile P. Francis	none	Francis
Toronto	James Gregory	none	D. J. McLellan
Vancouver	Norman R. Poile	none	V. J. Stasiuk

November 21, 1972—Poile hospitalized.
December 14, 1972—Poile succeeded by Harold R. Laycoe.
January 29, 1973—Goyette replaced by Earl T. Ingarfield (N.Y. Islanders had won 6—
lost 40—tied 4) and Autry R. Erickson named Assistant Coach.
February 5, 1973—Johnson replaced by Armand Guidolin (Boston had won 31—lost
16—tied 5).

West Division

Clubs	Games	Won	Lost	Tied	Points	Goals for	Goals against	Shut-outs
Chi. Black Hawks	78	42	27	9	93	284	225	4
Phila. Flyers	78	37	30	11	85	296	256	3
Min. North Stars	78	37	30	11	85	254	230	7
St. Louis Blues	78	32	34	12	76	233	251	2
Pitts. Penguins	78	32	37	9	73	257	265	5
L.A. Kings	78	31	36	11	73	232	245	5
Atlanta Flames	78	25	38	15	65	191	239	4
Cal. Golden Seals	78	16	46	16	48	213	323	2
						1960		32

	General-Mgr.	Asst. Gen.-Mgr.	Coach
Atlanta	Clifford Fletcher	none	B. Geoffrion
California	Garry F. B. Young	none	Young
Chicago	Thomas N. Ivan	none	W. T. Reay
Los Angeles	Lawrence E. Regan	none	R. J. Pulford
Minnesota	Wren A. Blair	John Mariucci	John Gordon
Philadelphia	C. Keith Allen	none	F. A. Shero
Pittsburgh	John T. Riley	Jack Button	L. P. Kelly
St. Louis	Sidney G. Abel	none	A. J. Arbour

November 7, 1972—Young replaced by Frederick A. Glover as General-Manager and Coach (California had won 2—lost 7—tied 3).

November 8, 1972—Arbour replaced by Jean-Guy Talbot (St. Louis had won 2—lost 6—tied 5).

January 12, 1973—Kelly replaced by Kenneth C. Schinkel (Pittsburgh had won 17—lost 19—tied 6).

Player Transactions

November 13, 1972—N.Y. Rangers sold Ronald Stewart to N.Y. Islanders

November 25, 1972—St. Louis waived Jean-Noel Picard to Atlanta

November 27, 1972—Atlanta traded William Hogaboam to Detroit for Léon Rochefort

November 29, 1972—Atlanta traded Ronald Harris to N.Y. Rangers for Curt Bennett

December 5, 1972—California traded Richard Redmond to Chicago for Darryl Maggs

December 14, 1972—Philadelphia traded Brenton Hughes and Pierre Plante to St. Louis for André Dupont

January 17, 1973—Detroit traded Robert Cook to N.Y. Islanders for Brian Lavender and Kenneth Murray

January 21, 1973—Los Angeles traded Paul Curtis to St. Louis for Francis St. Marseille

February 12, 1973—Atlanta traded Ernest Hicke to N.Y. Islanders for S. Arnold Brown

February 13, 1973—Atlanta traded Normand Gratton to Buffalo for Ernest Deadmarsh

February 19, 1973—N.Y. Islanders waived James Mair to Vancouver ($30,000.)

February 26, 1973—Chicago traded Daniel Maloney to Los Angeles for Ralph Backstrom

February 27, 1973—Pittsburgh acquired Andrew Brown from Detroit

March 1, 1973—Minnesota bought J. Donald Blackburn from N.Y. Islanders

March 2, 1973—Boston traded Garnet Bailey to Detroit for Gary Doak

March 2, 1973—N.Y. Rangers acquired Sheldon Kannegiesser from Pittsburgh

March 2, 1973—N.Y. Rangers traded Albert DeMarco to St. Louis for Michael Murphy

March 4, 1973—Boston acquired J. Jacques Plante from Toronto

March 5, 1973—N.Y. Rangers acquired Albert Marshall from California

March 5, 1973—N.Y. Islanders traded Terrance Crisp to Philadelphia for Jean Potvin

1973 Stanley Cup

Montreal Canadiens

Pierre Bouchard
Yvan Serge Cournoyer
Kenneth Wayne Dryden
Réjean Houle
Guy Damien Lafleur
Joseph Jacques Hugues Laperriére
Guy Gerard Lapointe
Claude David Larose
Charles Thomas Lefley
Jacques Gerard Lemaire

Francis William Mahovlich
Peter Joseph Mahovlich
Robert John Murdoch
Joseph Henri Richard
James Wilfred Roberts
Larry Robinson
Serge A. Savard
Marc Tardif
Murray Wilson

The first and fourth and second and third place clubs in each division met in a 4 out of 7 game series. The winner of the first and fourth place clubs in the East Division then met the winner of the second and third place clubs in the West Division and the winner of the first and fourth place clubs in the West Division then met the winner of the second and third place clubs in the East Division in a 4 out of 7 game series. These winners then met in a 4 out of 7 game series.

Montreal (first in East Division) vs. Buffalo (fourth in East Division)

April	4, 1973	at Montreal	Montreal	2	Buffalo	1
April	5, 1973	at Montreal	Montreal	7	Buffalo	3
April	7, 1973	at Buffalo	Montreal	5	Buffalo	2
April	8, 1973	at Buffalo	Montreal	1	Buffalo	5
April	10, 1973	at Montreal	Montreal	2	Buffalo	3*
April	12, 1973	at Buffalo	Montreal	4	Buffalo	2

*Rene Robert scored at 9:18 in overtime

Boston (second in East Division) vs. N.Y. Rangers (third in East Division)

April	4, 1973	at Boston	Boston	2	N.Y. Rangers	6
April	5, 1973	at Boston	Boston	2	N.Y. Rangers	4
April	7, 1973	at New York	Boston	4	N.Y. Rangers	2
April	8, 1973	at New York	Boston	0	N.Y. Rangers	4
April	10, 1973	at Boston	Boston	3	N.Y. Rangers	6

Chicago (first in West Division) vs. St. Louis (fourth in West Division)

April	4, 1973	at Chicago	Chicago	7	St. Louis	1
April	5, 1973	at Chicago	Chicago	1	St. Louis	0
April	7, 1973	at St. Louis	Chicago	5	St. Louis	2
April	8, 1973	at St. Louis	Chicago	3	St. Louis	5
April	10, 1973	at Chicago	Chicago	6	St. Louis	1

Philadelphia (second in West Division) vs. Minnesota (third in West Division)

April	4, 1973	at Philadelphia	Philadelphia	0	Minnesota	3
April	5, 1973	at Philadelphia	Philadelphia	4	Minnesota	1
April	7, 1973	at Minnesota	Philadelphia	0	Minnesota	5
April	8, 1973	at Minnesota	Philadelphia	3	Minnesota	0
April	10, 1973	at Philadelphia	Philadelphia	3*	Minnesota	2
April	12, 1973	at Minnesota	Philadelphia	4	Minnesota	1

*Gerhardt Dornhoefer scored at 8:35 in overtime

Montreal (eliminated Buffalo) vs. Philadelphia (eliminated Minnesota)

April	14, 1973	at Montreal	Montreal	4	Philadelphia	5*
April	17, 1973	at Montreal	Montreal	4*	Philadelphia	3
April	19, 1973	at Philadelphia	Montreal	2	Philadelphia	1
April	22, 1973	at Philadelphia	Montreal	4	Philadelphia	1
April	24, 1973	at Montreal	Montreal	5	Philadelphia	3

*Richard MacLeish scored at 2:56 in overtime
*Larry Robinson scored at 6:45 in overtime

Chicago (eliminated St. Louis) vs. N.Y. Rangers (eliminated Boston)

April 12, 1973 at Chicago	Chicago 1	N.Y. Rangers 4
April 15, 1973 at Chicago	Chicago 5	N.Y. Rangers 4
April 17, 1973 at New York	Chicago 2	N.Y. Rangers 1
April 19, 1973 at New York	Chicago 3	N.Y. Rangers 1
April 24, 1973 at Chicago	Chicago 4	N.Y. Rangers 1

Chicago (eliminated N.Y. Rangers) vs. Montreal (eliminated Philadelphia)

April 29, 1973 at Montreal	Chicago 3	Montreal 8
May 1, 1973 at Montreal	Chicago 1	Montreal 4
May 3, 1973 at Chicago	Chicago 7	Montreal 4
May 6, 1973 at Chicago	Chicago 0	Montreal 4
May 8, 1973 at Montreal	Chicago 8	Montreal 7
May 10, 1973 at Chicago	Chicago 4	Montreal 6

National Hockey League Champions   1972–73   Montreal Canadiens

League Leader 1972–73   Goals Philip Esposito   Boston Bruins   55
                          Assists Philip Esposito   Boston Bruins   75
                          Points Philip Esposito   Boston Bruins
                                 (55 goals—75 assists)   130

Trophies 1972–73

Clarence S. Campbell Bowl	Chicago Black Hawks
Prince of Wales Trophy	Montreal Canadiens
Frank Calder Memorial Trophy	Stephen Vickers, N.Y. Rangers
Dr. David A. Hart Memorial Trophy	Robert Clarke, Phila. Flyers
Lady Byng Memorial Trophy	Gilbert Perreault, Buffalo Sabres
James Norris Memorial Trophy	Robert Orr, Boston Bruins
Lester Patrick Trophy 1973	Walter L. Bush
Arthur H. Ross Trophy	Philip Esposito, Boston Bruins
Conn Smythe Trophy 1973	Yvan Cournoyer, Mont. Canadiens
Georges Vezina Memorial Trophy	Kenneth Dryden, Mont. Canadiens

Stanley Cup Winner   1973   Montreal Canadiens

Most Times Stanley Cup Winner   Montreal Canadiens   18

World's Amateur Champions 1973   Russia   played at Moscow, Russia

Allan Cup Champions   1973   Orillia Terriers

Memorial Cup Champions   1973   Toronto Marlboros

26th All-Star Game: January 30, 1973 at New York
East Division All-Stars 5   West Division All-Stars 4

1972–73

1st All-Star Team			2nd All-Star Team	
Kenneth Dryden	—Montreal	goal	Anthony Esposito	—Chicago
Robert Orr	—Boston	defence	D. Bradford Park	—N.Y. Rangers
Guy Lapointe	—Montreal	defence	William White	—Chicago
Philip Esposito	—Boston	centre	Robert Clarke	—Philadelphia
Michael Redmond	—Detroit	right wing	Yvan Cournoyer	—Montreal
Francis Mahovlich	—Montreal	left wing	Dennis Hull	—Chicago